ALSO BY EVAN THOMAS

THE VERY BEST MEN:
Four Who Dared: The Early Years of the CIA

THE MAN TO SEE:
Edward Bennett Williams
Ultimate Insider; Legendary Trial Lawyer

THE WISE MEN:
Six Friends and the World They Made
(with Walter Isaacson)

Evan Thomas

A TOUCHSTONE BOOK
PUBLISHED BY SIMON & SCHUSTER

NEW YORK • LONDON • TORONTO • SYDNEY • SINGAPORE

ROBERT KENNEDY

HIS LIFE

TOUCHSTONE
Rockefeller Center
1230 Avenue of the Americas
New York, NY 10020

Copyright © 2000 by Evan Thomas
All rights reserved,
including the right of reproduction
in whole or in part in any form.
Touchstone and colophon are
registered trademarks of Simon & Schuster, Inc.
First Touchstone Edition 2002
For information about special discounts for bulk purchases,
please contact Simon & Schuster Special Sales:
1-800-456-6798 or business@simonandschuster.com
Designed by Edith Fowler
Manufactured in the United States of America

10 9 8 7 6 5 4 3 2 1

The Library of Congress has cataloged the Simon & Schuster edition as follows:
Thomas, Evan.
Robert Kennedy : his life / Evan Thomas.
p.   cm.
Includes bibliographical references and index.
1. Kennedy, Robert F., 1925–1968. 2. Legislators—United States—Biography.
3. United States. Congress. Senate—Biography. I. Title.
E840.8K4 T49 2000
973.922'092—dc21
[B]   00-041995

ISBN 0-684-83480-4
       0-7432-0329-1 (Pbk)

ACKNOWLEDGMENTS

My FIRST AND GREATEST DEBT is to my researcher, Michael Hill. Mike is tireless, responsive, and resourceful. He approaches all challenges with boundless good cheer and zest. He is a true partner and friend.

This book draws heavily on interviews with RFK's friends and colleagues. Kennedy was forty-two years old when he died; three decades later, most of his associates are in their sixties and seventies. With few exceptions, the men who served Kennedy were forthcoming. I want to thank, in particular, Joe Dolan, Richard Donahue, Fred Dutton, Peter Edelman, Ed Guthman, Frank Mankiewicz, John Nolan, John Reilly, and John Seigenthaler, all of whom read and commented upon drafts of the manuscript. They did not all like, or agree with, my conclusions, but they tried to be fair-minded in their comments. Many others, listed in the source notes, helped me as well. There is a rich lode of oral histories in the Kennedy Library, and I wish to thank Jean Stein for allowing me to see the oral histories she conducted with George Plimpton for their book *American Journey*.

Over the past thirty years, the Kennedy family has only slowly and sparingly made public RFK's papers. That is one reason Arthur Schlesinger's magisterial 1978 biography has remained definitive. Schlesinger had exclusive access to all of RFK's papers. I am, I believe, the first author since Schlesinger to be allowed to see the most significant of the closed RFK papers at the Kennedy Library, RFK's confidential file as attorney general, and his family correspondence. Kennedy's official files are still not fully declassified, but the material I reviewed included some important documents, including his original handwritten notes from the Cuban Missile Crisis, which have never before been made public. I am grateful to Maxwell Taylor Kennedy for giving me access on behalf of the Robert Kennedy family, and thankful as well to John Nolan and John Seigenthaler for recommending that he do so. I am also grateful to Paul Kirk for his role in granting me access to the family correspondence and to Charles Daly of the Kennedy Library Foundation for his advice and guidance.

I benefited from another resource that has long been kept closed, some ninety hours of tape-recorded reminiscences by RFK and JFK's close aide and friend Kenneth O'Donnell, originally intended for a book on the so-called Irish mafia by NBC newsman Sander Vanocur. My thanks to Kenny O'Donnell Jr. for giving me permission to listen to those tapes and to quote from them, and to Helen O'Donnell for first telling me about the tapes and their contents and for sharing her recollections of her father.

During the last decade, many CIA and FBI documents have been made public under the federal government's maddeningly slow declassification program. These documents allowed me to go beyond earlier treatments of RFK's dealing with the Mafia, Cuba—and perhaps most important—the FBI's J. Edgar Hoover. The documents do not always cast RFK in the best light, but I believe that I was able to debunk some of the conspiracy theories that continue to swirl around his involvement in assassination plots. The Kennedy Assassination Records Act was a very useful prod in forcing the bureaucracy to release documents that had too long remained secret. My thanks to Judge John Tunheim, Jeremy Gund, and Tom Samoluck of the Assassination Records Act Review Board for their assistance and guidance. I also want to thank Peter Kornbluh and the National Security Archive for helping me find and understand key documents relating to Cuba. For an overview of RFK's handling of the Cuba crisis and foreign policy generally, my thanks to Philip Zelikow and Timothy Naftali at the Miller Center at the University of Virginia, and to Professor Ernest May of Harvard. The Miller Center was of enormous assistance to me in understanding and making use of the Kennedy White House tapes.

I would describe the Kennedy family's attitude towards this book as wary but ultimately helpful. In 1997, I met with the late Michael Kennedy to discuss access to his father's papers at the Kennedy Library; the meeting was not fruitful. But over several years, his brother Max overcame his own doubts to give me the access I sought. Kathleen Kennedy Townsend and Eunice Kennedy Shriver granted me useful interviews. Dr. Robert Coles, the Harvard psychiatrist and RFK's friend in the last years of his life, offered me thoughtful analysis and perspective during the course of one three-hour conversation early in the project. Thanks, too, to Melody Miller of Senator Edward Kennedy's staff for her guidance.

For insights into Kennedy's schooling and a tour of Portsmouth Abbey, my thanks to Dom Damian Kearney, OSB; for guiding me to his Harvard football teammates, Wally Flynn; for helping me understand his dealings with the Cuban community in Havana, Roberto San Román and Rafael Quintero.

Mike Hill and I benefited from the patience and professionalism of a number of archivists and librarians. At the Kennedy Library, Megan Desnoyers was patient, considerate, and a steady source of intelligent help; my thanks to her and the terrific staff at the JFKL: June Payne, Maura Porter, Stephen Plotkin, Rosie Atherton, Jim Cedrone, Allan Goodrich, James Hill, and Stuart Culy, and, especially, Mary Kennefick and Stephanie Fawcett, who fight the good fight on declassification. Thanks as well to Jeffrey Flannery, Mary Wolfskill, and David Wigdor at the Manuscript Division of the Library of Congress; Steven D. Tilley, Steven Hamilton, and Martha Murphy of the Assassination Records Review Board, National Archives; L. Rebecca Johnson Melvin of the Special Collections Department, University of Delaware; Dale C. Mayer of the Herbert Hoover Presidential Library,

West Branch, Iowa; Chris Carberry and William Fowler of the Massachusetts Historical Society; Carol Bowers of the American Heritage Center, University of Wyoming; Sean Noel and Charlie Niles of the Department of Special Collections, Boston University; Mitsuko Coliver of the Department of Special Collections, Frank Melville, Jr., Library, SUNY at Stony Brook; Linda Seelke, Claudia Anderson, and Philip Scott at the LBJ Library, Austin, Texas; and Bonnie Olson at the Karl E. Mundt Historical and Educational Foundation. Two very promising students, Emily Johnson and Ulka Anjaria, did research projects for me. Mike wishes to thank as well Rebecca Purdy and Kevin Kertscher. And I owe a debt of gratitude to David McCullough, the gifted historian, for sending me Mike Hill.

I wish to thank the authors of other Kennedy books who shared information and insights: Arthur Schlesinger, Ronald Steel, Richard Reeves, Jack Newfield, C. David Heymann, Doris Kearns Goodwin, and Robert Dallek. There is a wealth of RFK literature, of varying quality. A recent important and somewhat overlooked volume is James Hilty's *Robert Kennedy: Brother Protector*.

I have been blessed to have the best agent and the best editor in publishing. This is my fourth book with Amanda Urban at ICM and Alice Mayhew at Simon & Schuster. I feel incredibly lucky to have them on my side. At S&S, I have been fortunate as well to work with Alice's assistants, Brenda Copeland and Anja Schmidt. Charlotte Gross was a masterly copy editor.

As always, I have counted on the wise counsel of friends and family. Michael Beschloss provided support and sage advice, as only he can. At *Newsweek*, I depend on Ann McDaniel and Jon Meacham, and I hope they depend on me. They were early and sound editors of this book. My debt is great as well to my bosses at *Newsweek*, Rick Smith and Mark Whitaker, who graciously put up with my moonlighting. Thanks, too, for editing tips from my old friends Sven Holmes and Stephen Smith, and to Marshall Hornblower for his sharp eye. I rely every day on my *Newsweek* colleagues Gail Tacconelli and Steve Tuttle, whose efficiency, intelligence, and thoughtfulness have helped me over and over again.

I could not have written this book without the love and support of my wife, Oscie, and our daughters, Louisa and Mary. Oscie has always been one of my most perceptive editors, and Louisa has saved me from more than one clunky or flat topic sentence. Mary offered many happy distractions. One of the nice things about writing books is that I get to do it at home.

TO OSCIE

CONTENTS

ROBERT KENNEDY

His Life

PROLOGUE

ROBERT KENNEDY liked to plunge into cold water. He swam in the surf off Cape Cod in February and in white water in upstate New York in May. Sailing off the coast of Maine on rainy, foggy days, he would egg on family and friends to follow him into the fifty-degree ocean. George Plimpton, the writer and amateur sportsman, once watched as Kennedy jumped into cold rapids on a rafting trip in the Grand Canyon. Taking an icy dip before lunch was a WASP ritual that Plimpton understood and appreciated: you would let out a gleeful whoop and then down a martini. But Kennedy, Plimpton observed, was grimly silent.

On this particular day, in late June 1967, the river guides tried to stop Kennedy. The white water was too rough, they warned; a swimmer might hit a rock and drown. But Kennedy, strapping on a life jacket, went anyway. Plimpton recalled anxiously watching Kennedy, "just his head in a great wash of water." Plimpton, who—as a stunt—had once climbed into the ring against a champion professional boxer, was afraid to join him. So was Jim Whittaker, the first American to conquer Mount Everest. Kennedy had brought along Plimpton and Whittaker as fellow adventurers, but they had less to prove.

Kennedy camping trips were rollicking and fun, with famous athletes and celebrities along for entertainment—humorist Art Buchwald cracked jokes, and crooner Andy Williams led the campfire sing-along—but the fainthearted rarely came back a second time. Kennedy's custom was to arise from his tent in the morning, scan the surrounding mountain peaks, and announce his intention to climb the highest one. On the morning of July 1, Kennedy set forth on a seven-mile climb out of the Grand Canyon. The temperature at noon was 110 degrees. Some of the entourage begged off and flew out with the younger children by helicopter instead. The march was so demanding that one of the professional guides dropped out. At one point, Whittaker, who by then was half carrying a couple of young Kennedys, asked if the group should turn back. Kennedy answered by reciting a few lines of the St. Crispin's Day speech from Shakespeare's *Henry V.* "We few, we happy few, we band of brothers," Kennedy orated. "For he today that sheds blood with me shall be my brother. . . ." "Say the whole thing," urged his wife, Ethel. Kennedy did once, and then a second time when the group was again flagging. Plimpton was reeling like a drunk by the time they neared the end. Andy Williams, unable to go on, had to be carried on a donkey. Considerate in his way, Kennedy stopped the donkey near the summit to let Williams walk the last few hundred yards, and thus not lose face.

Kennedy believed that one should mock fear, not show it. He adopted the studied casualness, the effortless grace of a New England prep school boy of the 1930s and 1940s, but beneath the offhand manner was ferocious determination. The speech from *Henry V* was delivered half—but only half—in jest. As attorney general and right-hand man to the president, Kennedy made light of dire predicaments, often using a gallows twist, and he expected his subordinates to join in the joking. In September 1962, several of his top aides, sent by the Department of Justice to gain the admission of a black student to the University of Mississippi, were besieged by angry men, armed with shotguns and squirrel rifles, who had poured into the college town of Oxford from the outlying hills and dirt-poor farms. The mob began by throwing rocks and bottles; soon, shots rang out. From a pay phone in the university administration building, where the feds were surrounded, Ed Guthman, a trusted aide, called the attorney general, who was back at his office in Washington. "It's getting like the Alamo," said Guthman. Kennedy dryly replied, "Well, you know what happened to those guys." Less than a month later, CIA spy planes discovered Soviet ICBMs tipped with nuclear warheads in Cuba. It was the moment of maximum danger for America and the world, the most perilous showdown of the Cold War. At a very tense briefing at the White House, CIA photo interpreters described the deadly missiles and their range. Robert Kennedy mordantly piped up, "Can they hit Oxford, Mississippi?"

The black Irish humor, like the prep school cool, was for show, to keep up a brave front. In truth, Kennedy revered courage in a romantic, sentimental way that his friends found touching and revealing. In his daybook, where he dutifully recorded inspirational sayings, Kennedy quoted Winston Churchill's epigram that courage is "the first of human qualities because it is the quality which guarantees all others." In his well-thumbed copy of Emerson's *Essays,* he underlined "It was a high counsel that I once heard given to a young person, 'Always do what you are afraid to do.' "

Kennedy made a cult of courage. He collected brave men. General Maxwell Taylor, who had commanded a division of paratroopers on D-Day, was a frequent tennis partner and visitor to the Kennedy house, Hickory Hill. Mountain climber Whittaker and astronaut John Glenn often came, along with various professional athletes and Olympians. Kennedy would quiz them about their experiences. The questions were precise and practical, but aimed at eliciting deeper truths about the nature of valor.

Courage was a moral test that his enemies always failed. Lyndon Johnson was a "coward," Nelson Rockefeller had "no guts," Chester Bowles was a "weeper." To RFK, there could be no greater reward than a Congressional Medal of Honor for bravery under fire. In 1963, President Kennedy hosted a reception at the White House for all of America's surviving Medal of Honor winners. Over 250 heroes from America's wars gathered in the Rose Garden, chatting and joking with President Kennedy. JFK, a war hero himself who handed out tie clips fashioned in the shape of his old PT boat, basked easily in the reflected glory. RFK, on the other hand, stood off at the edge of the crowd, watching silently. His eyes, observed White House aide Kenneth O'Donnell, were "full of fascination." The younger Kennedy, who kept a copy of General Douglas MacArthur's World War I Medal of Honor citation in his desk drawer, often spoke reverently of his own brothers' bravery.

Robert Kennedy missed combat in World War II. In 1946, he served as a seaman, second class, aboard a destroyer named after his brother, Joseph P. Kennedy Jr., a naval aviator who had perished after volunteering for a virtual suicide mission. Perhaps in part because he had never seen the real thing, Kennedy glorified war. He felt diminished that he had never been tested in battle. At a Georgetown dinner party in about 1960, when the guests played a parlor game, if you could do it all over, what would you be? Kennedy answered, "A paratrooper." He was thrilled when the president's military adviser, General Taylor, told him that he would have made it in his old unit, the 101st Airborne.

Left behind, unable to catch up to his war-hero brothers, he reconciled himself to a supporting role. He extolled their exploits, advanced the family cause, and carefully polished the Kennedy myth. The Medal of Honor ceremony at the White House was Robert Kennedy's idea. It was in keeping with the role he had created for himself, as the stage manager who worked behind the scenes, who sublimated his own ambitions to the larger cause of his family's success.

Kennedy, for much of his young life, was an acolyte. As a youth, he had been proud to be trained as an altar boy. He liked to be part of the ceremony, to help reenact a great drama, to serve the priest. Attending Catholic Mass as a grown man, he sometimes stepped over the rail to help out if he saw that an altar boy was missing and the priest needed a hand. He served his father, Joe, and his brother John in the same faithful, unembarrassed way, attending to them, celebrating them, helping them produce the grand drama of their lives. He outgrew his altar boy role; to his foes he sometimes looked more like Cardinal Richelieu, lurking behind the throne. He was without question a forceful executor of his brother's will. Yet he did not often or easily imagine himself succeeding his brother as president.

Then, with brutal suddenness, Robert Kennedy stood alone. JFK was dead. Their father, crippled by a stroke, could only utter the word "no." Robert Kennedy had no one left to serve and protect. He had to remake himself, to find a new role. He escaped into brooding for a long time, then slowly rejoined the world. Events pulled at him, forced him to weigh his capacity to lead—and his courage. Anguished, uncertain, he hesitated, pulled back—then lunged forward. His entry into the 1968 presidential race—criticized as belated and opportunistic at the time—required an act of tremendous personal will. Kennedy was able to transform himself from follower and behind-the-scenes operator to popular leader in part by conveying, in an urgent, raw way, his identification with the underdog.

THIS IS THE STORY of an unpromising boy who died as he was becoming a great man. There was very little about young Robert F. Kennedy that foretold a grand or tragic destiny. Overshadowed by his more glamorous and accomplished siblings as a little boy, he was small, clumsy, and fearful. His father slighted him, while hovering about the older children, particularly Joe Jr. and John. Desperate to win his father's attention and respect, Kennedy became a hard man for a long while, covering over his sensitivity and capacity for empathy with a carapace of arrogance. But never entirely: his humility was always a saving grace. He might have made an unusual and gifted national leader, one who was able to both feel for and challenge his people.

He lives on in our imagination of what might have been. Robert Kennedy is one of history's great what-ifs. He was a Zelig of power—at the vortex, it seemed, of every crisis of the 1960s, a decade that sometimes felt like one long crisis. He was centrally engaged in most of the great epics of the postwar era—McCarthyism, the civil rights movement, the superpower confrontation, Vietnam. He was an essential player in the most severe test of the Cold War, the Cuban Missile Crisis. He had vast influence when JFK was in the White House. His brother gave him virtually unlimited discretion—and he exceeded it. Sure of his standing with the president, he scorned yes-men and surrounded himself with confident achievers. He did overreach at times, and he could be a bully. Yet in tight spots, under pressure, he often demonstrated that rare and ineffable quality, good judgment. He was at once honorable and cunning. At certain critical moments in his brother's presidency—and the nation's history—he both connived and stood fast to advance the causes of peace and justice. Nonetheless, he never had the chance to develop and carry out his own vision.

He seemed so young when he died. He *was* young—only forty-two, a year younger than JFK had been upon his election as the second-youngest president in the nation's history. But Robert Kennedy somehow seemed younger, more boyish. With his buck teeth and floppy hair and shy gawkiness, he sometimes came across like an awkward teenager. At other times, he was almost childlike in his wonder and curiosity. RFK was regarded by many as "ruthless," and though the adjective stung, it often fit. Yet with children, his own as well as anyone else's, he was tender. When he spoke to them, he didn't feign affection. Children could feel his identification; they would follow after him, wrapping their arms around his leg and climbing into his lap.

"He had a child heart," said his friend, filmmaker George Stevens. "A gentleness and playfulness and a trace of innocence." Robert Coles, the child psychiatrist who became a friend of RFK's through their shared interest in poor children, observed that even as boys, the older Kennedy siblings were expected to behave like men. RFK, on the other hand, was allowed to be a child, and in some ways never grew up. As an adult, Kennedy retained childlike mannerisms. Put off by someone or something, he would stick out his tongue or make a face. Sitting on a podium listening to a speaker he did not like, he would squirm and look petulant or bored. He was "a little boy in his enthusiasms," said Coles, capable of showing childish delight over something so simple as licking an ice cream cone. Kennedy once engaged Coles in an animated conversation debating the relative virtues of different flavors of ice cream—vanilla, strawberry, and chocolate (RFK's personal favorite). On the campaign trail, Kennedy liked to end the day by eating a big bowl of ice cream (while at the same time sipping a Heineken beer). Kennedy was not unself-aware. Once, as a crowd pressed in on Kennedy, someone cried, "There's a little boy there! Watch out!" The person was referring to a small child who had become caught in the crush, but Kennedy felt the identification instantly. Without missing a beat, he remarked, "Yes, he's a U.S. senator."

And yet, at other times—for days at a time—he seemed prematurely aged, possessed by morbidity. "Doom was woven in your nerves," Robert Lowell wrote in a poem about him. He seemed especially haunted after JFK was assassinated in 1963. Kennedy had never been very forthcoming about his feelings, but now, with his brother killed, he seemed to be holding back, almost as if he were hiding something. He would withdraw, staring out into space, or lose himself in reading. He seemed to be searching, groping for an answer. Mary Bailey Gimbel, a friend since school days, recalled him lugging around a heavy tome of Western literature "like a football." The only writing he liked in it, he told her, was a story about a French poet named Gérard de Nerval who walked with a lobster on a leash. In the story, a friend asked the poet why. The poet replied, "He doesn't bark, and he knows the secrets of the deep."

Kennedy had his own secrets. He was known for his candor—indeed, for his bluntness. But at the same time he carefully compartmentalized information. His closest aides understood that he rarely, if ever, told everything to any one person. He had learned, partly from his father, to use private back channels to accomplish difficult or sensitive tasks. He routinely circumvented the bureaucracy in his relentless pursuit of the Mafia and Cuban dictator Fidel Castro, not trusting even the CIA to keep his secrets. For public consumption, Kennedy accepted the finding that JFK was not the victim of a conspiracy, but rather had been killed by a deranged lone gunman. Privately, RFK could never quiet his fear that his own enemies had struck back by killing his brother.

On the night JFK died, a friend heard RFK, alone in a White House bedroom, cry out, "Why, God?" His Catholic faith in a good God was shaken. In visible pain—"like a man on the rack," said one friend—he cast about for a way to make sense of the despair he felt. At the suggestion of his brother's widow, Jacqueline Kennedy, he began reading the plays and writings of the ancient Greeks. In the plays of Aeschylus and Sophocles, Kennedy discovered fate and hubris. He began to wonder if the Kennedy family had somehow overreached, dared too greatly. In his copy of Edith Hamilton's *The Greek Way*, he had underlined Herodotus: "All arrogance will reap a harvest rich in tears. God calls men to a heavy reckoning for overweening pride." Comparing oneself to an actor in a Greek tragedy may seem pretentious, and inconsistent with RFK's customary self-deprecation, but Robert Kennedy had an epic sense of his own family. The Kennedys *were* the House of Atreus, noble and doomed, and RFK began to see himself as Agamemnon. RFK also saw himself as Shakespeare's Henry V. When Robert Lowell derided the comparison as trite, Kennedy argued with the poet, pulling down a volume of Shakespeare's Histories and reading from Henry IV's deathbed scene. ("For what in me was purchased,/Falls upon thee in a more fairer sort. . . .") "Henry the Fourth," said Kennedy, without apparent irony, "that's my father."

Fate was to be accepted—but not passively, resignedly. The former C-student regarded as a black-and-white dogmatist by his foes began carrying Albert Camus in his pocket. He became an existentialist, without at the same time abandoning his faith in God. He refused to accept the bleakness of a godless world, though he was troubled that God could allow a Hitler or the suffering of small children. He had been a romantic Catholic who believed that it was possible to create the Kingdom of Heaven on earth. He lost the certainty of his faith but never the hope. He believed that one had to keep trying. His philosophy, which he urged on others and truly tried to live by himself, was: we may all be doomed, but each man must define himself anew each day by his own actions. Action relieved Kennedy from dwelling on his fate, while leading him to it.

THE YEAR 1968 was one that cried out for action. It was a time that, in retrospect, seems overripe and overwrought, but to ordinary Americans watching the disturbing images on TV—young people burning the flag, soldiers burning villages, blacks burning their own neighborhoods—the feeling was ominous, pre-revolutionary. In Vietnam, the generals had stopped giving speeches about the light at the end of the tunnel. Now, as the Viet Cong's surprise Tet offensive exploded in February, Walter Cronkite was joining the longhairs looking for a way out. In Detroit and Newark in "the long hot summer" of 1967, snipers had opened up on firemen, and President Johnson had sent in paratroopers and tanks. In the summer of 1968, many whites feared angry blacks would try to burn the cities down. The national crisis called for a leader who was unafraid, who could bring together angry blacks and students and the blue collar workers who feared and loathed them. At once a radical and a moderate pragmatist, Robert Kennedy cast himself as the only one who could reach across the divide.

Yet he balked. He thought and talked incessantly about running for president, but he could not bring himself to declare. He liked to say that his brother's favorite quote was from Dante, that the hottest places in hell are reserved for those who in times of moral crisis preserve their neutrality. But through the winter of 1967–68 he equivocated. He did not want to destroy the Democratic Party, said his protectors. He did not want to start a civil war with President Johnson that would ruin his own political future and in the end elect Richard

Nixon and prolong the war. Beware of hubris. Do not invite a second tragedy. He was, for all his activism, a prudent man, and he had no time for lost causes.

Or possibly, he was afraid. Kennedy would have made a courageous small-unit commander in combat, the kind who slept with the troops and led the charge. But as a politician, he could appear shy and small and slouched; his hands trembled; he recoiled from the backslapping and insincerity of election-eering. Curiously, for someone whose family helped invent mass media poli-tics, he was terrible on TV. He was too intense, not facile, and the camera caught the haunted look. More profoundly, he had not been raised to be a leader in the grand or visionary sense. If he overreached for power, would he tempt his brother's fate? Kennedy was fatalistic in the extreme. If the police passed on a threat, and his aides tried to hustle him out the back, he would insist on leaving by the front door. Yet he could not entirely hide his fear. His administrative aide in the Senate, Joe Dolan, would not tell Kennedy about most threats, but if there was a really serious one, Dolan would try to be nearby to warn and pro-tect. "I was always the angel of death," Dolan recalled. "I wouldn't show up at his events unless there was a real threat." Kennedy understood this and was not at all glad to run into his loyal aide unexpectedly. Once, as he was leaving a polling place in Manhattan, he stumbled across Dolan standing in line outside. Kennedy visibly flinched at his angel's shadow.

As he dithered in the winter of '67–'68, the crowds and the pundits taunted him. He saw a protester waving a sign, "Kennedy: Hawk, Dove—or Chicken." He hated it. He kept a letter in his wallet from a journalist friend re-minding him of the photos of John F. Kennedy that hung on the walls of poor people around the world. "This is your obligation," the letter implored. His wife, Ethel, urged him to run, despite the obvious dangers. As fierce in her own way as her husband, she understood that he had to run. Ethel preferred to look at the world in black and white, the good guys (her husband, always) versus the bad guys (her husband's foes). A determined optimist, she would not permit herself to contemplate gloomy outcomes. RFK, by contrast, was a brooder who could easily imagine the worst. But he knew that his wife was right—that if he did not run, he would never be able to live with himself. And so, on March 16, 1968, he declared his candidacy.

Viewed three decades later, the films and photographs of Robert Kennedy's eighty-one-day campaign seem feverish, almost hysterical. Not just the jumpers and screamers waving signs that said "Bobby Is Sexy," "Bobby Is Groovy," "I Love You Bobby," but the farmers and workers and housewives who closed in on him, clutching at him, pulling him from his car, and (twice) stealing the shoes off his feet. They came out, at first, to cheer the myth of Camelot restored. They saw instead a raw, sometimes reticent young man struggling to be honest with them and with himself. His speeches were effec-tive not so much for their words, which, when scripted, were usually bland, or their delivery, which was often flat or awkward, but for something more ineffa-ble: the body language, the aura, the emanations of compassion and under-standing that Kennedy conveyed. Inarticulate but urgent and sincere, Kennedy could reach poor and dispossessed people who themselves had difficulty articulating their needs and anxieties. People loved him even though he challenged, even baited them, to overcome their fears and narrow self-interest. He would embarrass middle-class college students—whose support he desperately wanted—by belittling their draft deferments, pointing out that the casualties in Vietnam were disproportionately suffered by minorities and the poor. When a medical student asked him who would pay for better care for the poor, he answered bluntly: "You will." Measured by the poll-driven caution of the stereotypical politician, Kennedy's willingness to speak hard truths seems almost quaint. But it worked to inspire many voters, particularly those most alienated from conventional politics.

The intensity was so great, the yearning and devotion so palpable, that the inevitability of Kennedy's victory in 1968 has become an enduring political myth. In fact, as his campaign entered the final day before the California primary that June, his advisers were very worried. "We were losing altitude, though the Kennedys today don't like to admit it," recalled Fred Dutton, Kennedy's top aide on the campaign plane. Defeated by Eugene McCarthy in Oregon, way behind Vice President Hubert Humphrey in the delegate count, Kennedy himself understood that if he failed to win California, he was out of the race.

KENNEDY'S SOLUTION, as always, was to try harder. On the Monday before the Tuesday vote, he intended to travel from Los Angeles to San Francisco, back to Watts and Long Beach, on to San Diego, and back to L.A.—1,200 miles in thirteen hours. His aides wanted to hit the three major TV markets in a single news cycle. Kennedy, whose father took home movies as footage for the family myth and whose brother spent hours choosing which photographs to release to the press, understood the practical necessities. But at times he drifted along in a dreamy reverie. From time to time he would think of the Ulysses of his favorite poem by Tennyson, which he often quoted in his slightly self-dramatizing way—wishing "to sail beyond the sunset, and the baths of all the western stars, until I die."

Generations of office seekers have tried to model themselves on Robert F. Kennedy, as politicians able to exude sensitivity, moral force, and a touch of glamour—while doing whatever it took to win. Beyond warmed-over rhetoric, haircuts, and hand gestures, none have succeeded. Kennedy was one of a kind. He was consumed by an inner flame. On this last day, he seemed on the verge of burning out.

As the motorcade crept through San Francisco's Chinatown that Monday morning, there was a series of loud pops. In any Kennedy motorcade post–November 1963, a sound that seemed to echo gunfire was an instant source of panic. Ethel Kennedy "dove for the bottom of the car," recalled Bill Eppridge, a *Life* magazine photographer in the car just ahead of the Kennedys. Robert Kennedy, standing on the rear hood of a convertible, remained upright and continued to wave to the surging crowd. But Karl Fleming, a *Newsweek* correspondent who was running alongside the motorcade, saw Kennedy's knees buckle. The campaign entourage and traveling press were all "scared to death," remembered Eppridge. "Everyone remembered Dallas." The explosions were only firecrackers. Seeing that Ethel was badly shaken, Kennedy asked a newspaper reporter, Richard Harwood of the *Washington Post*, to comfort her. Harwood climbed into the car and held her hand.

After Chinatown and another rally at Fisherman's Wharf, Kennedy flew to Los Angeles. Burgeoning, fast-forward California was in many ways the perfect test for Kennedy. It was a vast mixing bowl in danger of becoming a cauldron. The first of the urban race riots of the 1960s had erupted in Watts in 1965. The white middle classes in their bungalows and tract houses, the voters who had elected Ronald Reagan governor, feared that the fire next time would be in their backyards. To some, Kennedy was a peacemaker, but to others he was merely an instigator. He needed to challenge and soothe all at once, a tricky task for someone who still had to steel himself to appear in large public forums. In Long Beach, Kennedy was engulfed by six thousand people. As usual, the crowd was enormous and edgy. An agitated man kept calling out, "How 'bout your brother? Who killed your brother?" Kennedy stumbled; his delivery was flat, his attempts at humor forced. "He seemed spaced-out, like he had gone off someplace," observed *Newsweek*'s Karl Fleming, who was watching from the crowd. Back in the car, Fred Dutton, who understood Kennedy's low tolerance for insincere flattery, told the candidate that his speech had not gone well. "I don't feel good," said Kennedy. Dutton was taken aback. Kennedy subsisted on four hours a night of sleep, almost never got sick, and never complained if he did.

The motorcade headed down an avenue in the black inner-city neighborhood of Watts, where the stores were still burnt out from the rioting three years before. The Los Angeles Police Department was nowhere to be seen. The mayor of Los Angeles, Sam Yorty, regarded RFK as a subversive. In downtown L.A. a few days earlier, a policeman had improbably given the Kennedy motorcade a ticket for running a red light. Security, such as it was, was provided by a militant group called Sons of Watts. Ethel, sitting in Kennedy's car, did not seem reassured. Her customary sunniness had, for the moment, clouded over. "I looked into her face," said Marie Ridder, a friend and journalist who was working as a reporter for campaign chronicler Theodore H. White. "It was a mask of such concern and fear—fear is not the right word—it was tenderer than that. It was: what's going to happen?"

Dutton was eager to get out of the ghetto. "We knew that coming to Watts would look bad on TV that night. California is full of Okies and Iowans. TV is a cool medium and we were too hot, too emotional." Dutton and other top advisers had been trying to tone down the campaign. "Bob understood this, rationally, when he was sitting in a hotel room," said Dutton. "But out there. . . .." Dutton paused as he recollected; he seemed suddenly weary, as if he had gone back thirty years in time and was trying, futilely, to reason with a force of nature. Shy and uncertain, Kennedy fed off the crowds.

Fortunately, the candidate was, as usual, running behind schedule; Dutton was able to steer the motorcade into a quiet residential neighborhood to make up time—and escape the mob. As the press bus raced down a deserted street, assistant press secretary Richard Drayne asked aloud, "What is this? Are we going house hunting?"

IN SAN DIEGO, night was falling. In the semi-darkness, black children squealed "Bobby! Bobby!" as the motorcade pushed through Logan Heights, a poor district on the edge of downtown. Kennedy's driver was Stuart Bloch, a young onetime volunteer. Bloch had simply been given a credit card in the name of Joseph P. Kennedy ("that's how we charge everything," an aide had explained) and been told to rent a white convertible. Greeting Kennedy at the airport, Bloch was surprised by his weak handshake. "It was like a noodle. He seemed shy, mousy. He kept looking at the ground." In the car, Ethel scolded Bloch to watch out for the children. Kennedy seemed to revive, rejuvenated by the squealing kids, whose natural energy seemed so out of place in the dusty, exhausted streets. Kennedy's bodyguard, Roosevelt Grier, an all-pro tackle for the Los Angeles Rams, held Kennedy by the waist as the candidate leaned out, his arms stretched wide so he looked like a human cross, swinging from side to side. The children squealed and waved and smiled, their teeth flashing white in the gloaming. After a while Kennedy, spent, fell into the front seat with Ethel, who anxiously stroked her husband's forehead, feeling for fever.

The motorcade arrived at Kennedy's last rally of the campaign three hours late. About three thousand people had crammed into a ballroom at the El Cortez Hotel. A few minutes into his speech, Kennedy nearly collapsed. He abruptly sat down on the stage and put his head in his hands. Grier hustled him into a bathroom, where he threw up. He lay on the floor while Grier knelt and mopped his head. He rose and walked back into the ballroom and finished his speech, ending, as he always did, by paraphrasing George Bernard Shaw. Kennedy's talents as an orator may have been limited, but his Boston twang became more resonant as he delivered his familiar peroration: "Some men see things as they are, and ask why," said Kennedy. "I dream of things that never were, and ask why not."

It was nearly midnight when he took off for Los Angeles. "He just shriveled up," said Bloch. On the plane, Ethel told the staff and the reporters to leave them alone. The usually boisterous press corps quieted. Kennedy rested. He was not really ill, just done in. He had given all he had. In a few hours, he would learn if it was enough.

HISTORIANS HAVE ARGUED ever since that night about what Kennedy might have become, just as journalists and commentators in his lifetime debated who he really was. The Good Bobby/Bad Bobby dichotomy, limned by cartoonist Jules Feiffer, became a cliché even before he died. Was he the hard, bullying, McCarthyite, wiretapping, Hoffa-Castro–obsessed hater forever scowling and vowing to "get" his enemies? Or was he the gentle, child-loving, poetry-reading, soulful herald of a new age? Liberals and conservatives have laid equal claim to his legacy. If Bobby had lived, he would have united the races and—at the cost of billions, but worth every penny—saved the cities, cured rural poverty, and uplifted the American Indian. No, if Bobby had lived, he would have ended welfare, abolished racial preference, and made personal responsibility the crucible of rich and poor alike. Hawks and doves have tugged and pulled: he drew the world back from the abyss in the Cuban Missile Crisis and would have yanked every American soldier out of Vietnam; no, he was the original war lover who turned for foreign policy advice to generals who were intellectually self-confident, and hence the most dangerous kind. Then, of course, there is the endless debate—it sputters and flares decades later—over whether Bobby really changed. He was *always* changing, goes the argument; he had an experiencing nature that led him to constantly reexamine and transform himself. Nonsense, counter many of his oldest friends (and most of his family). He was born gentle—and also born tough.

None of these images is wholly right; none wholly wrong. Only two Bobbies? asks Robert Coles. Why not four or five? Without thinking hard, Coles began ticking them off: Bobby the idealist. Bobby the plotter. Bobby the adventurer. Bobby the family man. How about Bobby the chief law enforcement officer who saw himself as a juvenile delinquent? Categorizing him is a futile exercise; the contradictions too confusing. There is no model that suffices to encompass the varieties of his nature, plain and half hidden.

A better way to understand him is to examine his fear. Kennedy spent most of his life struggling to face down demons from within and without. He was brave *because* he was afraid. His monsters were too large and close at hand to simply flee. He had to turn and fight them. Kennedy, who romanticized guerrilla fighters, became one himself. The self-destructive frontal assaults of his youth gave way to more clever and sometimes devious raids and insurgencies. He became a one-man underground, honeycombed with hidden passages, speaking in code, trusting no one completely, ready to face the firing squad—but also knowing when to slip away to fight again another day. Although he affected simplicity and directness, he became an extraordinarily complicated and subtle man. His shaking hands and reedy voice, his groping for words as well as meaning, his occasional resort to subterfuge, do not diminish his daring. Precisely because he was fearful and self-doubting, his story is an epic of courage. He did not give in.

Kennedy's "house had many mansions," said Coles. "Bobby had to live with complexity and contradiction to survive in the world—and in his own family. It gave him great flexibility, and the ability to live with secrets." We know some of those secrets, and, over time, we will learn more. But we will never know them all. We will not know about the cryptic conversations with Joe Sr. and Jack, the almost nonverbal signals between family members who communicated by grunts and through indirection. Unlike his cautious kinsmen, however, Robert Kennedy was a plunger and risk taker, a seeker open to the new. Because he could be raw and unguarded—his emotions so close to the surface that he seemed to visibly itch—we can see honest struggles suppressed by others of his clan. He is the light in the family cave.

Unlike his older brothers, Robert Kennedy was not born and raised for power, so he was not required to hide behind a mask of command. His sensitivity was not, like theirs, sealed over by premature adulthood. In his vulnerability, he found strength. He was rarely happy, certainly not content. But he never lost his childlike wonder and capacity for awe, for tenderness, and for rage. In his family, he was the most fierce and the most vulnerable, the Kennedy who most intensely experienced the range of human emotions. He was, in a way, the lucky one.

CHAPTER **1** RUNT

FOR ALL HIS DESIRE to shape and promote his children, Joseph P. Kennedy does not seem to have paid much attention to the schooling of his third son and seventh child. In September 1939, Kennedy Sr. enrolled thirteen-year-old Robert at St. Paul's School, an establishment training ground, but within a month RFK was gone. St. Paul's was too Protestant for his mother, Rose. In early October, Ambassador Kennedy wired Rose that it would be acceptable to send Bobby to the local day school near their house in Bronxville, New York. Instead, Rose sent Bobby to Portsmouth Priory, a small boys' school run by Benedictine monks. There is no record that Joe objected, or even particularly noticed.

The ambassador was intensely preoccupied at the time. On September 1, a few weeks before Bobby entered St. Paul's, Germany invaded Poland. Ambassador Kennedy, who had hoped to hold back Hitler with appeasement, called President Franklin Roosevelt and cried out, "It's the end of the world, the end of everything." Kennedy was intensely fearful that his two draft-age sons, Joe Jr. and Jack, would be swept away by a world war. He was not unduly concerned with whether his third son was reading from a Protestant prayer book at morning chapel.

Set on a windswept hillside above Narragansett Bay in Rhode Island, Portsmouth Priory aimed to funnel the sons of well-to-do Catholics to Harvard and Yale, not Holy Cross or Fordham. Supported by newly prosperous Irish families in Boston and New York, the school flourished at first. But when the Depression hit in the '30s, the money for a second brick dormitory dried up. The boys lived in wooden prefabs so drafty that they hung blankets in the windows and mockingly called their school Beaverboard Prep.

Bobby was ill-suited to life in a boys' dormitory. Not yet fourteen, he was shy and sweet. He had been very attentive to Luella Hennessey, his nanny. She recalled his making a great show of asking the police to stop traffic in busy London intersections so that she could cross the street. When she returned to the ambassador's residence after a free afternoon, Bobby would rush past the footmen and swing open the door for her. Bobby was even more considerate to his mother. In the evenings, when Rose Kennedy went out, as she often did, he would wait by the front door to tell her how beautiful she looked. Years later Hennessey wondered if Bobby, sensing his mother's loneliness and isolation, was trying to comfort her. "He was so close to her," said Hennessey, adding, in an unguarded moment, "Someone had to be."

Within his family, Bobby was described, with some derision, as his mother's "pet." To be allied with Rose was to be at the wrong end of the table in the Kennedy household. Within the Kennedy family there was a clear hierarchy of talents and expectations. The older boys and their sister Kathleen ("Kick") were the "golden trio," the children deemed most likely to succeed. Bright, athletic, outgoing, they shone in their father's eye. His boundless ambitions lay with them, especially the oldest boy, Joe Jr. Lost in a crowd of younger girls—Eunice, Pat, and Jean—Bobby, born in 1925, ten years after Joe Jr. and eight years after Jack, had to turn to his mother for attention. Vivacious and intelligent as a young girl, Rose Fitzgerald Kennedy was a proper and ambitious matron. But she had been subtly undermined, first by her dominating father, who denied her heartfelt wish to go to Wellesley and sent her to a convent school instead, and then by her husband, whose show of marital respect did not include fidelity. By the time Bobby was a boy in the early 1930s, Rose was somewhat fey and emotionally detached, consoling herself against Joe's indiscretions by piety and periodic withdrawal into a make-believe world of fashion and royalty. Rose could join in the dinner table teasing and she still "managed" the family, setting schedules and acting as day-to-day disciplinarian, but Joe was the vital center. At family dinners, while Joe argued politics with Joe Jr. and John (switching sides from time to time to keep the debate alive), Bobby sat quiet and apart with the younger girls. Bobby's grandmother, Josie Fitzgerald, worried about Bobby's spending so much time surrounded by women. She feared he would become a "sissy." Rose, too, worried that RFK would become "puny" and "girlish." Joe Sr. seems' to have written him off. Joe Kennedy wanted his sons to be conquerors, strong and independent men who could push their way into the Protestant establishment but owe loyalty to no one save their family. There was no room in this plan for a sweet momma's boy. Lem Billings, Jack's Choate roommate, remarked to Joe Sr. that Bobby was "the most generous little boy." Joe Sr. gruffly replied, "I don't know where he got that." The only similarity between father and son that Billings could discern was in their eyes, a kind of icy pale blue.

The Kennedy household was full of laughter, but it was often at someone else's expense. The older children learned to give back as good as they got. As a little boy, Bobby was not quick. He suffered in awkward silence or turned his humor on himself. Bobby was, in his father's description, the "runt" of the family. He was not only smaller and slower than his brothers, he *looked* afraid.

He lacked the jaunty, glowing air of a young Kennedy. A group portrait taken in about 1935, when Bobby was ten, shows the other Kennedy children looking sporty and sure. Bobby, however, perches by his mother's side, his face tense with anxiety. His siblings cut him no slack. Teased hard, Bobby would look crushed. Rose would console him. "You're *my* favorite," she would say, in a half-kidding tone. In about 1939, the same year RFK left for boarding school, a friend asked his sister Eunice how the Kennedy brood was doing. All very well, except for Bobby, came the reply. He was "hopeless" and would "never amount to anything." Many years later, Robert Kennedy seemed to have felt the same way about himself. He told writer Jack Newfield, "What I remember most vividly about growing up was going to a lot of different schools, always having to make new friends, and that I was very awkward. I dropped things and fell down all the time. I had to go to the hospital a few times for stitches in my head and my leg. And I was pretty quiet most of the time. And I didn't mind being alone."

At Portsmouth Priory, he was known as "Mrs. Kennedy's little boy Bobby," said David Meehan, his fourth form (sophomore) roommate. Robert would bring his mother around and gravely introduce her to the other boys, who predictably made fun of him and her. Bobby was hotly defensive of his mother. A boy in the class below, Pierce Kearney, passed along a mild dig he had heard from his own mother—that Mrs. Kennedy used so much lipstick she looked "like a Hollywood star." Bobby screamed at Kearney, "How can you say such a thing!" and chased the younger boy out of the dormitory. Kennedy defended himself with a temper and a contemptuous air. He was regarded by most as standoffish. "He didn't invite friends," recalled Cleve Thurber, a classmate. "He wanted to be alone. This was his choice, but people saw it as snobbery." In the survival-of-the-fittest world of an all-boys school and in the even more Darwinian competition of his own family, RFK discovered sarcasm as a defense. Eager to please, he was sweet. Unable to please, he was caustic. Kennedy was "not arrogant," said another classmate, Frank Hurley, "but he had a sarcasm that could be biting."

The monks who ran the school regarded him as a moody and indifferent student. "He didn't look happy, he didn't smile much," said Father Damian Kearney, who was two classes behind RFK and later became a teacher at Portsmouth Priory (the school was renamed Portsmouth Abbey in 1967). According to Father Damian, who reviewed RFK's records, Kennedy "was a poor-to-mediocre student, except for history." He was a dogged but uncoordinated athlete. "Bob had trouble with his hands," said Father Damian. "He dropped things. It was recommended that he squeeze a tennis ball. He was self-conscious about it until he was told that [heavyweight boxing champion] Gene Tunney did it." (Kennedy's tendency to drop things was "not a physical problem," recalled his sister Eunice. "He just didn't pay attention.") Kennedy's records show considerable correspondence between Mrs. Kennedy and the school. "She was intensely concerned about the minutiae. Nothing was too trivial," said Father Damian. "Bob's handwriting was atrocious. Couldn't the

school get a calligrapher for him?" Bobby Kennedy enjoyed a brief moment of
fame when he spotted a fire in the barn then being used as a gym. Joe Kennedy
Sr. gave the school $2,000 towards a new gym, almost enough, said Father
Damian, "to build a squash court."

Mostly, though, Bobby stood out for his religiosity. As a little boy, he had
served as an altar boy at St. Joseph's Roman Catholic Church in Bronxville. He
was more pious than his siblings, showing off to them his knowledge of church
Latin. Kennedys were taught that they belonged on a great stage. They were
introduced by their ambitious father to the president, the pope, and the queen
of England. They posed for newspapers and absorbed their father's gospel of
winning. The older, more confident children were clearly groomed to take their
rightful place alongside the movers and shakers. For Bobby, the overlooked
"runt," the future was perhaps not so clear. But as an altar boy, he was able to
play a small but indispensable role in reenacting the greatest drama in the history of the Christian world, Christ's Last Supper. As he swung the censer and
smelled the incense, waving the perfumed smoke in the processional, or ringing the bell as the priest consecrated the bread and wine into the body and
blood of Christ, Kennedy could forget, for a moment, his insignificance at the
family dinner table. He had found a place, a minor and subservient part, to be
sure, in support of more blessed and worthy men, but still essential and
charged with mystery and meaning.

At Portsmouth, where "most boys wore the Catholic mantle very lightly,"
said his classmate Frank Hurley, Bobby went to mass more than the required
three times a week and was often seen lingering afterwards, as if seeking
refuge. He once prayed for three straight hours, though he was careful to mask
the experience in self-deprecating sarcasm when he wrote home. "I feel like a
saint," he wrote, trying to be droll, lest anyone think he was taking himself too
seriously.

Bobby could be dryly funny, but he was not lighthearted. He lacked the
careless charm of his older siblings, who mocked him for his heaviness. His
brother Jack, the Kennedy who worked the hardest at being effortless, called
him Black Robert. In a later era of child-rearing, RFK would have been described, perhaps diagnosed, as depressed. In the summer of 1940, a few weeks
after Bobby came home from his first year at Portsmouth, Rose wrote an anxious letter to Joe Sr. at the American embassy in London. Their son Jack, who
had just graduated from Harvard, was having "the most astounding success"
with his college thesis-turned-bestseller, *Why England Slept*, Rose reported.
But "Bobby is a different mold. He does not seem to be interested particularly
in reading or sailing or his stamps. He does a little work in all three, but no special enthusiasm. . . ." On July 11, she wrote Joe, "I am trying to get Bob to do
some reading. He doesn't seem to care for sailing as much as the other boys. Of
course he doesn't want to go to any of the dances. . . ." To not do the "work" of
sailing at Hyannis was a significant dereliction. Kennedys were supposed to
win on the water. In 1937, her first summer working as a nanny for the
Kennedys, Luella Hennessey crewed for Jack in a race. When the wind began to

die, he told her to jump overboard to lighten the boat and allow it to go faster. "He wasn't kidding," she recalled.

Other families muttered about the Kennedys' win-or-else ethic. Joe Kennedy had brought his family to the low-key summer colony in the mid-1920s from slightly tonier Cohasset after he had been blackballed by the Cohasset Golf Club. The WASPs of Hyannis were somewhat more accepting, but anti-Irish prejudice lingered. The comfortable white-shingled house bought by Kennedy for his family was locally known as the Irish House. Decades later, members of the yacht club grumbled that the Kennedy children—frequent trophy winners in the 1930s—had cheated by adding extra canvas to their sails. The older siblings by and large ignored the sniping. But Bobby was more easily wounded. From an early age, he seems to have been the most self-consciously Irish of the brood, the one who identified most closely with the Irish history of oppression. In 1967, in an article in *Look* magazine, Bobby suggested that his father had left Boston in 1927 because of the signs that said "No Irish Need Apply." An editor at another magazine wrote to gently chide him for exaggerating, pointing out that when Joe Kennedy's family left Boston that year, it was in a private railway car. "Yes but—It was symbolic," Bobby wrote back. "The business establishment, the clubs, the golf course—at least that was what I was told at a very young age. . . ."

Extremely defensive about his family, he seemed to have responded to his own low standing in the family hierarchy by adopting a rigid and fierce protectiveness about the family name. He was in awe of his father and older siblings; feeling insignificant, he may have felt that the family name was all he had. In the fall of 1940, his second year at Portsmouth, Joe Kennedy became the object of intense public scorn. The ambassador was increasingly pessimistic about the war raging in Europe. That November, he foolishly told some newspapermen, "Democracy is all done. . . . Democracy is finished in England. It may be here." The remarks finished Kennedy as ambassador to England. At school, in angry shouting matches and sometimes with his fists, Bobby defended his father against charges of defeatism. When Kennedy Sr. slightly redeemed himself with a speech defending President Roosevelt's lend-lease program for England in January, Bobby optimistically wrote his mother from school, "I listened to Daddy['s] speech last night and I thought it was wonderful. I think it was the best speech that he ever made. I thought he really cleared himself from what people had been saying about him. . . ." Bobby had apparently been receiving some hate mail himself. In the same letter, he told his mother, "I got another one of those Post cards telling me like the last one how awful we Catholics are."

From his spare and chilly dormitory, Bobby watched apprehensively as his family entered a bleak time in 1941. His post untenable, Joe Sr. came home in February. Roosevelt would not give his disgraced ambassador another appointment, at least not one Kennedy deemed worthy enough, so he brooded. Sitting with a friend in Palm Beach, he gloomily watched the ocean undermine the seawall in front of his house. He wasn't going to fix it, he said. Let it go. The world was collapsing anyway. His oldest daughter, Rosemary, now twenty-three, was increasingly given to tantrums and outbursts. Kennedy was afraid that she would become uncontrollable and was especially fearful that she might throw herself at a man. That summer, he arranged to have her undergo a radical new medical procedure, a lobotomy, to cut off the frontal lobe of her brain. Something went wrong with the operation. Rosemary emerged not just quieter but zombie-like. Totally unable to care for herself, she had to be institutionalized.

Kennedy did not tell his own wife the nature of the operation. Rose was informed only that Rosemary, whom she had struggled to give a near-normal life, was being sent away, and that Rose—for her own good—would not be able to visit her for a long time. The rest of the family was told almost nothing. Their sister simply disappeared.

A mystery so strange and awful can haunt a family for generations. Yet the Kennedy children, Robert included, were accustomed to living with secrets. Joseph Kennedy was a secretive man. His phone was equipped with a special cupped mouthpiece to thwart eavesdroppers. He never discussed his business activities with his children. They could see him sitting in his "bullpen," an enclosure that allowed him to conduct business while he sunbathed in Palm Beach or Hyannis. But they could only wonder to whom he was talking on the phone. He didn't want them to know. His job was to make the money that would free them to follow more noble pursuits.

There were other secrets less well kept. Since the day in 1929 when Joseph Kennedy landed in Hyannis in an amphibious plane and stepped out with Gloria Swanson, his older children could not miss the parade of women on his arm. After his barely concealed affair with the movie goddess, there were more actresses and models and "secretaries" sitting beside Joe in the movie theater he built in the basement of the Hyannis house. In 1941, Jack casually talked to a friend about his father's infidelities. He observed that Joe bought off Rose with presents, "a big Persian rug or some jewelry."

Bobby probably knew less about his father's indiscretions. But in his eagerness to please, he was keenly attuned to the moods of his parents. He must have sensed their remorse—and their alienation from each other—in the summer and fall of 1941. Like many sensitive children, he may have in some way blamed himself and tried even harder not to disappoint. His behavior in these months displays classic signs of teenage depression: withdrawal, overcompensation, then a self-destructive outburst to get attention.

Bobby was very down over Christmas vacation in Palm Beach during his third year at Portsmouth. His shyness became reclusiveness. Bobby is "very unsociable and should step out a little more," Rose wrote Joe just after New Year's 1942. "He absolutely refused to go to the Bath and Tennis [Club] and when he has gone out he doesn't seem to like any of the boys here." A week later, Bob's dismal grades from school arrived. "I was so disappointed in your report," Rose wrote her "favorite." "The mark in Christian Doctrine was very low . . . Please get on your toes," she instructed. "I do not expect my own little pet to let me down." It is doubtful that she realized how anxious he was to please her—and even more so, his indifferent father. Shortly after this scolding, he tried to prove his faithfulness by sending his pious mother "two or three recommendations about serving mass." He longed to correspond with his father about world events—he knew that Joe Jr. and Jack had routinely received missives from the ambassador. To prepare himself, Bob made his roommates quiz him every Sunday night on current affairs from the *New York Times* News of the Week in Review. But his father did not write. In Rose's chatty, newsy missives to her children, Bobby is mentioned only in passing, usually after the exploits of the older children.

While generally inarticulate and diffident, Bobby was capable of sudden, almost wild acts that can be seen as cries for help. His father insisted on punctuality, so Bobby was, his mother recalled, "spectacularly prompt." As a very little boy, rushing to make it to the table on time for dinner, he crashed through a glass partition, badly cutting his face. Slow to learn to swim, he apparently decided to hurry the process by plunging off a yawl into Nantucket Sound. His older brother Joe fished him out. "It showed either a lot of guts, or no sense at all, depending on how you looked at it," remarked his brother Jack. It was the first of many extreme shows of courage, or recklessness. His sister Eunice recalled watching Bobby stand on the edge of a very high cliff above a swimming grotto at Cap d'Antibes on the Riviera when he was about ten years old. "He'll never jump," she thought. But he did. In the winter of 1942, Bobby vanquished fear on the ski slopes at Lake Placid by skiing in a headlong way that was dangerous to himself and anyone near him. His oldest sister, Kathleen, commented on his performance with a kind of caustic wit familiar to visitors at the Kennedy dinner table. "Dearest Robert," she wrote,

> To say the descriptions of your escapades in the snowy hills of Northern New York are vivid would be putting it mildly. It sounds to me as if you left no poor man unscarred, and that anyone within a mile of your ski poles was subject to a hit or a narrow escape. Where did you ever get the idea you could ski in the first place? I never whispered such a fact into your large, cauliflower-like ear. Maybe the younger members of the clan said something like it but don't believe them—they're just a bunch of little liars.

Back at school, Bobby struggled to improve himself. He was on the sailing team, but "my sailing so far has been awful, and I lost a race yesterday in which I sailed poorly," he reported. He quit sailing to run track, he wrote home, "to see if I can't run faster." He hopefully reported that "our grades come out sometime this week and I think I did quite well and passed everything," but a week later his marks showed no improvement from the level that had so "let down" his parents.

His weak academic record was not the product of carelessness. Rather, he was famous as a grade-grubber. "Bob wanted to please his father—that was very important," recalled Frank Hurley. "He needed to get his grades up, and that was his motivation." "Bob would haggle over grades," recalled Father Julian Stead, a classmate who became a monk and returned to teach at Portsmouth. "If he got a 77, he would argue for a 78 and not give up. He was remembered for that quality more than any other student in the history of the school." Kennedy was clearly not stupid, but paralyzed by the prospect of failure, he could not pull his grades out of the 60s or 70s. He seemed to be flailing, not studying. In the late spring of 1942, as final exams approached, Bob Kennedy considered other, more drastic means.

"There was a lot of cheating," remembered Father Julian. "Many boys had no conscience about it. They cheated easily." The monks despaired over one boy, a southerner, who was such a sinner that he seemed consumed with hellfire. "If you threw holy water on him, he'd go up in smoke," the fathers joked. Years later, according to Father Julian, Bobby ruefully told a priest at the school, "All we thought about at school was cheating." Bobby himself did not "cheat easily." He was generally seen as a stickler for rules. Playing touch football (even then, a passion), he would preach "fairness," said Nick Reggio, who was a class above Kennedy. "He was always saying, 'That's not fair.' " He also obeyed the schoolboy code of never ratting on your mates, to the point of sacrificing himself. When a friend was caught using an automobile—strictly against the rules—Bobby insisted that he had been the one at the wheel. The other boy was already in disciplinary trouble and at risk of being thrown out. So Bobby took the rap and was put on bounds—confined to campus on the weekends. At sixteen, Bob was developing a sense of duty and honor. But he was also desperate.

At the end of his fourth form year, Robert Kennedy was caught in a cheating scandal. The incident was a poor end to his career at Portsmouth Priory, but it may also have given him an early lesson in scandal management and the importance of hiding embarrassing secrets. The facts are somewhat murky: a dozen schoolmates interviewed about the incident offered different details and disagreed over the degree of Kennedy's culpability. But his involvement appears beyond dispute.* Before finals that June, a purloined copy of an exam

---

* In 1997, I wrote to all the surviving members of the classes of '43 and '44 at Portsmouth. I received letters from or spoke to fourteen of his schoolmates. The very first I spoke to, a member of the class of '43 and Kennedy's roommate in the fall of 1941, insisted that RFK had stolen an English exam from the sock drawer of Harold E. Coogan, one of the masters in "New," Kennedy's dorm, and shown it to "half the class—8 to 10 boys." Kennedy "brought it back and let us all look at it. We all got A's. Because someone smelled a rat, he confessed and they kicked him out that day." Another member of the class, however, said that his classmate did not have his facts right. "Yes, there was an exam stolen from Mr. Coogan's underwear drawer and it was passed around. Everyone was caught, including me. The only person who was kicked out was not RFK. It was a southerner and he 'fessed up and was kicked out. Bob may have shared seeing it but he didn't take it. The exam was passed around the dorm. They didn't discharge the kids who saw the exam. We were put on probation and allowed back next term. There were eight to ten boys involved. I'll swear on a Bible." According to another classmate: "Yes, there was an exam taken—a math test taken out of the trash. I don't believe Bobby would have stolen it. He may have shared it and admitted it." Yet another

began making its way around Kennedy's dormitory. Pierce Kearney explicitly remembered handing the stolen exam to Kennedy. "I went into Bob's room and said, 'Bob, we have the exam!' He got so nervous. Should he take a peek? His hands were shaking. They shook like hell. I remember that. He was very, very uncomfortable." But the temptation was too much, the need was too great. He took the exam. Kennedy's roommate, Mike Egan, recalled Bob offering to share the test with him. Egan was a new boy from Savannah, Georgia. "I didn't know a soul." Kennedy sympathized with the younger newcomer. "Bob could be biting and sarcastic, and he wasn't appealing from a distance. But he was kind to me." As Egan recollected the story, "Someone passed the test on to Bob. He showed me the test, offered it to me. I was a goody-goody and refused."

Predictably, the cheating was found out. "We were caught because we did so well on the test," said Cleve Thurber, who said he was one of the "eight to ten boys involved." The scandal "got hushed up quickly," said Thurber. It is not clear who, if anyone, among the boys was kicked out. But Kennedy left school right away. Paul Wankowicz, a schoolmate, recalled seeing a large black chauffeured limousine pull up at Kennedy's dorm and remove Kennedy and his luggage before the end of the term. Wankowicz had heard that Kennedy had been kicked out, though he wasn't sure why (one improbable rumor: Kennedy had been caught sneaking into the "Portuguese maids' quarters" at night). Father Damian, who reviewed Kennedy's records at the school before agreeing to be interviewed by the author, said there was no record of Kennedy's involvement in a cheating scandal. In Kennedy's otherwise thick file, said Father Damian, there is only an "abrupt" letter from Joseph Kennedy's secretary informing the school that RFK would not be returning in the fall. That summer, Egan visited his former roommate at Hyannis. Aware that Kennedy was not coming back to school, Egan made a cryptic reference about the cheating incident in front of Bobby and two of his sisters, Eunice and Jean. "I met with total damnation," Egan recalled. "They [Eunice and Jean] said it never happened and I should never say that it did." In September, Rose wrote Jack and Joe Jr. to say that Bobby was going to a new school, Milton Academy. She explained that Bobby "did not seem to like" the headmaster at Portsmouth Priory and "did not seem to make much headway in his classes last year; that is, he did not show any particular effort. . . ."

SHY, PRICKLY, AND DEMORALIZED, Robert Kennedy arrived at Milton, his sixth school in ten years, in the fall of 1942. Milton was a traditional feeder school for Harvard, which recommended it to Ambassador Kennedy, but the tone and culture were High WASP, unwelcoming to Catholic new money. Milton could have been a disaster for Bobby Kennedy. He arrived knowing no one and made

---

reported: "I think it was [another name] who stole the exam. Bob got mixed up in it but cleared." Another had yet another variant: "They broke into the school safe and stole the exam and distributed it. Bobby was the ringleader. He was expelled." Another confirmed: "Bobby was kicked out." The most convincing eyewitnesses, I believe, are Kearney and Egan, whose accounts are quoted.

little attempt to learn anyone's name. He simply called the other boys "fella," as in, "hey, fella." Kennedy was instantly, and not affectionately, nicknamed Fella. In the recollections of his classmates, he was deemed to have "a chip on his shoulder," "a short fuse," and, just as unacceptable, "the wrong clothes." There were a few Catholics on campus, but most of them worked in the kitchen or made beds. Almost all the students came to the school in eighth or ninth grade. Bobby entered in eleventh grade, after the cliques had already formed. His schoolmates insisted, somewhat defensively, that Milton was free of prejudice. "There were no ugly incidents," said Joy Luke, who went to the coordinate girls' school across the street. "But we were all aware his father was a bootlegger." RFK could have remained an outcast, but for a friendship he formed while playing football.

At Portsmouth, Kennedy had been a slow, small, but inordinately determined second-string halfback. As he neared his seventeenth birthday, Kennedy had filled out and hardened. He still looked scrawny in street clothes and walked head down, "like a bird in a storm," as one of the Milton girls described him. But he was taut and wiry. While his legs were short and stubby, his torso was long and muscled, and his arms, particularly his forearms, were well developed. "Bobby is going to be the most robust and Jack practically admits to us— though not to Bobby—that Bobby could throw him now," Rose wrote Kathleen and Joe Jr. At football practice at Milton, he tore into tackling dummies "as if his life depended on it," recalled Sam Adams, another would-be halfback trying out for the team. Adams and Kennedy both made the second backfield, along with a younger boy, a tenth grader named David Hackett.

Hackett would become a schoolboy god, Milton's best football and hockey player ever, his schoolmates swore decades later. Little boys would follow him around, "like the Pied Piper," recalled Mary Bailey Gimbel, who was at the Milton Academy girls' school at the time. Hackett's appeal to Kennedy, however, was less as a boy hero than as an anti-hero, a romantic renegade. In his famous coming-of-age novel, *A Separate Peace*, John Knowles would use Hackett (whom he had met at summer school at Exeter) as the model for his doomed golden boy, Phineas. Phineas possessed a "scatterbrained eloquence," a "calm ignorance of the rules with a winning urge to be good." He was a "model boy who was most comfortable in the truant's corner." So, in real life, was Hackett. "Hackett was offbeat," said Joy Luke. "If he couldn't find the right words, he'd try a different way." Hackett was an astonishingly graceful athlete and "a wild man. He'd do anything and get away with it, in a charming way," said Tom Cleveland, the more traditional campus "big man" of the era.

Hackett took an immediate shine to Kennedy. "We were both misfits," he later recalled. Hackett liked Kennedy's "impulsiveness and fearlessness," he said. He enjoyed his irreverent humor and admired the fact that, in a world of conformity, Kennedy was "willing to embarrass his friends." Bobby made no attempt to downplay his Catholicism; indeed, he tried to expose others, urging Hackett to join him at Sunday mass. Hackett was enormously impressed one Sunday when Kennedy, seeing that an altar boy was missing, suddenly hopped over the prayer rail. Quite unself-consciously, it seemed to Hackett, Kennedy began attending to the priest. Hackett was impressed with Kennedy's unwillingness to compromise to gain acceptance. Kennedy would not join in dirty jokes. He disliked bullying and would step in when an upperclassman tried to push around a younger boy.

Hackett gave Kennedy his first real taste of friendship. They roughhoused together and played practical jokes. Hackett would be Kennedy's friend for life, long after the adolescent hero worship wore off. For once, Kennedy had a sense of belonging, even a measure of stature in Hackett's reflected glory. Kennedy's confidence grew; his grades improved from D to C with an occasional B. He began to court, however timidly, the girls at the school across the street. He nurtured a crush on one girl for a whole year and never spoke to her. But then he mustered up the courage to approach a Milton girl named Piedy Bailey (Mary Bailey Gimbel). Gimbel has offered a touching picture of Kennedy walking her home after chapel on Sunday night, "four feet behind; head down. Everything was buried, including the bones of his face." Kennedy was still "moon-faced" as a seventeen-year-old. Gimbel was very fond of Bobby, remembering him "one foot resting on the other foot; hands way down in his pockets," peering out from under a shock of hair. He was "very appealing," she said. "Funny, separate, larky; outside the cliques; private all the time."

Hackett, curiously for someone so exalted by his peers, shared Bobby's outsiderness. A day student who lived not in the dorm but with his genteel, threadbare family in nearby Dedham, Hackett identified with the dispossessed. He and Bobby earnestly questioned why they should be the privileged ones; when Milton played the local public school, Hackett said he felt as if he was on the wrong side of the ball. Something stirred inside Kennedy as well. He had always sided with the downtrodden at school. Now he began to notice inequity in the wider world. On a trip home to Hyannis Port, Bobby began questioning his father about the poverty he glimpsed from the train window. Couldn't something be done about the poor people living in those bleak tenements? Kennedy Sr. dismissed his son's show of social conscience.

Increasingly, as time wore on, the talk between Bobby and Hackett was about joining the marines. The world war was never far away, even from a cloistered prep school. The chapel tower was manned as an observation post, to spot any enemy planes that might be flying nearby. Maps of the Southwest Pacific and North Africa—American battle zones—were hung in classrooms. Almost as soon as he arrived at Milton in the fall of '42, Bobby began agitating with his father to allow him to enlist. He wanted to catch up to his brothers.

JOE JR. AND JACK KENNEDY were distant and romantic figures in Bobby's childhood. Engaged in a war for primacy, they were more absorbed in fighting each other than in coddling their younger siblings. "I used to lie in my bed at night sometimes," Robert recalled, "and hear the sound of Joe banging Jack's head against the wall." Bobby tried, fitfully, to catch his brothers' attention, to join in their private contest. In Palm Beach, he would swim after them, falling behind as they raced each other out into the ocean. Although he revered Joe, the chosen one, the destined heir, handsome and athletic and outgoing, Bob seems to have been more drawn to Jack. While Joe was bluff, at times bullying, Jack was more thoughtful and mentally playful. Often bedridden with one illness after another, Jack was a voracious reader. He disappeared into a romantic world of historical fiction and derring-do. Partly as a result of coping with frequent pain and suffering, he had learned to keep his true feelings to himself. He made little effort to really get to know his little brother. Even so, after school, he would occasionally take Bobby on walks, telling him the stories of his heroes, educated swashbucklers like T. E. Lawrence, the dashing and mystic Lawrence of Arabia.

A favorite author was John Buchan, spinner of spy yarns like *The Thirty-Nine Steps*. Buchan's secret agent, Richard Hannay, was a precursor of James Bond. Together, Jack and Bobby were riveted by Hannay's intrigues in the "queer subterranean world of the Secret Service." The books had a lasting impact on both brothers. Buchan's autobiography, *Pilgrim's Way*, published in 1940 when Jack was twenty-three and Bobby was fifteen, reads like a primer for the values most esteemed by the New Frontier. Jack Kennedy called *Pilgrim's Way* his favorite book. He identified with Buchan, an outsider from Scotland who made his way into the Edwardian establishment, winning a peerage (as Lord Tweedsmuir) and proving himself as an intellectual-adventurer in the twilight days of empire. The Kennedys found inspiration in Lord Tweedsmuir's description of statesmen who were "debonair and brilliant and brave"—and died young in battle—who "held to the old cavalier grace and wherever romance called . . . followed with careless gallantry." Two hours before he was shot to death in 1968, Robert Kennedy quoted Lord Tweedsmuir to a gaggle of newsmen standing outside his hotel suite in Los Angeles. "I like politics. It's an honorable adventure," Kennedy said. "That was Lord Tweedsmuir. Does anybody here know who he was?" The half-dozen reporters looked back in baffled silence.

War allowed the Kennedys to emulate the dashing aristocrats of Buchan's novels. In 1942, Jack Kennedy, a lieutenant in naval intelligence, volunteered for duty in PT boats, the rough-riding torpedo craft that were sure to torture his bad back. Bobby was soon begging his father to let him join as an enlisted man. From the Pacific, Jack counseled against it. "To try to come steaming out here at 18 is no good. . . . It's just that the fun goes out of war in a fairly short time and I don't think Bobby is ready to come out yet." Bobby was just as eager to follow Joe Jr. into naval aviation. On a visit to Norfolk, where Joe was learning how to fly bombers, Bobby was allowed (against regulations) to fly with his older brother, even hold the controls. The younger Kennedy was "hard-up for conversation," reported Joe to sister Jean, but thrilled that his brother would take him on such an adventure.

Joe Sr. was decidedly not. With two sons already headed for combat, Joe was loath to put another at risk. Bobby was permitted to enlist in December 1943, during his last year at Milton. But it was understood that Bobby would join the V-12 program—training for naval officers—at Harvard in March 1944. That would keep him out of war for a couple of years. A picture of Bobby's swearing-in appeared in the newspaper. In a letter from the front, Jack gently condescended to his little brother for still playing schoolboy games while the real men were at war:

> The folks sent me a clipping of you taking the oath. The sight of you up there, just as a boy, was really moving, particularly as a close ex- amination showed that you had my checked London coat on. I'd like to know what the hell I'm doing out here while you go stroking around in my drape coat. . . . After reading Dad's letter, I gathered that the cold vicious look in your eyes was due to the thought of that big blocking back from Groton. . . . Well, black Robert, give those Grotties hell. . . .

Joe Jr. also patronized his little brother with a sly reference to his clumsi- ness. It was fortunate, the oldest son wrote home, that the war would be over by the time the third son could earn his wings: "The only thing he will have to be careful of is spinning himself in, and with his good steady head, he won't have any trouble with that, or will you, Bobby?"

RFK spent part of the summer of 1943 working on a farm "not too enthu- siastically," Joe Sr. wrote Jack. While Bobby attempted to learn how to milk a cow, his older brothers were engaged in a quietly desperate competition for glory. "Dear Children," Rose wrote in February 1943, "Jack brought me a miniature Torpedo Boat done in silver in the form of a tie clip. He is terrifically jealous of the fact that I wear Joe's gold wings all the time and is bound that I have one of his insignias, and so I am to turn this tie clip into a pin some way or another." Thus, out of sibling rivalry was created what would become one of the memorable symbols of the New Frontier. Jack won the race to become the first family war hero. In August 1943, when his PT boat was cut in half by a Japanese destroyer, Lieutenant Kennedy showed true bravery trying to rescue his men. "Kennedy's Son Is Hero in Pacific" was the headline of a page-one *New York Times* story. Rose reported to the children that the family was "all terribly excited by Jack's feat of glory. . . ." (She mentioned in passing that Joe Sr. had known that JFK had been missing in action for several days without telling her.) From Joe Jr., there was silence for several days, which was "consid- erably upset[ting]" to Joe Sr., who wondered why his eldest did not call. Joe Jr. finally weighed in unconvincingly that he had been too busy to call. Jealousy is a more plausible explanation. Writing home that he had received a "countless number of paper clippings about our young hero"—brother Jack—Joe sardon- ically announced "the battler of the wars of Banana River [Florida], San Juan, Virginia Beach, New Orleans, San Antonio, and San Diego, will now step up to the microphone and give out a few words of his own activities. . . ." The wave of adoration for Jack washed over Bobby as well. In Hyannis, strangers rushed up to the younger brother, mistaking him for Jack, "with effusive words of praise,"

Rose wrote the other children. "Bobby was so bowled over that he didn't have time to explain."

IN MARCH 1944, Robert reported to his "ship"—Harvard's Eliot House. He rose at reveille, ran two miles, dressed in a sailor's suit, and then went to class, like any other student. At his first physics lecture, a group of student/sailors began joking about Ambassador Kennedy. A student sitting right behind Bobby called him "Bastard Kennedy." Bobby whirled around and grabbed the heckler by his shirtfront. Other boys pulled them apart.

One of them was a former Middlesex School football player, Fred Garfield, who had played against Bobby at Milton. Garfield and Kennedy became friendly. Garfield found Kennedy to be at once earnest and sardonic, with a disarming sense of humility. The ex-ambassador's son did seem a little too slavish in his devotion to Joe Sr., who was referred to by his children as "the Ambassador," even though he had resigned in 1941. Garfield was put off when Kennedy used an anti-Semitic slur to describe Jews, but he figured that Kennedy was just reflecting his father's prejudices. Kennedy told Garfield about some of his experiences at court, such as dancing with Elizabeth, the future queen. (Garfield: "What was she like?" Kennedy: "Just another girl.") Kennedy seemed uncomfortable around girls, said Garfield, and never joined the dormitory chatter about sex. He was physically unable to sit through the compulsory film describing, with graphic slides, the consequences of venereal disease. That summer, Garfield and Bobby went on a double date in New York City. The evening was entirely arranged by "the Kennedy organization," recalled Garfield. The boys met at the Kennedy apartment at the Carlyle, picked up two prearranged dates (professional models) at the Barbizon, dined at "21," and danced (awkwardly) at the Copa. The club photographer asked for permission to take a snapshot. Garfield said yes; Kennedy said no. "In tomorrow's paper," Bobby explained, "there would be a picture of the ambassador's son living it up while other sons are dying in the war."

Bobby was acutely aware of the importance of image. He had seen public relations preached and practiced by his father. That same summer at Joe Sr.'s instigation, *Reader's Digest* reprinted a gripping article by John Hersey in *The New Yorker* detailing Jack's exploits in the Pacific. When Garfield visited Bobby at Hyannis, he saw stacks of the *Reader's Digest* reprints lying around the house. "Rose handed them out to anyone who came through the door," Garfield recalled. In England, Joe Jr. was determined to best his brother. After hearing JFK toasted as "our hero" at a Boston banquet, Joe had vowed to himself, "By God, I'll show them. In July 1944, he volunteered for a virtual suicide mission: flying a bomber filled with high explosives against the Nazis' secret V-1 launching pads near Calais and parachuting before detonation. The plane blew up on the way to the target.

Robert was home in Hyannis on an oppressively hot Sunday afternoon in August when two priests appeared bearing a telegram from the War Department. Joe Sr. assembled the children on the front porch and read the grim message that Joe had been lost. He told the children to be brave and to go ahead and race their sailboats. Jack ignored his father's wishes and went to walk alone on the beach. Bobby dutifully followed orders and trudged off to the yacht club. Ambassador Kennedy collapsed, locking himself in his room.

Bobby, ever solicitous of his negligent father, tried to protect him. In September, Jack brought some of his war buddies and their wives out to the house on Cape Cod. Chafing at the ambassador's one-cocktail-before-dinner rule, Jack, his sister Kathleen, and their guests went rummaging for liquor in the kitchen. Bobby found them sneaking Scotch and threatened to tell Joe Sr. One of the wives recalled a "scrawny little guy in a white sailor suit" who was "very upset." Bobby, fearful and censorious, tensely faced his older siblings. "Kathleen handled him," the guest recalled. "She told him to get lost." Jack and his friends went out to the front lawn and began to sing and clap. Joe Sr. leaned out his bedroom window and called down, "Jack, don't you and your friends have any respect for your dead brother?" Joe's old friend, *New York Times* columnist Arthur Krock, suspected more than grief was eating at Joe. The ambassador's prewar support for a policy of appeasement had prompted whispering that he was "yellow." Joe had wanted to erase the family stain and died trying. "His father realized it," said Krock. "He never admitted it, but he realized it."

Joseph Kennedy was too consumed with his own grief to notice a subtle reordering in his own household. With Joe dead, Jack became the heir apparent. Jack was more independent minded than Joe, more likely to resist his father's wishes, or to keep his distance even as he acquiesced. Joe Jr. had always been more pliable. In family debates before Pearl Harbor, Joe Jr. had reflexively joined his father's side to argue that America should stay out. Jack had split away, arguing that the United States needed to come to the rescue of England. In the years ahead, Jack would accept his father's mandate, but he would stage small rebellions to show his independence. Increasingly, it would fall to Bobby to mediate, to protect father and son from each other. When Bobby in his sailor suit had tried to quiet Jack and Kathleen and their carousing friends, he had been dismissed as a meddlesome spoilsport. But his true purpose had been to avert the inevitable filial confrontation with Joe Sr., brooding in his room upstairs. Bobby went largely unnoticed in these years. Ignored on his return from school one summer by Jack and his friends, who were chatting in the living room, Bobby paused on the stairs and forlornly asked, "Aren't you glad to see me?" In the grieving over Joe Jr.'s death, Bobby remained invisible. But the death of the oldest son meant that Bobby had moved up a notch, and though no one was paying attention, begun to step tentatively into a role that would in time make him indispensable.

It is doubtful that RFK himself noticed these changes. Feeling his father's anguish, wrestling with his own feelings of inadequacy, Bobby too was shattered. "He looked like death walking around," recalled Garfield. Bobby's religious faith was briefly shaken. That September, as they rode the subway into Boston, Bobby asked Garfield, "Fred, do you think there's a God?" Back at Harvard for the fall, he failed to make the football team. "Dad's kind of disap-

pointed," Bob wrote Hackett, who was finishing Milton. "Maybe I'll make the
B team and that will please him, for as you all know all he wants is his 9 chil-
dren to do well." Bobby ended with an attempt at bluster: "Say hello to all the
Irish Catholics for me, and tell [th]em that next to John F. Fitzgerald and J.P.
Kennedy I'm the toughest Irishman that lives which makes me the toughest
man that lives."

In November, Bobby was sent to Bates College in Maine to continue his
officer training. The Maine woods seemed awfully far from the front. Bobby
was increasingly manic about getting into the fight. He wrote Hackett in late
January 1945, "Things are the same as usual up here, and me being my usual
moody self I get very sad at times. . . . If I don't get the hell out of here soon I'll
die." Kennedy was writing his old teammate at an army base in Georgia, where
Hackett had gone to become a paratrooper. More and more of Bobby's classmates were going overseas and leaving Bobby behind. The thought that one of
them might get into combat before him "makes me feel more & more like a
Draft Dodger or something." Just as irksome was the shirker's mentality of
some of his mates in V-12 at Bates. Kennedy complained to Hackett, "the attitudes of some of these guys really makes [sic] me mad especially after Joe being
killed."

Kennedy's anger finally exploded. That spring, the war in Europe was ending; in the Pacific, Japanese island bastions were falling, though at great human
cost. At dinner, one of Kennedy's bunkmates proclaimed, "I won't be the last
man killed." Kennedy, morose, looked up. "That's not the right attitude to
have," he said. The man growled back, "Anyone who says that is a jerk."
Bobby's eyes smoldered. "My brother didn't feel that way," he said, a bit cryptically; most of the other men at the table, including the man mouthing off, had
no idea who his brother was or that he had been killed in action. The other man
kept on pouring gasoline: "Your brother is a jerk," he said. Bobby leapt from his
seat and grabbed the man by the neck. An officer candidate named Richard
Daly witnessed the confrontation. "He would have killed him if we didn't pull
him off. We had to pry Kennedy's fingers off his neck," said Daly. "It really
scared us."

In March, Kennedy wrote Hackett that he would try to get into flight
training school so that he could have his "wings of gold." He added, however, "I
am not sure, between you and me, just how much I go for flying. . . ." He recounted an exceedingly melancholy weekend alone in New York, visiting the
zoo and taking solitary walks in Central Park. He had made a date to see his father that weekend, but he was disappointed. Joe Sr. was so intently involved in
his children's lives that he once said, "my work is my boys." He was referring
to Jack and Joe, not Bobby. On this March weekend, the ambassador stood up
his third son at the last minute. Bobby went to New York anyway and wandered about morosely. Then in May, RFK learned that he had flunked his aptitude test for flight school. In the depths, he wrote his father suggesting that
maybe he should just flunk out of officer's candidate school and enlist. Joe Sr.
counseled against such rashness. Perhaps something else could be arranged. In

July, a 2,200-ton destroyer, the *Joseph P. Kennedy, Jr.*, was launched; Ambassador Kennedy had quietly lobbied his friends in the Pentagon to name a ship after his fallen hero son. The ambassador stood erect and tearful as the warship slid down the ways. Bobby was allowed to resign from officers' candidate school and become an ordinary sailor aboard the *Kennedy*. It is not clear whether young Kennedy asked to go aboard the *Kennedy* or if his father arranged the berth for him. In any case, the assignment seems almost designed to reinforce Kennedy's feelings of inferiority and subordination. He shipped out in the winter of 1946.

He had missed the war. He chipped paint, and then chipped paint some more. The ship steamed to Cuba, where Kennedy grew bored by the sunsets. His only pleasure was swimming. Against regulations, he dove off the bow of the ship as it rested at anchor in Guantánamo Bay. An officer upbraided him. "I fell in," Kennedy sulkily responded. His shipmates regarded him as a quiet loner and barely noticed when he left the ship. In May 1946, Seaman Second Class Kennedy was discharged from the navy.

Robert Kennedy was twenty years old. He had been sidelined from the greatest test of his generation, failing to pass flight aptitude in the Maine woods while other young men were fighting and dying all over the world. In an earlier moment of moral weakness—and a rare instance of going with the crowd—he had reached for the stolen exam. He was inarticulate and moody and a mediocre student. His own family continued to judge him a failure. Asked about Bobby, one of his sisters had answered, "Forget Bobby. Let's talk about Joe and Jack." Kennedy seemed to regard himself as a loser. His letters to his friend Hackett are so mordant that his self-deprecation is almost embarrassing.

He was far too harsh on himself. Despite, or because of, his adversity, he was developing a sense of himself and a code of personal integrity. He was not the spoiled rich boy he might have been. Rather, he showed a genuine curiosity about, and nascent concern for, the less fortunate. More easily than his princeling siblings, he could identify with working people. His mother understood that he had learned a useful lesson as an enlisted man: "I enjoyed what you said about the officers not understanding the point of view of the men unless they had done the work themselves," she wrote him while he was at sea. "After your rubbing and scrubbing these months, you will never again be in that position." RFK could be funny, especially about himself. He was not a conformist. He had the courage to defy convention—as Hackett admiringly put it, to "embarrass his friends." Realizing that he could not be popular, he did not try to ingratiate and was thus made free to follow his own conscience. He had shown raw physical courage on the football field and self-discipline in his personal habits. He had a strong and even rigid moral sensibility. Though in his letters to Hackett he joked about alienating the waiters and bartenders of New York by refusing to imbibe, he was the only one of the Kennedy boys to meet his father's challenge of not smoking or drinking until the age of twenty-one (the reward was $1,000). Though lonely, he had shown a capacity for friendship. He was, if anything, too loyal. In his search for a role that would please his father, he was already finding one—as family protector. He would at last become a true family member, though at a cost: his independence of spirit would be sublimated, his more sensitive and winning qualities covered over in a hard defensive shell.

CHAPTER **2** TOUGH

GLOOMILY WAITING to get into the war, Robert Kennedy would from time to time accompany his grandfather, former mayor John F. "Honey Fitz" Fitzgerald, on walking tours of Boston. Honey Fitz would take Bobby and his little brother Teddy to climb aboard *Old Ironsides* or mount Bunker Hill. Honey Fitz, "the little Napoleon of Ward Six," is remembered as an Irish pol full of blarney and cunning, but he tried not to play on ethnic jealousies. He was an Irishman proud of Boston's Yankee history. As a candidate for mayor in 1905, Fitzgerald inveighed against parochialism. His fellow Catholics should not set up special schools, he implored, but "go to school with the superior men, read their words, listen to them, talk to them." Many of his fellow Hibernians bridled at the description of Yankees as "superior men," and to be sure, Honey Fitz had no admiration for the Brahmins of his day who, fearful of the immigrant tide, were retreating into their clubs on Beacon Hill. Nonetheless, he revered their Yankee ancestors, the eighteenth-century merchant princes who were the founding fathers of Boston. All that separated the Cabots and the Fitzgeralds, he liked to say, is "the difference of a few ships."

Honey Fitz preached civic virtue and the myths of Boston's proud past to his grandchildren. On those long and winding walks, he took the boys past monuments of the Revolutionary War—to the old North Church, where he would recite "The Midnight Ride of Paul Revere," and out to Concord, where he would stand on the "rude bridge that arched the flood" and proclaim "the shot heard round the world." Honey Fitz's patriotic reverence affected all the grandchildren, even "Black Robert." Bobby Kennedy liked to play the tough Irish "mick," especially around Brahmins. He would enrage his WASPy classmates at Harvard by defending Irish neutrality in World War II. At the same time, he loved America in a deep and sentimental way. All his life, as he traveled around the country, RFK would make a point of visiting the birthplaces of presidents and other historic monuments and shrines.

Joe Kennedy shared his father-in-law's admiration for the Yankee aristocracy—not the modern-day snobs but their forebears. At a St. Patrick's Day speech in 1937, he antagonized some of his audience by chiding the Irish for lacking the "family tradition adequate to win the respect and confidence of their puritan neighbors." Joe Sr. wanted his sons to not only belong to the ruling class, but to rule. Joe and Honey Fitz shared the same boundless ambition for the next generation and zeal for promotion. Within moments of the birth of Joe Jr., Honey Fitz had raced to the phone to call the newspapers, jocularly boasting, "Well, of course, he *is* going to be President of the United States." With Joe's death, Jack became the nominee of the Kennedy Party, whether he wanted to be or not. As a first step, Jack was to run for Congress. "I can feel Pappy's eyes on the back of my neck," Jack confided to his friend Paul "Red" Fay in 1946. "It was like being drafted. My father wanted his eldest son in politics. 'Wanted' isn't the right word. He demanded it. You know my father."

Characteristically, Joseph Kennedy cleared the way by spreading money around. By paying off his debts and promising to generously support his campaign for mayor, Kennedy persuaded the incumbent congressman from the Eleventh Congressional District, rogue politician James Michael Curley, to vacate his seat so that Jack could take it. Kennedy went on to hand out somewhere between $250,000 and $500,000—vast sums in those days—for billboards, newspaper ads, and radio broadcasts. "We're going to sell Jack like soap flakes," he cheerfully confided to a friend. No one was ever sure how much money Joe spent, or exactly how he spent it. Dave Powers, who became a charter member of Jack Kennedy's so-called Irish mafia, recalled the secretive way Eddie Moore, Joe Kennedy's henchman, handed out the cash: by inviting the recipient into a pay toilet. "You can never be too careful in politics about handing over money," Moore explained.

Just returning from the navy in the late spring of 1946, Bobby was probably only dimly aware of the machinations behind his brother's congressional campaign. A family friend recalled Bobby walking on the beach at Hyannis with the younger children, a safe distance behind Honey Fitz and Jack, who were engaged in an animated one-way conversation: "Fitz [was] talking about a mile a minute to Jack, you know, crowding him with information, crowding it into him—just hammering it into this guy's skull." Jack Kennedy ran as a member of the "new generation," appealing to the returning vets. Movie-star handsome, he certainly appealed to their sisters, who crowded around him squealing "Sinatra!" But he loved and respected his grandfather and listened carefully to his instructions for survival in the back-stabbing byways of Boston politics. We can only guess at what Honey Fitz was telling his favored grandson. But one of the lessons can surely be found in Thomas H. O'Connor's political history, *The Boston Irish*, which observes that "old-time politicians—and quite a few young ones, too—generally observed the well-known dictum . . . that a wise politician never puts anything in writing. 'Don't write when you can talk; don't talk when you can nod your head.' " O'Connor notes that like most politicians of their era, Patrick Kennedy (Joe Sr.'s father) and John F. Fitzgerald left behind no compilation of official documents or personal papers. Certain rules of silence—the importance of compartmentalizing information, of knowing when to look the other way—fit naturally with the Kennedy clan's insularity. In time, these lessons would be passed along to Robert, who would make them his own.

Joe Sr. could be just as secretive as Honey Fitz, but in his free-spending eagerness to elect Jack, he was a little heavy-handed. Jack Kennedy's main opponent, Mike Neville, was complaining to newsmen that the Kennedy strategy was "Buy them out or blast them out!" In the late spring of '46, with the decisive Democratic primary approaching in June, Joe Kennedy's lavishness was beginning to backfire. The press jeeringly referred to his son the candidate as "Jawn the Pawn." The Kennedys responded by throwing family into the breech. Eunice, Pat, and Jean were assigned to drive and pass out leaflets and pour coffee. Bobby, fresh off the *Joseph P. Kennedy, Jr.* and still in his sailor suit, was told to report to headquarters for his assignment.

Dave Powers recalled Bobby's appearance at Jack's smoky, slightly seedy room at the Bellevue Hotel. "Bobby turned to me and said very quietly and sort of in a shy way, 'How is my brother going to do in Charlestown?' " Powers said he'd do fine; Charlestown, a gritty blue-collar area, admired courage. Bobby looked at Powers and said worshipfully, "My brother has more courage than anyone I have ever met."

Jack Kennedy was less romantic—or gracious—about his brother's help. "I can't see that sober, silent face breathing new vigor into the ranks," he told his navy friend Red Fay, who had volunteered to help on the campaign. One photograph of the two brothers standing together for the newspapers would do, said Kennedy. It "will show that we're all in this for Jack. Then," Kennedy instructed Fay, "you take Bobby out to [the] movies or whatever you two want to do."

It is striking, given the closeness of their later relationship, that JFK was so dismissive of his little brother. The older Kennedy was too caught up in his complicated relationship with his father—at once defiant and dependent—to pay much attention to the worshipful kid brother in the sailor suit. At this stage of his life, JFK wanted worldly friends who could joke about life in the world-weary way of war veterans. He had no use for a former altar boy who might run off and tell Dad if his older brother did something rebellious or naughty.

Fay took Bobby to a vaudeville show. Bobby was monosyllabic on the way to the show, dead silent inside. He did not laugh at any of the jokes. "From his expression," Fay later wrote, "he might have been paying last respects to his closest friend."

Bobby was farmed out to another friend, Lem Billings, JFK's old Choate roommate. Billings was in charge of some tough wards in Cambridge. Bobby asked to set up his own get-out-the-vote operation in the most remote and unwinnable of the wards, and he almost never came to headquarters thereafter. He was put off by the old hacks hanging around swapping lies and smoking cigars. He preferred playing softball with neighborhood kids in East Cambridge. Nonetheless, he worked hard chasing votes, and when Jack won the primary in June, he lost East Cambridge by smaller margins than expected.

As a favor to the family, Billings took Bobby on a trip through Latin America that summer. Still teetotaling, Bobby would drink Cokes and want to hurry Billings along from cocktails to dinner. He was abashed when South Americans asked him what he did in the war. He had nothing to say. "I used to kid him about it," said Billings. "He didn't think it was especially funny." Instead, he compensated. In the black of night, he insisted on swimming at Copacabana Beach in Rio, despite warnings about a severe undertow. Skiing in the Andes, he demanded to hike beyond the lifts, in order to hurl himself down steeper and untracked pitches. Back in New York, Billings took Bobby to lose his virginity at a Harlem whorehouse, the same one, Billings later claimed, where Jack had lost his virginity some years before. Bobby reported to Billings that the experience "wasn't bad, but it wasn't fabulous either." Joe Sr. reimbursed Billings for the cost.

Still three semesters shy of a college degree, Robert was back at Harvard in the fall. He had been admitted to Jack's undergraduate social club, the Spee, partly on the strength of his Milton pedigree. JFK had been grateful to gain admission to the Spee. Both Joe Sr. and Joe Jr. had been turned away by Harvard's "final clubs," with their Brahmin prejudice against Irish Catholics. JFK (whose election had been a close thing) welcomed the entree into the company of stylish and pedigreed young men. But Bobby quit the Spee when his snobbish clubmates blackballed an Irish Catholic. He was more comfortable across the river at Dillon Field House with the football team. Most of the players were older, returning vets on the GI bill. The large majority were not prep school boys; they had names like Rodis and Flynn and Drvaric and would not have known where to find the Spee Club. Kennedy was drawn to the best player, Kenneth O'Donnell, a combat veteran of thirty bombing missions over Germany. "I think it was the streetfighter in Kenny that attracted Bobby," recalled Sam Adams, Bobby's old Milton friend who was also on the team. O'Donnell had a sharp tongue, strong opinions, and a democratic instinct. Together O'Donnell and Kennedy entertained their teammates with lively debates at the Varsity Club while conspiring to get the coach, Dick Harlow, fired. O'Donnell regarded Harlow as a capricious martinet. Bobby's motives were more personal. Coach Harlow had denied Joe Jr. his letter by keeping him on the bench during the 1937 Yale game. Joe Sr. had been so outraged that he had climbed down on the field after the game and angrily berated the startled coach. Harlow became a Kennedy family bête noire. In a letter to his parents, Jack Kennedy sarcastically referred to the Harvard coach as "our good friend Dick Harlow," and clucked over a coaching blunder "which pleased us all, as it made Gentleman Dick look a little sick."

RFK was playing for his father, not Harlow. In the copious family correspondence, the first positive mention of Bobby by Joe Sr. came in the fall of 1943, when Bobby, a Milton senior, was a blocking back and sometime receiver for the fleet Dave Hackett. Joe approvingly notes in letters to Jack and Joe Jr.

that Bobby "played a swell game against St. Mark's" and a "whale of a game Saturday" against Nobles. Joe Sr. did attend a Harvard practice or two to watch Bobby play and saw him catch a touchdown pass in an early-season rout of Western Maryland. But the real respect won by RFK was that of his teammates, who admired his physical courage.

At five feet ten, 155 pounds, Kennedy was too small and too slow for college football, but he was a fearless hitter. He insisted on tackling the 230-pound fullback, Vinnie Moravec, head-on. "For Christ sakes," Moravec told the coach, "stop him before he gets killed." Another player, Wally Flynn, looked up in the huddle after one play to see tears streaming down Kennedy's face. He had broken his leg and, bravely or foolishly, kept on playing.

Kennedy did not just play furiously. He was furious. His anger boiled over at the slightest provocation. Shortly after his twenty-first birthday, Kennedy celebrated by buying his first beer. Soon he was buying rounds for everyone in the bar. Some of the patrons began singing "Happy Birthday" to someone else, and Kennedy, inebriated for the first time in his life, became enraged at their ingratitude. He smashed a beer bottle over one man's head and refused entreaties by O'Donnell to apologize. Bobby was easily enraged by moral impurity, especially in his fellow Catholics. In his dorm at Milton, one of the masters had been a rare Catholic in a WASP school. A former Jesuit seminarian, the dorm master smelled of alcohol and tobacco. Bobby treated him with contempt. At Harvard, the campus Catholic priest, Father Leonard Feeney, was a bigot who denounced the university as a "pest-hole" for Jews and atheists. Kennedy publicly challenged him, writing the cardinal that Father Feeney should be removed from his post.

Rose Kennedy was shocked when RFK came home and denounced Father Feeney at the dinner table. Her little Bobby, her altar boy son, was challenging the authority and reputation of a priest. Kennedy's attack on Father Feeney was telling. Just a few years ago, he had mindlessly aped his father's anti-Semitism. Now he was openly attacking an anti-Semite. His outspokenness showed an independence of spirit, a willingness to question the establishment, that belied his youth and former timidity. There may as well have been unconscious forces at work. It is common for rebellious youths who find some indirect way of proclaiming independence—typically through music or dress or radical causes—rather than risk a frontal confrontation with their parents. Consciously, Kennedy worshipped and built up his family, overlooking or forgiving the slight interest his older siblings and father showed in him. He remained respectful to his mother for all his life, but he may have quietly resented her condescension to him as her "pet." During his career as a congressional investigator and then as attorney general, Kennedy would channel fury at targets in a way that seemed disproportionate to the task at hand.

Outwardly, RFK was in no way a heretic or wild-eyed rebel. He remained religiously devout. A football teammate, Emil Drvaric, was startled to burst into Kennedy's room one night and find him on his knees, praying. RFK was also, his trip to Harlem notwithstanding, prudish. There was considerable mirth on the team when someone arranged for Bobby to go on a date with Miss Lynn, Massachusetts, of 1946. What should I do with her? he anxiously asked. Buy her a drink, came the answer. Kennedy frowned. When he returned to the Varsity Club that night he was mortified. "I kissed her and she opened her mouth," he explained to his teammates, who made no attempt to stifle their laughter.

Bobby's priggishness was amusing, but, again, it may have been a revealing psychological reaction to feelings he probably felt or understood only dimly. He was in all likelihood overcompensating, rebelling against his own family's licentiousness. By now, he was well aware of his father's and brother's reputations as lotharios. He seemed determined to go in the opposite direction, while perhaps envying their conquests. His vexation and confusion about romance were aggravated that winter of 1946–47, when his first true love was stolen by his brother Jack.

Kennedy had fallen hard for a beauty of the day named K.K. Hannon. Dave Hackett had introduced him to Hannon, whose family was middle-class Irish Catholic. Hannon, who physically resembled Lauren Bacall, had a steady stream of Harvard clubmen as suitors. One of them, George Plimpton, recalled the "odd sight" of Bobby sitting in the Hannons' dining room in Brookline, working on a term paper as a wild party boiled around him. "I don't think he got a lot of studying done," recalled K.K. Hannon. "He wanted to be there, but he didn't feel part of that crowd, the P.C. and A.D. Club boys who had gone to Groton and St. Mark's. Their conversation was quick, and he couldn't keep up. But he thought he could outwait them." After the swells had left, Bobby would shyly mumble to K.K., "Do you want to go to the movies?"

Years later, she recalled RFK as "not tough at all. He was gentle. Mummy thought he was sweet, though she hated his father. I liked him. He was a touching person, really. He was wry and very dear. He was interested in everything, curious. He didn't have good manners, but he tried. He was like a ten-year-old in a grown-up's suit. There was nothing hale-fellow. His shoulders were a little bit hunched. He didn't seem happy in his own skin."

One night that winter, the two of them sat in Kennedy's "junk heap" of a car after a movie. "My hands were freezing. 'We can go in,' I said. 'Please stay,' he said. 'You can put your hands on my chest.' " The gesture was intimate but "it didn't seem sexual," said Hannon. "He just wanted to talk, and he was trying to make me comfortable."

Kennedy asked her to marry him. Hannon demurred. "I wasn't in love with him or ready to get married. I didn't see my future with him." A little later, Bobby and Hannon passed brother Jack on a Boston street. Bobby and K.K. were on their way to a movie. Jack was walking along with two of his aides—"thugs from Charlestown," in Hannon's description. Jack took one look at K.K., sexy and stylish in her fur coat, and said to his hangers-on, "Okay, fellows, good night." As Hannon recalled, Kennedy turned around and accompanied his little brother and his brother's girl to the movies. Hannon sat between them. "The next morning, Jack called up," Hannon recalled. "I thought he was terrific. That was the end of Bobby. It was very awkward." Bobby did not express any of the anger or jealousy he must have felt. He deferred. "He just sort of peeled off," said Hannon.

Hannon went to visit Jack at Hyannis a half-dozen times that spring and summer of 1947. She felt a little intimidated. "The Kennedy girls frightened me to death. They were brazen. Mrs. Kennedy would disappear halfway through lunch. Joe was tough and terrible, but he had a real interest in what his kids thought." After dinner one night, Joe took K.K. aside and told her she had picked the wrong Kennedy. "You should marry Bobby," she recalled him saying. "*That* one." Hannon said that she mumbled "something like, 'You never know.' " Joe may have felt that Hannon was not quite grand enough for Jack. Though she was ardently pursued by the club crowd at Harvard, her own background was relatively modest. In any event, Jack soon moved on to other women; his romance with Hannon was "not serious," recalled Lem Billings.

But it is significant that Joseph Kennedy was at least considering the romantic fortunes of his third son. Bobby was still very much a low man on the family totem pole. "Eunice and Pat didn't give him much of a chance, and Jack condescended to him," said Hannon. But Joe Sr. had finally begun to pay attention to his third son. In part, the patriarch may have been reacting to Jack's rebellious streak. JFK had accepted his father's draft to be the family standard-bearer and office seeker, but he grumbled and rebelled. At times, Hannon recalled, Jack Kennedy was barely speaking to his father. Bobby, by contrast, was willing to do anything to get his father's respect. Hannon could see that Father Joe appreciated Bobby's dutifulness. In Hannon's observation, "Joe showed more respect for Bobby than for Jack, in a funny way. Joe was afraid of what Jack would do. Jack was a loose cannon. Bobby was more pliable. It was Jack who could say no and mean it. Bobby didn't challenge his father. He knew he couldn't change his mind. Bob was never an instigator in the conversation. His role was to be solicitous. The others didn't give a hoot."

For Bob, just getting his father's attention was a triumph. As an officer candidate up at Bates in January 1945, Bobby had at last scored some decent marks. "I congratulate you, . . ." his father had written. "Let me know if there is anything I can do for you." Bobby responded like a drowning man to rope: "I wish, Dad, that you would write me a letter as you used to Joe & Jack about what you think about the different political events and the war as I'd like to understand what's going on better than I do now." Joseph Kennedy wrote back a two-page, single-spaced letter. "Thanks very much for your letter, Dad, which is just what I wanted," Bobby wrote back.

RFK uncritically regurgitated his father's political views to his football mates at Harvard. Kenny O'Donnell, his debating partner and an ardent pro-Roosevelt New Dealer, thought that Bobby was a mouthpiece for his father's too-cautious approach to the postwar world. Just as he had wanted to avoid American entry into World War II, Kennedy Sr. wished to avoid U.S. engagement in a cold war. In beery debate at the Varsity Club, Bobby hotly, if not always persuasively, repeated these admonitions against foreign entanglements.

Bobby's friends, many of them war veterans with rough manners, scoffed at RFK's deference to his father. O'Donnell regarded the senior Kennedy as a martinet, a "drill sergeant" who pushed around his sons, or tried to. RFK began bringing his football mates to Hyannis, where they mixed uneasily with the Kennedy clan. Bumptious and loud, the footballers smoked JPK's cigars and sampled his liquor and behaved boorishly towards Kennedy's siblings. Eunice Kennedy recalled that Bobby would bring home friends who were "not at all like Jack's friends," whom she described as "Long Island sophisticates." O'Donnell and the other Varsity Club men teased Bobby about his father's pretensions. When they saw the senior Kennedy parading about the house in a robe emblazoned with a coat of arms, they asked RFK if his father sported a coat of arms on his underwear as well. They were amused when the salty Honey Fitz told off-color stories and JPK left the room in disgust. And they badgered RFK to stand up to his autocratic father. "Why don't you tell him off once in a while?" O'Donnell baited Bobby. "Oh, you tell him off," RFK replied. "I like it the way it is."

RFK was not ready to openly defy his father. He was grateful to have found a role. He was the reliable one, dutiful, helpful, and "tough." Kennedy Sr. was very impressed that Bobby had won a varsity H at Harvard, something Joe Jr. and Jack had failed to do. At last, he had his father's grudging admiration. In March 1948, just as Bobby was graduating from Harvard, Joe Sr. wrote Lord Beaverbrook, the British press baron: "He is just starting off and he has the difficulty of trying to follow two brilliant brothers, Joe and Jack. That in itself is quite a handicap, and he is making a good battle against it." More important, Joe Sr. had begun to recognize himself in Bobby. He had been so focused on creating a next generation that could rise above the station to which Joe Kennedy had been consigned by the Harvard snobs that he had failed to notice his true kinship with his third son. The elder boys had been by and large accepted into the Protestant elite. But Bobby, defiantly Irish, had his father's outsiderness, the drive that comes from resentment.

Following his brothers did not, at that point, mean going into politics or public service. Bobby had idly told friends that he might go into business, but he seemed unenthusiastic. Secure in his father's fortune, RFK does not appear to have given much thought to making, keeping, or spending money. Kenny O'Donnell was shocked one day to find Joseph Kennedy's reward to RFK for not drinking or smoking until age twenty-one—a check for $1,000—carelessly tossed in a corner of Bobby's footlocker, uncashed after three years. Kennedy was not ascetic; he had become accustomed to a fairly luxurious upper-class lifestyle. Indeed, he was spoiled in the fashion of most wealthy children. He had to show up for meals on time and have carefully read the newspaper to participate in table talk, but he was not required to make his bed or clean his room or do household chores. As he grew up, RFK did not so much demand a certain level of service and comfort as take it for granted. There is not much evidence that he even noticed his grand environs at home—the broad lawns and gardens of the Kennedy houses in Riverdale and Bronxville, the gilded ambassador's residence in London, the seaside villa in Palm Beach, the roomy, airy "cottage" on Cape Cod. He was not at all fastidious about his appearance. His clothing can best be described as shabby-preppy: ratty sweaters and torn khakis. "He did not care about the amenities," recalled his sister Eunice. For most of his youth he was oblivious to fashion, culture, and society. Beyond a vague wish for adventure, he had no ambition, save one: to please his father.

In the summer of 1943, Bobby had wanted to go to sea and work on a fishing boat, but his mother had demurred; she already had two boys off in dangerous places. So Bobby had faithfully worked on a farm, then as an office boy at the same bank in East Boston where Joe Sr. had started out. Bobby was bored by the drudgery, though he enjoyed taking the subway and encountering, for the first time, common folk. He lacked any entrepreneurial instinct. As a little boy, he had started a paper route once, but tired of it quickly and began delivering his papers from the family's chauffeured Rolls-Royce. Law school was a possibility, but his grades, mostly C's and D's, were too low for Harvard Law School. He considered Harvard Business School, then said to be partial to football players, but his D in introductory economics did not bode well. Finally, the University of Virginia Law School took him in, with the warning that he would have to greatly improve his academic performance.

As Kennedy slipped deeper into his father-pleasing, tough-guy persona, he became more insensitive and selfish around his peers. At Virginia, a school with a gentlemanly cast, Kennedy was known for his rudeness. His landlord complained that he ruined the floors with football cleats. His few friends griped that, in the manner of the careless rich, he carried no money and that he seldom paid anyone back. His genteel classmates were offended when he picked up meat with his hands and put his muddy feet on the table. He kept unleashed a large German police dog who liked to bite. An impatient golfer, he cut ahead of slower players at the country club. The once-considerate little boy, it appeared, had become a bit of a lout, his inner sweetness by now well concealed.

As ever, he spoiled for fights. When his father came down to the law school to speak and urged isolationism, the law school paper ran an editorial headlined "Mr. Kennedy, the Dinosaur Is Dead." Kennedy showed up in the paper's offices "ready to punch someone in the nose," recalled Allison Page, who was the only person in the office at the time. With some difficulty, Page persuaded Kennedy that it would do no good to hit him, since he had not written the article. Kennedy's most spectacular confrontation came over a more worthy cause. The University of Virginia was whites-only and its seat, Charlottesville, was segregated. With an eye, perhaps, on tweaking the southern dandies in his law class, Kennedy in the spring of 1951 invited Ralph Bunche, who as a UN peace negotiator had won a Nobel Prize, to address the university. Bunche, an African-American, refused to address a segregated audience. Kennedy was determined he should come and that the university should open its doors. When other student leaders balked, Kennedy stood up and shouted, "You're all gutless!" He became so enraged addressing the university's governing board that

he was virtually incoherent. But Kennedy's insistence worked: Bunche spoke
to an integrated audience, open to the public.

It is reassuring to see the stirrings of Kennedy's social conscience in these
early episodes, and there is no doubt that he was sincere in his identification
with the downtrodden. But he had trouble relating to people in ordinary
human ways. He was so absorbed in pleasing his parents that he was heedless of
others. In her memoirs, Rose Kennedy unwittingly reveals a small but telling
story of how her once thoughtful boy now thought mostly about himself.
Bobby had taken a friend, who could not sail, out in one of the family sailboats.
The wind was fading, and as lunchtime approached, Kennedy realized that they
might not make it ashore in time for lunch. Obsessed with his father's insistence on punctuality, he simply dove overboard and swam for shore, leaving his
helpless crewmate to fend for himself. After flailing about, the friend was rescued by a passing boat. Kennedy made no attempt to apologize. Bobby was not
a boy at the time. The incident occurred in 1948, when he was twenty-two
years old and headed for law school.

Bobby had shown little interest in girls after K.K. Hannon at Harvard.
There was one, however, who was interested in him. During Jack Kennedy's
congressional campaign in the spring of '46, Jean Kennedy had brought along
as a volunteer her roommate at Manhattanville College of the Sacred Heart.
Ethel Skakel was a bubbly, headstrong young woman who loved to tease and
who wanted, as much as any Kennedy, to win. She greeted everyone, "Hiya
kid," and distracted the nuns at Manhattanville with her gags and practical
jokes. A tomboy, she had been indifferent to boys. Working with Bobby in East
Cambridge that June, however, she developed a crush. Bobby did not recipro-
cate. He was more romantically inclined towards Pat Skakel, Ethel's older sister.
Ethel was determined to win him away. When Bobby invited Pat down to Palm
Beach for Easter, Ethel got herself invited by Jean. More athletic and outgoing
than Pat, she "turned the tide," Jean Smith later reported. By the time Bobby
was at law school, he was regularly flying up to visit Ethel on the weekends. At
Hyannis house parties, Ethel, sporty and joshing and ebullient, became difficult to distinguish from the Kennedy sisters.

A fling briefly diverted Kennedy on the way to the altar. After he had
graduated from Harvard in the spring of 1948, Bobby went alone on a grand
tour of the Middle East and Europe before starting at Virginia in September.
While he was in Italy, recovering from a case of jaundice, his sister Kathleen
died in a plane crash in the south of France. In deep mourning, Kennedy wandered on to London, where he gloomily attended a popular play called *The
Chiltern Hundreds*. The play was based partly on the much-publicized drama
of Kathleen's marriage, outside the faith and against her mother's wishes, to
the son of the Duke of Devonshire. In the starring role—as the American mil-
lionairess who marries the son of an earl—was a blond twenty-seven-year-old
actress named Joan Winmill. Smitten, Kennedy asked Winmill out to dinner
the next night. She later recalled his boyishness—his freckles and toothy
smile—and the intensity of his stare. The two began a secretive and slightly

lugubrious romance, visiting Kathleen's grave and her late husband's ancestral home, Chatsworth. Inevitably, Joe Sr. found out and disapproved. He would not have his son marry a showgirl. Promising he would return, Bobby said good-bye to Winmill in August. According to Winmill's memoirs, Bobby wrote her often, sending her chocolates and perfume and hand-me-down dresses with expensive labels from his sisters. She considered herself "in love," she later wrote, until she received a letter from him in the summer of 1949. The letter said, "I am getting married to Ethel Skakel."

Ethel had her own distractions. She had been raised as a strict Catholic by her mother, whose piety rivaled Rose Kennedy's. Ann Skakel kept a prie-dieu and font of holy water in her house for daily prayer. In the fall of 1949, Ethel briefly considered entering a nunnery. "How can I fight God?" Bob wondered aloud as he walked the beach at Hyannis. Ethel's absolute and literal faith in the Catholic Church complemented RFK's devotion, which was not quite as unquestioning, but still strong. The former altar boy and the would-be nun were joined more closely by the mysteries of the faith. In Ethel's purity Kennedy may have found refuge from temptation. Despite his dalliance with a British showgirl, Kennedy openly scorned "loose women," recalled a University of Virginia classmate, Endicott Davison. To friends, Ethel and Bobby seemed more matey than romantic, but the affection was real, and it deepened to love.

By winter they were engaged. "My fiancee [sic] followed me down here," Robert wrote his sister Pat from Charlottesville in the spring of 1950, "and wouldn't let me alone for a minute—kept running her toes through my hair & things like that. You know how engaged couples are." Robert and Ethel were married that June in a huge society wedding in Greenwich, Connecticut, attended by 1,200 guests. The heat that day was stifling. Rose carried a parasol made from the same cloth as her Paris designer dress. Bobby's groomsmen, most hulking linemen from the 1947 Harvard football team, sweltered in the cutaways that RFK had rented for them. The bride and groom, with their toothy smiles and dark tans, could easily have passed for cousins. They had no financial worries. In addition to RFK's trust (probably about a million dollars) Ethel had family money. Her father, a midwestern industrialist, once quipped that his hobbies were "old money and new money." The Skakels were a flamboyant and rambunctious clan. Mixed and stirred with alcohol, Ethel's reckless and headstrong brothers and Bobby's lumbering ushers created a critical mass. Earlier that week, Bobby's free-for-all bachelor party had wreaked thousands of dollars of damage on the Harvard Club of New York. At the wedding, all the bridesmaids were thrown in the pool.

That fall, one of Bobby's football friends, Wally Flynn, paid a surprise visit on the newlyweds in Charlottesville. The kitchen was "an unbelievable mess," he recalled. Dirty dishes were stacked in the sink and the refrigerator was empty, save for some frozen steaks. Tidiness was not one of Ethel's fortes. Nor was thriftiness. She was extravagant in her buying habits, showering Bobby with expensive presents. She was also unstinting in her affections. Ethel believed, as she herself put it, in "goodies and baddies." To her, Bobby was perfect. A law school classmate, E. Barrett Prettyman Jr., remarked that Ethel "looked at Bobby like she did at God. God did inexplicable things, but he was never wrong." Ethel lifted her husband's spirits and made him meet people. She would launch into a story, then turn to her husband and say, "Bobby, *you* tell it." She was an inexhaustible source of good cheer, and she put up with his moods. She gave him the one thing he had never had before: unconditional love. For Kennedy, who had spent his life at a table where the major portions of love and respect were passed to others, Ethel's utter devotion marked the end of a long emotional fast.

JACK KENNEDY was the best man at Bobby's wedding. In shaky health from chronic disease, overcome by heat, he fainted before the service. That night, he rallied, taking an attractive young socialite, Mary Pitcairn, to *Gentlemen Prefer Blondes* and a late dinner at "21." But he kept thinking about the solemnity of the occasion he had just witnessed. Throughout the evening, Pitcairn later recalled, Jack "couldn't get over the seriousness of the vows Bobby had taken. . . . He kept going on and on about it. The fact that his little brother had agreed to do all these things and had committed himself for life to this girl. He just couldn't leave it alone, all evening." For a moment, at least, Bobby had won his older brother's attention and, possibly, his envy.

The relationship between the two men, so central to their later lives, was still distant in 1951. Both men remained focused on their father—Jack at keeping the patriarch at arm's length, Bobby at winning his attention. They were neither rivals nor partners, but rather remote planets orbiting the same sun. The paths of the two brothers did not really cross, their interests did not coincide, until 1952, when JFK ran for the Senate and needed someone who could handle his overbearing father.

Jack Kennedy's election as a U.S. senator that year, against difficult odds, made the oldest surviving Kennedy son a national figure, a contender to fulfill Father Joe's dream of a Kennedy in the White House. The race was equally important for Robert Kennedy in the politics of the Kennedy family. No longer the "runt," RFK had already begun to win his father's respect for toughness and steadiness. But his role in electing Jack to the Senate permanently defined Bobby in his father's eyes. It secured his place as brother protector. Joe came to see Bobby as the reliable one, fiercely loyal (in contrast to the detached, more free-spirited Jack), willing to sacrifice himself, to do the messy and hard jobs for the greater glory of the family. After initial reluctance, Bobby seemed to embrace this role, burying, for the time being, any resentment that he had been required to sublimate his own ambitions.

JFK's opponent was Henry Cabot Lodge, a Brahmin scion whose grandfather by the same name had been senator from Massachusetts before him. An incumbent, Lodge was heavily favored to win reelection. At the outset, the Kennedy for Senate campaign was "an absolute disaster," according to Kenny O'Donnell, Bobby's football pal, who, bored by law school, had gone to work as a political aide to Jack. Joe Kennedy had taken charge of getting his son elected, throwing money about the state and catering to "elder statesmen who knew nothing about politics," said O'Donnell. Kennedy Sr. was about twenty years out-of-date in his knowledge of the Massachusetts political scene, O'Donnell later scoffed, but he was "such a strong personality that no one dared argue with him." Eager to assert his independence, Jack was barely speaking to his father. O'Donnell, caught in the middle, felt helpless. The campaign, he recalled, was in a state of "utter chaos." Realizing that "the only one who can talk to Kennedys is another Kennedy," he called Bobby and begged him to help.

After graduating in the middle of his law school class, Robert Kennedy had, with his father's help, secured a job at the Justice Department. He had just been given his first real case, a political corruption investigation in New York, when O'Donnell called and asked him to join the campaign. Bobby angrily resisted. He said that he didn't know anything about politics or Massachusetts. "I'll just screw it up," he told O'Donnell. A week later, RFK called back, sounding resigned. "Okay," he said, "I guess I'll have to do it." It may be significant that Kennedy took a week to decide, and accepted his duty only grudgingly. He must have struggled with some stirrings of independence, some desire to strike out on his own and forge a career that was not entwined with the empire building of his father or the political aspirations of his brother.

Helping his brother get elected—and mediating between domineering father and rebellious son—was, at the outset at least, a thankless task. John Kennedy was not glad to see his little brother when he arrived in Boston in late May. The candidate berated O'Donnell for meddling. JFK apparently believed that Bobby's presence would just irritate Joe Sr. and make him more intrusive. "Jack was very upset that I'd called Bobby," O'Donnell remembered. "He was irritated with me." O'Donnell discovered, to his surprise, that the brothers were not at all close: "Bobby didn't know what Jack was doing, Jack didn't know what Bobby was doing, and neither one cared very much what either one was doing. I had been under the impression that they were peas in a pod. They certainly weren't."

Born eight years apart, possessing very different temperaments, John Kennedy and Robert Kennedy were not considered close even by their own siblings. "All this business about Jack and Bobby being blood brothers," their sister Eunice remarked, "has been exaggerated." She noted that they had "different tastes in men, different tastes in women." At their father's insistence, the two brothers had traveled together on a seven-week tour of the Far East in the fall of 1951. Jack fretted beforehand that Bobby would be "a pain in the ass." Jack had never chosen to socialize with his little brother and may have felt that he had been drafted to play tour guide and baby-sitter by his father. It was Bobby who ended up as caretaker. Jack became critically ill on the trip. In Okinawa, he was rushed to a military hospital with a temperature of 106 degrees. In the family tradition, Bobby had teased Jack about his susceptibility to illness, joking that if Jack were bitten by a mosquito, the mosquito would die. But to sit alone by his brother's bed on a remote Pacific island while a priest read the last rites had to have been a jarring experience for RFK. "Everyone expected him to die," he later recalled.

Always sickly, Kennedy had been diagnosed in 1947 with Addison's disease, a failure of the adrenal glands that could lead to weakness, weight loss, vomiting, and circulatory collapse. Not properly cared for, the disease could be fatal. In 1950, cortisone was found to be an effective treatment, and Joe Kennedy immediately began stashing the drug in safe-deposit boxes around the country so that Jack would never run out. But the cortisone was not a cure-all, and it had some disturbing side effects, including inducing a state of euphoria. Addison's disease was not Kennedy's only health problem. His unstable back, damaged by war and football, also caused him excruciating pain.

In the 1952 Senate race, Kennedy's health was his greatest campaign vulnerability. Had voters known how truly sick the handsome war hero was, his political career could have been a nonstarter. The Kennedys were determined that the voters would never find out. His recurring fevers from Addison's were passed off as mild flare-ups of malaria from his wartime service in the Pacific. Kennedy's healthy tan, refreshed by a sunlamp, kept up a mask of false vitality. Although Kennedy needed crutches to get around much of the time, voters rarely saw him hobbled. The crutches were left in the car. "Those who knew him well would know he was suffering only because his face was a little whiter and the lines around his eyes were a little deeper, his words a little sharper," Bobby Kennedy said. "Those who did not know him well detected nothing." It's doubtful that Kennedy regarded his brother's brave show as a cover-up. He was, in any case, accustomed to keeping family secrets. His personal prudishness did not stand in the way of his willingness to act as a procurer for his father. Kay Halle, a Washington socialite and family friend, recalled being approached at a restaurant by both Jack and Bobby Kennedy in about 1950. Their father was in town and needed some discreet help finding a girl for the night, the Kennedys told a startled Halle. Did she know of any?

RFK became the manager of JFK's Senate campaign "by elimination more than design," recalled Kenny O'Donnell. After Bobby arrived at campaign headquarters on Kilby Street in Boston, Charlie Bartlett, a Palm Beach friend of the family's who had volunteered, heard Bobby talking on the phone to his father. "Yes, Dad," Bobby kept patiently saying. "Yes, Dad." Bobby was not so much acquiescing to his father as humoring him. He had learned how to placate and temporize.

RFK was no longer a mere agent for his father's wishes. His brother-protector role cast him more as a mediator, a go-between who could keep peace between controlling father and stubborn oldest son. At several important moments during the campaign, RFK rejected his father's advice. Joe Kennedy wisely did not push too hard. Shrewdly, and because he was truly more ambitious for his son than for himself, Joe Kennedy learned to lower his profile. He understood the risk of being identified as the man behind the curtain, the cardinal to the dauphin. Joseph Kennedy was acutely PR conscious and justifiably prided himself as a clever image maker. He understood that the whisperings about his alleged criminal associations and shady dealings on Wall Street created an image problem for his son, whose political appeal rested partly on running as a standard-bearer for the "new generation" of war veterans. Joe Kennedy did not want to read stories about "bootlegger's son" John Kennedy.

Bobby's active presence in the campaign allowed Joe to step back into the shadows. With Bobby's arrival, Joe stayed strictly in the back room, concentrating on his own special interests. The senior Kennedy busied himself with the advertising and television (not much in those early days) and kept the money flowing. His other job—an important one—was to handle Senator Joe McCarthy. The demagogue from Wisconsin was at the height of his power in 1952, and his appearance on behalf of the Republicans would have sunk Kennedy. But the fearsome red hunter never came to the Bay State. A large donation to the McCarthy campaign from Kennedy Sr. and a few quiet words from the Catholic hierarchy in Massachusetts—from Richard Cardinal Cushing, at Joe's behest—kept him out.

Unable to abide laziness or freeloaders, Bobby goaded the campaign out of its lassitude. He was curt and dismissive to the hacks who hung about headquarters waiting for handouts from Joe. He banned the usual freebies of sandwiches and coffee and derisively told the old boys that if they were looking for something to do, they could start addressing envelopes. A former mayoral candidate who had once campaigned by traveling around Boston in a sound truck singing "Danny Boy" was taken aback when Bobby did not know his name. Kennedy threw him out for using profanity around female staffers. Bobby recoiled from the backslapping and glad-handing of the hustings. "I don't know how you stand it," he said to Larry O'Brien, a shrewd campaign organizer who had signed on (and would remain, with Kenny O'Donnell and several others, the Kennedys' "Irish mafia"). Kennedy used the word "politician" as a form of disparagement. In a confrontation with the headquarters hangers-on, he shouted, "I don't want my brother to get mixed up with politicians!" The politicians felt nearly the same way about Bobby. "The candidate's brother," as he was usually introduced, just shrugged. "I don't care if anyone around here likes me," he muttered, "as long as they like Jack."

Jack was more than happy to let his brother play the heavy. JFK liked to remain above the fray, coolly elegant and sardonic. He let Bobby deal with the hacks and favor-seekers, as well as run interference with their father. From the start, the Kennedy campaign had declared its independence from the state Democratic organization. At first, there had been no objection from the incumbent governor, Paul Dever, who regarded young Kennedy as a drag on the ticket. But in the September primaries, their fortunes reversed; Kennedy ran ahead of Dever, who had sweated and stumbled through a nationally televised speech at the Democratic convention in August. Now Dever wanted to join forces with Kennedy and share headquarters. A believer in making deals with the party bosses, Joseph Kennedy wanted to go along with Dever for the sake of party unity. Believing that a new generation of voters were tired of the old politics, O'Donnell and O'Brien regarded Dever as a creature of a dying order and did not want him running under the same banner. JFK sided with O'Brien and O'Donnell and decided to deny Dever's request. "Don't give in to them," instructed JFK, "but don't get me involved in it." It was Bobby's job to deliver the bad news—first to his father, then to the governor. With Dever at least, Bobby was blunt. When RFK left his office, Dever angrily grumbled, "Keep that young kid out of here."

Bobby threw himself into creating a political organization that was separate and apart from the existing party structure. "We couldn't win relying on the Democratic political machine," Robert Kennedy later recalled, "so we had to build up our own machine." Kennedy wanted civic-minded amateurs who were not tainted by the old ways. Larry O'Brien went to work recruiting three hundred campaign "secretaries" in cities and towns around Massachusetts. Many were young veterans and some were Republicans or not even registered to vote. It all had the feel of newness and freshness, "new politics" for a "new generation," except that the basic animating principle was old. Back in the late nineteenth century, when the Irish immigrants were slowly undermining the political power of the Yankees, they had created a system of "ward bosses"— Honey Fitz had been one—to act as a shadow government on the real one.

Bobby was "not a very good organizer," recalled Richard Donahue, a young lawyer from Lowell who would join O'Donnell and O'Brien in the Irish mafia. "He was not good at follow-through and he was not always realistic. He would say, 'Let's have a tea for five hundred people tomorrow in Worcester.' " Kennedy's failings as an organizer—his impatience, his amateurism, his predilection for going outside channels—would become problematic. But for the time being his shortcomings were hidden by the sheer force of his determination. Bobby was still softhearted in some ways. He hated to fire anyone whose family depended on a paycheck. He was solicitous of the many young women who, starstruck by the candidate, volunteered to work for the campaign. "Bobby admired women," said Joe Gargan, RFK's twenty-two-year-old cousin who bunked with him at a rooming house on Marlborough Street. "He wanted women in the campaign because they were the workers." RFK instructed Gargan to walk female volunteers to the subway if they worked late. Some evenings, the campaign manager would take a carload of volunteers over to the Ritz for ice cream sundaes.

Such chivalry and courtliness notwithstanding, the image of Bobby Kennedy as "ruthless" probably began during his brother's 1952 Senate campaign. He was "the enforcer," said Donahue. He made sure tasks got performed, no matter how trivial. He was extremely demanding, but of no one more than himself. If a campaign poster needed to be tacked up a little higher, Kennedy would be the one to perch precariously on the ladder. He would personally go door-to-door handing out a campaign tabloid newspaper extolling JFK's virtues, which he had ordered printed up at great expense. Joe Kennedy was perplexed and a little vexed by Bobby Kennedy's costly pursuit of each and every voter. By the judicious application of a $500,000 loan to the cash-poor publisher of the *Boston Post*, the patriarch had switched the paper's influential endorsement from Lodge to Kennedy. Why was Bobby wasting money on an expensive tabloid that required hand delivery? RFK stood up to his father and pushed ahead with the canvassing, climbing the steps of rotting double-deckers on the poor backstreets of Dorchester to knock on doors. "Bobby had never seen tenements before," recalled Kenny O'Donnell.

By far the most effective family enterprise was "the Kennedy tea." During Jack's 1946 congressional campaign, Rose and the Kennedy girls had hosted a tea party for women voters at the Commander Hotel in Cambridge. The response was overwhelming. Traffic in Harvard Square was tied up for hours. Women by the hundreds, mostly middle class but dressed carefully in gloves and hats, turned out to listen to the wife of the ambassador to the Court of St. James's describing her stay at Windsor Castle as the guest of the king and queen. For the upwardly mobile Irish, the Kennedys held the promise of arrival. Jack Kennedy was the man they wanted their daughters to marry. In the summer of 1952, some of Kennedy's aides cautioned against holding a tea in the blue-collar stronghold of South Boston. Too "highfalutin," they warned. But Bobby knew better. Kenny O'Donnell later joked that the tea caused "the biggest run on new dresses in the history of Boston."

As election day approached, Kennedy still trailed in the polls. There were no real issues to speak of. Kennedy's slogan was "Kennedy Can Do More for Massachusetts." Lodge countered with "Lodge Has Done More for Massachusetts." Though the front-runner, Lodge wanted to debate. Bobby Kennedy and Kenny O'Donnell feared a trap. Lodge could ask leading questions about Kennedy's tepid support for the new state of Israel, hoping to evoke responses that would remind Jewish voters of Joe Kennedy's well-known anti-Semitism. Kennedy's answers, taped at the debate, could be made into negative ads. To protect JFK, Bobby demanded that the Lodge forces agree not to record the debate. Lodge's advisers appeared to agree, but a Lodge supporter arrived at the debate, at Waltham High School, carrying a tape recorder. Furious, Bobby, O'Donnell, and O'Brien urged JFK to walk out and cry double cross. Jack Kennedy told his advisers to relax. Onstage, he was cool and offhand as he verbally sparred with his opponent. Lodge, by contrast, sweated and his hands shook. The Irishman had shown up the Brahmin at the WASP art of effortless grace.

The Republican presidential candidate, Dwight D. Eisenhower, won Massachusetts in a landslide. Governor Dever lost. On election night, at dinner with his father at the family apartment on Beacon Street, JFK teased and joked with his sisters, pretending to ignore the early poll results forecasting a Republican sweep. At campaign headquarters, as the returns began to show a close race between Lodge and Kennedy, the crowd cheered and danced. The only family member who looked worried, recalled JFK's Harvard friend Torbert Macdonald, was Bobby. At 4 a.m., Macdonald found RFK in a bedroom, bitterly complaining about campaign workers, especially those from organized labor, who had "just given lip service and hadn't done what they should have for Jack."

Shortly after 7 a.m. on the morning after election day, Kennedy was declared the winner by seventy thousand votes. For the Kennedys, the revenge was sweet. A half century earlier, Lodge's grandfather, the first Henry Cabot, had introduced a bill in the U.S. Senate to keep out Irish immigrants by imposing a literacy test. When John F. Fitzgerald, then a young congressman, had spoken out against the bill, Lodge had scorned him as "an impudent young man." Honey Fitz's daughter Rose celebrated her son's conquest of Henry Cabot Lodge II by entertaining Larry O'Brien with a devastating imitation of the patrician Lodge, who was bitterly grumbling to reporters that Kennedy had "floated into the Senate on an ocean of tea." Governor Dever pronounced Jack the "first Irish Brahmin." Bobby, he added, was "the last Irish Puritan."

Bobby had worked seven days a week since June, opening up headquarters at 8 a.m. and closing it after midnight. He looked pale and gaunt, having shed ten pounds from his slender frame. He had won his brother's confidence. "I don't think [Jack] was aware," recalled Lem Billings, "that Bobby had all this tremendous ability." JFK would not always enjoy RFK's company in the future, but he would no longer ignore him. RFK was grateful to have finally garnered the attention of his older brother. But the real prize—his father's approbation—was more elusive. There can be no doubt that Joe Kennedy appreciated RFK's labors. He would not have stepped back and allowed Bobby to take over the campaign had he not trusted his judgment and efficacy. With his newspaper friends and cronies, Joe could be effusive in his praise of Bobby. But Joe Kennedy was a demanding father, almost cruelly so in the eyes of some of Bobby's friends. "Bobby had a deep respect for his father, tinged with fear. They never showed any emotion. There certainly wasn't any cuddling," recalled Gerald Tremblay, a friend of Kennedy's from the University of Virginia. Over Thanksgiving, a couple of weeks after the election, the Kennedys invited Larry O'Brien and his wife to Hyannis for the weekend. During some cheerful cocktail-time chatter, O'Brien recalled, Joe Kennedy turned to Bob and abruptly demanded, "Well, what are you going to do now?"

"What do you mean?" asked Bob.

"You've got to get to work," said Joe Sr. "You haven't been elected to anything."

IN JANUARY 1953, Bobby went to work as a lawyer on the staff of the Senate Permanent Subcommittee on Investigations under its chairman, Senator Joseph McCarthy. His father got him the job by picking up the phone and calling McCarthy. (The senator from Wisconsin was soon joking to an aide that he wasn't sure Joe's campaign contribution was worth it.) In later years, the Kennedys would struggle to explain how RFK could have worked for the most reckless red-baiter in history. McCarthy's reputation for smears was well established by 1953. "I just cannot understand how you could ever have had anything to do with Joe McCarthy," the writer Peter Maas said to Bobby Kennedy in the mid-1960s. "Well, at the time, I thought there was a serious internal security threat to the United States," Kennedy responded, ". . . and Joe McCarthy seemed to be the only one who was doing anything about it." After a pause, Kennedy added, "I was wrong." Some Kennedy true believers were so incredulous that by the liberal late 1960s they were engaging in outright denial. Bobby Kennedy "didn't know Joe McCarthy from a cord of wood," Kenny O'Donnell told an interviewer shortly after Kennedy's death in 1968.

Actually, McCarthy was reasonably close to the family. An affable, hard-drinking Irishman, he took Pat and Jean out on dates. He warmed up by discussing communists for a half hour or so, then "kissed very hard," Jean remembered. He was invited up to Hyannis, where he joined, or rather became, the fun. A family friend recalled watching the Kennedy kids laughing and taking home movies as they threw McCarthy, who couldn't swim, off the dock. Bobby invited McCarthy to speak to the law students at the University of Virginia. At dinner at Bobby's house, McCarthy became sodden with drink and pawed a woman. Bobby helped him to bed, but he refused to be embarrassed for him. It is likely that Bobby Kennedy sympathized and identified with McCarthy. Black Irish and, beneath the bluster, vulnerable and eager to please, McCarthy may have been a bully, but to Bobby he was at the same time an underdog who enjoyed provoking the establishment. McCarthy's Catholicism strengthened the bond. The Wisconsin senator had been a lazy and directionless first termer when a group of Catholic priests from Catholic and Georgetown Universities suggested to him that chasing communists would be a worthy cause, as well as politically profitable. The church's ferocious anticommunism appealed to RFK's black-and-white moralism.

Kennedy did not like McCarthy's chief aide, Roy Cohn. Joe Kennedy had asked McCarthy to appoint his son as staff director of the Investigations Subcommittee, but McCarthy had instead chosen Cohn, a young red-chaser who as an assistant U.S. attorney had helped convict atomic bomb spies Julius and Ethel Rosenberg. Francis "Frip" Flanagan, a Senate staffer close to both the Kennedys and McCarthy, warned Cohn that Robert Kennedy was "disturbed" that he had lost out to Cohn as chief counsel. At their first meeting, Kennedy sullenly looked over his rival. According to Cohn, Kennedy belligerently began, "You puzzle me very much. Mort Downey [a famous entertainer and friend of Joseph Kennedy] thinks you're a great guy. But a lot of people think you're no good. I don't know which side to believe." RFK quickly joined Cohn's detractors. There was much to fault in Cohn: McCarthy's chief henchman was a bully and smear artist. But Kennedy's loathing may have been more personal. He would from time to time display deep homophobia, and Cohn's homosexuality was unacknowledged but obvious. Cohn, heavy lidded and malevolent, returned the antipathy. He called Kennedy a "rich bitch" and gave him menial work. When Cohn and his fellow investigator and love object, David Schine, took a much-ridiculed inspection tour of American embassies in Europe, weeding out subversive literature and peering under beds for reds, Kennedy seethed with disapproval. He later said that he complained to McCarthy about the way McCarthy and Cohn were running the committee. "I thought it was headed for disaster. . . . I told him I thought he was out of his mind and was going to destroy himself." Then, Kennedy said, he quit.

Kennedy's account may be only part of the story. The full explanation for his departure from McCarthy's committee in July 1953, only five months after he signed on, is probably more complex. FBI documents show that McCarthy actually considered making Kennedy staff director in May, but that other staffers were opposed and FBI director J. Edgar Hoover—with whom McCarthy checked every move—was at best indifferent. The FBI's Hoover was beginning to cool on McCarthy, sensing that the senator was about to overplay his hand and become a liability to the anti-communist crusade. It is likely that Hoover shared his concerns with Joseph Kennedy. Kennedy Sr. was in close contact with Hoover—at one time in the 1950s he had tried to hire Hoover away from the FBI as his own personal "director of security." Father would have warned son, expediting his resignation.

Out of work, Kennedy settled for yet another job arranged by his father, as his father's assistant on a presidential committee on government reform, headed by former president Herbert Hoover. Bobby spent his time impatiently listening to old men argue about reorganizing the Department of Agriculture. He quit after a couple of months and went back to work on the Investigations Subcommittee, this time as a counsel for the minority Democrats, who by now had turned on McCarthy. RFK's seat on the committee dais gave him a shot at Roy Cohn as McCarthy was self-destructing during the Army-McCarthy hearings in the spring and early summer of 1954. RFK stayed in close touch with Joe Sr.: "Bobby telephones his father regularly and, of course, everybody is listening to the McCarthy hearings," Rose wrote her daughter Pat on June 2.

Cohn would later claim that RFK returned to the committee for the precise purpose of "getting" his old nemesis. Cohn recalled:

> He came back not to fight McCarthy, but to fight me. . . . He found Mary Driscoll [McCarthy's secretary] in the beauty shop and said give him [McCarthy] a message: "I'll do nothing to hurt him. But I'm going to get that little son of a bitch Cohn." He always had that little smirk on his face, designed to get under my skin, and it did.

Sitting behind Senator Henry "Scoop" Jackson of Washington, Kennedy fed questions to the senators designed to embarrass Cohn about a grandiose anti-communist plan of action written up by his friend David Schine. Cohn grew angrier and angrier as he watched Kennedy snickering and laughing while Senator Jackson picked apart the "plan." During a recess, Cohn stormed across the hearing room to Kennedy and threatened to "get" Senator Jackson. "You can't get away with it, Cohn," Kennedy snarled. The conversation rapidly deteriorated. "Do you want to fight right here?" Cohn demanded. He started to swing at Kennedy, but aides pulled them apart. With a tight smile, Kennedy turned away. The papers found sport the next morning: the headline in the *New York Daily News* was "COHN, KENNEDY NEAR BLOWS IN 'HATE' CLASH." For all his bravado, Kennedy was shaken by the confrontation. After he left the hearing room, he went to find his brother Jack. His brother had warned Bobby against working for McCarthy. An aide saw them huddled together, speaking in low tones.

CHAPTER 3 MORALIST

ROBERT KENNEDY'S PROPENSITY to pick fights, always pronounced, was becoming manic. Intemperate and reckless, Kennedy seemed to welcome bad odds. Larry O'Brien recalled watching Kennedy play touch football with his brother Teddy in a park in Georgetown in the spring of 1954. Some students from the university, playing softball nearby, kept hitting fly balls into the middle of the Kennedys' game. Ted Kennedy yelled at them to stop. A confrontation ensued, and Teddy, a lineman on the football team at Harvard, squared off with one of the bigger opponents. Bobby pushed aside his younger brother and insisted on single combat against the man, who was about thirty pounds heavier. The fight was "uneven," O'Brien recorded, "which was no doubt what Bob wanted." The two punched and chased each other around the park until they could no longer raise their arms. At dinner that evening, Ethel saw Bob's bloody face and remarked, "That must have been a rough game of touch." Robert barely looked up from dinner. "Yeah," he mumbled.

It was a time of "bad doldrums" for Bobby, recalled Lem Billings. When he went out in the evening, Kennedy seemed determined to provoke embarrassing arguments. Many of them were waged over Joe McCarthy. Disgraced by the Army-McCarthy hearings, the Wisconsin demagogue was fast becoming a pariah, which seemed to make Bobby fierce in his defense. His football friends from Harvard recalled an angry blowup between Ken O'Donnell and Bobby after the 1954 Harvard-Yale game. Perplexed at Bobby's stubborn refusal to recognize the shame of McCarthy, O'Donnell pleaded, "What the hell is wrong with you?" In January 1955, CBS newsman Edward Murrow, whose exposé helped topple McCarthy, spoke at a banquet honoring the Junior Chamber of Commerce Ten Outstanding Young Men of 1954, one of whom, thanks to his father's finagling, was Bobby. Grim-faced, young Kennedy walked out during the speech. At a dinner table argument at Charlie Bartlett's, Kennedy an-

nounced that he admired McCarthy so much that he had asked him to be his
own child's godfather.* The only one unperturbed by Bobby's vehemence was
Joe Kennedy. "That's pretty tough company he's travelling with," observed
Robert Lovett, a former secretary of defense, who disliked McCarthy. "Put
your mind to rest about that," responded Kennedy Sr. "Bobby is just as tough
as a bootheel."

Joe should have been the uneasy one. There is more than a trace of adolescent defiance in Bobby's acting up in the early 1950s. In ways large and small,
Kennedy had never quite grown up. He was approaching his thirtieth birthday,
but he wore white sweat socks with his suits to work. He may have just been
slovenly—he was a notoriously indifferent dresser. Or, in a petty act of resistance, he may have been purposefully ignoring his mother's stern injunction
that a gentleman never wears white socks with business attire. At his brother
Jack's wedding to Jacqueline Bouvier in September 1953, Bobby had behaved
like a naughty teenager, stealing a policeman's hat. Joe Kennedy was furious.
He summoned Bobby and his co-conspirators, his brother Teddy and some
younger cousins, and gave them a lecture about disgracing the family name.
When Bobby tried to speak up, Joe snapped, "No. You keep quiet and listen to
me. This is childish behavior, and I don't want anything more like it."

Bobby's defiance of authority, his desire to break away, was so puerile that
it signaled something more than the commonplace angst of a young man uncertain about his future. These times in Kennedy's life were not so much the
doldrums, as Lem Billings described them, as days of rage. Kennedy seemed to
be swinging wildly, yet unable to connect. Even his natural curiosity was sacri-
ficed to fearful introspection. To show him life behind the Iron Curtain, Joe
Kennedy recruited Justice William O. Douglas to take Bobby on a tour of the
central Soviet republics in 1955. Douglas later told his wife that Bobby had
trudged along glumly, suspiciously eyeing his hosts. He had refused most food
and even, when he became seriously ill, declined to be treated by a "communist
doctor." (He may have been less careful in other ways: an intelligence file on
Kennedy in the Kremlin foreign office, made public in 1997, reports that he
asked his Intourist guide to send a "woman of loose morals" up to his hotel
room.) When he returned, Kennedy gave a speech and a slide show on his trip
at Georgetown University. His faithful secretary, Angie Novello, later described his performance:

> I was appalled. I thought, "Oh, no!". . . . I was sitting in the middle of
> the auditorium and I could hardly hear him because his voice was
> very high pitched and he'd slur his words and go down to nothing.
> When we got back, Bob said, "How did you think it went?" I said,
> "The pictures were great, but I think you could have spoken better

---

* Rumors persisted for years that McCarthy was Kathleen Kennedy's godfather. Jean
Kennedy Smith later denied these rumors to Kennedy biographer Arthur Schlesinger.

than that." And Ethel said, "I thought he was very good!" Bob sort of smiled.

Kennedy was grateful for his wife's support. Ethel remained the one true believer in RFK. But she could not rescue him from brooding. Encouraged by Ethel, RFK quietly entertained hopes of seeking elected office. Chatting one day with his friend Gerald Tremblay, Kennedy ventured that he might even run for president one day. Tremblay suspected that Kennedy was just trying out the idea, that he wasn't terribly serious. For the most part, RFK had to swallow his ambitions. He knew he was a poor speaker who lacked his brother's glamour and air of authority. Possibly, Kennedy lashed out during these years because he felt thwarted, wishing to be something greater than his brother's helper, yet recognizing that his own role—a seasonal one at that—was in service to the family dynasty at election time. From time to time, he dreamed of escape. He talked to one friend about working for the Atomic Energy Commission in Colorado, in part, he admitted, to be close to the skiing. He suggested to a Senate aide that he might run for the Senate "somewhere like Nevada." Running for office in Nevada would give him an excuse to get away from the East Coast with all its rigidities and expectations. In June 1953, after he quit working for Joe McCarthy, he settled—briefly—on moving out west to work in the oil business and maybe run for Congress. "Bobby is going to New Mexico," Rose wrote daughter Pat. "They [Bobby and Ethel] seem to think it will be a good spot as it is near the oil wells. It is also a good spot for a Democrat with a lot of Spanish Catholics around. . . . They could come up here for the summer as usual. I think you should all try different states myself." New Mexico fell through, and when Kenny O'Donnell and Larry O'Brien urged him to run for attorney general in Massachusetts in 1954 (partly as a way of keeping greased the new Kennedy machine), Bobby begged off.

Joe Kennedy was quoted as saying that Bobby was more like him than any other child because "he hates like me." Kennedy Sr. later denied the remark. Whether he said it or not, Bobby was not at heart a hater. His anger in this period made him offensive to others and upsetting to his friends, but his better side had not been entirely eclipsed. He wanted to be a good family man. Ethel was bearing children at the rate of one every year or so, beginning with Kathleen (1951), Joseph II (1952), Robert Jr. (1954), and David (1955). Kennedy's co-workers on the investigations subcommittee recalled him racing home to see them at precisely five-thirty every afternoon. Bobby had rented a soon-to-be-overflowing house in Georgetown for $400 a month, about $70 less than his monthly salary. Friends described an innocent, almost pure atmosphere at the Kennedy home on S Street: the doors of every room were always open, and Ethel kept no liquor or ashtrays in the house (hard to imagine in 1955). While often cross with adult humans, Bobby was tenderhearted about animals: JFK's friend Chuck Spalding recalled an evening in Hyannis when Bobby accidentally struck a dog with his car. He spent the rest of the night walking door-to-door, looking for the dog's owner. He could be rude and insensitive to strangers, but he was at the same time a loyal friend who would go out of his way to care for a sick colleague: LaVern Duffy, a Senate staffer, remembered Bobby's coming to his house when he fell seriously ill. Bobby insisted on taking Duffy to a hospital where he could be cared for by Kennedy family doctors. At home, RFK was grateful for Ethel's unquestioning love and support. At dinner party arguments over Joe McCarthy, Ethel fiercely defended her husband for defending McCarthy. When friends brought up McCarthy's reckless red-baiting, Ethel hotly interjected, "Name one person he has hurt."

RFK was warm and playful with his ebullient wife, reciprocating her affection. But if, as a couple, they shared their deepest fears and doubts, such intimacy was not readily apparent to friends. Ethel was not the sort to dwell on hurts and longings. In October 1955, her parents died in an airplane crash. Her father had been taking instruction as a Roman Catholic, fulfilling a lifelong wish of Ethel and her Irish Catholic mother, Ann. George Skakel planned to convert when he returned from a business trip to California that October. The refurbished B-26 bomber he used as a company plane exploded in the air over Oklahoma. Skakel was given a big Catholic funeral, with twenty-five priests on the altar, a great consolation to Ethel. At the funeral and wake, Ethel coped by laughing and smiling instead of crying. She never spoke of her parents' death with friends.

Although RFK was emotional as a young man, his anger so close to the surface that it showed as clench-fisted rage, he did not show many signs of self-awareness. He felt strongly, but it is doubtful that he understood his own passions. He would, in later years, seek to understand human nature, including his own, by reading and thinking. But as a thirty-year-old, he was more reactive than reflective. Without quite realizing why, he seemed to be searching, with a kind of grim determination, for an outlet for his anger—for an enemy he could attack.

When the Democrats won back control of the Senate in 1955, Bobby became chief counsel of the Senate Permanent Subcommittee on Investigations. With communist hunting out of favor in the wake of McCarthy's excesses, Kennedy steered the committee towards government corruption. But he discovered his true interest in the netherworld of organized crime.

During an investigation into government procurement fraud in New York in 1955, Kennedy stumbled across the common practice of gangsters' extorting protection money from employers and unions. Kennedy became intrigued, and he began asking federal investigators about extortion and racketeering. In those days, the FBI stayed away from mobsters. Fearing that his G-men might be corrupted by the mob, Hoover steadfastly denied the existence of organized crime. The Bureau of Narcotics was less fastidious and less blind. It was to the "narcs" that Bobby first turned for a tour of the underworld.

Since at least the 1920s, the Sicilian Mafia had been exporting its trade to the United States. The mobsters entered the usual rackets—loan-sharking, extortion, prostitution, gambling, and, during Prohibition, bootlegging. Some gangsters also moved into the potentially lucrative market for narcotics. In the mid-1950s, a pair of narcotics agents, Angelo Zurlo and Joe Amato, put together an elaborate "family tree" of the Sicilian mobsters who ran the strongest crime organizations. As he asked around about organized crime, Kennedy met Zurlo and Amato, who in turn introduced him to street agents. Bobby began riding at night with narcotics agents on their raiding parties. "He liked being a police-man," recalled Howard Diller, a Bureau of Narcotics agent who would see Kennedy around headquarters downtown at 90 Church Street. "And he loved Irish detectives." The intelligence division of the New York Police Department was dominated by Irishmen. Self-consciously Irish, admiring Irish "tough-ness," Kennedy enjoyed the company of the NYPD detectives, who had a loose alliance with the Federal Bureau of Narcotics. Making ten or so busts a night, the Bureau of Narcotics used New York City cops to kick in doors. In that pre–civil liberties era, local police had a freer hand than the feds, who, at least in theory, were restricted by the Bill of Rights. As a practical matter, "defendants had no rights," recalled Diller. During his forays around Manhattan in 1955 and 1956, Bobby saw some shocking atrocities, on all sides. One night in Harlem, he was out with a flying squad that caught a man sexually abusing a two-year-old. As Bobby watched, the police threw the man out a window.

Joyriding with the cops at night exposed Kennedy to a Runyonesque world of cops and thugs and hookers. Kennedy learned some street skills of sur-vival. Mel Finkelstein, a police photographer for the tabloids, recalled a drunk in a bar, who, recognizing Kennedy's photo in the papers from the McCarthy hearings, called him a "rich kid" and said worse things about his father. Bobby asked the man to step outside. "I thought, Christ, the guy is going to murder Bobby," Finkelstein recollected. But as the man turned around, Kennedy hit him in the face, breaking his nose. Kennedy's nocturnal ramblings among the lowlifes touched a side of Kennedy that had been well concealed. Sin held a fas-cination for the prudish son who, unlike his brothers, had been abstemious enough to win his father's $1,000 reward for not drinking or smoking until age twenty-one. Kennedy never bragged to friends about his bar-fighting tri-umphs; he kept his night life in New York well hidden from his family. In later years, his friends were slightly puzzled by Kennedy's fondness for colorful rogues; it seemed somehow out of character with the straightlaced moralist. But like William Gladstone, the nineteenth-century British prime minister who wished to save the souls of the ladies of the night by interviewing them in his rooms, Kennedy was drawn to the flame he wished to snuff out.

RFK was not out cruising into the small hours merely to flirt with danger or the pleasures of the night. He wanted to conquer evil. As he quizzed the narcs and the detectives in the intelligence division of the NYPD about crimi-nals and their connections, he was getting at least a glimpse of the larger, darker forces behind street life in the city.

His education was furthered by newspapermen. Then as now, congres-sional investigators often got their best tips from newspapermen. In the sum-mer of 1956, Kennedy began hearing from muckraking reporters who were writing stories about corruption in the trade union movement. Unions, with their vast pension funds and need for muscle, made ideal targets of opportunity for organized crime. Ever since the Kefauver hearings in 1951, the public had been at least dimly aware that labor was being infiltrated by the mob. *On the Waterfront*, the 1954 movie about corruption in the Longshoremen's Union, dramatized the problem. But it took some muckraking reporters to begin to expose the vast reach of labor racketeering.

Uncovering mob ties to the unions was a dangerous business. In April 1956, some hoods threw acid into the eyes of a crusading labor reporter, Victor Riesel. The chief suspect, Johnny Dio (Dioguardi), was by coincidence the subject of an investigation by Kennedy's subcommittee into extortion schemes by mobbed-up unions against some government contractors, textile factory owners in New Jersey who made uniforms for the military. The New York prosecutors asked Kennedy to hold off on Dio while a grand jury took testimony in the Riesel maiming (the mobster later beat the rap). But reporters began nudging Kennedy: Shouldn't his congressional investigators take a look at the broader problem of labor racketeering? Kennedy hesitated. He was only just beginning to see the dimensions of the threat. Anyway, he wasn't sure his committee had jurisdiction. The Senate Labor Committee was jealous of its purview, but its members were also leery of offending Big Labor, which generously donated to the political parties.

A relentless and abrasive newsman named Clark Mollenhoff found the key to Kennedy: he baited him for being gutless. Was Kennedy scared? Mollenhoff taunted. Afraid of the power of the unions? He didn't have to ask if Kennedy was physically afraid. Kennedy took the bait. In August 1956, he got the members of the investigations subcommittee to authorize a preliminary look into racketeering by the labor unions.

Although he could not yet see the scale of his crusade or where it would take him, Kennedy had at last found an enemy worthy of his passion. But, as usual, family duty came first. Before RFK could take on a thorough rackets investigation, he had to attend to his brother Jack's political ambitions. Already plotting his path to the White House after four years in the Senate, Jack Kennedy wanted to make a try at getting on the ticket with Adlai Stevenson, the Democratic nominee who was making a second run for the presidency in 1956. Rather than name his running mate, Stevenson had thrown the choice open to a vote of the delegates at the party convention in Chicago in August. Just as in 1952, when Jack campaigned for the Senate, Bobby was expected to postpone his own career and come to his brother's side.

There was an element of rebellion in Senator Kennedy's last-minute grasp at the vice-presidential nomination. His father had warned him against openly campaigning for the vice presidency. If he lost, Kennedy Sr. predicted, JFK might squander his shot at the head of the ticket in 1960. And even if he won and got on the ticket, a Stevenson defeat in November might be blamed on his Catholicism. But at the Chicago convention, Jack Kennedy was seduced by a press corps that gushed over his vitality and glamour. He had brought Bobby along to Chicago (typically, Bobby refused to stay in the suite of his brother-in-law Peter Lawford because it was too grand). Jack made Bobby play the role of bad-news bearer to Joe Kennedy. "Call Dad. Tell him I'm going to go for it," JFK instructed from a safe corner of his hotel room. Kenny O'Donnell, who was in the room with the two brothers, could hear Joe's profanities spewing out over the phone line. "Whew, is he mad!" Bobby exclaimed when he hung up the phone.

Kennedy's impromptu campaign for the number two spot was done in by clumsy amateurism. Bobby and O'Donnell irked some party elders by tactless pressure and offended others by slighting them. As the balloting began, the neophytes barged about the convention floor, unsure where the real power lay and often guessing wrong. "Bobby and I ran around the floor like a couple of nuts," said O'Donnell. "We didn't know two people in the place." JFK lost, narrowly, to Senator Estes Kefauver, the Tennessee senator who had first won national attention with televised hearings on organized crime in 1951.

John Kennedy was disconsolate afterwards, fearing that he had damaged his political career by ignoring his father's warnings. Bobby went to commiserate with his brother in his room at the Stockyards Inn, near the convention hall. "You're the luckiest man in the world," Bobby declared as he walked in the room. Ken O'Donnell, watching this scene, observed that Bobby was joking "as Kennedys always do," in difficult times. In part, Bobby was taking his cue from his father. Joe Sr., who could be rough on his sons, also knew when to buck them up. At low moments, the patriarch was a cheerleader, telling them they could do no wrong. In fact, JFK's defeat really had been a blessing. Stevenson's campaign was doomed. But JFK had established himself as the bright young face of the party's future, the hope to recapture the White House in 1960.

For Bobby Kennedy, the abortive campaign at the Chicago convention had at least three positive results. It further established him in the role of go-between, the buffer between Joe and John Kennedy who could absorb the insults and prevent a real clash or break between father and son. The frantic floor effort gave Bobby a dry run at rounding up delegates at a national nominating convention. And the victory of Estes Kefauver, whom RFK had dismissed as a drunken lightweight, opened his eyes to another possibility—a way to make a name and win headlines while chasing bad guys.

Right after the balloting, a disappointed Bobby had run into Clark Mollenhoff, the newspaperman, on the convention floor. Mollenhoff argued that Jack Kennedy could enhance his stature in the Senate by investigating racketeering. Kefauver had made a national reputation with his hearings on organized crime. "Well, goddamn it. Do you believe me now?" Mollenhoff demanded. Kefauver "did his investigations five years ago and it got him enough clout to beat your brother's butt." Bobby's reaction is unrecorded. But Mollenhoff's remarks may have allowed RFK to see a way to further his own ambitions at the same time he served his brother's.

Duty kept Bobby tethered to politics for another three months. At JFK's request, Bobby spent most of the fall presidential campaign traveling with Adlai Stevenson. The Democratic nominee expected Bobby to help deliver the

Catholic vote. Bobby gave a few shaky speeches, but showed no loyalty to Stevenson, whom he regarded as weak and indecisive. He was only along to study the Democratic nominee's mistakes so that his brother would not repeat them in 1960. "Bob learned what not to do," said Newton Minow, a Stevenson aide and RFK's roommate on the campaign trail. "Adlai spent too much time writing his own speeches and not meeting people," said Minow. "Bob didn't like Adlai and he made no attempt to hide it." RFK was tender with Minow's daughter, who was in a wheelchair; otherwise, he was sullen and withdrawn. Newspapermen out on the campaign remembered Kennedy as hard-bitten and sour, but Minow observed a well-masked sentimental side. One day in Springfield, Illinois, Kennedy skipped a Stevenson speech and went instead to see the home of Abraham Lincoln. Minow recalled Kennedy's quiet reverence at the shrine. On election day, Kennedy voted for Eisenhower.

Then it was back to his new cause, investigating labor corruption. Kennedy saw a chance to top the 1951 Kefauver hearings by investigating the growing links between labor and organized crime. Such an investigation would be politically risky, given the power of Big Labor in the Democratic Party. Still, Kennedy started at the top: he picked as his first target the nation's largest and richest union, the Teamsters, the 1.3-million-man union that dominated the trucking industry. The union had been "mobbed up," quietly infiltrated by gangsters who saw the Teamsters' $250 million pension fund as a honey pot. In November, Kennedy traveled west under an alias (Mr. Rogers), talking to newspapermen who had written stories about labor corruption. With him was Carmine Bellino, an accountant and former FBI agent who, as a Senate staffer, had seen two previous congressional investigations of labor racketeering wilt under political pressure. "Unless you are prepared to go all the way," he advised, "don't start it." Kennedy replied, "We're going all the way." In Los Angeles, they heard grisly stories of strong-arm tactics. They learned about the union organizer who had been warned to stay out of San Diego by the jukebox operators. He went anyway and was knocked unconscious. When he awoke the next morning, "he was covered with blood and had terrible pains in his stomach," Kennedy wrote. "The pains were so intense that he was unable to drive back to his home in Los Angeles and stopped at a hospital. There was an emergency operation. The doctors removed from his backside a large cucumber. Later, he was told that if he ever returned to San Diego it would be a watermelon."

In Seattle, Mollenhoff sent Kennedy to see Ed Guthman, a Pulitzer Prize winner for the *Seattle Times* ("Can you trust him?" Guthman had asked Mollenhoff). Guthman directed Bobby to some Teamster dissidents. The renegades told Kennedy how the rank and file were being fleeced by the union bosses, who lived high (one of them used union trucks to transport his racehorses). The Teamsters' president, Dave Beck, was a self-important glad-hander who posed as a statesman of the union movement. He had built a grand headquarters in Washington known as the Marble Palace and won access to the Eisenhower White House. He was just the kind of puffed-up phony Kennedy delighted in exposing.

Through his newspaper contacts, Kennedy found a labor consultant named Nathan Shefferman, who had helped Beck buy a few items "wholesale." Kennedy and Bellino flew to Chicago and—with a subpoena—persuaded the affable Shefferman to show them his books. Bellino, an investigator with a nose for cooked books, spread the documents around their hotel room in the Palmer House. Bellino followed the money from union coffers to various improvements on Beck's lavish house in Seattle. After an hour, Kennedy later wrote, "we had come to the startling but inescapable conclusion that Dave Beck, the president of America's largest and most powerful labor union, the Teamsters, was a crook."

Kennedy was exhilarated when he returned home the next day, December 20. He was convinced that labor racketeering across the country "cried out for an investigation." For Christmas, Kennedy took his growing brood (five children, with the addition of Mary Courtney in September) and his crime-busting ambitions to Hyannis Port. He announced to his father and the rest of the clan that he would ask his Senate committee to probe the grip of organized crime on labor unions. The reaction was disappointing. No one cheered, and Joseph Kennedy was dead set against the idea. "He was really mad," sister Jean recalled. Such an investigation would be "politically dangerous. It would antagonize labor and lead to nothing," Jean recalled the patriarch arguing. "He was really, deeply emotionally opposed." The father-son debate raged on, dampening the holiday. Unable to make a dent, Joe Sr. recruited Justice William Douglas to talk some sense into his stubborn son. No luck, Douglas reported back. Bobby "feels it is too great an opportunity," Douglas told his wife.

An opportunity to do what, exactly? Was Kennedy risking his own brother's presidential ambitions by taking aim at the unions? Kefauver had capitalized on his organized crime hearings to become the running mate on a losing ticket in 1956. But Jack Kennedy aimed higher, and a Democrat would have a hard time winning the White House without the support of organized labor. Hearings that publicized the depth of union corruption hardly seemed like a way to make friends in the labor movement.

Some close observers of the Kennedy family, like historian Doris Kearns Goodwin, have wondered if some deeper, more Oedipal urge was driving RFK. Kennedy's fierce longing for his father's love, for so long withheld from the third and least successful son, and then meted out only slowly, could conceivably have provoked an equal and opposite reaction in Kennedy's psyche. Resentful and angry without quite knowing why, did Kennedy seek to attack the mob as a way, perhaps unexamined and unrealized, of lashing back at his father? As always, such psychological theories rest more on hints and intuitive feel than proof. There *is* a certain logic to the argument: Kennedy had as much reason to hate as to love his father. Directly attacking his father was unthinkable. But striking at his father's shadowy associations could be an indirect way of getting even. Certainly, it tempted fate. Bobby Kennedy's relationship to his father is the kind of human puzzle that fascinated the Greeks and Shakespeare. Still, in real life, there are some important pieces missing. Joseph Kennedy's shadowy ties to the underworld are the subject of much speculation and little

hard evidence. He was a liquor distributor whose clients were sometimes unsavory. Beyond that, little has been proved. In any case, it's not clear how much, if
anything, Bobby knew. He undoubtedly did hear the spiteful gossip from his
classmates that his father was a bootlegger. In the secretive universe of the
Kennedys, a world in which his own sister could simply vanish with the most
minimal explanation, Bobby Kennedy may have sensed, at least at some level,
that his father was the keeper of more dire secrets. Whether he did or not, the
fact remains: Robert Kennedy, after so many years of slavishly following his
father's wishes, had defied the patriarch. His stubbornness and independence
towards others had finally come home, provoking a family confrontation that
was, as sister Jean recalled, "the worst ever."

Kennedy's psychological motivations will always remain speculative, if
intriguing. More certain is Kennedy's dogmatic division of the world into good
and evil, his desire to stand up for the underdog, and his determination to test
his courage. In Jimmy Hoffa, Bobby Kennedy found the perfect foil.

HIS FATHER'S OBJECTIONS did not appear to slow down RFK even for a day. As
soon as he got back to Washington, two days after Christmas, Kennedy called
on Senator John McClellan of Arkansas, chairman of the investigations subcommittee, at his apartment, and laid out the evidence that he had collected
against the Teamsters. A crusty, righteous Baptist from a conservative southern
state, McClellan was perfectly willing to investigate racketeering by Big Labor.
To appease labor's defenders, however, a special committee would have to be
created, with four senators from McClellan's investigations subcommittee and
four from the more sympathetic and pliable Labor Committee. The new committee's mandate would be to look at wrongdoing by management as well as
labor. Thus, on January 31, 1957, was born the Select Committee on Improper
Activities in the Labor or Management Field, better known as the Rackets
Committee.

The creation of the select committee created an immediate dilemma for
RFK's brother. As the number two–ranking Democrat on Labor, Senator John
Kennedy was automatically entitled to join the Rackets Committee. He could
have ducked, following the example of Senator Henry "Scoop" Jackson, who
was fearful of crossing Teamster president Dave Beck, a powerful figure in
Jackson's home state of Washington. But JFK "reluctantly" agreed to serve,
writes RFK in his memoir of rackets-busting, *The Enemy Within*. According to
his brother, JFK initially felt that one Kennedy investigating labor was probably enough, a judgment Joseph Kennedy undoubtedly shared. JFK later said
that he went on the committee to keep off the next senator in line of seniority—arch-conservative Strom Thurmond of South Carolina—and because
"Bobby wanted me on that committee." But JFK was cagey. He may also have
wanted to keep an eye on RFK, to make sure his hotheaded little brother didn't
push too far and create a backlash that could jeopardize JFK's presidential ambitions. As one of his first acts as chief counsel of the Rackets Committee,
Bobby Kennedy asked his football buddy Kenny O'Donnell to come to Wash-

ington to serve as his administrative assistant. O'Donnell had been working for JFK in his Massachusetts office, preparing for JFK's 1958 Senate reelection campaign. JFK was irked when Bobby hired O'Donnell away, especially because RFK had failed to ask first. RFK and JFK were not so close that they were above spying on each other. Without telling Bobby, Jack Kennedy decided to use O'Donnell as an informer and governor on his brother's activities. He quietly implored O'Donnell to watch over Bobby and to stop him from doing anything impolitic. O'Donnell, who was personally closer to Bobby but politically ambitious for Jack, was in a somewhat awkward position. He resolved it by convincing himself that he was actually doing a favor for Bobby, whom he regarded as politically naive. O'Donnell was squirrelly and shrewd. Other staffers noted that, in the Irish tradition, he never wrote anything down. In the office, the old Harvard teammates often tossed around a football as they talked strategy. But O'Donnell tried to steer RFK away from any rash moves, and he kept Senator Kennedy informed.

RFK was already involved in his own intrigues. Eddie Cheyfitz, a Washington lawyer-fixer-PR man, had been hired by Dave Beck to polish the image of the Teamsters. Cheyfitz had invited RFK over to the Marble Palace and boasted of Beck's clout with leading politicians. Secretly, however, Cheyfitz was working for the man who wanted to push Beck aside and take over the Teamsters—Jimmy Hoffa, a hard-eyed, fire-plug-shaped former warehouseman from Detroit. Eager to see Beck brought down, Hoffa was quietly feeding damaging information about the Teamster president to Kennedy through Cheyfitz, who acted as the middleman and cutout.

Cheyfitz figured that Kennedy and Hoffa would get along because they were in many ways alike. Tough, competitive, suspicious, tightly wound, congenial when they felt like it and rude when they did not, Jimmy Hoffa and Robert Kennedy did have much in common, including wearing white socks with their suits. Arrested and convicted of assault, conspiracy, and extortion, a veteran of many bloody labor battles, Hoffa had always played rough. "Guys that tried to break me up got broken up," he bragged. He also flaunted his ties to gangsters. Union bosses who did not use underworld muscle, he scoffed, were "fools." But unlike Dave Beck, Hoffa was not a high liver, and he had—like Bobby Kennedy—his own sense of rough honor. He had lived with his wife and family in the same modest working-class house in Detroit for twenty years. When he traveled, he refused to let bellhops handle his luggage or hail him a cab. He never smoked or drank. And he saw himself as the champion of the underdog, standing for the rank and file against the free-loaders in the Marble Palace. Cheyfitz wanted to persuade Kennedy that Hoffa was a reformer who would clean up the Teamsters. Hoping that the two driven men would see their similarities and not their differences, Cheyfitz invited Hoffa and Kennedy to dinner at his house on a snowy evening on February 19, 1957.

Kennedy went, but with his guard up and his suspicions high. Unbeknownst to Cheyfitz, Kennedy had been tipped off that Hoffa was trying to subvert the Rackets Committee. On the night of February 12, a week before his

scheduled dinner with Hoffa and only two weeks after the creation of the committee, he got a call from a New York lawyer named John Cye Cheasty. "I have
information that will make your hair curl," Cheasty announced. "In those
days," recalled Kennedy, "there were few people I talked with who did not claim
to have information that would make my hair stand on end, and I tried to see
them all." Kennedy invited Cheasty to Washington. The next day, munching a
sandwich, he listened to Cheasty tell his story. He soon stopped eating. Cheasty
told him that he had been given $1,000 in cash as a down payment to get a job
as an investigator with the Rackets Committee. Hoffa wanted Cheasty to act as
a spy. Kennedy immediately hired Cheasty to act as a double agent.

   Kennedy was late to dinner at Cheyfitz's on the nineteenth because he had
been waiting in his office for a phone call from the FBI, reporting on a secret
meeting between Cheasty and Hoffa on a snowy street corner late that afternoon. At Cheyfitz's ornately decorated house, Kennedy and Hoffa said hello
and eyed each other warily. Kennedy noticed that Hoffa was short (five feet
five) and solidly built, with eyes that were small, bright green, and hard. Hoffa
was struck by Kennedy's weak handshake. He later told a reporter, "I can tell by
how he shakes hands what kind of fellow I got. I said to myself, 'Here's a fella
thinks he's doing me a favor by talking to me.' " Both men refused Cheyfitz's
offer of a drink. Kennedy began quizzing Hoffa about his ties to Johnny Dio,
the New York gangster charged with throwing acid into the eyes of labor reporter Victor Riesel. Hoffa brushed off the questions and bragged about his
toughness. "I do to others what they do to me," he blustered at Kennedy. The
union boss talked about his police record (sixteen arrests) and the brutal fights
he had waged against management. He said that he had destroyed employers
who tried to pick on him. "Maybe I should have worn my bullet-proof vest,"
Kennedy bluffed back. Kennedy always tried to deal with tense situations by
cracking wise jokes. The forced quality of his humor this evening suggests how
tense he felt. During the course of this uncomfortable evening, both Hoffa and
Cheyfitz revealed a knowledge of the Rackets Committee's inner workings that
could only have come from Cye Cheasty. Kennedy was tempted to drop
Cheasty's name, just to test the reaction, but decided not to risk tipping his
hosts off to Cheasty's double agent role.

   At about nine-thirty, Ethel called the Cheyfitz home to say that someone
had skidded into a tree outside the Kennedy house in McLean, and that her husband was needed at home. Hoffa chided, "Better hurry up, Bob. She probably
called to see if you're still alive." Kennedy called Ethel back and said, with more
labored humor, "I'm still alive, dear. If you hear a big explosion, I probably won't
be." "He's a damn spoiled jerk," Hoffa told Cheyfitz when Kennedy was gone.

   In his car driving home, Kennedy thought of how often Hoffa had said he
was "tough." The word had talismanic meaning to Kennedy, but he felt that
men who really were tough did not have to boast about it. Kennedy concluded
that Hoffa was "a bully hiding behind a facade."

   Less than a month into his investigation, Kennedy was reasonably confident that he could bring down not only Dave Beck, but also his would-be

usurper Jimmy Hoffa. Beck was vain and selfish, Kennedy believed, but Hoffa was more sinister. Kennedy was especially interested in Hoffa's ties to the mob and his use of "muscle" to keep discipline in the union and intimidate employers. From his friends in the New York police force, Kennedy had wiretaps of Hoffa making deals with Johnny Dio. Now, with Cheasty, he had his own lure to catch the Teamster boss.

On March 13, the FBI set a trap. As the government's hidden cameras whirred, Cheasty was seen handing over a manila envelope to Hoffa outside a hotel on Dupont Circle in downtown Washington. Hoffa stuffed $2,000 in fifty-dollar bills into Cheasty's hand. The gumshoes moved in, and Hoffa was arrested and charged with bribery.

Kennedy was waiting for Hoffa when he was arraigned at the courthouse after midnight. Hoffa glared at Kennedy "for three minutes," Kennedy recalled. Kennedy bridled when Hoffa addressed him as "Bobby" and told him to mind his own business. Then the men engaged in a debate over who could do the most push-ups. Ethel had come along to the courthouse. "I've never been to an arraignment before," she explained to a reporter. This one was "very exciting." Ethel was not there as a mere spectator. She had alerted the press, drawing fifty reporters to the scene. A little too cocky, Bobby told the reporters that he would "jump off the Capitol" if Hoffa were acquitted.

Kennedy was riding high, confident he could remake the Teamsters all at once. As he waited for the Hoffa bribery trial to start, he turned his attention back to Beck. At the end of March, the Rackets Committee called Beck to appear as a witness. The hearings began ponderously. The Teamster president blustered, offering rambling philosophical answers to his equally windy Senate inquisitors. Then, towards the end of the afternoon, it was the turn of the committee's chief counsel. Kennedy tipped his hand right away. "Can you tell the committee what your relationship had been with Mr. Nathan Shefferman?" Kennedy began. Beck immediately looked for cover. He invoked the Fifth Amendment privilege against self-incrimination. Kennedy was dryly sarcastic in his pursuit:

> MR. KENNEDY: Do you feel that if you gave a truthful answer to this Committee on your taking of $320,000 of union funds that might tend to incriminate you?
>
> MR. BECK: It might.
>
> MR. KENNEDY: Is that right?
>
> MR. BECK: It might.
>
> MR. KENNEDY: You feel that yourself?
>
> MR. BECK: It might.
>
> MR. KENNEDY: I feel the same way.
>
> CHAIRMAN: We will have order, please.
>
> MR. KENNEDY: I want to know, breaking that money down, Mr. Beck, did you use union funds to purchase five dozen diapers for some of your friends at $9.68?

Kennedy went on to list all the items that Nathan Shefferman had bought for the Beck family with union funds: undershirts from Sulka's of New York, golf balls and clubs, football tickets, twenty-one pairs of nylon stockings, outboard motors, love seats, a gravy boat, a twenty-foot deep freeze, etc. Over the next few weeks, Kennedy was able to prove that Beck was stealing money from the widow of his best friend. Beck was finished. He was eventually indicted and convicted of larceny and income tax evasion and sent to prison.

Hoffa was next. The Teamster boss's bribery trial began three months later, as the Washington heat rose in late June. Hoffa had hired the best criminal defense lawyer in the country, Edward Bennett Williams, who knew that he had a difficult case—the prosecution had movies of his client handing an envelope stuffed with cash to a federal employee. But Williams was extremely resourceful. He argued that Cheasty was not Hoffa's spy, but rather his lawyer. He had been retained to help Hoffa defend himself from the congressional probe. The argument was clever, if disingenuous, and it was buttressed by Williams's flagrant playing of the race card.

Having purposefully chosen a jury that was two-thirds black, Williams hired a black lawyer to sit at the defense table. An article extolling the lawyer was delivered to the homes of several jurors. Outrageously, the defense team brought heavyweight champ Joe Louis into court to greet the Teamster boss. The Justice Department prosecutor, by contrast, performed clumsily, putting on a weak and fumbling case. RFK, in the judgment of everyone except his loyal wife, was underwhelming as a witness. The jury voted to acquit.

Kennedy was conducting a committee hearing when the verdict came down. A reporter watching his face saw Kennedy blanch. Kennedy's secretary, Angie Novello, dreaded her boss's return to the office. Kennedy walked in, sensed the defeated mood, and said, "Come on now. We've got a lot of work to do. No sitting around." Kennedy was furious about the Joe Louis gambit, and he sent his best investigator, Walter Sheridan, to confront the ex-heavyweight champ. Touchingly, Kennedy's sentimentality and hero worship interfered with making an example of the old boxer. Kennedy asked Sheridan to bring back Louis's autograph for his son Joe, age five. When Louis gladly obliged, Kennedy couldn't bear to bring him to Washington to expose him as a Teamster shill before a congressional committee.

Kennedy finally summoned Hoffa himself to appear before the committee in August. The ornate Senate Caucus Room filled with spectators who looked forward to a showdown. The senators on the committee leaned back in their chairs. McClellan called the hearing to order in his slow, sad voice. Kennedy sat tense, on the edge of his chair, nervously pushing his horn-rimmed glasses up on his forehead. Hoffa was breezily confident. He began by addressing Kennedy as "Bob." He made a mockery of poor memory: "To the best of my recollection, I must recall on my memory, I cannot remember . . . I can say here to the Chair that I cannot recall in answer to your question other than to say I just don't recall my recollection. . . ." Hoffa and Kennedy would lock eyes and stare at each other for several minutes at a time. Then Hoffa would wink. "I used to love to bug the little bastard," Hoffa recalled.

None of this amused Kennedy. He later said he detected in Hoffa "absolute evilness." Kennedy portrayed the Teamsters as a threat on a par with communism. The Teamsters—"the most powerful institution in this country, aside from the United States government itself"—had the power to squeeze the lifeblood from the country by controlling the nation's transportation network. He warned Americans, "Quite literally, your life—the life of every person in the United States—is in the hands of Hoffa and his Teamsters." This was hype: Hoffa never dreamed of the kind of general strike that could choke the country. Still, he was a baleful force in the labor movement.

Kennedy was convinced that Hoffa had beaten, if not killed, union dissidents, stolen millions in union funds, and shaken down employers. But proof was hard to come by. Records had vanished, along with Hoffa's memory of key events. Kennedy hoped to grind Hoffa down, slinging charges at him until one stuck. Though obsessed with his foe—and obsessed is not too strong a word—Kennedy strangely underestimated Hoffa. Kennedy was so sure of the rightness of his cause that he could not see that Hoffa felt the same way about his own. The Teamster leader was accustomed to being prosecuted and, as he saw it, persecuted. Hoffa could easily regard himself as the friend of the working man unfairly assaulted by a showboating millionaire's son.

Day after day, the two antagonists went at it. A Civil War buff, Kennedy rather grandly compared himself to General Ulysses Grant, "slugging it out" in the Wilderness Campaign, where the fog of war lay heavy, fighting was chaotic, and casualties were high. Kennedy tempered his grandiosity with wry, self-deprecating humor. "My first love is Jimmy Hoffa," he told one reporter, John Bartlow Martin. Martin, who was profiling the Kennedy-Hoffa feud for the *Saturday Evening Post*, was driving with Kennedy down Capitol Hill on the way home one night when Kennedy noticed that the lights still burned at Teamster headquarters. Never to be outworked, Kennedy turned the car around and went back to his office. Hearing of Kennedy's reaction, Hoffa saw an opportunity for more winking mischief. He began leaving the lights turned on in his office after he went home at night.

The Hoffa hearings became a kind of trench warfare, exhausting and inconclusive. Hoffa lost his blitheness. "You're sick!" he snarled at Kennedy. "That's what's the matter with you—you are sick." But Hoffa managed to stay a step ahead of the law. Indicted for wiretapping in New York, he escaped with a hung jury—eleven to one to convict. Retried, he was again acquitted in the spring of 1958. One day, Hoffa and Kennedy ran into each other in the elevator of the federal courthouse. Kennedy asked how the trial was going. "You never can tell with a jury," said Hoffa. "Like shooting fish in a barrel." (When Hoffa was finally convicted in 1964, the crime was jury tampering.)

Even Kennedy began to weary of the chase. He desperately cast about for a smoking-gun document or a turncoat witness. John Bartlow Martin found Kennedy in his office one day in the late summer of 1958, tired and dispirited, eating lunch at his desk as he tried to cajole a prospective witness. "Sol, can I get you to come over here and testify?" Kennedy pleaded. "It would make a real difference." Kennedy waited and prodded some more: "Are you going to let him stand up here and kick everybody around?" Then, discouraged: "Okay, Sol." He slammed down the phone and glumly drank his milk.

On September 20, 1958—over a year after Hoffa first appeared before the committee—at the end of a long afternoon of circular questions and answers, Chairman McClellan called a truce. Mournfully puffing on a cigarette, the chairman proposed a recess. Kennedy, "bushed," smiled wearily. Hoffa, standing across the table, snickered, "Look at him, look at him! He's too tired. He just doesn't want to go on." Kennedy wrote in his journal:

> I am mentally fatigued—more than during any other hearing. We
> have been going on for a long time without a break & I have about
> had it. I shall be happy when Hoffa is finished next week. McClellan
> also very tired. This year seems to have been tougher than last. Plod-
> ding grind. . . . I feel like we're in a major fight. We have to keep
> going, keep the pressure on or we'll go under.

It was characteristic of Kennedy that his response to fatigue and frustration was not to pull back, but to try harder. He needed to find a way to work more quickly, to pore through the documents flooding his office. Ever the self-improver, he somehow found time to travel to Baltimore once a week to take a speed reading course. (His brother John went with him for a while, then, bored, dropped out.) He expanded the scope of the rackets investigation. In between chipping away at Hoffa, he had begun looking at the whole of organized crime. Not much was known in the mid-1950s. The word "Mafia" had been used to describe the Italian crime families, but not widely. Kennedy was just asking a witness about the existence of the Mafia on November 13, 1957, when the next day local police in the upstate New York hamlet of Apalachin began wondering why there were so many limousines with out-of-state licenses parked outside a secluded estate. When the police approached, dozens of well-fed men with pinkie rings and dark glasses emptied out of the house and ran into the woods. The cops had stumbled across a gangland convention of most of the top mob leaders in America. The dons had been meeting, undetected and unperturbed, every five years or so since 1931. Hearing about the raid, Kennedy demanded FBI files on the conventioneers. He was shocked to find, he later said, that Hoover's men "didn't know anything, really, about these people who were the major gangsters in the United States." His friends over at the Bureau of Narcotics, by contrast, had "something on every one of them."

Kennedy decided to do some investigating of his own. Characters out of the movies, like Joseph "Crazy Joey" Gallo, attired from head to toe in black, began raising their right hands in the Rackets Committee hearing room and then asserting their constitutional right to remain silent by "taking the Fifth." Kennedy was fascinated and even amused by the lowlifes of the underworld with their Runyonesque names like Cockeyed Dunn. When Joey Gallo visited Kennedy's office, he felt the rug and said, "It would be nice for a crap game." Kennedy bombarded them with questions, sometimes accompanied by sneers.

The star witness was Momo Salvatore "Sam" Giancana, heir to the Capone gang in Chicago. Giancana had hung people on meat hooks, but he was an upscale mobster who counted top entertainers among his friends, including Frank Sinatra. Questioned by Kennedy if he disposed of opponents by stuffing them in the trunk of a car, Giancana seemed amused. Kennedy was not:

MR. KENNEDY: Would you tell us anything about any of your operations or will you just giggle every time I ask you a question?

MR. GIANCANA: I decline to answer because I honestly believe my answer might tend to incriminate me.

MR. KENNEDY: I thought only little girls giggled, Mr. Giancana.

Tense and awkward as a questioner at first, speaking in convoluted or incomplete sentences, Kennedy improved over time and gradually became a clear and forceful interrogator. He learned to be patient, and he was always tenacious. He developed a sly, mocking style. When a witness gave him a long-winded and obviously phony answer, a *New York Times* reporter observed, Kennedy "reacted with a long, silent look and then grunted, 'Oh!' with an attitude of mock surprise. The witness shrugged his shoulders helplessly." Kennedy played the bullyboy at times, especially when witnesses tried to take him on. "Don't give me that shit," a union boss swore at him under questioning. Kennedy, who was generally not profane, tried to goad him further. With the mike off, Kennedy kept hissing at the witness, "You're full of shit."

For all the frustrations of dealing with forgetful or belligerent witnesses, Kennedy was fundamentally happy to have a calling at last. "He wasn't the angry man any more and he was much more pleasant to be around because he hadn't this terrible feeling that he wasn't contributing," said Lem Billings. Kennedy even allowed himself to be privately content. In the fall of 1957, Senator Lyndon Johnson complimented Kennedy by saying that Congress could successfully investigate Russia's head start in space—with the launch of *Sputnik*—only if there was "someone like young Kennedy handling it." In his diary, Kennedy dryly noted, "Am very pleased with myself." Committee staff noted that RFK became "a little keyed up, a little tense," as one put it, on the rare occasions when Joseph Kennedy showed up in the hearing room to watch his son. But mostly they felt well led by Kennedy; indeed, most of Kennedy's large staff came to worship him.

They felt drawn in by him, sucked into the vortex of his energy. His office in the basement of the Old Senate Office Building was strewn with papers piled on overstuffed chairs. Men worked in shirtsleeves and secretaries called their bosses by their first names, unusual familiarity in the 1950s. The atmosphere was casual but frenetic. On his office wall, Kennedy hung a quotation from Churchill, "We shall not flag or fail . . . we shall never surrender." Someone pasted a cartoon on a filing cabinet urging, "If at first you don't succeed, file a subpoena." Kennedy rushed in and out, always running up and down stairs.

His staff was expected to scramble, too. He hired Walt Sheridan, a former

FBI man, as he was racing up a flight of steps to a committee hearing. There-after, most of Sheridan's conversations with Kennedy seemed to take place on the move. "He seemed more relaxed when he was going somewhere," Sheridan recalled. Sheridan once made the mistake of scheduling a plane flight around noon. Kennedy scolded him: "I never go anywhere at noon! It wastes the whole day." Kennedy gave Sheridan wide discretion, and Sheridan, quiet and persis-tent, returned total loyalty. The two shared doggedness, a love of football, and the same birthday. When Kennedy was shot in 1968, Sheridan remarked, "I felt a little funny that we didn't die on the same day. But in a way, we did."

Kennedy had a way of deflecting people at first, sometimes with insults, yet then giving his total attention to those he liked. John Seigenthaler's experi-ence was characteristic. An able newspaperman for the *Nashville Tennessean*, Seigenthaler wanted to share information that he had dug up on the Teamsters. Flying to Washington, he found Kennedy glowering and stalking up and down in his office. "You're late. You southerners are always late," said Kennedy. Seigenthaler, who was ten minutes early, tried to protest, but Kennedy told him to talk to one of his assistants. It took three brush-offs before Kennedy finally looked at Seigenthaler's work, but when he did, he read every word. Kennedy flew to Nashville to talk to Seigenthaler, who soon revised his estimate of Kennedy as a "rich snob." In the car, one of Seigenthaler's friends inquired about Bobby's siblings. Bobby said that in addition to his brother Jack, the sen-ator, he had an older brother, Joe Jr. Where was Joe? the friend innocently in-quired. "In heaven," Bobby replied. Seigenthaler noted that Bobby was simple and direct, yet mysterious: "You never knew if there was a smile there or not." On the way back to the airport, Kennedy said he wanted to see the home of President Andrew Jackson. There was another plane leaving for Washington in two hours. Kennedy became so preoccupied with talking to Seigenthaler and soaking up the history of Old Hickory at the Hermitage that he nearly missed the second plane as well.

Home and work blurred for RFK. He liked to be home on the weekends to be near his children, so he instructed his staff to join him. He would come home and immediately change his shirt, which he would wear half unbuttoned with the tails hanging out. His staffers had to come prepared to ride horses or play touch football. John Bartlow Martin observed that "Kennedy saw nothing in-congruous about a millionaire's meeting beside the pool on his Virginia estate with former policemen and ill-paid lawyers and accountants to set traps for a Teamster from the Indiana coalfields." Ethel was very much a part of the scene. Although "she sometimes seemed a little overwhelmed," noted Martin, she at-tended hearings and the Hoffa trial as an avid partisan. During Hoffa's cross-examination, she could be heard exclaiming, "Give it to him!" When Kennedy was cross-examined, she muttered, "They have no right to ask those ques-tions."

The thirty-three-year-old Kennedy had a virtually free hand with the Rackets Committee. Chairman McClellan was fond of RFK and shared his moralistic sense of good and evil. He stepped in only when the chief counsel became entangled in his own questions. Kennedy's staff grew and grew until it had over a hundred investigators, by far the largest staff on Capitol Hill. Kennedy's men were encouraged to be resourceful. Pierre Salinger, a bonvivant magazine writer who joined the staff, recalled getting a housemaid drunk so that he could reach under her mattress and remove some Teamster documents hidden there. Kennedy himself would go out on wild goose chases, on one occasion digging in an Illinois cornfield for the body of an alleged Teamster victim (never found). Sensitive to the abuses of the McCarthy Committee (and his own taint by association), Kennedy was careful not to fling around baseless charges or haul up witnesses before first checking out the allegations against them. It is true that Kennedy's scattershot method produced many more headlines than indictments. The evidence adduced at the hearings was rarely strong enough to prompt the cautious Eisenhower Justice Department to bring a criminal case. But no one has turned up any evidence of illegal overreaching by Kennedy. FBI reports noted that Kennedy's committee employed a well-known wiretapper, but Hoover's men made no allegations of warrantless eavesdropping.

There is little proof that Kennedy played politics on the committee, at least not in a heavy-handed way. Any attempt to make him "go easy" on a witness was likely to have the opposite effect, even if the request came from his own brother. In 1958, Kennedy's investigators began to look into sweetheart contracts between a grocery workers union and Food Fair, a supermarket chain. Union officials pressured Senator John Kennedy to rein in the committee's chief counsel. Eager as ever to avoid confrontation, JFK instructed an aide, Myer Feldman, to "talk to" RFK. Just as Feldman arrived in Kennedy's office, RFK took a phone call from a union official warning him to back off the investigation if he cared about Senator Kennedy's political future. Coldly, RFK informed the caller, "Maybe I'll ask you to come and testify to that fact." RFK was "extremely tough," Feldman noted, when he questioned a Food Fair executive before the committee. Union officials with ties to the Democratic Party were subjected to the same grillings.

Still, the Republican minority naturally chafed. Senators Barry Goldwater of Arizona and Karl Mundt of South Dakota began writing each other, complaining bitterly that "the Kennedy boys" had hijacked the committee. They saw a Democratic plot: by focusing on Hoffa and the Teamsters, Kennedy was covering up for the real labor outlaw, Walter Reuther and the United Auto Workers, a union that typically backed Democratic office seekers. Goldwater referred to Reuther as the "leader of Soviet America, more dangerous than *Sputnik*." The Republicans demanded that the committee investigate the UAW, especially its role in a violent four-year strike against the Kohler Company, which manufactured plumbing supplies in Sheboygan, Wisconsin.

Kennedy disdained Goldwater and Mundt as craven. "They have no guts," he wrote in his journal. "They just complain to newspapermen. Never to me personally." Nonetheless, he was in a difficult position. Investigating the UAW would be politically risky. The UAW was a major cog in the Democratic Party.

If RFK alienated Reuther, he could bid farewell to his brother's hopes of winning the Democratic presidential nomination in 1960. Still, he had little choice. The Republicans were beginning to score political points by leaking to the press that the Kennedys were fronting for Reuther and covering up for the UAW. Actually, relations between the Kennedys and Reuther were not particularly warm. In 1956, Reuther had opposed JFK's last-minute run for the vice-presidential slot. He frostily told the junior senator, "Young man, you're going to have to change your voting record."

Boxed in, Kennedy announced that the Rackets Committee would investigate the UAW. Kennedy himself traveled to Sheboygan in January 1958 to look into the bitter strike. He found wretched conditions for the workers and a labor-hating management. Kennedy was saved by Reuther's essential honesty. Reuther could be long-winded and flowery. But, unlike many Teamster officials, who offended RFK with their gold rings and sweet-smelling cologne, Reuther lived and dressed simply. He did not consort with gangsters. He was—important to Bobby—physically brave, having been shot by mobsters and dumped into the Detroit River. Fortunately for the political future of the Kennedys, Reuther resisted the temptation to cash in on his power. Reuther's representative in Washington, Jack Conway, himself a tough Irishman like Bobby, opened up all of Reuther's financial records. Kennedy's accountant, Carmine Bellino, with his expertise at sniffing out phony bookkeeping, could find nothing wrong. Reuther didn't even expense account his dry cleaning. The investigation exonerated the UAW. The Republicans were left spluttering. "You were right," Goldwater honestly admitted to Kennedy. "We never should have gotten into this matter."

Joe Sr.'s fears had not been realized. The Kennedys had not antagonized organized labor. Big Labor would never fully embrace the Kennedys—especially RFK—but the union bosses never sought to wreck JFK's progress towards the White House. "Attacking Hoffa was good politics," said Paul Schrade, a top UAW official who became close to the Kennedys. "The AFL-CIO was going after corrupt unions anyways and expelled Hoffa." During the investigation, the Kennedys showed a "more than usual" curiosity about how the Auto Workers were organized around the country. The UAW's Conway suspected they were "feel[ing] out a potential alliance." After the investigation, the Kennedys openly courted the UAW's support. While Reuther kept the union officially neutral, top UAW officials, particularly Conway, quietly worked to get JFK nominated and elected. In retrospect, the Rackets Committee worked so well to the Kennedys' advantage that it seems carefully orchestrated. It wasn't. "Bob and Jack didn't know it was going to be good politics," said Schrade. "What the hell did they know about unions? Not much." Clark Mollenhoff, the reporter who helped goad Kennedy into investigating labor racketeering, also saw risk rewarded. "It happened that . . . it made them front-page figures for about four years; but it could have . . . dynamited them at the very outset."

The Rackets Committee did offend some powerful local politicians, most

notably Mayor Richard Daley of Chicago, whose backing was critical to secur-
ing the Democratic nomination for JFK. In 1959, Daley told a Kennedy ally that
he didn't appreciate Bobby Kennedy's "approach . . . coming to town throwing
subpoenas around and calling everyone crooks," Kenny O'Donnell later recalled. Jack Kennedy wrote his father, warning that Daley was telling people,
"I'm not sure we want a prosecutor as a president." Worried that Daley might
slip away, John Kennedy called Hizzoner and invited him to a World Series
game that October. Daley and JFK barely spoke during the ball game, but by
publicly showing his respect for the Democratic powerbroker, JFK mollified
Daley. Behind the scenes, Joseph Kennedy, who as owner of the Merchandise
Mart was an important Chicago constituent, carefully cultivated the mayor.

And what of the risk that RFK's investigative zeal might somehow backfire against Joe Sr.? As he surveyed the underworld, did RFK ever trip across his
father's traces? The available record discloses nothing significant, only a hint or
two. On August 15, 1957, the committee called Johnny O'Rourke, a stooge installed as the head of a "paper local" by Hoffa and his mob associate Johnny
Dio. Kennedy got up and left the questioning to his assistant counsel.
O'Rourke, a power on the New York waterfront, took the Fifth Amendment
fifty-seven times. Later, a rumor circulated among newsmen that O'Rourke
was close to Joe Kennedy Sr., and Bobby had agreed to go easy on O'Rourke out
of deference to his father. But it was just a rumor. The only reference to Joe
Kennedy on the record came from the superintendent of a building, owned by
Joe Kennedy, where several of the unions under investigation kept their offices.
Subpoenaed by the committee, the superintendent said, "I take my orders from
the father, not the boys." Hoffa got in a few digs, telling reporters that he had
cut no more corners than Joe Kennedy and suggesting that the money allegedly stolen from the Teamsters' pension fund was nothing compared to the
money Joe Kennedy made "selling whiskey."

Most of the publicity, however, added luster to the family name. In the
summer of 1957, as Bobby's face-off with Hoffa began attracting national attention, the glossy magazines began running glowing spreads. "Young Man
with Tough Questions" headlined *Life* on July 1. "Rise of the Brothers
Kennedy" answered *Look* on August 6. "The Amazing Kennedys" topped the
Saturday Evening Post on September 7. Constitutional scholars, writing in the
smaller magazines, did question RFK's inquisitional style and tactics. They
grumbled about "Profiles in Bullying" and wondered if RFK was transforming
the Fifth Amendment into a tacit admission of guilt. But most newsmen were
Kennedy's supporters, if not virtual camp followers. Kennedy traded information with reporters and gave them tremendous access. They, in turn, often
showed him what they planned to write before publication. Kennedy was surprised and bothered when John Bartlow Martin wrote, in an otherwise flattering profile, that Kennedy resembled Hoffa in many ways. To his credit,
Kennedy did not ask Martin to take out the offending passage. But Kennedy
was quite conscious that he was manipulating reporters. He told Martin—in a
passage that Martin *did* cut out of his article—"Our committee is more power-

ful than the old McCarthy committee . . . newspapermen don't watch us as
closely as they did at first." Kennedy, Martin wrote in another passage he cut
from the piece, "has carefully cultivated closer relations with the press and
some newspapermen, having covered the hearings for more than two years, attend staff parties almost like members of the staff. Some, indeed, share the
staff's zeal for getting Jimmy Hoffa. . . ."

Kennedy's many friends in the press chose not to reveal everything they
saw. When Bobby attended the funeral of Senator Joseph McCarthy, who died,
a broken drunk, in 1957, he asked reporters not to disclose that he was at grave-
side. The reporters honored the request, sparing Kennedy an embarrassing
identification with the disgraced demagogue. Allowed to roam freely in
Kennedy's office, *Life*'s Hugh Sidey observed that Kennedy enjoyed the fruits
of his wealth. Bobby did not fancy Senate food, so at lunchtime his butler
would drive into town with a wicker basket full of his favorites, grilled lamb
chops and chocolate ice cream with chocolate sauce. But Sidey left out that kind
of potentially eye-opening detail when *Life* profiled Kennedy's personal life in
April 1958 with a sweet article about the christening of Kennedy's sixth child,
Michael. "A Debut in a Burgeoning Family" shows Bobby assembled with his
brood and his dog, a scene of happy domesticity.

It was a reasonably accurate picture. Kennedy worked outrageous hours
and rarely saw his children on the weekdays. But he adored them. Unlike his
own parents, who never physically demonstrated their affection, Kennedy
hugged and roughhoused with his, playing games of "tickle-tumble" that left
the little ones squealing with delight. John Bartlow Martin, observing this
scene close hand—and hanging on as Kennedy, hair flying, drove too fast in his
convertible—concluded that Kennedy was possessed less by zeal than sheer
youthfulness. While Kennedy's wardrobe continued to look like a rummage
sale, he did live very comfortably. In 1956, after Jackie Kennedy lost her first-
born child, the John Kennedys sold to Bobby and Ethel a large estate they had
bought in McLean, Virginia. Called Hickory Hill, it soon had horses, a pool and
a tennis court, and a retinue of gardeners, grooms, cooks, nurses, and a butler.
Ethel had a large household budget which she routinely overspent. At Christmas 1959, an exasperated Joe Kennedy complained that his children and in-
laws were spendthrifts. "And you," he said, turning to Ethel, "are the worst!"
In tears, Ethel fled from the table. Bobby chased after her and comforted her.
Rose, too, became impatient with Ethel's carelessness about money. "Grandpa
[Joe Sr.] told me yesterday that Bobby had again requested that somebody
from the office go down to your house to go over the bills," she wrote on January 15, 1960. "And my first thought was that you and Bobby should sit down
and go over your household expenses each month, as I believe I have already
suggested to you." Rose was irked to find children's clothes lying about and
Ethel's new tennis racket uncovered in the damp pool house. "As you know,
dear Ethel, I have a great deal to do and I get rather tired of picking up after all
of you. . . ." Rose also remonstrated with Bobby to not disturb his father at
dinnertime: "This is just to remind you again to please not telephone your fa-

ther around 7:15 p.m., as we have dinner then and if he gets too excited before dinner, as he did the other night when he talked to you about labor legislation, it is not very good for his little tummy."

Despite Rose's chiding, RFK had at last won his family's full attention. Ethel was a cheerleader for Bobby with her in-laws. "The hearings are great—despite the poor coverage in the Times and Trib," Ethel wrote Rose in the summer of 1957. "Everyone in the Caucus Room cannot help but be impressed by the tons of work behind them—and how very smart some people were marrying the chief counsel." When Hoffa was acquitted that summer, Ethel suffered with Bobby and shared his determination to fight on. "We're all sick to death about Hoffa," she wrote Rose and Joe Sr. "But we are relying on Carmine [Bellino], Clark Mollenhoff, and Bobby and Jack to hit one for our team. . . . Even Ena and Josie [Ethel's black housekeepers] are ashamed of Joe Louis." Rose shared Ethel's pride and engaged in some mild revisionism about Bobby's childhood prospects for success. "I know how excited and thrilled you must be about Bobby as we all are," she wrote Ethel, "but I always expected great things from my seventh-born."

Kennedy was emerging as a national figure in his own right. His ambitions, however, were for his older brother. By early 1959, Jack and Bobby and two or three close aides like Kenny O'Donnell "were running for president in our office after five o'clock in the evening," observed a committee staffer, Ruth Watt. In September 1959, after 1,525 sworn witnesses and more than 500 hearings produced 46,150 pages of testimony, Robert Kennedy resigned as chief counsel of the Senate Rackets Committee. Kennedy took time in the summer of '59 to draft a book about his investigations called *The Enemy Within*. Sensitive to the charges that Jack's Pulitzer Prize–winning book, *Profiles in Courage*, had been ghostwritten by committee, RFK wrote his own, in indecipherable longhand. *The Enemy Within* was, briefly, a bestseller. Although overheated, it captures Kennedy's crusading passion. It might have launched him on a political career of his own. But family duty called.

CHAPTER 4 MANIPULATOR

I<small>T WAS "UNDERSTOOD"</small> that Robert Kennedy would manage his brother's campaign, wrote Rose Kennedy. Bobby was not eager for the job. He was impatient with politics, and he loathed the glad-handing and backslapping. In some unacknowledged way, he may have resented being once again forced to subordinate his own ambitions to his brother's. Standing by Joe Kennedy's pool in Palm Beach in December 1959, RFK harangued his brother Jack about the slow start of the campaign. It was "ridiculous" how little work had been done, Bobby complained. Jack turned to his friend Paul "Red" Fay and asked, "How would you like looking forward to that high whining voice blasting into your ear for the next six months?"

Jack was teasing, in the manner of Kennedy siblings, using humor to defuse a tense moment and to establish his own posture as the cooler head. Jack and Bobby had not somehow become better friends through their long hours at the Rackets Committee. Their two families rarely socialized, partly because Ethel and Jackie were not well matched. (Ethel and the Kennedy sisters, who had much in common, referred to Jackie as "the deb.") Still, the Kennedy brothers shared a family bond that sometimes froze out all others and made the clan look, from the outside, like a secret society. JFK's Senate aide, Ruth Watt, recalled on a visit to Hyannis Port in the late 1950s that the conversation between RFK and JFK at breakfast was so exclusive that it seemed as if the other guests did not exist.

The two brothers had distinct roles to play, defined in large measure by their father. Jack was noble, Bobby was tough. Jack was the visionary, Bobby the enforcer. Jack's job was to move forward, Bobby's to cover his back. Their close friends had a more subtle understanding. Many years later, JFK's friend Chuck Spalding tried to sort through the complexity of their relationship. "Jack thought Bobby was too serious, a severe figure, and tried to lighten him up. At the same time, he thought Bobby was . . ." He paused. "The sacred one. He felt protective about him." Bobby was a moralist, "straightlaced." He disapproved of his brother's sexual philandering. But his role as minder and scold to JFK stopped outside the bedroom door. "He didn't accept Jack's infidelity. But," Spalding added, "he didn't try to stop it." Largely through Joe Sr.'s cultivation of the press, ably abetted by his sons, certain myths about the two brothers became enshrined during this period. JFK was generally portrayed as a Prince of Enlightenment, intellectual in a dashing sort of way—a liberal-minded humanist in warrior's garb. Bobby was seen as a more medieval figure, comfortable in a black cowl, far harsher and dogmatic in his judgments. Like most myths, there was some truth to both of these images. But they distorted and disguised essential elements of character kept hidden from public view. In some ways, the truth about the two Kennedys was a mirror opposite from their media personas. In 1964, after JFK died, filmmaker Charles Guggenheim was interviewing Kenny O'Donnell for a documentary about RFK. While he was changing film, Guggenheim asked O'Donnell if Bobby was "ruthless." The office was dark in the late-afternoon gloom, and O'Donnell's "eyes drifted off," Guggenheim recalled. "Jack was the tough one," said O'Donnell. "Not Bobby. Jack would cut you off at the knees. Bobby would say, 'Why are we doing that to this guy?' "

Bobby's tough-guy act provided useful cover for JFK. It freed him to float above the muddy arena. Jack Kennedy's preferred mien was cool detachment. When Norman Mailer outdid the fawning press corps by describing JFK as an "existential hero," JFK remarked, "It really runs on, doesn't it?" Bobby's protectees included Jack's wife. Jacqueline's first baby had been stillborn while Jack was off cruising in the Mediterranean with two of his fellow pleasure-seekers, his brother Ted and Senator George Smathers. Jack did not rush back. But Bobby, alerted by Rose Kennedy in the middle of the night, rushed to be by his sister-in-law's bedside. When she awoke from the anesthetic, he told her that she had lost the baby. Bobby took care of the child's burial. "Senator Kennedy on Mediterranean Trip Unaware His Wife Lost Baby" was the headline in the *Washington Post*, and later accounts criticized JFK for not rushing back. In fact, JFK had been left undisturbed "on Bobby's advice," Rose wrote her daughter Pat. The decision shows how other family members—including the patriarch, Joe Sr.—deferred to RFK on sensitive family questions. RFK believed, Rose wrote Pat, that "it would be better for him [JFK] not to be told as he would want to go home immediately, and Jackie is so depressed it would be very tragic for both of them."

Jackie Kennedy increasingly relied on RFK. "You knew that, if you were in trouble, he'd always be there," recalled Jacqueline. She saw through the Ruthless Robert myth as well as anyone else. His determined efforts notwithstanding, Bobby was, she observed, the son "least like his father."

Other family myths have been long since debunked. The Kennedy campaign of 1960 was not the "well-oiled machine" it seemed at the time. It was chaotic and opportunistic, more instinctive than planned. It was driven by momentum, not carefully drawn lines of authority. Its organization was mysterious even to those close to the inner circle. "The Kennedy operation was very loose. The Kennedys wanted it that way," recalled Fred Dutton, a young political organizer recruited to bring the Kennedys some of the new media strategies used to elect Pat Brown governor of California in 1958. "The only real architecture was the family, but even they manipulated each other and used us [staffers] as buffers between them."

The central figure of mystery was Joe Kennedy. He had been an overbearing presence in JFK's first congressional campaign, but as time went on, he preferred inscrutability. Asked why he didn't tell his sons what he was doing for them, he answered, "I don't want them to inherit my enemies." Dutton, like other staffers, often wondered what Joe Kennedy was up to—"how much was the ambassador freelancing? How much was he spending? Was he doing things that Jack didn't want to be held accountable for?" Actually, Joe Kennedy's maneuvering may have been less vigorous, and less nefarious, than has been popularly imagined. His self-assigned role seems to have been bucking up JFK by telling him that he was doing a great job even if he wasn't, and providing money. His fortune at the time was generally (although perhaps not accurately) estimated at about $400 million; the children, who had all been provided with generous trust funds, were expected to tithe to Jack's campaign. The manner of spending was largely delegated to son-in-law Steve Smith, Jean's husband. Joe liked Steve because he was "as tough as Bobby." Unlike Bobby, who regarded money as something that Ethel spent, Steve was tightfisted. Campaign vendors learned to get their bills paid before election day. Afterwards was too late.

The campaign strategy, clearer in retrospect than at the time, was a flanking maneuver. Jack was not a favorite of the party elders. He had not been a member in good standing of the Senate Club, and his religion and his father put off the traditionalists. ("It's not the pope I'm afraid of, it's the pop," cracked Harry Truman.) Political power in 1960 was still largely in the hands of the bosses—Richard Daley of Chicago, John Bailey of Connecticut, David Lawrence of Pennsylvania. A single man could control large hunks of delegates at the political nominating conventions. Candidates were still chosen in smoke-filled rooms, not by state primaries. The Kennedys correctly sensed, however, that the party machinery was rusting. As in 1952, the best course was to end run the old guard and appeal to the "new generation" of voters. Kennedy's best hope was to make a good grass-roots showing in the primaries and force the hand of the barons. The strategy was never either/or, the masses or the bosses. The actual campaign was a more subtle, evolved process that at times seemed contradictory and confused. The aim was to sway and nudge party leaders, not to replace or alienate them, an injunction Bobby sometimes had trouble remembering while dealing with slow-moving hacks. Money helped, in all directions. The Kennedys were able to deliver bags of cash where "walking-around" money was required and to spend $300,000 to hire a full-time pollster to help measure—and manipulate—public opinion.

An old prejudice stood in the way. America had never elected a Catholic president. Bobby, defensive, initially wanted to hide Jack's religion. Jack, urbane, wanted to shrug it off as an irrelevancy. They delivered their lines with telling shades of emphasis. Jack, coolly but firmly: "Nobody asked me if I was a Catholic when I joined the United States Navy." Bobby, hotly, and on one occasion, tearfully: "Did they ask my brother Joe whether he was a Catholic before he was shot down?" The first test was Wisconsin, where Bobby's first act was to move the location of Milwaukee campaign headquarters away from the Catholic cathedral across the street. In a state with a disproportionately large Catholic population, JFK won with 56 percent—not enough. On election night, CBS reported that Republican Catholics were crossing over to vote for Kennedy, but that in other, less Catholic states, he would be in trouble. When CBS anchor Walter Cronkite asked JFK about his Catholicism, the answer was more frigid than cool. As soon as the lights dimmed, Bobby burst into the studio and accused Cronkite of breaking a promise not to bring up religion. Cronkite replied that he had made no such promise. RFK, who truly could be ruthless, did not stop there. He called Tom Watson, the president of IBM and a family friend, whose computers were supplying CBS with election analysis. The next day, a pair of Columbia University professors who had analyzed the returns were ordered to "justify" their results. Appalled by Kennedy's unsubtle hand, the Columbia professors quit the CBS election team.

In RFK's universe, there were only two sides: his and the enemy's. The president of the Young Democrats of Illinois, Bill Rivkin, was friendly with Hubert Humphrey, Kennedy's main primary opponent, but he also wanted to keep his ties open to the Kennedys. On election night in Wisconsin, Rivkin wandered from Humphrey's suite to Bobby Kennedy's room. "What are you doing here?" Bobby demanded, and slammed the door in his face. Back at Palm Beach, Joe Kennedy heard of Bobby's hardball approach and was pleased. Gesturing at Jack in the pool, Joe Kennedy said, "I don't understand it. He's not like me at all. . . . But Bobby is like me." Jack and Spalding were on the way to the Caribbean for a few days of relaxation. Bobby, who had shed a pound a week trudging through the snows of Wisconsin for much of the winter, was off to West Virginia, to gird for the next and possibly last test. The primary in the poor mining state, coming in May towards the end of the primary season, was a must win. For Kennedy, it was the place he would have to prove that he could overcome anti-Catholic prejudice.

As always, Bobby wanted straight answers from the Kennedy organization on the ground. Meeting with volunteers in Charleston, West Virginia, on the day after the Wisconsin primary, he asked, "What are our problems?" A man stood and said, "There's only one problem. He's a Catholic. That's our goddamned problem!" RFK seemed to be "in shock," reported Kenny O'Donnell, who was watching. Kennedy showed the same tolerance for slow-moving or free-loading political hacks that he had demonstrated during his brother's Senate campaign in Massachusetts in 1952. He demanded that the Kennedy workers get out of the bars and smoky clubhouses and go look for votes.

He went, too, and was shocked by the raw poverty he saw in the Appalachian hollows and raw mining towns.

At first, RFK was so shaken by the anti-Catholic prejudice in West Virginia that he thought his brother should drop out of the primary. Too late, argued JFK. The best hope was to lean on Humphrey to disavow religious bigotry. Hoping to enlist Big Labor in the cause, JFK quietly appealed to George Meany of the AFL and Walter Reuther of the UAW. As Kenny O'Donnell later recalled, the bosses did call on Humphrey to smooth over the religious issue. But Humphrey, already resentful of Kennedy's seemingly bottomless campaign war chest, refused to be labor's "tool." He made no effort to defuse the anti-Catholicism. The Kennedys were furious—"in a white heat"—O'Donnell recalled. They conveniently decided that HHH was a "cheap, cunning politician" who was "deceiving the people," said O'Donnell. JFK and RFK felt justified to hit back. Or, as O'Donnell put it, "Dirty tricks would be met with dirty tricks."

Politics was a rough sport in West Virginia, and Bobby played accordingly. Humphrey was soon complaining that someone was handing out anti-Catholic literature and trying to blame it on him. The immediate suspect was a Kennedy operative named Paul Corbin. Short, swarthy, resourceful, and belligerent, Corbin had a quality that forever endeared him to Robert Kennedy: he was unthinkingly, unswervingly loyal. He would do anything Kennedy wanted, regardless of whether Kennedy asked. Corbin was born Kobinsky, but he seemed to remind everyone of an Irish rogue out of *The Last Hurrah*. In a way, he had made himself Irish, converting to Catholicism so that he could make Kennedy his godfather. Corbin was at once outrageous and effective. In Catholic areas, he used priests to get out the vote by knocking on doors; in Protestant areas, he asked Catholic seminarians canvassing for Kennedy to wear sport shirts. He handed out promises he couldn't deliver on, offering to make several upstate New York pols ambassador to Ecuador. He handed out postmasterships, a prized form of federal patronage, like bumper stickers. He was the sort of advance man who could go anywhere—once. Years later, Secretary of Defense Robert McNamara got so mad at Corbin over some minor matter that he wanted to put Corbin on a lie detector. Bobby just laughed: "Lie detector? He'd break the machine!" No one could ever be sure if Corbin was carrying out an order from Kennedy or operating on his own. Kennedy preferred it that way.*

---

* RFK was entertained by the rogue politics of West Virginia. Almost three years after the election, when Kennedy was attorney general but already thinking about JFK's reelection in 1964, the Justice Department's civil rights division brought a case against a Wayne County constable—a Democrat—for falsely arresting a Republican election official (on trumped-up charges that the poll worker had raped the constable's wife) and locking him up in jail in the early hours of election day 1960. RFK teasingly wrote his civil rights chief, Burke Marshall, that the Justice Department should stay out of West Virginia politics: "Burke, this is the kind of thing that could lose West Virginia for us, too. You and your people have lost their sense of humor. You just don't seem to understand how things are done in West Virginia. P.S. I do. P.P.S. If you didn't, you wouldn't be where you are."

The most notorious dirty trick in West Virginia was not perpetrated by Corbin, but by a far more distinguished figure. Joseph Kennedy persuaded Franklin D. Roosevelt Jr. to lend his father's still-strong aura to JFK. Roosevelt's most powerful message was not an invocation of the New Deal, but rather a shameless allusion to Hubert Humphrey's failure to fight in World War II. Humphrey had been exempted from the draft for a physical disability. Someone anonymously mailed Humphrey's records, which appeared to show that he had ducked the draft, to the Kennedy campaign staff. The staff intended to hold the material as a weapon of last resort, leaking it only in extremis. Roosevelt, however, came right out and strongly insinuated that Humphrey was a draft dodger. Both Kennedys insisted that Roosevelt was acting on his own. Roosevelt claimed he had been goaded into it by Bobby Kennedy. The whole truth will always remain murky; the Kennedys certainly made no effort to stop Roosevelt.

Votes were sold in West Virginia, and the Kennedys paid for them. One local boss, Raymond Chafin, recalled asking the Kennedy campaign for $3,500 to be spread around to drivers who helped voters get to the polls. The Kennedy campaign misunderstood; they thought his request for "thirty-five" meant $35,000. Chafin received two suitcases full of cash at the airport. Usually, RFK was astute about money, recalled one of his county campaign managers, David Fox. "He had done his homework and he knew just how much money it was going to take." On election day, campaign chronicler Theodore White stood with Richard Donahue, the Lowell, Massachusetts, lawyer who was working with the Kennedys, watching voters flock to the polls. "Isn't democracy wonderful!" White exclaimed. "Yeah, Teddy," agreed Donahue, who, unbeknownst to White, had delivered $25,000 to the poll workers. ("They divided it up into little bundles," he recalled.)

The money was probably not decisive. Kennedy's war hero record, his appeals to sweep out the old guard, and his answers on religion, at once direct and nonchalant, had more to do with the 61 to 39 margin. But Kennedy's open checkbook thoroughly rattled Hubert Humphrey, who fell off the high road and began accusing the Kennedys of trying to buy the election. Sleeping in his bus at night, Hubert would hear a plane fly overhead and pretend it was the *Caroline*, the Kennedy plane. "Come down here, Jack, and play fair!" he would cry out.

On election night in West Virginia, JFK was in Washington, killing time by watching a racy film showing at a theater a few blocks from the White House. Every twenty minutes, recalled his friend Ben Bradlee, a *Newsweek* reporter who spent the evening with JFK, the candidate would get up and call Bobby at campaign headquarters in West Virginia to get the latest results. The results were good: Humphrey lost, knocking him out of the race and opening the way for Kennedy to secure the nomination.

Late that night, Robert Kennedy paid a visit to Humphrey's hotel room. As he entered, Humphrey's workers cleared a path. Kennedy made for Muriel Humphrey and leaned down to give her a kiss on the cheek. "I thought she was going to hit him," recalled Joe Rauh, a Washington lawyer and Humphrey aide who was in the room. At 3 a.m. that morning, Kennedy called Bill Rivkin, the Illinois Young Democrats leader in whose face Kennedy had slammed a door just a month earlier. "Okay," Bobby said abruptly. "Jack won. Are you with us?" He was, and so were a majority of the delegates going to the Democratic National Convention in Los Angeles.

THE OPPONENT Jack Kennedy had feared most in 1960 was Lyndon Baines Johnson, the powerful Senate majority leader who owned a stack of political IOUs and had access to unlimited campaign funds. Johnson was effusive, glad-handing, boastful, and canny. Only in this last respect did he have anything in common with Robert Kennedy.

LBJ and RFK had met in the Senate during the early '50s and taken an instant mutual dislike. Johnson's aide Horace Busby recalled seeing Kennedy sitting, silent and scowling, at the customary table of Senator Joseph McCarthy in the Senate Office Building cafeteria. When Senator Johnson stopped by to pay his respects to McCarthy, young Kennedy just glared. Johnson recalled that he would say hello to RFK in the hallways, but his patronizing greeting "Hi, sonny!" would hardly have warmed up RFK, who saw the Texas senator as a threat to his brother's presidential ambitions.

At one time, Joseph Kennedy Sr. had tried to leverage JFK's political future on LBJ's back. In the papers of Thomas ("Tommy the Cork") Corcoran, the famous New Deal figure who became a Washington fixer, LBJ biographer Robert Dallek found evidence of an extraordinary offer from Joseph Kennedy to Senate majority leader Johnson: if LBJ ran for president in 1956—and agreed to make JFK his running mate—Joe Kennedy would "arrange financing for the ticket." But LBJ demurred, sensing—correctly—that the senior Kennedy was just trying to use him as a stalking horse. JFK figured Johnson would lose to President Eisenhower, but wanted to establish his son's name nationally so that he could run on the top of the ticket in 1960. Jack Kennedy was calm and "circumspect" about LBJ's rejection of this convoluted plot, Corcoran recalled, but Robert Kennedy was "infuriated. He believed it was unforgivably discourteous to turn down his father's generous offer."

In the late fall of 1959, JFK dispatched Bobby to Johnson's ranch in Texas to sound out the powerful Senate majority leader: Was he running? And, if not, would he stand in Kennedy's path? RFK put those questions to Johnson in his usual prosecutorial way. Johnson assured young Kennedy that he had no designs on the presidency and planned to remain on the fence in 1960. Then Johnson took Bobby deer hunting. The recoil from the shotgun knocked Bobby on his back and cut his cheek. Johnson patronizingly reached down to give Kennedy a hand. "Son," he said, "you've got to learn to handle a gun like a man." Kennedy glared back. In his later retelling of the story, RFK was equally patronizing, mocking LBJ's practice of shooting deer from an elevated concrete platform. "This isn't hunting," he said, "it's slaughter."

Johnson's plan was to avoid the primaries, let the other candidates destroy each other, and then graciously accept the nomination from the party elders at the convention. Too late, he realized that he had miscalculated and that Kennedy would come to Los Angeles with just enough delegates to win on the first ballot. On the eve of the convention, Johnson launched a thinly veiled "stop Kennedy" campaign. His surrogates leaked to reporters that JFK was terminally ill with Addison's disease, kept alive only by regular drug injections. At a news conference, LBJ made cutting asides about Joseph Kennedy, referring to the father as a "Chamberlain umbrella man" who had appeased the Nazis. Bobby Kennedy was apopletic: on the eve of his family's moment of triumph, here was Johnson reneging on his word to remain neutral, trying to spill the best kept of Kennedy family secrets, and, equally unforgivable, maligning the patriarch. Kennedy held a press conference to present a phony medical report on his brother's health ("superb"). At a conventioneer's hotel, he sought out LBJ's closest aide, secretary of the Senate Bobby Baker. According to Baker, RFK leaned over LBJ's right-hand man and, with fists clenched, hissed, "You'll get yours."

Jack Kennedy, meanwhile, was blithely hinting to newspaper reporters that he would choose LBJ as his running mate. Johnson was in many ways the obvious choice: he could deliver Texas, call in congressional markers, and help in the South. Bobby was dead set against putting Johnson on the ticket and, prematurely as it turned out, reassured labor leaders and northern liberals that LBJ wasn't even on the short list. What happened next has been a source of historical debate for many years.

The story that Robert Kennedy told, as related by historian Arthur Schlesinger and other Kennedy chroniclers, was one of confusion and accident. On the morning after he secured the Democratic nomination, JFK had gone to see LBJ to offer him the number two spot—but only as a matter of pro forma courtesy. " . . . [JFK] never dreamt that there was a chance in the world that he [LBJ] would accept it," Bobby told Schlesinger in 1965. Why, after all, would Johnson want to give up his immensely powerful post in the Senate for four years of gilded impotence? At about 11 a.m., Jack Kennedy arrived back in his suite greatly disturbed, according to Bobby's account. "You just won't believe it," said a dazed Jack. "He wants it!"

"Oh, my God!" Bobby exclaimed.

"Now what do we do?"

Kennedy's allies in the labor movement were beside themselves when they heard that the southern, still-conservative Johnson would be JFK's running mate. Jack Conway, the UAW political operative whom Bobby had carefully cultivated during the rackets investigations, was as blunt with RFK as RFK might have been with a lazy campaign volunteer: "If you do this," Conway warned, "you're going to fuck everything up." But the Kennedys had done it.

Unless, of course, they could undo it. That afternoon, Bobby later recounted, his brother sent him as an emissary down to LBJ's suite to fix what Bobby was calling "this terrible mistake." After one or two rebuffs by Johnson's wary advisers, Bobby was ushered before LBJ "to see," as Bobby described his mission, "if I could get him to withdraw." Bobby explained to the proud Texan that the liberals were threatening to bolt, perhaps stage an ugly floor fight on national TV. Wouldn't LBJ really prefer to be chairman of the Democratic National Committee? Johnson looked crestfallen, humiliated. "I thought he'd burst into tears," RFK recalled. "He just shook, and tears came to his eyes, and he said, 'I want to be vice-president, and if the president will have me, I'll join him in making a fight for it.' " Bobby squirmed, but he was trapped. "Well, then, that's fine," Kennedy glumly replied. "He wants you as vice-president if you want to be vice-president, we want you to know."

That was Kennedy's story, but it wasn't the whole story or, the evidence suggests, an entirely accurate account. A half hour *before* Robert Kennedy appeared in LBJ's suite, Jack Kennedy himself had been on the phone with Lyndon Johnson, reassuring him that the vice-presidential nomination was his and no one else's. When a Johnson intermediary, understandably perplexed by the mixed signals from the Kennedy camp, asked JFK what was going on, the older brother blandly answered that Bobby was "out of touch." So what *was* going on? Robert Kennedy later said the complete story would never be known, but that may be because he hoped it wouldn't. Jack Kennedy relied on his brother, trusted him, needed him, but he didn't always tell him everything he was thinking or doing. There is considerable testimony in the memoirs of journalists and other politicians that JFK had for some time wanted LBJ as his running mate and that he didn't quite level with RFK. It is possible that JFK was tense and uncertain and changed his mind, perhaps several times, during the course of the day. The ferocity of Bobby's response probably did give JFK second thoughts about choosing Johnson. But it may also be that JFK was—not for the first time—using his brother as a stalking horse. Fred Dutton, the longtime Kennedy political adviser well versed in the family dynamic, said, "I always suspected that Jack didn't tell Bobby everything about LBJ because Jack figured Bobby would try to stop him. The Kennedys followed an old political rule: always leave 2 percent for the double cross, even if it's your brother."

Bobby was desolate that evening as the exhausted brothers repaired to the ornate Spanish-style mansion rented by their father in Beverly Hills. "Yesterday [when JFK won the nomination] was the best day of my life," Bobby told Charlie Bartlett, the newspaper columnist and family friend. "Today is the worst day." Jack Kennedy was also a little downcast and remote, distantly reading a newspaper spread over the hood of a car. Bartlett recalled the scene: The sun was setting, Bobby's children were splashing in the fountain, and Joseph Kennedy Sr. was resplendent in a red velvet smoking jacket. The patriarch had deliberately stayed away from the convention hall, lest his presence detract from his son's moment of glory. Conscious of his unsavory image, the elder Kennedy refused to be photographed. His deliberate low profile showed considerable self-awareness and self-discipline. His fulfillment now came entirely through his sons. He was generous with his praise, a cheerleader whenever the game seemed to be turning sour. "Don't worry, Jack," he soothed his fretful son. "In two weeks they'll be saying it's the smartest thing you ever did." Back at his hotel suite, Lyndon Johnson was still ranting about "that little shitass" Bobby Kennedy, whose loathing he now returned.

AFTER THE CONVENTION, the Kennedys repaired to Acapulco to relax, each in his own way. Together with his Milton chum, David Hackett, who had joined the campaign, Bobby went scuba diving. Though he had never dived before, he strapped himself with weights and went over the side. "He just jumped in and went right to the bottom," Hackett recalled. Uneasily following his competitive schoolmate, Hackett became anxious as he plunged over a hundred feet into the depths—"it was pitch black"—and hastily decided to swim back to the surface. Interviewed years later, Hackett remarked that Bobby's unschooled plunge had been "crazy," yet he couldn't help admiring his "tremendous courage."

The vacation was brief. "You can rest in November," Kennedy told the campaign staff. Theodore White recalled sitting at Kennedy headquarters in Washington, chatting with some aides and gathering material for *The Making of the President*, when the campaign manager, in short sleeves, burst in. "What are you doing?" he demanded. "What are we all doing? Lets's get on the road. Let's get on the road tomorrow! I want us all on the road tomorrow!" He slammed the door without waiting for an answer.

Far-flung campaign workers learned to dread Kennedy's arrival in town. At the airport in Houston, John Singleton, a lawyer active in Democratic politics, handed Bobby some talking points for the candidate to say about tax breaks for the oil and gas industry. Bobby read the paper, tore it up, and threw it on the ground. "We're not going to say anything like that," Kennedy told the embarrassed Texan. "We put that son of a bitch [LBJ] on the ticket to carry Texas and if you can't carry Texas, that's your problem." Riding in from the airport in St. Louis, a local coordinator, John Graves, said to RFK, "We've got to talk about the religious issue." Kennedy fixed him with a stare. "There will be no religious issue," he stated. Around the country, local party officials nervously joked, "Little Brother Is Watching You." Bobby professed not to care. "I'm not running a popularity contest," he told Hugh Sidey of Time-Life. "It doesn't matter if they like me or not. Jack can be nice to them. . . . Somebody has to be able to say no."

Kennedy operated with a mix of starchy principle and expediency. He found a superb advance man in Jerry Bruno, a gruff pixie, and a clever political operative in Dick Tuck, a merry prankster with many tricks, including the "spaghetti barricade," designed to break at the right moment. At the convention, Lyndon Johnson's aides complained that Kennedy's men had cut their phone lines on the convention floor. They had no proof, however; certainly nothing implicating the Kennedys directly. It has never been clear how much Bobby Kennedy knew about the pranks of Tuck or the more malign connivances of Paul Corbin. Kennedy may have preferred not to ask too many questions. Yet at other times, Kennedy inquired very closely. That fall, some anti-Catholic literature was traced to a press in a building on Long Island owned by Texas oilman H. L. Hunt. A little later, when Hunt made a generous campaign donation, Bobby ordered the money returned. He explained that, if elected, the Kennedy administration might want to prosecute the press owner for publishing hate mail.

Nowhere was the Kennedy calculus of moral pragmatism more evident than in the campaign's courtship of the black vote. It is likely that Kennedy did not have a clearly thought-out plan, but rather adjusted and adapted as he went along, especially as he learned and experienced more about racial inequity. The political equation was difficult to solve. In 1960, the segregated South was still solidly Democratic. John and Robert Kennedy had to be careful not to offend local sensibilities. On the other hand, a growing population of black voters, concentrated in northern cities in key swing states like New York, Pennsylvania, Ohio, and Illinois, was there for the wooing. To the happy surprise of liberal activists, Bobby took a hard line in favor of a pro–civil rights platform at the convention. "Don't fuzz it up," he instructed. And on a trip through Georgia in September, he behaved like Sherman. In Savannah for a political dinner, he insisted on being driven through the black part of town. Any blacks coming to the dinner? he inquired. No, he was told, by a somewhat irritated aide to the governor; Kennedy, the staff man knew, was well aware that the local hotels were segregated. No blacks, Kennedy responded, no dinner. Kennedy wasn't just looking for black votes; not that many blacks in the South were registered to vote. Segregation offended his natural sense of justice.

And yet, at the outset, Kennedy was cynical about the black vote. It was a commodity, to be bought. The usual procedure was to find a local black political leader or clergyman and get a local white politician to hand him a wad of cash. At the suggestion of Mayor Daley, Bobby had installed Congressman William Dawson, a well-known shakedown artist from Chicago's notoriously corrupt Second Ward, as chairman of the campaign's civil rights section. Dawson was given a specially constructed office known among the staffers as Uncle Tom's Cabin and rarely spoken to again. "Bob didn't want to get into a bidding war for the black vote," recalled John Seigenthaler, the Tennessee newspaperman who had signed on to help Kennedy with the South. Richard Nixon's running mate, Henry Cabot Lodge—the Brahmin vanquished by Kennedy in '52—was promising that the Republicans would put a black in the cabinet. Kennedy, said Seigenthaler, didn't want to have to promise two blacks. Getting out the black vote was described by Congressman Frank Thompson, who headed up efforts in Newark, Philadelphia, and Baltimore, as "hauling coal." Congressman Adam Clayton Powell, the charismatic Harlem preacher, told Kennedy that, for $300,000, he would establish a nationwide get-out-the-vote drive. Kennedy's shrewd black adviser, Chicago publisher Louis Martin, laughed out loud. The money would go straight into the Reverend Powell's pocket, he told Bobby. Kennedy settled by giving Powell $50,000 for ten speeches, pay-per-performance.

The strains of genuine decency and hardheaded pragmatism met in arguably the most important moment of the campaign, the effort to get Martin Luther King Jr. out of jail. Just two phone calls—one by JFK, one by RFK—

decided the outcome of the election and determined the course of racial politics for decades to come. The story told and retold in various Kennedy biographies and memoirs is an uplifting tale, but it is also partly myth. It needs to be re-examined twice—first as a moral impulse and second as realpolitik.

King was not a partisan. The great black civil rights leader, whose nonviolent crusade was still gathering momentum in 1960, eschewed taking sides in the election, though he had praised the Republican nominee, Richard Nixon. The Kennedys had made no real effort to cultivate Dr. King. Had he not been arrested for sitting-in at a segregated lunch counter in Atlanta on October 19, just two weeks before the election, they might never have spoken. The precipitating event was an outrage: a local judge, on a thin legal pretext, sentenced King to four months' hard labor. A few days later, in the early-morning darkness, King was hustled off in chains to a state prison deep in the Georgia backwoods. King's wife, Coretta, five months pregnant, was distraught. She called Harris Wofford, a Kennedy campaign aide who handled civil rights. "They are going to kill him," she cried. "I know they are going to kill him." Wofford called Sargent Shriver, Kennedy's in-law (married to Eunice) and Wofford's liberal ally out on the campaign trail. In an airport lounge at Chicago's O'Hare Airport, Shriver pleaded with Jack Kennedy to call Mrs. King and at least extend his sympathy. "Why not?" shrugged the candidate. "Do you have her number?"

News of Kennedy's phone call to Mrs. King soon leaked. It didn't take long for Wofford and Louis Martin, who had also pressed for the call to Mrs. King, to get a summons from a worried-sounding John Seigenthaler at campaign headquarters. "Bob wants to see you bomb throwers right away," said Seigenthaler. At headquarters, Bobby Kennedy "turned on us," Wofford recalled, "with fists tight, his eyes cold blue." RFK stated, in a way that invited no response, "Do you know that three southern governors told us that if Jack supported Jimmy Hoffa, Nikita Khrushchev, or Martin Luther King, they would throw their states to Nixon? Do you know that this election may be razor close and you have probably just lost it for us?" Kennedy told Wofford that the civil rights section "isn't going to do another damn thing in this campaign." Louis Martin tried to explain that the judge had refused to allow King to make bail. The civil rights leader had been sent to prison for violating his probation on an earlier trumped-up charge—driving without a license (King had been driving in Georgia with an Alabama license). Kennedy listened doubtfully. "How could they do that?" he asked. "You can't deny bail on a misdemeanor." "Well, they just did it," said Martin. Kennedy paused. He seemed distracted, overwhelmed, Martin suspected, by his multiple burdens. "Uh, goddammit," Kennedy muttered.

Kennedy seemed to fret about what to do as John Seigenthaler drove him to the airport early that afternoon. He was flying to New York for a campaign event. Maybe, he told Seigenthaler, he should take the heat off his brother and act as a "lightning rod" by calling the judge himself. Seigenthaler, whose phone had been ringing all morning with the calls of angry southern politicians protesting JFK's call to Mrs. King, urged Bobby to stay out of it. Bobby wearily agreed.

The next day, a press aide told Seigenthaler that the wires were reporting that the judge had released King—at the intervention of Robert Kennedy. Can't be true, Seigenthaler said; Kennedy had assured him he wouldn't call the judge. But it was true. Seigenthaler called Kennedy, who sheepishly disclosed the call. He said that, on the plane to New York, he had got to thinking about the whole matter. It was "disgraceful. . . . It just burned me up," Kennedy said. "It grilled me. The more I thought about the injustice of it, the more I thought what a son of a bitch the judge was." So Kennedy called the judge and gave him a lecture on the constitutional right to make bail, and the judge agreed to release King. Later, speaking with Wofford, Kennedy said he told the judge, "If he was a decent American, he would let King out by sundown. I called him because it made me so damn angry to think of that bastard sentencing a citizen to four months of hard labor for a minor traffic offense."

The impact of JFK's call to Mrs. King and RFK's intervention with the judge was immense. Daddy King, Martin Luther King's father, an extremely influential Baptist preacher, openly shifted his endorsement from Nixon to Kennedy. The Kennedy campaign brilliantly exploited the symbolism of the phone calls with a *samizdat* campaign in the black community. Careful not to tout the Kennedy-King connection in the popular mainstream press, lest southern voters take umbrage, the Kennedy campaign published hundreds of thousands of leaflets and handbills that were distributed at black churches and bars. On one side, a flyer read: "Jack Kennedy called Mrs. King." On the other side it said: "Richard Nixon did not." Many political analysts believe that this PR offensive decided the election. In a half-dozen states in the East and Midwest carried by Kennedy by very narrow margins on election day, black turnout made the difference. Richard Nixon's chauffeur understood. "Mr. Vice-President," he told his boss after the election, "you know I had been talking to my friends. They had been all for you. But when Mr. Robert Kennedy called the judge to get Dr. King out of jail—well, they just all turned to him."

RFK's phone call to the judge, his act of impetuous decency, has long been seen as a defining moment in Kennedy's life and political career. But, like the tale RFK spun about Lyndon Johnson and the vice presidency, the version told by Wofford, Seigenthaler, and Kennedy omits some important facts. What actually happened is more complicated and revealing about Kennedy's character and his way of doing business.

When King was arrested on October 19 and sentenced to hard labor, Jack and Bobby Kennedy discussed the political ramifications of trying to get him out of jail. While the risks were probably clearer than the rewards, doing nothing was not a good option, either. King's incarceration was an embarrassment to the Democratic power structure down South. It was an invitation to the Republicans—"the party of Lincoln"—to take the moral high ground. Better, then, to set King free—but quietly, if possible, without provoking a backlash. The Kennedys had been warned against making public statements by their southern allies, including Georgia governor Ernest Vandiver. This was a matter that called for the utmost discretion. At 6:30 a.m. one morning a few days after King's imprisonment, Senator Kennedy telephoned Governor Vandiver. Kennedy asked, couldn't the governor do something to get King out of jail? Vandiver, awakened at the executive mansion by JFK's call, said he couldn't do anything publicly—he was a segregationist himself and needed political cover. But he wanted Kennedy to win the presidency, and he understood and appreciated the political embarrassment of sentencing King to the rockpile over a traffic ticket. Vandiver agreed to make some phone calls. He reached George D. Stewart, the secretary of the state senate, who also happened to be a close friend and classmate of the DeKalb County judge in the King case, Oscar Mitchell. The judge consented to release King, but added that he needed his own political cover. Judge Mitchell had to be able to say that he let King out of jail only after being called on the phone by Senator Kennedy or his brother.

Vandiver relayed all this to Jack Kennedy. Kennedy, in turn, instructed Bobby to call the judge. RFK was *not* operating on his own initiative. He was carrying out his brother's orders. The timing remains uncertain, but Bobby—increasingly steamed over the injustice of King's punishment—probably placed the call to Judge Mitchell from a phone booth in New York shortly after he had assured Seigenthaler, as they drove to the Washington airport, that he would not. Following a brief cordial conversation with RFK, the judge released King. That intricate chain of events, long kept secret, is the more nuanced story behind Kennedy's impulsive blow for justice.*

The full story did not come out until Vandiver broke his own silence in 1993 and told the background details to Jack Bass, a biographer of federal judge Frank Johnson. Vandiver repeated his version to the author in 1998. Vandiver's account came as something of a surprise to Seigenthaler, who, left out of the loop, had been one of the main sources for the more heroic version of RFK's

* Actually, RFK himself hinted at this fuller explanation in an off-the-record oral history he gave *New York Times* correspondent Anthony Lewis in 1964. Kennedy, almost in passing, revealed that he had called Mitchell *at the suggestion of Governor Vandiver*. Furthermore, in Kennedy's 1964 retelling, his call to the judge had not been the cry of moral outrage he had conveyed at the time to Seigenthaler and Wofford. Rather, Kennedy had politely asked if King would get out on bail, and Mitchell had replied, "Bob, it's nice to talk to you. I don't have any objection about doing that." Later, when scholars, engaged in trying to reconstruct the story, read Bobby Kennedy's somewhat cryptic reference to the "suggestion" from Governor Vandiver, they were perplexed. While working on his biography of RFK in 1976, Arthur Schlesinger wrote John Seigenthaler and asked him whether Kennedy had spoken to Vandiver. No, Seigenthaler responded, he felt quite sure that Kennedy had spoken to no one else. Perhaps Kennedy was "confusing" the call with some earlier call to the governor. Other historians have tried to rationalize Kennedy's second, more toned-down version of the call to Judge Mitchell. Possibly Kennedy, who at the time of the interview with Tony Lewis had recently stepped down as attorney general to become a U.S. senator, had become more sensitive to appearances and did not wish to look as if he was trying to privately arm-twist a judge. He had only called the judge, he wanted to emphasize, to ask a simple question about making bail.

moral impetuosity. Trying to sort through the conflicting accounts in 1999, Seigenthaler still clearly recalled how angry Bobby had seemed about the injustice done to King by the judge. Kennedy's words and actions that day remain difficult to decode. Why, if he and his brother were already maneuvering to get Dr. King out of jail, did he so angrily berate Wofford, Shriver, and Martin for wanting to reach out to Mrs. King? In this instance, Kennedy's fury may have been largely fueled by a frustration that he had lost control over his minions. The Kennedy campaign was, in appearance at least, free-form and nonhierarchal, but Bobby Kennedy hated freelancers, especially on matters as sensitive as this one. Here the Kennedys were working on a discreet plan to get King out of jail, and the bleeding hearts had blundered in and unwittingly threatened to upset a delicate negotiation. Kennedy's anger was often plain to see, but the reasons for it were sometimes hidden. He was probably aware of his own mixed motives. After the election, when the results were in and it was clear that the black vote had helped elect JFK, columnist Murray Kempton asked Kennedy if he was glad he had called King's judge. "Sure I'm glad," Kennedy said and added cryptically, "but I would hope I'm not glad for the reason you think I'm glad." Thinking over the story of Kennedy's call to Judge Mitchell, Seigenthaler finally concluded that RFK must have been operating on twin tracks— moral impulse *and* pragmatism.

Kennedy was fully capable of such internal contradictions—not contradictions, really, but parallel instincts that coexisted within him, sometimes in conflict, sometimes carefully compartmentalized. Two other aspects of the King story are characteristic of the Kennedys. One: Bob and Jack kept their back-channel operation a secret, even from a trusted aide like Seigenthaler. Two: the Kennedys methodically sought to identify key inside players—in this case, Governor Vandiver—who could get them what they wanted. "That's the Kennedy family m.o.," said Joe Dolan, a longtime Robert Kennedy aide. "Case it out. Who knows somebody? Who can talk to someone? Often they didn't make just one approach, but several. They got it from the old man. Joe was no respecter, he was never in awe. He never trusted one man." The Kennedy's use of back channels and secret go-betweens would become a basic modus operandi in the White House.

As they had with the Massachusetts "secretaries" in 1952, the Kennedys set up their own private political campaign organization, Citizens for Kennedy, to run parallel to the existing Democratic Party. Kennedy discovered that he couldn't depend on party regulars even when they were Irish Catholic—in New York State, perversely *because* they were Irish Catholic. In New York, recalled CUNY professor Richard Wade, who helped organize the campaign upstate, almost all the Democratic committee chairmen were Irish Catholics. But they resented JFK for proving that a Catholic politician could climb to the top. They had built their own base by playing off anti-Catholic prejudice—and reconciled their own lack of advancement to a glass ceiling. JFK's ascendancy gave lie to their victimology. Remembering the hangers-on from JFK's congressional campaigns, Bobby Kennedy just shook his head over the old Irish pols.

"They're the worst kind," he told Wade. He instructed Wade to set up a separate Kennedy organization in upstate New York.

At the same time, the Kennedys, including Father Joe, courted some old-time party bosses, like Jesse Unruh of California and John Bailey of Connecticut—the ones who could still really deliver. If there was one man the Kennedys needed more than any other in 1960, it was Richard Daley, the mayor of Chicago. Illinois would likely be a critical swing state, and Daley's machine could deliver about a half-million votes, including some from the graveyard. Joe Kennedy, who owned the single largest retail operation in Chicago, the Merchandise Mart, had been cozying up to the mayor for years. Bobby Kennedy was careful to pay homage to Hizzoner as he traveled through the Midwest. "Bob thought he understood Daley because he understood his dad—the same age, the same culture, the same Irish Catholic determination to get results," said John Nolan, another veteran Kennedy campaign aide.

The Kennedys knew they would need every vote. According to most polls, Kennedy and Nixon were dead even as the campaign began in late August. Lurking in the background was the religious issue. The Kennedys wanted both to stimulate the Catholic vote—a quarter of the nation's electorate and potentially decisive in a number of large northern states, where Catholics had been moving into the GOP column since the 1940s—and to convince Protestants and Jews that a vote based on religious preference was a ballot for intolerance. RFK's own thinking had begun to change on the religious issue. In a pattern of decision making that would become familiar, Kennedy's initial and sometimes rash visceral instincts gave way to shrewd calculation and measured boldness. During the primaries, fearful of backlash and bigotry, he had wanted to run away from JFK's Catholicism. But during the general election, he took a different, more considered approach. Ted Sorensen, JFK's speechwriter and close aide, recalled RFK flying from Washington in early September to join the candidate on a whistle-stop swing through California. JFK had been invited to speak to the Houston Ministerial Association to address the religious issue on the night of September 12. Nixon had declined to appear before the ministers. Should Kennedy go? His brother argued that he should. "Bobby said something like, 'This is the place to confront the issue. Let's do it,' " recalled Sorensen. In Houston, Jack Kennedy gave one of the best speeches of his life, calmly affirming the separation of church and state and declaring that he would resign if he thought his conscience—meaning his religious beliefs—ever conflicted with the national interest. His high-minded statement effectively salved a wound that might otherwise have festered. RFK, meanwhile, barnstormed through the Catskills, telling Jewish voters that an attack on Catholics could presage an attack on them.

As the campaign entered the last lap, it appeared that television, still a fairly new medium, would be the testing ground. The candidates had agreed to a series of four televised debates during the final six weeks of the campaign. The Kennedy camp was anxious, fearful that Nixon's superior grasp of the issues would make him a formidable debater and show up JFK's relative lack of experience. The Kennedys knew they would have to win partly on style points. The Kennedy camp did not plan on psychological warfare, but in their opportunistic way, the Kennedys were quick to exploit Nixon's personal insecurities.

The opening debate was televised nationwide from Chicago on September 26. At the studio, asked by a CBS producer if he wanted to be made up, the ruddily tanned Kennedy replied, "No." Standing nearby, Nixon was listening. Trying to show the same manly indifference, the sallow-faced vice president also turned down the offer of professionally applied cosmetics. Back in his dressing room, Kennedy was discreetly tended to by his own makeup man with a light face powder. Nixon clumsily applied a "Lazy-Shave" makeup "stick," hastily bought at a drugstore out on Michigan Avenue, to paste over his chronic five o'clock shadow. In the TV control room, an uneasy Nixon aide asked Bobby Kennedy how he thought the vice president looked. "T'rific," Kennedy lied. "T'rific."

During the debate, JFK coolly stared straight into the camera while Nixon, sweating through his chalky makeup, kept darting his eyes towards his rival. The effect on TV viewers was devastating. As reporters clustered around Nixon afterwards, a woman posing as a Nixon supporter piped up, "That's all right. You'll do better next time!" The woman had been planted in the crowd by Dick Tuck, the Kennedy campaign prankster hired by RFK. During the next debate in Washington, Nixon's team insisted that the studio be kept cold. Determined to make Nixon sweat, Bobby Kennedy stormed into the control room, demanding that the heat be turned up.

In RFK's brother-protector role, no detail was too small. Before the first debate, Bobby instructed his brother to take a nap. (Whether JFK did or not is unclear: pollster Lou Harris found the candidate relaxing by playing Peggy Lee records, but Ted Sorensen recalled JFK on his bed dozing beneath a mound of briefing materials.) As usual, RFK attended to Jackie as well as Jack. At the fourth debate in New York, Nixon's limousine was parked in front of Kennedy's limousine in an alley outside the TV studio. RFK asked Nixon's advance man, John Warner, if the Kennedy limo could switch places and go first. Jackie Kennedy was eight months' pregnant, RFK explained, and might need to make a quick getaway.

In the last week, both Kennedys began to worry that JFK's narrow lead over Nixon was eroding. Bobby feared a resurgence of anti-Catholic prejudice. Fearing that Nixon would find some nefarious way to exploit it, he instructed Bill Haddad, a *New York Post* investigative reporter he used as one of his occasional sleuths and troubleshooters, to work with Carmine Bellino, Kennedy's trusted accountant from the Rackets Committee, to build a file of negative research on Nixon. Years later, Haddad claimed that the file was chock-full of dirt on Nixon, including illegal land deals with Nixon's friend Bebe Rebozo. Kennedy may have wanted to maintain some kind of insurance policy he could use to leak to reporters, just in case Nixon was caught playing too rough. Still, there is no evidence Kennedy ever used his file on Nixon. In fact, the opposite: singer Frank Sinatra, seeking to curry favor with the Kennedys, gave the

Kennedy campaign a report from a private investigator supposedly documenting that Nixon had been treated by a psychiatrist in New York. RFK instructed
his aide John Seigenthaler to return the file to Sinatra, unused.

As the campaign wound down, the greatest threat to JFK's chances was out
in the open: President Eisenhower, who had slighted Nixon earlier in the campaign, had finally begun to campaign effectively to keep the GOP in the White
House. Fearful that the election was slipping away, both Kennedys staggered,
exhausted, through the last hours. Passing in a remote airport, each on his way
to another whistle stop, Robert wearily called out, "Hi, Johnny. How are you?"
The candidate replied, "Man, I'm tired." "What the hell are you tired for?"
asked the campaign manager. "I'm doing all the work."

On election night, RFK established a command center in the sunporch of
his large cottage, next to his father's and his brother's, in Hyannis Port. After
playing touch football in the afternoon, he studied the polls and early returns
with the campaign's private pollster, Lou Harris. "We're being clobbered," he
moaned at 7:15 in the evening. Yet only minutes later, he let out a whoop of joy.
John Bailey had called in; John F. Kennedy was sweeping Connecticut with a
heavy turnout.

Up and down through the night the results seesawed, along with emotions
in the Kennedy household. "Oh, Bunny, you're president now!" cooed Jackie
Kennedy at about 10:30 p.m. "No . . . no . . . it's too early yet," cautioned her
husband. In other rooms, the Kennedy sisters mercilessly, somewhat cruelly,
teased little brother Teddy, who had been in charge of the Rocky Mountain
states and now seemed on the verge of losing them all. To Kenny O'Donnell,
RFK seemed "very calm" and, unlike his sisters, worried about the bruised feelings of his brother Ted. In the early-morning hours, Bobby was in frequent
touch with Mayor Daley in Chicago. The downstate vote was coming in
strongly Republican. Not to worry, the mayor reassured Bobby; Illinois would
wind up in the Democratic column.* At 4 a.m., Jack Kennedy went to bed, still
unsure about the outcome. One by one, drained aides and advisers fell out,
until only Bobby remained awake and vigilant. At about 7 a.m., Secret Service
men took up their places around the home of the new president-elect. Robert
Kennedy fell into bed beside Ethel, too weary to remove anything more than
his shoes.

During the course of the campaign, the brothers had grown closer. JFK no

---

* One of the more persistent conspiracy theories is that organized crime, working with
Joe Kennedy, delivered Chicago and hence Illinois and hence the presidency to JFK. FBI
bugs did pick up bragging to this effect from Chicago boss Sam Giancana. Regardless of
whether Giancana was somehow working for the Kennedys—a dubious claim—there
are at least two problems with the mobster's boast. First, the Kennedys did not need Giancana, who controlled possibly one or two wards (which voted heavily Democratic
anyway), because they already had Daley, who could deliver the entire city (voter
turnout in Chicago on election day 1960 was over 90 percent). Second, even if Nixon
had won Illinois (and there was plenty of GOP vote stealing downstate), Kennedy still
had enough electoral votes to win the election.

longer condescended to little brother. He accepted him into his fraternity of macho irony. As JFK walked onstage for the first of the crucial presidential debates, RFK eased the tension with some good-natured profanity. "Kick him in the balls," he said, and Jack smiled at the bluffery. JFK sometimes had to soothe newsmen and campaign workers ruffled by his brother's bluntness. In a German restaurant in Milwaukee on the night before the Wisconsin primary, RFK had asked NBC's Sander Vanocur, "How do you think we'll do?" Vanocur had answered, offhand, "I think you'll carry the Catholic vote." Oversensitive to the religious issue, RFK blew up. On the way out of the restaurant, Vanocur grumbled to JFK, who was standing by the door, "That brother of yours has no manners." With a shrug, JFK replied, "Ignore him." From time to time JFK had to rein in RFK's combative instincts. In August, RFK became exercised because baseball great Jackie Robinson was backing Richard Nixon. "Tell Bobby that we're running against Nixon, not Jackie Robinson," Senator Kennedy instructed.

Still, JFK was profoundly and forever grateful for his brother's all-out devotion to the hard and sometimes dirty job of running a presidential campaign. "I don't know what Bobby does," JFK told Charlie Bartlett, "but it always seems to turn out right." What Bobby did for his brother was everything, from hiring the media expert—a brand-new niche in 1960—who told JFK to wear just the right light makeup for the debates, to shutting down potential sexual blackmailers. Working with Father Joe, RFK found trustworthy lawyers to fend off extortion schemes from Kennedy's old girlfriends and scam artists. Yet, quietly and with little notice, he grew in his own right. In the coalfields of West Virginia he saw for the first time—and, with his experiencing nature, felt—abject poverty. He came to understand that race in America was about more than buying votes. And he discovered, in a most demanding arena, that he could lead. To be sure, his style of leadership was somewhat unconventional. He was not a commanding physical presence, and his insistent, at times hectoring, tone put off more than a few followers. But he was clever and totally focused and his judgment was sound. He could be belligerent, but he could also change his mind without embarrassment. His ability to sublimate his ego made him more effective. He did not need to posture or stand on points of pride. Still, his ego was in harness; it had been tamed, but not eliminated. Beneath the selfless devotion to his brother's political ambitions burned a desire to strike out, on his own, against evil as he saw it.

CHAPTER **5** PROTECTOR

ROBERT KENNEDY'S DESIRE for independence flickered, briefly, in the first few weeks after the election. He didn't want a position in the White House. Working directly for his brother would have been "impossible," he told Arthur Schlesinger in 1965. "I had to do something on my own." He toyed with the idea of going to Massachusetts to run for governor, or taking a job in the Defense Department, or at State. But his father was adamant: Bobby would become attorney general. "Nobody's better qualified," Joe Sr. told Jack Kennedy, who had his doubts. The president-elect could hear the outcry on the editorial pages if he chose, as the nation's top lawyer, his thirty-five-year-old brother who had never practiced law. The patriarch was thinking, as always, about protecting his family. He had urged—instructed—Jack to reappoint FBI director J. Edgar Hoover, along with CIA director Allen Dulles, as his first official act. A sultan is never satisfied with his tribute, however, and Hoover was soon grouching that the phone call to Dulles was made before the phone call to him. The surest way to protect Jack from his enemies, in and out of government, Joe Kennedy believed, was to make Bobby the attorney general.

Playing golf with a *New York Times* reporter on November 19, JFK casually floated Bobby's name for the job. The reaction in the press was quick and mostly negative. The *Times* editorialized against nepotism and accused the Kennedys of sullying an office that was supposed to be above politics. Bobby's own survey of Washington elders—Justice William Douglas, Senator John McClellan, columnist Drew Pearson, the FBI's Hoover—brought more warnings. Only Hoover told him he should take the job, and Bobby suspected, correctly, that the top G-man was being insincere. At dinner with John Seigenthaler at Hickory Hill in early December, Bobby seemed torn and anxious. Father Joe had been leaning hard; Bobby was resisting. Finally, RFK resolved that he would tell his older brother that he did not want to be attorney general. As he

reached for the phone, he muttered, "This will kill my father." To Jack, he argued that if he took the job, the newspapers would "kick our balls off." The
president-elect stalled. "Don't tell me now," he said. JFK was ambivalent about
making his brother attorney general, but he was also mindful of his father's
wishes. The president-elect told Bobby to meet him for breakfast in the morning. Over bacon and eggs at his house on N Street in Georgetown, JFK insisted
that he would need a cabinet member who would tell him "the unvarnished
truth, no matter what." John Kennedy didn't want to hear any arguments from
his little brother. There were restless newsmen waiting outside. "So that's it,
General," said the president-elect. "Let's grab our balls and go." But first, JFK
instructed his thirty-five-year-old brother, who was no longer a teenager but
looked like one, to go upstairs and comb his hair. In the newsreel clips of their
appearance on the snowy sidewalk, JFK looks debonair and confident and
Bobby, his brow furrowed, looks like a guilty ninth-grader who has been summoned to see the headmaster.

At lunch later that day with Arthur Schlesinger, Bobby seemed "rueful and
fatalistic," Schlesinger writes. Kennedy did not let on why, but he may have realized that his father, not for the first time, had misread his fundamental character. More intuitive than articulate, more feeling than reflective, Kennedy
could sense, only dimly perhaps, the inevitability of collisions ahead. Though
sensitive to his clan obligations, Bobby Kennedy was not about to turn the Justice Department into a Kennedy family citadel. He aimed to sally forth. It was in
Kennedy's nature to quest and experience, to challenge orthodoxy and to tempt
fate. He could surely foresee some, if not all, of the consequences of an activist
attorney general. During the campaign, Bobby had been struck by the fact that
Eisenhower's attorney general, William Rogers, didn't dare get off the plane
when he visited South Carolina with Richard Nixon. At a time when the Justice
Department was just beginning to enforce the law of the land on school desegregation, the federal government's chief law enforcement officer was already
persona non grata south of the Mason-Dixon line. The Eisenhower Justice Department had actually been quite slow-going and cautious. Kennedy must have
understood, even then, that he would push much harder—and that his brother
the president would have to bear the consequences.

But few others could see that far ahead. In the faculty room at Bobby's
alma mater, the University of Virginia Law School, the announcement of RFK's
appointment as attorney general was greeted with a "roar of incredulity," recalled Mortimer Caplin, Bob Kennedy's old tax professor (and soon-to-be Jack
Kennedy's commissioner of internal revenue). In the newsroom at the *New
York Times*, the law correspondent, Anthony Lewis, felt a sense of disappointment. He remembered Bobby from Harvard, where they were classmates, as
sullen and anti-intellectual, a bit of a lout. He did not think Kennedy would
make a very good attorney general.

Jack Kennedy affected a bemused attitude towards the grumbling. At dinner on January 20, the newly inaugurated president jokingly told his friends,
"I don't know why people are so mad at me for making Bobby Attorney Gen-

eral. I just wanted to give him some legal experience before he practiced." After dinner, Bobby came up to Jack, Charlie Bartlett observed, "with his fists clenched." RFK accosted his older brother, "Jack, you shouldn't have said that about me." JFK tried to lighten him up. "Bobby, you don't understand. You've got to make fun of it, you've got to make fun of yourself in politics." Bobby was not mollified. "You weren't making fun of yourself," he said. "You were making fun of me."

THE NEXT MORNING, Robert Kennedy was sworn in at a family ceremony in the second-floor residence of the White House. He made his way to the reception downstairs by sliding down the banister of the massive curving stairway, followed, in similar fashion, by several of his children. "Oh, Mr. Kennedy!" cried out the children's nurse, Ena Bernard, ". . . [Y]ou'll never grow up!" The Justice Department staffers waiting for him in the East Room were not impressed by the man they beheld. The new attorney general slouched and seemed smaller than his five feet ten; he spoke in a high, reedy voice; his hands shook; and he was painfully shy.

Byron White, Kennedy's number two, had "a bad impression" of his new boss, according to Louis Oberdorfer, whom White hired as assistant attorney general for taxation. Oberdorfer, like most of the senior staffers recruited by White, shared his misgivings. Most of the top men knew Kennedy mainly as the bullyboy from the Rackets Committee. "I thought he was an absolute disgrace," said Joe Dolan, a Denver lawyer hired by White as one of his assistants. "I thought I was going back to Washington to save the country from Robert Kennedy." White—the famous Whizzer White, all-American football player and Rhodes scholar, the first and unquestionably last man to finish first in his class at Yale Law School in the same year (1940) he led the National Football League in rushing yardage—was really more Jack's choice than Robert's. White, the head of Citizens for Kennedy during the campaign, had known JFK in the Pacific during the war. JFK hinted that White would earn the first available seat on the Supreme Court if he first helped out Bobby at Justice.

White recruited a superb staff, possibly the most impressive group ever assembled in the top jobs of one government agency. Typical was Nicholas deB. Katzenbach, in charge of the office of legal counsel. A graduate of Exeter, Princeton, Oxford, and Yale Law School (editor in chief of the *Law Journal*), he had flown as a bombardier in World War II and survived a German POW camp before teaching law at the University of Chicago. Bobby Kennedy, with his penchant for hero worship, was pleased to be surrounded by such men, Rhodes scholars and combat veterans who were at once self-effacing and action-oriented. Kennedy set out to make them his own.

It is very much to RFK's credit that he wanted a strong staff—that he did not feel threatened or upstaged by men who had more experience, credentials, and in some cases a greater aura of command than their boss. As the president's brother, Kennedy's authority was never in question. Kennedy liked to be in control, but at the same time he believed in delegating responsibility, often to greenhorns. William Geoghegan, a young aide who worked for Byron White, was summoned to Kennedy's office on a Saturday afternoon. There are race riots in Danville, Virginia, Kennedy told Geoghegan. Go deal with them. Kennedy did not offer much in the way of instruction or advice, and he accepted no excuses— but he unwaveringly supported his charges against outside criticism. Kennedy turned to his old Milton friend, Dave Hackett, and said, "There's a problem"— juvenile delinquency—"would you like to get into it?" "Yeah," said Hackett. Years later, Hackett laughed, "I don't think he knew any more about it than I did, and I didn't know anything." Sending well-intentioned amateurs out to handle complex crises was risky. But for these veterans of World War II, many of whom had been given life-and-death responsibility as very young men and now, as thirty-five-year-olds, chafed to take over the civilian world, the atmosphere in the Kennedy Justice Department was heady.

Kennedy could seem impetuous, but his closest aides said he was actually quite deliberate. "His initial reaction was often off the mark, but if you said, 'Listen a few minutes, Bob,' he really did listen and think," said Archibald Cox, a Harvard law professor recruited to serve as solicitor general. Kennedy would bore in on a problem, reading sheaves of documents and making pointed comments in his small, squiggly handwriting. ("The madder he got, the smaller the handwriting," said Joe Dolan.) Kennedy was overextended, increasingly so as time went on and his brother drew him closer as an adviser. But Kennedy was able to zero in on what really mattered. "He had a better sense of what was important, and what was not, than anyone I ever met," said John Nolan, a former marine and U.S. Supreme Court clerk who served as his administrative assistant. "Once he realized something was significant, he became the most deliberate, most thoughtful, most intense man." Whenever he had a spare moment, he roamed the halls of the department, bursting into the offices of shocked career lawyers, most of whom had never seen an attorney general up close. There was rarely any small talk. He would start quizzing them on their work. "Almost done with that?" he would inquire, in a manner designed to discourage dawdling. If a staffer didn't seem to be doing anything worthwhile, Kennedy would hand him a copy of *The Enemy Within* to read.

His staffers, who called him Bob (at Kennedy's wish; the more boyish-sounding Bobby was for his family), came fairly quickly to accept his insistent nature. They understood that he was most demanding of himself. They felt honored to be counted among his "band of brothers," as Ed Guthman, the Pulitzer Prize–winning reporter Bobby recruited as his spokesman, romantically characterized Kennedy's inner circle. Joe Kraft, a journalist who was close to Kennedy, observed that Kennedy's top men weren't really his social friends. They shared a "special kind of stoicism," said Kraft; they admired his "willingness to take unpleasant tasks upon himself."

Kennedy's integrity was tested almost right away. In New York, State Supreme Court Judge J. Vincent Keogh was caught taking a bribe in a complex case that involved one of Bobby's old nemeses, Tony "Ducks" Corrallo, a Teamster nicknamed for his ability to duck subpoenas. Politically, the case was highly sensitive. Keogh's brother, Congressman Eugene Keogh, was a powerful

Irish machine boss and close friend of Joseph Kennedy's, credited by the Kennedy family with delivering New York's delegates at the 1960 Democratic convention. In a late-night meeting in the attorney general's office in the late spring of 1961, Byron White presented the somewhat murky facts to Kennedy. "You have *got* to prosecute this," said the upright White. Kennedy, who had been pacing around the room, sat down, put his face down on the big desk, wrapped his elbows around his head, and said, "Goddammit, I told my brother I didn't want this job." Kenny O'Donnell, who had become White House appointments secretary, tried, as he usually did, to protect the president's political interests. Couldn't Judge Keogh just be allowed to resign? At a White House reception, several Justice staffers watched as a heated argument broke out on the stairway (the same one Bobby had slid down several months before). O'Donnell pressed his case to allow the judge to quietly step down. Byron White cracked an acerbic joke about the attorney general dragging his feet. Bobby's face lost color. "How could you say that?" he demanded of White. Shaking with anger, Bobby walked away. The case was prosecuted. Judge Keogh went to jail for two years, and Keogh's brother never forgave RFK.

The cafe society columnist Igor Cassini, who wrote under the pen name Cholly Knickerbocker in the Hearst papers, was closer to Joseph Kennedy than the Keogh brothers. Cassini entertained the elder Kennedy, swapped tidbits of gossip with him, and, according to investigative reporter Peter Maas, procured women for him. Cassini's brother, Oleg, designed dresses for the first lady and went to White House parties. In late 1961, Maas, who was then writing for the *Saturday Evening Post*, began looking into allegations that Igor Cassini had been hired—for $200,000—as a secret agent of Dominican dictator Rafael Trujillo, to use his influence with the Kennedys. Maas took the charges to the attorney general, expecting RFK to try to protect his father by offering to make a trade: if Maas sat on the Cassini story, Kennedy would give him some other scoop. ("I was willing to make a deal," Maas recalled.) At first, Kennedy protested that Cassini was innocent, but when Maas had finished laying out the evidence, all Kennedy said was, "Thank you very much." The next day, two FBI agents showed up at Maas's door, wanting to see the reporter's notes. After checking with his editor, Maas cooperated with the feds. Cassini was indicted, pleaded nolo contendere, and paid a $10,000 fine. "Cholly Knickerbocker's" career as a gossip columnist was ruined. Maas was surprised and impressed that RFK had not tried to cover up for his father's friend. (President Kennedy, on the other hand, was very upset and tried to get the story killed, dispatching White House press secretary Pierre Salinger to plead and wheedle with Maas.) Maas was puzzled by RFK's willingness to cross his own father. Some years later, after they had become friends, Maas asked RFK why he had not tried to block the Cassini exposé. "What's right is right," answered Kennedy. Maas was skeptical. "I didn't buy that," he recalled. "I think he was so enraged that a guy like Cassini would jeopardize JFK's administration [by secretly flacking for Trujillo], I think that's why he went after him."

The president was, as usual, content to let his brother play the heavy. In the first year of his administration, JFK was besieged with entreaties from a

corporate tycoon who had been a major contributor to the Democratic Party.
The man was under investigation by the Justice Department for antitrust vio-
lations. JFK tried to pass him off to a White House staffer, Myer Feldman, but
the corporate executive insisted that he was "entitled" to see the president. JFK
acquiesced, and promptly hid behind RFK. "You're a good friend and I'd like to
help you," JFK told the Democratic fat cat. "But I'm afraid we have an attorney
general we can't fix."

Robert Kennedy's men loved his ferocious dignity. Yet, they couldn't help
noticing that he was, in the manner of the very rich, rather spoiled. He was a
penny-pincher: he insisted on traveling coach and booking medium-priced
hotel rooms. But because he rarely carried money, his staff or traveling companions often had to pick up the check. Once, sitting in church with RFK, Maas
dutifully pulled out a dollar to place in the collection plate for RFK. "Don't you
think I'd be more generous than that?" Kennedy inquired. Kennedy was forever
leaving his coat or his briefcase behind, expecting that someone would bring it
along. He was blessed to have a secretary, Angie Novello, who could tease him
and take care of him. "It would be *extremely* helpful if the Attorney General of
the United States . . . would notify his immediate staff of his whereabouts at all
times," she chided in one memo. Kennedy scrawled back, "What if I'm lost.
Love." Other staffers were less amused about getting his laundry. For all his
slovenliness, Kennedy (like his brother Jack) changed his shirt three or four
times a day. His ambitious aides were expected to play valet. "If you want to be
secretary of state, you have to know how to get those shirts out of their plastic
bags," a slightly miffed handler told *New York Times* reporter Richard Reeves.

If Kennedy was a prince, most Justice Department officials were proud to
be his liegemen. They knew they were at the center of things. There was an
aura of action, of movement, of freewheeling openness around Kennedy. His
offices, decorated with busts of Winston Churchill and his children's splotchy,
stick-figure drawings, had a kind of rough-and-ready glamour. The men near
Kennedy began looking like him, their ties askew, sleeves rolled up. They were
young, handsome, vigorous. A reporter would later observe that Kennedy's
personal staff, Guthman and Seigenthaler, who had signed on as administrative
assistant, looked like "Marlboro Men." Even the stern Whizzer White was
spotted by a reporter tossing a football with Kennedy in his cavernous office
one day in March 1961. The *New York Times* reported the game of high-
echelon catch in the next morning's paper.

Kennedy was mindful of the imagery. He devoted many hours to the
press. Asked how he spent his first four months, he answered, "For the most
part, seeing newspaper people." He enjoyed the company of reporters and
columnists at breakfasts and cookouts at Hickory Hill, and he was open with
them. But not too open. "Remember," his father had warned, "reporters are not
your friends." Kennedy was friendly, but cagey. The Kennedys would routinely
grant access to journalists from mass-market magazines, but demand to review
the story before publication. When Teddy Kennedy consented to be profiled by
Redbook, Bobby insisted on seeing the article and sent his younger brother an
extraordinarily detailed list of changes to request ("You will want to have them

eliminate the quote on what [Teddy's wife] Joan said about 'never meeting a Jew'. . . . On page 24, eliminate the sentence: 'Ted loves his family but there are times when he likes to be away from them' "). Journalists worried less in those days about getting too close to their sources. Seigenthaler often watched Bobby seduce reporters with candor: "In a calculated way, he'd ask them about substantive issues, usually off the topic they'd come to see him about. He'd ask, 'What would *you* do?' By the time he was through, he'd got them."

Bobby was not above pitching to Hollywood. During 1961, he often talked with Budd Schulberg, who wrote the screenplay to *On the Waterfront*, about making a movie of *The Enemy Within*. Paul Newman was supposed to play the role of RFK. Bobby may have been engaging in a bit of sibling rivalry; Hollywood was at the time producing *PT 109* with Cliff Robertson as the young JFK. In any case, the major studios were too intimidated by the Teamsters to make a movie with Jimmy Hoffa as the bad guy.

Still, there was nothing contrived or fake about Bobby Kennedy's willingness to take on hard cases against tough foes, and right away. The casualness was studied, but the urgency was real. He had a "horror of wasting time," wrote *Life* magazine reporter Paul O'Neil, who described Kennedy's unsuccessful efforts to conceal his impatience: in the presence of anyone even slightly long-winded, Kennedy would "clasp his hands as if in prayer," stare at his knuckles, and begin patting the arm of the chair in "slow and feverish rhythm" while staring away with an expression of "muted despair." No wonder his aides communicated in grunts, and Byron White had a duodenal ulcer by mid-February.

Within two weeks of taking office, Kennedy had declared "war on crime." He meant organized crime. He wanted to find a way to prosecute the hoodlums he had summoned before the Rackets Committee. From his old allies in the Federal Bureau of Narcotics, he had obtained a thick, black book on eight hundred mobsters. He handed the book to a task force of lawyers created to handle organized crime cases. "Don't tell me what I can't do," he instructed them. "Tell me what I can do."

THE MAIN OBSTACLE was not Jimmy Hoffa or talented defense lawyers like Edward Bennett Williams, who represented the Teamsters and mob bosses like Sam Giancana. The greatest impediment to Kennedy's war on crime was the director of the FBI, J. Edgar Hoover. The top G-man's resistance was passive and cunning, but it undermined Kennedy's effectiveness.

As RFK knew from his racket-busting days, Hoover had long denied the existence of a "Mafia." The FBI had instituted a Top Hoodlums Program after the raid at Apalachin exposed the meeting of a mob "commission" in 1957. But when Kennedy took office, the FBI was still lagging. In New York, Kennedy asked for the FBI's files on organized crime and got mostly newspaper clips. The New York office had four hundred agents out looking for communists and ten devoted to the mob. Kennedy was scornful. By 1961, the American Communist Party had only a few hundred members, Kennedy knew, and most of them were undercover FBI agents.

Kennedy had been instructed by his father to treat Hoover with respect. FBI reports indicate that Kennedy was uncooperative with the bureau during his early days as a Senate investigator, but Hoover's correspondence file shows that RFK sought to make amends in late August 1956 (right after JFK's failed run at the vice-presidential nomination). "I hope the United States continues to enjoy your leadership for a long period," Bobby wrote, "Mr. Hoover." RFK's mash note may have been prodded by his father. Bobby is "more enthusiastic than ever about J. Edgar Hoover and the FBI," Joe Sr. gushed to "Edgar" in April 1957. After Jack began campaigning for the presidency in 1960, Hoover's files show more encomiums from the candidate and his father, who expressed "deep admiration for the Director." Hoover's files also show that the director was gathering the sort of raw gossip about the Kennedys that could be useful if a Kennedy became president. A July 13, 1960, FBI memo to one of Hoover's aides reported, with a sinister tone but without specifics, that "allegations have been received concerning immoral conduct on part of [John F.] Kennedy and hoodlum connections of Kennedy."

The Kennedys knew they had something to fear from Hoover, and the director lost no time in reminding them. On January 30, 1961, just ten days after the inauguration, Hoover received a field report that a woman named Alicia Purdom claimed to have been JFK's lover. "Send memo to A.G.," Hoover jotted at the bottom. Once every two or three months, similar missives would arrive in Bobby's office from the director, not-so-subtle signals that Hoover was keeping, and regularly updating, a file on the president. Blackmail was an efficient means towards Hoover's true end, the preservation of his own power. Having an activist attorney general, the president's brother to boot, made the director nervous. On January 31, the day after Hoover posted his first notice about the president's sexual past, RFK provoked a comical cascade of memos in FBI headquarters just by trying to make use of the Justice Department gym, which, like so much else in the department, was under FBI control. Kennedy wanted to use the sunlamp (he was vain about his tan, and wanted to refresh it during the winter months) and get a massage. The attorney general was informed that the masseur was only for agents who had sustained injuries. On one of the several long memos reporting Kennedy's attempted invasion of the gym, Hoover repeated his earlier warnings about the need for agents to refrain from "horseplay" and to be "properly attired" at all times. "No one knows when and where the A.G. will appear," Hoover wrote ominously.

The A.G. appeared unannounced in Hoover's office while the director was taking his afternoon nap. Kennedy had insisted on a direct phone link to Hoover. When Hoover's secretary answered, Kennedy icily announced, "When I pick up this phone, there is only one man I want to talk to. Get this phone on the director's desk." On several occasions, Kennedy had the temerity to "buzz" Hoover to come to his office. This was not done to the director; in theory, Hoover reported to the attorney general, but in practice, attorneys general came to him.

Kennedy wanted to change the practice. In the beginning, he halfheartedly tried to pay court to Hoover, promising the director a private lunch once every couple of months with the president and calling him Edgar at staff meetings, but he could not hide his disdain. On some salutations, he actually crossed out the Edgar and wrote in Mr. Hoover. A chasm in style and attitude yawned between thirty-five-year-old Kennedy and the sixty-six-year-old director. Kennedy's informality in dress and habit grated on the compulsively orderly Hoover. Bobby's dog Brumus, a large and ill-tempered beast who relieved himself on the carpets and bit strangers, was a particular source of irritation. Kennedy insisted on bringing Brumus to work because, he explained to Angie Novello, the dog was "lonely" at home. The director once called a meeting of his twelve top assistants to see if there was legal justification to ban Brumus from the building. Kennedy, consciously or not, aggravated relations. The attorney general once conducted a conversation with the FBI director while throwing darts at a board hung on the wall of his formal office. From time to time, Kennedy would miss, embedding a dart into the oak paneling. Hoover fumed to his aides that Kennedy was "desecrating government property." Behind Hoover's back, Kennedy cursed the director and vowed that—after JFK was reelected—Hoover would be out of a job. The attorney general made cutting jokes about Hoover's faithful live-in assistant, Clyde Tolson. Told that Tolson had just undergone an operation, Kennedy quipped, "What for? A hysterectomy?"* Ethel, ever the loyal prankster, did not help. After sparring with Hoover at a Justice Department reception, she put an anonymous note in the FBI's "suggestions" box proposing that the director be replaced by the Los Angeles police chief, William Parker, whom Hoover loathed.

Word inevitably got back to Hoover, who feared he might lose his job at any moment. Hoover understood that he could not simply refuse to do Kennedy's bidding on major enforcement initiatives, like organized crime. But he was determined to do it in his own way, under FBI control, with minimal interference from the attorney general. An attorney general can prosecute—he or his minions can impanel grand juries and seek indictments—but only the FBI can investigate. Although Kennedy, over Hoover's fervent objections, brought the IRS, the Bureau of Narcotics, and other agencies into the crime fight, the attorney general was still dependent on Hoover's G-men for most investigations. It was up to Hoover to decide the best way to penetrate organized crime.

The method he chose was the use of electronic eavesdropping devices—so-called bugs. Hoover's men knew very little about the Mafia in 1961. A very quick way to catch up was to listen in on the private conversations of mobsters. It is estimated that during Bobby Kennedy's three years as attorney general, Hoover's men installed almost eight hundred bugs, usually by "black bag jobs," breaking into homes and bars and barbershops and planting the small transmitters under a chair or in a light socket. With an eye towards bureau aggrandizement and professional self-preservation, Hoover was more interested in

---

* Despite this gibe at Hoover's "wife" and cracks about Hoover's virility ("He has to squat to pee"), RFK did not take too seriously the rumors that Hoover was a practicing homosexual, according to William Hundley, the chief of the organized crime section.

gathering intelligence than bringing cases. Hoover saw the FBI as a rival to the CIA, not as a mere police force. He did some of his most effective spying on American public officials. The director was particularly eager to learn of mob ties to politicians, whom he could then blackmail. Hoover did not widely share the gleanings from these bugs, and when he did, FBI memos referred vaguely to "extremely reliable sources" or "informants."

The legal authority for such blatant invasions of privacy was murky in the early '60s. Hoover claimed to have a blanket authorization dating from Kennedy's predecessors as far back as the FDR administration. Kennedy later insisted that he knew nothing about the bugging. The evidence does not support his claim. He was informed of FBI electronic surveillance in at least one memo and played tapes from the bugs on two or more occasions. He later protested that he thought the FBI was playing him tapes from recording devices planted by local police. His aides argue, none too convincingly, that Kennedy was inept at all things mechanical, that he couldn't "tell the difference between a spark plug and a generator," much less understand the difference between wiretaps on phones—which by law clearly required his approval*—and electronic bugging devices. But Kennedy's own records show him seeking to learn more about electronic eavesdropping techniques, and officials at the FBI and IRS insisted that Kennedy pushed them to use both wiretaps and bugs as tools in his war on organized crime. Early in the Kennedy administration, the attorney general met with a Treasury Department official who was charged with instructing agents on the proper technique for wiretapping and bugging, including how to break into a house without detection. Normally, Treasury taught the course to fifteen people a year. Kennedy demanded the number of "students" be increased to fifty. Too many, argued the Treasury official. Kennedy turned on the man and said, "You look old to me. You should think of retiring." The man did retire, and the electronic eavesdropping course was expanded.

It is probable that Kennedy was not informed of specific acts of bugging, at least in advance. Most likely, he did not want to know. As one aide explained, "He became a civil libertarian later."

When the FBI's routine practice of bugging suspected criminals first publicly surfaced in 1966, Kennedy became caught up in a finger-pointing exercise with Hoover. The debate was framed almost entirely in terms of civil liberties. But the real cost was greater, and not generally remarked upon at the time or even later. By using bugs to gather intelligence on organized crime, Hoover compromised Kennedy's ability to prosecute criminals. None of the evidence collected by those bugs was admissible in court. The Supreme Court was still evolving its doctrine on inadmissible evidence in the early '60s, but it was a rea-

---

* Kennedy approved six hundred wiretaps, mostly for "national security." He thought electronic eavesdropping should be regulated, but he favored it. In March 1961, as he discussed wiretapping legislation with an aide, Kennedy asked, "Do you mean to tell me, that if your little girl were kidnapped, and a tap might get her home safely, you still wouldn't approve?" The aide mumbled, "Hard cases make bad law." On the taps Kennedy authorized, he kept no records and placed no time limits.

sonable guess that evidence gathered by illegal trespass and surreptitious eavesdropping was not going to pass constitutional muster. "We knew you couldn't use it," said Organized Crime Section Chief William Hundley. Indeed, as we shall see, when a bug was discovered in Las Vegas in 1963, it blew any chance of bringing cases against dozens of Las Vegas mobsters for illegal skimming operations. The most thoroughly bugged Mafia boss was Momo "Sam" Giancana. But Giancana was never prosecuted by Kennedy. Part of the reason was that Kennedy's brother—the president—had foolishly opened himself up to blackmail by sharing a girlfriend, Judith Exner, with the mobster. But even if Exner had never existed, the FBI's main evidence against Giancana—his own admissions that he had murdered, bribed, and extorted—was unusable in a court of law. It had been gathered by illegal eavesdropping. Kennedy never let up in his push against Giancana or other top gangsters. But his ability to put them behind bars was severely constrained by the tactics used by his FBI colleague down the hall at the Justice Department. Kennedy's failure to inquire more closely into Hoover's methods remains one of the mysteries of his tenure as attorney general. Kennedy rarely hesitated to pick up the phone to learn more, and he was not easily intimidated. But when it came to Hoover's invasive and self-defeating investigative tactics, he chose to remain ignorant.

AT HIS FATHER'S URGING, John Kennedy had put his brother in the cabinet to be available as an all-purpose *consigliere*. John Kennedy may have felt that he didn't really need to consult his brother on foreign affairs. He already had the best and the brightest to advise him, men like Robert McNamara, the president of Ford Motor Company who became secretary of defense, and McGeorge Bundy, the Harvard dean who became Kennedy's national security adviser. In the first two months of the New Frontier, as the Kennedy era was jauntily described, Robert Kennedy functioned much as any other cabinet member, attending meetings and talking to the president from time to time on the phone. But the relationship quickly deepened when the new administration sailed into its first crisis, a fiasco born of the hubris of the spymasters at the Central Intelligence Agency and the romantic naiveté of the amateurs at the White House.

The Kennedy brothers shared a fascination with secret operations and spy stories. As schoolboys, they had first read about the derring-do of secret agents in John Buchan's *The Thirty-Nine Steps*. As adults, they moved on to Ian Fleming's James Bond. JFK was such an aficionado of Fleming's novels that, by enthusing about them, he helped make the British thriller writer a top bestseller in the United States. At the Central Intelligence Agency, then at the peak of its power, the Kennedys were pleased to find real-life James Bonds. At least, the agency men played the part. High-ranking covert operaters like Tracy Barnes and Desmond FitzGerald were everything J. Edgar Hoover was not. Charming and smooth, wellborn and well-taught, they seemed to blend effortless grace and schoolboy panache. The CIA was quick to ingratiate itself with the Kennedys. Des FitzGerald loaned his Georgetown house to Robert

Kennedy's family for the inauguration festivities. In early February, CIA director Allen Dulles hosted a small dinner for the top men of the new administration and the agency at the Alibi Club, a small, exclusive men's club a few blocks from the White House. After a three-martini cocktail hour, Richard Bissell, the CIA's chief of covert operations, stood up and declared, with just the sort of tongue-in-cheek macho the Kennedys loved, "I am a man-eating shark."

On April 12, 1961, Bissell appeared in Robert Kennedy's office at the Justice Department to brief him on the most spectacular covert operation ever attempted by the CIA. In a few days, a secret CIA armada planned to land a clandestine army in Cuba to start a revolution. When the 1,300 CIA-trained Cuban exiles stormed ashore at the Bay of Pigs, Bissell predicted, the Cuban people would rise up and overthrow their communist dictator, Fidel Castro. The plan had been conceived during the Eisenhower administration, which had considered Castro's revolutionary regime, recently brought into Moscow's orbit, to be an intolerable threat off the Florida coast. President Kennedy had signed off on the operation, but it was essentially a CIA invention, pushed hardest by the agency's brilliant and extremely self-confident Richard Bissell.

Bissell, who liked to breezily quantify the odds, told Kennedy that the chances of success were about two out of three. And if the Cuban people did not rise up? Then the invading force would slip into the jungle and become guerrilla fighters. The attorney general, who had been aware of the planning for the invasion but not deeply involved, did not quiz Bissell closely. That Friday night, RFK tipped off Hugh Sidey, Time-Life's man, at a party at Hickory Hill. "Hugh," he casually asked, "do you have anyone in Cuba? Big things are about to happen. Better get someone there."

The first invaders landed shortly after midnight on Monday morning, April 17. A few hours later, Bob Kennedy was summoned by his anxious brother. "I don't think it's going as well as it should," said the president. Poor communications between the overly secretive CIA and the White House kept JFK from knowing the full extent of the disaster. Castro's planes had blown up the secret army's ammunition ship, and Cuban tanks were already bearing down on the landing beach. On Tuesday morning, McGeorge Bundy reported that the situation was "not a bit good." Bobby Kennedy began casting about for a way to control the damage. As he had with Governor Vandiver during the 1960 election campaign, he looked for one man who could be counted on to run a back-channel operation, reporting personally to the Kennedys. The hardest charger he could find was Admiral Arleigh "31-Knot" Burke, a World War II hero commanding destroyers in the Pacific, who had become chief of naval operations. Kennedy found Burke swearing ("Balls!") in the Situation Room and drafted him on the spot. Burke was to send U.S. carrier fighters over the invasion beach to gather intelligence, Kennedy instructed. He was to deal directly with the president, no one else. Burke was taken aback at being commandeered in this way. Contemporaneous notes of his reaction, made by the admiral's aide, capture Burke's unease:

Then Bobby Kennedy called me up and said the President is going to rely upon you to advise him in this situation. I said it is late! He needs advice. He said the rest of the people in the room weren't helpful. [Burke takes a call from the President.]

What do you do. He is bypassing [General Lyman] Lemnitzer, the Chairman [of the Joint Chiefs of Staff], the SecDef, the SecNav, CIA and the whole works and putting me in charge of the operation. That is a helluva thing. We had better watch this one.

Cdr Wilhide [Burke's aide]: He must realize what he is doing.

Adm Burke: I told Bobby Kennedy this was bypassing. He said he knew.

That night, President Kennedy hosted a gala reception for members of Congress. Dressed in white tie and tails, entering the room while the Marine Band played "Mr. Wonderful," Kennedy went to look for his old crony Senator George Smathers. "The shit has hit the fan," the president told Smathers. The Florida senator suggested that it was time to send in the marines. Bobby, who was standing nearby, said, "What? Are you crazy?" But JFK was desperate to do something. After midnight, the president, still in his formal dress, convened his top advisers. General Lyman Lemnitzer offered that the time had come for the invaders to "go guerrilla" and fade into the mountains. The CIA's Bissell had to sheepishly admit that the mountains were eighty miles distant, across a swamp, with 20,000 Cuban troops in the way. Admiral Burke, quietly prodded by RFK, put forth a plan of action: provide the Cuban invaders with an hour of air cover in the morning to try to shoot down Castro's air force. Haltingly, clinging to the futile hope of launching a "secret" invasion, President Kennedy agreed. But he went to the absurd precaution of ordering the navy to paint out the U.S. markings on its war planes, as if the Cubans and the rest of the world wouldn't know who had sent them.

John F. Kennedy had been in office less than three months and he was faced with a failure of monumental proportions. The moods among the president's men in the Cabinet Room at 3 a.m. ranged from despair to fury. Bobby was among the most emotional. As the president rose from his seat, Robert Kennedy clapped his brother on the shoulders and pleaded, "We've got to do something! They can't do this to you!" The president turned away and walked into the Rose Garden. For about an hour, he paced in the wet grass. JFK was in tears when he awoke in his bed a couple of hours later.

Unable to sleep, Robert Kennedy composed a memo to his brother. RFK's first attempt at formulating foreign policy, the memo is revealing of his best and worst instincts. The document, hastily dictated sometime in the early-morning hours and revised in Kennedy's nearly illegible scrawl, is a template for his future thinking. The United States cannot return to the status quo of "waiting and hoping for good luck," he wrote. "Something forceful and determined must be done." An invasion by U.S. troops was going too far. But some kind of covert action was called for. He suggested staging a provocation: pretend that Cuban MiGs had attacked the Guantánamo, the naval base at the tip of Cuba still held by the Americans. Kennedy was to return to this idea of a staged provocation repeatedly in the years ahead. The provenance of Kennedy's sleight of hand is unclear: possibly, he was recalling the sinking of the *Maine*, which gave the United States an excuse to invade Cuba and liberate the Spanish colony at the turn of the century. Fortunately, the suggestion never caught on with his more prudent brother, and RFK was forced to settle for less dramatic covert operations. Yet with Kennedy's rash proposal on this bleak April morning came genuine foresight: he predicted that if the United States failed to act, Cuba would very soon become a base for Soviet missiles. His judgment was at least a year ahead of American intelligence experts.

At the Bay of Pigs on Wednesday morning, Burke's air cover plan failed. Because of a communications snafu, the carrier-based jets arrived an hour late, and the aging B-26 bombers supplied by the CIA to the Cuban exiles were all shot out of the sky. By early that afternoon, the invaders were being driven into the sea, begging for the American warships and planes that rested just over the horizen. Bobby Kennedy was at his most anguished. Pacing back and forth in the Cabinet Room, he kept repeating, "We've got to do something, we've got to do something." Pausing, he glared at the glum CIA and military officials sitting around the table. "All you bright fellows have gotten the President into this, and if you don't do something now, my brother will be regarded as a paper tiger by the Russians." There was little they could do. The American destroyers could not draw close to the beach and risk being fired upon. Trapped and abandoned on the beach, the Cuban freedom fighters fired angrily and futilely at the wakes of the departing American warships.

Bobby was proud when his brother took full responsibility for the failed invasion at a press conference. Assistant Attorney General Louis Oberdorfer was standing beside RFK in his office watching on television. "Bobby put his fist in his palm, as if to say, that's right, this is the way to do it," recalled Oberdorfer. At the same time, RFK was a harpy to anyone else who tried to duck. He snapped at Lyndon Johnson when the vice president started to say that he had been kept out of the loop, and he almost assaulted Chester Bowles, the under secretary of state who had wisely opposed the invasion. Jabbing his finger into Bowles's chest, Kennedy "savagely," as Bowles recalled, informed Bowles that he had been all *for* the invasion, and not to forget it.

Kennedy seemed to take an almost vindictive pleasure in berating Bowles. He regarded the under secretary, a Stevensonian Democrat who favored diplomacy over force, as "soft" and "ladylike," as a talker, not a doer. On April 22, Bowles presented a State Department white paper on Cuba at a White House meeting. The document concluded, correctly, that short of an invasion there was little the United States could do to change the Castro regime. Bowles's delivery, verbose and circular, infuriated RFK. "That's the most meaningless, worthless thing I've ever heard," he exploded as others around the table gaped. "You people are so anxious to protect your own asses that you're afraid to do anything. All you want to do is dump the whole thing on the president. We'd be better off if you just quit and left foreign policy to someone else." Watching Kennedy's tirade was a young White House aide named Richard Goodwin. The observant Goodwin noticed that while RFK ranted, the "president sat calmly, outwardly relaxed," gently tapping his teeth with a pencil. "I became suddenly aware," Goodwin later wrote, ". . . that Bobby's harsh polemic reflected the president's own concealed emotions, privately communicated in some earlier, intimate conversation."

The Bay of Pigs was a severe lesson. It taught the president, Bobby Kennedy later said, "that he could not substitute anybody else's judgment for his own." Lacerating himself for blindly following the CIA, the president repeatedly asked, "How could I have been so stupid?" (And, more wryly and ruefully, "Why couldn't this have happened to James Bond?") JFK determined that he needed his brother to protect him. After the Bay of Pigs, Bobby Kennedy noted, "I then became involved on every major and all the international questions." Actually, RFK deserved at least some of the blame for the fiasco. He had not quizzed Bissell in his usual blunt and probing fashion. His bias for action and romantic awe of spies had caused him to let down his guard. Still, from this point on JFK would rely on his brother more than anyone else. Their family friend Lem Billings recalled, "Up until that time, Jack more or less dismissed the reasons his father had given for wanting Bobby in the cabinet as more of that tribal Irish thing. But now he realized how right the old man had been. When the crunch came, family members *were* the only ones you could count on. Bobby *was* the only person he could rely on to be absolutely dedicated. Jack would never have admitted it, but from that moment on, the Kennedy presidency became a sort of collaboration between them."

For a moment, JFK suggested that RFK take over as director of the CIA. The clandestine service was the president's action arm in the Cold War, and Kennedy needed to be able to trust it. But Bobby knew better than to position himself as chief spy. The reason is illuminating: in that age of aggressive skulduggery, the president had to be able to deny the "black operations" of the nation's spies. This doctrine of "plausible deniability" is unworkable in a democracy, too often abused as a license for recklessness. But "plausible deniability" was national security cant in 1961. The doctrine fit neatly with the maxim Joseph Kennedy had imparted to his sons. In 1962, Bobby Kennedy was explicit in a letter to John McCone, Allen Dulles's successor as CIA director. He wrote, "As my father always told me, 'never write it down.' "

At his brother's behest, RFK agreed to join a four-man commission to clean up after the Bay of Pigs. It became an article of faith among old CIA hands that the so-called Taylor Commission, named after its chairman, General Maxwell Taylor, was a whitewash. The CIA men argued that the invasion failed because President Kennedy, in a misguided effort to keep down the "noise level," canceled a bombing mission on the eve of the invasion aimed at destroying Castro's air force. Unprotected against Castro's small fleet of jets and old prop planes, the Cuban exile brigade was badly chewed up on the beach. Both Grayston Lynch, a CIA guerrilla who went ashore with the invaders, and Stan-

ley Gaines, who ran the CIA's covert air operations, recalled Bobby Kennedy
trying to steer the Taylor Board's questioning away from the president's role.
"Bobby Kennedy sat there with his feet up and his tie down. He was sullen and
defensive," recalled Lynch, still bitter thirty-five years later. Kennedy's handwritten notes show that he thought that the CIA and the military failed to adequately warn JFK of the consequences of canceling the strike. The final report,
though hedged and written in dry bureaucratese, does not excuse anyone. The
Kennedys were persuaded, and later historians have agreed, that the invasion
would have ultimately failed even if the Cuban exile force controlled the skies.
But rancor in the ranks of the CIA would dog RFK in the years ahead.*

Kennedy's mentor during the investigation and writing of the report was
Maxwell Taylor. A retired general who had led a paratrooper division in the D-
Day landings, Taylor had expected his fellow commissioners—in addition to
Kennedy, CIA director Dulles, and Admiral Burke—to try to fudge the findings
about their respective institutions. He was impressed that Kennedy wanted to
make the report tougher. It was then that Taylor flattered Kennedy by telling
him that he thought Kennedy could have made it in the 101st Airborne: "You're
the kind of guy we wanted around to take a hill or hold a trench." Kennedy, in
turn, was so impressed by Taylor, a handsome warrior-intellectual whose retire-
ment job was running the Lincoln Center for the Performing Arts, that he
brought him back into uniform and later named a child after him. Taylor was
Kennedy's beau ideal: he had been nicknamed Mr. Attack as wartime commander of the Screaming Eagles of the 101st Airborne, yet as superintendent of
West Point after the war, he broadened the curriculum to make the cadets read
the dissenting opinions of Justice Oliver Wendell Holmes and the poetry of
T. S. Eliot. Bobby Kennedy was such an avid student of military tactics and
strategy that Taylor jokingly offered him "a field marshal's baton." Working
closely with Taylor in the months ahead, Kennedy would become a marshal
in mufti.

Kennedy made one more important friend as he picked through the rub-
ble of the failed invasion. One of the few members of the Cuban Brigade who
had not been killed or captured, Roberto San Román, appeared before the Taylor Commission in late May. He and twenty-two other soldiers had escaped

---

* Four American pilots, air national guardsmen temporarily assigned to the CIA to help
train the Cuban émigrés, were shot down and killed during air battles over the Bay of
Pigs. The daughter of one of the pilots, Janet Weininger, told the author that the CIA's
Richard Bissell made a shocking admission to her before he died in 1994. As the invasion was collapsing, Bissell went to the Oval Office and revealed to the president that
American pilots had been shot down. He wasn't sure if they had been killed or captured
alive. The president was angry. No American personnel were supposed to have participated in the invasion. Bobby Kennedy, listening in on Bissell's report, jumped in. "This
better not be another Francis Gary Powers," he said (referring to the CIA spy plane pilot
who was shot down over Russia in 1960 and put on a show trial). "Those Americans,"
said Bobby Kennedy, "better be dead." A CIA official involved in the Bay of Pigs, Jake
Esterline, confirmed Weininger's story, but Bissell's family denied it.

from the Bay of Pigs in an open boat. They had drifted for nineteen days; ten men died. Finally rescued by an American naval ship, he was hustled to Washington to testify before the Taylor Board. San Román broke down. "How could you send us and leave us there?" he asked, weeping. Kennedy came around from behind the table and shook his hand. "Anytime you have something to tell me," he told San Román, "anytime you need me, you can come see me."

Kennedy felt an enormous sense of personal responsibility for—and guilt about—the fate of the 114 Cubans who died and the 1,189 Cubans who were captured and now languished in Castro's jails. The president's brother could not hide his personal anguish. Rowland Evans, a newspaperman who had befriended Kennedy, was at a dinner at Steve Smith's with Kennedy shortly after the Bay of Pigs. Abruptly, Kennedy rose from the dinner table and announced that he was going for a walk. He disappeared into a raw and wet spring night. He was not just brooding. He was planning revenge. On June 13, Taylor submitted his report to President Kennedy. The report concluded: "There can be no long-term living with Castro. . . ." Bobby was more blunt. After the investigation, he declared, "We will take action against Castro. It might be tomorrow, it might be in five days or ten days, or not for months. But it will come."

6 TESTING

Robert Kennedy had become, in effect, chancellor to an empire. America's commitments and obligations, and the confidence to meet them, peaked with his brother's inaugural address in January 1961. Kennedy's concerns could never be parochial. He was forced, by the unique nature of his job and the age in which he lived, to think globally. Everything he did had to be measured not only against the particular—and burdensome—duties of chief law enforcement officer, but in the larger context of helping his brother rule, as they saw it, the "free world." In the spring of 1961, Kennedy became engaged, warily, with the civil rights movement. The experience would have been trying enough, were he not at the very same moment trying to sort through the wreckage of the Bay of Pigs and run a private diplomatic channel to the Kremlin.

On April 22, four days after the collapse of the beachhead at the Bay of Pigs and on the same day he terrorized Chester Bowles for his flaccid presentation on Cuba, Robert Kennedy hosted a small lunch at the Mayflower Hotel in downtown Washington. The lunch was off the record, a secret closely held by a few officials at Justice and the White House. Service was buffet, in order to eliminate the need for waiters who might overhear and gossip. The guest was Martin Luther King Jr.

The Kennedys may have been willing to help get King out of jail, but they weren't ready to embrace him and his cause, publicly at least. King had not been invited to a meeting of civil rights leaders in the attorney general's office on March 6. He was regarded as a troublemaker and, more annoyingly, difficult to control. King himself asked for an appointment with the president ten days later and was rebuffed, informed that the chief executive was too busy with the press of the "present international situation." Civil rights was not of deep concern either to JFK, who did not even mention the subject in his famously expansive inaugural address, or to RFK. "I won't say I lay awake at night worrying about civil rights before I became Attorney General," Kennedy acknowledged in 1964. RFK rejected Harris Wofford, the "bomb thrower" who had helped persuade JFK to call Mrs. King, as chief of the civil rights division. Rather, at the suggestion of Byron White, he chose a corporate lawyer, Burke Marshall, who represented clients like Standard Oil and knew no one in the civil rights community. There was little eagerness in the Kennedy administration to try to push through federal civil rights legislation, though it was much needed in the still-segregated South. The Kennedys were too afraid of the congressional barons.

Still, RFK's conscience was pricked by the racial inequity he experienced close at hand. He was embarrassed that only ten of the Justice Department's 950 lawyers were black. He was contemptuous that Hoover's only black FBI agents were his chauffeurs, office boys, and manservant. Ashamed that his men's club, the Metropolitan, refused to take blacks, he quit in protest. RFK's liberal friends chipped away at any residual Kennedy prejudice. When Arthur Schlesinger sent him an editorial in a Catholic magazine inveighing against racial discrimination in private clubs, RFK replied deadpan, "We Catholics are really coming along nicely, don't you think?"

In his role as chief law enforcement officer, he was frustrated with the southern governors who disregarded the law of the land and refused to integrate their schools and universities. With typical pugnacity, he would travel into the heart of the opposition, to the University of Georgia in early May, to announce (with hands shaking) that the Justice Department intended to enforce the law. Just how was another matter. The Kennedys had a vivid recollection of Eisenhower's 1957 use of paratroopers, in combat gear with fixed bayonets, to integrate a high school in Little Rock, Arkansas. The pictures, the Kennedys believed, had humiliated the United States around the world and provided fodder for Soviet propaganda. In the national priorities of the federal government in 1961, containing communism far outweighed integrating schools. At the Justice Department's civil rights division, the day-to-day focus was on the enforcement of the voter registration laws, an incrementalist approach with political dividends: most of those new black voters were Democrats.

Martin Luther King wanted more. He wanted to end the stifling hold of Jim Crow in the South. His method was massive, peaceful civil disobedience. Blending religious teachings from Gandhi to Christ, King preached nonviolent protest and led boycotts and sit-ins that got his followers arrested and beaten—and that sometimes, eventually, brought down the Whites Only signs. King desired something for himself as well. He wanted the respect of the white elites. He was a prince of the black church, his father a famous preacher. For graduation from high school, he had been given a convertible, a remarkable luxury for a Negro teenager in the postwar South. He summered on Martha's Vineyard and dressed in fine clothes. King was fascinated by the Kennedys (he once used as his code name JFK) and a little envious. He wanted to be treated with dignity, as an equal.

Surprisingly, he was not so treated, at least in the beginning. RFK, it's true, liked to be able to control people, but he also admired courage and respected men who stood up to him; indeed, he almost demanded it. King was in some respects similar to him. He, too, admired courage and showed it. As King's longtime friend and associate Stanley Levison observed, King shared Kennedy's guilt about his privileged background. But culturally, the two men were far apart. And because of small, seemingly superficial differences, matters of taste and humor and style, Bobby Kennedy and Martin Luther King passed by without ever really understanding, or liking, each other. They *should* have been mutual admirers; they might have become the great black-white alliance of the 1960s. But, though they came to share the same cause, they remained cool—respectful but distant. These human differences were important. To Kennedy, politics and policy were intensely personal. If he liked someone, he was much more inclined to like what they stood for. Because Kennedy did not warm to King the man, he was slower to recognize the dignity and power of his dreams.

Burke Marshall, the seemingly bland lawyer who became a highly effective champion of civil rights, saw and regretted the cultural mismatch from the beginning. Talking to Marshall or other subordinates, King was easy and natural company. But when he was ushered in to see Kennedy, his voice and manner changed. He became the grave preacher, speaking in slow cadence with rising intonations and lofty expressions of high ideals. Kennedy, who was sympathetic to those ideals but preferred dry humor and self-deprecation, would sit stonily. It would be "the Reverend King" and "Mr. Attorney General." One of King's young disciples, John Lewis, also noticed the disconnect. King, like Kennedy, could be playful and sly, he observed. But when King met with any high government official—a mayor or a police chief or especially the attorney general—he took on "a different air," said Lewis, more formal and proudly earnest. The difference in style between Kennedy and King emerged in that first lunch at the Mayflower. King adopted a preacherly, high-minded tone that Kennedy barely responded to. Afterwards, Kennedy and his men concluded that Dr. King was either a saint or a pushover.

At least he had not been too demanding of the Kennedy administration. Dr. King seemed safe enough to be shown to the president. He was ushered in to see President Kennedy in a secret meeting at which JFK tried to explain why it was too soon to seek civil rights legislation. The president went back to worrying about Cuba, Laos, and the Soviet Union. Robert Kennedy returned to revisiting the Bay of Pigs.

Bobby Kennedy's true initiation into the civil rights movement came as a surprise. He first learned of the Freedom Riders—thirteen idealistic young protesters, seven black, six white, schooled in nonviolence—from a black journalist who visited the attorney general's office in late April. Preoccupied with the Bay of Pigs, Kennedy forgot all about the protesters until they turned up in the newspapers. On May 4, the Freedom Riders set out by bus to test a Supreme Court ruling that banned segregation in facilities used for interstate transportation. On May 14, near Anniston, Alabama, they were dragged from their seats and beaten by an angry mob. The bus was firebombed. Like many Americans, Bobby Kennedy was shocked by the violence. His brother was angry at the militancy of the Freedom Riders. "Tell them to call it off!" JFK angrily instructed Harris Wofford, his special assistant for civil rights. "Stop them! Get your friends off those buses!" Bobby shared the view that the Freedom Riders had brought on their own woes, but he also felt duty-bound to protect them. He dispatched John Seigenthaler, his administrative assistant, to Alabama to "hold their hands." Then he tried to reach the governor, John Patterson, to arrange safe escort. Patterson, who had been, in Kennedy's words, "our great pal in the South" during the 1960 election, was unavailable. The governor, an aide said, had "gone fishing." The Greyhound Company, meanwhile, couldn't find a bus driver willing to continue the dangerous journey of the Freedom Riders. Impatient and increasingly irritated, RFK impulsively called the bus company himself. "Do you know how to drive a bus?" he demanded from a Greyhound official. "Surely, somebody in the damn bus company can drive a bus, can't they?" Kennedy told the superviser to get in touch "with Mr. Greyhound or whoever Greyhound is and somebody better give us an answer to this question. I am—the Government is—going to be very much upset if this group does not get to continue their trip." Secretly tape-recorded by the state of Alabama, the phone conversation soon leaked—and southern whites believed that Robert Kennedy was the moving force behind the Freedom Riders. From that moment on, as historian Taylor Branch has noted, "Bobby" became an epithet in the South.

"Mr. Greyhound" complied with Kennedy's demand, but as the bus pulled into downtown Montgomery, Alabama, there was an eerie silence around the terminal. Suddenly, dozens of men armed with lead pipes and baseball bats emerged from the shadows and set upon the passengers, screaming, "Get those niggers!" A Justice Department official who happened to be working on a voting rights case from an office across the street looked out in horror. The official, Deputy Assistant Attorney General John Doar, picked up the phone and called Kennedy's office. "It's terrible! It's terrible!" he cried. "There's not a cop in sight." The local police had stepped aside for the Ku Klux Klan. Warned by their informants in the Klan, FBI agents were watching. But their orders from Hoover were to gather intelligence, not to intervene. RFK was not told of the FBI's presence at the scene. John Seigenthaler drove by and tried to rescue a woman from the mob. He was knocked cold with a metal pipe and left lying in the street.

Bobby Kennedy was summoned from his Saturday-morning touch football game. Learning that his friend and closest aide had been hospitalized with a cracked skull, he was indignant. As always in crisis, to sublimate his own fear and rage, he turned to gallows humor. He called Seigenthaler and dryly thanked him for helping to win the black vote. Groggy, his head splitting, Seigenthaler tried to riposte, weakly telling RFK that he should rule out running for governor of Alabama.

Martin Luther King arrived in Montgomery that Sunday. Kennedy asked him not to go, but he ignored the attorney general. The civil rights leader intended to hold a mass meeting in support of the Freedom Riders. Grudgingly, the Kennedys realized that their hand was being forced. Recalling the unfortunate images of paratroopers in Little Rock, they wanted to use federal troops only as an intervenor of last resort. Byron White suggested putting together a force of U.S. marshals in civilian clothes. Bobby Kennedy and his men scrambled to patch together a makeshift army. Drawing on federal prison guards, border patrolmen, and Alcohol, Tobacco and Firearms agents—"revenooers" normally devoted to busting up the stills of moonshiners—a force of four hundred men was mustered at an air force base outside Montgomery. There was an informal, almost homespun air to this motley assemblage. Their leader was Jim McShane, the former New York City cop who had worked as a Rackets Committee investigator for RFK and as a bodyguard to Jack Kennedy and, before that, as a sometime chauffeur for Ethel Kennedy's family, the Skakels. Also pressed into duty was the Justice Department civil division chief, William Orrick, who had made the mistake that Saturday of sticking his head into the attorney general's office and asking if there was anything he could do to help out. Feeling a little over his head, Orrick tried to remember his army training from World War II as he shuffled the men into platoons. Eyeing the redneck ATF agents, Byron White dryly remarked, "I wonder which side they'll take on."

On Sunday night, King holed up with several of the battered Freedom Riders and about 1,500 sympathizers in the First Baptist Church downtown, with a thin line of fifty U.S. marshals out front. "Be quiet and proud as possible," the worshippers were told. A howling mob of about 3,000 surrounded the church and tipped over a parishioner's car, setting it ablaze. Crude Molotov cocktails sailed towards the church, where the parishioners began singing, fervently, "We Shall Overcome" and "Love Lifted Me." By now, Kennedy, still dressed for weekend touch football, had set up a command post in his office at Justice. King called the attorney general and asked for help. Kennedy sought to reassure him by saying that more marshals were on the way. He tried to find some common ground with the reverend, recounting the stories his grandfather had told of anti-Catholic mobs burning convents in nineteenth-century Boston. King was not interested in the Irish history lesson. He wanted to know: when was help arriving? Kennedy, who wasn't exactly sure where the marshals were, trotted out his mordant humor: "As long as you're in church, Reverend King, and our men are down there, you might as well say a prayer for us."

King did not think Bobby was funny. "If they don't get here immediately," King said, "we're going to have a bloody confrontation." The rioters, he explained, with rising urgency in his voice, "are at the door now." King seemed "panicky" and "scared," recalled Burke Marshall, who was listening in. But King's fear was entirely justified and shared by others in the church. "There was one minute in which I could see only panic and slaughter for many people," said the Reverend Wyatt Tee Walker, one of King's aides. But by allowing himself to show fear, by not following Kennedy's prep school code of mocking danger, King at that moment failed to win Kennedy's respect. The failure was more RFK's than King's—the goal of the civil rights leader at that moment was to get desperately needed help, not win machismo points with RFK.

Fortuitously, the marshals did arrive as King and Kennedy were talking. In an effort to appear unmilitaristic, they were incongruously hiding in red-white-and-blue mail trucks. Firing tear gas, they pushed the crowd back—but only temporarily. From his office in Washington, Kennedy glumly began to discuss with Byron White, who was stationed at Maxwell Air Force Base outside Montgomery, the possibility of sending in federal troops. After eavesdropping on these conversations through the local switchboard operators, Governor Patterson finally sent in the Alabama National Guard. The marshals gladly withdrew, but the crisis was not over. The national guardsmen, local boys whose commander reported to the governor, had little sympathy for the Freedom Riders. Waving Confederate flags, the Alabama guardsmen kept the parishioners, at bayonet point, trapped in the church. Exhausted, angry, besieged all night in a steamy tear-gas-filled building with 1,500 frightened parishioners, King called Kennedy, who was conducting a post-midnight interview with a *Time* reporter in his office in Washington. "You shouldn't have withdrawn the marshals," King protested, so loudly that Kennedy held the receiver away from his ear. In a weary voice, Kennedy told King that he had talked to the chief of the state police and the commander of the national guardsmen, and that he had confidence in them. King was disbelieving and bitter and told Kennedy that he felt betrayed. "Now, Reverend," RFK said. "You know just as well as I do that if it hadn't been for the United States Marshals, you'd be dead as Kelsey's nuts right now!" There was silence over the phone. Turning away, King asked, "Who's Kelsey? Anyone know Kelsey?"*

After dawn, the Justice Department finally negotiated safe passage for the hostages in the First Baptist Church. A convoy of state troopers and marshals escorted a busload of Freedom Riders on to Jackson, Mississippi, where they were promptly arrested and put in jail. But more Freedom Riders descended on the scene, this time with northern white liberals including Yale chaplain William Sloane Coffin. Kennedy was fed up, especially with white liberals, whom he described to the president as "honkers." "It took a lot of guts for the first group to go," he was quoted as saying, "but not much for the others"— sweeping in King with the "honkers." By prolonging the crisis, they made "good propaganda for America's enemies." Kennedy was worried about his brother's upcoming summit with Charles de Gaulle and Nikita Khrushchev. In his first formal statement, he told reporters that he "feared" that "continuing international publicity about ugly race riots would send the leader of the free world into European palaces with mud on his shoes."

Robert Kennedy and Martin Luther King were talking past each other. Kennedy offered to arrange bail for the Freedom Riders still held in the Jackson, Mississippi, jail. But the Freedom Riders refused the offer. King tried to ex-

---

* Kennedy apparently garbled an obscure Boston Irish expression, "as tight as Kelsey's nuts," meaning cheap.

plain why to Kennedy: "Our conscience tells us the law is wrong, and we must resist, but we have a moral obligation to accept the penalty." Kennedy suspected a ploy and bridled: "The fact that they stay in jail is not going to have the slightest effect on me." King pushed a little harder: perhaps the attorney general would be affected if students "came down here by the hundreds—by the hundreds of thousands." Kennedy was coldly angry now: "Do as you wish, but don't make statements that sound like a threat. That's not the way to deal with us." King, hearing the steeliness, backed off. "I'm deeply appreciative of what the Administration is doing," he said. He became the preacher again: "I see a ray of hope, but I am different from my father. I feel the need of being free now!" Kennedy was unmoved. He reiterated his offer to get the Freedom Riders out of jail. "They'll stay," said King. Kennedy was hopping mad. He called Harris Wofford to vent: "This is too much! I wonder if they have the best interests of their country at heart. Do you know that one of them is against the atom bomb?"

As he testily tried to hold down the clamor from Dr. King and the Freedom Riders, RFK comes across as intolerant and narrow-minded. He alienated another leading civil rights figure in this period, Thurgood Marshall, the black lawyer who had won the NAACP's landmark school desegregation case, *Brown v. Board of Education*, in 1954 and by the spring of 1961 was up for a well-deserved federal judgeship. Kennedy wanted to make Marshall a district court judge, but Marshall was holding out for the higher court of appeals. "That's the problem with you people," RFK hotly told Marshall that May. "You want too much too fast." Such condescension would have been unthinkable in the later Robert Kennedy. But Kennedy should not be judged too harshly. During the siege of the First Baptist Church, when Governor Patterson had whined that the demonstration was jeopardizing his political career, Kennedy took the high ground. "John," he said, "it's more important that those people in the church survive physically than for us to survive politically." RFK wanted to help the civil rights movement, but he wanted to do it on his own terms, in a way that did not detract from his brother's waging of the Cold War. Voting rights was the way: enforcing the right of blacks to exercise their franchise in the South. Meeting with civil rights leaders on June 16 (three days after he handed his brother the Taylor Report on Cuba), he told them that the Freedom Rides were no longer productive. But he offered to do everything he could to support and protect civil rights activists who wanted to register voters. The Negro leaders in his office were understandably skeptical. Was he just trying to get them off the street? But Kennedy's offer of support was real—and lavish. He said that he was already working, behind the scenes, without publicity, to arrange for private foundations to fund their efforts. He had intervened with the new head of the IRS—Mortimer Caplin, his University of Virginia Law School tax professor—to arrange a tax exemption. Later, he would confidentially promise that the administration would arrange draft exemptions for young civil rights workers, so long as they worked quietly on voter registration. Secretly, privately, under control. That, Kennedy believed, was the way to get things done.

• • •

KENNEDY'S TESTINESS with King, his apparent fear that King's morality play would undermine the Cold War effort, can be explained in part by RFK's simultaneous dealings with a character of a different kind, Soviet agent Georgi Bolshakov. Publicly, Bolshakov was a middle-tier diplomat in the Soviet embassy in Washington, the editor of a glossy English-language monthly on Soviet life. Under cover, he was a colonel in the GRU, Soviet military intelligence. From their first meeting until he was replaced during the Cuban Missile Crisis in October 1962, Bolshakov was RFK's direct back channel to the Soviet regime in Moscow. Through this back door, Bobby Kennedy entered a high-stakes diplomatic realm for which he was unprepared and seemingly ill-suited.

Unlike others in the stodgy, flat-footed Soviet diplomatic corps, Bolshakov was a convivial man about town, "a tubby, bouncy little guy," said Charlie Bartlett, one of his several friends in the American press corps. Bolshakov was "engaging, clownish, offhand. He would make jokes to disarm the Yanks," said James Symington, one of Bobby Kennedy's aides. Bolshakov was very well connected: his patron in Moscow was Aleksei Adzhubei, Chairman Khrushchev's son-in-law. In late April 1961, one of Bolshakov's American newspaper pals, Frank Holeman of the *New York Daily News*, casually suggested that the Soviet diplomat might like to meet the brother of the president, face-to-face. Eager for intrigue and status, the GRU agent readily agreed. Holeman passed on Bolshakov's interest to Kennedy's spokesman, Ed Guthman, who immediately went across the hall and asked his boss. RFK, always on the outlook for promising go-betweens, did not hesitate to say yes.

On the afternoon of May 9, Bolshakov was escorted to the southwest corner of the Department of Justice. He found the attorney general sitting on the granite steps outside. The jolly, fat Russian and the spare, taciturn American strolled down Constitution Avenue towards the Capitol. As Bolshakov recalled their conversation a quarter century later, Kennedy said, "Look here, Georgi. I know pretty well about your standing and about your connections with the boys in Khrushchev's entourage. . . . I think they wouldn't mind getting truthful firsthand information from you, and I presume they'll find a way of passing it on to Khrushchev."

Sitting on a park bench, the two men talked for four hours, until they were chased inside by a downpour. Kennedy carefully told the Soviet agent that the president was "concerned" that the Soviet government "underestimated the capabilities" of the U.S. government. This was Kennedy's guarded way of expressing his fear that the Soviet Union would regard America as a "paper tiger" after the Bay of Pigs. In April, Moscow and Washington had at least tentatively agreed that the time had come for a summit meeting. There had not been such an encounter between the leaders of the superpowers since 1955; the last scheduled summit, in 1960, had been aborted after the Soviets shot down an American spy plane and captured the pilot, Francis Gary Powers. The Kennedys were uneasy. A summit could bring détente, but it could also be a trap, a forum for the belligerent Chairman Khrushchev to try to bully the green American

president publicly into concessions on Laos, Cuba, and, most importantly,
Berlin. The Soviets had captured Berlin in World War II; they regarded the former German capital as a trophy of war. With the belligerence of an insecure ex-
pansionist power, they wanted to drive out the Americans, who, with the
British and French, had occupied the Western half of the city. Bobby Kennedy
was speaking to Bolshakov because his brother wanted to learn more about Soviet intentions before meeting with the Kremlin leader. The president wanted
to know the chances for a nuclear test ban treaty. During the 1950s, both nuclear powers had detonated ever-larger H-bomb blasts. Parents worried about
schoolchildren drinking radioactive fallout in their milk.

The Kennedys were, in the family manner, bypassing normal channels.
The U.S. ambassador to the Soviet Union, Llewellyn "Tommy" Thompson, was
a savvy and balanced expert on Soviet affairs. But the Kennedys did not yet
know Thompson well enough to trust him, and they scorned the State Department bureaucracy. As young men, they had been warned by their father not to
believe in men in striped pants; the elder Kennedy felt he had been betrayed
by the professional diplomats during his rocky ambassadorship to Great
Britain. Jack Kennedy was impatient with any rigid structure or hierarchy. He
had decided that cabinet meetings were a "waste of time" after two of them.
The White House viewed the State Department as slow-moving and lightweight. "They're not queer, but well," the president said, "they're sort of like
Adlai. . . . " His brother Bob regarded UN ambassador Stevenson as "an old
lady" and was almost as contemptuous of the man JFK had appointed secretary
of state, Dean Rusk, whom RFK described as "rather a weak figure."

As always, the Kennedys looked for ways to cut through the red tape and
to maintain personal control. Georgi Bolshakov became an important go-
between in America's most critical arena, the tense nuclear standoff with the
Soviet Union. Robert Kennedy later estimated that he saw Bolshakov about
twice a month. They would meet in his office, or in a doughnut shop near the
Mayflower Hotel, or take walks along Constitution Avenue. The meetings
would be set up by Frank Holeman, the newspaperman who brought them together, and Kennedy spokesman Ed Guthman. The signal was not exactly in
code: "My guy," Holeman or Guthman would say, "wants to meet your guy."

Back channels can be useful, especially in a deadlocked negotiation or a
crisis. But they have serious drawbacks as a substitute for regular diplomacy.
They can create confusion and misunderstanding, and cut out expertise and
sound judgment. The Kennedy-Bolshakov back channel had additional shortcomings. Because RFK was the president's brother, the Russians considered his
word binding on the United States government. Bolshakov, on the other hand,
was a mere intelligence apparatchik. The Kremlin could simply disavow him.
Bobby had the president's writ, but he came with little grounding in the subtleties of arms control or alliance politics. His inarticulateness was an impediment: the Soviets were sometimes baffled by his colloquial utterances. He
never kept the State Department informed. He later regretted following his
father's no-paper-trail dictum in his dealings with Bolshakov: "Stupidly, I

didn't write many of the things down," he admitted in a confidential oral history in 1964. "I just delivered the messages verbally to my brother, and he'd act on them. I think sometimes he'd tell the State Department—and sometimes he didn't."

Not surprisingly, the foreign policy professionals at State were very dubious about the Kennedy-Bolshakov back channel. So was Mac Bundy, the president's national security adviser, though he knew it was useless to protest. The Bolshakov channel, he later said, was one of the "unshareables," one of the secrets that the Kennedy brothers kept to themselves. Documents recently released from Soviet archives show that the Kremlin, too, had some misgivings about the back channel. The conservative Soviet bureaucracy did not like to operate outside of the normal chain; indeed, when Bolshakov first suggested meeting alone with RFK, his superior in the GRU forbade it. Bolshakov, who was brash, went anyway, figuring, correctly, that his patron in Moscow, Aleksei Adzhubei, would approve. Aside from his tie to the president, RFK was regarded as a suspect emissary. He was seen as more belligerent than his brother and virulently anti-Soviet. His sullenness towards the Soviets, which he made no effort to hide on his unhappy tour of the Soviet central republics with Justice Douglas in 1955, is amply documented in the Kremlin's intelligence file on RFK. "Kennedy was rude and unduly familiar with the Soviet people he met," wrote the KGB. He quizzed KGB agents with tendentious questions, asking how many people were in forced labor camps and informing his hosts that he wished to learn about Soviet wiretapping methods and their means of punishing foreign spies.

At first, the Kremlin was not quite sure what to make of RFK's off-the-record feelers about a summit. Waiting for word from Moscow, the GRU agent took more than a week to get back to the attorney general. On May 16, the Soviets formally invited Kennedy to a summit meeting in Vienna. Two days later, Bolshakov, no longer freelancing but under strict Kremlin control, met secretly with Kennedy to give him a preview. The Kennedys must have been disappointed with his dry recitation of foreign office talking points. In their initial conversation on May 9, Bolshakov had indicated, or so RFK thought, that Khrushchev might be willing to negotiate a test ban treaty. Kennedy, with his untrained ear for diplo-speak, may have misheard Bolshakov, or the ebullient Russian agent, excited to be talking to the brother of the American president, may have exaggerated his masters' willingness to compromise. In any case, there was little in what Bolshakov said now, in their second meeting on May 18, to encourage American hopes for arms control. Signals were muddled from the American side as well. During their first chat on the park bench, Bobby Kennedy had meant to rule out any summit discussions about Cuba. But the way he put it—that Cuba was a "dead issue"—confused the Soviets. Did he mean, the Kremlin now wanted to know, that the United States would stop meddling in the Caribbean island? Bobby Kennedy relayed Bolshakov's answers to the president on the same weekend in May that the Freedom Riders crisis was boiling over—hardly the best timing for a considered response. But it was already too late. The United States could not very well back out. The summit was scheduled for the end of May. The Kennedys' apprehensions grew a couple of days later, on May 24, when Khrushchev signaled through the American ambassador in Moscow, Tommy Thompson, that the Soviets might squeeze harder in Berlin. The Soviet premier was just as enigmatic in his choice of words about Berlin as RFK had been about Cuba. Khrushchev spoke vaguely of "belt tightening." For the president, very anxious that the Kremlin would force a confrontation in Berlin, Khrushchev's signal was fuzzy, but disturbing.

The Vienna summit in early June went badly, at least as far as the Kennedys were concerned. Khrushchev blustered and threatened. Kennedy, trying to show that he could not be intimidated, vowed "a cold winter." The president was very low when he met with RFK back in Washington. The parley with the Kremlin leader, he bleakly joked, was like "dealing with Dad: all give and no take." For a moment, JFK's detachment crumbled. He began to talk about nuclear war. "We've had a good life," he told his brother, "we're adults. We bring these things on ourselves." But, he went on, beginning to tear up, "The thought, though, of the women and children perishing in a nuclear exchange. I can't adjust to that."

Robert Kennedy later remembered that summer as a "tougher, harder, meaner period" than anything he had experienced. The Kennedy brothers believed that nuclear war was close, perhaps "a one chance in five," RFK recalled. The popular magazines were full of advice for doomsday. "How You Can Survive Fallout" headlined *Life*, showing a man garbed in a "civilian fall-out suit," seeming to wave goodbye. The magazine offered diagrams for backyard shelters, with helpful hints: "the inside walls of the shelter [should be] painted bright colors to add a note of cheerfulness." The article was accompanied by a letter from President Kennedy urging citizens to read it. The president's own bunker was a mountain in Maryland; for a quick escape from Hyannis, the navy in the summer of 1961 built JFK a secret shelter on the nearby island of Nantucket.

The experts estimated that, in a holocaust, a nationwide nuclear shelter program could save 20 million lives—but that 60 million or so would still die. Robert Kennedy did not want to even hear such ghoulish calculation. He opposed the shelter program, even though among the president's advisers, he later acknowledged, he was "a minority of one." His own defense was gallows humor. In late August, the National Security Council gloomily considered what to do about the Soviets' decision to resume nuclear testing. Khrushchev was vowing to detonate a 100-megaton "superbomb," so awesome, *Life* wrote, that its fireball would "appear bigger than the moon, from London to Berlin." After the meeting, RFK told his brother, "I want to get off." "Get off what?" the president asked. "Get off the planet," said Bobby. RFK's mischievous friend Paul Corbin had been jokingly urging Bobby to run against his brother in 1964. Bobby now dryly announced that he had decided to reject Corbin's advice. "I don't want the job," he said. A former ethics professor at Georgetown University, Father L. C. McHugh, argued in a Jesuit journal that shelter owners had a moral right to kill their neighbors clamoring to get in. When Arthur Schlesinger lamented the *"sauve qui peut* [every man for himself] ethic" at a meeting of Kennedy advisers, RFK sourly interjected, "There's no problem here. We can just station Father McHugh with a machine gun at every shelter."

Both Kennedys were very skeptical of the high-ranking generals and their elaborate war plans for devastating the Soviet Union. Air Force General Curtis LeMay, who had commanded the firebombing raids against Japan in World War II and gone on to create an Armageddon force under the Strategic Air Command, was particularly obnoxious. "LeMay believed in devastation," recalled Paul Nitze, a high-ranking official at Defense. "He thought nothing of burning 100,000 people. He had done it before, in Tokyo in 1945." When LeMay badgered Kennedy for more military control of nuclear weapons, Kennedy instructed, "I don't want that man near me again." The Kennedys' response to overbearing and balky generals, typically, was to hire their own general—Maxwell Taylor, RFK's ally on the Bay of Pigs investigation—in the new, outside-the-chain-of-command role of military adviser to the president. Taylor had resigned from the military in the late '50s in protest against the Pentagon's overreliance on "massive retaliation" with nuclear weapons. In *The Uncertain Trumpet,* an influential book carefully read by JFK, Taylor called for "flexible response," strengthening conventional forces to allow the United States to resist a Soviet invasion of Western Europe without immediately resorting to nuclear weapons. Taylor would remain close to the Kennedys and particularly RFK, although the upright general was careful not to play the toady.

Kennedy also went outside the bureaucracy on the thorny question of Berlin. To advise him, the president brought in Dean Acheson, the former secretary of state, who had argued for standing up to the Soviet threat back in the Truman administration. Acheson was an outspoken hawk: he believed that the Soviets only understood force or the genuine threat of military action and that a too-ready willingness to negotiate would be seen by the Kremlin as a sign of weakness. Bobby Kennedy was respectful of Acheson's power of persuasion, but he disliked him personally, partly for clannish reasons. The Groton- and Yale-educated Acheson thought that Joseph Kennedy was a disreputable bootlegger and made no effort to hide his caustic opinions, which quickly got back to RFK.

Personality counted for more than ideology with RFK. His personal likes and dislikes could make him capricious, but they also freed him from orthodoxy. The "assistant president," as he was now sometimes called behind his back, was remarkably free of Cold War cant. This may seem surprising from Joe McCarthy's former aide, the onetime suspicious tourist to the Soviet Union who refused to be treated by "communist doctors." But as his brother's secret emissary, Robert Kennedy quite quickly developed a more balanced, nuanced way of dealing with the Kremlin. On the one hand, he urgently reminded the Soviets that his brother would go to war rather than see West Berlin fall into Soviet hands. In July, at a lunch arranged by Bolshakov with the dour Soviet ambassador, Mikhail Menshikov (known as Smiling Mike by the White

House), Kennedy became so enraged by Menshikov's airy dismissal of American resolve that he almost stalked out of the room. At the same time, usually through his Bolshakov back channel, he looked for face-saving escape routes in time of crisis. Indeed, the bullyboy of the 1940s and 1950s, so quick to pick a fight, became a secret peacemaker when it really counted, during the nuclear face-offs of his brother's administration. Part of this moderation, of course, came on the direct orders of his brother, who was consistently more cautious in his actions than his rhetoric. But RFK's flexibility and pragmatism in his dealings with the Soviets also suggest the complexity of his character. While his first instinct was to strike a blow, his second was to listen carefully. He was romantic and at times naive, but he was also result-oriented, willing to settle for the least-bad option.

Perhaps to foster the myth of Kennedy "toughness," RFK, in his public statements and later oral histories, played down his willingness to negotiate—or hid it altogether. The most spectacular example of secret deal-making would come later, during the Cuban Missile Crisis in October 1962. But there are hints in the odd newspaper article in the summer of 1961, as well as from the sketchy record of the Bolshakov contacts, that RFK, acting on his brother's orders, was willing to bargain from the beginning. On July 27, just two days after the president gave a hard-line speech to the nation vowing to stand fast in Berlin, the *New York Herald Tribune* reported that President Kennedy would be interested in signing "some kind of 20- to 50-year nonaggression pact" with Khrushchev. The story vaguely referred to "State Department officials" as the source. The author of the story, Marguerite Higgins, was routinely on the receiving end of RFK's leaks. Kennedy's phone logs show her calling RFK on July 25—two days before the story appeared in the paper. Three weeks later, Higgins called again to say she had just finished an article called "My Favorite Kennedy" and to invite RFK for dinner. "If you don't accept the dinner invitation," the message, taken by a secretary, continued, "she would like an appointment to see you to discuss Berlin." Higgins was so close to the attorney general that she asked him to be the godfather to her child.

More dramatic, though speculative, is the suggestion, first raised by presidential historian Michael Beschloss, that RFK might have signaled through Bolshakov that the United States would not react drastically if the Soviets erected the Berlin wall. When the wall went up in mid-August, dividing the Soviet-controlled Eastern sector from the free Western sector, the response from the Kennedy administration was surprisingly muted. After a couple of weeks, a battle group of 1,500 American troops was marched up the autobahn from West Germany to the enveloped city, but it was a token force, meant to boost the morale of the West Berliners, not hold off the Red Army. Though the wall was a cruel affront to liberty, and became a dramatic symbol of the East-West tension, its immediate impact was to defuse the Berlin crisis, since it stopped the daily exodus from the Soviet bloc. No evidence has emerged yet from Soviet archives of an explicit back-channel deal over the wall, and some Cold War scholars doubt that Bolshakov had the independence and stature to engage in such high-stakes diplomacy. Nonetheless, Bolshakov and Kennedy may have, in some subtle and deniable way, at least touched on the question of closing the border between East and West Berlin before the Soviets took this dramatic step.

The RFK-Bolshakov channel may have played a role in ending a very tense standoff at the wall a few weeks later. In late October, the blustery local American commander, General Lucius Clay, began on his own authority to test the right of American civilians to pass into East Berlin. The East German border guards balked, and a dangerous confrontation quickly loomed at "Checkpoint Charlie." For the first time, American tanks faced off against Soviet tanks, their cannon barrels leveled at each other only a hundred yards apart. (The American tanks also had bulldozer blades. Again without asking Washington's permission, General Clay had ordered his tankers to practice knocking down a replica of the wall.) Quietly, the Kennedys moved to disarm the face-off. According to an oral history RFK made in 1964, he told Bolshakov that if the Russian tanks drove away, the Americans would follow suit within twenty minutes. The tanks rumbled off. In private correspondence passed through the Bolshakov channel that fall, Kennedy and Khrushchev began tentatively discussing areas of confrontation and accommodation. By December, Berlin began to cool as a flash point, though it would flare up again.

JFK was eager to use RFK as his counselor and emissary, but without fanfare. Just as he did not wish to appear too soft on the Russians, JFK went to some lengths to demonstrate that he was not overly reliant on his brother. In conversations with anxious professionals who had been browbeaten by the attorney general, JFK would make light of his brother's belligerence and hectoring zeal. While the president and much of the national security hierarchy had been away at the Vienna summit at the end of May, rebels deposed the Trujillo regime in the Dominican Republic. Striding into the operations center at the State Department, RFK, who had remained in Washington, began issuing orders. He wanted to send the American fleet steaming into Dominican waters, preparatory to landing the marines. Under Secretary Chester Bowles—RFK's punching bag after the Bay of Pigs—prudently and rather bravely protested. RFK shouted at him: "You're a gutless bastard." Bowles appealed to the president, forthrightly asking, "Who's in charge here?" JFK, who had no stomach for armed intervention in the Caribbean less than two months after the Bay of Pigs, answered, "You are." "Good," said Bowles. "Would you mind explaining that to your brother?" Bowles won the battle but lost the war: a few months later, he was shipped out of Washington as a roving ambassador.

Meeting with his friend columnist Joe Alsop in London after the summit, the president said that he had received "frantic" cables from his brother about the situation in the Dominican Republic. JFK used one of his more cutting putdowns. Bobby's cables, he said, were "boring." When he asked General Clay to lead the battle group up the autobahn to Berlin in early September, Clay said he would do it on one condition: under no circumstances would he ever deal with the president's brother. The president would gently mock his brother before the entire National Security Council. The attorney general usually sat along the wall of the Cabinet Room, back with the staff, during NSC meetings, but his moods were transparent. The president concluded one discussion, about building a dam in Africa, by remarking, "The Attorney General has not spoken but I can feel the cold wind of his disapproval on the back of my neck."

Yet, at the same time, the president quietly delegated great authority to his brother on the newest, hottest front of the Cold War. In January, just before JFK's inauguration, Khrushchev had given a much-noticed speech predicting that the global struggle against capitalism would be won not by conventional warfare—because modern wars could too easily escalate into nuclear war—but rather by wars of "national liberation." In the Third World, from Vietnam to Algeria to Cuba, Khrushchev vowed, communist insurgencies would over-throw their colonialist oppressors. JFK required all his foreign policy and military advisers to read Khrushchev's speech. Almost overnight, a new and faddish weapon was added to the Cold War arsenal: counterinsurgency. If the communists were going to lead guerrilla uprisings, then the West would have to learn how to fight back. Unconventional warfare became the rage among New Frontiersmen: Special Forces, wearing rakish green berets, were trained to fight "people's wars." To win the "hearts and minds" of the people—and deny their allegiance to the communists—soldiers and diplomats were instructed in civilizing missions that ranged from land reform to child delivery. Everyone, from ambassador to grunt soldier, was supposed to get in the spirit. The president himself surprised his wife one weekend by quoting, out of the blue, from Mao Tse-tung: " 'Guerrillas must move among the people as fish swim in the sea.' " There was a certain logic, even common sense, to counterinsurgency. Enacting land reform or building irrigation systems or providing better health care was, certainly in theory, a better way to defeat communist movements in the Third World than by bullets and bombs. The actual experience, however, became a lesson to Robert Kennedy in the limits of power, his own and America's. His stubbornness and contempt for bureaucrats made him a slow learner.

CHAPTER 7 GOAD

ROBERT KENNEDY was a true believer in counterinsurgency. He coined the term, according to Michael Forrestal, a national security staffer (and son of the first secretary of defense, James Forrestal) who often worked with him. "Counterinsurgency might best be described as social reform under pressure," Kennedy wrote. Combating communism by building roads and hospitals appealed to his idealism and sympathy for the downtrodden. Training guerrilla fighters played to his storybook sense of history and reverence for "toughness"; among his heroes was Francis Marion, the Swamp Fox, whose hit-and-run tactics had bedeviled the British during the Revolutionary War. Kennedy soon had Special Forces troops showing his children how to swing from the trees at Hickory Hill. On his desk at the Justice Department, the attorney general kept a green beret.

Kennedy had a romantic and naive faith in the possibilities of "psychological warfare" and "political action," as the CIA defined its covert attempts to stir the masses. RFK could not accept the fact that the KGB was better at these black arts than the CIA. When the Soviets resumed nuclear testing at the end of August, RFK demanded to know why the CIA couldn't bring angry hordes into the streets of Europe, shouting against Soviet war-mongering. He summoned David Murphy, the head of the CIA's East European division, and demanded an explanation. Murphy tried to explain that the CIA could not simply order up a street protest. "Kennedy didn't understand our limitations," recalled Murphy. "He just pouted."

Other government officials could see not only the limitations of trying to win the war of "hearts and minds," but also the dangers of trying. One of RFK's pet ideas was to try to train the police forces of developing countries, particularly those of Latin America. On September 11, 1961, RFK sent a memo to the president urging him to order the FBI and Pentagon to "determine whether all necessary steps are being taken by the internal police to deal with communist infiltration and whether the military or police are prepared to deal with mob riot, or guerrilla bands that may become active. . . ." In January 1962, the White House set up the Special Group (CI) ("CI" stood for "counterinsurgency") to prod the various government agencies into greater efforts in the struggle against communist subversion. "He thought that by making their cops more like ours, we could stop communism," said Charles Maechling, a State Department official who served as staff director of the Special Group (CI) and had the thankless task of communicating RFK's wishes. The State Department diplomats had their doubts. They knew, from firsthand observation, that the fragile democracies of Asia and Latin America had "no control over their security services," said Maechling. By making them more "professional," the well-meaning Americans risked simply making them more efficient engines of repression.

"There was no evidence that Bob saw the risk of this," said Maechling. He did not want to hear the doubts of the quavering diplomats summoned before the Special Group (CI). Feet up and tie down, he would sullenly greet equivocations with hostile, somewhat random questioning. "He was not so much abusive as abrupt and off-the-wall," said Maechling, who witnessed many interrogations. "He rarely swore. He was just inarticulate. The bureaucrats would react with panic." Kennedy, with his fondness for policemen (Chief William Parker of Los Angeles was a particular favorite, in part because he was a bitter foe of the FBI's Hoover), would bring in police chiefs from the heartland to train their foreign counterparts from Latin America and Asia. The "academy," where RFK would show up to deliver graduation addresses, was an old car barn in Georgetown. Inside, men in dark glasses with pitted faces blasted away on the shooting range at large cardboard cutouts of men, each one stenciled Subversive. "We didn't teach them to torture. We tried to teach them not to," said Maechling. "But they didn't want our advice. They wanted our equipment." Armed with walkie-talkies and American record-keeping systems, the Latin policemen became more effective at propping up local oligarchies by chasing down leftist students and labor organizers. Along the way, the "reform" impetus vanished.

It is more than a little ironic that Robert Kennedy, who naturally identified with radical students challenging the establishment, should have unwittingly provided technical assistance for their oppressors.* But as attorney

---

* Convinced that the State Department was not doing enough to identify and cultivate the "leaders of tomorrow" around the world, Kennedy set up the Inter-Agency Youth Committee. Every American embassy was required to set up "youth programs" to "spot" future leaders. "It was a floating crap game," said Lucius Battle, an assistant secretary of state picked by RFK to run the committee. "I liked Bobby, but he was very difficult to work with. He neither read nor listened. Everyone was scared to death of him." The program, which faded out after the Kennedy administration, was deeply resented by career diplomats, but it did spot some future leaders, including Anwar Sadat, then a rising young Egyptian politician, who was sent on a cultural tour of the United States

general and the president's all-purpose number two (or Number One-and-a-Half, as he was also known by reporters fascinated by the brother act), Kennedy was spread too thin to really notice. At the Justice Department, where he could count on loyal deputies and had time to ponder and follow up, he was a truly effective leader. But as a member of the Special Group (CI)—nominally, not even the head of it—he was nothing more than a shrill goad. He usually arrived late, often without having read the background materials. His lack of sophistication, impatience, and messianic impulse overcame his natural shrewdness and empathy. George Ball, who replaced the unfortunate Chester Bowles as undersecretary of state and regarded counterinsurgency as overintellectualized and often counterproductive, objected when RFK demanded that the United States do something to stop the spread of Chinese communist subversion in Zanzibar. Ball responded with a memo that, he recalled, said something like, "God watches every sparrow that may fall, so I don't see why we have to compete in that league." Kennedy, said Ball, "got his back up." RFK could be truly petulant, once knocking over a chair in anger. On another occasion, right after a newspaper story called him "Washington's No. 2 Man," the Special Group (CI), in a rare moment of open defiance, failed to do Kennedy's bidding on a minor matter. "Well, shit," Kennedy sulked, "the second most important man in the world just lost another one." He slammed down his notebook and walked out of the meeting. The effect of this puerile behavior was predictable: Some bureaucrats passively resisted. Others overcompensated and tried to do too much. Robert Amory, the head intelligence analyst at the CIA, recalled that "the Chief of Staff of the Army said that every school in the army should devote a minimum of 20 percent of its time to counter-insurgency. Well, this reached to Finance School and Cooks and Bakers School, and they were talking about how to wire typewriters to explode . . . or how to make apple pies with hand grenades inside them. It just really was a ridiculous thing. . . ."

RFK's private memoranda reflect his frustration with the bureaucracy. He was pleased when more than a hundred Cuban refugees declared their wish to be trained as policemen in the United States, and thoroughly vexed when the State Department ruled that the Cubans would be "unqualified," while the Department of Health, Education, and Welfare refused to get involved in a matter deemed "outside its jurisdiction." Fuming at "bureaucracy at its worst," Kennedy wrote in exasperation to an aide, "The fact that 113 [Cubans] want to be Police could be extremely useful to us!" He despaired over counterinsurgency training courses that were a "waste of time" because they dealt in generalities, not specifics. "It is just incredible to me after all this time, talk and effort we still haven't gotten through," he wrote Mike Forrestal of the National Security Council. "I hope you will raise a real fuss about it. Would you let me know when that happens?" Kennedy sometimes complained directly to the president when the bureaucracy balked. In March 1962, the American ambassador to

(on $12 a day). "Sadat was enchanted," said Battle, who was later U.S. ambassador to Egypt.

Guatemala wanted to reward the right-wing regime in Guatemala with modern riot-control equipment—water cannons and CS grenades that were more powerful than tear gas. At the State Department, the Agency for International Development (AID) refused the ambassador's request, deeming the water cannons and gas grenades to be "repressive equipment." AID tried to compromise by proposing to send the Guatemalans water-tank trunks that could be used to disperse crowds with ordinary fire hoses. This was not good enough for RFK. He sent President Kennedy a memo from a Pentagon official whom General Maxwell Taylor had assigned to look into the matter. "In choosing between the water cannon and CS grenades versus fire hoses and tear gas," the Pentagon man wrote, "the issue here is whether we want to go first class or not." RFK, who wanted to go "first class," wrote JFK that AID's refusal to go along with the Guatemalans' request for more effective riot-control equipment "demonstrates quite clearly how damaging certain bureaucratic decisions can be."

When Kennedy could not get what he wanted from the bureaucracy, he worked around it. Long before Oliver North, the maverick marine colonel on President Ronald Reagan's national security staff, popularized the term "off-the-shelf operation" during the Iran-contra hearings of 1987, Robert Kennedy was running private, custom-made covert actions. A small but illustrative example is his handling of American support for a revolutionary leader named Eduardo Mondlane, whose Liberation Front was trying to free Mozambique, still an African colony, from the Portuguese in the early '60s. Mondlane came to Washington in the spring of 1963 to lobby for support, essentially setting up a Cold War auction (he was already getting aid from East Bloc countries). At the State Department, Dean Rusk would not see the African revolutionary: the United States could not back a rebellion against Portugal, a NATO ally. But RFK met with Mondlane and was impressed with his charisma. He needed to find a way to funnel money to Mondlane while preserving the "deniability" of the United States government. A rare Dictabelt recording of a telephone conversation between RFK and JFK, made public in 1998, shows the almost offhand way these matters were handled in the Kennedy administration. The president and attorney general were discussing sundry personnel matters when Robert Kennedy abruptly brought up Mondlane and the need for deniability. "Now one other thing," RFK began. "Uh . . . I've had some conversations the last couple of weeks with a fellow named Mondlane. . . . He's a terrifically impressive fellow." Secretary Rusk, RFK explained, had "to be able to sit down with the Portuguese and say none of these people [Mondlane and the Mozambique Liberation Front] are getting any money." The attorney general suggested that a private foundation could be enlisted to provide some of the cash, but the rest would have to come "from us" (all told, about $100,000; RFK mentioned the Ford Foundation as a possible resource). RFK proposed that either Averell Harriman, an under secretary of state, or John McCone, the head of the CIA, could oversee the operation—not in their formal capacity as State Department or CIA officials, but "just as someone to use their own judgment." (Both Harriman and McCone were personal friends who maintained direct contact with the attorney general.) RFK said that Mondlane would be meeting with the heads of some African nations at an upcoming meeting. The president's taping system* recorded the following exchange:

> THE PRESIDENT: 'Course, we wouldn't want him [Mondlane] to be saying that he got anything from us.
> RFK: No, but you wouldn't have that, you see. You'd have it through some private foundation.
> THE PRESIDENT: Yeah.
> RFK: Then they could have cutouts on it.
> THE PRESIDENT: I see.
> RFK: And John McCone can handle it. So it wouldn't have to come from the Agency.

This sort of frank talk about cutouts, go-betweens to mask the true source of the money and thus preserve deniability, is the sort of exchange the Kennedys would record only by happenstance and never write down. But it was integral to their relationship and operating style.

The Special Group (CI) was an add-on to the Special Group, the formal body of top officials from State, Defense, and CIA who met every week to review and approve, or disapprove, of all U.S. covert actions. The Special Group had been revitalized by Kennedy after the Bay of Pigs, at the recommendation of Maxwell Taylor, to bring some order and military-style planning discipline to the president's free-floating decision mode, which was deemed partly responsible for permitting the CIA's botched invasion of Cuba. But the Kennedys—particularly Bobby Kennedy—could not resist subverting their own creation. After the Special Group met at 2 p.m. on Tuesdays, the Special Group (CI) with most of the same members—plus RFK—would convene to plot counterinsurgency. Then, beginning in January 1962, a second shell-within-a-shell was carved out, called the Special Group (Augmented). This benignly named "augmentation" was concerned with only one topic: Cuba. The proclivities Kennedy showed at the weekly meetings of the Special Group (CI)—his scorn for the bureaucracy, his zest for covert action, his misplaced idealism and identification with the underdog, his restless insistence on action as well as his carelessness about the consequences—would intensify when Kennedy turned his attention to the impossible mission of getting rid of Fidel Castro.

"THE CUBA MATTER is being allowed to slide," Robert Kennedy wrote in a memorandum to himself on June 1, 1961, as the Taylor Board was wrapping up its

---

* Like most modern presidents in the pre-Watergate era, JFK recorded some of his conversations and phone calls. By pressing a button, he could activate a Dictaphone system that recorded conversations on plastic Dictabelts. Kennedy recorded about 250 hours of meetings and 12 hours of phone conversations during the second half of his presidency. (Richard Nixon's voice-activated system, by contrast, recorded 3,700 hours.) At least two tapes have been tampered with and several are missing.

investigation of the Bay of Pigs. "Mostly because nobody really has the answer to Castro." An all-out invasion of the well-populated, increasingly well-armed island would cost thousands of casualties. (Laid out across a map of the United States, Cuba stretches from Washington to Chicago.) U.S.-backed subversion was becoming problematic as Castro cracked down on dissent with East German–trained secret police. But the fact that there was no good "answer" to Cuba did not stop RFK from trying to find one. In the fall of 1961, RFK increasingly turned his attention to fomenting a secret proxy war against the Caribbean stronghold. Off and on during the Kennedy administration—in between chasing mobsters, trying to integrate the South, and attending to the president's official and personal needs—Bobby Kennedy looked for ways, sometimes outlandish, to eliminate the bearded revolutionary dictator who had overthrown the right-wing regime of Fulgencio Batista in 1959.

In later years, veterans of the Kennedy administration would look back at the Kennedys' Cuba obsession, and their own role in abetting it, with wonder and some shame. "We were hysterical about Castro at the time of the Bay of Pigs and thereafter," said Robert McNamara, the defense secretary who was Robert Kennedy's close friend. The president's national security adviser, McGeorge Bundy (less enamored with RFK, whom he described as a "terrier of a man"), suspected that RFK was trying to avenge his brother's humiliation at the Bay of Pigs. "It was almost as simple as, goddammit, we lost the first round, let's win the second," said Bundy. In terms of its importance to national security, Bundy regarded Cuba as a sideshow to Berlin, but he couldn't avoid it: Visitors noted two boxes on Bundy's cluttered desk. One was labeled "President's box" and the other was "Cuba."

It is difficult, decades after Castro's revolution, to imagine how threatening it seemed at the time. In June 1961, *Life* magazine ran an enlarged close-up of Castro's eyes and intoned, "The Messianic eyes of Fidel Castro, hypnotic and hungry for power, summon up a new and nightmarish danger for the U.S." A four-part series warned how the "Bearded One" was spreading revolution "everywhere in Latin America." The editors of *Life*—and the Kennedy administration—may have hyped the danger, but they were not merely imagining monsters. Castro *was* trying to spread the revolution—and the weaponry to wage it—around Latin America. He was quickly arming Cuba with Soviet hardware, including MiG jet fighters and tanks, that would make a U.S. invasion ever costlier. In 1958, Castro's ragtag rebel force—maybe 800 men—had defeated a professional army of 30,000 soldiers to take power. In 1961, Castro had driven the CIA's invaders back into the sea. He was a shrewd and charismatic leader. With his tendency to romanticize guerrilla fighters, RFK saw Castro as a formidable adversary, especially now that he had the backing of the Soviet Empire. Writing his early-morning memo to the president as the Bay of Pigs beachhead was collapsing on April 19, RFK had been both early and right in predicting that Castro's arsenal would one day—soon—include nuclear-tipped missiles aimed at the United States. For all the talk of vengeance, Kennedy also felt a humanitarian moral obligation: during 1961 and 1962, he spent as much, if not more, time trying to free the more than 1,000 Cuban exiles captured at the Bay of Pigs than he did trying to "get rid" of Castro. Nor was Kennedy wholly unrealistic about the difficulties involved in dislodging Castro. At a meeting on Cuba at the White House at noon on November 3, 1961, RFK wrote in his own hand:

> My idea is to stir things up on the island with espionage, sabotage, general disorder, run & operated by Cubans themselves with every group but Batistaites & Communists. Do not know if we will be successful in overthrowing Castro but we have nothing to lose in my estimate.

Kennedy's mistake was in assuming that "we have nothing to lose." He failed to appreciate the power of his own words—or even more compelling, his body language—on junior diplomats and career professionals. Though sensitive to others when he wished to be, he could not, or would not, put himself in the place of a lowly government employee, summoned before the president's brother, staring woefully into those icy pale blue eyes, hearing that insistent high whine challenging, at least by implication, the witness's patriotism and his manhood. Kennedy could not empathize in part because he often felt thwarted and flummoxed by inert bureaucrats. The more clever ones did know how to deflect his flailings. But others marched right off the cliff. Kennedy's scattershot interrogations, delivered with the general hope of getting things "moving," had unintended consequences that would have been comical if they had not been dangerous.

The Central Intelligence Agency, which had swaggered through the 1950s, staging coups throughout the Third World, had been badly demoralized by its spectacular failure at the Bay of Pigs. Richard Bissell, the chief of covert operations who had sold himself to the Kennedys as a "man-eating shark," was on the way out in the late fall of 1961, forced to resign after a decent interval. Already banished was Allen Dulles, the gung-ho director known as the Great White Case Officer for his love of skulduggery. When his replacement, John McCone, arrived in November, he found the agency to be in a "condition of shock."

Bissell was present at the White House meeting on November 3 at which RFK, as the attorney general put it in his jottings, vowed to "stir things up" in Cuba. Kennedy began by stirring up the CIA. Afterwards, returning to the office he would soon be vacating in the CIA's shiny new headquarters in Langley, Virginia, Bissell complained to one of his assistants that he had just been chewed out by Bobby Kennedy, told it was time to "get off his ass" on Cuba. RFK kept hectoring the lame-duck Bissell. Over Thanksgiving weekend, RFK repeatedly called Bissell at home to ask him what he was doing to get things "moving" on Cuba. (RFK spent much of the rest of the weekend in Hyannis Port playing touch football in the rain. Burke Marshall, the head of the civil rights division at Justice, had come to Hyannis to talk to RFK about much-needed new legislation to enforce voting rights in the South. Preoccupied with Castro, RFK seemed bored by civil rights.)

Robert Kennedy was at the moment driving Cuba policy in the administration. The brainy young New Frontiersman Richard Goodwin had written a memo to the president on November 1 arguing that RFK would be "the most effective commander" of a major new covert operations program to overthrow Castro. RFK was too busy to take on the job full-time, as well as sensitive to the need to maintain deniability. When Goodwin sent him a draft of a strategy paper on Cuba on November 22, Kennedy wanted no paternity. He wrote on Goodwin's cover note, "Eliminate my name." As a "commander," Kennedy wanted an experienced guerrilla fighter, a modern-day Swamp Fox—but one who would be personally loyal to him.

In Kennedy's handwritten notes from the November 3 meeting on Cuba, he listed the participants, mostly familiar names from State, Defense, and CIA, like Bissell. But a new name also pops up, identified by RFK as "Ed Lansdale (the Ugly American)." Kennedy's inclusion of the nickname is significant. To run the new secret war on Castro, Kennedy had seized on a figure straight out of a novel; indeed, two novels. Edward Lansdale was a legendary CIA operative whose covert machinations had been instrumental in suppressing a communist uprising and electing a democratic leader in the Philippines in the early 1950s. A cross between a Boy Scout and a street hustler, at once corny and cunning, the gung-ho Lansdale was the model for both Graham Greene's *The Quiet American* (1956) and William Lederer and Eugene Burdick's *The Ugly American* (1958). The portraits, especially Greene's, were far from uncritical (Greene's Lansdale—Alden Pyle—is a well-meaning menace), but the subtleties seem to have been lost on RFK, whose weakness for hero worship sometimes eclipsed his discernment. Kennedy handpicked "the Ugly American" to overthrow Castro. Within the CIA, Lansdale was seen as a loner, a free spirit who did not take orders well—and a bit of a con man who promised more than he could deliver.

Eager to make Lansdale his own man, RFK found him languishing in a Pentagon office, where he had been shuffled from the CIA. Kennedy briefly considered headquartering the "get Castro" project in the Justice Department but decided that such proximity to the president's brother was too close to home. Lansdale's first impressions of Robert Kennedy had been condescending. He had watched the attorney general performing during the Taylor Board investigation of the Bay of Pigs in May. "I wondered what that youngster was doing sitting in the meeting and talking so much," Lansdale later recollected. But the Ugly American knew how to win over his new boss. He played to the Kennedys' shared disdain for slow-moving bureaucrats. A handwritten note from Lansdale to RFK on December 7, describing an early meeting with the CIA's Cuba hands, is full of folksy, all-American, can-do spirit: "I decided to lay it right on the line on what it will take to win against the Communist team," Lansdale wrote. "I'm not sanguine that even a heavy whip will put the right spirit into bureaucrats, but doggone it we have to work with what we have."

The "bureaucrats" tried to warn Kennedy that the Cuban people were not likely to rise up against Castro. A National Intelligence Estimate by the CIA on November 28 flatly declared: "The Castro regime has sufficient popular support and repressive capabilities to cope with any internal threat likely to develop within the foreseeable future." But in a memo on November 30, Lansdale urged Kennedy to ignore the intelligence experts: they were just playing bureaucratic warfare, Lansdale insinuated, sending up false warning flags to discourage Kennedy from setting up a separate command that would be outside agency control. Kennedy was easily swayed by Lansdale, in part because he was still so angry at the CIA for the Bay of Pigs. The attorney general "resented CIA resistance to this idea [the new anti-Castro operation]," noted John McCone, the new CIA director, in a memo to the record on November 29.

Kennedy's resentment and too-easy infatuation with Lansdale led him into precisely the trap that had doomed the Bay of Pigs. Before the ill-fated invasion, the swashbuckling Bissell had also ignored a National Intelligence Estimate warning that the Cuban masses were unlikely to unseat Castro. But Kennedy's only lesson from the Bay of Pigs was to keep trying, though in a more underhanded way. He failed to heed several blinking red lights, including the failure of a couple of small CIA-run Cuban exile raids against the island in December. The botched missions were case studies in how these adventures can, and often do, backfire. In one, the Cubans' boat broke down; in the other, two of the raiders were captured and made to "confess" on Cuban TV.

Kennedy just pressed on. On January 19, he gave a pep talk to various agency representatives to the new Cuba project, code-named Mongoose, that left no room for doubt about his desires. As recorded by the CIA's new director of operations, Richard Helms, Kennedy announced that overthrowing Castro was "the top priority of the United States Government—all else is secondary—no time, money, effort, or manpower is to be spared." The attorney general invoked what is known at the CIA as "Higher Authority"—that is, the president. RFK went on to say that his brother had told him just the day before that " 'the final chapter on Cuba has not been written'—it's got to be done and will be done." Helms recorded Kennedy's words in a memo to his new boss, McCone, but the CIA's covert operations chief didn't believe for an instant that overthrowing Castro would, or could, "be done." He was just making a record.

The official record, gradually fleshed out as documents have been slowly declassified over the last thirty years, is full of such moments when the notetaker (sometimes the same man whose job it was to implement the order) swallowed his incredulity. The gap between words and actions, between aims and realities—often wide in government—was vast when it came to the Kennedy administration's program to remove the Castro regime. Filing cabinets filled with contingency plans that were laughably unrealistic and instructions from "Higher Authority" that could never be carried out. Real orders were often not written down. The need for deniability and secrecy mixed with bureaucratic rivalry to create court intrigues straight out of a fifteenth-century doge's palace. Examining the often opera-buffa interplay between Kennedy and his grudging servants at the CIA is, on one level, entertaining, but it is also essential to understanding his role in the secret war against Castro. Kennedy apologists and their inevitable opposites, the debunkers and conspiracy theorists, have distorted this critical chapter of RFK's life. They tend to picture RFK as either an innocent do-gooder or a cold-blooded would-be murderer, neither of which he was. The first step to getting beyond these fictions and obfuscations is to understand the quirky and outsized characters he had to deal with.

The day before RFK's pep talk, Lansdale had unfolded his plan of action to eliminate Castro: thirty-three "tasks" that would steadily build towards "the Touchdown Play" when a rebel column would march triumphantly into Havana in October (conveniently, just before the November congressional elections in the United States). Lansdale's plan was grandiose, a fantasy, and it was immediately ridiculed by CIA subordinates, who began mockingly calling Lansdale "the FM"—for field marshal. Lansdale's fascination with "psywar"— psychological warfare—gave agency wags plenty of comic material. A particular favorite was Lansdale's plan to surface an American submarine just over the Havana horizon to fire star shells into the night sky, in the hopes of convincing the Cubans that the Second Coming was imminent, thus spurring them to get rid of the anti-Christ—Castro. The jokesters called this plan "elimination by illumination."

Lansdale was a general, but he still needed an army, so he depended on CIA handlers and their Cuban exile foot soldiers, whose barracks were safe houses scattered about Miami. Sam Halpern, the executive officer of Task Force W, the CIA team designated to carry out Operation Mongoose, knew the pitiful state of his forces. Of the CIA's two dozen or so agents inside Cuba, only about half were still in communication with the agency, and several of those were probably double agents feeding back disinformation. Halpern went to the CIA's new chief of covert operations, Dick Helms, to tell him, "We don't have anything."

Helms was a spook of a different kind than his predecessor, Richard Bissell. Within the agency, Helms was the leader of the so-called prudent professionals, career intelligence officers who scorned and resisted the cowboy antics of the dashing Ivy League amateurs like Bissell, a former Yale professor. (Bissell had tried and failed to get Helms, a true survivor, fired.) But while careful, Helms was also ambitious. He had just climbed over Bissell's body, and already he had his eye on the director's office. Helms was just as aware as Halpern of the weakened state of CIA forces arrayed against Cuba; indeed, Helms was partly responsible for their thinness. In late 1960 and early 1961, sensing disaster ahead, he had quietly advised up-and-comers at the agency to avoid serving in the Bay of Pigs operation if they valued their careers. Now, reviewing the resources available to meet RFK's new demands on Cuba in early January 1962, Helms just shook his head. The staff list for Task Force W included many of the CIA's mediocrities, eccentrics, and burnouts. Still, Helms, whose nickname among his detractors was the Eminence Grease, knew how to play the game. He told Halpern to write a memo to Lansdale and Kennedy that was "forward-leaning." Surely, Helms told Halpern, he could find a way to give the *appearance* of action. "There are 500,000 words in the English language," instructed Helms. "Use them."

Helms needed to pick a commander for Task Force W. He knew about the Kennedys' fondness for Ian Fleming's spy novels. "They want James Bond?" Helms said to Halpern. "We'll give him Bill Harvey." Helms was being droll. Harvey shared a love of guns and martinis with 007, but not much else. Bug-eyed, frog-voiced, and pear-shaped, Harvey was secretive to the point of paranoia. He had been Berlin station chief during the 1950s, when the divided city was a battleground for Soviet and Western spies, so he was experienced at espionage—though not with Cubans, who were regarded as hopelessly garrulous by their gringo handlers at the agency. Harvey was also a serious alcoholic who from time to time nodded off in meetings after lunch. He always carried two guns because, he explained, he knew so many secrets. When he went to meet the president for the first time in January, he handed his firearms to a startled Secret Service agent at the door of the Oval Office. JFK was equally taken aback with the man who was supposed to be the battlefield commander in the nation's most important secret war. "So you're our James Bond?" the president inquired, clearly unconvinced.

Since RFK had decreed that "no time, effort, money, or manpower" was to be spared in the assault on Castro, the CIA quickly spent about $100 million to create a base for clandestine operations out of Miami. Code-named JM/WAVE, the Miami station had hundreds of agents, exotic weaponry, and its own fleet of airplanes and speedboats. But it didn't accomplish much. The real work of building an intelligence network, a prerequisite to staging a popular uprising, is slow and painstaking and probably impossible in a true police state like Cuba. But there was not time to even try. The Kennedys, as Halpern put it, wanted "boom and bang" on the island—raids that would produce tangible results, like blowing up bridges and factories. Perversely, the Kennedy drive to avenge the Bay of Pigs ran straight into the reforms enacted to prevent a recurrence of the Bay of Pigs. Harvey's Task Force W had to clear all of its covert actions with the Special Group (Augmented). The chairman of the Special Group (Augmented) was General Taylor, who turned out—unsurprisingly for a military man, but apparently a shock to Robert Kennedy—to be a stickler for detail. Though himself a daring paratrooper in World War II, Taylor held a low opinion of unconventional warriors. The first time he saw a soldier in a green beret, he instructed, "Take that silly headgear off." Taylor wanted to hear specifics from Harvey, but Harvey, vague and squirrelly with information (and, after lunch, drunk), was reluctant to share CIA secrets with a "uniform."

The tensions between Harvey and Taylor were exceeded by the bad blood between Harvey and Bobby Kennedy. The short, fat Harvey and the short, wiry Kennedy were equally proud and tempestuous. RFK once slammed a chair to the floor in the Special Group; Harvey kicked in a door while visiting JM/WAVE in Miami. Kennedy was impatient and Harvey patronizing. Both were sarcastic. "Why can't you get things cooking like 007?" Kennedy face-

tiously asked Harvey. When Harvey tried to explain that a certain infiltration
had been delayed because the agents were not yet properly trained, Kennedy
supposedly suggested that if the CIA couldn't train these men, he'd take them
to Hickory Hill and do it himself. And what will you train them in? inquired
Harvey. Baby-sitting? Unguarded over his martinis at lunch, Harvey casually
referred to the Kennedys as "fags" and RFK as "that fucker." With that kind of
teamwork behind them, it was unlikely that the Cuban masses were going to
rise up in time for the "Touchdown Play" in October.

THE MOST DIRECT WAY to remove Fidel Castro from office was to kill him. In fact, the CIA had been plotting to assassinate Castro since at least the summer of 1960, several months before John F. Kennedy's election as president. The Kennedys made clear their desire to "get rid" of Castro. But did they order an attempt on his life? A 1975 congressional investigation into CIA abuses, the Church Committee, turned up eight separate plots to kill Castro between 1960 and 1965, some of them cockamamie—a cigar for the Cuban leader, dipped in poison; an exploding seashell for El Jefe to discover while skin-diving—and some of them jaw-dropping, such as the CIA's outsourcing of the job to infamous gangsters. But the senators could never decide whether President Kennedy or his brother directed the CIA to try to kill Castro. The investigators were thwarted by agency officials invoking, often with winks or pained expressions, the doctrine of plausible deniability, and a parade of Kennedy aides swearing up and down that neither Kennedy would even consider anything so sordid as attempting to murder a foreign leader.

There is something so unbelievably reckless about the United States government hiring the mob to try to kill a head of state, no matter how noxious, that our fascination with the CIA's botched attempts in the early '60s lives on, amplified and embellished in the retelling. It is the moment of stranger-than-fiction reality that sustains decades of far-out fantasy. The debate over the Kennedys' involvement—and the consequences thereof—has raged on in books and magazines and movies. The Kennedy defenders, led by Arthur Schlesinger, insist that RFK in particular was too noble—and too devout a Catholic—to engage in attempted murder. Mainstream historians for the most part scoff at this defense, arguing that the Kennedys must have been involved, while admitting the evidence is circumstantial. Conspiracy theorists go much further. In some gothic finales, the mob turns on JFK when his brother refuses to back off his dogs at the Justice Department. In Oliver Stone's 1991 film *JFK*, not just the Mafia, but all the others stung by Bobby's lash—from renegade Cubans, to the embittered CIA, to the jealous Lyndon Johnson, to the war hawks on the Joint Chiefs of Staff—congeal in a giant blob of a plot. Lee Harvey Oswald is a mere patsy in Stone's imagined but widely credited docudrama; the real killers are shadowy figures on the Grassy Knoll.

The truth is unknowable, lost in a maze of dissembling, obscured by the demands of art, commerce, and politics. But trying to untangle the web is worth the effort for what it shows about Robert Kennedy and his fraught relationship with the FBI's J. Edgar Hoover. The drama of the assassination plots has been overstated: in reality, the plots were more silly than sinister, known only to a few people who doubted from the beginning that they would ever work. The real significance of the scheming against Castro lies in the way the cloak of secrecy, particularly about the Mafia's involvement, was manipulated by the director of the FBI. Thanks to a small and clumsy mistake by the plotters, Hoover was able to learn about the CIA connection to the Mafia. With his zest for scavenging secrets that could be transformed into tools of blackmail, the ever-curious Hoover began pulling on a string that, incredibly, led him to discover a nugget that, for Hoover, was pure gold: President Kennedy's affair with a woman who was a friend of the same mobsters hired by the CIA to kill Castro. The CIA-Mafia plots never came close to killing Castro, but, by a perverse ripple effect, they had a great impact on others, most especially on Robert Kennedy. A careful examination of the evidence suggests that Kennedy may or may not have been a perpetrator of the assassination plots—enabler is probably a more accurate term—but he was definitely the victim—not physically, but rather psychically. It appears most likely that RFK's involvement in the plots was at worst peripheral—but that, after his brother died in 1963, he became very fearful about what they might have wrought.

The CIA's breathtakingly foolish decision to hire the Mafia to kill Castro was made by Richard Bissell, the spy agency's then-chief of covert action, in August 1960, while Dwight Eisenhower was still president. The atmosphere at the agency in the summer of 1960 appears to have been murderous: Bissell also launched a scheme to poison the new president of the Congo, Patrice Lumumba. Bissell, an extraordinarily self-confident figure, was not acting on direct orders from anyone. He believed that the Eisenhower administration wanted to eliminate Castro, and he figured that the mafiosi, as professional killers who had an interest in reclaiming their Havana gambling casinos from Castro, were the right men for the job. He informed his boss, CIA director Allen Dulles, that he had subcontracted with the mob, but only in the most "circumlocutious" terms, naming no names. When Dulles did not say no, Bissell went ahead, and working through a cutout, an ex-FBI agent named Robert Maheu, recruited Johnny Rosselli, a mid-ranked Las Vegas mobster, who in turn lined up Momo "Sam" Giancana, the boss of Chicago, as well as Santos Trafficante, the Miami gangster who handled the mob's gambling interests in Havana.

Bissell testified that he never spoke to either Kennedy brother about the plan to kill Castro. He assumed that Dulles had briefed the Kennedys after JFK was elected in November 1960, but he never asked. Scholars generally assume that JFK was in the know—the Bay of Pigs makes a lot more sense if Castro was to be eliminated at about the time of the invasion. But proof is elusive. Senator George Smathers of Florida said in a 1964 oral history that President Kennedy, walking the White House grounds in about March 1961, had asked him if "people would be gratified" if Castro were assassinated. In a 1988 interview, Smathers told historian Michael Beschloss that the president told him that he had been "given to believe" by the CIA that Castro would be "knocked off" before the invaders hit the beaches at the Bay of Pigs.

Bissell himself said that he never had high expectations that the Mafia plots would succeed, and he had pretty much given up hope before the Bay of Pigs. Bissell had originally contemplated a traditional gangland-style execution. Too dangerous and too bloody, cautioned the mobsters; poison would be better. The CIA whipped up a batch of lethal pills, to be dropped in Castro's drink, but the Cuban recruited to deliver them got "cold feet." There are indications that Giancana and company did not try very hard to kill Castro. The dons were more interested in collecting IOUs that could be presented to government prosecutors who might later wish to send them to jail. In any case, the poison pill plot, if it was ever serious, petered out by April 1961.

But along the way an accident happened—the sort of minor, faintly ridiculous screwup that makes a mockery of cloak-and-dagger and illustrates the perils of hiring clumsy outside help to accomplish delicate inside jobs. Giancana, it appeared, was worried that his girlfriend, popular singer Phyllis McGuire, was two-timing him with comedian Dan Rowan. As a favor, Giancana asked his CIA cutout, former FBI agent Maheu, to arrange to have the phone tapped in Rowan's hotel room. Predictably, the private investigator hired by Maheu to install the wiretap got caught by a curious hotel maid. When the police arrived, the private investigator pointed to Maheu. Maheu's alibi: he was working for the CIA.

In due course, J. Edgar Hoover discovered the opportunities for mischief in this Keystone Cops caper. Since wiretapping is a federal offense, the FBI took over the investigation. In early May 1961, one of Bissell's CIA colleagues, Sheffield Edwards, told the FBI that the CIA had indeed hired Maheu to be a cutout to Sam Giancana. The agency, Edwards explained, had hired the "underworld" to conduct clandestine efforts against the Castro government. Bissell's underling couldn't say what those efforts were, exactly. The clandestine work was, he explained, "a dirty business." Hoover no doubt lit up when he read his field agent's report on the case. Here was an opportunity to strengthen the director's hand by weakening his opponents'. In the spring of 1961, the FBI director was under unrelenting pressure from the attorney general to stop dragging his feet on organized crime. Without question, Hoover realized he had an excellent tool to embarrass his rivals at the CIA and put the attorney general in a tight spot. On May 22, the FBI director sent Kennedy a memo informing him that the CIA had hired the mob to try to do some "dirty business" in Cuba.

Kennedy's response was prompt. "Courtney[,] I hope this will be followed up vigorously," the attorney general wrote on the top of Hoover's memo. "Courtney" was Courtney Evans, an FBI agent who had worked closely with RFK on the Rackets Committee and now had the thankless job of acting as an intermediary between the attorney general and the FBI director. The written record, however, does not reveal how "this" was "followed up," and memories, including Evans's, had conveniently faded by the time congressional investigators began asking questions a decade later. There was a June 6 memo from Evans to one of his bosses at the FBI, saying that the bureau was still investigating, and that the attorney general would be "orally informed." But then nothing. There is no evidence that Kennedy asked another question for the next four months.

This seems passing strange. To be sure, Kennedy's lieutenants pointed out that the attorney general was extraordinarily busy at the time. Indeed, Hoover's May 22 memo arrived on a Monday after RFK had been up all that Sunday night, trying to keep an angry mob from burning down the Montgomery, Alabama, church with Martin Luther King and 1,500 others in it. On the same weekend, the attorney general had learned that his back channel to Georgi Bolshakov had done little to lay the groundwork for a productive summit meeting between the president and Khrushchev, less than a fortnight away. Those crises required immediate action. Jack Miller, the chief of the Justice Department's criminal division, also received a copy of Hoover's May 22 memo. Interviewed in 1999, he noted that Kennedy was not required to do anything about the Maheu case. In August, the U.S. attorney in Las Vegas notified the Justice Department that he was unlikely to bring a wiretapping case against Maheu and the hapless private investigator who got caught. The case was legally weak, and in any event, not worth compromising the CIA.

All true. But Miller's explanation seems disingenuous. No matter how busy he was with the Freedom Riders and the summit, Kennedy must have been shocked to learn that the CIA had hired the mob for some "dirty business" against Castro. Giancana was enemy number one in RFK's new assault on the mob, and the attorney general was at that moment investigating the CIA's failures against Castro at the Bay of Pigs. Kennedy never hesitated to pick up the phone and reach way down the chain of command to learn more about a Justice Department case or a counterinsurgency operation. "Bob would talk to anyone," acknowledged Courtney Evans. It is simply inconceivable that he would not have wanted to dig deeper into a report of "dirty business" against Castro.

Unless, of course, he already knew about it. During the Church Committee hearings in 1975, Bissell testified that, while briefing Kennedy about Cuba operations during the Taylor Board inquiry in May 1961, he had told the attorney general that the CIA was using "underworld elements against the Castro regime." Bissell's testimony was dodgy and murky. He said he never came out and told Kennedy that the CIA hired Giancana to try to kill Castro. Pressed by a senator, Bissell surmised for a moment that from his "circumlocutious" remarks Kennedy must have inferred as much. But then, sensing perhaps that he had just crossed a fine and shadowy line, the former chief of covert operations backed off. He was just speculating, he said.

What did RFK really know? A better question might be, how much did he want to know? In his office, along with the busts of Churchill and Lincoln and the green beret, Kennedy kept a carved ivory statue of a blind monkey, inscribed at the base, "See No Evil." There were times, in that age of plausible deniability, when it was best not to see too much. Kennedy may have asked enough questions to know that the CIA-backed Mafia assassination plots against Castro had fizzled out by then, late May 1961; better, then, not to inquire too closely what went wrong.

When Kennedy finally did get around to asking about the Maheu wiretapping case, the timing raises more questions. On October 5, Justice Department records show, the attorney general inquired about the "status" of the wiretapping case against the CIA's cutout. On the same day, in another part of the Kennedy forest—a meeting of the Special Group on Cuba—the CIA was instructed to prepare a "contingency plan in connection with the possible removal of Castro from the Cuban scene." The Special Group chairman, General Taylor, instructed the CIA man transmitting the request that "the President's interest in the matter not be mentioned" to anyone else. It is an interesting coincidence that on the very same day that the attorney general—for the first time in four months—asked about a case that risked exposing CIA plotting against Castro, the administration requested a study on the likely effect of removing Castro—and further ordered that the president's interest in this subject be kept quiet. That October, the Kennedy brothers had just turned their attention to Cuba in a serious way for the first time since the collapse of the Bay of Pigs six months before. There can be little doubt that they discussed assassination as at least an option, however sordid. The clearest indication is a conversation that JFK had at about that time with *New York Times* reporter, Tad Szulc.

On November 8, Robert Kennedy summoned Szulc to lunch at his office in the Justice Department to talk about Cuba. The Spanish-speaking Szulc had walked the battlefield of the Bay of Pigs with Castro in June, and he had a good reporter's feel for Latin American politics. At the end of a general conversation about Castro, RFK, almost shyly, asked, "Would you mind seeing my brother?" The next day, Szulc was escorted into the Oval Office. After some general conversation about Cuba, the president abruptly asked, "What would you think if I ordered Castro to be assassinated?" The newsman, taken aback, said that killing Castro would be immoral and impractical; it would not change the Cuban system. According to Szulc, the president said, "I agree with you completely." Back home that night, making some notes about this remarkable exchange with the commander-in-chief, Szulc wrote, "JFK said he raised question because he was under terrific pressure from his advisers (think he said intelligence people, but not positive)." It is hard to know which "intelligence people" might have been badgering the president in November 1961. The CIA was on the defensive: Dulles was gone, and the once-mighty Bissell was a lame duck, on his way out. Interviewed in 1998, Szulc said, "Now, as I look back, I don't think he meant intelligence officials. I think he was talking about Bobby."

The meeting between Szulc and JFK was on November 9. Just five days before, RFK had told Bissell to "get off his ass" on Cuba. Wearily returning to his office, Bissell told his aide, Sam Halpern, that Kennedy wanted him to "get rid" of Castro. Any limits? asked Halpern. "No limits," said Bissell. On November 16, Bissell summoned William Harvey to his office. About nine months before, Bissell told Harvey, he had been instructed by "the White House" to set up an "executive action" capability, agency jargon for assassination. Using the code name ZR/RIFLE, Harvey had put a professional hit man on the agency payroll, but ZR/RIFLE had never been activated. Now, Bissell instructed Harvey to take over the CIA's Mafia connection and fold it into ZR/RIFLE.

Did President Kennedy or his brother explicitly order Bissell to revive the assassination plots against Castro? In an interview with the author in 1994, Bissell repeated what he had told the Church Committee, that he never discussed assassination with either Kennedy. Bissell used plausible deniability as a license to do pretty much whatever he wanted. A wink or a nod was authority enough. "They never told me *not* to," Bissell said, with an owlish smile. Being told to "get off his ass" was to Bissell what a formal "warning order" is in the military: not an order to launch an attack, but a signal to get ready to. Bissell wasn't telling Harvey to try to assassinate Castro, just telling him to be prepared, if the order came.

Harvey was in no rush to get the green light. He waited until April 1962 to approach Johnny Rosselli, the initial mob contact, about making another try against Castro. A few weeks later, he gave Rosselli some poison pills and left a U-Haul van, with the keys in it, full of weapons and bomb detonators in a parking lot in Miami. In the meantime, Harvey discussed the assassination plot with his new boss, Richard Helms. Neither man was enthusiastic, to say the least. Harvey regarded the Mafia plot as a "damn fool idea." Too many people knew about the failed 1961 attempt. Harvey, who liked to maintain tight operational control, eliminated Maheu and other cutouts and dealt directly with Rosselli (the mobster and the spy became friends; they would dine together, watched by FBI men sent by Hoover to shadow them). Harvey remained doubtful that anything would come of his mob ties. Helms was even more dubious. He considered the assassination plan to be "feeble," a "big zilch."

So why did Helms and Harvey go ahead and supply Rosselli and his henchmen with pills and guns? Interrogated by the Church Committee in 1975, both men squirmed and ducked. Helms is a particular puzzle. Unlike Bissell, who defied gravity, Helms was a careful climber. But incredibly, in hindsight, the covert operations chief did not even discuss the assassination plot with *his* boss, John McCone. Helms had trouble explaining why, except to say that he wanted to insulate his masters (more deniability) from such an "unsavory business." McCone was an outsider, a West Coast businessman recruited by the Kennedys, not an agency hand. Helms seems to have figured and half hoped that nothing would come of the Harvey-Rosselli connection, that if he said and did nothing, it would just whither away—as it eventually did in 1963.

Helms testified that he was continually pressured by RFK to "get rid" of Castro, but that the two men never discussed assassination. "You haven't lived until you've had Bobby Kennedy rampant on your back," Helms told the author in 1993. Harvey also testified that he never talked to Kennedy about killing Castro. Loathing Kennedy, resenting the attorney general's intrusion into spy work and his unwillingness to appreciate the difficulty of mounting covert actions against a police state, Harvey told the attorney general as little as possible. John McCone also testified that he knew nothing about Harvey's "executive action" machinations. One would think that Edward Lansdale, the chief of Mongoose, would have been "witting" to the plots, but he, too, testified that he knew nothing.

Journalists and historians have had a hard time believing that the Kennedys were not directly running an assassination program right out of the White House. They point to a meeting of the Special Group on August 10, 1962. At the meeting, Defense Secretary McNamara openly suggested that Mongoose consider the "liquidation of leaders." Lansdale put McNamara's suggestion on paper—and Harvey had a fit, furiously objecting that such things should never be openly discussed or written down. CIA director McCone grew red in the face and exclaimed that, as a practicing Catholic, he could be excommunicated for trafficking in murder. These furious protests are seen by some historians as a telling slipup, the moment when the administration's dark plots leached out on to the record and guilty officialdom scrambled to erase the stain. Actually, the incident tends to prove the opposite. If Bobby Kennedy was aggressively trying to kill Castro, he surely would have let Lansdale in on the secret. And if Lansdale was "witting" to the CIA's Mafia operation, he hardly would have written a memo about "liquidation of leaders." What the August 10 flap really demonstrates is that the second phase of the Castro assassination plots, the Harvey-Rosselli connection, was small, feckless, and closely held. The Kennedys may have discussed the idea of assassination as a weapon of last resort. But they did not know the particulars of the Harvey-Rosselli operation—or want to.

ONE HIGH PUBLIC OFFICIAL knew a great deal about the dalliance of these CIA officials with mobsters and wished to learn more. J. Edgar Hoover had been officially brought into the loop sometime after Robert Maheu, the CIA cutout to the mob, was caught in the ludicrous wiretapping foul-up risible even to the mob. (Told of the incident, Sam Giancana "laughed so hard he almost choked on his cigar," according to a CIA informant.) In all likelihood, J. Edgar Hoover had been closely tracking the assassination plots for months. He was looking for intelligence that could be put to good use, not against the enemies of the United States—the mob or Castro—but rather against Hoover's rivals for power, the CIA and the Kennedys. Hoover's role in the story of the CIA-Mafia assassination plots has to be understood in the context of the director's basic mode of operation—and the Kennedys' vulnerability to it. As always, Hoover's number one goal was not defeating communism or organized crime, but preserving his own power. Collecting the secrets of his foes, in and out of government, was the surest means of self-preservation. Throughout his tenure as attorney general, Robert Kennedy would receive missives detailing what Hoover knew (or had heard from informants of varying reliability) about the connections of organized crime, not only to the CIA, but to the president and to his father.

Hoover had been keeping a file on John F. Kennedy for years—ever since the FBI wiretapped Lieutenant (junior grade) Kennedy, a young naval intelligence officer in 1942, while he was romancing Inga Arvad, a woman suspected of spying for the Nazis. Kennedy's womanizing made him vulnerable to Hoover's snooping. Joe Kennedy's careful cultivation of Hoover maintained a veneer of good will, but the FBI director was always trawling. In February 1960, just as Senator Kennedy was beginning his presidential campaign, FBI informants spotted JFK cavorting with the "Rat Pack," Frank Sinatra's clique of sybarite entertainers, at the Sands Hotel in Las Vegas. "Show girls from all over town were running in and out of the Senator's suite," the informant reported. Sinatra had been ingratiating himself with actor Peter Lawford, Kennedy's brother-in-law. In addition to actors and their politician-in-laws, Ol' Blue Eyes liked the company of hoodlums; he found them raffish and exciting. The political implications of a Sinatra-Kennedy relationship were obvious to an anonymous FBI informant in a March 29, 1960, report to Hoover. The source told the G-men that he "would hate to see a pawn of the hoodlum element such as Sinatra have access to the White House." Sinatra may or may not have been a Mafia "pawn," but he kept bad company. The worst was Sam Giancana, the very same Mafia don who had patriotically agreed to help the CIA try to kill Castro. The Chicago gangster wore a sapphire pinkie ring given to him by Sinatra. Giancana claimed to "own" part of Sinatra, as well as several other famous nightclub entertainers. The connection between Sinatra and Giancana was of great interest to Hoover, especially since Sinatra—in this strangely small world—was a friend of the Kennedys.

Kennedy's close friends would later argue that Kennedy wasn't a big fan of Sinatra but that he had strung along the powerful entertainer out of family loyalty in order to help the acting career of his brother-in-law Lawford, who was married to sister Pat. Maybe so, but Kennedy was willing to overlook political risk to spend time with Sinatra. JFK liked not only the showgirls he shared, but also Sinatra's aura of hard-edged glamour. Amused and relaxed by Hollywood gossip, he was—like his father before him—drawn to the glitz and raciness of show business. So, curiously, was straightlaced Bobby Kennedy, though for slightly different reasons. In part RFK was pleasing his wife, Ethel, who liked parties and celebrity and wanted to have famous actors out to Hickory Hill. A family friend, Joan Braden, was excited but not really surprised to find Sinatra playing the piano and singing in the Robert Kennedys' living room in September 1960. With his choirboy's interest in sin, Bobby may also have been intrigued by the roguishness of the Rat Pack. He liked to visit Peter Lawford in Los Angeles, flirt with the ubiquitous starlets, and joke with Sinatra's playboy pals. As attorney general, Kennedy enjoyed introducing Rat Packers,

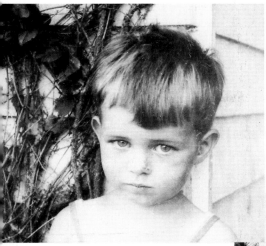

1

LEFT: The third son and seventh child, Robert did not receive the attention lavished on Joe Jr., Jack, and Kathleen. Joe Sr. called him the "runt" and Rose worried that he would become "puny" and "girlish." His sister Eunice said that Bobby would "never amount to anything." RFK recalled, "I was very awkward. I dropped things and fell down all the time . . . and I was pretty quiet. . . . I didn't mind being alone."

BELOW: His family hoped to toughen up Bobby with boxing lessons.

2

BELOW: As the ambassador to the Court of St. James, Joseph Kennedy represented the United States at the coronation of Pope Pius XII in March 1939. Robert, thirteen, is to the left of his mother, Rose. (Only Joe Jr. is missing from this family picture.) The most pious of the boys, Robert tried to please his mother by sending her "recommendations" for serving Mass.

3

G. Felici-Ro

4

ABOVE: The Kennedy family created a lively world of their own in Hyannis Port on Cape Cod. RFK (far left, at about age seven) struggled, sometimes recklessly, to keep up with family competition. Slow to learn to swim, he tried to hurry it up by plunging off a yawl into Nantucket Sound. His older brother Joe fished him out. "It showed either a lot of guts or no sense at all, depending on how you looked at it," said his brother Jack.

6

5

ABOVE: After RFK was sworn into the navy in December 1943, just after his eighteenth birthday, Jack wrote him from the Pacific, where he was a PT boat commander: "The sight of you up there, just as a boy, was really moving, particularly as a close examination showed you had my checked London coat on." RFK missed combat, serving in 1946 on a destroyer named after brother Joe, who died in the war.

RIGHT: Jack, Bobby, and little brother Ted at Hyannis right after the war.

RIGHT: RFK married Ethel Skakel in a society wedding in Greenwich, Connecticut, attended by 1,200 guests in June 1950. Sporty, joshing, and ebullient, Ethel fit in easily with the Kennedy clan. She had briefly considered becoming a nun, and her purity appealed to RFK, who scorned "loose women" to his friends. Housekeeping was not Ethel's forte, nor was thrift. But she was unstinting in her affection towards RFK. A moralist like her husband, Ethel believed, as she put it, in "goodies and baddies." To her RFK was perfect. Ethel gave RFK the unconditional love that he had never received from his own family. A classmate of RFK's at the University of Virginia Law School remarked that Ethel "looked at Bobby like she did at God. God did inexplicable things, but he was never wrong." The Kennedys bought their McLean, Virginia, estate, Hickory Hill, in 1956 and turned it into a vibrant center of parties and games for friends, guests, and their eleven children.

BELOW LEFT: Touch football with Ethel and Teddy in Acapulco in 1960.

BELOW RIGHT: Reading documents at the Justice Department as attorney general. RFK was a relentless self-improver. He listened to Shakespeare while shaving in the morning and carried books of poetry and Greek plays in his briefcase.

7

8

9

RIGHT: In 1953, RFK became an aide to Republican senator Joseph McCarthy of Wisconsin. The infamous red hunter was a family friend of the Kennedys (on dates, he discussed communism for a half hour, then "kissed very hard," recalled Kennedy's sister Jean). McCarthy was a bully, but RFK liked the way he provoked the East Coast establishment. Kennedy hated and quarreled with McCarthy's chief aide, Roy Cohn, who called RFK a "rich bitch."

LEFT: As chief counsel on the Senate Rackets Committee from 1957 to 1959, RFK said that Teamster boss Jimmy Hoffa embodied "absolute evilness." "You're sick!" Hoffa snarled at Kennedy when he appeared before the committee. Hoffa and Kennedy would lock eyes for several minutes at a time. "I used to love to bug the little bastard," said Hoffa.

BELOW: Family patriarch Joe Kennedy warned that RFK's investigations into labor racketeering could harm the presidential ambitions of Senator John F. Kennedy, who sat on the Rackets Committee.

TOP RIGHT: RFK played the tough guy managing JFK's 1960 presidential campaign, allowing JFK to seem above the fray.

CENTER RIGHT: RFK, who loved ice cream, takes a break from campaigning in West Virginia.

BELOW: President Kennedy appointed his brother to be attorney general at the insistence of Joe Kennedy Sr. RFK had his doubts, but he chose a superb staff and accomplished a great deal in the fields of civil rights and organized crime. He was blessed to have a secretary, Angie Novello (shown here outside RFK's office), who could tease him and take care of him. "It would be *extremely* helpful if the Attorney General of the United States . . . would notify his immediate staff of his whereabouts at all times," she chided in a memo. Kennedy scrawled back, "What if I'm lost. Love." RFK was not only hard to find, he was secretive, often not telling staffers what he was up to. The Kennedys "got it from the old man," said longtime aide Joe Dolan. RFK routinely used back channels on sensitive matters.

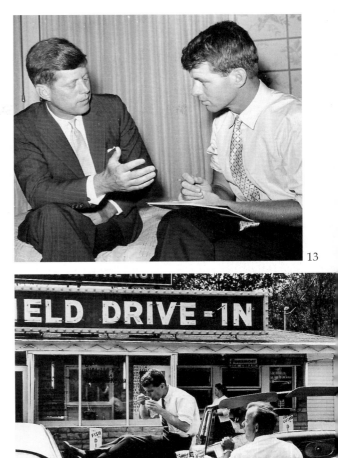

13

14

15

RIGHT: Kennedy worked nights and weekends at the Justice Department. Staffers sticking their heads into his office on a Saturday could suddenly find themselves on a plane to a crisis. Kennedy's own willingness to take on the hard jobs inspired great loyalty. His aides learned to put up with his quirks. Since Kennedy never carried cash, someone else was always picking up the bill. In church, a friend threw a dollar in the plate for RFK. "Don't you think I'd be more generous than that?" Kennedy inquired.

1

17

LEFT: President Kennedy communicated with his brother through a verbal shorthand of quips and cryptic asides.

BELOW: Strolling together towards the Rose Garden. Before JFK made his historic speech in June 1963 calling for a civil rights bill outlawing discrimination in public places, RFK urged the president to speak "in moral terms," recalled RFK's aide Burke Marshall. "Perhaps because we're brothers, we didn't make speeches at each other," RFK remembered. The president, he said, "made notes on the back of an envelope or something."

1

LEFT: RFK meets with White House press secretary Pierre Salinger (right), family adviser and brother-in-law Steve Smith (left), and political aide Larry O'Brien (far left).

BELOW: Jack and Bobby sailing with Ethel, Jackie, and John Jr. off Cape Cod. RFK sometimes played conciliator. Once, when Jack made a circus catch playing touch football and exclaimed, "Hey, Jackie, did you see that?," Jackie, reading, ignored him. Bobby implored her, "It would help if you could say something nice. It would mean a lot to him."

20

9

BELOW: RFK with the ExCom, the group of top advisers summoned by President Kennedy to meet during the thirteen days of the Cuban Missile Crisis in October 1962. "He sometimes wouldn't even sit at the cabinet table," recalled McGeorge Bundy, the president's national security adviser. "But it didn't make much difference," said Bundy, "because . . . wherever he sat was one of the most important places in the room."

21

LEFT: RFK comforts his children on the afternoon President Kennedy was shot. He was thinking about threats from the mob and the Cuban exile community. To his aide Ed Guthman he said, "I thought they'd get one of us. . . . I thought it would be me." Kennedy, who had been pushing hard to prosecute the Mafia, immediately used a back channel to try to learn whether the mob had assassinated his brother (he was told no), and that afternoon he personally called Cuban exiles working for the CIA and said, "One of your guys did it."

BELOW: Leaving the Capitol with Caroline, Jackie, and John Jr. after viewing the president lying in state. The night before, his friend Charles Spalding at the White House heard Kennedy cry out, "Why, God?"

RIGHT: RFK flanked by Jackie and Rose Kennedy at JFK's funeral. For months afterwards, RFK appeared wasted and gaunt. He tried gallows sarcasm. "Been to any good funerals lately?" he asked a friend. On winter nights he arose before dawn to drive around in his convertible, with the top down, sometimes to his brother's grave. Often, in the afternoon, he went to Jackie Kennedy's house in Georgetown to sit by the fire and talk about religion and philosophy. "All things are to be examined & called into question," RFK wrote in a note to himself.

24

25

26

ABOVE: RFK and Ethel at Hickory Hill in 1967 with nine of their eleven children. RFK welcomed the tumult that greeted him when he walked in the door at night. He was uneasy with newborns, seemingly fearful that he would drop one, but he loved to roughhouse as the children grew older. If a boy cried, Kennedy would hug him, but not in a coddling way. "Hush now," he'd say. "A Kennedy never cries."

LEFT: RFK huddles up with two of his boys for touch football. "The whole idea" of Hickory Hill "was to relax in a violent fashion," recalled a friend.

28

LEFT: RFK shows deceptively good form on the slopes. Speed over grace was usually his style. He sometimes dressed in old clothes, and a day of skiing was incomplete without a spectacular crash. On horseback, he rode flat out. Even tennis was a moral challenge. "He had a ferocious forehand—very straightforward—but no backhand at all. Too duplicitous," said George Plimpton.

27

BELOW: RFK on a rubber raft in white water in the Grand Canyon, June 1967. He later led a hike out of the canyon in 110-degree heat. As the climbers flagged, he stopped to recite the "band of brothers" speech from *Henry V.*

ABOVE: RFK became the first person to reach the summit of Mount Kennedy, named for his brother by the Canadian government, in March 1965. RFK, who was afraid of heights, told his guide that he had trained by running up and down the stairs at home, practicing crying, "Help!"

29

RIGHT: Senator Robert Kennedy visits hungry children in the Mississippi Delta in the spring of 1967. He was "ashen faced" when he walked into dinner at Hickory Hill, recalled his daughter Kathleen. To Amanda Burden, he said, "You don't know what I saw! I have done nothing in my life! Everything I have done was a waste! Everything I have done was worthless!"

BELOW: Kennedy may have been the last white politician to be idolized by blacks. "There was a strangeness that caused blacks to love him," said black militant Sonny Carson. "He was this younger brother full of pain."

BELOW: Lyndon Johnson described RFK as "a grandstanding runt," while RFK described LBJ as "an animal in many ways." LBJ was an effusive, long-winded arm-grabber, while RFK was terse and recoiled at clutchers and touchers. Both had sympathy for the underdog and a keen sense of deal-making, and they might have been wary allies under different circumstances, but LBJ saw RFK as a rival and RFK saw LBJ as a usurper.

LEFT: Fred Dutton with RFK in Indiana. Dutton went everywhere with Kennedy in the spring of 1968. Dutton and other top advisers worried that Kennedy's crowds were too hot and emotional, that Kennedy's campaign looked like a "traveling riot" to voters who were frightened by social unrest in that tumultuous year. Dutton tried to tone down the candidate, making RFK's speeches more measured, even dull, and staying away from black or poor areas that were particularly clamorous. "Bob understood this, rationally, when he was sitting in a hotel room," recalled Dutton. But Kennedy couldn't help himself. "He wanted big crowds, and he was mad if he didn't get them." Kennedy liked to challenge audiences. When a group of medical students in Indiana wanted to know who would pay for Kennedy's national health insurance plan, RFK answered, "You will."

BELOW AND OPPOSITE: RFK is overwhelmed by the crowd in California before the June primary. At times, he was pulled from the car. His cufflinks were routinely torn from his shirt. He chipped a tooth and had a shoe stolen—twice.

33

34

35

36

37

38

ABOVE: RFK with farmworkers'
leader Cesar Chavez in March 1968
at the end of Chavez's twenty-five-
day hunger strike. After breaking
bread with him, Kennedy climbed on
the roof of his car and cried, with his
thick Boston accent, "Viva la
huelga [Long live the strike]."
Kennedy made up his mind to run
for president that day.

RIGHT: Black children often ran
alongside Kennedy's car when his
motorcade passed though the inner
city. "Kennedy needed children as
much as they needed him," observed
journalist Mary McGrory.

BELOW: Kennedy liked to campaign
with his dog Freckles.

39

LEFT: Kennedy existed on about four hours of sleep a night. He took massive vitamin B$_{12}$ shots. At forty-two, he "did not look young," said campaign aide John Bartlow Martin. "He aged more than he should have since his brother's death." His body was still hard from exercise, but varicose veins protruded from his legs. At dinner, Ethel counted out the pills, about a dozen in all, mostly vitamins and medication for his damaged voice. Unable to sleep some nights, he would come down to the bar to talk to the photographers, to ask them what they saw in the crowds. In low moments, he compared himself unfavorably to President Kennedy. After losing an audience one night in South Dakota with a flat, rambling speech, he told George McGovern, "I just am not Jack."

BELOW: RFK's mood, often irascible, improved when Ethel came on the campaign plane.

43

RFK in Los Angeles a few days before he was shot. "He always looked . . . so alone, so vulnerable, so fragile," said John Bartlow Martin.

who were often under FBI surveillance because of their gangster friends, to Courtney Evans, the FBI agent who was Hoover's official liaison to the attorney general. On a trip to visit the FBI field office in L.A., Kennedy brought Evans out to cocktails at Lawford's Malibu beach house. "You ought to meet this guy!" he said, introducing Evans to actor and comedian Dean Martin. "Jesus, no," said Martin. "I have enough trouble with the feds."

In public, the Kennedys were careful to keep some distance from Sinatra. The president was not to be photographed at play with the singer. When Sinatra visited Hyannis Port in August 1961, reporters were instructed that he was a guest of Peter Lawford and Teddy Kennedy, not of the president or the attorney general. RFK was nervous that the show biz idol might somehow dishonor his brother. Sinatra had sung for the president-elect at a preinaugural gala in January, but Bobby had muttered in a low voice to Red Fay that he hoped Sinatra would "live up" to the respectability the Kennedys had bestowed on him. (When Fay tried to relate that anecdote in his White House memoir, *The Pleasure of His Company*, Bobby ordered it deleted from the manuscript.)

Bobby never forgot that reporters and FBI agents were watching. During his time as attorney general, he tried not to fatten Hoover's secret files. But he could not have anticipated the serendipity that allowed Hoover to link Sinatra, Giancana, and the president with a woman who, at one time or another, was the lover of all three. RFK's role of brother's keeper was severely tested by the Judith Campbell Exner story. The tale is a twisted one, a weave of several different plot threads that have to be untangled to appreciate the subtle pressures at work on Bobby Kennedy in the fall, winter, and spring of 1961–62. The story begins with the Castro assassination plots and Hoover's discovery of the part played by Sam Giancana.

The relative ease with which Hoover learned of the Mafia plots underscores the essential riskiness of such operations. In September 1960 (two months before John Kennedy was elected president) the FBI learned from an informant that Giancana was bragging to friends that Castro would soon be dead, poisoned by an assassin. The mob boss made no mention of his CIA relationship, which was formalized at a meeting with the agency cutout, Robert Maheu, at Miami's Fontainebleau Hotel earlier that month. But Hoover was able to connect the dots in May, when Sheffield Edwards of the CIA acknowledged to FBI agents investigating the Maheu wiretapping case that the agency had hired Giancana for some "dirty business" in Cuba. Hoover promptly sent Robert Kennedy a memo—the May 22 wake-up call that provoked Kennedy to call for a "vigorous" follow-up—putting the attorney general on notice that Hoover knew about the mobster–spy agency connection and that he was watching closely.

Hoover used the Maheu wiretap case as an excuse to crowd Giancana and learn more about the gangster's relationships in high places. In July, Hoover's men confronted Giancana face-to-face. In the lounge of the Phoenix airport, several FBI agents approached the mobster, who was traveling with his girlfriend, singer Phyllis McGuire, and began asking questions about the Maheu wiretap. Giancana exploded at the G-men. "Why aren't you investigating the communists?" he demanded. "I love this country and I would sacrifice my life for it. I proved this not long ago," he declared, hinting about his role in the anti-Castro plot. Giancana told the agents to report his patriotic declaration back to their "super boss" and their "super super boss." Who? the agents asked. "I mean the Kennedys. I know all about the Kennedys and Phyllis knows a lot more about the Kennedys, and one of these days we are going to tell all!"

Giancana was angry at the FBI because he had been led to believe that he would be given a free pass. He had hoped that his service to the CIA would buy him some protection (Giancana had refused the CIA's offer of a $150,000 cash retainer; he and Rosselli told Maheu, the CIA cutout, that they were motivated by love of country). Giancana also believed that he would be insulated by the friends-of-his-friend—by Sinatra's palship with the president. Incredibly, Giancana believed that Frank Sinatra had given him an "in" with the Kennedy family. The singer had foolishly bragged that he could persuade the attorney general to go easy on his friends in the underworld.

Both Sinatra and Giancana were disappointed. At Kennedy's request, Giancana was a target of constant FBI surveillance and tax and criminal investigations. FBI files reflect incessant pressure from the attorney general to probe Giancana for federal crimes. Ever since their 1959 confrontation in the Rackets Committee hearing ("I thought only little girls giggled, Mr. Giancana"), Kennedy had regarded Giancana as the devil in a sharkskin suit. FBI agents recalled that on his visits to the bureau's field office in Chicago, the attorney general would barrage them with questions about the gangster who had achieved Capone's stature in the underworld. With "the face of a gargoyle and the personality of a viper," Giancana personified evil to RFK, who as ever saw his job in personal and moral terms. The mobster "was violent, crazy, unstable as an animal. He'd kill people for kicks. He wasn't like the Mafia leaders in New York," said William Hundley, Kennedy's chief of the organized crime section. Kennedy was determined to behead the Mafia's leadership. He was not about to lighten up on Giancana to please Frank Sinatra.

Kennedy was well aware that Hoover was looking over his shoulder (and, he suspected, listening to his phone calls). As early as April 1961, Kennedy demonstrated to the FBI director that he was not Sinatra's patsy. In a meeting at which both sides were undoubtedly aware of the larger implications, Hoover reported to the attorney general that Giancana's top lieutenant was trying to secure a liquor license for his Las Vegas restaurant. Hoover recounted that Giancana's friend Frank Sinatra had interceded with the local authorities to make sure that Giancana's henchman got the license. Kennedy asked, couldn't something be done about this? Probably not, replied Hoover; the Las Vegas authorities were "venal." Kennedy made a point of registering his disapproval and requesting that Hoover instruct his Las Vegas field office that the attorney general personally requested a full investigation. The message was clear: no favors for Sinatra.

In time, it dawned on Giancana as well that Sinatra's boasting was empty, that he could not "deliver" the Kennedys. Furious, the Mafia don cried betrayal. In early December 1961, an FBI electronic eavesdropping device picked up a conversation between Giancana and another one of his sidekicks, Johnny Formosa, discussing the singer's failure to win protection from the Justice Department. The exchange was very revealing, not only because it graphically demonstrated Giancana's rage over the "heat" he was feeling from the feds, but because there are several provocative allusions to Joseph Kennedy Sr., as well as braggadocio that organized crime helped elect JFK in 1960.

In the bugged conversation, Formosa recounted to Giancana that he had just been to visit Sinatra at his home in Palm Springs. Formosa had quizzed Sinatra: had he made any progress interceding with the Kennedys on behalf of Giancana? Sinatra said he had tried to persuade the attorney general to back off. "I took Sam's [Giancana's] name and wrote it down and told Bobby Kennedy, 'This is my buddy, this is what I want you to think, Bob.' " But "Bob" wouldn't listen. Formosa asked if Sinatra had tried to work on the sons through their father. Sinatra was in contact with Joe Sr.—indeed, Formosa reported, the elder Kennedy had called Sinatra on the phone three times during the course of his short visit to the entertainer's Palm Springs home. But no, Sinatra complained, Jack and Bobby were not "faithful" to Joe Sr.

Giancana listened to Formosa's report with rising fury. He aimed his scorn at both Sinatra ("One minute he says he talked to Robert and the next minute he says he hasn't talked to him. So, he never did talk to him. It's a lot of shit") and the Kennedys. As FBI agents monitored the bugged conversation, Giancana vowed not to give "one penny" towards JFK's 1964 reelection campaign. The Chicago don would see to it that the president was denied Illinois. "That [obscene] better not think of taking this [obscene] state," Giancana ranted. The mob boss claimed that he was not getting his "money's worth" out of Kennedy. "If I got a speeding ticket," Giancana spewed, "none of those [obscene] would know me." The mobster went on to bitterly complain that he was being harassed by the FBI. "I was on the road with that broad [Phyllis McGuire]. There must have been up there at least twenty guys. They were next door, upstairs, downstairs, surrounded all the way around. Get in the car somebody picks you up. I lose the tail, boom, I get picked up someplace else. Four or five cars with intercoms, back and forth, back and forth." Formosa asked, "This was in Europe, right?" Giancana exclaimed, "Right here! In Russia, Chicago, New York and Phoenix!"

The FBI's Chicago office sent a cable to Hoover reciting Formosa's account of his meeting with Sinatra and Giancana's ravings. A Hoover aide wrote on the bottom, "Memo to AG being prepared." Hoover scrawled next to that: "& promptly." It is easy to understand why Hoover would be eager to share such details with Robert Kennedy. The intelligence demonstrated that the FBI had Giancana, literally, surrounded. And while RFK came off as an upright and unswayable chief law enforcement officer, there was the strong implication that his brother's election had been fixed and that the father was still currying favor with Sinatra, conceivably as an entree to Giancana. One wonders about those three phone calls from Joe Sr. to Sinatra. What were the two men discussing? No solid evidence has ever emerged to prove either that Joseph P. Kennedy was "mobbed up" or that Giancana delivered Illinois to JFK as his part of a bargain. It is conceivable, as various less-than-reliable sources have reported, that the elder Kennedy met at one time or another with members of the so-called Chicago Outfit and discussed support for JFK's presidential effort in 1960. Over the years, Joe Kennedy's shadowy business practices have been the source of much rumor and little proof. A 1964 summary of FBI files, declassified in 1998, indicated that "numerous sources" reported that "prior to the last [1960] presidential election," Joseph P. Kennedy "had been visited by many gangsters (not identified) who had gambling interests." The summary referred vaguely to a "deal" that gave Sinatra and various Rat Packers interests in the Cal-Neva Lodge, "a lucrative gambling establishment" near Lake Tahoe. But the report does not make clear what role Joe Kennedy played in this "deal"; it simply states that JPK was staying in the hotel at the time. This is typical of raw FBI intelligence files—intriguing, but inconclusive and fodder for smears. Nothing more solid has so far surfaced in government files.

Hoover reported the essence of Giancana's bluster, including the reference to Joseph Kennedy Sr. and Giancana's alleged role in the 1960 election, in a memo to the attorney general on December 11 ("this is being furnished for your personal information"). Robert Kennedy's reaction has gone unrecorded. Nor is it known if RFK spoke to his father. If he did, it was one of their last conversations: a week later, on December 19, Joseph Kennedy Sr. suffered a massive and debilitating stroke.

FOR RFK, THE SHOCK of his father's stroke was severe. Joseph Kennedy had seemed perfectly fit, cheerfully waving goodbye to the president just that morning as JFK left Palm Beach after a weekend trip. RFK was overwhelmed with his multiple burdens, but he dropped them immediately to fly to his father's side. Any narrative of the complex dance between the attorney general, the mob, and J. Edgar Hoover must pause to consider the incapacitation of such an important, if mysterious, player in the story and touch on the larger implications for RFK's life.

The circumstances surrounding his stroke, like so much about Joseph Kennedy, remain somewhat murky. Feeling ill on the golf course on the morning of December 19, the patriarch managed to struggle home to bed, and apparently discouraged a call for the doctors. Rose Kennedy was so unconcerned about his condition that she went off to her own golf game. But the elder Kennedy slipped into a coma and an ambulance rushed him to the hospital around 2 p.m. RFK was in his office at the Justice Department when the call came that his father was seriously ill. The attorney general immediately called the president, and the two brothers flew down to Palm Beach on Air Force One later that afternoon.

Joseph Kennedy was "one breath away" from death when his sons arrived, according to family friend Lem Billings. "The doctors came to the family and said, 'Look, this strong, virile man is going to be imprisoned in a body that won't work even if it recovers.' It was an opportunity to pull the plug. But Bobby said no, let him fight for his life." His father lived, but the doctors' warnings were borne out. At seventy-three, Joseph Kennedy was left essentially speechless. All he could clearly say was "No," which he repeated angrily, "No, no, no, no."

RFK was losing a central figure in his life, however ambivalent his feelings about him might be. True, he had defied his father, but he had never stopped seeking his attention. Robert Kennedy may have forged ahead with the Rackets Committee investigation over Joe Sr.'s protests, yet throughout the hearings he habitually called his father on the telephone for advice and, one suspects, approval. For his part, the father had learned to restrain his impulse to direct the lives of his sons. JFK's friend Chuck Spalding recalled Joe Kennedy waiting anxiously by the phone for a call from the White House. "It was really touching if you knew Mr. Kennedy, who was a terribly aggressive individual, the way he would hold himself in check," said Spalding. Yet both Kennedys had continued to call their father and seek his counsel.

The emotional pull remained strong even after Joe Kennedy's stroke. RFK's administrative aide, Jim Symington, remembered driving to the hospital with the attorney general to visit his father. Kennedy was still and silent and on the verge of tears. What was he thinking? Kennedy's innermost thoughts about his father remain one of the unknowns in his life. If he confided his true feelings to anyone, discretion has kept them private. We are left to wonder about many things, but most immediately what, if anything, RFK might have said to his father about his relations with Sinatra—and Sinatra's friends—and the fact that the FBI was reporting on them. The timing of Joe Kennedy's stroke is curious, coming so soon after J. Edgar Hoover put RFK on notice that his father was keeping bad company, and that the FBI was watching. The coincidence may be mere happenstance; no evidence has been found to suggest otherwise. Still, the suspicion remains that RFK did pass on word of Hoover's interest to his father, and that Joseph Kennedy was badly jolted by the news and its possible ramifications.

WHATEVER THE INTERACTION between father and son, nothing changed in the attorney general's single-minded pursuit of Giancana and his cohort. The mobsters continued to squeal that they had been double-crossed by the Kennedys. On February 2, the FBI's bug in Giancana's "headquarters"—the Armory Lounge in Chicago (which the agents had named "Mo," after Momo, Giancana's first name)—recorded the don in a virtual state of surrender. He was despairing with John D'Arco, the mob-owned alderman of the First Ward. "Tell everyone that everything is off. This is it because of the G," cried Giancana; the pressure from the "G"—the federal government—had disrupted the mob's bookmaking, extortion, and loan-sharking operations. D'Arco, who was moaning "We are through, there's no place to go" over the sound of the jukebox, recounted to Giancana that one of his cronies had angrily told his FBI interrogators that "President Kennedy can thank the Italian ward politician for delivering the Illinois vote . . . and the thanks they get is investigation of Italians."

These bleats should have been gratifying to the FBI director. But cracking the mob was Robert Kennedy's priority, not Hoover's. Hoover was paranoid as ever that Kennedy was about to fire him. In December, at about the same time the FBI was overhearing Giancana rant about Sinatra, Hoover's spies reported to him that RFK was thinking of ousting Hoover and replacing him with the State Department's director of security. On January 6, columnist Drew Pearson predicted on a radio broadcast that Hoover would be "eased out if there is not too much of a furor." The report was mostly conjecture. Despite RFK's unhappiness with Hoover, the Kennedys weren't quite ready to overthrow him, and indeed sought to signal reassurances. On January 11, before a group of congressmen, President Kennedy praised the FBI for its "coordinated and hard-hitting effort." On January 13, JFK sent word through Courtney Evans that he "desired to speak with Mr. Hoover," granting the director his first White House audience in a year. But Hoover wasn't taking any chances. He needed an insurance policy. The meandering Maheu wiretap investigation, which, thanks to Hoover's persistence, was still alive in February 1962, gave him one.

Even though the U.S. attorney in Las Vegas had signaled back in August that the Maheu case was too weak to prosecute, Hoover had forged ahead, sending his agents out to investigate the mobsters who were working for the CIA. Reviewing the phone records of Johnny Rosselli, the gumshoes came across a woman named Judith Campbell. Tracing *her* phone calls led them first to Frank Sinatra—and then to Evelyn Lincoln, the personal secretary of the president of the United States. Campbell placed two calls to the White House, on November 7 and November 15, 1961. A background check revealed that Campbell, a divorcée, had worked in public relations for comedian Jerry Lewis in Hollywood and now described herself as a "freelance artist." Interviewed by the FBI in early February, she was reluctant to talk, but she revealed another surprising "association" with a powerful man: Sam Giancana.

For Hoover, this was too good to be true. He prepared two memoranda, dated February 27. One went to the president's appointments secretary—and RFK's old football friend—Kenneth O'Donnell. "My Dear Mr. O'Donnell," it began, "I thought you would be interested in learning of the following information. . . ." The letter informed the president's aide of the telephone calls from Judith Campbell to Mrs. Lincoln. The letter added, "Information has been developed that Campbell has been in contact with Sam Giancana, a prominent Chicago underworld figure." The other memorandum, stating essentially the same information, went to the attorney general.

At the time, Robert Kennedy was on his way back from a three-week around-the-world tour. He had met with heads of state in Asia and Europe and spoken to students in Japan. In Djakarta, reporters saw him engrossed in a copy of the latest James Bond novel, *Diamonds Are Forever*. In Rome, the pope gave him rosaries for his children, and Ethel showed off for cheering reporters by riding a motor scooter around a traffic circle, until she crashed into a parked car, bruising her leg. In Paris, a friendly newspaper columnist warned him that the Italian press, with its looser standards, might print a scurrilous story that President Kennedy had concealed a secret first marriage.

Robert Kennedy was accustomed to such gossip by now. Hoover continued to send him reports, written in flat bureaucratic prose, about his brother's sexual indiscretions, as well as some implausible rumors about RFK's. He was generally dismissive. When one of Hoover's informants reported that the president had been secretly married to a girl in Palm Beach, Kennedy told an aide, "Tell him that was one of Joe's girls." When another of the director's numerous and unreliable sources reported that the attorney general was having an affair with a woman in El Paso, Kennedy instructed the aide, "Tell him I've never been to El Paso." With his own men, RFK's approach was to shrug or make sarcastic fun.* He and Kenny O'Donnell were particularly mordant together. They told and retold an amusing anecdote about the unfortunate ambassador who had been caught with his pants down jumping out a lady's bedroom window. Hoover wanted to know what the White House planned to do about it. O'Donnell answered, "Hire faster ambassadors." For the most part, Hoover's implied threats of blackmail were not as dangerous as they might have been in a later, more prurient and scandal-obsessed age. In 1961, newsmen were often entertained by tales about the sexual escapades of politicians, but they did not publish them.

The memo about Judith Campbell that landed on Robert Kennedy's desk on February 27 was on a different order of magnitude. Reporters who might laugh off JFK's persistent skirt chasing would react less benignly to the news that the president was sleeping with the girlfriend of a mobster who was on the FBI's "Top Hoodlum" list. Judith Campbell was a true threat to Robert Kennedy's war on organized crime and to his brother's presidency. The kind of woman found in hotel lobbies frequented by famous entertainers, she had been a sometime girlfriend of Frank Sinatra's as well as Johnny Rosselli's. On February 7, 1960, Sinatra, eager to share a favor with a friend, had introduced her to Senator John F. Kennedy at the Sands Hotel in Las Vegas, where the Rat Pack was staying while filming a movie. According to FBI reports, Las Vegas police bugged the romantic interlude between the senator and the self-described "freelance artist." The FBI discovered Campbell's two calls to JFK in November 1961, then two more, then a call on February 14. White House phone logs would eventually show that Campbell placed some seventy phone calls to the

---

* In a 1964 oral history, RFK was asked about Hoover's file-keeping by *New York Times* reporter Anthony Lewis. Kennedy answered with careful nonchalance: "I suppose every month or so he'd send somebody around to give information on somebody I knew or a member of my family or allegations in connection with myself. So that it would be clear—whether it was right or wrong—that he was on top of all these things and received all this information. He would do this also, I think, to see what my reaction to it would be. . . ." Lewis: "You think he is dangerous?" RFK: "Yes. But it was a danger that we could control. . . ."

White House over a two-year period (many of these, it should be noted, were not returned). Campbell, remarried as Judith Exner, would eventually—and not believably—claim that she had served as a courier between the president and Giancana, carrying cash and messages about assassination plots. But those lurid tales would come later. In the winter of 1961, the FBI had heard only from a questionable informant that Campbell was the woman who was "shacking up with John Kennedy in the East."

The identity of that informant, Fred Otash, was further grist for Hoover's gossip mill—and another warning signal to the attorney general that the latest FBI reports could not be just laughed off. Otash was a Los Angeles detective who had been approached by one of Jimmy Hoffa's sidekicks, a man described by the FBI as a "notorious wiretapper." The Hoffa sleuths were looking for prostitutes who had slept with members of the Kennedy family. The attorney general was duly notified by the FBI that Hoffa was hoping to use the president's womanizing to "bury the Kennedys." RFK had received all sorts of threats from Hoffa, including death threats, but this one, delivered by the prying Hoover, had to be taken seriously. The attorney general moved to contain the damage, to cut off the Rat Pack and end his brother's relationship with Judith Campbell.

Shortly after he returned to Washington at the end of February, RFK summoned Joe Dolan, a top Justice Department aide whose discretion he valued, and handed him a brown folder. Inside was a summary of the Maheu wiretapping case and a list of the known phone calls from Judith Campbell to the president's secretary, Evelyn Lincoln. "Tell me what you think of this," said RFK matter-of-factly. Dolan went back to his office for an hour and read the folder. He quickly understood that the president had taken a mistress of unsavory provenance and that further investigation into the Maheu wiretap risked exposing a parade of horribles. When he returned to Kennedy's office, Dolan, in the studied low-key manner of Kennedy lieutenants, said, "Mrs. Lincoln shouldn't take calls like that." Expressionless, Kennedy inquired: "Well, what do you think?" Dolan replied, "I think I'll write Mrs. Lincoln a little memo." Kennedy nodded. "Do it today," he ordered. (Mrs. Lincoln's reply was, "Joe, I'm shocked.")

Dolan later wondered about RFK's indirection. "He didn't have the guts to tell his brother. He wanted me to do it," Dolan recalled. After RFK was elected to the Senate in 1964, he made Dolan his administrative assistant. Dolan learned that although RFK was famously fearless about delivering bad news, he sometimes preferred to have others (usually Dolan) handle the chores if a family member or close friend was on the receiving end. Kennedy was blunt with his brother and his brother-in-law on the subject of Frank Sinatra, however. The president was scheduled to stay with Sinatra in Palm Springs at the end of March. In early March, the Palm Springs Police Department was notified that JFK would be staying with a different local celebrity—Bing Crosby—instead. Furious and humiliated, Sinatra dispatched the pliant Peter Lawford to plead with the attorney general. RFK coldly turned him away. RFK called Sinatra on the phone and told the singer, "He [President Kennedy] just can't do it." Sitting in the attorney general's office at the time was *Saturday Evening Post* reporter Peter Maas, who had become a close family friend and a privileged insider. Maas could tell that Sinatra was yelling imprecations at the other end of the line. RFK listened impassively. The FBI had provided Kennedy with a report on Sinatra's mob ties that included a warning that the entertainer might be brazen enough to invite Giancana as a houseguest on the same night as President Kennedy.

Armed with the FBI report, RFK told the president that his playtime with the Rat Pack was over. "Johnny," said RFK, addressing his brother (usually "Mr. President") with an affectionate diminutive reserved for private moments, "you can't associate with this guy." In Palm Springs, Sinatra had built a concrete landing pad to accommodate visits by the president's helicopter. In a rage, the singing star seized a sledgehammer and went out and began smashing the concrete platform.

Sinatra was gone, but Hoover remained. As a gesture of appeasement, RFK granted the FBI director a rare private lunch with the president on March 22. The president's appointment calendar shows a last-minute appointment with the attorney general squeezed in just before Hoover arrived for lunch. No record survives of what was said between the FBI director and the president. Hoover brought with him a briefing paper detailing Campbell's calls. It is likely that Hoover, who did not like confrontations, was blandly bureaucratic—the ever-dutiful servant—and that the president hid his anger (and apprehension) behind a cool demeanor. When he left, JFK told Kenny O'Donnell, "Get rid of that bastard. He's the biggest bore." But as the president understood, now better than ever, Hoover was going to be as hard to "get rid of" as Castro.

Hoover was moving, after a period of retreat, to consolidate his power. He advanced on several fronts, including a new one—an assault on the dignity and reputation of Martin Lurther King. In December, the top G-man had been galled by RFK's offhand comment to a British journalist that the Communist Party in America "couldn't be more feeble and less of a threat, and besides its membership consists largely of FBI agents." Hoover devoted a good deal of the bureau's budget to the communist threat: the FBI had 1,500 informants within the Communist Party on its payroll and roughly ten times as many agents chasing spies as gangsters, a ratio RFK was admirably trying to reverse. Hoover was far more comfortable attacking communism—no matter how chimerical—than putting his agents at risk in the murky world of organized crime, or alienating the bureau's allies in police departments in the South by enforcing the civil rights of black men. He needed a way to make communism at home appear menacing again. In early January 1962, he found one.

Stanley Levison, who acted as a financial adviser and ghostwriter for Martin Luther King, had once been a follower of the Communist Party. He had broken away in 1955, but no matter; to Hoover, once a communist, always a communist. On January 8—interestingly, two days after columnist Drew Pearson predicted that RFK was trying to "ease out" Hoover—the director sent a memo to RFK warning of Levison's subversive influence. Kennedy does not appear to have replied. RFK's deputy, Byron White, asked to see Levison's FBI file. Too secret, responded the bureau; the FBI's source was too vital to risk any exposure. By invoking "national security," Hoover was able to conceal the fact that his information was more than five years old. But to learn more, the bureau wanted to wiretap Levison's office.

RFK acquiesced and signed off on a wiretap. Hoover may have overstated the threat of the American Communist Party, but to the Kennedys—as well as to most Americans in 1962—communist subversion, directed by the Kremlin, remained a genuine threat. Kennedy's willingness to tap Levison was in this sense unremarkable, consistent with the national security obsessions of the time. Still, it is likely that other considerations weighed on the attorney general. Hoover asked for the authority less than a week after Robert Kennedy returned home from Europe and his around-the-world trip. The director's timing was fortuitous—and probably not a coincidence. RFK had just received Hoover's ominous memo about Judith Campbell's phone calls to the White House. If he ever had any reservations about authorizing Hoover's request for a wiretap on Martin Luther King's most valued friend and adviser, the image of Judy Campbell, hovering over Hoover's shoulder like Banquo's ghost, probably banished them. Kennedy lent his signature—and a long and dirty campaign commenced to smear the leader of the American civil rights movement.

Hoover was difficult to control, in part because Kennedy couldn't very well do his job without the FBI. No task was too petty to become a battleground between bureaucratic rivals. On April 12, the attorney general complained that the television set in his office had poor reception. Couldn't the FBI technicians do something about it? No, responded Hoover when one of his assistants passed along the attorney general's request. "I don't like getting into this," Hoover scrawled on the memo. "If the set breaks down, henceforth the FBI will be completely to blame. . . ." That same morning, at about 3 a.m., Hoover's agents had added to Kennedy's problems. The Kennedy administration was locked in a test of wills with the chief executives of the nation's steel companies over a price hike that President Kennedy considered unconscionable and unpatriotic. With his father's distrust of businessmen, JFK could not understand how Big Steel could be jerking up prices at a time the president was calling for Cold War sacrifice. As usual, the president had employed his brother to play the heavy: the attorney general had ordered an immediate price-fixing investigation, bullying steel executives with subpoenas and threats to investigate their expense accounts. Bobby Kennedy's reputation for "ruthlessness" was greatly aggravated by the steel crisis, but Kennedy had Hoover partly to blame. Seeing an opportunity to embarrass the attorney general by taking his orders a little too literally, Hoover had ordered his gumshoes to call the steel executives at home in the middle of the night. With particular malice aforethought, he sent FBI agents out to awaken newspaper reporters just before dawn, demanding to see their notes about some comments made by the head of one of the steel companies. The "knock-on-the-door" was a public relations disaster for RFK—the press cried about "Gestapo police state tactics" and blamed Kennedy, not Hoover.

The fencing between Hoover and RFK finally came to a head over Hoover's unwillingness to let go of the Maheu wiretap investigation—with its deep potential for embarrassing the CIA and the risk that it might raise questions about the Kennedys' role in the Castro assassination plots. All winter and into April, the memos had flown back and forth between FBI, CIA, and Justice Department officials. Although the Las Vegas U.S. attorney had indicated back in August that he would not prosecute the case, Hoover wanted to force the issue. He demanded, through a drip-drip of memoranda, that the CIA go on record invoking national security, and that the Justice Department—the attorney general himself—formally decline to prosecute. As always, Hoover wanted to make a record that might, one day down the road, prove useful.

Kennedy's precise feelings about Hoover's gamesmanship on the Maheu case are unknown. Interviewed in 1998, Jack Miller, the chief of the criminal division whose name is on several of the memos that rattled back and forth between the bureau, the agency, and the department, could not recall ever discussing the matter with the attorney general. This seems hard to believe, though Kennedy was extremely careful to compartmentalize information and Miller, too, was cagey about not wanting to know too much. But the record does finally show what Kennedy did, which was to make his own record.

On May 7, 1962—at his request—Kennedy was formally briefed by the CIA on the assassination plot against Fidel Castro. At four o'clock that afternoon, Sheffield Edwards, the CIA's security chief who had recruited Maheu as a cutout and handled the initial attempt to poison Castro in the winter of 1961, came to the attorney general's office, along with CIA counsel Lawrence Houston. Edwards later testified that he briefed RFK "all the way." Actually, he briefed him halfway. The CIA man told Kennedy about offering the mob a $150,000 contract to dispose of the Cuban dictator, and said the operation had failed and been terminated after the collapse of the invasion at the Bay of Pigs. The unwitting Edwards did not, however, inform Kennedy that the Mafia channel had been revived only several weeks earlier by William Harvey (indeed, Harvey was handing over poison pills to Johnny Rosselli at just about the moment Edwards—himself cut out of the loop—was standing in the attorney general's office).

Kennedy made no comment about the assassination operation. But he was obviously angry at the CIA. "If you have seen Mr. Kennedy's eyes get steely and his jaw set and his voice get low and precise, you get a definite impression of unhappiness," Larry Houston later testified. Kennedy told his visitors from the CIA, "I trust that if you ever try to do business with organized crime again—with gangsters—you will let the attorney general know."

Two days later, Kennedy paid a call on J. Edgar Hoover. Only Hoover's record of the meeting survives, but it must have been a painful moment for Kennedy. Even Hoover's bland recitation of the facts cannot hide his feelings of triumph and pleasure at Kennedy's discomfort. The director's memo to the record began:

> The Attorney General told me he wanted to advise me of a situation in the Giancana case which had considerably disturbed him. . . .

Kennedy related the dreary facts: that the CIA had approached Giancana with a $150,000 contract to kill Castro; that the operation had failed; that the agency cutout, Maheu, had been caught in a ludicrous attempt to help Giancana catch his girlfriend cheating on him by bugging the other man. Hoover was shocked:

> I expressed astonishment at this in view of the bad reputation of Maheu [Hoover considered the ex-FBI man to be an apostate] and the horrible judgment in using a man of Giancana's background for such a project. The Attorney General shared the same views.

Kennedy told Hoover that he had "issued orders to CIA to never again in the future take such steps without first checking with the Department of Justice." All very well, but now the damage had been done. With his usual unctuousness, Hoover rubbed in the larger ramifications:

> I told the Attorney General that this was a most unfortunate development. I stated as he well knew the "gutter gossip" was that the reason nothing had been done against Giancana was because of Giancana's close friendship with Frank Sinatra, who in turn, claimed to be quite close to the Kennedy family. The Attorney General stated he realized this. . . .

Prosecuting Giancana would now be difficult, Kennedy conceded. As Hoover put it in his memorandum to the record, "Giancana could immediately bring out the fact that the United States Government had approached him to arrange for the assassination of Castro." But, according to Hoover, Kennedy said, "We should keep after him."

The next day, RFK instructed the CIA to prepare a memorandum recounting what had been said at his May 7 briefing. Hoover had forced him to play his game, to make a written record that could be produced in case the bureaucratic warfare ever broke out in the open. The "record," of course, was Kabuki theater. It neglected to mention that Kennedy had been informed *a full year earlier*, on May 22, 1961, that the CIA had hired Giancana to engage in operations against Cuba that Sheff Edwards himself had described as a "dirty business." The whole experience galled Kennedy and weighed on him. It was just about exactly at this time—on May 2—that RFK wrote CIA director John McCone and quoted his father: "Never write it down." The context had been innocuous—Kennedy was thanking McCone for sending him a copy of Richard Nixon's self-serving memoir, *Six Crises*. But Kennedy was undoubtedly thinking about the trap set by J. Edgar Hoover.

Giancana was never indicted by the Kennedy Justice Department. Prosecuting Giancana under federal law was always going to be difficult, and not just because of the threat of blackmail. Lacking the anti-racketeering laws of a later age, the feds had to stretch to find jurisdiction over crimes like murder and extortion. Kennedy had initially hoped to bring a tax case against Giancana, along the lines of the prosecution that finally sent Giancana's infamous predecessor, Al Capone, to jail in the 1930s. But a mole was discovered in the IRS leaking information to Giancana, who had already learned to evade the tax man by leaving no paper trail (the mobster used cash and declared $50,000–$90,000 "miscellaneous" income on his taxes). The evidence of other crimes gathered from the FBI's bugs was unusable. The FBI could continue to harass Giancana with round-the-clock surveillance—at Kennedy's prodding, agents began to follow the gangster right onto the golf course—but the Justice Department could not bring him to court.

RFK was handcuffed in other ways. Staff attorneys in the Justice Department's organized crime section were agitating for a tax investigation of Frank Sinatra. In late May, shortly after he met with Hoover, the attorney general rejected their arguments. The case against Sinatra was weak—"he liked to hang around mobsters, but there was nothing there," said former U.S. attorney Robert Morgenthau, who examined the evidence. Still, Kennedy could not get over the "gutter gossip," as Hoover had put it, that the Kennedys were reluctant to take on Sinatra.

The messy collision of Kennedy's war on crime with his war on Castro, aggravated by his brother's poor taste in paramours, is the worst chapter in an otherwise noble career of public service. The costs were high. Whether or not Robert Kennedy ordered the CIA to assassinate Castró, his unusual lack of curiosity about the agency's activities had harmful long-term consequences, however unintended. The atmosphere in the spy service at the time was "anything" goes. Kennedy encouraged the CIA's recklessness when he should have been finding out more about it. Kennedy aides somewhat defensively protested that he really wasn't so gung-ho about "getting" Castro, that the agency men misconstrued his natural agitation and innate impatience as license-to-mayhem. But that was precisely the problem. The CIA needed to be watched closely and reined in, not handed more rope.

It has long been speculated that the CIA's secret war against Cuba risked setting off World War III. By provoking the Soviet Union to defend Cuba with nuclear missiles, the argument goes, the CIA's adventurism touched off the Cuban Missile Crisis in October 1962. Recent scholarship in the Soviet archives suggests that Khrushchev was motivated by other considerations— chiefly, a reckless wish to force the West out of Berlin by aiming missiles at America's underbelly. Still, the CIA's bumbling did feed Castro's paranoia. His fear that the CIA's ill-concealed machinations with mobsters and Cuban exiles in Miami presaged more plots and perhaps another invasion attempt may have made the Cuban leader more willing to accept nuclear missiles into his growing Soviet-built arsenal.

There were more subtle but long-reaching byproducts from the foolhardy attempts to kill Castro and the underlying and bizarre subplots. The story may have been grossly magnified by Hollywood and the conspiracy theorists, but the public has been understandably credulous. Most insidious, the failed attempt to kill Castro has been inextricably linked to the successful attempt to kill John F. Kennedy. Hard evidence that one plot led to another is lacking. Most of the conspiracy scenarios cannot withstand close scrutiny. But the public knows only what they see: a poll taken after Oliver Stone's far-fetched movie *JFK* appeared in the early '90s showed that most Americans believe that Kennedy was killed as a result of a conspiracy—and many believe that the CIA was in on the plotting. By allowing the CIA to run free, the Kennedys, who did so much to elevate public faith in government in their lifetimes, perversely added to public cynicism about the national security state. The final irony is that among those who worried most about a plot, after his brother's death, was Robert F. Kennedy.

CHAPTER **9** PLAY

WITH HIS ROMANTIC FAITH in a few good men and his distrust of the bureaucracy, Robert Kennedy kept searching, in the spring and summer of 1962, for effective freedom fighters in Cuba. As usual, he went outside the chain of command to look for brave mavericks who would be personally loyal to him. Kennedy does not appear to have consciously tried to skirt the elaborate infrastructure created by Operation Mongoose, but his natural and impulsive instinct led him to recruit a band of restless Cubans exiles who, in time, would become a small private army.

In early April, while he was fencing with J. Edgar Hoover and hounding steel executives, RFK asked to see a Cuban exile spy who had returned to Miami after hiding out on the Caribbean island for four months. Rafael "Chi Chi" Quintero had slipped in and out of Cuba twice between December 1960 and April 1962. The first time he escaped from prison; the second, he fled a step ahead of Castro's secret police. Flown to Washington, he was taken to see General Maxwell Taylor, the chairman of the Special Group (Augmented) handling the covert war on Cuba. The no-nonsense general took off his watch, put it on his desk, and announced to Quintero, "You have ten minutes." Quintero, a proud, intense man who felt the weight of his people's oppression, informed Taylor, "I can't tell you about Cuba in ten minutes." The general, a busy man, dismissed the Cuban patriot.

The reception in the attorney general's cavernous office, with its clutter of children's drawings, was a good deal more personal. Kennedy seemed to be in physical pain as Quintero poured out the grievances of the Cuban exiles, over a thousand of whom—the Bay of Pigs prisoners—were still rotting in Castro's jails. "You could see he was angry, in his face," Quintero later recollected. "He felt hurt that we felt betrayed." Kennedy directly asked Quintero if his people believed that they had been let down by President Kennedy. "I said yes and he jumped he was so agitated," said Quintero. The attorney general asked about setting up an underground in Cuba. Impossible, answered Quintero, not until the United States was serious about liberating the island. Kennedy feverishly took notes. "I could see that what I was telling him didn't gibe with what he had been hearing. He had been led to believe there was an organized underground. There wasn't. Just me."

Quintero told Kennedy of his friends who had been rounded up by the increasingly efficient, Soviet-trained Cuban security service and shot. He said that the Cubans had lost all faith in American intervention. Even his own grandfather, a ninety-three-year-old farmer, had refused to harbor him. Quintero had told his grandfather, "The Americans are behind me," and the old man had responded, "You've got to be shitting me. You have to get out of here tonight before the police come." Quintero tried to use his CIA radio to be extricated from the island—and twice the militia showed up, somehow tipped off. Finally, on an open phone line from Havana, he called a friend in Miami, who came and rescued him by boat.

Tie loose, face drawn, Kennedy leaned forward as Quintero talked. "For two hours we went on like this," said Quintero. "Kennedy didn't like what he was hearing, but he listened." Kennedy had refused to believe earlier intelligence reports by faceless CIA analysts (one as recent as March 21) that an internal uprising was highly unlikely in Cuba. He had chosen to put his faith instead in Ed Lansdale's fantasies about the "Touchdown Play" by October. But Quintero, by personalizing the hard truth, got Kennedy's attention. RFK knew that an invasion of Cuba was out of the question; the president had made that clear in private meetings with his advisers. But he felt an intense personal motivation to do *something* to avenge the Bay of Pigs and relieve his moral guilt—not just his, but his brother's—about the members of the Cuban Brigade captured and imprisoned by Castro.

Kennedy's sense of urgency grew on April 8 when, after a grotesque show trial, Castro sentenced all 1,189 members of the brigade to thirty years' hard labor for treason—and set the ransom at $62 million. In Miami, the families of the prisoners were wild with fear and resentment. One of the survivors of the Bay of Pigs, Roberto San Román, who had escaped off the beachhead and floated for three weeks in an open boat before rescue, scraped together $500 and flew to Washington. Coldly put off at the State Department, he impulsively jumped in a cab and went to the attorney general's office. He had no appointment, but he remembered that RFK had been by far the most sensitive of the government officials who had interrogated him after the Bay of Pigs. Kennedy, in his shirtsleeves, came out and greeted San Román in the waiting room. A quiet, dignified man from a middle-class Cuban family, San Román was surprised by the informality of RFK's greeting and his direct manner. After the chilly diplomats at State, "it was like talking to a Brigade man," said San Román. Kennedy asked sympathetically after the families of the brigade prisoners and told Román to call him "ten times a day if you have to."

Kennedy's relationships with San Román and other Cuban exiles are revealing—not just because they demonstrate once more RFK's weakness for do-it-yourself operations and his yen for heroes, but because they display his basic decency. San Román could not get over Kennedy's warmth and sensitivity, his lack of pretense and obvious feelings of moral obligation. Thirty-five years later, his feelings towards RFK bordered on reverence. "He suffered for me," said San Román. The Cuban exile—who had nearly died in a doomed invasion ordered by RFK's brother—became part of Kennedy's extended family in 1962 and 1963, joining the odd-lot ménage surrounding Robert and Ethel Kennedy at their rollicking and chaotic home at Hickory Hill.

San Román began to call Kennedy, as the Cuban soldier later recalled, "day and night." Despite the enormous demands on him that spring of 1962, Kennedy was patient and thoughtful with San Román and several other Cuban exiles who came to him for help. "I was used to rank in the Latin world. People above you were arrogant. I couldn't believe how humble and open and sincere he was. It was a shock," said San Román. In Kennedy's office, then at his home at Hickory Hill, the two men talked about the Cuban situation. "He never created false hopes," said San Román. "He said he wanted a 'second shot' at Castro, but that it would not be easy."

Kennedy was willing to entertain very cold-blooded outcomes. Once, while they were driving to Hickory Hill, and San Román was describing how hundreds had been lined up and shot by Castro after he took power, Kennedy remarked, "Isn't it too bad someone won't shoot the son of a bitch." San Román explained that he would be a difficult target, sleeping in a different bed each night. According to San Román, Kennedy did not push the assassination option.

But San Román did push it that June, as the two men sat, alone, in the living room at Hickory Hill. San Román said he had heard rumors about the CIA's assassination plots in Miami. "He acted like he didn't know," said San Román. "But he wasn't against it." San Román asked RFK directly if he would help the Cuban exiles kill Castro. "Why do you think about me?" Kennedy responded. "It was as if I was asking him personally," said San Román. "He said, 'Couldn't you get five or ten Cubans to do it?' " Kennedy wondered why a rich Cuban family couldn't be found to help with such a plot. "He was saying, 'Don't think of me,' " said San Román. "His reaction was, it's not my job, it's not something the United States would do, but if the Cubans can, fine. I wanted to know if he would confirm [the rumors about the CIA's assassination plots] but his reaction was, hey, you know, a lot of Cubans have money. Why can't they do something?" According to San Román, Kennedy mentioned the names of "two or three" prominent Cuban exile families, wealthy sugar plantation owners who had fled to Miami. San Román said the talk ended there. "I was a soldier," he said, "not a terrorist," and Kennedy was "guarded, careful."

Kennedy wanted to help the Cubans in other ways, if he could. Through San Román, Kennedy met other exile leaders. RFK had little use for the CIA- and State Department–sanctioned Cuban Revolutionary Council, which he regarded as fractious and bombastic, speechifiers not fighters. He preferred more

self-effacing types, quiet warriors like San Román, Chi Chi Quintero, and particularly a Bay of Pigs veteran named Enrique Ruiz-Williams ("Harry
Williams"). Wounded while fighting valiantly at the Bay of Pigs, Williams was
released by Castro in mid-April 1962 to negotiate a ransom for the other prisoners. An engineer schooled in the United States, the burly Williams was
straightforward, especially about his desire to topple Castro. To the despair of
their CIA handlers, Kennedy formed a private bond with Williams and San
Román. ("The CIA was paying me but didn't like me," said San Román. "They
thought I was Kennedy's spy.") When the Cubans told Kennedy about some
potential underground fighters inside Cuba who needed arms and supplies,
Kennedy ordered the CIA to secretly supply them through the American naval
base at Guantánamo. A CIA official tried to explain to RFK that the Special
Group had decided not to use Guantánamo as a base for covert actions. "We'll
see about that," Kennedy snapped.

Although initially reluctant to pay Castro's extortionate ransom, Kennedy became increasingly preoccupied with trying to free the imprisoned
brigade. He was willing to reach out to some disreputable characters to help.
Justice Department files identified drug runners and smugglers who had contacts in Cuba. A CIA case officer, Charles Ford, was given an Italian pseudonym—Fiscalini—and sent undercover. He would be called by Angie Novello,
RFK's personal secretary, and dispatched to meet with characters like Bubbles
Abdullah, a suspected drug dealer whose lawyer was trying to get him a lighter
sentence by cooperating with the feds. Abdullah and a man later identified by
the CIA's Ford as the "manager of the Hotel Theresa" in Harlem were to go to
Havana to plead for the prisoners. Nothing came of these shadowy contacts, but
they show the lengths to which Kennedy was willing to go to help free the
Cuban Brigade.

RFK's Cuban friends—bitter CIA men called them his "pet Cubans"—
were embraced by Kennedy's own family. San Román recalled his amazement
when he was first invited out to Hickory Hill in May 1961, just days after
he had escaped the carnage at the Bay of Pigs. Arriving at a pool party, he
was gaily handed a Cuba Libre (rum and Coke) and blithely quizzed by Ethel:
was America's failure to provide air cover to blame for the debacle? San
Román almost choked on his drink. That was precisely the question the
Taylor Board—and Ethel's own husband—had seemed intent on ducking at
the hearings earlier in the day. "She is a wonderful woman," concluded San
Román.

San Román had trouble understanding RFK at first. In April 1962, as the
newspapers reported the attorney general's heavy hand during the steel crisis,
Kennedy was widely described as calculating and "ruthless." Driving San
Román out to Hickory Hill one evening, Kennedy showed him one such attack
and asked him if he agreed with it. "Yes," answered San Román. "I thought it
was a compliment—that a great leader should be ruthless. But he hated it."

Kennedy was anything but ruthless with San Román and the other Cuban
exiles. He asked after San Román's children—by name—and spoke to his

mother on the phone. San Román watched as Kennedy played affectionately with his own children. "I was a typical Latin father, too proud to be that way with my children. I realize now that he made me a better family person," said San Román in 1997. "I took better care of my kids because I saw how he took care of his."

San Román was taken aback and then charmed by the comfortable (though competitive) informality of Kennedy's friends. He was invited to a skating party, where he watched in disbelief as the attorney general, the president's national security adviser, and the secretary of defense wobbled about on skates, playing tag and crack the whip, racing, falling, and laughing with their children. Then everybody piled into family station wagons for hot chocolate and marshmallows. "They all behaved like kids. There was such enthusiasm. I kept wondering, where is the security? Where are the follow cars?"

SAN ROMÁN was perhaps an exotic outsider among the WASPy families of the New Frontier, but he was not out of place among those invited to Hickory Hill. Anyone who had done something daring or truly memorable was eligible. Ethel Kennedy's parties, thrown at any excuse, were famous for their eclectic guest lists, denominated only by celebrity or achievement. She liked to mix and match: aristocratic diplomat Averell Harriman might be seated next to migrant labor organizer Dolores Huerta; actress Shirley MacLaine could draw defensive tackle Roosevelt Grier. Though the seating arrangements could produce awkward silence, they more often provoked laughter and surprise. There was an offbeat spontaneity to parties at the Kennedys', a refreshing contrast to the staidness of more conventional Washington dinners. Teddy White, the presidential chronicler, recalled the "sweetness" of parties at Hickory Hill:

> First of all, if the party was outside, all the little kids would be . . . standing around peeping over the hedge, barefooted in those little nightgowns. Wherever it was, anytime you'd walk in they'd say, "This party is for *you*."

By the summer of 1962, Hickory Hill had become a symbol of the New Frontier—its informality and glamour, its brainy playfulness, and, as more guests were pushed into Ethel Kennedy's pool, its occasional overindulgence. Teddy White giddily described a typical evening at Hickory Hill. On the terrace, calypso singer and civil rights activist Harry Belafonte taught guests how to do the twist, while off in a corner State Department Sovietologist Charles "Chip" Bohlen debated East-West relations with Kremlin back channel Georgi Bolshakov. Eunice Shriver wandered about raising money for retarded children. In the meantime, Robert Kennedy challenged anyone to a push-up contest. Huffing and puffing on the flagstones, the attorney general took on his old Harvard teammate Kenny O'Donnell, then Teddy White, then Byron "Whizzer" White, who had just been elevated to the Supreme Court. Bolshakov, not to be outdone, challenged Kennedy to an arm-wrestling contest. A crowd gathered round. RFK, who was wiry and determined, began to press the Soviet agent's arm to the table. "We're winning! We're winning!" chanted Ethel, in the Cold War spirit. Bolshakov, raising his elbow from the table, pushed back. "He's cheating! He's cheating!" shouted the hostess. At 3 a.m., nobody wanted to leave. Finally, Kennedy, who had to go to work in a couple of hours, shouted, "Everybody out!"

To a guest, Hickory Hill was a "wild, informal mixture of a children's playground, menagerie, upbeat discotheque, and a humming political head-quarters," write two longtime Kennedy friends and aides, William vanden Heuvel and Milton Gwirtzman. Set on a gentle rise in the verdant horse coun-try of Virginia, the Kennedy's comfortable white mansion had been the Union Army headquarters of General George B. McClellan ("He didn't press," scoffed RFK). Bought from the John Kennedys in 1956 when Ethel was about to have her fifth of eleven children, the house was brightly decorated—Ethel favored lush sherbet colors, shocking pinks, pale aquas, raspberry reds—noisy, and often chaotic. A baby sea lion lived in the pool until it wandered down the road to the neighbors; a giant land turtle, an anteater, and various other creatures in-habited Bobby Jr.'s zoo in the basement. Children were forever hurtling from tree to tree on a zip wire copied after the paratrooper training course at Fort Bragg, or "watching you go by, owl-like, with grave, proprietary eyes," recalled George Plimpton, the amateur sportsman and writer who was a frequent guest. "This house is 'hellzapopping'!" exclaimed André Malraux, France's minister of culture, as he walked in the door.

At her parties, Ethel loved pranks and games. Playing sardines, cabinet secretaries would squeeze into closets with pretty young actresses. At a dinner for poet Robert Frost, Ethel handed out pencil and paper and instructed guests to write their own poems. There was no lounging about on the weekends. Vis-iting at Hyannis, where the pace was just as feverish, José Torres, the light heavyweight boxing champion of the world, kept trying to take a nap, but was pressed into nonstop sailing, swimming, tennis, touch football, etc. Finally, one of the Kennedy children handed him boxing gloves. "Box Daddy, José! Box Daddy!" they cried. Reluctant to flatten the attorney general, Torres bobbed and weaved while RFK swung wildly. The next morning, Torres, unable to stand any more relaxation, announced that he had to leave.

"The whole idea was to relax in a violent fashion," recalled Gerald Trem-blay, the friend from law school who often visited Kennedy. Justice Department aides, invited out to Hickory Hill for a sandwich, would end up, still in their gray flannels and street shoes, chasing down the lawn after Kennedy children, large and small, holding footballs. The touch football was ferociously competi-tive; everyone was expected to give their all. "Bobby would really chew you out if you wouldn't leave your feet to make a tag," recalled family friend Red Fay. George Plimpton remembered being scolded because he was talking to Justice White (who was playing in his black stockinged feet) about Mickey Mantle in-stead of going out for passes. In another game, Plimpton recalled, Ethel bit him in the ankle.

The games were fun, but a little relentless and wearing. "If you were going out for a pass, you had to fly," said Plimpton. "Bobby was sour if you missed one." Plimpton was glad to catch the Hickory Hill wave, but he felt a kind of undertow. "He was always judging you, somehow. You had to make the clever remark or catch the great pass." Plimpton, who wrote engagingly about his experiences pitching against major league baseball players and quarterbacking in an NFL exhibition game, understood that he was a prize, an object of curiosity to RFK. "I think he liked me because I had been in a game with the likes of Rosie [Roosevelt] Grier [the all-pro L.A. Rams lineman who also frequented Hickory Hill]," said Plimpton. Fascinated by their achievements, searching for the magic ingredient, Kennedy quizzed the heroes he collected at Hickory Hill. From New York Giants halfback Frank Gifford, he wanted to know: what was the great running back Jimmy Brown really like? With Colonel John Glenn, the marine fighter pilot and first American to orbit the earth, Kennedy burned to know, what does it feel like to be weightless? What did Glenn think about just before the booster took off? What did the sunset look like? "A thousand and one questions," recalled Glenn.

Kennedy could be funny and engaging. He could also be self-absorbed and rude. He was at once keenly attuned to the poor and careless in the manner of the very rich, a habit reinforced by Ethel. Anyone who traveled with the Kennedys was apt to see both sides. On their round-the-world trip in the winter of 1962, a young foreign service officer named Brandon Grove had the task of acting as a kind of official minder for the attorney general and his wife. Grove liked and admired Kennedy, but he had experienced the attorney general's impatience with protocol on an earlier trip to West Africa. In receiving lines, the president's brother had failed to understand why he should be required to wait in line behind the head of state of smaller, less powerful countries. The three-week trip to Asia and Europe in February revealed how Kennedy could be at once sensitive and demanding. In an elevator at their hotel in Tokyo, RFK was horrified when a slight Japanese girl in a white kimono dropped to her knees and began polishing his shoes. "Oh, no, *please*," Kennedy cried softly. Grove and another aide quickly lifted the girl to her feet. It occurred to Grove that Kennedy was at once appalled by the girl's abject subjugation and worried that when the elevator doors opened, awaiting photographers would snap an awkward picture. In Djakarta a few days later, it was Grove's turn to be embarrassed. During an interminable state dinner, Kennedy insistently signaled his State Department escort that he wanted to leave. Grove kept shaking his head and whispered that it would be impolite. At the end of a long, graceful, but dull display of Indonesian native dance, Kennedy announced that the Americans would demonstrate one of their native dances. He turned to Grove and instructed him to do the Charleston with one of Ethel's friends, Susie Wilson. Doing their best without benefit of accompanying music, they felt uncomfortable, "to put it mildly," Grove later recalled. "Bobby had a cruel streak," said Grove. "It was just 2 percent, but it was there." On the last day of their stay in Indonesia, Grove was again thrust into a difficult position. Their

Pan Am flight was scheduled to leave at 5 p.m. Missing it would set off a chain reaction of disruption for the rest of the trip. As the departure hour approached, the Kennedys had not even returned to the hotel, much less packed. In his memoirs, Grove recalls what happened next: "In discouragement and trepidation, and with the daring of the desperate, I began to pack [Ethel's] varied belongings and had nearly finished when she burst on the scene and asked what I was doing. 'Ethel,' I began slowly and I hope thoughtfully, 'this is a real world with real people and real airplanes. Pan Am isn't going to hold the plane for us!' She wasn't pleased but she said nothing more about it." Yet when Grove returned, the Kennedys invited him to a reunion at Hickory Hill. "With a sweet smile," recalled Grove, Ethel slipped the young foreign service officer a tiny leather box. Inside were two gold cufflinks, one inscribed "Real World," the other "Real People." On the backs were Grove's and Kennedy's initials. Grove was won over. "The Kennedys do that, wear you out to a frazzle and then do something lovely for you," he recalled. He began going to parties "two and three times a week" at Hickory Hill and remained a close family friend.

Puzzled, sometimes irked by the contradictions, Kennedy's friends coped. Hostesses at dinner parties smiled with clenched teeth when he disrupted their seating arrangements by switching around place cards in order to place himself next to pretty girls. He offended a social gathering by behaving preemptorily towards elder statesman Harriman. Discussing some minor matter, Kennedy was heard coldly ordering, "Well, get on it, Averell. See that you do it tomorrow." (Harriman, a tough old coot who was nicknamed the Crocodile for his ability to snap off heads in meetings, was not long offended; he admired RFK's brusqueness.) RFK's Brumus, a dog loved only by his owner, became a symbol—joked about and indulged, but also resented. The pony-sized Newfoundland who drooled, smelled bad, and snapped at children once lifted his leg on two matrons at a Hickory Hill party. Kennedy fled inside the house, where comedian Art Buchwald accosted him for profiles in courage. Kennedy was determined to take Brumus everywhere, including to the office of the secretary of state. The dog reared up and pawed the dignified Rusk, slobbering on his face. "Bobby thought it was funny," recalled Rusk's son Robert. "My father was embarrassed."

Yet at the same time, Kennedy could be sensitive while others were unfeeling. Nick Katzenbach, Kennedy's valued assistant attorney general, regaled a party by describing how his son got sick smoking his first forbidden cigar. Everyone laughed except for Kennedy, who asked in a pained voice, "How is he feeling?" Actress Judy Garland—Dorothy from *The Wizard of Oz*—came to Hickory Hill when her career was waning. She looked unwell and seemed to be a little lost, sadly standing off to one side. No one seemed to speak to her, or even notice her, until Kennedy took her in his arms and began to dance. The past-her-prime actress and the shy dancing-class dropout performed a gentle soft shoe together. Garland lit up, touched by Kennedy's kindness.

Such grace notes were sometimes drowned out by the roar of the party. Ethel's exuberance could exceed her judgment. The Hickory Hill regulars among the three hundred guests who came to a party for Astronaut John Glenn on the night of June 16, 1962, could sense mischief just from the seating arrangements. Mrs. Kennedy had erected a catwalk across the pool and placed a table for two on it. The chair legs were inches from the edge. Glenn, a certified national hero since his orbit in February, was supposed to sit with Mrs. Kennedy on the precarious platform. Glenn knew better; he never came near the pool. (At one point in the evening, he attached a note to a helium party balloon—"Help! I'm a prisoner of the Kennedys!"—and let it float into the night sky.) Predictably, someone went in, clothes and all—first, Arthur Schlesinger in his tuxedo, then Ethel in her evening dress, then a friend of Ethel's, Sarah Davis. The dunkings made the newspapers, first the society pages, then the *New York Times*. Staid *U.S. News & World Report* ran a full-page story, "Fun in the New Frontier: Who Fell, Who Was Pushed." Some people were amused, but many (especially the uninvited) were not.

Gerald Tremblay was watching while the guests splashed into the pool. "Sarah Davis came out dripping wet in a clinging evening dress. She slung her arms around Bob and said something like, 'Look what they've done to me.' And, boy, he really pushed her aside. It really irritated him. That's one of the only times I've seen him angry," Tremblay said (Davis did not recall trying to embrace RFK). Kennedy liked to flirt, but on his own terms.

RFK would stand off from the hijinks when they got out of control. Every summer, the Kennedy family sailed off on cruises with friends up the rocky coast of Maine. The Kennedy style left the sailing purists aghast. "They used to sail with road maps, not even proper charts. Why they didn't end up on a rock, I'll never know," said Douglas Dillon, the Treasury secretary whose Maine summer house was one of their ports of call. "Normally, when you cruise, it's all very tight and taut, and there are just the right number of people for the boat, slim rations, and everything is highly controlled," said Kay Evans, wife of columnist Rowland Evans and a close Kennedy friend. "On the Kennedy cruises, it's quite unlike that. There are too many people and thousands of suitcases. And then all that food that Ethel brings . . . turkeys and hams and chocolate cakes . . . and sometimes a dog." Michael Forrestal, the national security staffer who was a very salty sailor, came across the Kennedys and their entourage sailing out of the mists in a large blue yawl off Rockland, Maine. "As their vessel approached . . . it seemed as if there was a circus on board," recalled Forrestal. "There were not only a great many people on the boat, some in costume, but also a menagerie of animals. We came alongside . . . I found Bobby in the bow, standing outboard of the genoa, really looking as if he wanted to have nothing to do with this turmoil that was going on on the deck behind him. He shouted something like, 'I'll bet you rather wish you'd never met us, Forrestal!' "

Kennedy was embarrassed by too much hilarity. But he relished the brushes with danger, the bracing plunges, the tests of fortitude and endurance—all wrapped up as vacation fun. In an oral history, Kay Evans related an epiphany, how she came to understand why Kennedy loved these chaotic

outings, the wilder the better. She described a harrowing night of clawing up
the Maine coast with the Kennedys and a too-large crew of friends aboard a
borrowed yacht. As she anxiously watched the surf burst on nearby reefs in the
moonlight, an old Kennedy football buddy, Dean Markham, tried to navigate
the boat with amateur elan ("I'm steering just a little bit to the left of the
moon"). The radio didn't work and the stove wouldn't light, so there was nothing hot to eat. She remembered:

> All we ate that day were doughnuts and Danish pastry. The ones who
> weren't scared the way I was were either exhausted, because there
> weren't enough places to sleep, or hungry, because there was nothing
> to eat or furious, because they had agreed to come on the expedition,
> or seasick. . . . There were only two people who were having a good
> time . . . one was Bobby, who just loved the whole thing, and the
> other was Ethel, who was happy because Bobby was. The rest of us
> were wrecks. When we got to the Watsons' [Thomas J. Watson Jr.,
> chairman of IBM] that night it was like getting to heaven after a
> hideous time in purgatory . . . everything was so beautiful at the
> Watsons'. We took hot baths and had a wonderful lobster dinner. At
> that dinner, I said to Bobby, "That was the most terrified I've ever
> been in my life, last night." And he said, "But doesn't it just make it
> twice as wonderful that we're here? Aren't you having twice as good
> a time because you did that last night?" And then I began to see the
> whole thing. . . .

Sport for Bobby Kennedy was less a relaxation than a cleansing ordeal.
Though initially skittish around horses, he became an avid, if undisciplined
rider. "If you got to a flat place where he could gallop, he just took off," said
Marie Ridder, a frequent riding companion. Ethel was a strong horsewoman,
and their eldest daughter became a champion in the ring ("You go in there to
win," Kennedy instructed Kathleen). A day on the ski slopes was incomplete
without at least one spectacular crash. Old movies of Kennedy on skis reveal an
absence of form and a surfeit of speed. He could even make tennis a moral challenge. "He had a ferocious forehand—very straightforward—but no backhand
at all. Too duplicitous," said George Plimpton. Yet RFK would try to psych out
his opponents, unexpectedly rushing the net, and he was impatient with dally-
ing partners, including Ethel. "Ethel, what's the matter? We're playing tennis
out here, aren't we?" he would demand if she became too chatty with the opposition.

Kennedy was indifferent to cold, wet, or fashion. A friend described him
hurtling down the slopes of Stowe looking like a ragman. Yet when he was not
wearing a hair shirt, Kennedy could be a sensualist. He enjoyed the small lux-
uries of wealth like good cigars and expensive restaurants in New York, and he
indulged himself with chocolate sundaes. He was careful to maintain his tan
with a sunlamp in the winter and long hours by the pool at Hickory Hill. Al-

though he pushed away Sarah Davis in her wet dress, he enjoyed teasing and flirting and always sought out, as he described them, "pretty girls."

If Kennedy was aware of these internal contradictions—the kind boy within the rude man, the pleasure-seeker within the puritan—he did not dwell on them, not at this stage of his life. He substituted action for self-reflection. Indeed, one suspects he used his constant self-testing and agitation to keep at bay dimly understood (but strongly felt) urges and fears. His self-defense kept him from opening up too much with friends. "He never discussed intimate problems," said Gerald Tremblay. "He did discuss his relationship with his father, but in a kidding sort of way—intimating that his father was a little bit of a tyrant in the household." While all politics and policy were personal for RFK, in his own friendships, he avoided the too-personal. His empathy and his immense curiosity ended when friendly conversations became too intimate or self-revelatory, especially if he detected self-pity. "He didn't like anybody to gripe. He didn't like any kind of a heavy situation. He hated to be bored," said Tremblay. When conversations did veer towards the confessional, he was sometimes rescued by Ethel. "She was always clowning around, keeping things light," said Tremblay.

Kennedy's compassion was deep, but it was also, in a way, distant. He felt the pain of the world, but not always that of his friends. His concern for the poor, so pronounced in his later life, had already begun to take hold by 1962. Within a few months of becoming attorney general, he had taken a walking tour of Harlem with his friend Dave Hackett and been shocked by the despair and degradation. His mission to Hackett to "do something" about the problem of juvenile delinquency was really aimed at helping poor young blacks. In addition to everything else he was doing, Kennedy had made a private project of Washington, D.C.'s large poor black population, forced to attend wretched schools and denied basic services. Unannounced, the attorney general would show up at local schools or parks, chatting playfully with the kids while terrorizing sleepy city bureaucrats. It outraged Kennedy that the swimming pool at Dunbar High had been closed for eight years for want of $30,000 for repairs. Kennedy privately raised the money himself. Right after chewing out a cowering supervisor in the recreation department (the shallow end of the pool is too deep for small children! how do you expect them to swim?) he walked slowly among the children, smiling, squeezing their hands, rubbing their heads.

Yet Kennedy did not want to hear about the suffering of his closest friends. In part, he and Ethel wanted to look on the bright side, but there was, especially in Ethel's determined positivism, a degree of avoidance. If a friend complained of physical weakness or illness, Bob and Ethel would steer the conversation someplace else. RFK "didn't want to hear people's individual problems. Now, he was great with the problems of a group, like Indians, colored people, or people that were being religiously oppressed or the poor. But as far as a one-to-one basis, that wasn't his cup of tea at all," said Tremblay.

Bob would never complain of his own ailments to a friend. The only person he sought out for comfort was Ethel. Not one for deep self-reflection, she did not invite him to analyze his woes, while treating her own as God's will. But she showered him with absolute and undying love. "She adored Bobby. He couldn't do anything wrong. She brought him out of his shell," said Red Fay, who vacationed with the Kennedys every year through the 1950s. Robert and Ethel were joined by a deep Catholic faith. In 1951, right after they were married, Bobby scribbled, from memory, these words from the Book of Ruth for his wife: ". . . for whither Thou goeth I will go; and where Thou lodgest I will lodge; Thy people shall be my people and Thy God my god. When Thou diest then will I die and we will be together forever." Religion was the way and the salve. The Kennedy household brimmed with piety. Bobby Jr. recalled that his mother

> always carried a rosary and led our kneeling family through the decades each evening. We made a morning offering and attended daily mass with her throughout the summer and on holidays, sometimes twice. We fasted on Sundays, fainted from hunger at High Mass, ate fish on Fridays, and bracketed every meal with prayers. We read about the lives of the saints and prayed with particular fervor to St. Anthony and St. Francis of Assisi. . . . My father, whose devotion rivaled my mother's, read us the Bible every night.

Whenever Ethel was away, Bobby missed her desperately. In August, when his wife and children were at the Cape, Kennedy was morose, returning gloomily each night to an empty house. It was that summer, August 1962, when RFK began bringing Brumus to his office at the Justice Department, causing J. Edgar Hoover to summon his deputies and consult the federal statutes banning dogs from government buildings. Kennedy explained to the *New York Times* that the kids and Ethel were gone and "Brumus gets lonely. So I bring him down here to get pretty girls to take him for walks." (The newspaper showed a photograph of an attractive secretary from his office, dutifully hanging on to the brutish dog.) Brumus was not the only lonely one, of course. Kennedy was too.

Kennedy would become exasperated with Ethel from time to time, especially on the subject of money. "Oh, Ethel," he would say, surveying the stack of bills. The household accounts were such a shambles that Kennedy had to bring in Carmine Bellino, the sharp-eyed accountant who had deciphered the phony books of mobbed-up unions for the Rackets Committee. When, in 1959, Joe Sr. had sent Ethel fleeing in tears from the dinner table with his caustic remarks about her profligacy, Bobby tried to step in, saying, "Dad, I think you have made your point." As Ethel bolted, he went after her. When she returned to the table, JFK cracked, "Ethel, don't worry. We've come to the conclusion that the only solution is to have Dad work harder." When Jackie Kennedy, to much fanfare, redecorated the White House, the ever-competitive Ethel wanted to keep up. She demanded a formal dining room to entertain in the Justice Department, including a pattern of Lenox china with the department seal. Salvatore Andretta, the career assistant attorney general for administration, was dumbfounded. "Where the hell am I going to get unauthorized money to pay for unauthorized china for an unauthorized dining room?" he asked. Kennedy shrugged and told him, "Listen to her but don't pay any attention."

A steady stream of cooks and governesses, some close to hysteria, left Hickory Hill. But Robert Kennedy seemed oblivious. He stood apart when someone made a scene or grumbled, as skiers waiting in the lift lines at Stowe sometimes did when the Kennedy entourage clambered across their ski tips to the head of the line. He loved the tumult that greeted him when he walked in the door at night. In an age when children were still seen but not heard by wealthy parents, RFK could not get enough of his. To be sure, his long hours and the sheer size of his family limited the amount of individual attention he could devote, and on occasion he was observed struggling to remember all their names as they lined up in identical blue blazers and short gray flannel pants or skirts. As the father of newborns, he seemed reluctant to hold his babies, as if fearful that he might, with his shaking hands, drop them. But as the children grew older, he was an embracing and loving, if sometimes stern, parent. The little ones climbed on him when he shaved in the morning, squirting shaving cream and yelling with delight. Though Kennedy disliked physical affection from his friends—bridling if anyone slung an arm around his shoulder—and rarely touched Ethel in public, he was immensely tactile with his children. He played a game called tickle-tumble, rolling about on the ground, pretending to fight. If a boy cried, Kennedy would hug him, but not in a coddling way. "Hush now," he'd say. "A Kennedy never cries." Warren Rogers, a newspaperman who became a family friend, once watched as Kennedy, while rough-housing, lightly slapped one of his sons across the face. Wasn't he being a little rough with the boy? Rogers asked. No, Kennedy explained, boys had to get used to being hit unexpectedly. That was the way of the world.

Young Kennedys were always in training. The breakfast table was a classroom. Kennedy would test his children on current events, just as he had seen his father do with the oldest favorites, Jack and Joe and Kathleen. Unlike his father, Kennedy was careful to include all the children, the youngest and smallest, too. The Kennedy children lived in a shrine as well as a funhouse. They were lectured on the martyred saints by their father, standing beneath a portrait of his dead brother in uniform, the flak-filled London sky silhouetting his bomber. On the walls, to inspire and remind, hung autographs of war leaders—Churchill, FDR, Douglas MacArthur—along with Lincoln's Emancipation Proclamation and their uncle Jack's inaugural address. Kennedy was determined that his children should be ready and worthy to pick up the family burden. At bedtime prayers, all the children would say, "And please make Uncle Jack the best President ever, and please make Daddy the best Attorney General ever." Punishments in the Kennedy household included memorizing poetry.

Kennedy did not neglect his own self-education. His tastes still ran to popular biography and military history—Bruce Catton on the Civil War, Barbara Tuchman's *The Guns of August*, and tomes like Paul Horgan's *The Conquista-*

dors in North American History and E. S. Creasy's *Fifteen Decisive Battles of the World.* But he was dutiful about his reading, and just beginning a process of intellectual discovery that would, in time, take him in surprising and unimagined directions. Possibly trying to compensate for the Harvard education he missed while hanging around the Varsity Club, he began nudging the Harvard professor-turned-White House aide Arthur Schlesinger to set up some informal seminars along the lines of the Aspen Institute. The acerbic Schlesinger was skeptical at first, but pressed by Ethel (who wanted what Bobby wanted), he organized a kind of Big Thoughts seminar that quickly became known as Hickory Hill Academy. The lecture meetings, accompanied by drinks and dinner for sixty or so, called on famous educators and thinkers, who were flattered to be asked to tutor cabinet officers and Supreme Court justices. There were occasional duds and a few awkward moments. Mortimer Adler bored Ethel by droning on about his Great Books. She wanted to hear from the next-in-line, her entry for the evening, Father Francis Cavanaugh of Notre Dame. And Bobby Kennedy was indignant when a well-known psychiatrist, Dr. Lawrence S. Kubie, lectured on "Urban Problems and Poverty Children." Kubie tried to explain the plight of poor children in psychoanalytic terms. Revealing perhaps more about himself than he intended, Kennedy burst out, "That's the biggest bunch of bullshit I've ever heard. You're trying to tell us that people can't help being what they are." Ethel chimed in, "Everything isn't sex." The baffled and humiliated professor cut short his presentation and made a hasty retreat. But for the most part the Hickory Hill seminars were deemed a success. Washington matrons began to vie for the honor of hosting them at their own homes. "There was nothing precious about these lectures," recalled Alice Roosevelt Longworth, the often acid-tongued grande dame. "It was all sorts of fun, that was all. Fun to watch all the people who were there."

ONE PRIZE GUEST who very rarely came was John F. Kennedy. He made gentle fun of his brother's earnestness—to worldly JFK, the Hickory Hill seminars were too reminiscent of the "self-improvement schemes" that Mother Rose had tried to impose, like purgatives, on her brood. While enjoying the gossip about Ethel's battles with the eggheads, the president generally steered clear of entertainments at Hickory Hill. A place card had been set for him and the first lady at the John Glenn swimming pool party in June, but, anticipating his sister-in-law's unbridled sense of fun, he begged off at the last minute. "That was a party to miss," he told a friend, Mary Bailey Gimbel, Bobby's old friend from Milton days. (Gallup polls registered a negative public reaction to guests-in-the-swimming-pool; to Ethel Kennedy, JFK simply ordered: "Enough.") In regretting invitations to Hickory Hill, the president argued political prudence—he did not want the New Frontier to look any cozier than it already did—but Gimbel suspected that JFK simply did not wish to go.

The president and the first lady seldom invited Bobby and Ethel to informal social gatherings at the White House. JFK wished to be diverted; he did not want to be nagged by his brother. The two brothers had a very different approach to socializing. Though JFK was debonair and loved to gossip, and RFK was shy and sometimes socially uncomfortable, RFK was a more open and welcoming host. At Hickory Hill, RFK's aides, friends, celebrities, and mere acquaintances passing through for the night were "all thrown together in a common hopper and mixed around very nonselectively," recalled William Walton, the society painter, who was close to both Kennedys. Ethel Kennedy sometimes did not know who was coming for dinner until the guests arrived on her doorstep. JFK, on the other hand, rigidly divided his relationships, separating staff ("the Irish mafia" and Ted Sorensen) from his social friends like Charles Spalding and Ben Bradlee. RFK was, in a sense, staff: Though he increasingly trusted RFK as a wise adviser and valued his role as a gadfly and prod to the bureaucracy, the president did not find his brother to be relaxing company. They remained essential opposites, the older brother, in Arthur Schlesinger's famous description, "a realist brilliantly disguised as a romantic," the younger "a romantic stubbornly disguised as a realist." Their wives had nothing in common save a married name. In public, they were "polite, but not cozy polite," said one of their frequent hostesses, Susan Mary Alsop. Privately, Ethel regarded Jackie as snooty and fey and Jackie regarded Ethel as noisy and gauche. JFK had little patience with RFK's boisterous and too-numerous offspring. At a rare family gathering, he stood at the head of the stairs as various Robert Kennedy children squealed and squabbled below, and declared: "I am the president of the United States and I say, 'Out! Out!' "

The Robert Kennedys were included in most formal state dinners. Kennedy was an anxious guest, always vigilant. The White House social secretary, Letitia Baldrige, described RFK "circling, watching. At outdoor events, he was like a Secret Service man, always casing the crowd." In conversation, "he was talking to you but not talking to you. He was doing it for his brother. He was always cruising, talking to people because he had to. When he did talk, he was untouchable. He might speak with two or three people, but the body language was always a closed circle. It said: Don't interrupt us!"

RFK saw himself as guardian not just to the president, but to his extended family. He was not in constant touch with his mother, but he remained the Kennedy offspring most attentive to Rose, who turned seventy in 1960. RFK's devotion to self-improvement came straight from his mother. (During dinner conversation, Mrs. Kennedy would sometimes produce a small notebook in which she jotted down new vocabulary words.) Her "pet" naturally and easily returned her affection. "When he said 'Mother,' you could hear it in his voice," said Joe Gargan, RFK's cousin. "He was the one who could relax with her and joke with her, more than the others," recalled William vanden Heuvel, a regular visitor at Hyannis Port. While Kennedy's siblings sometimes condescended to their mother, rolling their eyes when she corrected their grammar, RFK told vanden Heuvel that his mother had been a real source of strength in the family, keeping track of the details in her children's busy lives. Still trying to bring discipline and impose punctuality on a household teeming with grandchildren, Rose Kennedy would appear at breakfast and launch a formal discussion of the morning papers. Gently and lovingly, RFK would "tease her out of it," vanden Heuvel recalled.

RFK was the acknowledged paterfamilias. He organized masses for his late sister, Kathleen—"the best of the sisters." He helped his little brother Edward get elected to the United States Senate from Massachusetts. Running Teddy to fill Jack's old seat was father Joe Kennedy's idea; worried about charges of nepotism, both Robert and Jack were initially lukewarm, but came around when their father insisted. Edward Kennedy's election was not a shoo-in. He had to run for the nomination against the nephew of House Speaker John McCormack, and the *Boston Globe* revealed that he had been caught cheating as a student at Harvard in the 1950s. But in August 1962, as Ted Kennedy anxiously prepared for his first debate before the September primary, RFK appeared and breezily announced in an exaggerated Boston accent, "Have no feah, we are heah." Well coached, a natural politician in his own right, Teddy won the primary, then the election by a comfortable margin in November.

Less successful was the painful attempt to rehabilitate Joe Kennedy, crippled and speechless from his stroke in December 1961. "Bobby would fly down to Palm Beach at 6 a.m. and be back at noon, just to say hello for fifteen minutes," said Baldrige. On one visit, determined to show that he could walk, Joe Sr. rose from his wheelchair but staggered. Quickly, Bobby caught him. Family members watched in horror as the old man, enraged by helplessness, began swatting RFK with his cane. Bobby tried to laugh and tease and plead. "Dad," he said, "give me your arm and I'll hold you till you get your balance. . . . That's what I'm here for, Dad. Just give me your hand when you need it. You've done that for me all my life, so why can't I do the same for you now?" But the outbursts—his father would cry, "No, no, no, no," over and over again—and the false hope of therapy wore down RFK. "The only time I ever saw him show emotion," recalled his aide Joe Dolan, "was when his father suffered a relapse."

RFK's protectorate extended to his brother's wife. RFK understood that his brother appreciated Jacqueline—her cultural sophistication, her cool elegance, her whimsy and toughness—even if JFK sometimes seemed to take her for granted. Jackie is "good for Jack," RFK told *Look* reporter Laura Bergquist, "because he knows she's not the kind of wife, when he comes home at night, she's not going to say, 'What's new in Laos?' " Reverting to his childhood role of helpmate and family conciliator, RFK tried to ease the periodic tension between JFK and Jacqueline. Early in their marriage, JFK showed off at touch football, making a circus catch and exclaiming, "Hey, Jackie, did you see that?" Jackie, reading, ignored him. Bobby came over to her lawn chair and sweetly implored, "It would help if you could say something nice. It would mean a lot to him." During their first summer in the White House, the first lady was irritated when the president permitted a *Look* magazine photographer, Stanley Tretick, to take pictures of her children romping about Hyannis over the Fourth of July weekend. While JFK forbade Tretick to photograph his quarters in Air Force One—lest voters think it a "rich man's plane"—he was not overly concerned about his children's privacy. It fell to RFK to ask Tretick not to publish the photos. (When they appeared anyway a year later, RFK recalled that his father had warned him not to trust magazine editors. JFK only pretended to be mad: "He knew damn well his image would be burnished by good, heartwarming pictures," recalled Bergquist.)

Bobby's defensive alacrity was demonstrated in a much-gossiped-about incident with writer Gore Vidal at a White House dance in November 1961. Vidal, a little unsteady from drink, availed himself of Jackie's bare shoulder for support as he arose from a crouched position by her chair. The ever-wary RFK swept in and removed Vidal's hand from his sister-in-law's shoulder. Startled, thinking he had done nothing inappropriate (he and Jackie were old friends and had the same stepfather at different times), Vidal walked over to Bobby Kennedy and instructed, "Don't ever do that again." Words and insults were exchanged, and Vidal was never invited back to the White House.

RFK had always protected his brother's secrets, from the time he hid JFK's crutches in the car during the 1952 Massachusetts Senate campaign. In the summer of 1962, he had to contend with his brother's twin addictions—his promiscuity and dependence on painkillers. Since the fall of 1960, JFK's bad back had been treated by Dr. Max Jacobson, known to his New York society clients as Dr. Feelgood. Jacobson regularly traveled with the president, injecting him with a mysterious pharmaceutical cocktail of steroids, amphetamines, vitamins, and vegetable oil. Kennedy's other doctors were suspicious of the unkempt, rather creepy Jacobson, and complained to Bobby. The long-term effects of amphetamines were not well understood in 1962, but RFK, sensitive to his brother's moods, may have noticed the swings of euphoria stimulated by Dr. Feelgood's shots. RFK demanded that his brother get Dr. Jacobson to turn over samples of his elixir, to be tested, Jacobson was informed, by the Food and Drug Administration. Actually, Bobby sent several vials to the FBI labs. Noting the attorney general's "intense personal interest," the Justice Department aide passing along the request speculated that the drugs were for RFK's father. On June 7, the FBI lab reported back that the sample was too small to thoroughly analyze. The sample did not test positive for narcotics, but then Jacobson never used opiates. The FBI apparently did not test for amphetamines. JFK told Jacobson that his injections were now government-approved. To his skeptical brother, the president said, "I don't care if it's horse piss. It works."

At just about the same time RFK was investigating Dr. Feelgood's potions, he was dealing with JFK's most celebrated liaison, with Marilyn Monroe. In late May, the White House heard that the troubled actress was spreading stories around Hollywood of her purported affair with the president. At the president's birthday party on May 19, Monroe, sewn into her sequined skin-colored dress, sang a sultry "Happy Birthday, Mister Pres-i-dent" to JFK and 15,000 others at Madison Square Garden. After chewing hard on his cigar, JFK took the microphone and winkingly thanked Monroe for her "wholesome" rendition. In late March, denied the use of Sinatra's house by his cautious brother, JFK had compensated by inviting Monroe to join him at Bing Crosby's for the night. Kennedy enjoyed flirting with danger, but Monroe really was dangerous—a borderline paranoid who abused drugs and alcohol. Marrying baseball legend Joe DiMaggio, then playwright Arthur Miller, she played pathetic dramas of seduction and abandonment with high-profile heroes. After the Madison Garden display, JFK realized that he needed to distance himself from Monroe, whose behavior was increasingly rocky. Although the press had overlooked his indiscretions, this one, fanned by the Hollywood gossip mill, risked breaking into print. Friends with newspaper connections were dispatched to quietly deny the affair to New York editors, while Kennedy's old partner in skirt chasing, Senator George Smathers, had a quiet word with the actress.

RFK's role in this damage-control mission remains murky. A small publishing industry has grown up devoted to proving, or at least insinuating, that RFK not only slept with Marilyn Monroe, he then arranged to have her snuffed out—and covered up the sordid mess. Although widely believed, these conspiracy theories have no real evidence to support them. They are based on the testimony of discredited or unbelievable witnesses or the fantasies of writers. One of Kennedy's alleged trysts with Monroe was said to have occurred on a date when they were not even in the same country. All that is certain and provable is that RFK knew Monroe and saw her on four occasions, probably never alone. It may be that RFK's feelings for Monroe were more than protective. At once repulsed and fascinated by sin, Kennedy appears to have fluttered briefly around Monroe, but without flying too close.

Robert Kennedy met Marilyn Monroe in early October 1961 at a dinner at the Peter Lawfords' in Los Angeles. Arriving in an intentionally provocative dress with a mesh bodice, she departed drunk on champagne, driven home by Robert and his press aide, Ed Guthman. Kennedy saw her again at a dinner party at the Lawfords' home on February 1, 1962, as he was headed west on the first leg of his around-the-world tour. In a letter she wrote to her father the next day, Monroe enthused that RFK had a "wonderful sense of humor." Joan Braden, a guest at the dinner, recalled that Monroe, seated beside RFK, read aloud questions that she had written out in lipstick on a napkin. The queries were pedestrian: What is it like to be attorney general? Kennedy, she said, seemed uncomfortable.

Their next encounter came at a party at the home of a wealthy New York Democratic donor, Arthur Krim, on the night in May when Marilyn serenaded the president with "Happy Birthday." Arthur Schlesinger described RFK hovering about Monroe: "Bobby and I engaged in mock competition for her; she was most agreeable to him and pleasant to me—but then she receded into her own glittering mist." To one of the women present, Helen O'Donnell, wife of Kenny O'Donnell, Marilyn looked like a "cornered animal," surrounded by predatory males. RFK was sensitive enough to see the crush and asked Mrs. O'Donnell to try to help Monroe.

From that evening, some kind of friendship emerged. The Kennedys—Robert and Ethel—invited Monroe to the John Glenn swimming pool party that June (the Lawfords were also guests of honor), but she declined. RFK saw her one more time for dinner in late June at the Lawfords', then went to see her new house in the morning. Less is known about this encounter, except that Kennedy's tight schedule seemed to preclude romantic interludes. At any rate, Monroe began to call RFK. Her phone records show eight calls at the end of June and early July. The calls were brief—a minute or two. Kennedy's secretary, Angie Novello, later said that Monroe was upset—she was quarreling with her movie studio at the time and no doubt distraught that the president was now incommunicado. Novello insisted that RFK wanted to protect Monroe, a suggestion that brought hoots from Kenny O'Donnell, who told his family, "Bobby discovered girls." But O'Donnell did not say that RFK was foolish enough to sleep with Monroe.

Sometime on Saturday night, August 4, Monroe overdosed on barbiturates. The conspiracy theorists place RFK lurking in the shadows nearby. Actually he was about 350 miles away, with Ethel, at a ranch owned by some friends outside San Francisco, an hour from the nearest airport or five hours by car. His hosts have attested to his presence throughout the weekend. His Justice Department aide Joe Dolan picked up RFK in San Francisco on Monday. If the attorney general had been engaged in nefarious plots over the weekend, he did not show a trace of anxiety, reported Dolan.

Still, the rumors persist. In 1999, John Miner, a former deputy district attorney and liaison to the Los Angeles Police Department's crime labs, told the author that he had listened to some incriminating tape recordings made by Monroe before her death. At the request of her psychiatrist, Dr. Ralph Greenson, Monroe had spoken her stream-of-consciousness thoughts into a tape recorder as part of her therapy. In the course of the medical examiner's inquest into her death, Miner listened to those tapes. The former prosecutor remained silent about them for thirty-five years, until Dr. Greenson's family permitted him to speak up to exonerate the late psychiatrist from charges that he had a hand in murdering Monroe. The tapes strongly insinuate that both JFK and RFK had physical relationships with Monroe. Before he died, Peter Lawford told author David Heymann that he, too, had listened to the tapes and heard Monroe speak of a sexual relationship with both Kennedys.

Lawford's testimony can be discounted. Plagued by problems with drugs and alcohol, he went through a hostile separation from Pat Lawford in 1963, rejected and scorned by the Kennedy family, particularly RFK. Miner's account is harder to dismiss. Still, it is entirely possible—even likely—that Monroe was engaging in fantasies when she recounted love affairs with both Kennedy brothers. Sick and drug-ridden, she may have been the least reliable witness of all.

If Kennedy had taken up with Monroe, it seems likely that J. Edgar Hoover would have learned of the relationship and filed the information away for later use. But only one mention of RFK and Marilyn Monroe has emerged from Hoover's files, and the source was RFK himself. The date was August 20, two weeks after Monroe's death. Hoover was engaged in his usual routine, sending the FBI's Justice Department liaison, Courtney Evans, to tell the attorney general of "information that we have received alleging that he was having an affair with a girl in El Paso." After replying that he had never been to El

Paso, Kennedy said that he "appreciated our informing him," and took the opportunity to knock down a more sensational bit of gossip. According to Evans's memo of the meeting, Kennedy "said he was aware that there had been several allegations concerning his possibly being involved with Marilyn Monroe since she was a good friend of his sister, Pat Lawford, but these allegations had a way of growing beyond any semblance of the truth." Kennedy never forgot that Hoover was watching and listening. At the Seattle World's Fair the day after he learned of Monroe's death, Kennedy told reporters that the FBI director had done an outstanding job of controlling the Communist Party in the United States. "I hope," he added, speaking to an audience of one, "he will serve the country for many, many years to come."

CHAPTER **10** CRISIS

J AMES MEREDITH, the first black student to enroll at the all-white University of Mississippi, would later say that he had been inspired by John F. Kennedy's inaugural address. He may have overlooked JFK's failure to mention civil rights in the speech. The administration's commitment to integrating the nation was still fairly tepid in September 1962 when Meredith, represented by the National Association for the Advancement of Colored People (NAACP), won a court order banning the segregationist governor from interfering with his enrollment at "Ole Miss," a school drenched in nostalgia for the Lost Cause. Meredith, a twenty-nine-year-old air force veteran, announced that he would drive to school in his new gold Thunderbird automobile. Kennedy's self-effacing civil rights chief, Burke Marshall, advised Meredith to rethink his mode of conveyance. "Boy," RFK later reflected, "that's all we needed was to have him arrive on the campus with a gold Thunderbird." In the end, to keep him there required an occupying army.

The integration of the University of Mississippi in late September 1962 was a near disaster for the Kennedys. RFK's impatience, lack of careful preparation, romantic amateurism, and weakness for backdoor diplomacy almost resulted in a second Fort Sumter, or to use the analogy that occurred to both RFK and JFK in the small hours of a riotous night, another Bay of Pigs. Until that night, Kennedy's aide Ed Guthman said, the Kennedys did not understand the depth of opposition to racial integration in the Deep South. The battle of Ole Miss was a hard way to learn, but the Kennedys—correctly—sensed they had to act. There was no simple solution. White Mississippian politicians wanted to talk forever, while their bloody-minded constituents were ready to fight. Bringing in bayoneted troops from the beginning might have just made martyrs of them all. Kennedy's improvised middle course, sometimes bumbling, sometimes nimble, broke through in a single night that was violent, but could have been much worse.

Despite his crack about Meredith's Thunderbird, Bobby Kennedy was not at all insensitive to the hopes and dreams of young black men like James Meredith. Quick to identify with disaffected youth, RFK was one of the first white leaders to see the drift towards Black Power, the growing militancy of black activists impatient with compromising leaders and official timidity. But he was fearful of setting off conflagrations that would sacrifice forever the votes of the Democrats' once-solid South, and of doing anything that might embarrass his brother's administration in the eyes of the world. Both Kennedys still recoiled at the prospect of using federal troops to enforce the law of the land. Above all, RFK wanted to maintain control, an almost impossible task in an arena awash with suspicion and hatred.

Standing in the way of James Meredith was Ross Barnett, the genial racist governor of Mississippi who vowed to go to jail before allowing "that boy" to attend Ole Miss. On September 25, 1962, Barnett personally stopped Meredith from registering at the university. "Which one is Meredith?" he asked, looking right past the only black man in the room. Then, as a souvenir, he gave Meredith a copy of the governor's proclamation barring his admission to Ole Miss. Robert Kennedy at first regarded Barnett as a "loony," later as "an agreeable rogue. Weak." RFK thought he knew how to deal with rogues. Willing to use any weapon at his disposal, he hoped to squeeze Barnett financially by getting him held in contempt for defying a federal court order and fined $10,000 a day. (Kennedy's informants had told him that Barnett was saddled with hefty mortgage payments on a new office building.) But the governor seemed to enjoy posturing too much to worry about his bank account. Kennedy needed to find another approach. As always, he looked for a back channel, a discreet go-between, a man he could trust to talk reason with the enemy.

Kennedy fastened on a Mississippi lawyer named Thomas Watkins. A Phi Beta Kappa graduate of the University of North Carolina, Watkins was a society lawyer in the state capital of Jackson. His law office, the best in town, was next door to the governor's mansion; the headquarters of the Citizens Council, the white supremacist organization that dominated state politics, was just across the street. Watkins had a taciturn manner, reassuring to the Kennedy Justice Department accustomed to dealing with hotheads and rednecks in civil rights cases. A close friend and adviser to Governor Barnett, Watkins was the discovery of Burke Marshall. As a private corporate lawyer, Marshall had used Watkins as local counsel to try a case in Mississippi for the American Can Company in 1959. ("I did the work," Marshall recalled. "He watched TV.") Putting his faith in individuals, Kennedy trusted Marshall to find him able ones. "Marshall had impeccable taste in men," said Teddy White about the soft-spoken and usually wise civil rights chief. Watkins's role as back channel was supposed to remain a secret. In 1964, historian Walter Lord was given complete access to the Justice Department staff to write a chronicle of the integration of Ole Miss. But Marshall appeared surprised and displeased when Lord found out about Watkins, possibly because Watkins did not quite turn out to be the solution that RFK had hoped for.

"Bob may have thought Watkins was a good go-between but I didn't," said Marshall in 1998. Kennedy's aides were generally dubious about RFK's penchant for back channels. "Bob used to do this [use private contacts for government negotiations]," said Nicholas Katzenbach. "He used Prince Radziwill [married to Lee Bouvier, Jaccqueline Kennedy's sister] for diplomatic matters. I said, 'Jesus, Bobby!' And Bob said, 'Yeah, he is pretty dumb.' " Trying to manipulate Governor Barnett through a back channel was "stupid," said Katzenbach. "Barnett was dumb and paid attention to the last person he talked to. That was okay as long as it was Watkins, but then Barnett would talk to someone else."

RFK's negotiations with the Mississippians—a score of telephone conversations in September, secretly tape-recorded by Kennedy—eventually verged on farce. In the beginning, Watkins was useful. He dissuaded the governor from arresting Meredith, averting an immediate state-federal clash. But then Watkins tried to engineer a complicated face-saving arrangement to make it appear that Governor Barnett was backing down because of overwhelming federal force. In a deal worked out between Marshall, RFK, and Watkins, two dozen armed U.S. marshals would accompany Meredith to the gates of Ole Miss. Only then would the governor step aside. Initially, Marshall suggested that one marshal pull his gun. Not enough, said Watkins. How about if the marshals put their hands on their holsters? asked Marshall, who was feeling increasingly uncomfortable about the charade. Watkins said he would have to consult with Barnett.

Negotiating directly with RFK on Thursday, September 27, Barnett insisted that *all* the officers pull their guns. Kennedy was uneasy with this arrangement, but he accepted it in return for a guarantee that the governor would take responsibility for "preserving law and order." Both sides wanted plausible deniability. As soon as they had agreed to a secret deal, Barnett said, "You understand we have no agreement." Kennedy, an old hand at this game, answered, "That's correct." Accompanied by a phalanx of marshals, Meredith flew by helicopter towards Ole Miss.

Events on the ground, however, threatened to sweep aside the elaborate playacting. Roughnecks in pickup trucks carrying coolers of beer and hunting rifles began descending on the college town of Oxford. Over and over, the local radio station played "Dixie"—the Confederate rallying song that doubled as a fight song for the Ole Miss teams, the Rebels—and a Jackson newspaper urged its readers to memorize the words to a new song, "No, No, Never." At 6:35 that evening, Barnett called Kennedy. "General, I'm worried—I'm nervous, I tell you. You don't realize what's going on. There are several thousand people here in cars, trucks. Several hundred are lined up on the streets where they [Meredith and his escorts] are supposed to land. We don't know these people."

Frustrated, Kennedy agreed to turn around Meredith's convoy and call off the attempt to register him—that day. Barnett continued to fret: "There are dozens and dozens of trucks loaded with people. We can't control people like that. A lot of people are going to get killed. It would be embarrassing to me."

Kennedy had heard the same sort of political calculation from Governor Patterson of Alabama during the Freedom Rides, and he had the same indignant response: "I don't know if it would be embarrassing—that would not be the feeling." Barnett, still posturing: "It would be bad all over the nation." Kennedy, wearily: "I'll send them back."

The next day, the federal courts found Barnett in criminal contempt and gave him four days to open the university door to Meredith. While generally trying to insulate his brother from such messy confrontations, RFK decided to roll the president into action against Barnett. The Oval Office that Saturday afternoon, September 29, brimmed with macho bluster. "Go get him, Johnny boy," said RFK, burlesquing a fight manager, as he prepped his brother for a phone conference with the balky governor. JFK joined the in-jokiness, rehearsing a mock greeting, "Governor, this is the President of the United States—not Bobby, not Teddy, not Princess Radziwill." But Barnett, when he came on the line, refused to swing back. He blandly proposed that Tom Watkins—"really, an A-1 lawyer"—come to Washington to talk things over with the president. Then the governor thanked the president for his interest in Mississippi's poultry program. Baffled, not sure whether to laugh or curse, JFK hung up. "You've been fighting a soft pillow all week," he said to his brother. Later that afternoon, Barnett and Watkins trotted out a new trick play: register Meredith for Ole Miss in the state capital of Jackson, and allow Barnett to claim that the feds had snuck him in. The Kennedys went along, unhappily, but grasping for a way out.

That Saturday night, Barnett went to an Ole Miss football game, circling the field in a white convertible at halftime before a hysterical crowd that chanted "We want Ross!" "I love Mississippi!" cried Barnett as 50,000 people roared. "I love her people!" Louder roars. "I love our customs!" Pandemonium. It was, Taylor Branch writes, "the last militant race rally among respectable whites for at least a generation." In Washington, the White House got the word late that night: the deal was off again. Barnett couldn't go through with it.

The time had come to play hard. By secretly recording all of his phone conversations with Barnett, RFK had set a trap, which, on Sunday morning, he sprung. President Kennedy would have to address the nation that night, the attorney general coldly informed Barnett, announcing that the president had federalized the National Guard to secure the admission of Meredith to the University of Mississippi. And in his speech, he would disclose that he had called out the troops because Barnett had broken yesterday's agreement to register Meredith.

No longer syrupy and unctuous, Barnett fairly squealed. "That won't do at all!" he exclaimed.

"You broke your word to him," Kennedy insisted.

Gasping, Barnett said, "You don't mean to tell me the President is going to say that tonight?"

"Of course he is," said Kennedy, explaining, "we have it all down"—a complete record of all their secret dealing.

It was Barnett's turn to beg. Stalling no more, he now proposed to hurry up: to steal a march on the mob forming in Oxford, oiling their guns for the court's Tuesday deadline for admitting Meredith. How about flying Meredith into Oxford *this afternoon?* he asked. Then he could claim that he had been bamboozled by the conniving Kennedys.

Quick action suited the Kennedy spirit. As if picking sides for touch football, the attorney general, who had been restlessly tossing a pigskin in his cavernous office with Burke Marshall, immediately began throwing together a team to go to Oxford. Lawyers were drafted as they walked down the hall. An old Harvard football pal of the Kennedys, Dean Markham, had been in town for a conference on narcotics; he wound up on the plane to Mississippi. Harold Reis, a scholarly lawyer in the Office of Legal Counsel, stuck his head into Kennedy's office and asked if he could help. "Are you ready to go?" asked Kennedy. Reis thought he meant to the federal courthouse downtown; he discovered in the car to the airport that he was going to Mississippi. "The next time," Reis later joked, "I'll ask, 'Go where?' " Kennedy was in his gallows humor mode. As Katzenbach left the office, RFK called out, "Hey, Nick, don't worry if you get shot. The president needs a moral issue." The troops loved the amateur elan. When Katzenbach and his team arrived (the government jet had to jettison fuel to land on Oxford's too-short runway), they walked into the Ole Miss administration building, the Lyceum, and one of Katzenbach's men dropped a dime into the pay phone and called the Justice Department collect. A few days later, after the army had been upbraided for poor communications during the crisis, a general asked Katzenbach how the Justice Department had maintained such clear and strong signals to Washington. Katzenbach reached into his pocket and pulled out a dime.

The Kennedys were completely reliant, however, on forces beyond their control. RFK always looked for tough cops in tight spots, and in Alabama, during the Freedom Rides, he had found one in Floyd Mann, the courageous chief of the state police who had stopped the Montgomery bus station riot by firing his pistol in the air. Mann had worked with his opposite in the Mississippi highway patrol, Colonel T. B. Birdsong, to convoy the Freedom Riders safely from Montgomery to Jackson. Now Kennedy was counting on Colonel Birdsong to be another Mann, a faithful servant of the law. He was to be disappointed: Birdsong took his orders from Mississippi politicians.

Escorted by marshals, Meredith arrived at Ole Miss at about 6:30 p.m., picked out a room in a deserted dormitory—and began pulling out textbooks from his suitcase. He wanted to get a head start on studying for class the next day. The Kennedys were beginning to think they had pulled it off. Kenny O'Donnell called his old teammate RFK "Mandrake the Magician" for so skillfully sneaking Meredith onto campus. But surly knots of students were swirling about outside, chanting, "Go to Cuba, nigger lovers!" and, more ominously, "Just wait'll dark!" As he walked about outside the administration building, one of the Kennedy aides pressed into service that afternoon, Joe Dolan, was struck by the ferocity and vocabulary of the pretty co-eds, screaming obscenities in his face.

Unprepared and ignorant of local lore, the Kennedy team blundered in its choice of a place to stand. A command post was established in the Lyceum in the heart of the Old Miss campus, and white-helmeted U.S. marshals, in business suits and yellow riot vests, were picketed outside, facing a tree-shaded lawn known as the Grove. The Lyceum and the Grove were sacred ground at Ole Miss. Katzenbach later realized they might as well have decided to bivouac in Robert E. Lee's tomb.

To avoid using federal troops, Kennedy had quickly assembled a force of U.S. marshals, federal prison guards, and border patrolmen. In the rush to get to Ole Miss, they had left their bullhorns behind at the airport. Some of the border patrolmen forgot their tear gas and gas masks. The feds were counting on Colonel Birdsong's highway patrolmen, arrayed behind the jeering students, to act as a buffer. But at 7:25 p.m., the Border Patrol monitored orders crackling across the short wave, telling the state police to withdraw. At first, the students flicked cigarette butts and gravel at the marshals' trucks. Then, as the state police drifted away, rocks and bricks and even a jar of acid, stolen from the chemistry lab, flew at the marshals themselves, standing exposed in front of the hallowed Lyceum. Shortly before 8 p.m., a Molotov cocktail—a Coke bottle filled with gasoline—burst into flame near the picket line. Then a U.S. lawman was felled by a piece of steel pipe. The chief of the marshals, Jim McShane, gave the order to fire tear gas. The first victim was one of the few remaining Mississippi highway patrolmen, hit in the head from behind by a shell casing and nearly killed by the gas.

In Washington, where it was just after 10 p.m., Burke Marshall tried to reach the president before he began his nationwide address from the Oval Office. He was too late. The president was already telling the American people that Meredith was safely on campus, that no troops had been called out, and that the rule of law was prevailing. He praised the Mississippians for their "honor and courage, won on the field of battle, and on the gridiron, as well as the university campus." The president had just finished his speech and joined his aides in the Cabinet Room when RFK arrived to announce that the demonstrators outside the Lyceum were "throwing iron spikes." The president's secret recording system was on; hidden microphones picked up the next three hours of pleading, plotting, and grim joking among a half dozen of the president's men, including RFK. Though the New Frontiersmen for the most part maintained a studied calm, anxiety crept into their voices with each worsening bulletin from the front. It was, RFK would later say, "the worst night I ever spent."

With his reverence for gridiron heroes, RFK at first seized on a somewhat far-fetched idea to disperse the angry crowd: bring in the popular Ole Miss football coach, Johnny Vaught, to tell the students to go back to their dorms. This suggestion was greeted with incredulity by a few in the room. "Huh, he won't believe it," a voice piped up. Understandably, Vaught proved difficult to find and sent back word that he wanted to "keep his squad out of it." Several times during the night, RFK's aides would inquire, a little forlornly, if the coach had been heard from. "This reminds me a little bit of the Bay of Pigs," said Kenny O'Donnell. "Yech!" responded RFK. "We have riots just like this at Harvard because some guy yells. . . ." said JFK, trying to sound jaunty.

At about 9 p.m. (11 p.m. daylight saving time in Washington), a shotgun blast rang out from the Grove. A marshal dropped, buckshot in his neck. Then came the crack of a high-powered rifle and down went another marshal, wounded in the leg. The students in crew cuts and T-shirts began to scatter; the boys from the hills had taken over, hard-eyed men with ducktail haircuts and missing teeth. Joe Dolan made his way through the skirmish line to the college infirmary and tried to explain to the doctor on duty that he had wounded men who needed medical attention. The doctor gave him forms to fill out, then more forms. Finally, he told Dolan, "We've got to take care of our people first." In Washington, RFK gloomily announced that General Edwin Walker had arrived at the scene of the riot. A Korean War hero, Walker had become a rabble-rouser. JFK interjected, "Imagine that son of a bitch having been commander of a division." The president and his men began discussing a recent bestseller, *Seven Days in May*, about a military coup in the United States. "It's not any good," grumbled the president. "The only character that came out at all was the general. . . ."

RFK brought the conversation back to reality. General Walker, he said, "is getting them all stirred up. If he has 'em march down there with guns, we could have a helluva battle." "Thugs," said Burke Marshall. The president tried to maintain his ironic detachment with mordancy: "I haven't had such an interesting time since the Bay of Pigs. . . ." RFK picked up the gallows humor, acknowledging that this time the noose was around his neck. Ole Miss was his responsibility, not the CIA's or the Pentagon's. RFK pretended to be reading from a press release: "The attorney general announced today, he's joining [former CIA director] Allen Dulles at Princeton Univers. . . ." He was interrupted by raucous laughter.

At 10 p.m. (midnight in Washington), the bulletins seemed truly desperate. "They're storming where Meredith is," announced RFK. The would-be freshman had been stashed away in a dormitory in a remote corner of the campus, but some rioters had apparently found him. Kenny O'Donnell raised the prospect on everyone's mind: "You don't want to have a lynching," he said. A dozen marshals defending Meredith were armed with sidearms. "They better fire, I suppose," RFK concluded, heavily. "They gotta protect Meredith." The president rang up Governor Barnett, who was at the governor's mansion in Jackson. JFK reported to his brother that Barnett wanted to move Meredith out of the dorm for his safety. For the first time, a note of the slightest panic enters RFK's voice. "I can't get him out. How am I gonna get him out?" he asked no one in particular.

The siege was worsening at the Lyceum, too. Two more marshals went down with gunshot wounds. Bullets were splatting against the walls of the graceful, colonnaded building. Under fire with the marshals, Ed Guthman, RFK's spokesman and a combat veteran from World War II, "is so scared he can't talk," reported O'Donnell. (It was Guthman who famously told Kennedy, "It's getting like the Alamo down here" and elicited his cheerful response, "Well, you know what happened to those guys.")

McShane, the chief marshal, wanted authority to open fire to keep the Lyceum from being overrun. Ramsey Clark, who normally handled Indian claims cases at the department but now commanded the crisis "communications center," reluctantly passed along the request. For Kennedy, the moment of decision had arrived. Say no to defensive fire and he risked sacrificing his men—several of them dear friends—and letting the mob string up Meredith from one of the gracious oaks in the Grove. Say yes and he risked provoking a second civil war. Robert Kennedy huddled with his brother. The answer was no. The marshals could open fire only if the rioters stormed Meredith's room and threatened his life. They could not use their weapons to protect themselves at the Lyceum. RFK called Katzenbach, the senior man at the Lyceum, to deliver the cold verdict. We do not have a recording from Katzenbach's side of the conversation, but, judging from RFK's halting and pained words, it must have been an anguished exchange:

> Hey, Nick? . . . Oh, uh, I just got, uh, Ramsey just asked me for, if they have permission to fire back? . . . Do you have to do that? . . . Well, can't they just retreat into that building [the Lyceum] . . . Is he [Meredith] safe over to your place [Kennedy was asking if the marshals had moved Meredith out the dorm over to the Lyceum]? . . . Uh, I think that they can fire to save *him* . . . But, uh, uh, uh, uh . . . Now, uh, if you can hold out for an hour there? . . . Can you hold out if you have gas? . . . Is there much firing? . . . Is there any way you could figure a way to scare them off? . . . [This apparently provoked some exasperation by Katzenbach] . . . Sorry, but I, I think if we start a, uh, battle. . . .

Katzenbach, a former army air force bombardier who had survived the Luftwaffe (his plane had been shot down over Germany), was not eager to open fire, either. But something had to be done to lift the siege. With reluctance, he asked Washington to send in federal troops. Shortly after midnight, the Pentagon was told to began airlifting a force of MPs from a base in Memphis. The military's cumbersome chain of command could not adjust to RFK's impromptu demands, or just as unforgivable, give straight answers to the insistent attorney general. "Damn army!" exclaimed RFK at about 1 a.m. "They can't even tell if the MPs have left yet." O'Donnell wisecracked: "I have a hunch that Khrushchev would get those troops in there fast enough." As the army dithered, uncrating rifles by flashlight on the tarmac, the battle of Ole Miss raged on. The rioters tried to break the marshals with a bulldozer, then a fire truck, then by aiming an unmanned '53 Chevy—with the accelerator held down by a rock—into their midst. With remarkable discipline, the marshals held fast—and never opened fire. When the army finally arrived at the Lyceum at 2:17 a.m., 160 marshals had been wounded, 28 by gunfire. The mob had shot and killed a reporter for Agence France-Presse who tried to take a photograph of some rabble-rousers unloading guns, as well as an unlucky local jukebox repairman who caught a stray round.

RFK knew that there would be recriminations. "Sure is a great day," he muttered in the early-morning hours. Speaking on the phone with press secretary Guthman while the bullets were still flying, he asked, "What are we gonna say about all this, uh, uh, Ed? . . . We're gonna have a helluva problem about why we, uh, didn't handle the situation better." But Kennedy was a good leader to his troops: he praised Guthman and the men at the Lyceum and took the responsibility for failure on himself: "You did terrific," he told Guthman. Privately, RFK recognized that "we were lucky to get out of it" without greater loss of life. Furious at the military for its tardy rescue, President Kennedy chewed out Secretary of the Army Cyrus Vance and the general. As they did after the Bay of Pigs, JFK's poll ratings went up in the immediate aftermath of the battle. It might have been a temporary boost, a momentary show of rallying around the commander in chief. The public did not have long to dwell on Ole Miss. In little more than a fortnight, they were held spellbound by the worst and most dangerous crisis of the Cold War.

WITHIN A FEW DAYS of the Ole Miss riots, 23,000 federal troops had descended on Oxford, Mississippi—three times the college town's population. Scorned by classmates and surrounded by marshals, Meredith attended classes and ate in lonely isolation. Worried commanders in the occupying army ordered the black soldiers in their units to stay in their tents, lest they offend the local whites. The troops were on such a heightened state of alert that when some college boys serenaded a sorority on October 11, 10,000 soldiers scrambled to guard against any rioting.

By then, RFK had already plunged back into an arena that continued to concern him more than civil rights. Cuba still vexed Robert Kennedy. It reminded him of his brother's worst defeat and greatest humiliation, made him suffer for the Bay of Pigs prisoners still in Castro's jails, and provoked him to want to take unreasonable chances. On the subject of Cuba in the early fall of 1962, RFK was by turns disagreeable, foolhardy—and far-seeing.

After seven months, Kennedy's secret war—Operation Mongoose—was hopelessly bogged down, riven by personality clashes, incapable of producing the "boom and bang" that Kennedy wanted to see on the island. On October 4, just four days after the Battle of Ole Miss, Kennedy played his familiar hectoring role with the Special Group (Augmented), the top officials from State, Defense, and CIA charged with getting rid of Fidel Castro. The president was dissatisfied, RFK stated. The commander in chief wanted "massive activity" on the island. Maybe a program of sabotage and subversion was not enough, and more "direct action" was called for, said RFK. The attorney general demanded "dynamic" and "imaginative" solutions. RFK's own idea—a bad one, fortunately never implemented—was to mine Cuban waters with "non-attributable mines."

The other top men in the room listened wearily. For the most part they were resigned to RFK's rants—and to failure in Cuba. Mac Bundy, the president's national security adviser, believed that the choices were invading Cuba—which he ruled out—and "learning to live with Castro." Bundy and Secretary of State Rusk worried that too high a "noise level" on Cuba would provoke Soviet retaliation in Berlin, which they rated as a more essential Cold War battlefield.

In his fulminations over Cuba, RFK had only one true ally, John McCone, the director of the CIA. McCone's abiding fear was that the Soviets would turn Cuba into a missile base. A former assistant air force secretary and chairman of the Atomic Energy Commission, McCone was a devout believer in strategic superiority. To him the arms race was essential and never-ending; the United States could never be too far ahead. McCone, a wealthy California businessman and a Republican, had been recruited to run the CIA after the Bay of Pigs by the Kennedys, who wanted a smart, tough outsider not easily snowed by the agency old guard. McCone was a blunt and prickly man and a literal-minded Catholic moralist, all of which appealed to Robert Kennedy. The bond was cemented when McCone's wife died almost as soon as he took over the agency, and Ethel Kennedy became a close and faithful mourner and comforter.

Like RFK, McCone was a Cassandra on Cuba. In August, the CIA director warned that an unusual number of Soviet ships were entering Cuban harbors, dispensing heavy loads. CIA analysts were certain that the Cubans were installing Soviet ground-to-air missile defense systems. McCone extrapolated that those little missiles heralded bigger ones—ballistic missiles, tipped with nuclear warheads. Nonsense, responded all of the other government experts. Khrushchev would never be so stupid as to put nuclear missiles ninety miles away from Florida. The only one who heeded McCone's warnings was RFK. The president's brother had predicted nuclear missiles in Cuba back in April 1961. RFK had a healthy capacity to ask the hard and painful question, the one that others did not want to hear. In March 1962, he had requested contingency plans for U.S. reaction to a Soviet missile base in Cuba. Nothing was done in response, the State Department later ruefully noted, because "it was decided that the possibility was too remote to waste time on."

To McCone, the only solution was to invade before the Soviets could make Cuba a launching pad. RFK could not be quite so openly belligerent. He knew his brother was very reluctant to hurl tens of thousands of U.S. Marines and paratroopers against Castro's island stronghold. But he shared McCone's sense of urgency. At a meeting on Cuba at the White House on September 9, RFK gloomily doodled during a discussion of the Soviet threat. On a scrap of White House notepaper, he wrote "surface to surface" (meaning nuclear missiles that could reach the United States from Cuba). Then he wrote the word "invasion" and heavily underscored it.

In one sense, Kennedy was being realistic. The United States could not easily tolerate Soviet missiles in Cuba. But he was more willing than most of the president's national security team to contemplate a full-scale invasion. The devious portion of his mind returned to spinning scenarios that would give the United States an excuse to intervene. Back in April 1961, in the anguished memo he wrote his brother during the Bay of Pigs fiasco, RFK had imagined a provocation. Perhaps, he had suggested, the United States could pretend that the navy base at Guantánamo had been struck by Cubans flying Soviet MiGs. No doubt stimulated by RFK's thinking, contingency plans drafted for Operation Mongoose began coming up with harebrained schemes for staging a provocation. In one, Operation Bingo, the CIA would simulate a firefight at Guantánamo to justify an invasion; in another, "a 'Remember the *Maine*' incident could be arranged . . . we could blow up a US ship in Guantánamo Bay and blame Cuba." RFK himself again raised the possibility at a meeting of all the top national security officials on August 21. According to McCone's notes of the meeting, "the Attorney General queried the meeting as to what other aggressive steps could be taken." RFK's own tentative suggestion was to stage "an action against Guantánamo which would permit us to retaliate. . . ."

No one was listening. At the end of August, the president (not nearly so gung-ho as RFK portrayed him to be with the Special Group) essentially equivocated, approving a "stepped up" program of sabotage against Cuba, but most of his advisers were wary of raising the "noise" level. McCone, who had just remarried, counseled RFK to keep the pressure on. Then he went on his honeymoon to the French Riviera. Without McCone around to press, the national security bureaucracy became even more quiescent about Cuba. Fearful that the CIA's high-flying spy plane, the U-2, would be shot down by Castro's new Soviet-made air defense missiles (SAMs), Secretary of State Dean Rusk canceled U-2 flights over Cuba in September. RFK was outvoted and his reaction was typically ad hominem. "What's the matter, Dean?" he snarled, as the other officials around the table looked on uncomfortably. "No guts?"

His petulance notwithstanding, RFK was absolutely correct to want to keep the U-2s flying. Unknown to the United States, those Soviet freighters seen docking in Cuban ports in August and September carried medium- and intermediate-range ballistic missiles capable of hitting at least half the cities in the United States. On October 4, as RFK was browbeating the Special Group (Augmented), demanding more action, the Soviet freighter *Indigirka* arrived in the Cuban port of Mariel. It unloaded 45 one-megaton warheads for ballistic missiles, a dozen atom bombs, and 48 tactical nuclear weapons (to be used to repel an invasion)—all told, twenty times the explosive power dropped by Allied planes on Germany in World War II.

Robert Kennedy, like the American intelligence community, was in the dark. But he sensed a brewing crisis in U.S.-Soviet relations. On October 5, the very next day, RFK met with his Soviet back channel, Georgi Bolshakov. Entering the attorney general's office, Bolshakov immediately noticed that Kennedy appeared distant and tense. Gone was the shirtsleeved, teasing RFK who had invited him to arm-wrestle at Hickory Hill. Kennedy sat gravely behind his desk, with his suit jacket buttoned up. Bolshakov repeated a promise from Chairman Khrushchev that the Soviets were only putting defensive weapons in Cuba—

"exclusively defensive weapons intended for protecting the interests of the Cuban revolution." Kennedy anxiously asked Bolshakov to repeat the part about defensive weapons, and then took careful notes while the GRU agent spoke.

Bolshakov was not telling the truth, though he didn't know it. He was totally unaware of Operation Anadyr, Khrushchev's secret plan to install nuclear missiles in Cuba. Bolshakov's unwitting deception illustrates the drawbacks of operating through go-betweens and back channels. Kennedy and Bolshakov had grown close over the past year and a half. They had met a dozen times and conducted some useful behind-the-scenes diplomacy, including a secret agreement to remove U.S. troops from Thailand in exchange for Soviet help in enforcing a peace accord in Laos. Bolshakov had drunk with Kennedy and his friends at Hickory Hill, and Bolshakov had asked Kennedy to vacation with him in the Caucasus Mountains (the Kremlin nixed that idea). But Bolshakov was still a Soviet agent and closely controlled by his spymasters in Moscow. A friendly journalist, Warren Rogers, then with the *New York Herald Tribune*, thought that Bolshakov might be induced to defect if he brought his family— his wife and nine-year-old son—to the United States. When Rogers asked why he didn't ask his family to join him in Washington, Bolshakov replied succinctly, "I can't." Rogers understood: the GRU agent's family was being held hostage back in the Soviet Union.

Kennedy's friendship with Bolshakov was genuine enough, and, with his acute sensitivity, Kennedy probably could tell by now when Bolshakov was not telling the truth. But his instincts didn't do much good if Bolshakov didn't know himself.

Kennedy, tutored by Soviet experts like Ambassadors Chip Bohlen and Llewellyn "Tommy" Thompson, knew that *something* was up. Ever since late spring, the Kennedy administration had felt a new chill in U.S.-Soviet relations. "Tell me, Georgi," asked RFK, as he sat in the sunshine at Hickory Hill with Bolshakov on the first Sunday in June, "is there anyone in the Soviet leadership who advocates a decisive clash with the United States?" Kennedy suspected that hard-liners in the Soviet military were pushing Khrushchev to become more belligerent. The attorney general was projecting his own fears. In Moscow, Khrushchev was in control; putting missiles in Cuba had been entirely his idea. But in Washington, the Kennedys remained extremely wary of the war hawks like Air Force General Curtis LeMay. In his casual conversation with Bolshakov, RFK was remarkably indiscreet about his worries. He told the GRU agent that the Joint Chiefs of Staff had "offered the president a report in which they confirmed that the United States is currently ahead of the Soviet Union in military power and that *in extremis* it would be possible to probe the forces of the Soviet Union." Kennedy's loose use of the word "probe" predictably set off alarms in the Kremlin. Did he mean that the Pentagon was considering a preemptive strike? This was exactly the kind of provocative talk that drove the arms race and deepened the Cold War. Khrushchev was in awe of nuclear weapons. He called them "the new Gods of War." Rockets and superbombs had elevated the Soviet Union to superpower status. Worried about his country's shaky economy and localized dissent (there had been food riots in a city near the Black Sea), suffering uneasy relations with the Chinese and East Europeans, he wanted to show his muscle. "Why not throw a hedgehog at Uncle Sam's pants?" he had suggested to his advisers in April, just before launching Operation Anadyr. Installing missiles in Cuba would show the world—and guarantee against any more foolish invasions by the Americans.

Cuba was only one of Khrushchev's concerns. The Kremlin leader was perhaps more intent on Berlin. The on-again, off-again Berlin crisis was heating up. Khrushchev wanted the West out of the divided city, and he seemed ready to force the issue by staging a confrontation. He was willing to hold off until after the November elections in the United States, in order not to catch Kennedy at a politically awkward time. But he wanted to be ready to play nuclear brinksmanship. It remains unclear whether Khrushchev was much of a strategic thinker. Still, the Kremlin leader may have worked out a rough nuclear equation that would tip the balance in Berlin. The Soviets believed that President Kennedy, pushed by the war hawks in the Pentagon, was capable of striking first with nuclear weapons. Khrushchev knew as well that his small and unreliable force of intercontinental ballistic missiles—ICBMs based in the Soviet Union—was vulnerable to being wiped out before they could be fired in retaliation, and that his aging bomber fleet was next to useless. The Soviets did have many tested and proven medium-range missiles—MRBMs with a range of about a thousand miles—but no platform close enough to the United States from which to aim them. Cuba, so close to the Florida shore, could be transformed into a Soviet aircraft carrier and launching pad. With such a dagger pointed at his heart, President Kennedy would never risk a first strike to keep Berlin out of Soviet hands. Or so Khrushchev was apparently willing to bet.

The MRBMs were scheduled to be operational in Cuba by the end of October. Khrushchev did worry that he would get caught before the missiles were in place. American spy planes routinely flew low right over Soviet freighters as they plied the ocean between the Black Sea and the Caribbean. In the summer of 1962, Khrushchev developed a ploy to throw off the American snoops. He would send a false message, with Bolshakov as carrier pigeon. Bolshakov was instructed to tell the Kennedys that the best way to improve superpower relations was to call off the "piratical" American flights over Soviet shipping.

President Kennedy took the bait. On September 4, Bolshakov was summoned to the Oval Office and told that the United States, as a gesture of good faith, was calling off aerial surveillance of Soviet ships en route to Cuba. "Tell him [Khrushchev] that I've ordered those flights stopped today," said JFK. In the alleyway between the White House and the Old Executive Building, an agitated RFK implored Bolshakov to tell his masters not to try anything provocative before the congressional elections in November. Senator Kenneth Keating, Republican of New York, was making speeches accusing the Kennedy administration of weakness in the face of the Soviet buildup in Cuba. "Goddamn it, Georgi, doesn't Premier Khrushchev realize the President's position?" demanded Kennedy. JFK was under attack from hawks on the right. It would be a mistake to play into their hands by creating a blowup before November. Then he startled Bolshakov by suggesting that "they"—the right-wingers—might "go to any length." His brother's safety was never far from his mind. He asked the FBI to examine some wine sent by the Russians to Kennedy as a gift. The lab reported no poisons or mind-altering drugs and, perhaps in mild mockery, that "the wine was consumed in the examination."

The United States had been blinded and deceived. In early October, Mc-Cone returned from his honeymoon and immediately demanded the resumption of U-2 flights over Cuba, the SAM sites be damned. Refugees fleeing Cuba had reported seeing trucks bearing round objects as long as palm trees in the San Cristóbal region. Heavy tarpaulin-covered trucks were knocking over phone poles as they navigated tight turns on the country roads. On October 9, Washington authorized the first U-2 flights over Cuba in six weeks. The weather socked in for four more days. At 11:30 p.m. on the night of Saturday, October 13, a U-2 finally took off from Edwards Air Force Base in California, flying at 70,000 feet, heading south and east. The pictures taken by the spy plane over San Cristóbal, in western Cuba, brought the world to the brink.

CHAPTER 11 BRINK

Shortly after he arrived at his Justice Department office on the morning of Tuesday, October 16, 1962, Robert Kennedy received a phone call from his brother at the White House. "We have some big trouble," said the president. "I want you over here." At about 9 a.m., RFK burst into the small, cluttered office of National Security Adviser McGeorge Bundy. A CIA man handed the attorney general some blown-up aerial reconnaissance photographs and explained that the images revealed Soviet ballistic missiles in Cuba. Robert Kennedy rarely used expletives, but he did now. "Oh shit. Shit! Shit!" he exclaimed, pounding his fist into his palm. "Those sons a bitches Russians."

RFK examined the photos carefully. "What I saw appeared to be no more than the clearing of a field for a farm or the basement of a house," Kennedy later wrote in his memoir of the Cuban Missile Crisis, *Thirteen Days*. He was relieved to hear that other nonexperts were equally mystified. Viewing some slightly sharper photos, the president thought he was looking at a football field. The photo-interpreters from the spy agency identified four missile launchers and eight canvas-covered trailers carrying medium-range ballistic missiles. RFK's mordant humor did not fail him. "Can they hit Oxford, Mississippi?" he asked.

He was working to control his fury. He had been completely, if perhaps unwittingly, deceived by his Soviet friend Georgi Bolshakov. "It had all been lies, one gigantic fabric of lies," RFK wrote. To ease Cold War tensions, the Kennedys had acceded to the Kremlin's request to stop American spy planes from flying over Soviet ships bound for Cuba; now, it appeared, the Americans had been snookered. The president felt equally betrayed. He had been still in his pajamas when McGeorge Bundy brought him the news at about 8 a.m. "He [Khrushchev] can't do this to me!" the president shouted. After nearly two years of plotting and strategizing about Cuba, and all that private and public diplomacy to carefully manage the superpower rivalry, this was what they had to show for it. With Castro's help, Khrushchev was building a base for missiles that could, within a few minutes of launch, vaporize not only Oxford, Mississippi, but also Washington, D.C.

RFK's predictable immediate reaction was to get even, to want to strike back. He gave way to those feelings—but only for about a day. Then he calmed down and his shrewder instincts took over. The worst of times brought out the best in Robert Kennedy. On the whole, his advice and judgment during the thirteen days of the Cuban Missile Crisis were supple and discerning—and critically important to his brother. He blended high moralism and shifty pragmatism in a peculiarly Kennedyesque way to edge the United States and the Soviet Union back from the abyss. He made believers of men who expected less of him. "I was very much surprised by his performance," said George Ball, the under secretary of state.

> I had always had a feeling that Bobby had a much too simplistic and categorical position toward things—either you condemn something utterly or you accept it enthusiastically . . . and there seemed no intermediate positions. He reflected this rather determined view that you always acted decisively and that you always went in and damned the torpedoes . . . even though it might cause an awful lot of problems elsewhere in the world. But he behaved quite differently during the Cuban missile crisis.

His approach was subtle and variable, depending on the moment and the need. In the meetings of the ExCom, the name given the policy advisers gathered by President Kennedy to help him through the crisis,* RFK often played the role of prod and gadfly. He asked awkward questions (sometimes awkwardly; stress did not improve his syntax) and tested and quarreled with assumptions. Based on the transcripts of the ExCom meetings (about half of them, the ones held in the cabinet room, were recorded by the president's secret taping system, known only to JFK, RFK, and a few technicians), it is sometimes difficult to pin down exactly where RFK stood on important questions. He did not hesitate to reverse field or rethink an answer, in part to stimulate discus-

---

* The group was formally designated the Executive Committee of the National Security Council. In addition to the Kennedys, its members included Secretary of State Dean Rusk, Secretary of Defense Robert McNamara, Secretary of the Treasury Douglas Dillon, CIA director John McCone, National Security Adviser McGeorge Bundy, presidential counsel Theodore Sorensen, Under Secretary of State George Ball, Deputy Under Secretary of State U. Alexis Johnson, Chairman of the Joint Chiefs General Maxwell Taylor, Assistant Secretary of State for Latin American Affairs Edwin Martin, Soviet experts Charles Bohlen (who left to become ambassador to France after the first day) and Llewellyn Thompson, Deputy Secretary of Defense Roswell Gilpatric, Assistant Secretary of Defense Paul Nitze, and—intermittently at various meetings—former secretary of state Dean Acheson, former secretary of defense Robert Lovett, Vice President Lyndon Johnson, Ambassador to the UN Adlai Stevenson, special assistant to the president Kenneth O'Donnell, and USIA deputy director Donald Wilson.

sion, but also because he was working his own way through an extraordinarily complex set of problems. At other times, especially when his brother was not in the room, he became a consensus-maker, finding the middle ground between hawks and doves. Despite some unwise and intemperate remarks on the first day, one can always sense him trying to think a few steps ahead, working hard to calculate the unintended consequences, and then trying to head them off. That summer, the Kennedy brothers had both read Barbara Tuchman's *The Guns of August*, chronicling the blind rush of the great powers into the First World War. Tuchman quotes Germany's chancellor, Prince von Bülow, asking his successor, "How did it all happen?" "Ah," came the reply, "if only we knew." RFK chose this rueful exchange to end *Thirteen Days*. On the last night of the crisis, when war seemed very near, the Kennedys explicitly discussed the lessons of Tuchman's book. They were determined not to back Khrushchev into a corner.

As usual, the Kennedys operated on several levels, compartmentalizing information and using hidden back channels. JFK and RFK were secretive and cagey about their exit strategy, both during the crisis and in the postmortems. RFK, on his own behalf and for his brother, preferred to maintain a veneer of toughness and resolution. Having been a bully, RFK knew how to push back against bullies. But the younger Kennedy also showed a less obvious but equally fundamental aspect of his character, that of peacemaker and conciliator. As he searched for a way out—a means to allow the Russians to back down and save face—the RFK that comes to mind is not the fierce inquisitor of Jimmy Hoffa or the hothead who picked so many fights for the honor of his family (or for no particular reason at all). One thinks instead of the less well-known but true Robert Kennedy, the oversensitive little boy who cringed at night as he listened to Joe Jr. bang Jack's head against the wall—the "pet" who saw his beloved mother suffer her husband's dalliances by retreating into faith—the unsure young man in the sailor suit who told his siblings to keep quiet lest they disturb their grieving father—the solicitous younger brother who tried to make Jackie show a little appreciation for Jack's skill as an athlete—the eager-to-please son who withstood the blows of his crippled father and still begged to help. RFK never wanted to look soft, never wanted to be seen backing down, but he always maneuvered to avoid the kind of final showdown that could destroy a family—or, in a nuclear age, whole nations. Just two weeks before the Cuban Missile Crisis, he had been willing to go through the most elaborate charade to accommodate the political posturing of Governor Ross Barnett. That exercise had ended in near disaster, but it was useful training for averting a far greater catastrophe.

The battle of Ole Miss cost Kennedy only one sleepless night. The Cuban Missile Crisis was a two-week ordeal that stretched RFK and the other members of the ExCom to the limits of physical and emotional endurance. Five hours after learning about the missiles, Kennedy was still seething when he walked into the regularly scheduled weekly meeting of the Special Group (Augmented) at 2:30 p.m. on Tuesday afternoon, October 16. Icily, the attorney general told the get-Castro committee that the president was "dissatisfied" with the progress of Operation Mongoose. The operation had been under way for almost a year and still had produced no significant sabotage in Cuba. The attorney general stated that he intended to give Mongoose more of his "personal attention." From now on the Special Group would meet every morning at nine-thirty. He approved of the CIA's latest sabotage plans, which, he said, showed more "push" than earlier efforts. (The plans included an underwater demolition attack by Cuban frogmen on shipping in a Cuban port, a hit-and-run raid to set afire a tanker in Havana harbor, and a grenade attack on the Chinese embassy in Havana.) Kennedy pointedly asked how many Cubans would rise up and fight Castro if Cuba was invaded.

At 6:30 p.m. that evening, at the end of an unseasonably warm and muggy day, the government cars began to pull up at the White House, delivering every major foreign policy adviser to the president. For the second time that day (a briefing had been hastily summoned at noon), the ExCom gathered in the cabinet room to discuss what to do about the missiles. The mood was shaky; the advisers were still stunned. "How much time do we have?" the president asked the CIA. The agency analysts weren't sure; it was impossible to tell if the Soviet missiles were armed and ready to fly. To President Kennedy, and to most of his advisers, leaving the missiles in Cuba was out of the question. The politics, domestic and international, demanded action. Kennedy had publicly declared in September that the United States would not tolerate offensive missiles in Cuba. Republicans, already carping about administration "softness," would never allow him to forget that pledge. Most worrisome, Khrushchev could be expected to try using his new rockets as a club or a bargaining chip to drive the West out of Berlin.

A showdown was coming. President Kennedy could wait and face Khrushchev on the testing ground of Berlin, where the Soviets were spoiling for a confrontation. Or Kennedy could make his stand now. He understood that if he hesitated and allowed the Soviet missiles to remain in Cuba, his ace-in-the-hole in defending Berlin—the threat of an American first strike against the Soviet Union—would be less credible. MRBMs in Cuba would do more than reduce the warning time of a Soviet missile attack on the United States from a meager ten minutes to a pitifully brief two to three minutes. The Cuban missiles would mean that, as a practical matter, the United States would have a more difficult time launching a preemptive attack by wiping out Moscow's small and primitive nuclear force, its twenty or so ICBMs and fleet of obsolete bombers. As soon as the Soviet MRBMs became operational, the strategic balance would tilt, not fundamentally perhaps, but enough to affect the odds in the game of brinksmanship. As Kennedy lamented a few days later, "We're going to have this knife stuck right in our guts." If Washington did not move now, Moscow might be emboldened later. At least by hitting Cuba immediately, Kennedy could use conventional forces. If he waited for the showdown to erupt in Berlin, his only option would be to go nuclear. In the first hours of the crisis, a military strike against Cuba seemed nearly inevitable. To his advisers arrayed around the long table in the cabinet room on the evening of October 16, the president flatly declared, "We're going to take out those missiles."

But how? A "surgical" strike to cut out the missiles was tempting, but not realistic. Since even a single missile launched in retaliation would cost an American city, air strikes could not afford to miss any target. Yet the air force could not guarantee the destruction of each and every missile—even assuming that all the launching sites on the cloud-covered island had been found. "It'll never be one hundred percent," cautioned General Maxwell Taylor, whom Kennedy had recently made chairman of the Joint Chiefs of Staff in the hope of exercising a tighter rein on the military's top brass. The Pentagon generals did not want to strike without controlling the air over Cuba. But massive bombing raids to knock out Castro's air force—rapidly improving with the addition of Soviet MiGs—would require over a thousand sorties by American warplanes and risk killing many Cubans as well as Russian soldiers on the ground. As for storming the 800-mile island with marines and paratroopers, casualties would be high and victory hard-won. An invasion, General Taylor prudently warned, would be "deep mud." Finally, an air strike or an invasion, even if successful, might set off the Berlin crisis JFK was trying to avoid: Khrushchev might be provoked into snatching Berlin in retaliation.

The adviser who seemed most taken with the idea of an all-out invasion was Robert Kennedy. "If we go in, we go in hard," he scribbled on a piece of White House note paper sometime after 9 p.m. that Tuesday evening. Kennedy was not one to wait. Listing the reasons to act in a private note a few days later, he began, "We are going to have to act in Berlin anyway." Late in the discussion on the first evening of the crisis, after most others had held forth, RFK weighed in with his own gloomy assessment. Even if the air force could knock out all of the missiles, RFK asked, what was to stop Khrushchev from just sending more? Better, he suggested, to "get into it, and get it over with, and take our losses. And if he [Khrushchev] wants to get into a war over this . . ." He paused, trying to think through the unthinkable. "Hell, if it's war that's going to come on this thing, or if he sticks these kinds of missiles after the warning [Kennedy's declaration in September that offensive weapons in Cuba would be intolerable], then he's going to get into a war six months from now, so. . . ."

RFK's logic, at this point, tracked straight into the void. It boiled down to: if Khrushchev wants war, we'll give it to him. Not a satisfactory answer, since the war would be thermonuclear, but RFK was still burning with rage that he had been deceived by Bolshakov and the Soviets. Kennedy's next impulse, both ignoble and reckless, was to fight deception with trickery. Perhaps, he offered, the United States could stage an incident as a further pretext for invading. As RFK put it:

> . . . We should also think of whether there is some other way we can get involved in this, through Guantánamo Bay or something. Or whether there's some ship that . . . you know, sink the *Maine* or something. . . .

"Sink the *Maine* or something. . . ." Kennedy had been toying with the idea of this provocation for months. But one senses, listening closely to his remarks as recorded by JFK's secret taping system, that he knew the idea was a shaky one. His voice became slightly quavery, like that of a naughty boy trying to talk his way out of a lie by telling a bigger one. Robert McNamara, the clearest mind that evening, the one who did the most to help the group weigh the consequences of precipitous reaction, watched his friend struggle. On the first night of the thirteen days, McNamara later recalled, "RFK was a hawk in his head and his heart, because of that damn Mongoose thing. But," said McNamara, "he changed." RFK often followed a pattern: an initial burst of belligerence and intransigence, followed by a willingness to listen and change. This became his pattern during the Cuban Missile Crisis as well. Still in the process of becoming at the age of thirty-six, RFK grew faster during the thirteen days. One morning during the first week of the crisis, his assistant Joe Dolan walked into RFK's office at Justice to get his boss to sign some papers. Kennedy just stared straight ahead. "Something is different in here," said Dolan, who was unaware of the crisis. "I'm older," said Kennedy.

JFK and his advisers needed time to decide a course of action, but they feared the news of their discovery would leak, forcing premature declarations and allowing events to spin out of control. After talking to his brother, JFK decided that it would be prudent to maintain his public schedule, or at least a semblance, to lull the press, the public, and the Russians. On Wednesday, October 17, the president attended lunches for the crown prince of Libya and the foreign minister of West Germany, then flew to Connecticut to campaign for Abe Ribicoff, who was running for the Senate. RFK also believed that the ExCom would engage in more open and honest debate without the president presiding; government officials, RFK argued, tend to fall into line behind the chief executive and ape his opinions. After "a fight," RFK recalled, JFK agreed to absent himself from many of the ExCom deliberations.

In the president's absence, someone needed to step in as leader. The logical candidate might have been the secretary of state, but Dean Rusk was reticent and—inexplicably, to a scornful RFK—preoccupied with other diplomatic duties. The attorney general became the de facto chairman of the ExCom. RFK never actually took the chair. "He sometimes wouldn't even sit at the Cabinet table," recalled Mac Bundy. "I can remember times when he would deliberately put himself in one of the smaller chairs against the wall. . . . But it didn't make much difference; because, in a generic way, wherever he sat was one of the most important places in the room." During the thirteen days, the ExCom met in the cabinet room, in the oval room on the second floor of the White House, and in Under Secretary of State George Ball's conference room on the seventh floor at the State Department. "In all these rooms," said Bundy, "RFK was really the senior person. . . ."

RFK's style was never to dominate. Though he browbeat lowly bureaucrats and was sarcastic towards alleged "weaklings" like Chester Bowles, he was democratic and consensus-minded with the cabinet officers, top military and intelligence officials and old Cold Warriors summoned to join the ExCom. "We all spoke as equals. There was no rank," writes RFK in *Thirteen Days*. Discussion was "uninhibited and unrestricted." Kennedy preferred a swirling, almost Darwinian competition of ideas, secure in the knowledge that when the debate was over, he and his brother would decide. This freewheeling approach had been (and would be) RFK's campaign mode, but it made some around the table uneasy and insecure.

The eldest statesman of the ExCom, Dean Acheson, was appalled by the lack of discipline when he joined the group on Wednesday. Though the president had found Acheson to be overly hawkish and prickly during the Berlin crisis, he had summoned back Harry Truman's brilliant and acerbic secretary of state for his experience at dealing with the Soviets and for his formidable intellect. In his old age, Acheson was getting more rigid, and his sufferance of fools, always low, was now nonexistent. Acheson wanted to be in charge; failing that, he wanted to be heard above the din. With the president missing on Wednesday, the ExCom looked to him, he later recalled, like a "floating crap game." Discussion meandered about, ideas were ventured, discarded, then dredged up again. People wandered in and out as randomly as the coffee and sandwiches were delivered.

Acheson was clear in his own mind about the proper course of action. The United States should strike immediately and without warning. The missiles must be taken out, right away. By catching the Soviets in the act of sneaking missiles into Cuba, the United States had an opportunity to teach the Kremlin a lesson. The Russians were like an animal, "their tail caught in a screen door, and we ought to twist it," said Acheson, who enjoyed vivid metaphors, especially his own.

RFK warily watched Acheson perform that Wednesday. With his bristling guardsman's mustache, his clipped Groton accent, his too-sure manner, Acheson reminded Kennedy of the Brahmins who had kept his father out of the clubs at Harvard and in Boston. Acheson seemed cold-blooded, like a British pasha who wanted to teach the natives a lesson. As always, policy was personal for RFK. Acheson's hawkishness helped make a dove out of RFK. Less than twenty-four hours after he had suggested starting a war with a trumped-up provocation—"sinking the *Maine*"—Kennedy was suddenly seized with moralism. At some point, as he listened to the drumbeat for a surprise attack on Cuba, RFK passed a note on a slip of paper to JFK's speechwriter and counsel, Theodore Sorensen: "I now know how Tojo felt when he was planning Pearl Harbor."

The analogy was not his own. George Ball had mentioned Pearl Harbor at the ExCom meeting Tuesday evening. Later that night, Ball had written his fellow members of the ExCom a passionate memo: "We tried Japanese as war criminals because of the sneak attack on Pearl Harbor." A surprise attack, "far from establishing our moral strength . . . would in fact alienate a great part of the civilized world by behaving in a manner contrary to our traditions." On Wednesday, RFK picked up the refrain in testy exchanges with Acheson. "My brother is not going to be the Tojo of the '60s," said Kennedy. For the United States to stage a surprise attack would be a "Pearl Harbor in reverse."

To Acheson, this was so much poppycock. The animus between Kennedy and Acheson was mutual: The former secretary of state, who had been hounded by red baiters in the early '50s, remembered well that RFK had once worked for Senator Joe McCarthy. To the lawyerly, logical Acheson, RFK was all emotion and intuition. "Pearl Harbor in reverse," Acheson would later write, was a "thoroughly false and misleading analogy." Cuba was ninety miles away from Florida; Pearl Harbor was thousands of miles across an ocean from Japan. The United States had been pledged to defend the Caribbean since the Monroe Doctrine and had recently and explicitly warned the Soviets against placing offensive missiles in Cuba. With his own fondness for metaphor, Acheson derisively asked if it was "necessary to adopt the nineteenth-century method of having a man with a red flag walk before the steam engine to warn cattle and people to stay out of the way." On Thursday afternoon, Acheson was granted a private audience with President Kennedy in the Oval Office. When JFK brought up the Pearl Harbor analogy, the old statesman rebuked the young president for repeating "his brother's clichés." Such arguments were "silly" and "unworthy" of the president, said Acheson.

If not an air strike or an invasion, then what? Bob McNamara and others had proposed a naval blockade of Cuba, to keep the Soviets from delivering any more missiles and warheads and to demonstrate seriousness of purpose. A blockade was not a final solution—RFK glumly described it as "very slow death" on Thursday morning. He foresaw high seas' confrontations with the Russian navy and worried that as each day passed, the Soviets would have more time to hide and camouflage—or prepare to launch—the missiles already on the island. But as he contemplated the chain reaction of reprisals for an air strike—the Soviets grabbing for Berlin or bombing American missiles in Turkey, the United States shooting back, then "general war," that is, nuclear holocaust—a blockade beckoned as the least bad alternative. Robert Kennedy did not by any means rule out an air strike. But after the excruciating night of waiting for the troops to arrive at Ole Miss, he had low confidence in the military's capacity to do anything with precision. "He knew there was no such thing as a surgical strike," said Douglas Dillon. And he wanted to buy time to look for other, less obvious escape routes.

By Thursday night, Kennedy was on board for a blockade, at least as a first step. That evening at about 7 p.m., RFK came into the Oval Office through the Rose Garden, to find his brother expecting a visitor. Waiting in the anteroom was Robert Lovett, a Wall Street investment banker and, as a top adviser in the Truman administration, one of the architects of the Cold War standoff with the Soviet Union. The president had high regard for Lovett. After the election he had offered Lovett his choice: secretary of state, defense, or Treasury. Citing poor health, Lovett had begged off. Lovett's grace and equanimity were helpful on this tense evening, because they enabled the aging Cold Warrior to ignore RFK's inexcusable rudeness. According to Dino Brugioni, a CIA analyst who was waiting to see the president in an anteroom along with Lovett, RFK leaned his head out the door of the Oval Office and growled at the elder statesman, "Hey, you!" From within Brugioni could hear the president cursing his brother's poor manners: "Goddamn, Bobby!" In his formal recollection of the Cuban Missile Crisis, Lovett made no mention of his harsh summons. He praised RFK for his acuity and recalled being charmed by his children when he met them a few days later. (With typical Kennedy informality, Ethel and a station wagon full of kids picked up Lovett at the airport on his return from a weekend home in New York.)

In the Oval Office on Thursday evening, the three men settled around the fireplace to talk. After asking several "searching questions," Lovett recalled, Robert Kennedy told Lovett that he agreed on the "necessity of taking less violent steps at the outset because we could always blow up the place if necessary." RFK told Lovett that the president was being pushed by the hawks in the military. Sympathetic to RFK's exasperation with generals—Lovett had been secretary of defense in the early '50s—the wise old hand commiserated on the frustrations of dealing with the Pentagon.

That night at about 10 p.m. after a meeting in George Ball's conference room at State, nine members of the ExCom piled into a limousine (so as to attract less attention; RFK sat on the lap of Deputy Under Secretary of State U. Alexis Johnson) and drove to see the president, sneaking in from the Treasury Department through the White House bomb shelter. By midnight, President Kennedy believed that a consensus was forming around the blockade or less belligerent-sounding "quarantine" approach, but by Friday morning disagreements had broken out anew. Fatigue and stress were beginning to show. "Minds and opinions began to change again, and not only on small points," recalled RFK.*

Meeting alone with the president on Friday morning, the Joint Chiefs virtually bullied the president to begin bombing. "If we don't do anything to Cuba, then they're going to push on Berlin and push *real hard* because they've got us *on the run*," pressed the ever-bellicose air force chief of staff, General Curtis LeMay. "You're in a pretty bad fix, Mr. President," said LeMay. "What did you say?" asked Kennedy, taken aback at his general's *lèse-majesté*. "You're in a bad fix," repeated LeMay, almost as if he was enjoying his civilian master's discomfort. Kennedy mumbled a joke, but he was not amused. "Those brass hats have one great advantage in their favor," JFK groused to Kenny O'Donnell. "If we . . . do what they want us to do, none of us will be alive later to tell them they're wrong."

After the chiefs departed, the president ran into his brother and Ted Sorensen in the hallway off the Oval Office. "This thing is falling apart," said the president. "You have to pull it together." Sorensen believed that JFK had already ruled out military action as a first step and decided he wanted a blockade. "That's not what he said to us," Sorensen later recalled. "But he didn't have to. He knew what Bobby and I thought." Perhaps, but JFK was intentionally

* At about this time, Kennedy privately counted up the votes on a piece of scrap paper. Under "Blockade," he wrote, "McNamara, Gilpatrick [*sic*], Rusk [with a plus sign], Thompson, Bohlen, Adlai, Nitze [with a question mark and an arrow pointing to the "Strike" column], Lovett, Ed Martin, Ball, Alexis Johnson, Sorensen." Under "Strike," he wrote, "Mac Bundy, Taylor, Chiefs, Acheson, Dillon, John McCone" [with a question mark and the notation "switched"].

opaque and liked to keep his options open. Earlier that morning, before he met with the Joint Chiefs, he had instructed his national security adviser, McGeorge Bundy, to keep arguing for the air strike option. "Have another look at that and keep it alive," said Kennedy, according to a private memo written by Bundy.

Bundy, who was Dean Acheson's fellow Groton-and-Yale man and possessed of some of the same hauteur, became Acheson's ally at the 11 a.m. meeting of the ExCom in George Ball's office on Friday morning. Bundy and Acheson squared off with the attorney general in the most decisive debate of the thirteen days. Acheson was brusque: "The sooner we got to a showdown the better," recorded the State Department note-taker, summarizing Acheson's views. "He favored cleaning the missile bases out decisively with an air strike." Bundy was more tentative. He had experienced a "sleepless night," he said, and "doubted whether the strategy group was serving the president as well as it might, if it merely recommended a blockade." Bundy let drop that he "had spoken with the president this morning, and he felt there was further work to be done. A blockade would not remove the missiles . . . an air strike would be quick and take out the bases in a clean surgical operation."

Hawks Acheson and Bundy had formidable allies. Dillon, McCone, and General Taylor all emphatically chimed in for air strikes. The doves seemed to reel for a moment; George Ball said he was a "waverer" between air strikes and a blockade. Then it was RFK's turn to speak. This time, he did not hang back or pretend that he was anything other than the president's brother. He stood up and began to pace around the room. Grinning, he said that he, too, had talked with the president—and more recently than Bundy. He reviewed the three options: doing nothing, which he said was unthinkable; bombing; and a blockade. The State Department note-taker captured some of Kennedy's eloquence as RFK made the case against air strikes and for a blockade:

> He thought it would be very, very difficult indeed for the President if the decision was for an air strike, with all the memory of Pearl Harbor and with all the implications this would have for us in whatever world there would be afterward. For 175 years we had not been that kind of country. A sneak attack was not in our traditions. Thousands of Cubans would be killed without warning, and a lot of Russians too. He favored *action*, to make known unmistakably the seriousness of the United States determination to get the missiles out of Cuba, but he thought the action should allow the Soviets some room for maneuver to pull back from their over-extended position in Cuba.

Obviously irritated by Kennedy's speech, Bundy, "addressing himself to the attorney general, said this was very well, but a blockade would not eliminate the bases; an air strike would," recorded the note-taker. But others were moved. Listening to the attorney general speak with "intense but quiet passion," Treasury Secretary Dillon felt that he was witnessing "a real turning point in history. The way Bob Kennedy spoke was totally convincing to me. I knew then that we should not undertake a strike without warning." Most of the others came around or at least softened their insistence on immediate air strikes. They would continue to argue and wrestle with the options, but RFK had carried the day for a blockade.*

ON SATURDAY MORNING, October 20, RFK called his brother in Chicago, where the president was maintaining his campaign schedule, and told him to come

---

* Three days later, on Monday, October 22, before the president addressed the nation, RFK jotted down a succinct private accounting of the reasons for seeking a middle course between doing nothing and striking Cuba. He was already writing in the past tense, as if preparing a justification for the president's course of action:

Do Invasion or Strike
  1. Couldn't be sure of getting them all.
  2. Perhaps some were in preparation and might have been fired.
  3. Other missiles on island and we had no knowledge where they were and they would have been put in place.
  4. Pearl Harbor.

Do Nothing
  Argument that we have been living under gun
  Argument that we are [crossed out] have been living under gun anyway and we can't guarantee getting them out.

Do Something
  For us to do nothing would produce chance that in last analysis we wouldn't do anything elsewhere i.e. Berlin
  We are going to have to act in Berlin anyway
  In S. America would have feeling that inevetability [sic] of Communism becomes apparent
  Maybe we would have to invade.
  What will be our response as work continues on these sites—
  what about if U-2 is attacked
  Better think about it and meet tomorrow to determine what we should do
  Did not give up on Strike until talked to Gen. Sweeney [tactical air commander] yesterday
  Recognize military problems giving—
  warning, but Pearl Harbor
  would have been such a shock
  that busted alliance

  Why we did not—earlier
  Throws Berlin into jeopardy
  without reason—Difficult to get
  OAS approval—would have to
  declare war
  Far departure from
  Soviet foreign policy
  2. Surveillance of island did
  not reveal missiles until
  last wk
  August 29 Nothing present
  won't allow Cubans on sites

home. Feigning a cold, JFK returned to Washington. His feet dangling in the White House pool as his brother slowly paddled by, RFK described the deliberations of the ExCom over the past twenty-four hours. Then the brothers repaired to the cabinet room, where the ExCom awaited the president's decision: blockade or air strike?

There was an addition to the group that Saturday afternoon, Adlai Stevenson, the U.S. ambassador to the United Nations. The diplomat, for years the leader of the dovish wing of the Democratic Party (Acheson was the chief hawk), wanted to urge a different course: a trade. He proposed swapping American missile bases in Turkey and the American naval base at Guantánamo Bay for the Soviet missiles in Cuba. He wanted to do the deal publicly, at a summit meeting run by the United Nations or the Organization of American States.

Both JFK and RFK were scornful of Stevenson. Recalling past political quarrels, RFK referred to the intellectual, often indecisive Stevenson as "so *un*tough," a "whiner," and a "pain in the ass." Stevenson had proposed trading American bases in Europe in a memo to the president on Wednesday, the second day of the crisis. "Tell me," JFK contemptuously asked Ted Sorensen, "which side he is on." At the ExCom meeting that Saturday afternoon, "everyone jumped on Stevenson," writes Arthur Schlesinger. Exhausted by the difficult, circular debate, the ExCom was ready for a decision, not a new departure. The president sharply dismissed Stevenson's proposal and embraced the approach suggested by his brother: a blockade, followed by air strikes if the Soviets did not give in. The commander in chief would announce his plan to the nation in a televised address Monday night.

Yet JFK and RFK did not reject Stevenson's negotiating ploy out of hand. Sacrificing the navy base at Guantánamo was going too far, especially for Robert Kennedy. The Jupiter missiles in Turkey were cheaper coin. Several times during the ExCom deliberations, Defense Secretary McNamara had predicted that the United States would probably have to give up the fifteen medium-range Jupiters based in Turkey to get out of the crisis. The Jupiters, already obsolete by the time they were made operational in 1962, were supposed to be replaced by submarine-launched Polaris missiles. President Kennedy was not inalterably opposed to swapping the Jupiters, but he thought it would be foolish to publicly offer right away to trade them. This was not the time to engage the Soviets in a negotiation. Public talks over a missile swap could easily become bogged down, while the Soviets forged ahead on making the Cuban missiles operational, a *fait accompli*. It was important to keep the pressure on the Soviets to remove the missiles, rather than slip into an open-ended bargaining session.

Robert Kennedy, with his natural impatience and desire to grasp the nettle, understood the importance of not dithering. But he was also shrewd about steering a middle course between immediate air strikes and drawn-out negotiations. His friend Robert McNamara was advocating a blockade followed by negotiations. Kennedy wanted a blockade, but also an ultimatum to the Kremlin: the missiles had to be removed, or the United States would strike. Public negotiations through the United Nations could too easily become muddled and protracted. RFK urged the ExCom to keep pressing the Soviets. As the State Department note-taker paraphrased his words on October 19, Kennedy argued that "in looking forward to the future it would be better for our children and grandchildren if we decided to face the Soviet threat, stand up to it, and eliminate it, now. The circumstances for doing so at some future time were bound to be more unfavorable, the risks would be greater, the chances of success less good." RFK, like his brother, did not want the showdown to come a few weeks later in Berlin. A trade might be necessary as a last resort to avoid war, but it should be handled discreetly and only as a reward for good behavior by the Soviets. Always determined to appear resolute—and fearful of splitting the NATO alliance by selling out the Turks—President Kennedy wanted to hold the Jupiters back as a last card to be played in the end game, and not before.

Still, President Kennedy quietly kept his options open. On Saturday night, after the ExCom meeting broke up, the president privately instructed his brother and Sorensen to start looking into the possibilities of a deal with the Kremlin. Sorensen drafted, then scrapped, a paragraph about a negotiated trade in the president's Monday night address to the nation. "It just wouldn't write," recalled Sorensen. RFK, meanwhile, convened a meeting of State Department experts Sunday night in the Situation Room at the White House to talk about diplomatic initiatives. The idea of trading the Jupiters was discussed—and shelved, for the time being. The general consensus was that too precipitous a trade would look "weak and defensive," wrote the State Department note-taker.

And yet, the idea of a trade stayed alive. It was pushed with particular vigor by an old hand at U.S.-Soviet relations, Averell Harriman. The aristocratic, proud Harriman was miffed at being cut out of the ExCom. As Roosevelt's envoy to Stalin in World War II, he knew and understood Russia —better, he believed, than any other American diplomat. Invited to join the State Department group discussing diplomatic options on Sunday night, he made the most of the opening, and wrote a perceptive memo to Robert Kennedy on Monday morning. Harriman related to Kennedy that on his trips to Russia in the late 1950s, he had found that the American missiles in Turkey were a particular irritant to the Kremlin, whose rulers were historically paranoid about being "encircled" by the West. To permit a nuclear threat so close to Russia's borders was, Harriman wrote, "humiliating to Soviet pride."

Robert Kennedy respected Harriman and listened to him. While the crotchety, half-deaf old statesman had been relegated to a relatively minor post—assistant secretary of state for East Asia—by the young men of the New Frontier, RFK had come to admire Harriman's crustiness and drive. (Indeed, after the missile crisis, RFK persuaded his brother to promote Harriman to the number three spot at the State Department.) Kennedy had also been listening to Llewellyn Thompson, who had wisely warned against cornering Khrushchev. The Soviets needed an out, a way to pull back while saving face. A trade—Turkish missiles for Cuban missiles—could provide Khrushchev with cover.

The Kennedys needed a way to sound out Moscow without appearing to offer a concession. RFK's back channel to Georgi Bolshakov had been severely undermined by bad faith over the Cuban missiles. But Kennedy was not quite ready to cut off his old arm-wrestling foe, especially since he still needed a rear entrance to the Kremlin. On Tuesday, October 23, the morning after the president publicly revealed the missile crisis and announced a blockade, Bolshakov received a phone call from Frank Holeman, the *New York Daily News* reporter who had introduced Bolshakov to the Kennedys. Holeman was now working for Kennedy; temporarily unemployed because of the New York newspaper strike, he had taken a job with Ed Guthman, Kennedy's spokesman at the Justice Department. Meeting privately with Bolshakov, Holeman had a secret message to deliver. In 1993, historians Timothy Naftali and Aleksandr Fursenko found, in the papers of the Soviet foreign office in Moscow, Bolshakov's cable describing the conversation with Holeman: "R. Kennedy and his circle consider it possible to discuss the following trade: the U.S. would liquidate its missile bases in Turkey and Italy, and the USSR would do the same in Cuba." There was an important proviso: "The conditions of such a trade can be discussed only in a time of quiet and not when there is a threat of war."

At about the same time, Bolshakov reported to his bosses in Moscow, he was approached by another Kennedy friend, columnist Charles Bartlett, with the same message: the White House was thinking about a trade involving the Jupiters. At the same time, Robert Kennedy wanted to make sure that Bolshakov understood the depth of the Kennedys' anger. "Get ahold of Georgi and tell him how he betrayed us and how we're very disappointed," RFK told Bartlett. But Bartlett must have laid it on a little thick because five minutes after he hung up with Bolshakov, he was telephoned by RFK. The attorney general apparently had been listening in on a wiretap. "That wasn't very subtly done," Kennedy chided Bartlett. "I hope you can be a little more subtle." Kennedy's anger was vying with his shrewdness, and Bartlett had been caught in the middle.

On Tuesday evening at 7:10 p.m., sitting alone with JFK in the Oval Office (with the president's secret taping system on), RFK casually told the president that Frank Holeman had seen Georgi Bolshakov that day. "Holeman?" asked the president, sounding somewhat skeptical. "But he's not with us on this." JFK seems to have been referring to Holeman's earlier incarnation as a newspaper reporter who had covered, and been friendly with, Richard Nixon. RFK dodged the question about Holeman's loyalty. Instead he noted that Bolshakov was still trying to bluff. "He said this is . . ." Kennedy chuckled slightly, "this is a defensive base for the Russians. It's got nothing to do with the Cubans."

Curiously, RFK did not mention the real purpose of Holeman's (and Bartlett's) meeting with Bolshakov that day: floating a trial balloon to the Kremlin about trading away the Jupiters. Was RFK holding back something from his brother? Philip Zelikow, the scholar who has done the most to decipher and interpret the tapes of the Cuban Missile Crisis, suggests that RFK may have been freelancing and using the Bolshakov channel to float an idea that his own brother was not yet ready to embrace. It is clear from the president's other conversations at the time that he was not ready to trade the Jupiters, certainly until after the crisis had passed. Possibly, Kennedy saw no need to discuss the back-channel peace feeler. Or RFK may have exceeded his authority. In his dealings with bureaucrats and go-betweens, the impetuous and impatient Robert Kennedy occasionally spoke beyond his brief. When JFK grumbled about Holeman, RFK may have sensed that he had gone too far by sending out the feeler to the Soviets, however guarded and hedged (the message was delivered through cutouts; the conditions could be discussed "only in a time of quiet and not when there is a threat of war"). There is another, equally credible explanation for RFK keeping the president in the dark: he could have been trying to provide his brother with "plausible deniability," intentionally distancing JFK from any talk of a trade until the moment a deal needed to be cut.

The mood inside the Oval Office was bleak that Tuesday night. The weather had been mocking the gravity of the ExCom's deliberations: day after day of glorious Indian summer, crystalline blue skies and sunshine lighting up the foliage in the elms along the Ellipse. Inside, that afternoon, the ExCom had discussed how many of the 92 million people living within the 1,100-mile range of the Cuban missiles would survive a nuclear attack. Less than half, was the conclusion. "Can we, maybe before we invade, evacuate these cities?" asked the president. No one wanted to even contemplate the chaos and panic.

The death of millions seemed unreal, yet it wasn't. "This may end in a big war," Khrushchev told the Soviet Presidium on Monday, when he learned the Americans had discovered the missiles. The Soviet premier slept, fully clothed, in his office that night. Unbeknownst to the Americans at that moment, the Soviets had put dozens of tactical nuclear weapons into Cuba, and Khrushchev was prepared to use them. In an invasion, the marines clambering ashore on D-Day would be marching into the world's first nuclear battlefield. The escalating chain of events that might follow the detonation of Soviet nuclear warheads over an American fleet is appalling to contemplate.

The members of the ExCom did not know about the Soviet nukes awaiting an invasion force, but they felt the nearness of war. Since President Kennedy's speech on Monday night, the entire nation had been gripped by dread of a nuclear holocaust. Schoolchildren were practicing duck-and-cover drills. Kennedy's advisers for the most part were no less anxious. Like Khrushchev, some members of the ExCom were not even going home at night, preferring to sleep in their offices. (During the last week of the crisis, RFK slept very little, staying most nights at the White House.) On the morning after the president's speech, Dean Rusk greeted George Ball, bleary-eyed from a fitful night on his office couch: "George, we've won a great victory. You and I are still alive." At home, Ball wrote, his wife stockpiled a "meager and almost pathetic" stack of canned goods, bottled water, some books and a Bible "for our black cook, who was devoutly religious."

At the Justice Department, RFK told his aides to go home to be with their families. His personal assistant, James Symington, went to an outdoor supply store and bought a tent and some small knapsacks in the forlorn hope that, in the few minutes of warning before the missiles struck, his wife and children could flee into the countryside. At the cash register, he was spotted by another government official, similarly engaged. "Going camping, are we?" the other man inquired. The top White House officials were handed envelopes, to be opened in case of attack. Inside were directions to landing sites from which helicopters would supposedly whisk them to a mountain cave in Virginia. "I'm not going," RFK told Ed Guthman. "If it comes to that, there'll be sixty million Americans killed and as many Russians or more. I'll be at Hickory Hill."

The Kennedy brothers tried black humor. Standing on the Truman balcony Saturday night with RFK, the president had quipped, "We are very, very close to war. And there's not room in the White House bomb shelter for all of us." But even flat jokes had worn out by Tuesday evening. The next morning, the blockade would go into effect. American warships would be confronting the Red Navy on the high seas. As they sat alone in the Oval Office at about 7 p.m., John Kennedy said to his brother, "It looks really mean, doesn't it?"

RFK was trying to take discreet soundings to learn if the Soviets intended to honor the blockade, or as it had been more benignly termed, the "quarantine." Bolshakov had told Kennedy's intermediary, Charles Bartlett, that the Soviet ships would steam right on through. At about 9:30 p.m. Tuesday night, RFK slipped into the Soviet embassy in Washington to meet with the ambassador, Anatoly Dobrynin. A much more polished figure than his drab predecessor, Mikhail Menshikov, the silver-haired Dobrynin was eager to supplant the now-damaged Bolshakov back channel. But Dobrynin had some credibility problems of his own. Over tea in early September, he, too, had spun RFK the line about "defensive weapons." On Tuesday night, Kennedy was escorted to Dobrynin's sitting room on the third floor of the Soviet embassy, a turn-of-the-century capitalist's mansion near Dupont Circle. Meeting alone with the Kremlin's envoy, Kennedy was "in a state of agitation," Dobrynin recalled. Rambling and angry, RFK reviewed the history of betrayal by the Soviets as an uncomfortable Dobrynin listened and tried to parry. Finally, RFK "seemed to have calmed down" and asked Dobrynin what instructions the Soviet ship captains bound for Cuba had received from Moscow. Stiffly, Dobrynin said that the Soviets would not "bow to any illegal demands for a search on the high seas." Kennedy's parting words, as he stood in the doorway, were intended to be ominous: "I do not know how all this will end, but we intend to stop your ships."

At ten in the morning of Wednesday, October 24, the deadline for the blockade, two Soviet freighters drew near the quarantine line, five hundred miles from the coast of Cuba. The Pentagon went to Defcon 2 (Defcon 5 is peace; Defcon 1 is war), sending out the order in the clear over an open channel so that the Soviets would know. All 1,400 of America's nuclear bombers went on twenty-four-hour alert. In the cabinet room, Secretary of Defense McNamara informed the president that a Red Navy submarine had moved between the oncoming Soviet ships and the *Essex*, the American aircraft carrier manning the picket line. McNamara told the president that the Americans would have to try to surface the Soviet sub with depth charges. As Robert Kennedy watched, President Kennedy put his hand up to his face and covered his mouth. He opened and closed his fist. "His face seemed drawn," RFK recorded in his diary, "his eyes pained, almost gray. We stared at each other across the table. For a few fleeting seconds, it was almost as though no one else was there and he was no longer the President."

As the first naval engagement of the last war loomed, RFK fell into a reverie. His mind drifted to family tragedy. "Inexplicably," he recalled, "I thought of when he was ill and almost died; when he lost a child; when we learned that our oldest brother had been killed; of personal times of strain and hurt." The voices droned on, but RFK heard nothing, until his brother's voice broke through. The president wanted to avoid having to attack a Red Navy submarine. In calm tones, JFK began to discuss the next harrowing moves: The United States sinks a Soviet ship; in retaliation, the Soviets blockade Berlin. "What do we do then?" he asked. "We try to shoot down their planes," answered Assistant Secretary of Defense Paul Nitze. A discussion of the rest of the steps on the road to Armageddon was interrupted by the return of CIA director John McCone, who had left the room to check a report on the Soviet ships.

His news came as an enormous relief: the Soviet ships had stopped or turned back. Dean Rusk, not known for his public wit, leaned over and whispered to McGeorge Bundy, "We are eyeball to eyeball, and the other fellow just blinked."

But not for long. That night, a letter from Khrushchev, sent via the American embassy in Moscow, rattled over the teletype in the White House Situation Room. Khrushchev meant to challenge the quarantine—"we shall not be simply observers of piratical actions of American ships." The president wanted to avoid confrontation. On Thursday, an East German passenger ship and a Soviet tanker were allowed across the quarantine line. Finally, mostly for show, an American destroyer intercepted and boarded a Lebanese-registered ship under Soviet charter, the *Marcula,* carrying dry goods. The U.S. Navy destroyer (by coincidence, not design) was RFK's old ship, the *Joseph P. Kennedy, Jr.*

Meanwhile, American spy planes reported that the work on the Soviet missile sites in Cuba seemed to be quickening. American intelligence now estimated that twenty-four missiles were ready for launch. Disturbingly, reconnaissance planes also spotted Soviet short-range missiles along the coast—a clear sign that the Soviets were readying tactical nuclear weapons to greet an invasion. In the ExCom on Friday morning, the hawks were in ascendancy, pressing for air strikes by Monday or Tuesday morning. The blockade was failing. Hundreds of warplanes and tens of thousands of assault troops were moving towards southern Florida, preparing for the Battle of Cuba.

On Friday night, the Situation Room Teletype machines rattled again with another letter from Khrushchev. The tone this time was different. In rambling, anguished prose, the Soviet premier contemplated war—"only lunatics or suicides, who themselves want to perish and to destroy the world before they do, could do this." George Ball thought the letter was a "break in the clouds." "He's scared," said McNamara. Khrushchev suggested that, in return for lifting the blockade and promising not to invade Cuba, he would withdraw Soviet missiles from the island. As he drove home that night, RFK permitted himself "a slight feeling of optimism."

The feeling did not last. On Saturday morning, Khrushchev upped the ante in a much sterner letter: he demanded that the Americans withdraw their missiles from Turkey. Worse, he made the demand public in a radio broadcast. There was consternation among the frazzled, exhausted members of the ExCom. "He didn't really say that, did he?" one spluttered. President Kennedy understood the larger political realities: "He's got us in a pretty good spot here," JFK told the group. "Because most people would regard this as not an unreasonable proposal." Using an old Britishism, Kennedy could not see how the United States could have "a good war" when conflict might have been avoided by trading some useless missiles. Most other members of the ExCom, however, feared that a decision by the United States to withdraw the American Jupiter missiles from Turkey would split apart the NATO alliance. The doubters included RFK. "I don't see how we can ask the Turks to give up their defense," he said.

Kennedy knew what the others in the room, possibly including the president, did not: that the Soviet leader was very possibly responding to a secret signal sent by RFK—the suggestion, delivered by the Bolshakov back channel, that the superpowers engage in a trade, the missiles in Turkey for the missiles in Cuba. Khrushchev's thinking, as well as his timing, remain difficult to fathom. Why did he seem to capitulate on Friday, only to stiffen and demand the extra concession—the withdrawal of the Jupiters—on Saturday? Scholars of the missile crisis suspect that he may have been initially fearful that the United States was about to attack, but then gained heart when he saw that the American navy was only erratically enforcing the blockade. He is known to have read a column by Walter Lippmann on Thursday, proposing a missile swap. Khrushchev had high regard for Lippmann's clout and saw him as a spokesman for the Kennedy administration. But more influential must have been the cable from Bolshakov. Khrushchev knew that the GRU agent had a direct line to the Kennedys. By sending Khrushchev a back-channel peace feeler, did RFK unwittingly exacerbate the crisis, inadvertently emboldening the Kremlin leader to make new demands?

The ExCom struggled to formulate an answer to Khrushchev. Some, like George Ball, wanted to accept the missile swap. Others wanted to reject it outright. It was RFK who did the most to find a middle way, in essence saying "yes" to Khrushchev's *cri de coeur* proposal of Friday while finessing his hardline demand of Saturday. Working with Ted Sorensen as his wordsmith, RFK drafted a letter to Khrushchev accepting his first proposal—an agreement to remove the missiles from Cuba in exchange for a no-invasion pledge by the United States—while tabling for later his demand that the West withdraw the

Jupiters from Turkey. RFK was at his best in this confused and muddled debate, bringing judgment and nuance and looking for an answer that would keep the pressure on the Kremlin without foreclosing the possibility of a face-saving deal. He had to fend off some large egos, including his brother's. At one point, he scolded the president, "Why don't we try to work it out without you being able to pick it apart?"

That Saturday—"Black Saturday," October 27—was, if possible, grimmer than all the days that had come before. In the late afternoon, word reached the ExCom that an American U-2 spy plane had wandered into Soviet airspace and had been chased out by scrambled MiGs. The Cubans had opened fire on low-flying American reconnaissance planes over the island, hitting one. The Joint Chiefs were pressing for a decision: they wanted a massive air campaign against Cuba on Monday morning, said General Taylor, followed by an invasion seven days later. "Well, that was a surprise," piped up RFK, in a sarcastic deadpan. The room rocked with the giddy laughter of men under too much pressure.

Then came really troubling news. "A U-2 was shot down," announced Secretary McNamara. "A U-2 was shot down?" asked JFK, his voice now slightly tinged with anxiety. A Soviet surface-to-air missile had brought down an American spy plane over Cuba. "Was the pilot killed?" asked RFK, possibly thinking about prisoners as well as casualties. "Well, now, this is much of an escalation by them, isn't it?" said the president. He was in a box. The military wanted him to start bombing Soviet air defense batteries as soon as possible, which meant Sunday morning at dawn. The United States could not launch air strikes on Monday without up-to-the-minute intelligence, and the U-2s and other surveillance aircraft couldn't provide clear pictures if Soviet and Cuban batteries were shooting at them and downing aircraft.

Still, President Kennedy was determined to avoid war. At about 8 p.m., the United States publicly broadcast the letter drafted by RFK and Sorensen, pledging not to invade Cuba if Khrushchev removed the missiles, while putting off any decision on trading away the Jupiters in Turkey. Secretly, the president made plans to give up the Jupiters as well. At about 7 p.m. that evening, he gathered a small group of his closest advisers in the Oval Office. Their deliberations would remain secret for the next twenty-five years, until McGeorge Bundy described them in his memoir of the nuclear age, *Danger and Survival*. With little debate, the group quickly decided on a course of action: Robert Kennedy would sneak away to meet with Ambassador Dobrynin. He would deliver two messages. One was simple and stark: The Soviets would withdraw their missiles from Cuba. The United States would agree not to invade. Otherwise, as Bundy put it, "further action was unavoidable." The second message was more subtle. RFK would tell Dobrynin that, while there could be no public deal over the Turkish missiles, the United States was determined to pull them out and would do so after the Cuban crisis was resolved. The ten or so men in the room—Bundy, Rusk, McNamara, Sorensen, a few other top-level advisers—all swore to secrecy. If word of the missile trade leaked out, they feared it might tear apart the Atlantic alliance. Unspoken was the potential political cost of appearing to "appease" the Kremlin. RFK was also instructed "to make it plain to Dobrynin that the same secrecy must be observed on the other side, and that any Soviet reference to our assurance would make it null and void."

Thus armed, in his office at the Justice Department, Robert Kennedy met with Dobrynin at 7:45 p.m. Sitting behind his large desk in the cavernous, formal office, surrounded by telephones, Kennedy seemed less the supplicant than he had in Dobrynin's cramped study. Still, to Dobrynin, Kennedy looked exhausted, as if he had not slept for days. He informed Dobrynin of the U-2 shoot down and emphasized that the standoff was fast deteriorating and heading towards war. According to Kennedy's record of the conversation, he told the Soviet ambassador that "there was very little time left. If the Cubans were shooting down our planes, then we were going to shoot back. . . .

> I said that he had better understand the situation and he had better communicate that understanding to Mr. Khrushchev. . . . I said those missile bases had to go and they had to go right away. We had to have a commitment by at least tomorrow that those bases would be removed. This was not an ultimatum, I said, but just a statement of fact. He should understand that if he did not remove those bases then we would remove them. His country might take retaliatory action but he should understand that before this war was over, while there might be dead Americans, there would also be dead Russians.

Dobrynin did not argue. He asked: What about Turkey? RFK trotted out the non-deal deal: there could be "no quid pro quo." But, after a suitable time had passed—Kennedy mentioned four or five months—the American missiles would be withdrawn from Turkey. "The president can't say anything public in this regard about Turkey," RFK cautioned, according to Dobrynin's notes of the meeting. "R. Kennedy then warned that his comments about Turkey are extremely confidential: besides him and his brother, only 2–3 people know about it in Washington." Dobrynin was struck by RFK's anxiety. "I should say that during our meeting R. Kennedy was very upset," Dobrynin cabled Moscow. "I've never seen him like this before." The Soviet diplomat later told Khrushchev that the American president's brother was near tears. According to Dobrynin, Kennedy implied that he didn't know how much longer his brother could control the hawks and the military. "The generals are itching for a fight," Kennedy supposedly told Dobrynin. The Soviet ambassador immediately wrote up his account of the meeting and sent it—incredibly, there was no other means of immediate transmission—by Western Union. A young boy came by on a bicycle from the telegraph agency to pick up the message. Dobrynin watched him pedal off into the night, praying that he would not stop off for a Coca-Cola or to dally with his girlfriend.

Returning to the White House, RFK found his brother with Dave Powers eating chicken and drinking milk upstairs in the family quarters. He glumly reported on Dobrynin, without holding out much hope that the Russians would back down. "God, Dave," said JFK to Powers, "the way you're eating up all that chicken and drinking up all my wine, anybody would think it was your last meal." Powers, who enjoyed the role of court jester, replied that, in light of RFK's remarks, "I thought it was my last meal."

At 9 p.m., RFK returned to his strung-out comrades in the cabinet room. In the many hours of recorded debate by the ExCom, there is but one moment of personal solicitude. Late on Saturday night, as air force pilots were being handed their target folders for possible bombing runs the next day, Robert Kennedy could be heard asking his friend Robert McNamara—who had been working around the clock, meeting with the ExCom by day and into the night, helping plan the invasion of Cuba in the remaining hours—a simple question: "How are you doing, Bob?"

"Well," said McNamara, untruthfully. Watching the sun set, he had wondered if he would live out the week. "How about yourself?"

"All right," said Kennedy.

"You got any doubts?"

"Well, no, I think that we're doing the only thing we can do, and well, you know. . . ."

McNamara adjusted his armor. "I think the one thing, Bobby, we ought to seriously do before we act is be *damned* sure they understand the consequences. . . ."

The group began discussing an invasion and removing, once and for all, Fidel Castro. The talk turned blustery. "I would suggest that it would be an eye for an eye," said McNamara. "That's the mission," said Douglas Dillon. RFK interjected, "I'd take Cuba back. That would be nice." Another voice chimed in: "I'd take Cuba away from Castro." And, finally, to punch-drunk laughter, someone else cracked: "Suppose we make Bobby mayor of Havana."

At midnight the ExCom broke up to get some rest, await Moscow's answer—or prepare for war. The president and Dave Powers stayed up restlessly watching a movie, *Roman Holiday* with Audrey Hepburn. Robert Kennedy, who had given Dobrynin his phone number with instructions to call at any time, went to sleep, or tried to.

CHAPTER 12 CAUSES

KENNEDY HAD BARELY SEEN his family for two weeks. Early Sunday morning, he took his daughters to a long-promised horse show at the Washington Armory. Before 10 a.m., he was summoned to take a phone call from Dean Rusk at the State Department. The taciturn secretary had momentous news: the Soviets had agreed to dismantle and withdraw the missiles from Cuba. The Soviet premier's concession had been publicly broadcast over the radio. "In order to save the world," Khrushchev had declared to the Soviet Presidium, "we must retreat."

Why had Khrushchev finally caved in? Documents found in the Soviet archives reveal that Khrushchev made his decision on Sunday morning *before* he received the cable from Dobrynin with President Kennedy's proposal of a secret deal. The Soviet leader was apparently again gripped by war fears: Castro was recklessly urging him to launch a nuclear attack to stave off an imminent invasion, and Khrushchev feared that the situation might slip out of control. When he received the Kennedy administration's formal, public response sent out at 8 p.m. Saturday night (4 a.m. Sunday, Moscow time), offering a no-invasion pledge in return for withdrawing the missiles from Cuba, while at the same time leaving open the possibility that the Turkish missiles might be traded away at some later time, Khrushchev no longer hesitated. The Dobrynin cable, with its gloomy war tidings from "R. Kennedy," did have an impact. In signaling the Soviet stand-down, Khrushchev had not waited to send a letter to be laboriously translated and cabled from the American embassy in Moscow. The Kremlin leader ordered his retreat sounded over the public airwaves, lest there be any delay or misunderstanding.

So, abruptly, the crisis ended. RFK immediately drove to the White House, then to see Ambassador Dobrynin. The news was a "great relief," the president's brother said to the Russian. "At last I'm going to see my kids." Kennedy, who had told Dobrynin the night before that he was spending nearly all his time with his brother at the White House, joked that he had almost forgotten his way home. For the first time in the crisis, Dobrynin wrote, he saw Kennedy smile. At the 11 a.m. meeting of the ExCom, McGeorge Bundy, a hawk for many of the thirteen days, graciously acknowledged that "today is the day of the doves." As he walked out into the Rose Garden, bathed in golden October light, George Ball thought of Georgia O'Keeffe's painting of a rose growing through a skull. ExCom member Donald Wilson of the USIA "felt like dancing and singing." Only the Joint Chiefs were dejected. "We lost!" General Curtis LeMay bellowed at President Kennedy. "We ought to just go in there today and knock 'em off!" Kennedy could only splutter; his disdain for the Pentagon brass was now complete.

As JFK watched the network television correspondents declare an "American victory," he called his press secretary, Pierre Salinger. "Tell them to stop that," he ordered. Kennedy did not want to gloat or humiliate Khrushchev. That night, he made a strangely macabre joke. Remembering that Abraham Lincoln had been assassinated in Ford's Theatre shortly after his greatest triumph, the surrender of the South in the Civil War, JFK said to his brother, "This is the night I should go to the theater." RFK responded, "If you go, I want to go with you."

RFK, too, had a sense of history—his brother's and his own. He was determined that no one would find out about the secret arrangement on the Turkish missiles. On October 30, Dobrynin tried to hand RFK a letter from Premier Khrushchev confirming that the United States would remove the Jupiters from Turkey. RFK would not accept the letter. He simply handed it back to the Soviet diplomat. According to Dobrynin's cable home, Kennedy explained, with astonishing frankness, "Who knows where and when such letters can surface or be somehow published—not now, but in the future. . . . The appearance of such a letter could cause irreparable harm to my political career in the future." "Very privately," writes Dobrynin in his memoirs, "Robert Kennedy added that some day—who knows?—he might run for president, and his prospects could be damaged if this secret deal about the missiles in Turkey were to come out." In what one scholar has described as a "blatant falsification of history," Kennedy apparently also tried to cleanse the record in the files of the United States government. In the draft of an RFK memo to the secretary of state recounting his Saturday night conversation with Dobrynin, someone—RFK? JFK?—crossed out any mention of a deal on the Turkish missiles. Recalling, perhaps, their father's injunction ("never write it down"), the Kennedys wanted to make sure that no gremlins discovered a paper trail of the deal in the State Department files.

The Kennedys continued to shape (and bend) history in the popular press. In the days after the crisis, well-informed diplomats and reporters began to whisper about a secret deal on the missiles. The Kennedys decided to create a diversion. Michael Forrestal, the young and ambitious National Security Council staffer, was recruited as an agent of disinformation. At lunch with columnist Charlie Bartlett shortly after the crisis ended, Forrestal casually let slip that, during the deliberations of the ExCom, Adlai Stevenson had "wanted a Munich"—to appease the Soviets by swapping missiles in Turkey, Italy, and England. But President Kennedy, said Forrestal, had stood up to Stevenson and vetoed such a public cave-in. There was some truth to this account, but it was hardly the whole story and quite unfair to Stevenson who had (as even RFK recognized) shown some courage in standing up to the hawks. Indeed, President Kennedy himself had marveled at Stevenson's willingness to take such a political risk. Standing on the Truman Balcony with RFK and Kenny O'Don-nell right after Stevenson made his case to the ExCom on Saturday evening, October 20, JFK had remarked, "I wouldn't think a guy who's as smart a politi-cian would expose himself. There are a lot of bastards in there [the ExCom] who hate his guts and think he's an appeaser. To set yourself up to those guys is a pretty risky operation. . . ." That it was, especially since "the bastards" later slandered Stevenson at the direction of the president.

Bartlett, as he later acknowledged, was used. Teaming up with another Washington insider, columnist Stewart Alsop, he wrote an article for the *Sat-urday Evening Post* that became the widely read, and widely copied, first draft of the history of the missile crisis. President Kennedy insisted on seeing the ar-ticle before publication. He requested only one change: that the authors cut out a passage describing the role of Ted Sorensen on the ExCom (the article as pub-lished mentioned Sorensen only in passing). Sorensen had been a pacifist in World War II; it would not do to give him too prominent a role in the presi-dent's councils of war.

The resounding moral of the story—useful for defeating Republicans in 1964 but distorted and dangerous for future crises—was that toughness and unbending resolve were the ways to handle the Soviets. For the next two decades, the history of the Cuban Missile Crisis continued to be filtered through a political prism. When Robert Kennedy was writing *Thirteen Days* in 1967, he wanted to present himself as cool and rational, a wise peacemaker who could extricate the United States from Vietnam. So he allowed a strong hint of the Turkish deal to slip into his narrative, while omitting less well-considered moments, like his suggestion that the United States "sink the *Maine* or some-thing." (Not until 1989 did Ted Sorensen "confess" that he had "edited out" RFK's description of an "explicit deal" in his diaries when he was preparing *Thirteen Days* for publication after Kennedy's death in 1968.) Eager to show that RFK was "a dove from the start," Arthur Schlesinger in his 1978 biogra-phy overlooked RFK's initial belligerence—but he did reveal the Turkish mis-sile trade.

These omissions and elisions were unfortunate, but they do not eclipse a more basic truth: that Robert Kennedy performed extremely well during a crit-ical and brutally stressful time. His role in helping to steer the ExCom away from air strikes or invasion towards a blockade deserves to be celebrated. Throughout the thirteen days, he was an effective prod and synthesizer who, for the most part, showed instinctive good judgment about how hard to push the Soviets and when to ease up.

To be sure, it was a close thing. The Kennedys have been accused of playing brinksmanship by some thoughtful critics, who ask, with the benefit of hindsight, if the crisis was really necessary. What, they ask, was the rush to remove the missiles? And why *not* openly trade some obsolete rockets in Turkey? Reasonable questions, but the most recent scholarship tends to confirm the judgments of the men who were in the arena, struggling with imperfect intelligence, political pressures, and their own fear. Khrushchev was not a deep geopolitical strategist. While wily in some ways, capable of negotiation and compromise, he could also be a crude bully who liked to stamp his feet and wave his rockets as if they were war clubs. He needed to be met with firmness—and, at the same time, allowed to save face. It may be true, that as Dean Acheson groused, the Kennedys were saved by "plain dumb luck." But they were also served by an innate and cunning sense of when to give, when to take, and—just as important—how to be seen doing one while actually doing the other. On the tape recordings of the ExCom deliberations, one can almost hear the blending of their complementary talents, JFK steady and reasonable, RFK urgent and probing. Given the stakes and the pressure, their performance was remarkable. Some myths *are* true: this was their finest hour.

Their shared experience through the ordeal sealed forever the bond between them. They would always be different men, with different styles and temperaments. RFK continued to hector, JFK to lightly tease. With a faint hint of mockery, the president would gravely call his brother "Bob" in the presence of Justice Department staffers, knowing that RFK did not like to be addressed as "Bobby" by colleagues. Yet on the last night of the Cuban Missile Crisis, JFK said to Dave Powers, "Thank God for Bobby" and truly meant it. Watching the two men at a White House dinner a few weeks later, British statesman and historian Isaiah Berlin was intrigued. Though the brothers sat far apart at the table, they picked up on each other's jokes, asides, and glances. "They hardly had to speak with each other. They understood each other from a half word," Berlin recalled. "There was a kind of constant, almost telepathic, contact between them."

THE CUBAN MISSILE CRISIS spelled the end of Operation Mongoose—but not of Robert Kennedy's attempts to subvert Fidel Castro. President Kennedy's promise not to invade Cuba did not stop his brother from continuing to try to foment a revolution on the island. With his bias for action and informal (not to say loose and sometimes reckless) style of management, Kennedy was, at this stage of his career, better at dealing with sudden crises and emergencies than at addressing intractable problems. Though he was capable of vision—especially as he continued to mature—he was more adept at running political campaigns and inspiring a loyal staff than at shaping subtle long-term policies or directing, from afar, resentful bureaucracies. His handling of covert operations during and after the missile crisis illustrates the pitfalls and rewards of the Kennedy style. His "sink the *Maine*" blustering on the first day loosed an errant round that could have wrecked his later peacemaking machinations. Yet a few weeks after the crisis, he staged a magnificent and improbable rescue of the Bay of Pigs prisoners still held in Castro's prisons.

On the first or second day of the crisis, Kennedy called Roberto San Román, the Bay of Pigs veteran he had embraced as one of his allies in the Cuban exile community. Without telling San Román about the Soviet missiles, he sounded him out about the scenario he had rashly raised with the ExCom—staging an incident that would give the United States a pretext to invade. "We discussed creating a provocation, a way of drawing in the Cubans and Americans. Bobby asked me, 'What do you think you can do to provoke a situation?' I said we could badly damage a Russian ship approaching port," recalled San Román in a 1999 interview. RFK told San Román to talk to Ed Lansdale, the overall commander of Operation Mongoose. Lansdale had already suggested attacking a Russian tanker as one of the sabotage options considered by the Special Group (Augmented) on October 16. RFK approved this risky mission, along with other aggressive acts, including mining Cuban harbors—a blatant casus belli wisely vetoed by JFK. Had the attack on a Soviet tanker gone through—had CIA-trained and -backed guerrillas set ablaze a Soviet tanker in Havana harbor at the height of the crisis—tensions would have risen even closer to the breaking point. Fortunately, the CIA balked. Early in the crisis, the agency informed Kennedy that it opposed running high-risk sabotage operations "in view of the changed situation with regard to Cuba." Most of the sabotage operations, including attacks on Soviet shipping, were stood down. San Román and his hot-blooded mates, living in a CIA safe house behind a bowling alley in Little Havana, blustered among themselves about ignoring their CIA handlers and staging a seaborne raid against a Soviet ship in the hopes of provoking a war. But nothing came of the talk. "We were soldiers in our minds," said San Román.

Despite its reservations, the CIA did launch one sabotage operation in the midst of the crisis. For months, CIA-backed Cuban exiles had been trying to blow up the Matahambre mines near the Pinar del Río coast. The Cuban raiders had a record of missing this target; most recently, in September, three missions had failed, one because of a "navigational error," another because the radio man "fell and broke ribs," and a third after the raiders stumbled on a Cuban patrol and were driven back "after a brief fire fight." But, with RFK's approval, six Cuban exile commandos set off again on the night of October 19. Predictably, the two men chosen to do the actual sabotage were quickly lost, presumed dead or captured. Kennedy did not appear to have noticed. Despite his vow on the first day of the crisis to hold meetings on Operation Mongoose every morning, the president's brother was soon consumed by the ExCom and seemed to have forgotten about his insistent demands for more sabotage.

Sometime during the second week of the crisis, probably on Wednesday, October 24, or Thursday, October 25, RFK received a back-channel phone call from San Román in Miami. The CIA, San Román said, wanted to use some sixty Cuban exile guerrilla fighters to infiltrate the island and gather intelligence for a possible invasion. This apparently came as news to RFK, who did not like to be surprised. Picking up the phone, Kennedy learned that the CIA was already inserting reconnaissance teams into Cuba. Kennedy had not ruled out covert operations against Cuba as part of an invasion plan. But he was furious at Task Force W Chief William Harvey, the CIA man who had proved not to be James Bond, for jumping the gun. At 2:30 p.m. on Friday, October 26, with the blockade in its third day and the crisis lurching towards a climax, Kennedy called a meeting of the Special Group (Augmented) in the operations room of the Joint Chiefs at the Pentagon. The attorney general exploded at his old nemesis. What was Harvey doing sending Cuban exiles into Cuba at such a critical juncture without prior approval? The insular, suspicious Harvey had come to detest Kennedy. In September, he had been subjected to a ten-minute tirade by the attorney general over the failings of Operation Mongoose. (Harvey had not helped himself at this meeting by nodding off after consuming too many martinis at lunch.) Now, bullied again, Harvey hit back. The Cuban infiltrators were in support of the military's pre-invasion planning, he insisted. He didn't need to clear them with the attorney general. As voices rose, Harvey went over the edge: he said, in profane terms, that the Kennedys were to blame for the Bay of Pigs and the current crisis. RFK stormed out of the room. Later that day, CIA director John McCone told an aide, "Harvey has destroyed himself today. His usefulness has ended."

Mongoose was finished. Kennedy had also lost faith in Ed Lansdale, its chief architect. Before the crisis, Kennedy asked his aide, James Symington, to go talk to Lansdale at his office in the Pentagon and bring back some assessment of his effectiveness. Symington found the famed CIA operator to be effusive and thoroughly unbelievable. "I have just met Jack Armstrong, all-American guerrilla fighter," Symington wrote Kennedy. The attorney general did not think Symington was being funny, but too many others had scorned the "F.M." (Field Marshal), as Lansdale's CIA colleagues mockingly referred to him. Lansdale, like Harvey, was no longer useful to RFK.

Yet Kennedy had not given up on the counterrevolution. If the CIA couldn't do the job, then he would find some brave Cubans who could. Kennedy imagined a wholly separate subversive operation funded by the United States, but not run by the parochial bureaucrats at the CIA. Based in a Latin American country, the Cuban commandos would buy their own arms, train their own men, run their own raids—while operating under the protectorship of the attorney general. Within six weeks of the Cuban Missile Crisis, RFK was already planning, looking for the right men.

In early December, he summoned Rafael "Chi Chi" Quintero to see him at Hickory Hill. Quintero was the resourceful spy who, after narrowly escaping from Cuba in 1962, had come to Washington to lecture RFK on the difficulty of staging uprisings in a communist-controlled country. RFK had not heeded the lesson, but he liked Quintero. Now, in early December 1962, he invited the Cuban freedom fighter into his home to talk about new ways to overthrow Castro. They met on a Sunday morning in Kennedy's paper-strewn library, while Kennedy's children clamored outside that it was time to leave for the circus.

"He already had a plan in his mind," recalled Quintero. "He wanted a separate [non-CIA] operation. My feeling was that this was a man working behind the scenes, who wanted personal knowledge, not just what he was told by a government agency. He was very knowledgeable. He could talk about people and places on the map." Quintero complained, as he had before to Kennedy, that the Cubans had been betrayed by the U.S. government at the Bay of Pigs. With Castro reeling from the missile crisis, asked Quintero, wasn't this the moment to invade Cuba? Kennedy's answer was discouraging. "There was no chance [of an invasion] now," RFK said. The Cubans would have to create their own revolution against Castro. But the United States could help. Who, Kennedy wanted to know, could unite the Cuban opposition? Quintero suggested Manuel Artime, a charismatic doctor who had been one of the leaders of the brigade at the Bay of Pigs.

Artime, like 1,112 other brigade members, was still in prison in Cuba. Driven by stubbornness, honor, and guilt, RFK was determined to get them out. The U.S. government could not become openly involved in paying the $62 million ransom demanded by Castro, so Kennedy had to look to outsiders. His approach was typically haphazard and resourceful. He started with a friend in the counsel's office at the CIA, Mike Miskovsky, whom Kennedy had met at a Catholic retreat for Washington lawyers a few years before. Kennedy explained to Miskovsky that one of the Bay of Pigs veterans, Enrique "Harry" Williams, had camped outside his office, demanding that the United States rescue his mates in prison. "He won't go away," said Kennedy. Miskovsky suggested approaching a New York lawyer named James Donovan, who had negotiated the release of U-2 pilot Francis Gary Powers, shot down and captured by the Soviets in 1960. Miskovsky knew that Kennedy would be put off by Donovan's ego and volubility, but he won over the attorney general by suggesting that Donovan was "courageous" enough to stand up to Castro. Kennedy asked Donovan, and the New York lawyer immediately packed his bags for Havana.

As it turned out, Donovan and Castro got on famously. Both were Jesuit-trained and liked to talk for hours, and the Irish lawyer amused Castro with his outrageousness. (On greeting Castro, Donovan inquired, "Are you ready to defect yet?") Back in Washington, Kennedy had tried to arrange some discreet and deniable support. In September, he chaired a meeting of top government officials, including Rusk and Bundy, to discuss the Cuban prisoners. Bundy warned that, with the election coming up, it would be politically unwise to pay ransom to communists. Kennedy fixed Bundy with a stare. "I don't care if we lose every election until Kingdom come. We put those guys in there and we are going to get them out." He threw his pencil across the table and walked out.

The missile crisis stalled Kennedy's push, but in late November, when he heard from a cattle breeder who had visited Castro's jails that the prisoners were dying "like animals," he pulled together his top aides in Justice and told them to get the prisoners out—by Christmas. This was just the sort of assignment Kennedy and his "band of brothers" loved to undertake. It seemed impossible. "We're getting the prisoners out, Joe," Lou Oberdorfer told Joe Dolan, recently returned from trying to keep peace at Ole Miss. "Oh no," said Dolan.

He imagined clambering aboard a boat with Kennedy's other loyal lieutenants and sailing to Cuba to liberate the prisoners.

The task was only slightly less arduous. Donovan had persuaded Castro to accept $50 million in drugs and medicine in lieu of cash. Kennedy and his men leaned—hard—on the drug companies to make voluntary contributions. Tax breaks and antitrust exemptions helped. But Kennedy's amateurs, who knew nothing about shipping pharmaceuticals to a foreign country (much less a communist one), had two weeks to get tons of drugs to Havana. Sleeping on the couches in their offices, bluffing and hectoring public and private bureaucracies, they managed to move hundreds of shipments of drugs and medicine from all over the country to ships bound for Havana. "The laws we violated were unbelievable," said E. Barrett Prettyman, a Justice Department lawyer and old University of Virginia Law School classmate drafted by Kennedy to help with the prisoner release. (Actually, no laws were broken; Kennedy's lawyers obtained written waivers.) Somewhat dubious Cuban authorities had to be persuaded to accept cases of Listerine and Alka-Seltzer as well as antibiotics. The last hurdle, faced with only a day to go, was to find $2.9 million in cash demanded by Castro.

About half the prisoners had been loaded on planes for Miami when the question of money threatened to end the ransom operation. At 5 a.m. on the morning of December 24, John Nolan, a young lawyer hired to act as an aide to Donovan and a go-between to RFK (who was impatient with Donovan's long-windedness), called the attorney general at Hickory Hill to say that Castro was adamant: no cash, no prisoners. RFK played the tough bargainer to the end. He asked Nolan, "Are we in a stronger position one second after we turn over the money, or one second before?" Nolan, who later went to work for RFK as his administrative assistant, would come to appreciate Kennedy's careful probing. "He wanted to make sure we weren't just giving Castro the money to make him feel good," recalled Nolan. But once Nolan persuaded Kennedy that the Cuban leader was dug in, RFK immediately focused on getting the job done. "He would have done *anything* to get those prisoners out," said Nolan. Where to find nearly $3 million in cash in a few hours? Kennedy called Richard Cardinal Cushing in Boston. The cardinal produced $1 million, borrowed from wealthy Latin Americans. General Lucius Clay, the chairman of a citizens group working to release the prisoners, signed a personal note for the rest and later tapped rich American businessmen. On Christmas Eve, the last of the 1,113 members of the Cuban Brigade limped off planes into the arms of weeping, shouting family members at Miami airport. RFK was at Hickory Hill, sitting on the stairs in his front hall while various children stepped around and over him. In a characteristic pose, he was holding his hands on top of his head, waiting restlessly. When he heard the good news from his men at Justice, he dryly demanded, "All right you guys, what about Hoffa?"

The next day—Christmas—RFK consumed a large quantity of vodka, a rare occurrence. At a party with friends at Hickory Hill, he suddenly announced that he missed his friend Georgi Bolshakov and wanted to call him in

Moscow to wish him Merry Christmas. The White House operators were unable to find the Soviet agent. Bolshakov's name and back-channel role had been revealed in a column by Joe Alsop, who was well known as a friend of the Kennedys. The Soviets assumed that the Kennedys had intentionally blown Bolshakov's cover in their anger over being deceived about the missiles. Bolshakov's usefulness was finished. In Moscow, he was relegated to menial duties and took to drink.

Four days later, on December 29, President Kennedy spoke to a mass rally at the Orange Bowl in Miami to welcome back the Bay of Pigs prisoners. Bundy and Rusk had strongly urged JFK to stay away, but RFK had told his brother to go ahead. Kenny O'Donnell thought that the attorney general was trying to ease the president's guilt over the ordeal of the prisoners. The emotional veterans presented President Kennedy with their brigade flag, which the president promptly promised to return in a "free Havana." The president's rhetorical gesture—not scripted in advance—set off the crowd, which began roaring "Guerra, Guerra."

There was little appetite for war among the president's advisers. Bundy wanted to begin looking for diplomatic overtures. But RFK, partly out of loyalty to the Cuban exiles and partly from sheer cussedness, pushed ahead with his idea to help create a private Cuban guerrilla army. With funds funneled through the CIA, Dr. Artime bought several tons of weapons and ammunition, some small boats and planes, and established bases in Guatemala, Costa Rica, and Nicaragua. The CIA was very uneasy about a rebel force they could not control. "We told them where to buy guns without getting rooked, but this was Bobby's deal," said Sam Halpern, who helped run Cuban operations for the CIA from Langley headquarters. The agency bugged Artime's safe house in Maryland and decided that his girlfriend (who had also been Batista's mistress) was a security risk. The CIA case officers were contemptuous of Artime's operations, which accomplished very little except to sink a Spanish freighter by mistake. "Their camps were horrible," said Grayston Lynch, a paramilitary specialist. "There was no discipline, no nothing. I had spies in the organization. They went through $50 million in nothing flat, mostly on Managua R and R."

Kennedy still felt duty-bound to try to help the Cubans. He reached out to the Bay of Pigs survivors, trying to ease their reentry into American life. He arranged to win them commissions in the U.S. military and personally took care of the brigade's commander, Pepe San Román, Roberto's brother, who was suffering from severe depression. The Kennedys found a CIA safe house for San Román and his family near Hickory Hill in McLean. Ethel car-pooled the San Román children to school and bought clothes for them. Learning that San Román liked to ride, RFK appeared one day at his house on horseback and with a saddled horse. As startled morning commuters looked on, the attorney general and the former commander of the Cuban Brigade galloped down the wide green median strip of the Dolley Madison Highway, past CIA headquarters. Journalist Haynes Johnson, who was writing a book about the Bay of Pigs with the brigade leaders, observed, at close hand, Kennedy's complex relationship with the Cuban exiles. There was genuine feeling and affection, yet at the same time, "Kennedy wanted to control the Cubans," said Johnson. "He wanted to make them personally loyal to him. He didn't want them out there talking about betrayal." Johnson was at Pepe San Román's small frame house near Chain Bridge on a Sunday morning when RFK, wearing jodhpurs and puttees, rode up on his horse. After a pleasant chat, Kennedy, seeking to remount, casually snapped his fingers and put out his boot. "Pepe, the brave man, came over and raised Kennedy into the saddle," said Johnson. "It was an unthinking moment [for RFK], a bit of lord of the manor."

Kennedy did not treat Enrique "Harry" Williams that way. When the Bay of Pigs prisoners were returning to Miami on Christmas Eve, RFK feared they would emerge from the airplane denouncing the Kennedys for abandoning them at the Bay of Pigs. He asked Williams, a respected brigade veteran (released by Castro with some other wounded prisoners in April 1962), to fly with the prisoners, soothing their leaders by telling them how instrumental RFK had been in their release. "Bobby trusted Harry. He loved it that Harry was full of shrapnel from the Bay of Pigs. Harry was bluff, candid, blunt, and Catholic to the core," said Johnson. "He was willing to die at any moment. He had a one-track mind. He wanted to kill Castro, personally, if possible." Educated at Culver Military Academy and the Colorado School of Mines, Williams was "reliable. He showed up when he said he was going to, which is more than you could say about most of the other Cubans," said John Nolan, RFK's administrative assistant. Increasingly through 1963, RFK relied on Williams to be his top Cuban, organizing and motivating the others to keep the pressure on Castro.

RFK made little progress trying to interest his colleagues in the top echelons of the government in overthrowing Castro. A feeling of futility had set in by the winter of 1963. Still hawkish on Cuba, John McCone of the CIA was mildly hopeful of toppling the Cuban dictator, but he stood alone. JFK himself had little stomach left for tangling with Castro. On March 14, RFK wrote his brother urging action. "I would not like it said a year from now that we could have had this internal breakup in Cuba but we just did not set the stage for it." The president apparently didn't even bother to reply, because two weeks later, RFK wrote beseechingly, "Do you think there was any merit to my last memo? . . . In any case, is there anything further on this matter?"

RFK never stopped trying. On April 3, he suggested sending a 500-man raiding party storming up a Cuban beach. Had he somehow forgotten the Bay of Pigs? The proposal died without discussion. Cuba would remain a cause for Robert Kennedy. But in the spring of 1963, Kennedy's attention and moral passion were consumed by a more worthy cause, one that he could and did do much to advance: equal rights for black Americans.

CHAPTER 13 THREATS

Asked to chart a graph of Robert Kennedy's consciousness on civil rights, Burke Marshall shot his arm straight up. The more Kennedy saw of racial injustice in the South, the "madder he became," said Marshall, his chief civil rights assistant at Justice. Marshall might have been describing himself. A rational, methodical lawyer, Marshall was appalled by the chaos—the beatings, bombings, and burnings—that defied the rule of law in the Deep South in the early 1960s.

RFK's own progress was more complicated. Though infuriated by the resistance of the white know-nothings, he was also angry at the Negroes he was trying to help. The movement leaders were difficult to control and showed little gratitude for the political risks taken by the Kennedys. On one occasion, a group of black activists and artists was personally abusive to the attorney general. In his early and often tense encounters with blacks, they sometimes seemed utterly alien to him. They did not share any of the cultural norms Kennedy took for granted, particularly his brand of unquestioning love of country. Yet RFK did not turn away, as some other white leaders did. Kennedy's impetus to plunge, so dangerous in other realms, was a blessing in the realm of civil rights. Experience awakened emotion that logic and principle could not reach. Through anger, remarkably, he found his own empathy. Unlike his coolly detached brother, Kennedy allowed his emotions to disturb him, to rub raw until his own feelings of vulnerability were exposed, and he was able to identify with feelings of helpless rage. He did not achieve this transcendence easily or at once, and he was never able to articulate exactly what he felt. But in the spring of 1963, Kennedy was moved by the struggle of black Americans for equal rights. What had been an episodic annoyance, accompanied by twinges of his own conscience, became a passion and a cause.

John Kennedy's attitude towards the civil rights movement, at least up until May 1963, can best be described as avoidance. Asked to attend a commemoration of the hundredth anniversary of the Emancipation Proclamation, President Kennedy sent a tape-recorded message and went sailing. Passing his special assistant for civil rights, Harris Wofford, in the hallway, he would give a quick wave and a tight smile. "How are your constituents?" the president would ask and not wait for an answer. Frustrated, Wofford quit to join the Peace Corps, the New Frontier's idealistic youth army sent to dig wells and teach school in the developing world, in the winter of 1963. At a Lincoln's Birthday celebration in February 1963, President Kennedy flinched when he spotted Sammy Davis Jr. and his wife, Mai Britt. "Get them out of there!" he ordered; he did not want to be photographed with an interracial couple.

RFK was being slowly educated by Burke Marshall, who was in charge of bringing voting rights cases in the South. "We did not philosophize," said Marshall. "We argued." Marshall explained the perversity of justice in the rural South, where blacks trying to exercise their constitutional right to vote would be beaten by the police—and then arrested for disturbing the peace. Robert Kennedy was pessimistic about passing any civil rights legislation in a Congress still dominated by southern barons, but in February 1963 the Kennedy administration sent up a voting rights bill. (The president's role was nominal; "I don't think that we ever discussed it, particularly," recalled RFK.) The legislation decreed that a sixth-grade education was sufficient to fulfill a state literacy requirement. To keep blacks off the rolls, local officials had been ludicrously requiring them to analyze the U.S. Constitution, article by article. The Kennedy bill, like an earlier effort the year before, went nowhere. "Nobody paid any attention," he later complained.

Kennedy was impatient with the different and often rivalrous civil rights groups—the NAACP, the Southern Christian Leadership Conference (SCLC), the more militant Congress of Racial Equality and Student Nonviolent Coordinating Committee. At lunch one day in his private dining room at the Justice Department with columnist Murray Kempton, Kennedy irritably exclaimed, "If they would only pick one person and send him to me and *tell me what they want. . . ."* As his voice rose, Kennedy was oblivious to the black waiter pouring his coffee. Kempton caught the waiter's expression and half expected him to pour the pot of coffee over the head of the attorney general.

Martin Luther King was a source of particular exasperation. In the summer of 1962, King infuriated RFK by defying a federal injunction against marchers protesting racial segregation in Albany, Georgia. By violating a judge's order, Kennedy angrily argued to King over the phone, the civil rights leader was giving southern cities an excuse to do likewise: to ignore the federal courts when faced with a school desegregation ruling. The Justice Department had worked hard through the judicial system to desegregate schools in the South. Couldn't King see that? King was not moved. He accused Kennedy of creating problems by appointing segregationist judges to the federal bench.

Never easy with the Kennedys, Martin Luther King was feeling increasingly resentful by the late winter of '63. He continued to complain bitterly about the Kennedys' judicial appointments (the most infamous, Harold Cox of Mississippi, once from the bench described black defendants as "chimpanzees"). King wanted to do something dramatic to shake Washington from its torpor. His target was Birmingham, Alabama, a gritty blue-collar town where Jim Crow thrived. Blacks could not sit at lunch counters, use rest rooms, or get decent jobs at steel mills there. On April 3, King launched Project C—for confrontation—aimed at filling the city jails with blacks who tried to exercise the right to be served by public accommodations. After the first score of arrests, Burke Marshall informed King's aides that the attorney general disapproved of Project C, pronouncing the protests as "ill-timed." The Birmingham city government, he argued, was on the verge of reforms that would make it less ardently racist. King promptly got himself arrested. Possibly remembering Robert Kennedy's intervention to bail out King in 1960, King's wife, Coretta, called RFK and asked for help. Kennedy said he would look into it, but he told one of King's friends, "I'm not sure we can get into prison reform right at this moment." Behind bars, King wrote his magisterial "Letter from Birmingham Jail" in which he regretfully concluded that "the white moderate who is more devoted to 'order' than to justice" was a greater obstacle to Negro progress than "a Ku Klux Klanner."

Like his brother, RFK might have just withdrawn behind a screen of offhand jokes and political evasion. Instead, he went for a closer look at the forces oppressing blacks in Alabama. On April 25, he traveled to Montgomery to see George Wallace, the newly elected governor who had cried, "Segregation now! Segregation tomorrow! Segregation forever!" at his inauguration in January. Kennedy walked into a chaotic scene. At the state capitol, a woman threw her body across a mosaic commemorating the origin of the Confederacy, lest RFK tread upon it. As demonstrators waved signs such as "Koon Kissin' Kennedys," the attorney general climbed the steps of the statehouse, over which flew the Stars and Bars, not the Stars and Stripes. He stopped to shake hands with hard-eyed state troopers, one of whom jabbed him in the stomach with a nightstick. ("Not for laughs," Kennedy recalled.) In Wallace's office, he noted a tape recorder on the desk. He was being invited to say something inflammatory. He spoke guardedly, in a tentative, flat voice that Wallace's biographer Marshall Frady compared to the twang of a rubber band. From time to time during the conversation, Wallace tried to incite Kennedy, or at least make him speak up for the microphone ("I don't hear good," the governor complained). At the press conference afterwards, a local reporter asked the attorney general if he was a member of the Communist Party.

A hundred miles away, in Birmingham, King's Project C was fizzling. There were few arrests and no national press attention. On May 2, King turned to more desperate measures. Out of the Sixteenth Street Baptist Church that morning flowed a thousand children, some as young as six years old, to flood the department stores and lunch places downtown. Sheriff Eugene "Bull" Connor played his role. He turned high-pressured fire hoses and dogs on the children. Within a day, cameramen from every major network and a number of foreign correspondents had descended on Birmingham.

In Washington, Robert Kennedy was disgusted. How could King make martyrs out of little children? When Roger Wilkins, a USAID official and one of the few blacks in the Kennedy administration, attempted to argue that the children could learn from the experience, Kennedy wrote back, "That's very interesting, Roger, but after all, the children can get hurt." Briefing the president's cabinet, Kennedy was scornful of King. "The Negro leadership didn't know what they were demonstrating about." Burke Marshall later recalled, "I talked to King and I asked him what he was after. He didn't really know." But RFK's attention—and the machinery of the federal government—was now engaged—which was really what King had wanted all along.

The Kennedys' initial approach was the usual one: searching out a compromise through back channels. Burke Marshall "knew some lawyers down there and the editor of the paper," as he recalled, so he quietly slipped into town to mediate. Cabinet members were enlisted to call Birmingham businessmen and plead for peace. At Treasury, Douglas Dillon phoned the head of U.S. Steel, which owned the biggest plant in town. When King was arrested a second time, RFK raised the money to bail the civil rights leader out by calling on Walter Reuther of the Auto Workers and other union allies, who dipped into their slush funds for ready cash. By May 10, the patient and assiduous Marshall had worked out a deal with the city fathers to gradually desegregate lunch counters, rest rooms, theaters, and the rest. The children were released from the overflowing jails.

But the next night, sticks of dynamite exploded outside the home of King's brother and blew a door-sized hole in the motel where King was staying. It was Saturday night. Angry blacks poured out of the bars and into the streets, setting fire to cars, businesses, and homes. Blacks had begun calling Birmingham "Bombingham" and the black part of town "Dynamite Hill." "Let the whole fucking city burn!" cried one of the rioters. The disciplined Gandhian nonviolence that had distinguished the civil rights movement had given way. The protests had taken a different and more frightening form, and they were sure to spread.

At an emergency meeting at the White House on Sunday, Burke Marshall gloomily contemplated the destruction of his fragile peace agreement. "If that agreement blows up, the Negroes will be, uh . . ."

"Uncontrollable," said President Kennedy. Marshall nodded in agreement, adding, "And I think not only in Birmingham. . . ." Robert Kennedy, becoming sensitized to black anger, could already see the sparks in the wind. He began making his own investigations. On May 20, he reported that "major problems" were breaking out in a dozen cities. (By the end of July, the Justice Department would count 758 racial demonstrations in 186 cities.) The day before, RFK had told President Kennedy and his closest political advisers that Chicago's Mayor Daley had predicted "a lot of trouble." Negroes in "underworld bars who ordinarily would run" when a police car came down the street now would tell a police captain who came through the door to "go to hell."

RFK was worried about the northern cities. At a White House reception, he had met James Baldwin, the author of a widely read *New Yorker* piece, "Letter from a Region of My Mind," which concluded direly that while blacks lacked status in white society, they did have the power to create chaos. Kennedy invited Baldwin out to Hickory Hill for breakfast, then casually asked him if he could put together a group in New York to talk about the northern ghetto. On May 24, Baldwin brought an eclectic group of, as he later described them, "rowdy" friends to the Kennedy family apartment on Central Park South.

Robert Kennedy was in a testy mood. He had just been at an office in midtown trying to persuade the northern owners of chain stores to desegregate their lunch counters down south. Fearing that Kennedy would surprise them with reporters and cameras, the jittery businessmen had hidden a floor below until one of their number had signaled the all-clear. Arriving at his father's luxurious apartment, Kennedy walked into an ambush set by the friends of James Baldwin. "Kennedy expected experts who would talk about solutions; instead he got artists and activists who were mad," said Burke Marshall. Kennedy was in the midst of warning them against the extremism preached by Black Muslims when a young man with a bad stutter interrupted. "You don't have no idea what trouble is. . . . When *I* pull the trigger, kiss it goodbye," stammered Jerome Smith, who had gone south as a Freedom Rider two years before and been imprisoned and beaten bloody several times since. Fast losing his faith in Christian nonviolence, Smith was in New York receiving medical treatment. Just being in the same room with Kennedy, Smith spat out, made him want to vomit.

RFK turned away from the young man and resumed his address to the others. But playwright Lorraine Hansberry, the author of *A Raisin in the Sun*, forced his attention back on the angry young activist. Baldwin, perhaps inadvertently, aggravated matters by asking Smith if he would fight for the United States in a war against Cuba. "Never! Never! Never!" exclaimed Smith. Growing "redder and redder," RFK replied, "How can you say that?" He could not accept or understand a young man who refused to fight for his country. He proceeded to gall the assembled blacks by observing to them that the Irish had overcome prejudice. His grandfather had been an immigrant, he said, yet his brother was president. Barely able to contain his contempt for Kennedy's parochialism, Baldwin noted his family had been in America much longer than three generations and was still stuck at the bottom.

The conversation degenerated. Social psychology professor Kenneth Clark proposed that President Kennedy personally escort a student to a segregated school. RFK openly laughed at such political naiveté. He praised the Justice Department lawyers working on voting rights cases. The blacks laughed back. After two hours of haranguing, Kennedy sat tense and silent in his chair. Finally, led by Hansberry, the blacks got up and walked out. The whole experience had been excruciating. Baldwin told the *New York Times* that Kennedy was "insensitive and unresponsive." To some aides, Kennedy said unpleasant things about Baldwin, slurring the writer for his homosexuality. He made an equally tasteless remark about Clarence Jones, a King assistant who attended the meeting. Jones was guilty, Kennedy said, because he had married a white woman. Jones had fatally branded himself as a coward with Kennedy by telling him after the meeting that he appreciated the Justice Department's labors in Birmingham. "I wish you had spoken up and said something about that," Kennedy replied coldly. Kennedy asked for FBI dossiers on Baldwin and his friends. He sent them along with a snide note to Marshall, "He is a nice fellow & you have swell friends."

Kennedy's rage did not go away, but it found new outlets. He became obsessed with the failure of the federal government to hire more Negroes. Most agencies, including the Justice Department, hired blacks in token numbers. In Birmingham, Marshall reported, he could not even find a black sweeping the floor in the federal building. On May 29, five days after his rough handling by Baldwin's friends, RFK turned his rage on a favorite target, Lyndon Johnson, who chaired a sleepy and ineffectual committee on equal employment opportunity. Speaking in a quietly seething voice, Kennedy treated the vice president like the most feckless bureaucrat, challenging his "phony" statistics that showed hundred percent improvements in minority workforces that had expanded from one to two or two to four. "Bob just tore in," recalled one of the participants. "It was a pretty brutal performance." The vice president slumped in his chair, his eyes half closed. He never forgave Robert Kennedy for the public humiliation.

Kennedy's aides, worried by his anger, noticed a transformation from rage to outrage. "After Baldwin, he was absolutely shocked," said Nicholas Katzenbach. "Bobby expected to be made an honorary black. It really hurt his feelings, and it was pretty mean. But the fact that he thought he knew so much—and learned he didn't—was important." Katzenbach credited the quietly persuasive Marshall with helping Kennedy understand the "depth of anger" in blacks, but Marshall, in a separate interview with the author, said that Kennedy needed no tutoring. Most critically, RFK made the leap from contempt to identification. A few days after the Baldwin confrontation, he told Ed Guthman that if he had grown up a Negro, he would feel as strongly as the Baldwin group.

The connection—the bridge he crossed—may have been the experience of a lonely and despairing childhood. Children—his own and everyone else's—were always on his mind. Pondering segregated schools and rest rooms, "He'd always talk about how he'd feel if it was his children excluded from these places," Marshall recalled. Kennedy could remember growing up with a sense of exclusion and inferiority—not, certainly, in the way a black child can be made to feel oppressed, but still with an ache of lack of worth and nonrecognition. As a little boy, RFK at moments had felt invisible within his family. (His answer had been to plunge—first into Nantucket Sound, then into danger and controversy.) In a quite different context from Jerome Smith, RFK was an angry young man, too. One of his greatest gifts was his capacity to see from the other side. In a daybook where he jotted down quotes and famous sayings, he wrote, "The final lesson of the Cuban missile crisis is the importance of placing ourselves in the other country's shoes." The same intuition was allowing him to understand the Negroes' need to be free—now.

When his conscience engaged, Robert Kennedy had a certain voice that could irritate his brother but motivate his subordinates. "He had a way of creating the impression that, if he thought something was wrong, he'd do something to right it. He had a way of saying it, a certain lilt to his voice. I can still hear it, a little higher pitch, not in decibels, but in octaves. He said some rough things. It wasn't always rational, it wasn't fine-tuned, but he had a passion," said Louis Oberdorfer. RFK could also use a kind of heavy, brooding silence as a tool to shame others, including the president. In a recorded conversation among JFK, RFK, and some of the president's political advisers on May 20, Bobby's voice is edgy and irritable as he notes that a black college graduate who applied for federal employment in the South could hope for no better job than that of a mailman. President Kennedy interjected, "Pretty good job for a Negro in the South, though, letter carrier. . . ." There is a long pause before anyone speaks. One can almost feel RFK sulking. For years, JFK had kept his distance from Bobby precisely to avoid his moralizing. But John Kennedy was no longer pushing his little brother away.

RFK could feel the moment of moral crisis fast approaching. On a flight to North Carolina to give a speech in late May, the attorney general discussed with Marshall the need for laws that would, as he put it, get to "the heart of the matter." The time had come to kill Jim Crow, to outlaw segregation in all public accommodations—hotels, buses, restaurants, rest rooms. The president needed to send Congress a true civil rights bill and to persuade the nation that racial inequality was wrong.

RFK was well aware he would have difficulty persuading the president's political aides, Kenny O'Donnell and Larry O'Brien, that the political cost was worth the effort. Persuading his brother would also be tricky, but JFK's keen media instinct had begun to quiver. He saw the images in the papers and on television—of German shepherds leaping at black teenagers, of children being swept away by fire hoses—and he sensed that a turning point had arrived. John Kennedy would later describe the civil rights bill archly as "Bull Connor's Bill," after the Birmingham police chief whose brutal tactics shocked the conscience. But he was also aware that public opinion is fickle and confused, and moments of moral clarity can soon pass. He needed a single, defining image to use as a backdrop.

George Wallace gave him one. The governor of Alabama had vowed that he would "stand in the schoolhouse door" to prevent a Negro from attending the state university. A court order commanded him to step aside, and the Kennedy Justice Department, anxious not to reprise Ole Miss, began planning a strategy to avoid bloodshed. Fortunately, middle-class business owners and university trustees also feared rioting, and worked closely with Kennedy's men to ease the way. They reported that Wallace was "crazy and scared." The best course, Katzenbach recalled, seemed to be to let the Alabama governor posture for the cameras and then relent only because the "central government," as Wallace referred to Washington, "had the A-Bomb and he didn't." Still, ineptly handled, Wallace's grandstanding could blow up into another riot.

Perhaps because he had been through so many crises, or simply because he was now convinced of the rightness of his cause, RFK seemed completely relaxed on the morning of June 10, the day before a pair of black students were scheduled to integrate the University of Alabama. Kennedy had permitted a documentary film crew to record his family breakfast at Hickory Hill and follow him to work. The camera showed him cheerfully tousling heads and telling children to finish their milk. At the office, Kennedy spoke on the phone to Katzenbach, who had been deputized to act out the drama with Wallace at the university. Wallace seemed determined to physically block the Negro students from registering. It appeared that federal troops might have to literally carry the governor away. In their casual shorthand, Kennedy and Katzenbach discussed giving Wallace "a little shove," but neither man seemed comfortable about the prospect of a physical confrontation. Katzenbach had another idea: why not just go into the university administration building through a side door? Clever, but as Katzenbach realized, the humiliation might cause Wallace to act up in some other provocative way. RFK finally came up with the solution: Let Wallace have his show of defiance for the cameras. Then show up later in the day with troops—not regular army, but Alabama national guardsmen, placed under federal control—to order the governor to stand aside. Katzenbach suggested sending the two black students to their dormitories in the morning, in order to make clear that the students had come to stay. Though the situation was tricky, RFK seemed confident as he worked through the problem, looking for a solution that would force his adversary to back down while saving face to avoid a showdown. Kennedy had learned from past standoffs, particularly the Cuban Missile Crisis. By now, his aides were used to the drill. Katzenbach, smiling impishly at moments, seemed almost to relish the high-stakes gamesmanship.

On the morning of June 11, RFK still seemed calm as he plotted the final steps of the dance with Wallace. The visiting camera crew, documenting the crisis for ABC News, recorded three small Kennedy children dashing about the attorney general's huge office. RFK interrupted his council of war long enough to put little Kerry Kennedy, age three, on the phone with "Uncle Nick," who chatted with her. "Tell your father it's ninety-eight degrees down here," Katzenbach told Kerry in mock protest. "We're all going to get hardship pay." Kennedy came back on the phone to tell Katzenbach what tone of voice he should use with Governor Wallace. "Dismiss George Wallace as sort of a second-rate figure, wasting your time, wasting the students' time, causing a great fuss down there," said the attorney general. "Good luck," he said to Katzenbach, and added calmly, "You'll do well."

Shortly before 11 a.m., in the steaming heat, Katzenbach ambled up through a cordon of state troopers as the governor waited behind a lectern in the main doorway of the university's administration building. Standing behind a white line painted for the cameras, a microphone draped around his neck, Wallace held forth about the "usurpation of power" by the "central government." Bending forward, his arms crossed as he towered over the diminutive governor, Katzenbach ordered him to comply with the federal court order. Wallace fulminated; Katzenbach looked pained and mildly exasperated. Followed by camera crews, Katzenbach withdrew—but he proceeded to escort the black students into their dormitories across campus (he had obtained a key by saying that the feds had to check for bombs). In the afternoon Wallace, still carrying on about "military dictatorship," backed down before a general in the National Guard. There were no riots; everything went according to the script.

Listening to one of his aides describe the unfolding scene from the university campus, Kennedy had hunched forward over a speakerphone in his office, anxious. A sweat stain spread under his shirt. When the students were at last enrolled, Kennedy lit up a cigar and called his brother with the good news. Impulsively, the president announced that he would go on national TV that night to propose the civil rights bill. RFK later recounted, "He just decided that day. Called me up on the phone and said that he was going to go that night." He was trying to give his brother the credit. But the documentary filmmakers, allowed to follow RFK into the Oval Office, had recorded the attorney general pushing his brother to make a speech. On June 10, the day before the showdown with Wallace, when Ted Sorensen had asked the president if he wished to address the nation, JFK responded, "I don't think so. . . ." RFK broke in, "I think it would be helpful. . . . I don't think you can get by without it." RFK later conceded that among the president's advisers, he was the only one who urged him to send a civil rights bill to Congress and ask for the nation's support on television.

Burke Marshall had no doubt about the centrality of RFK's role. The president's political advisers—O'Donnell, O'Brien, and Sorensen—saw nothing but risk. "Every single person who spoke about it in the White House—every one of them—was against President Kennedy sending up that bill; against his speech in June; against making it a moral issue. . . ," Marshall recalled. The "conclusive voice within the government" was Robert Kennedy's. "He urged it, he felt it, he understood it. And he prevailed."

President Kennedy had only a few hours to prepare a nationwide address. His advisers were aghast, and even RFK was a little anxious over the prospect of the president's speaking off the cuff on national TV on a subject so weighty and so loaded. Sorensen was sent off to start drafting while JFK and RFK talked in their shorthand fraternal code. "Perhaps because we're brothers, we didn't make speeches at each other," Bobby recalled. JFK, he said, "made notes on the back of an envelope or something." Marshall, who was in the room, recalled that he urged his brother to speak "in moral terms." The president did. Reading from a half-finished speech and then just winging it, President Kennedy expressed his brother's passion far more articulately. "We are confronted primarily with a moral issue . . . as old as the Scriptures and . . . as clear as the American Constitution," the president declared. Reflecting Bobby's process of personal identification, the president beseeched Americans to try to put themselves in the shoes of blacks. "Who among us would be content to have the color of his skin changed and stand in his place? Who among us would be content with the counsels of patience and delay?"

After the speech, JFK quickly reverted to his habit of caution and jocularity. About "every four days," RFK recalled, JFK would half-kiddingly ask, " 'Do you think we did the right thing by sending the legislation up? Look at the trouble it's got us in.' " But the Kennedys were now committed. On the night of the speech, civil rights leader Medgar Evers of the NAACP was assassinated. Shot in the back by a sniper's rifle as he was coming home, he bled to death before his wife and children. RFK sat with Evers's brother Charles at the funeral. He gave Charles his personal phone numbers and told him to call anytime, night or day. "Whenever I had the need to call him," Evers later recalled, "I never found it too late or too early."

Robert Kennedy could be asked, but he would not be pushed. A few days after the Evers shooting, a crowd of about three thousand protesters formed outside the Justice Department. After about an hour, the attorney general appeared holding a bullhorn. A demonstrator asked why the Justice Department employed so few blacks—just the kind of question Kennedy had been asking inside the government. Writer Jack Newfield, who was in the crowd, recalled Kennedy's "hard, Irish face; alert, but without much character." Kennedy reminded Newfield of the Irish toughs who used to beat up little Jewish boys like him on their way home from school. Kennedy was tense, with "hostility radiating from his blue eyes. . . ." Through the bullhorn that made his voice even more abrasive, he answered, "Individuals will be hired according to their ability, not their color." It was not what the crowd wanted to hear. They booed him.

"WE'RE IN THIS UP TO OUR NECK," President Kennedy told a White House gathering of black civil rights leaders that June. His brother fretted that his own, deeper involvement in the struggle might drag his brother down. Because he had spoken on the Justice Department's duty to enforce the civil rights laws, RFK was now well known down south. "Bobby" was a curse word in parts of Dixie. A policeman shouted it aloud while bashing the head of a civil rights protester against the floor in Winona, Mississippi, in early June. RFK was naturally eager to try to exercise some control and restraint on a movement that could sweep his brother from office. Martin Luther King was proud and, with some justification, wary towards the Kennedys. He could hardly be ordered about. He might, however, be induced and maneuvered. With J. Edgar Hoover conniving in the background, two dramas evolved over the summer and early fall of 1963: one public and heroic—the march leading to Martin Luther King's "I have a dream" speech on the Washington Mall, and one secret and sordid—the wiretapping and bugging of King's private life.

King began talking about a March on Washington in late May. Exhilarated by the success of Birmingham, he wanted to stage "work stoppages" in other cities and hold a mass rally in Washington to keep the heat on the administration and Congress. "The threat may itself so frighten the president that he will have to do something," King told his confidant and adviser Stanley Levison on May 30. The FBI, tapping Levison's phone, was listening. The attorney general was informed the next day.

The FBI had been spying on King for a year and a half. Robert Kennedy had authorized the tap on Levison's phone in February 1962, a few days after the FBI director, up to his usual tricks, had informed him about the mysterious phone calls between the White House and Sam Giancana's girlfriend, Judith Exner. RFK may have been subtly pressured into wiretapping King's confidant; even so, the taps were proving useful. They provided advance warning of King's moves. Kennedy did not have direct access to the daily "take" from FBI wiretaps. Hoover doled it out when he wanted to look omniscient or remind Kennedy of his dependence on the director's fiefdom.

Unaware of the feds' electronic intrusions, King had asked for an audience with the president at the end of May and was surprised by a cool rebuff. The Kennedys had been determined to keep King at arm's length even before they were tipped off about his plans for more mass demonstrations. At their deliberations on May 20, RFK had suggested bringing scores of white and black business and church leaders to the White House, two or three times a week, to build support for civil rights legislation. The president had agreed, but instructed RFK not to invite King. "King is so hot that it's like Marx coming to the White House," he said.

In early June, when they learned of King's plan for a mass march on Washington, the Kennedys were very anxious. Reverting to his prep school/navy man profanity, the president wondered, "What if they pee on the Washington Monument?" Thousands of angry blacks massing at the doorstep of Congress could set off a backlash that would doom a civil rights bill. It was clear that the Kennedys could not stop the march, which had been suggested by a number of black leaders. They could, however, try to co-opt and control it. By mid-1963, Kennedy's men at Justice were old hands at ad hoc crisis management: in less than a year, they had enrolled blacks in two fiercely segregated universities and freed the Cuban prisoners, as well as achieved lesser miracles, such as making the white-governed District of Columbia open swimming pools for poor black kids and defusing potentially riotous standoffs in small towns around the South. Infighting and confusion among the civil rights leadership gave Kennedy's men an opening. The Negro leaders had done little to prepare for a march, other than to call for one at the end of summer. "It was very, very badly organized," recalled RFK. So the Justice Department quietly took over, planning the rally down to the smallest logistical details. To avoid a riot and reassure Washington's nervous whites, certain precautions were taken. All the bars and liquor stores in the District of Columbia would be closed on the day of the march. Using intermediaries in the labor movement, Kennedy's aides gently suggested that the march be aimed away from the Capitol and the houses of Congress at one end of the Mall and instead proceed to the Lincoln Memorial. Lincoln, of course, was the appropriate symbol for a rally celebrating freedom from bondage. Left unsaid was the fact that the marchers would be contained by the Potomac River and the Tidal Basin. Airborne units were kept on alert at nearby bases. The organizers also took steps to protect blacks from whites and avoid the horrific imagery of Birmingham. The D.C. police were persuaded not to use dogs.

RFK, as usual, delved into the specifics. "Where are they [the marchers] going to go to the bathroom?" he asked at a secret planning session. A Pentagon general suggested digging slit trenches, but portable toilets were arranged. If the oratory got out of hand, Kennedy aide John Reilly, stationed beneath the speakers' platform, had a phonograph record of Mahalia Jackson singing "He's Got the Whole World (in His Hands)," ready to pipe in over the loudspeaker system. Years later, Kennedy aides chuckled over the lengths to which they had gone to control a march that turned out to be a model of civility and decorum. They laughed about bringing in Mayor Daley's expert on staging parades in Chicago. "He'd fuck up a two-car funeral," joked Reilly. In Kennedy's compart-mentalized world, almost all the lieutenants were unaware of more drastic and secretive steps to keep a rein on King.

For months, Kennedy had been trying to persuade the civil rights leader to cut off his trusted adviser Stanley Levison, who also wrote speeches for King and helped him with legal and financial questions. A New York lawyer who had raised money for communist causes in the '50s, Levison was not very sinister. Indeed, after he broke with the American Communist Party in 1955, the FBI twice unsuccessfully tried to recruit him as a double agent. The file on Levison was thin: an FBI source by the code name Solo had identified Levison as a party member from the early '50s, but he was no longer on the party rolls (if he had ever been). No matter: Hoover's men decided that Levison must have gone un-derground as a *secret* communist controlled directly by Moscow. The G-men had no solid proof, but they didn't need any. Using the oldest of national secu-rity smoke screens, Hoover simply claimed that the bureau's sources were too secret to reveal to anyone, including the attorney general.

Kennedy's men, too, believed that Levison was a top Soviet agent. Only in hindsight does Soviet espionage against the United States in the 1960s seem relatively insignificant; at the time, the KGB was regarded as a mortal threat. "When I left the attorney general's office, I thought he [Levison] was at least a colonel in the KGB," said John Seigenthaler, Kennedy's special assistant who departed in the early spring of 1962 to be editor of the Nashville *Tennessean*. Before he left, Seigenthaler, on Kennedy's instructions, had warned King to drop Levison as a confidant and adviser. King's failure to do so was one of the reasons that Kennedy authorized the tap on his phone in February. On those taps, the FBI heard no evidence of Levison's taking orders from the Kremlin or even from the weak and demoralized American Communist Party. But in June 1962 the gumshoes were excited when Levison recommended Jack O'Dell, an expert fund-raiser with ties to the Communist Party, as an assistant to King at the Southern Christian Leadership Conference. Here, surely, was a communist conspiracy brewing. With well-placed leaks that October, the FBI made sure that several local newspapers uncovered the infiltration of a high-level com-munist into King's civil rights organization.

Kennedy was mindful of Hoover's blackmail game. Usually, it was not threatened but implied. Rarely did Hoover actually have to go public with the secrets he harbored as a kind of personal employment insurance. So when Kennedy saw Hoover's hand in the newspaper stories about communists in the

SCLC, he was very disturbed. He knew that Hoover had a powerful weapon to destroy King. The communist label was toxic in the early '60s, especially to congressmen faced with hard votes on civil rights. If the Kennedys allied themselves with a perceived communist dupe, civil rights legislation would be doomed and JFK's reelection chances severely wounded. Through various intermediaries, King had been warned to drop Levison and O'Dell. King did suspend O'Dell, or say that he would. But the FBI was pleased to report to the attorney general in November 1962 that King was still meeting surreptitiously with both Levison and O'Dell. Kennedy authorized another tap on Levison, this time on his home phone. "Burke," Kennedy wrote in January on an FBI report he passed along to Burke Marshall, "this is not getting any better."

Unaware that Hoover had marked him as an enemy of the public, King dismissed the warnings about Levison. The New York lawyer was a close friend. King knew the charges against him were bogus. It was his Christian and "pastoral duty," the reverend explained to a Kennedy intermediary in January, not to turn his back on such a friend. With the movement gaining momentum in the spring, King needed Levison more than ever.

On June 22, after some 1,500 business, religious, and civic leaders had already trooped through the White House in marathon sessions on civil rights, King finally received his invitation to see the president. But he was sandwiched in between Roy Wilkins of the rival NAACP and another group meeting, and the agenda was not the one he had in mind. First he was taken aside by Burke Marshall and flatly told that Levison must go. Marshall insisted that King's adviser was not just some old New York leftist, but "a paid agent of the Soviet Communist apparatus." King was disbelieving. So Marshall sent him on to the next level of persuasion, the attorney general. Kennedy had been coached earlier that week on how much he could and couldn't say about the FBI's sources to King. Naturally, Hoover's men had told him that he could disclose virtually nothing. Less credulous than the attorney general, King demanded proof. He lightly but pointedly observed that lots of people were called communists, Kennedy included. King's attitude irritated Kennedy. "He sort of laughs about a lot of these things, makes fun of it," Kennedy complained in a confidential oral history he made a year later.

Years later, Kennedy's aides insisted that RFK truly believed that Levison was a Soviet spy, just as they did. At the height of the Cold War, they observed, the communist menace seemed more real. Kennedy, the former Joe McCarthy aide, feared the subversive monolith. No doubt, in their top-secret briefings, the FBI spy chasers made a formidable impression, throwing around jargon and code names. Still, it seems out of character for Kennedy to have simply accepted their bureaucratic bluffery. True, he respected the professionalism of the FBI agents, but he knew that Hoover grossly exaggerated the communist threat; indeed, the attorney general was always nudging the director to move his agents away from infiltrating the moribund American Communist Party to investigating the real threat, organized crime. It seems odd that Kennedy did not press a little harder to see Hoover's evidence on Levison. Kennedy was a famously skeptical questioner of the bureaucracy. Little was off limits; certainly, he did not hesitate to grill the super-secret CIA. In the covert war on Cuba he demanded to see raw intelligence reports, and during the missile crisis he personally went to inspect the CIA photo analysis labs. About the only CIA plots he did not wish to uncover, it seems, were the ones involving assassination. Kennedy sometimes chose not to know too much.

Late in the morning of June 22, still shaking his head from his encounters with Marshall and RFK, King was asked to take a stroll in the Rose Garden with the president. JFK was just as adamant. "I assume you know that you're under very close surveillance," he said, tipping King off to Hoover's electronic sleuthing. Levison, said the president, was a Soviet agent of such importance that the details were classified. Levison was O'Dell's "handler," and O'Dell himself was the fifth-highest-ranking communist in America. Putting his hand on King's shoulder, the president whispered, "Get rid of them."

Incredulous, King tried to joke. O'Dell, he said, didn't have time to be a Soviet spy. "He's got *two* jobs with me." Kennedy tried to raise a different specter, one with special resonance for the president. "You've read about Profumo in the papers?" John Profumo was the British defense minister. He had been discovered consorting with a call girl who was also sleeping with a Soviet diplomat (not unlike the Giancana-Exner-Kennedy triangle). The scandal was all over the British papers and threatened to bring down the conservative government. Kennedy wanted King to appreciate the risk of his friendships undermining a worthy cause. "[Prime Minister Harold] Macmillan is likely to lose his government because he has been loyal to a friend [Profumo]," Kennedy told King as they strolled through the Rose Garden. "You must be careful not to lose your cause for the same reason." Then Kennedy got to his real concern: "If they shoot you down, they'll shoot us down, too. So we're asking you to be careful."

King said he wanted to see proof. Kennedy, tired of the debate, idly assured him that he could and broke off the conversation. The "proof" was delivered by Burke Marshall to King's associate Andrew Young a few days later in the federal courthouse in New Orleans. Marshall compared Levison to a famous Soviet spy, Colonel Rudolf Abel, but he offered no other evidence. Young suspected the underlying reason for the hocus-pocus: "They were all scared to death of the Bureau; they really were."

THE PROFUMO SCANDAL was much on the minds of both Kennedys in late June 1963. The president had been closely following the British government's faltering attempts to contain the damage. Watching, too, was J. Edgar Hoover. On June 21, the day before the president took his Rose Garden stroll with Martin Luther King, the FBI director sent the attorney general a memo with the "highlights" of the Profumo affair.

Though the president seemed careless about his sexual dalliances, he had to worry about exposure. Reporters, in a more discreet age, could by and large be trusted. But the Kennedys remained vigilant, lest any untoward suggestions seep into print. Hugh Sidey, Time-Life's man at the White House, recalled that the Kennedys paid especially close attention to small, gossipy items. Sidey was castigated for a "People" item in *Time* that reported the president doing the twist at the home of a prominent hostess. The item was not only untrue, the president indicated; it was not fit for publication.

Chief watchdog on the press was Robert Kennedy. In his role of brother protector, RFK continued to spend many hours cultivating and manipulating reporters. When the White House decreed that all Time Inc. correspondents must be "cut off" from their administration sources after *Fortune* magazine printed a CIA-fed article blaming JFK for the Bay of Pigs, Robert Kennedy wrote Sidey, "Hugh, come see me." The attorney general understood that Time-Life, like the Soviet Union, was too powerful to simply cut off. No matter how tense relations became between the president and the Luce press, Sidey and RFK always maintained a back channel.

But Sidey nearly broke it over sex. In March 1963, he sent a gossipy not-for-publication memo to his editors in New York recounting in vivid detail that the Kennedys had thrown a racy party in Palm Beach over the New Year, supposedly featuring black prostitutes from New York and—rather improbably—a gigolo for Rose Kennedy. RFK somehow got hold of a copy of the memo and angrily summoned Sidey to his office. "I thought you were a different kind of guy, Sidey," he said, disgustedly. "My *mother.*" Flabbergasted that his private, internal memo had leaked out to the attorney general, Sidey protested, "How did you get that?" Kennedy answered cryptically, "I have ways." Sidey effusively apologized—in writing—and was forgiven. "You have been a good friend of all of ours for a long time," RFK wrote back the Time-Life White House correspondent on April 23. "P.S., needless to say this was not mentioned to anyone else in my family."

RFK was always on patrol. In June, he had reason to fear that his brother would be dragged into the Profumo scandal. Along with Christine Keeler, the courtesan who was sharing her favors with the British war minister and the Soviet naval attaché, the names of two other women, high-class New York prostitutes, had surfaced. These women were telling reporters in England that they had serviced President Kennedy as well. One of them, Suzy Chang, supposedly dined with JFK at "21" while he was a senator. On Saturday, June 29, the story crossed the Atlantic and surfaced in the *New York Journal-American*, a Hearst tabloid. The front-page article reported that a "high elected American official" was a former paramour of Suzy Chang. RFK responded immediately, calling the publishers and summoning the *Journal-American* reporters to his office that Monday, July 1. The newspapermen told him that the "high elected American official" was "the president of the United States," according to a record made by Courtney Evans, Kennedy's FBI liaison, who was sitting in on the meeting. Kennedy angrily chided the reporters for publishing the story, "without any further check being made to get to the truth of the matter." The *Journal-American* never printed another word, though RFK continued to worry. The next day, he asked the FBI, "Have we learned what Christine [Keeler] and her friend did here in the U.S., when they were here?"

A day later, on July 3, the FBI presented RFK with a more direct threat. J. Edgar Hoover sent the attorney general word that an informant had told the FBI about another alleged sexual liaison between the president and a call girl. The woman, Ellen Rometsch, was a twenty-seven-year-old Elizabeth Taylor look-alike, and she was under suspicion by the FBI as an East German spy. RFK was accustomed to Hoover's gossip, but this was something else altogether. Unless RFK could head it off, President Kennedy now faced the prospect of his own Profumo scandal.

Rometsch was one of Bobby Baker's "party girls." Baker was secretary of the U.S. Senate, former right-hand man of Lyndon Johnson, and a well-known playboy about town. At Baker's Quorum Club at the Carroll Arms Hotel on Capitol Hill, senators and lobbyists caroused together. Baker provided them with girls. One of the regulars was Bill Thompson, a handsome ex-marine who represented southern railroads and pursued pleasure with his old college track teammate, Florida senator George Smathers—and, from time to time, with former senator John F. Kennedy. According to Baker, Thompson singled out Ellen Rometsch as a comely new arrival at the Quorum Club sometime in 1962 and took her on several occasions to the White House, where, according to Baker, she had sexual relations with JFK.

Interviewed several decades after this alleged tryst, Senator Smathers said he could not recall Rometsch's name, but went on, "there's no doubt that Bill Thompson [who died in 1970] was a good friend of Jack Kennedy's, and there's no doubt that Jack Kennedy attracted pretty girls. I knew all these people—I knew Baker—we all knew each other. Jack would invite girls to drop by the White House from time to time. It was easy for him to have pretty girls show up." President Kennedy's attitude was far more casual than his younger brother's, according to Smathers. "Bobby was Jack's self-appointed protector. Jack didn't ask him to do it. Bobby always worried about Jack's association with pretty girls. Bobby always tried to play nursemaid. Jack didn't like it. It was a pain in the butt. Bobby would say, 'You've got to be careful about these girls. A couple of them might be spies.' But Jack would just take them out on the boat [the presidential yacht, the *Sequoia*] and hug and kiss a little bit. It was very innocent really. No secrets were passed."

To Hoover, this "innocent" behavior was another opportunity to blackmail the Kennedys. When Hoover's warning about Rometsch arrived on July 3, Robert Kennedy instantly saw the danger. Courtney Evans, sent by Hoover to brief the attorney general, told RFK about the German-born call girl. Kennedy made "particular note of Rometsch's name," Evans reported back to Hoover. Evans did not elaborate, but the bare facts about Rometsch's background were enough to give pause to the president's brother. Rometsch had grown up in East Germany and become a member of communist youth groups before fleeing with her parents to the West in 1955. She had married an air force sergeant who was stationed in Washington at the West German embassy. In the capital, she allegedly decided to supplement her income as a high-end prostitute. In the end, the FBI never turned up any solid evidence that she was either spying for the communists or having sex with President Kennedy. Rometsch herself denied both the sex and the spying (possibly under pressure from the White House), and President Kennedy seems to have laughed off the allegations. But RFK was more defensive. From the outset, he understood that the merest whiff of a sex-and-spies scandal could be threatening to the president. Even after a preliminary report by the FBI in mid-July found no evidence that Rometsch had either spied for the communists or had sex with anyone at the White House, RFK took no chances. In August, at the direction of the attorney general, Rometsch was quietly deported to West Germany. She was accompanied on the trip by LaVern Duffy, the Senate investigator from the Rackets Committee who was so close to RFK that he baby-sat for the Kennedy children at Hickory Hill. Duffy, conveniently, had been having an affair with the German prostitute. Rometsch was gone, but she was not forgotten—by Kennedy, Director Hoover, or Bobby Baker, who would soon figure in a scandal of his own. Hoover filed the Rometsch case away, careful as always to make a record that could be of later use.

Hoover always covered his threats in a blanket of bureaucratic normalcy. Two days after Hoover helpfully alerted the attorney general to the specter of Ellen Rometsch, the director warmly congratulated RFK on the birth of a son, Christopher. "It is a pleasure to join your many friends in offering Mrs. Kennedy and you my heartiest congratulation . . . ," wrote "Edgar." Kennedy thanked "Mr. Hoover" for "your interest and all your good thoughts." Niceties aside, relations between Kennedy and Hoover were rancid in the summer of 1963. The rivalry between Justice and the FBI had turned into a vicious war of leaks and counterleaks, with damaging consequences to law enforcement. In later years, Kennedy's aides downplayed the friction with Hoover as a necessary, if unpleasant, cost of doing business with the bureau. The attorney general, they said, was annoyed but not moved in any significant way in pursuit of justice. The available facts do not support this view. Kennedy's actions on the mob and civil rights were inevitably affected by his relationship with Hoover. Kennedy was remarkable in his ability to act in many important arenas all at once, but he was distracted and sometimes hobbled by his complex relationship with the FBI director. The background is particularly important to understanding how Robert Kennedy took the next step in his tortured triangle with Martin Luther King and the FBI: personally requesting wiretaps on the civil rights leader. Although Kennedy tried to carefully keep separate his various crusades, the different strands would sometimes weave together in a web that entangled the attorney general. The war on organized crime, the pursuit of Castro, and the battle for civil rights—seemingly so disparate—periodically collided in strange ways. They did again in the spring and summer of 1963.

The first clash came over an electronic eavesdropping contretemps that went unreported at the time and remained unresolved. Perhaps the most important investigation of organized crime was in Las Vegas, where the mob was skimming the nightly take from the casinos and sending the money to bosses in Chicago and Miami. The FBI had been bugging the hotels but, with typical insularity, not sharing its intelligence with other investigative agencies, including the IRS. The attorney general wanted to investigate the mob-controlled casinos for tax evasion. In the spring of 1963, Kennedy finally insisted that Hoover send him a report on casino skimming that could be passed along to other agencies. The skimming report arrived at the criminal division of the Justice Department on Wednesday, April 24, 1963—and, incredibly, leaked right back to the mob by Monday. FBI agents, monitoring the bureau's bugs in the casinos, listened in horror as mobbed-up casino owners read aloud from the FBI's highly confidential report. The leak, never adequately explained, was a tremendous setback to the war on organized crime. It effectively blew any chance of making criminal cases in Las Vegas—indeed, the casino owners sued the FBI for violating their civil liberties. And it alerted the mob that the FBI was listening, making gangsters more circumspect and sensitive to hidden microphones. The blame for this fiasco went back and forth. Hoover insisted that the leaks proved that the Kennedys could not be trusted, insinuating that the attorney general himself was conspiring with gangsters. Kennedy's aides suspected a convoluted Machiavellian ploy by Hoover: anticipating that the mob would soon discover the bugs and blame the FBI, he had leaked their existence in a way that allowed him to blame the Justice Department.

While the feds were finger-pointing over the wreck of their most promising organized crime investigation, they were also squabbling over who deserved public recognition for uncovering the mob. In 1962, a gangster named Joe Valachi broke the code of *omertà* and began spilling the Mafia's secrets to federal investigators. Kennedy wanted to make a public show of Valachi and his story to prove, once and for all, that the Mafia truly existed as a force for evil. Before Kennedy could move, however, Hoover ordered up an article for *Reader's Digest* giving the bureau credit for discovering La Cosa Nostra, the Italian nickname that the FBI liked to use for the Mafia. Kennedy's spokesman, Ed Guthman, blocked the FBI publicity grab as too revealing of government secrets while the attorney general was feeding the more revealing Valachi story to writer Peter Maas of the *Saturday Evening Post*, who had come across the story through his own independent digging. Hoover was furious. "I never saw such skullduggery," he wrote on a May 23 FBI memo complaining that Kennedy's aides were "exploiting this whole situation for their own benefit."

The FBI-Justice rivalry reached ludicrous lows in July. The object of controversy was Kennedy's old nemesis, Chicago Mafia don Sam Giancana. Unable to prosecute the mobster without running the risk of exposing the Castro assassination plots and the girlfriend he shared with the president, RFK chose instead to embarrass Giancana with intense federal surveillance. In a rare end run on Hoover, Kennedy had met directly with the FBI agents tracking Giancana in Chicago. He encouraged them to lean hard on the Mafia boss, and they did, tailing Giancana right onto the golf course. Frustrated, one of Giancana's henchmen confronted his FBI shadows in Giancana's hangout, the Armory Lounge, in late June 1963. "If Bobby Kennedy wants to talk to me," said Chuckie English to the G-men, "I'll be glad to talk to him and he knows who to go through." (The gangster was referring to Frank Sinatra.) Giancana's answer was to sue the FBI for invading his privacy. He did not have to worry about being cross-examined by Justice Department lawyers; the attorney general would be much too afraid of what Giancana might say in open court about Castro and Judith Exner. Given a free shot, Giancana took the stand to describe his harassment at the hands of the federal government and, to the consternation of Washington, won an injunction from a federal judge requiring the FBI to keep a respectful distance. The judge openly criticized the FBI for "Russian spy–type" shadowing, infuriating Hoover, who hated any bad publicity for the bureau. RFK called the head of the Chicago field office to say "he was sorry he had put me to so much trouble in this matter," the agent reported to Hoover. The director angrily wrote on the bottom of the cable, "Nonetheless, it is the *FBI* which is publicly condemned in the court and by the press, not the A.G."

Kennedy, too, was "incensed" by the judge's ruling on July 16, according to Bill Hundley, the head of the organized crime division. His anger was not just directed at the judge, however. July 16 is one of those days in Robert Kennedy's frenetic, stretched-thin existence when the pressure became too intense, when too much crashed in all at once, and when a setback in one arena inevitably affected his mood as he dealt with a crisis in another. Bad news was coming in from two other fronts. In Chicago, headlines mocked the federal government's "Russian spy–type" pursuit of the hometown don. In Miami, newspaper stories revealed the existence of RFK's secret Cuban operations, the anti-Castro guerrilla bases in Central America. Kennedy's own role was prominently displayed. One article was headlined "Backstage with Bobby" and detailed RFK's supposedly secret conversations with the Cuban freedom fighters. RFK had been warned about the damaging publicity with a needling note from National Security Adviser McGeorge Bundy, who disliked Kennedy's freelancing in covert operations and now warned that security on the Cuban operations was "poor" and that "a little fire creates a lot of smoke." Kennedy's solution, as reported by a State Department note-taker, was devious: "The Attorney General suggested that we could float other rumors so that in the welter of press reports no one would know the true facts."

Kennedy's ruthless side was in command. On that same hectic day, he learned that Martin Luther King was still refusing to completely cut his ties to Stanley Levison. King sent one of his lawyers, Clarence Jones, to the Justice Department to outline an alternative plan. King would no longer speak directly to Levison, suggested lawyer Jones, but communicate instead through an intermediary. Jones himself could play the secret go-between. That way, explained Jones, the FBI, tapping Levison's phone, would be none the wiser. King's lawyer may have thought he had come up with a clever solution to outfox Hoover's wiretappers, but he misjudged the attorney general. Kennedy was in no mood for games or to be trifled with. Part of his exasperation, though he could not admit it, perhaps even to himself, was at his brother—for having let slip, during that Rose Garden stroll on June 22, that the feds were tapping

King's associates. To King and his men, the president's admission had come as a moment of communion between two of Hoover's victims; King not unreasonably assumed that Hoover must be bugging the president, too. But RFK was hardly disposed to start conspiring with King and his advisers to evade Hoover's snooping. He was already engaged with Hoover on too many other issues.

The uncomfortable fact is that Kennedy needed Hoover. While he loathed the FBI director, he depended on the bureau for intelligence and enforcement. He was even, from time to time, grateful for the bureau's work. Just that morning, the attorney general had been testifying on Capitol Hill in favor of the administration's civil rights bill. Southern senators were waving around a photograph that allegedly showed King teaching at a "training school" for communists in Alabama. During a break in the hearings, Kennedy rushed to find out whether the charges were true. The FBI was able to provide a quick answer knocking down the allegations.

Significantly, on that same July day, he received another favor of good tidings from the almighty director, this time about the sex-and-spying allegations involving President Kennedy and Ellen Rometsch, the East German call girl suspected of working as a communist agent. At a private briefing in the attorney general's office, Courtney Evans reported that the allegations against Rometsch were not checking out. This news must have come as a considerable relief to RFK, beleaguered as he was on so many other fronts. Whatever the actual facts regarding Mrs. Rometsch and the president, RFK had to worry that Hoover might somehow find an opportunity for mischief. For the time being, it appeared, Hoover was protecting the president. The bill would no doubt come later.

These were the pressures swirling around Kennedy on the afternoon of July 16; this is the context crucial to understanding what he did next, a decision that decades later still baffled and troubled Kennedy's aides and admirers. That afternoon, Kennedy listened impatiently as Burke Marshall described the proposal by King's lawyer, Clarence Jones, to outsmart the FBI's wiretappers by having Stanley Levison communicate with King through an intermediary. The proposal utterly backfired with the attorney general. The effect was to make RFK wish to crack down harder. Kennedy waited until Marshall was gone, and then, in irritation and frustration, proposed a draconian step. He told Courtney Evans of the FBI that he wanted wiretaps placed on the phones of both Jones and Martin Luther King. Interestingly, Kennedy did not tell Marshall, his trusted lieutenant, about his decision to tap King. He was compartmentalizing again. Possibly, he was ashamed, or felt that Marshall would disapprove.

Even Courtney Evans was surprised by Kennedy's request. Usually, the FBI initiated taps and the attorney general acquiesced, not the other way around. Evans warned Kennedy to think twice. What if his tap on King leaked out? The Kennedys would be finished with the civil rights movement. Kennedy would not listen. He was still too mad.

Over the next few days, RFK calmed down. By the time Hoover formally requested his signature on a wiretap on July 23, he had reconsidered. He said no to the tap on King. But he did authorize a tap on Clarence Jones, the counsel to King who also served as director of the Gandhi Society, one of King's fund-raising arms. Kennedy had a personal animus against Jones. He was still vexed at Jones for failing to stand up against the verbal assault administered to Kennedy by James Baldwin's "rowdy" friends in late May. His attitude towards Jones was not improved by the intelligence he had received from the FBI (gleaned from Levison's tapped phone) that Jones regarded RFK as "the worst illustration of white arrogant liberalism." Kennedy's motives in this episode can only be described as petulant.

Yet one can imagine the pressure he was under. FBI reports of rumors about the president's sexual indiscretions fell like a steady drizzle on RFK. Hoover's passive aggressiveness was "a pain in the ass, something you had to deal with all the time," said Ed Guthman. Kennedy doubted that Hoover would directly leak these rumors to the press, and he was reasonably confident that reporters would not print them. Still, he knew that Hoover was fattening his file. In early August, a Senate staffer close to Barry Goldwater, the likely GOP nominee in 1964, told the FBI that a private investigator was peddling salacious gossip that JFK had gotten a woman pregnant and offered to marry her before the 1960 campaign. RFK had heard the story before: it had been shopped around to other Kennedy foes—Lyndon Johnson and Jimmy Hoffa. Courtney Evans proposed orally advising RFK of the latest rumor attack, but Hoover ordered Evans to write a memo to file. The director wanted a record.

On the same day Hoover fattened his file on the Kennedys, RFK tangled, for the seventh time in a month, with Senator Sam Ervin of North Carolina before the Senate Judiciary Committee over the civil rights bill. Kennedy may have had morality and justice on his side, but Ervin's rhetoric was eloquent and lofty and the attorney general's was generally not. At a White House dinner during RFK's grueling testimony on the civil rights bill, Ethel Kennedy encountered Senator Ervin. With typical teasing bluntness, she asked Ervin, "What have you been doing to Bobby? He came home and went straight to bed." Kennedy was getting little rest. Family obligations pulled at him. On August 9, he flew to Boston where President Kennedy's infant child, Patrick, born prematurely the day before, was dying. At 4 a.m., when the child expired, Robert Kennedy was standing beside the president at the infant's crib.

Personal tragedy crowded in on Robert Kennedy that month. On August 3, *Washington Post* owner Phil Graham, a close family friend, shot himself after a long mental illness. The day before, James Landis pleaded guilty to tax evasion. Landis, former chairman of the Securities and Exchange Commission, Harvard Law School dean, and Kennedy family friend, had been a father figure to RFK, helping him pass his law school exams and write reports as a Senate counsel. More important, Landis had sought to persuade Kennedy's father that RFK was worthy of his respect and attention. As attorney general, RFK had wanted to put Landis on the Supreme Court. But Landis had a drinking problem and pathologically neglected his finances, including his obligations to the

IRS. The attorney general had recused himself from Landis's case, until a vindictive judge sentenced the old man to thirty days in prison. When Kennedy intervened to get Landis transferred from a filthy state psycho ward to a private mental hospital, his deputy, Nick Katzenbach, objected. The upright Katzenbach warned Kennedy that he would be criticized for favoritism. With one of his steely looks, Kennedy told Katzenbach that he didn't want his political advice. He just wanted to know if he had the legal power to order Landis's transfer to a more humane confinement. "This is the best friend I ever had," he told Katzenbach. "Do it."

Times of stress could bring out RFK's hard-bitten streak, but they could just as easily stimulate his compassion. Following Kennedy's trail as he raced from crisis to crisis in the summer of 1963, one is struck by an odd juxtaposition. On the one hand, Kennedy is cold-blooded and manipulative, ordering up wiretaps and misleading reporters. On the other, he seems sensitive to the suffering of friends and family. His attentions to Judge Landis and the first lady can be partly explained by clan loyalty, but Kennedy's softheartedness showed in other ways. On August 23, Kennedy traveled to Chicago to make the political rounds (an audience with Mayor Daley) and talk to prosecutors and the FBI, whom he quizzed about Giancana. In a cable to Director Hoover, the FBI's top man in Chicago noted that Kennedy had turned down a chauffeured limousine provided by a leading Chicago industrialist. Kennedy said he wanted to ride with FBI agents in their car. He asked to be given a tour of the "slum areas and was shown low-cost housing projects, boys clubs, integrated school and playground. Appeared to indicate dissatisfaction with youth development here," wrote Hoover's man in dry cablese. Kennedy often demanded to see the worst of it, the lost and forgotten, particularly abandoned youth. Earlier that spring, he had visited a state mental hospital "on a bright April day when you could have expected all the children to be playing outside," RFK later told a congressional committee. The children were inside, standing in a bare room whose floor was covered with urine. The scene resembled, he said, "a kennel." Somewhere on his travels, RFK discovered the most neglected of all populations, the American Indians. On September 13, he flew to Bismarck, North Dakota, where he told a gathering of Indian tribes that their treatment by the federal government was a "national disgrace." The Indians gave him a war bonnet and a name, Brave Heart.

CHAPTER 14 WORN

IN OCTOBER 1963, Robert Kennedy reversed himself again and gave the FBI authority to wiretap Martin Luther King. Kennedy's signature became a hunting license for J. Edgar Hoover. The FBI not only tapped King at his office and home, it also bugged his hotel rooms. In January 1965, when King returned from Oslo after accepting the Nobel Prize, his wife, Coretta, opened a package mailed anonymously by the FBI. Inside were transcripts and tape recordings of King speaking lewdly and engaging in sex. A crude letter suggested that King kill himself.

In later years, friends of Robert Kennedy would sense the remorse he felt over Hoover's grotesque smear campaign. John Seigenthaler recalled the "stricken" look in his eyes when RFK was asked in 1968 if he had authorized wiretaps on King. After his death, *New York Times*man Anthony Lewis, Kennedy's friend who had covered the Justice Department, described the "great distress" RFK felt over "Hoover's extraordinary attack on Martin Luther King." In Lewis's description, RFK seemed more sorry than guilty. "Bobby's reaction was, 'Isn't it awful? But isn't it part of life? Isn't it terrible that I can't do anything about that?' " Kennedy's attitude was not one of "violent fury," Lewis told an interviewer in 1968. Rather, "it was just a sense of the wrongness of things that this kind of thing could happen; but there it was! He really couldn't change it."

Actually, he could have—but only if he had been willing to stand up to Hoover. On his own, as chief law enforcement officer, he might have challenged Hoover's malevolent obsessions. But as guardian of his brother's political future, his position was intrinsically compromised. He always had to think ahead, to contemplate how Hoover might exact revenge or bring pressure to bear in other ways. Kennedy's aides suggest defensively that he authorized the taps by Hoover to resolve finally the question of King's communist ties. But after twenty months of eavesdropping on the telephone conversations of the Kremlin's alleged agent, Stanley Levison, the FBI had not produced a whit of evidence of communist influence on King. It is hard to see what was to gain by tapping King's phone. There certainly was much to lose: Kennedy hesitated because he knew that if the taps were uncovered, the Kennedy administration would be disgraced in the civil rights movement. As Taylor Branch has noted, Kennedy had *less* reason to tap King in October than he did in July. In the interim, King's "I have a dream" speech at the March on Washington in August had made Dr. King a hero to many Americans. And in September, the deaths of four little black girls in the bombing of a Birmingham church had created martyrs for King's cause.

Kennedy was not personally sympathetic to King. In August, on the tapped phone of King's adviser Clarence Jones, King was overheard talking lustily about loose women and the sexual habits of his colleagues. King worried that one of the organizers of the March on Washington, Bayard Rustin, who was homosexual, would have too much to drink and "grab one little brother." Hoover immediately ordered a memo prepared for the attorney general. It had the desired effect on the prudish and homophobic Kennedy. He passed the memo on to his brother with a note, "I thought you would be interested in the attached memorandum." At a Georgetown dinner party on the eve of the March on Washington, RFK said to Marietta Tree, the U.S. delegate to the United Nations and a prominent society figure, "So you're down here for that old black fairy's anti-Kennedy demonstration?" Mrs. Tree tried to change the subject to Dr. King. According to Mrs. Tree, Kennedy said, "He's not a serious person. If the country knew what we know about King's goings on, he'd be finished."

Protecting King's privacy was obviously not worth antagonizing Hoover. With his usual persistence and sense of timing, Hoover resubmitted a request to wiretap King's home and office on October 7. As it happened, Kennedy was at that very moment weighing the possibilities of a sex scandal engulfing his own brother. He was worrying that the name Ellen Rometsch, and the names of her more prominent clients, would surface in congressional hearings.

The proximate cause was Bobby Baker, the man who had allegedly provided Rometsch for JFK's pleasure. In late September, the Capitol Hill fixer had come under investigation by Republicans on the Senate Rules Committee for influence peddling. John Williams of Delaware, a stern moralist and self-appointed guardian of Senate ethics sometimes known as Whispering Willie, was demanding that Baker appear before his committee to answer questions about trading cash and sexual favors for contracts and votes in Baker's Quorum Club. That Monday, October 7, Baker later recalled, he "drank four martinis and resigned" his post as secretary of the Senate.

As the best fixer in the Capitol, Baker had many friends and IOUs, but he also had enemies, lawmakers and lobbyists he had crossed at one time or another. Robert Kennedy was believed to be among them. Rumors were swirling around town that RFK had been feeding damaging information about Baker to

Senate Republicans as an indirect way of hurting Baker's old patron, Lyndon Johnson. On Wednesday, October 9, Baker called RFK to ask if the rumors were true. RFK told Baker that he had nothing in his Justice Department files except a few old newspaper clips, and that he and his brother the president had only good wishes for Baker in his time of trial. "He told me he loved me, that his brother loved me," recalled Baker. "He didn't have to say anything about Ellen Rometsch." While it's doubtful that Robert Kennedy used the word "love" in talking to Baker, the attorney general had reason to make peace with the Capitol Hill fixer. Baker believed that Kennedy was seeking a truce. The terms, as Baker implicitly understood them, were a mutual nonaggression pact: The attorney general was signaling that he would not feed the congressional scandal threatening to consume Baker. In return, Baker would keep mum about Rometsch or any other call girl who might have serviced the president.

A wild card was Hoover, who knew all the rumors about Rometsch and the fact that the Kennedy administration had arranged to have her personally escorted out of the country in August. This was not a time for Robert Kennedy to cross the FBI director. On Thursday, October 10, the day after his conversation with Baker, Kennedy sent a cryptic note to his FBI liaison, Courtney Evans. It read simply, "Courtney, speak to me." That afternoon, Kennedy authorized a wiretap on Martin Luther King's home and office. Sometime later, he told a friend that "there would have been no living with the Bureau" if he had refused to sign. It is impossible to know the precise cause and effect of the Rometsch case and RFK's decision to authorize the King wiretaps. But there can be no doubt that Kennedy was particularly sensitive to Hoover's imperatives in this critical period.

Kennedy was not free of Ellen Rometsch. Someone else, a newspaper reporter with a close but complicated relationship with Robert Kennedy, was watching the offstage drama play out in the Bobby Baker investigation. A towering, bluff midwesterner, Clark Mollenhoff, was one of the leading investigative reporters of his day and an old friend of RFK's. It had been Mollenhoff who had baited Kennedy—by asking if he had the courage—to investigate labor racketeering in 1956. After the Jimmy Hoffa hearings in 1957, Robert Kennedy had written the Pulitzer Prize–winning newsman to offer thanks and full credit, and Mollenhoff had written back an equally flattering letter to "be on the record," as he put it, with praise for RFK. But relations between the two men had cooled by 1963. Badly injured in an auto accident in the summer of 1959, put in a body cast for a broken neck, Mollenhoff attended a party at Hickory Hill in the summer of 1960, just days after he had stopped wearing a neck brace. He was walking across a gangplank laid across the Kennedy swimming pool when RFK playfully leapt at him. Journalist Fletcher Knebel, watching from the patio, described the scene: "Out of nowhere came this form in swimming trunks with the spray all over him, like a young god coming out of the water." Mollenhoff lunged for the side of the pool, but caught his foot and fell hard on the side of the pool. As Mollenhoff's wife turned pale, others stopped and watched in disbelief.

What had motivated RFK to play such a rough prank on a man recovering from a broken neck? Kennedy so firmly believed that one should defy pain and sickness with action and stoicism ("Kennedys don't cry") that he sometimes applied his demanding standards to others outside his family. He was not unsympathetic; indeed, Kennedy went out of his way to visit friends in the hospital and help them secure the best medical care. Still, he did not like self-pity and expected hobbled friends to grin and bear it. He may have thought he was daring Mollenhoff to overcome his injuries. After all, Mollenhoff was willing to take a risk of walking across the gangplank—at Hickory Hill, an invitation to be pushed in. RFK was slow to realize that he had gone too far. Knebel recalled that "Kennedy kind of slumped back in the pool." RFK was grinning, though no one else was.

Mollenhoff, who was not seriously reinjured, never expressed any bitterness about the incident at the Kennedy pool. But as a journalist, he ceased to be a dependable Kennedy ally. In 1962, Mollenhoff battered the Kennedy administration with a series of investigative articles in the *Des Moines Register* probing Defense Department corruption in the awarding of contracts for a new military fighter plane, the TFX. Mollenhoff did not find any personal wrongdoing by the Kennedys, but his articles were a black mark on the New Frontier, and RFK began to regard Mollenhoff as disloyal.

Whether out of personal pique or not, Mollenhoff became dangerous to the Kennedys. Mollenhoff's diaries, made public with his personal papers after the veteran newsman died in 1991, show that he was closely watching the Baker case and its more interesting subplots. From unnamed sources, most likely in the FBI, Mollenhoff had picked up the trail of Ellen Rometsch. His calendar for October 7 shows these cryptic notes: "RFK/Bobby Baker. Baker— German girl in Embassy. Baker Resigns." Mollenhoff began sniffing about. His entries on October 17 show where the trail led: "Mrs. Rolf Rometsch. East German girl." Then a list: the names of two top White House aides, then "Smathers, JFK." The toughest investigative reporter in the country, one not afraid to cross the Kennedys, was fishing for a sex scandal in the White House.

Reporters and headline-seeking congressmen routinely trade tips. Mollenhoff had years of experience working closely with publicity-conscious lawmakers and their staffs, just as he had with RFK on the Rackets Committee. On October 25, Mollenhoff met with Senator Williams, the Senate Rules Committee member leading the probe into Bobby Baker. According to notes made by Senator Williams, Mollenhoff described Rometsch's East German background and offered other details, including her looks ("like Elizabeth Taylor") and measurements (35–26–35). Mollenhoff suggested that Williams summon the FBI to testify and ask why the "lesbian prostitute," as the newspaperman referred to Rometsch, had been so suddenly deported from the country in August. The FBI, Mollenhoff explained to Williams, had not verified Rometsch's boasting of sex with "high White House officials"—but then again, Hoover's men had not yet interviewed anyone at the White House. Mollenhoff wanted to use Senator Williams and the Rules Committee—with its subpoena power—to turn up the heat. Under oath, the real story might come out.

The next day, Saturday, October 26, Mollenhoff went public with as much as he felt safe to print. The headline that day in his paper, the *Des Moines Register*, read, "U.S. Expels Girl Linked to Officials." Mollenhoff reported that "an exotic 27-year-old German girl" had been deported in August, and that the Senate Rules Committee was examining allegations "regarding the conduct of Senate employees as well as members of the Senate"—a veiled reference to the cavorting at Bobby Baker's Quorum Club. Then came the paragraph sure to catch Robert Kennedy's eye: "However, the evidence also is likely to include identification of several high executive branch officials . . ." who associated with "the part-time model and party girl." The article continued that the "beautiful brunette" had been attending parties with "some prominent New Frontiersmen from the executive branch of the government." More ominously to the Kennedys, the woman is "reported to be furious because her important friends did not block her expulsion."

Such a story, printed in a more scandal-obsessed age, would have stirred a feeding frenzy with minute-by-minute updates on cable news networks. In 1963, the White House could depend on most reporters to steer clear of sex stories, so long as they were not put on a court record or testified to under oath at a congressional hearing. If Kenny O'Donnell's recollection is to be believed, President Kennedy was less anxious than bemused by Mollenhoff's muckraking. In an off-the-record oral history he gave newsman Sander Vanocur in the late 1960s, JFK's close aide claimed that the president called him that weekend in October when he first heard about Mollenhoff's story and asked—"rather humorously"—whether O'Donnell had ever been to Bobby Baker's house of ill repute. Assuming the president's bantering tone, O'Donnell flipped the question around to ask if the president himself had been to Baker's house. "He [JFK] said no, and we jested about it, actually," O'Donnell recalled. Kennedy stopped laughing long enough to instruct O'Donnell to get all the top White House aides on the record denying any involvement with Baker's call girl operation. "So," O'Donnell continued, "I did call each member of the White House staff and they all laughed; it was a rather humorous thing, but he [JFK] wanted the record clear. . . ."

We have no such personal testimony to describe RFK's response. But the attorney general does not appear to have been so lighthearted. RFK was compelled to turn to J. Edgar Hoover and the FBI for help. The FBI was not just passively standing by. Bureau files show that on the same day Mollenhoff's article appeared, the FBI had reopened its investigation of call girls and the Kennedy administration, and this time RFK himself was a target: "it was also alleged that the President and the Attorney General had availed themselves of services of partygirls," read one FBI document sent to J. Edgar Hoover on October 26. RFK moved quickly to contain the damage. FBI files show repeated requests by the attorney general's aides to persuade the FBI to use its influence with other journalists, in order to dissuade them from picking up Mollenhoff's story. On the fifth such request, one of Hoover's assistants noted, the attorney general's aide "told me the President was personally interested in having this story killed." The FBI told Kennedy's men they would take a "no comment" position with the press and investigate Mollenhoff's allegations. Kennedy had to worry about the FBI feeding rumors to newsmen like Mollenhoff. The greater worry, however, was a congressional investigation.

The White House phone logs suggest the sense of alarm and urgency that permeated the White House. RFK may have had an inkling of trouble brewing on Friday, October 25, the day before the Rometsch story broke. The attorney general called the president at 4:22 and 4:46. Kenny O'Donnell called at 4:48. At 4:58, the notation "Tell Kenny O'Donnell to get Mr. Hoover . . ." appears. At 5:30, the president's secretary, Mrs. Lincoln, noted a call from Bill Thompson, the railroad lobbyist who allegedly first spotted Ellen Rometsch among Bobby Baker's "party girls" and took her to the White House for the president's pleasure. When Mollenhoff's article appeared the next day, the wires burned up between RFK, O'Donnell, and JFK. The president's phone log shows calls from the attorney general at 4:26, O'Donnell at 4:42 and 5:24, the attorney general at 5:25 and 5:45, O'Donnell at 5:50, Ed Guthman at 6:44, and the attorney general at 6:50. At 8 p.m., RFK tried to reach Mollenhoff's publisher (and Kennedy friend) John Cowles. At 8:05, J. Edgar Hoover himself called the president. Then RFK again at 8:18, Guthman at 8:40, and O'Donnell at 8:45. Kenny O'Donnell's phone log shows two calls—at 4:50 and 8:50—from LaVern Duffy, Rometsch's boyfriend and RFK's old Rackets Committee investigator, who had accompanied Rometsch when she was flown to Germany on an air force transport in August. Duffy's brother, Wayne, told investigative reporter Seymour Hersh that the Kennedys had used Duffy to pay Rometsch for her silence. Correspondence between Rometsch and Duffy (who died in 1992) suggests that Duffy sent her money, but does not indicate the amount or the source. The only other evidence that survives is cryptic and hard to assess, given RFK's dry sense of humor. RFK sent his calling card—"The Attorney General"—to Duffy with a handwritten note: "Duffy—Another four years and you'll have this office—Bob."

RFK's dealings with J. Edgar Hoover are the most revealing piece of the puzzle. Usually, if he needed to see Hoover, the attorney general summoned the FBI director to his office. But on Monday morning, October 28, Robert Kennedy appeared, an uneasy supplicant, on Hoover's doorstep. He had a very big favor to ask. Kennedy told Hoover that the president urgently wished the FBI director to brief the Senate leadership on the dangers of the Rometsch case. If word got out that senators and executive branch officials were carrying on with a woman suspected by the FBI of spying, the integrity of the country would be damaged.

This was the kind of moment J. Edgar Hoover lived for. He already had RFK on his heels. Just four days earlier, the attorney general had signed off on four more wiretaps on Martin Luther King's office phones—a few days after Hoover had squeezed RFK a little harder by widely distributing to top officials at State and Defense an FBI report purporting to detail King's communist ties. Now the attorney general was, in effect, begging him to spare the Kennedy administration from a sordid scandal. Hoover let Kennedy squirm. The whole matter was distasteful to him, he said. Why shouldn't Kennedy speak to the Senate leaders himself? RFK was obliged to say aloud what Hoover wanted to hear: that only the legendary FBI director had the independent stature and authority to impress upon the senators the gravity of the situation. Outwardly reluctant, no doubt inwardly triumphant, Hoover agreed.

That day, seeking to avoid reporters, the FBI director met secretly with Senate majority leader Mike Mansfield and minority leader Everett Dirksen at Mansfield's home. He told them that an investigation had produced no evidence that Rometsch was a spy or that she had had sex with anyone at the White House. But then Hoover laid out, in convincing detail, the FBI's report on Bobby Baker's "party girls" and the senators they entertained. He had names, dates, and places. Shaken, the Senate leaders quietly informed the Rules Committee: the Bobby Baker hearings would stay away from sex. RFK covered his tracks for history. In a confidential oral history a year later, he told Anthony Lewis that Mollenhoff's story had been wrong about President Kennedy's involvement with Rometsch, but right about the senators. President Kennedy continued to make a joke of danger, jauntily telling *Newsweek*'s Ben Bradlee, "Boy, the dirt he [Hoover] has on those senators you'd never believe it."

Hoover's services were never free. He extracted from RFK a promise of lunch with the president and—more to the point—a testimonial from the attorney general that Hoover's job was secure. With obvious satisfaction, Hoover recorded Kennedy's avowal that any gossip about replacing the FBI director was "vicious" and baseless.

Robert Kennedy had lost control over Hoover. On November 1, the attorney general signed another of Hoover's wiretap requests, this time on Bayard Rustin, whose only secret ties were to other closeted homosexuals. Kennedy was supposed to review the taps on King within thirty days, by December 1, 1963. It does not appear that he ever did.

AT THE END OF OCTOBER 1963, Robert Kennedy's chronically divided attention was yanked back to an old worry—Cuba—and a new one—Vietnam. The underlying issue in both was the Kennedy administration's role in the overthrow—and assassination—of a head of state. Chastened by his nearly three years as foreign policy troubleshooter for the president, RFK approached the subject warily, with a growing appreciation of the difficulties of controlling violent acts in distant places.

Throughout 1961 and 1962, Vietnam had been largely a sideshow to RFK. When reporter Stanley Karnow had asked him about Vietnam in early 1962, Kennedy had shrugged and said, "We have twenty Vietnams a day." The attorney general had briefly stopped off in Saigon on his round-the-world tour in 1962 and mouthed some win-the-war clichés, but he had devoted little time or thought to Vietnam's simmering problems. Impressed with the "toughness" of the French paratroopers he saw in Vietnam on a trip with his brother Jack in 1951, he was doubly impressed when North Vietnam drove the French out in 1954. By 1962, American "advisers" were fighting alongside the South Vietnamese, but the United States had yet to commit combat ground troops. RFK had no desire to see the United States engage in a full-scale Asian ground war.

Politically, however, he knew that if his brother pulled out, he would be tagged by the Republicans in 1964 with "losing" Vietnam. Reluctant to wage a conventional war, the Kennedys looked for an easier and cheaper way to defeat the communists in Vietnam. Indulging their overoptimistic faith in counterinsurgency, the Kennedys demanded that the CIA wage an unconventional war in Vietnam—"stealing the thunder" of the enemy by using the same tricks of subversion and sabotage against the North that the North was using successfully against the South. Almost as soon as he took office, President Kennedy began pressing the CIA to conduct "black operations" against Hanoi. It was a fool's errand. As the CIA recognized, running spies and saboteurs against a tightly controlled totalitarian regime was destined to fail. His faith in the agency seriously eroded by the Bay of Pigs, JFK did not accept the CIA's realistic assessment of the low odds of secretly disrupting, much less overthrowing, the Ho Chi Minh regime. Instead, beginning in 1962, President Kennedy turned to the Pentagon to wage a secret war against North Vietnam. Though the Joint Chiefs of Staff were skeptical—suspicious of the mavericks and "snake eaters" who typically ran guerrilla operations—Secretary McNamara, evereager to be President Kennedy's action officer, took on the assignment. To organize the dirty war, he picked a tough marine general, Victor "Brute" Krulak.

Krulak was well known to the Kennedys. As a young World War II officer, he had led nighttime raids against the Japanese. On a mission in 1943, he had been rescued by a daring PT boat commander, Lieutenant John F. Kennedy. Lieutenant Kennedy gave Major Krulak a bottle of Scotch—which General Krulak gave back to President Kennedy almost two decades later at his inaugural in 1961. Krulak was soon invited to White House social events, where he met the president's brother. Krulak was just the sort of gung-ho marine RFK admired—bold, irreverent, unorthodox, and intellectual. At meetings of the Special Group during 1962 and 1963, RFK and Krulak became friends and allies. In 1963, as it became clear that the CIA was failing to stir up a covert war against North Vietnam, RFK pushed Krulak to come up with an ambitious plan of action. Krulak recalled RFK holding forth at meetings of the Special Group, insisting that if Hanoi could subvert the South, then why couldn't the Saigon regime and its American allies undermine the North? "Bobby," said Krulak, "was a get-even sort of guy." At Kennedy's prodding, Krulak began drafting an ambitious plan of spying, "psywar," and sabotage, known as OP-PLAN 34A. Wary of "special operations," the regular army officers in the Pentagon and at U.S. headquarters in Saigon were in no rush to fight a secret war against Hanoi. A toned-down version of Krulak's plan would not become operational until 1964.

While RFK was prodding the Pentagon to get moving on covert operations against the North in the summer of 1963, America's ally President Ngo Dinh Diem seemed headed for a collapse. Buddhist monks were burning themselves in the streets in protest against the strongman's repressive regime. The

American ambassador, Henry Cabot Lodge—the Brahmin senator unseated by JFK in 1952—argued that the corrupt Diem had to go. Over Labor Day 1963, RFK was summoned by his brother to bring order to a crisis that seriously divided the president's top advisers. In a series of errors and misunderstandings that proved, McGeorge Bundy quipped, "the danger of doing business on a weekend," Washington had authorized a coup against its client Diem. Confusion and recrimination reigned in the president's councils. In a moment of clarity, RFK actually asked whether "now was the time to get out of Vietnam entirely, rather than waiting." The question "hovered for a moment," writes Arthur Schlesinger, "then died away, a hopelessly alien thought in a field of unexamined assumptions and entrenched convictions."

Events lurched along through the early autumn, as the coup plotters in Saigon were on again, off again, amidst conflicting signals from Washington and the American embassy in Saigon. RFK was very uneasy about the coup plotting. At a White House meeting on Friday, October 25, he worried that Washington would be blamed if a revolt somehow went sour. "If it comes off and it's not effective, then obviously the United States is going to be blamed for it, particularly if some of these people are caught and they talk about the conversations they had with the United States," he warned. RFK proposed that the Americans use a cutout, an intermediary from a third country, to approach the coup plotters and learn more about their intentions. Somewhat contemptuously, JFK rejected his suggestion as overcomplicated and impractical. At a White House meeting on coup rumors four days later, on Tuesday, October 29, RFK came out flatly against a coup. He had just come through a difficult three days of dodging an incipient scandal over Ellen Rometsch; possibly, he was in no mood for risk-taking. More substantively, RFK had been influenced by his new friend Krulak, who took the side of another Kennedy ally, Chairman of the Joint Chiefs General Maxwell Taylor, against the anti-Diem faction in the American government. Taylor and most of the top brass at the Pentagon were still optimistic that the war could be won, given patience and more resources. Now was not the time to dump Diem. The CIA's McCone, too, argued against a coup. Prudent when he had to be, RFK saw the risks of a coup—instability in Saigon, power struggles, social unrest that could play into the hands of the Viet Cong. "We have a right to know what the rebel generals are planning," he insisted.

RFK was extremely wary of the role played by Ambassador Lodge, whom he regarded as a haughty, Irish-hating Brahmin and dangerous freelancer. Kennedy was convinced that Lodge was seriously jeopardizing the American involvement in Vietnam by backing mysterious coup plotters beyond the control of the Kennedy administration. "I may be in the minority," RFK argued on the afternoon of October 29, his anxiousness captured by the White House tape-recording system. "I just don't see that this makes any sense, on the face of it. We're putting the whole future of the country—and really, Southeast Asia—in the hands of somebody we don't know very well." If the coup failed, warned RFK, "they're gonna say the United States was behind it. I would think that we're just going down the road to disaster." But it was too late. On the morning of November 1, the generals attacked the presidential palace in Saigon. The next day, the White House learned that Diem had been assassinated. President Kennedy looked pale and shaken when he heard the news. "Pretty stupid," he muttered, speaking just above a whisper.

Unknown to his top advisers, save his brother, JFK was weighing another violent overthrow in early November. Through all the fitful attempts to unseat Fidel Castro by creating "boom and bang" in Cuba and the sometimes comic-opera plotting to kill him, the CIA had always lacked a truly effective "penetration agent," a mole working for the United States from deep inside the Cuban regime. Castro's inner circle had seemed impermeable. But in August 1963, a close Castro lieutenant and "hero of the revolution" had offered to defect to the United States. Disillusioned with Castro's repression and fealty to Moscow, Rolando Cubela Secades met with a CIA case officer on a trip to Helsinki and essentially offered his services—if the United States would do its share to overthrow Castro. Cubela said that he would be personally willing to "eliminate" Castro (he did not like the word "assassinate"). He had some experience in the elimination business: in 1959, he had helped kill the Batista regime's chief of intelligence. But he was very insistent: he would risk his life only if he was sure the United States would back a coup. The CIA gave him a tentative and conditional yes—American support *if* the coup was successful—and a code name, AMLASH.

On October 11, Cubela—AMLASH—met in Paris with his CIA handler. As a show of support and seriousness, Cubela demanded an audience with Robert F. Kennedy. That same day, RFK's phone records show a call from Desmond FitzGerald, the CIA's chief of operations for Cuba. FitzGerald, a clever and dashing Harvard man with a zest for covert operations, had taken over the Cuban account from William Harvey. In RFK's view, FitzGerald was a vast improvement. He had done a better job of staging some semblance of a secret war, organizing a few successful sabotage operations that autumn. Talking over a secure phone, FitzGerald and Kennedy often discussed covert operations against Cuba.

FitzGerald was excited about the AMLASH operations. Sending RFK to meet personally with a potential defector was out of the question—even for the risk-taking RFK—but FitzGerald himself agreed to sit down with the Cuban dissident. On October 29, the two men met in a CIA safe house in Paris. AMLASH asked for a high-powered rifle with a sniper's scope and a silencer. On November 19, the CIA sent back word that it would provide a "cache" of arms, including the rifle, on the island.

Except for a phone slip noting a call from FitzGerald on October 11, the day AMLASH met with his CIA handler in Paris, no written record has surfaced to document RFK's role in these decisions. Richard Helms, the CIA's chief of covert operations, has said that he never personally informed RFK of FitzGerald's mission to Paris. In his mordant way, Helms added that if he had told Kennedy about the Paris rendezvous with AMLASH, "Bobby probably would have gone himself." But another top CIA official, who was directly involved in the operation, told the author that Kennedy was fully informed of FitzGerald's dealings with AMLASH and approved the decision to provide AMLASH with an arms cache. "Des [FitzGerald] wasn't freelancing," said this official. "Not after Harvey got his head chopped off [after the Cuban Missile Crisis]. The word 'assassination' wasn't used, we danced around that. But there's no question that the coup was authorized."

There is little doubt that assassination plotting went on at lower levels of the intelligence and national security establishment. The imaginative Desmond FitzGerald suggested to his troops at the CIA that Castro, who enjoyed skin diving, might be killed with an exploding seashell. Another plotter inside the CIA suggested that, during the ongoing negotiations over returning a few remaining prisoners from the Bay of Pigs, Castro be presented with a gift—a new wet suit—lined with poison. David Ellis, a top Customs Department official who often worked with the CIA on covert actions, said that he served on a small working group in 1963 that came up with a plan to plant a bomb in the car of the Cuban dictator. According to Ellis, he hand-delivered the plan in a double-sealed envelope to Angie Novello, Kennedy's secretary, at the Justice Department. Ellis said that he never spoke to Kennedy, and that the plot—like most of the harebrained ideas cooked up by covert operators of this era—never got off the drawing board.

RFK's own views on assassination in this period have remained difficult to ascertain. There are no witnesses who know or will talk—with one prominent exception. In 1963, Joseph Califano, later a White House aide under Lyndon Johnson and a well-known Washington and New York lawyer, was counsel to the secretary of the army, Cyrus Vance. Califano served on an interdepartmental coordinating committee that planned covert operations in Cuba. The chairman of the committee was a State Department official, but the "real chairman," said Califano, "was Bobby Kennedy." At one meeting, probably in the summer of 1963, Kennedy "talked about knocking off Castro," Califano said in 1998. "I was stunned," said Califano. "He [RFK] was talking so openly, and there were other people in the room." Did "knock off" mean kill? Yes, said Califano, "no ifs, ands, or buts. No doubt." However, Califano's boss, Cyrus Vance, told the author he could not recall any such conversation, "nor did I have the sense he wanted to knock off Castro." Kennedy's closest aides flatly denied that he ever ordered an assassination or even discussed the possibility. John Nolan, RFK's administrative assistant in 1963, added that by the fall of that year, RFK was paying little attention to Cuban matters.

Whether or not they ordered an assassination attempt, the Kennedys—the president as well as RFK—did understand that a coup could involve bloodshed. In early November, the senior CIA official who participated in the AMLASH operation was sitting in Desmond FitzGerald's office at CIA headquarters in Langley, Virginia, while FitzGerald spoke on a secure phone directly to President Kennedy. This official overheard FitzGerald tell the president about the possibility of an anti-Castro coup in Havana. The CIA official could not hear

JFK's end of the conversation, but he sensed some hesitation—a "waffle," as he later described it—on the part of the president. The CIA official could tell from listening to FitzGerald that the CIA man was trying to deal with the president's anxieties: "Des's tone was, look, there may well be bloodshed. Castro may get killed. People get killed in coups." Possibly, after the death of Diem just a few days before, JFK had a greater appreciation of such risks.

JFK may have had qualms, but he did not "turn off the operation," said the former CIA official, who insisted on anonymity. A later investigation by the CIA's inspector general showed that the cache of weapons, including a high-powered rifle and silencer, was hidden on a farm in Cuba where the coup plotters could find them. On November 22, 1963, at a meeting at a safe house in Paris, a CIA case officer offered Cubela a poison pen he could use to kill someone from close range. At almost that precise moment Lee Harvey Oswald was taking aim at the back of John F. Kennedy's head.

FROM TIME TO TIME, Robert Kennedy was required to weigh the risk of his own death, and the death of his brother, at the hand of an assassin. FBI wiretaps would pick up occasional threats from irate mobsters, usually loose talk but nonetheless unsettling. That July, the FBI eavesdroppers had listened as Sam Giancana and several of his pals discussed playing golf. They all knew that JFK played golf; one mafioso asked if Bobby Kennedy did. Someone else suggested putting a bomb in the president's golf bag and the men laughed. After years of operating in secrecy and relative impunity, the Mafia bosses were bitterly complaining about pressure from the feds—a credit to the attorney general's persistence. The mob knew that the Kennedys, not Hoover, were to blame. On October 31, Buffalo, New York, mob boss Peter Maggadino railed into a hidden microphone, "They should kill the whole family, the mother and father, too!" The record does not make clear whether these threats were ever passed on to RFK. But the attorney general was well aware that Jimmy Hoffa wanted him dead. Kennedy had continued to pursue Hoffa with a unit known (though not in the Justice Department) as the Get Hoffa Squad, run by Kennedy's loyal top investigator, Walter Sheridan. In 1962, Sheridan's team had got a break when a disaffected Teamster named E. G. Partin agreed to cooperate with the government. Partin told Kennedy's men that Hoffa had asked him if he knew anything about plastic explosives. Partin quoted Hoffa as saying, "I've got to do something about that son of a bitch Bobby Kennedy." The Teamster chief marveled at RFK's almost defiant indifference to personal security. Hoffa told Partin that RFK had a lot of guts to swim alone in his pool and drive around in a convertible. Skeptically listening to Partin describe these threats, Walter Sheridan suggested that Partin be given a lie detector test. "What do we do if that fellow passes the test?" Kennedy asked.

RFK was fearless, but by the autumn of 1963 he was also tired, as he put it, "of chasing people." He had grown weary of dealing with Hoover. "I think the bitterness between him and J. Edgar Hoover took away a lot of the pleasure he got out of the Department of Justice," said his friend Gerald Tremblay.

Kennedy did not expect to be attorney general in his brother's second term. They had begun to talk about removing Dean Rusk as secretary of state and giving his job to Bob McNamara. RFK was an obvious candidate to succeed McNamara at the Pentagon.

First, however, RFK had to get his brother reelected. Worried that the Kennedy administration's stand on civil rights had lost the solid South for the Democratic Party, RFK tried to make up lost ground any way he could. On September 25, he instructed Kenny O'Donnell to schedule a visit by President Kennedy to the grave of General Robert E. Lee at Washington and Lee College in the spring of 1964. "By May of next year," RFK wrote the president's appointments secretary and chief political fixer, "I hazard a guess we might need Lee." A week later RFK sent the president a Pentagon report showing how defense spending was divided up around the country. The Kennedy administration, like all administrations, was not above trading pork for votes. "Note how well our Southern brethren, particularly Mississippi, have done. In doing more for Massachusetts and West Virginia," RFK dryly observed, "you have also done a good deal more for Mississippi."

Kennedy's wit masked a deep worry. RFK knew that he was a pariah in Dixie. That summer, he wrote North Carolina's progressive governor, Terry Sanford, "I hope I am not causing too much trouble for you down there. Just deny you ever met me—that is the only advice I can think to give you." JFK teased his brother for dragging him down in the South, where RFK was known as "Raoul" and "Little Brother." When the attorney general went south to speak, JFK urged him to come back soon—or not at all. RFK laughed, but he was, as always, sensitive to his brother's gibes. He was also exhausted by the grind of lobbying apprehensive congressmen to pass a civil rights bill. Every other week or so, Nicholas Katzenbach recalled, RFK would "play Mr. Host" to lawmakers from both parties aboard the presidential yacht, the *Sequoia,* offering "steaks and too much to drink." Kennedy "worked this like a son of a gun. He really wanted that bill," said Richard Donahue, a White House political aide. But stroking politicians was not something he naturally enjoyed. Katzenbach gave him a ride home after one cruise. RFK took his shoes off in the car and sighed, "What a shitty way to make a living."

RFK was badly overextended, yet he was always willing to take on more. He was becoming increasingly interested in national liberation movements in Africa and wanted the United States to embrace revolutionary leaders before the communists did. On October 20, he wrote a memo pushing national security adviser Bundy to get moving on Mozambique, South Africa, Angola, and Rhodesia: "Personally, I feel if we could take steps now, either through the CIA and/or making a concerted effort with students and intellectuals, we could head off some of the problems that are undoubtedly going to appear on the horizon in the next year or so."

The demands on RFK were taking a physical toll. Kennedy's confidential files suggest that he, or someone around him, was concerned that he was losing weight and energy. On November 5, White House physician Janet Travell wrote RFK, "Sustagen is a high protein, nutritional supplement which might be helpful to improve muscular endurance and to reduce fatigue in persons of light or subnormal body weight. . . . I suggest that you try this late in the afternoon to lessen end-of-the-day fatigue." The president himself knew that he was leaning too heavily on his brother. William Beggs, the editor of the *Miami News*, recalled suggesting to the president that RFK look into a difficult civil rights matter in Miami. JFK replied that his brother was already involved in "five or six enterprises" that were consuming "days" of his time. Beggs recalled that JFK paused and sighed, "I wish so very much I had two Bobbies."

He needed RFK more than ever in late November 1963. The specter of scandal persisted, now from a different quarter. Over the vociferous objections of many, Kennedy had protected Paul Corbin, his abrasive, meddlesome operative from the 1960 campaign, in a sinecure at the Democratic National Committee. Corbin rewarded Kennedy's loyalty by writing memos alleging that Kenny O'Donnell, RFK's old teammate and the president's close political aide, was stealing from Democratic campaign contributors. Corbin was a pathological liar who hated O'Donnell, but he had found an influential ally in Charles Bartlett, the newspaper columnist and presidential confidant, who was passing along Corbin's memos to the president. If RFK didn't do something about the Corbin-O'Donnell feud, it threatened to spill into the open.

On November 20, RFK turned thirty-eight. With deep lines around his eyes and flecks of gray in his sandy mop, he looked at once boyish and prematurely aged. At a surprise birthday party thrown for him at the Justice Department, he was in a particularly sardonic mood. He made a mock speech ticking off his contributions to his brother's reelection campaign, extolling his record as a Justice Department wiretapper and asking, "Who do you think clinched the South for President Kennedy? Robert Kennedy, that's who!" The secretaries tittered nervously. His friends gave him joke gifts, like a "hot line" to Paul Corbin. "That's funny," said RFK, in a dead flat voice, and no one laughed. Walking to the elevator afterwards, two of his top aides, John Douglas and Ramsey Clark, speculated that Kennedy would not be attorney general much longer. Douglas said that he thought Kennedy looked depressed. The birthday dinner at Hickory Hill that night was bright and lively, but Ethel gave an uncharacteristically subdued toast, simply raising her glass "to the president." As Byron White left, she said, "It's all going too perfectly."

CHAPTER **15** MOURNER

J. EDGAR HOOVER never called Robert Kennedy at home, so Kennedy knew right away that something was wrong. At 1:45 p.m. on November 22, 1963, RFK was summoned to the phone as he sat, eating a tuna fish sandwich with some Justice Department officials, on the patio at Hickory Hill. The day was warm and Indian-summery; Kennedy had swum in his pool that morning. Taking the telephone receiver, he identified himself and heard the FBI director intone, "I have news for you. The President's been shot." Kennedy asked if the wound was serious. Hoover said he believed so and would call when he knew more. Then he hung up.*

Kennedy's face contorted. He clapped his hand to his mouth and turned away. Ethel came and put her arms around him. He could not speak. Finally he forced out, "Jack's been shot. It may be fatal." The phone began ringing ceaselessly. "There's been so much hate," Kennedy muttered, wandering from one phone extension to another. To Ed Guthman, he said, "I thought they'd get one of us. . . . I thought it would be me."

His brother was probably dead, but he could not stop trying to protect him. Kennedy called McGeorge Bundy at the White House and instructed the national security adviser to change the locks on his brother's files, lest Lyndon Johnson rummage through them. The president's most sensitive files were removed to the offices of the national security staff in the Old Executive Office Building and kept under twenty-four-hour guard. RFK ordered the Secret Service to dismantle the hidden taping system in the Oval Office and the cabinet room.

---

* Kennedy later famously described Hoover's lack of emotion: the director sounded not quite as excited as if he had been reporting the discovery of a communist on the faculty of Harvard or of Howard, a mostly black university in D.C.

As he worked the phones and greeted family and friends, Kennedy never lost his composure, though Ethel handed him dark glasses to cover his red-rimmed eyes. When Hoover phoned around 2:30 p.m. and flatly declared, "The president is dead," Kennedy turned to Ethel and said, "He had the most wonderful life." He embraced his children as they returned from school and gently comforted them. His grace was touching, but a veneer. Grief would descend over Kennedy like a veil. In time, from long suffering would come transcendence and wisdom. But first, in the aftershock, Kennedy was seized by a desire to know who killed his brother.

Kennedy called CIA director John McCone and asked him to come to Hickory Hill, a few minutes away from agency headquarters in Langley. Bluntly, Kennedy asked the nation's top intelligence officer if the CIA had killed President Kennedy. The deeply Catholic McCone swore the agency was innocent. (RFK later told top investigator Walter Sheridan that he had asked McCone "in a way that he couldn't lie to me, and they [the CIA] hadn't," a possible reference to shared religious oaths.) Kennedy called Enrique "Harry" Williams, his favorite Cuban. Williams was meeting with a group of exile freedom fighters at the Old Ebbitt Hotel downtown, planning a series of raids from their guerrilla bases in Central America. Kennedy had just heard the first bulletins linking Lee Harvey Oswald, who had just been arrested in Dallas, to anti-Castro activities in New Orleans. "One of your guys did it," Kennedy spat out to the Cuban exile leader. As both men knew, the FBI had recently received threats from Cuban exiles angry at the Kennedys' perceived lethargy towards Castro. Taken aback, Williams said he knew nothing.

So many enemies, so many potential assassins: Southern bigots. Jimmy Hoffa. The Mafia. Castro. Kennedy called Walter Sheridan, who was in Nashville prosecuting Hoffa for jury tampering, and asked him to start making discreet inquiries. (Hoffa was pleased at the news, Sheridan reported back, but not guilty.) Kennedy himself spoke to Julius Draznin, a National Labor Relations Board lawyer in Chicago, who had good sources in the underworld. Draznin was part of an informal intelligence network maintained by RFK, a widespread web that included detectives in the Los Angeles Police Department, agents in the intelligence division of the IRS, and numerous journalists. Queried about sensitive matters in the past, Draznin had provided RFK with useful background on Frank Sinatra and Judith Exner. Now Kennedy asked the well-wired labor lawyer to find out whether the mob had shot his brother. "He was very subdued, low key," said Draznin. "He asked me, 'Do you have any angles on this? Can you tap in on this?' He wanted to know about Giancana. I called him back in a couple of days. There was nothing."

At twilight, as the shadows lengthened across Hickory Hill, RFK changed his shirt and headed for Andrews Air Force Base, to bring home his slain brother and widowed sister-in-law. Arriving a half hour before Air Force One, he saw a tangle of lights and cameras and hid in the back of a military truck. As the aircraft taxied in, he dashed out, his legs pumping up the gangway as it was wheeled to the plane door. Into the cabin he burst, not seeming to notice the new president of the United States as he ran by, mumbling, "Where's Jackie?" He found the former first lady, still in her blood-stained pink dress, and wrapped his arms around her. "I'm here," he said. "Oh, Bobby," she whispered.

In the hearse, the widow described the president's murder in gruesome detail. RFK did not want to hear it all, but he listened quietly, knowing that she needed to unburden herself. At Bethesda Naval Hospital, Ethel Kennedy arrived and tried to comfort her sister-in-law. Ethel was certain, she said, that the president had gone straight to heaven and "is just showering graces down on us." "Oh, Ethel," said Jackie, "I wish I could believe the way you do. Bobby's been so wonderful." "He'll always help you," said Ethel. Searching for some way to ease Jackie's grief, she blurted, "I'll share him with you."

RFK was a commanding figure at the hospital that night. He was the executive officer serving a dead captain, as if the new captain had not already taken over the ship of state. He gave orders in Jackie's name, just as he had in Jack's. The honor guard would include a member of the army Special Forces, the green berets. The choir would sing the Navy Hymn. The coffin would be closed. At one point Kennedy ordered, "Get me Mac Bundy." Told that Bundy was at a meeting and unavailable, RFK smiled ruefully; the new order had begun. Kennedy tried to be cheerful, at one point asking for a record player to be brought to the hospital's VIP suite. The president's non-Irish friends recoiled, but RFK said that some music might cheer up "the girls." Back at the White House, sometime before dawn, family friend Charles Spalding handed RFK a sleeping pill and wished him good night. "God, it's so awful. Everything was really beginning to run so well," said RFK. When the door closed, Spalding heard Kennedy finally break down and cry out, "Why, God?"

At 8 a.m., RFK walked alone around the South Grounds of the White House, misty in the gloom of a gathering easterly storm. At about nine, he found JFK's personal secretary, Evelyn Lincoln, sobbing outside the Oval Office, now occupied by Lyndon Johnson. "Do you know he asked me to be out by 9:30?" she said. "Oh, no!" RFK exclaimed.

Kennedy needed someone to attack, to blame. In his agony, Lyndon Johnson seemed more usurper than constitutional successor. During the Cuban Missile Crisis, RFK had regarded Johnson as a coward (for no cause that can be readily discerned from the transcripts of the ExCom meetings) and, as usual, had made no effort to hide his contempt. A couple of weeks after the crisis, at a White House dinner dance in mid-November 1962, LBJ had followed RFK into the family quarters and showed him his most pitiably needy side. Chuck Spalding, who was there, later gave a withering imitation of LBJ trailing after RFK, whining: "Now *yew* don't lih-ke me, Bobby. You do not lih-ke me. Your brother lih-kes me, your sister-in-law lih-kes me, and your Daddy lih-kes me, *but yew don't lih-ke me!*"

Encountering RFK outside the Oval Office on Saturday morning, November 23, LBJ delivered the full-Texas arm twist. He summoned RFK into the Oval Office and told him, as he had told everyone else that morning, "I need you more than he needed you." RFK wasn't listening. He wanted to know if it was really necessary for Johnson to move into the White House right away, while John Kennedy's rocking chair was stacked outside in the hallway and his body was lying in state in the East Room. Couldn't Johnson wait a few days? President Johnson, who was more gracious to RFK than RFK was to him, agreed to hold off—for a few hours.

Robert Kennedy would later use the word "nice" to describe the way he was treated in that desperate time: "They [the cabinet and Supreme Court] were all there, and it was nice." It was "nice" that Black Jack, the giant funeral horse, was restless; the speeches at the Capitol were "nice"; majority leader Mike Mansfield was "such a nice man." "Nice" is a word that would creep into RFK's vocabulary in a telltale way; in times of acute stress, he used the word almost dazedly, to deflect. It was such a bland and harmless word, and Kennedy so often felt rough and full of harm.

He was fastidious in his attention to the details of his brother's burial and coldly indifferent to the needs of his brother's successor. In the morning, wearing dark glasses in the driving rain, he selected a gravesite for his brother at Arlington Cemetery. He decreed that John Jr. would not wear white gloves. "Boys don't wear gloves," he explained to the boy's mother. But in the afternoon, he at first refused to attend the new president's first cabinet meeting. McGeorge Bundy had to plead with him. RFK arrived late, interrupting Johnson's opening remarks. Some cabinet members stood up when RFK came through the door, but LBJ remained seated. Kennedy stared at him with undisguised loathing. Johnson showed no expression, but he felt humiliated and believed that Kennedy had intentionally upstaged him.

At dinner at the White House, Bob McNamara looked at his wracked and turbulent friend and said, as an aside, to Jean Kennedy Smith, "Bobby should take a rest and go away and forget everything for a while. I'm afraid he'll get into a fight with Johnson." The mood among the Kennedy friends invited to the White House supper was punchy and manic. Someone yanked off Ethel's wig (which she wore when she had no time to get to a hairdresser) and passed it across the table. It ended up on the head of the secretary of defense. RFK got into an argument with Franklin Roosevelt Jr. over who was responsible for publicizing Hubert Humphrey's draft avoidance in World War II during the West Virginia primary. "Bobby, don't forget I did that on your instructions," said FDR Jr. RFK walked out of the room and paced the broad hallway of the executive mansion's second-floor residence.

Sunday morning dawned clear and mild for November. Peering out from a window of the White House, RFK was surprised at the number of people milling about in Lafayette Park, across Pennsylvania Avenue. Many in the crowd had been keeping vigil through the night. It is hard to know when Kennedy first sensed the enormity of his brother's myth and determined to nurture and enlarge it. But, through his grief, he was aware that his job as brother's keeper was not over and that certain appearances had to be maintained. At Bethesda Hospital on Friday night, the doctors performing the autopsy had been instructed by the White House physician, Dr. George

Burkley, not to make a written report on the slain president's adrenal glands, which had been atrophied by Addison's disease. Since Dr. Burkley was taking his orders directly from RFK, the suspicion arises that the Kennedy family wanted to avoid any public record of JFK's long-hidden illness. The autopsy was rushed, though not—as conspiracy theorists have suggested—to cover up some dark secret about the assassination, but rather because RFK was impatient to return the fallen president and his widow to the White House. Kennedy would be taking care of macabre chores for months and years to come. The president's brain, removed during the autopsy but apparently not buried with the president, had to be preserved (in a steel container, given to the president's secretary, Evelyn Lincoln; stored in the National Archives; and probably interred at a later time). The president's coffin from Dallas had to be quietly disposed of, sunk by the navy far out at sea, lest it become a ghoulish collector's item. (As late as February 1966, Kennedy was squabbling with the General Services Administration over who owned the casket—the government or the Kennedy family.)

The mythmaking machinery would soon enshrine President Kennedy, making him more far-seeing and bolder in death than he was in life. In mid-December, RFK wrote a posthumous foreword to *Profiles in Courage* that extolled JFK's personal bravery. "Courage is the virtue that President Kennedy most admired," RFK began, writing as much about himself as his brother. Leafing through JFK's papers in the weeks after the assassination, RFK found a scrap of paper from President Kennedy's last cabinet meeting. On it, the president had scribbled the word "poverty" several times and circled it. White House economic adviser Walter Heller had been urging JFK to begin thinking about programs to help the poor. No evidence exists to prove that President Kennedy intended to massively attack poverty in America; indeed, when he died, JFK was apparently cooling on the idea, fearful of alienating suburban voters he would need in 1964. But to RFK, the mere mention of the word "poverty" was a kind of last testament. He had the scrap of paper framed and kept on display in his office at the Justice Department.

In such moments, there are hints of the moral crusader that Robert Kennedy would become in his own right, reaching far beyond the cautious and realpolitik JFK. For someone defined by family duty, who subordinated his own ambition and ego for the sake of his brother's, the death of JFK was a cause for more than sorrow. Robert Kennedy would now have to redefine himself. RFK's tortured self-examination, his search for redemption and identity, would become all-consuming. Nonetheless, it is doubtful that he was thinking beyond the awfulness of the moment as he fretted over the details of memorializing his brother on the morning of Sunday, November 24, 1963.

Shortly after noon, Bobby escorted Jackie Kennedy into the East Room. The coffin lid was opened up and JFK's brother and widow looked, for the last time, upon the visage of the slain president, now waxen and grotesquely made up. It isn't Jack, it isn't Jack, Jackie thought to herself, as she later recounted to historian William Manchester for his authorized chronicle, *The Death of a*

President. She was glad that Bobby had agreed to keep the coffin shut while JFK lay in state. She placed three letters, from herself and her two children, in the coffin, along with a scrimshaw and a pair of cufflinks she had given her husband. Bobby Kennedy took off his *PT-109* tie clip and turned to Jackie. "He should have this, shouldn't he?" "Yes," she whispered. He pulled from his pocket a silver rosary that Ethel had given him at their wedding and a locket of his own hair and placed them, along with the tie clip, beside his dead brother.

Just a few minutes earlier, unbeknownst to JFK's widow and brother, the president's assassin, Lee Harvey Oswald, had been shot at point-blank range by Dallas nightclub owner Jack Ruby. The scene, at a Dallas jail, had been witnessed by millions on live TV. President Lyndon Johnson broke the news to RFK. Addressing Kennedy in his role of law enforcer as the attorney general, the president demanded, "You've got to do something, we've got to do something. We've got to get involved. It's giving the United States a bad name in the rest of the world." RFK would later wonder at Ruby's role as the assassin's assassin—had Ruby, who had ties to the mob, been sent to "silence" Oswald to cover up a conspiracy?—but at the moment, he could focus only on what he perceived as LBJ's continued insensitivity. "I thought at the time," he haltingly recounted to Manchester, "that . . . it [international embarrassment over the shooting] wasn't, it couldn't be, the thing foremost in my mind."

Kennedy's family obligations weighed heavily. He had made the most difficult phone call right after the shooting, reaching his mother in Hyannis. Rose Kennedy had just heard the news on the TV and sat trembling in a chair when her son told her, "It looks bad. . . . As far as I know, Jack can't pull through." Rose hung up, hugging herself. "I can't stand it," she said, "I've got to keep moving." She began pacing methodically. For hours she walked outside in the cold mist that had settled over Cape Cod, "too upset to even see her husband," according to William Manchester. It fell to Teddy Kennedy, who had flown up to Hyannis, to break the news to Joe Sr. At first, the youngest Kennedy son pretended that the television set was broken when the patriarch, suspicious about the hushed and muffled sounds around the house, demanded to see the news. Finally, on Saturday, Senator Kennedy stammered out, "There's been a bad accident. The president has been hurt very badly." Then: "As a matter of fact, he died." Later that day, Joseph Sr. demanded, with grunts and gestures, to be driven to the airport. His niece, Ann Gargan, obliged. They sat in the car for a time, then drove home. At Robert Kennedy's direction, Joseph Kennedy did not attend his son's funeral. RFK understood that the spectacle would be unbearable for his father.

Through the bleak pomp of the next two days, Robert Kennedy remained stoic and dry-eyed. With hundreds of millions watching on television, he marched, a slender, slightly hunched figure, behind his brother's flag-draped caisson as it was slowly drawn to the Capitol rotunda, to St. Matthew's Cathedral, and across the Potomac to the president's final resting place at Arlington Cemetery. On Sunday night at the executive mansion, where the lugubrious house party went on, RFK tried to join in some of the forced frivolity. Among the houseguests was Aristotle Onassis, the Greek shipping tycoon whom Jackie had befriended (and would later marry). At dinner, the Kennedy clan teased Onassis about his yacht and his riches. The attorney general drew up a kind of ersatz decree stipulating that Onassis divest himself of half his wealth to help the poor in South America. Going along with the joke, Onassis signed the document in Greek.

On Monday morning, the day of the funeral, RFK was somber and composed. Outside St. Matthew's, when little John F. Kennedy Jr. raised his tiny hand to salute his slain father, RFK's face could be seen constricting in pain. At the gravesite, he stood erect in his tailcoat while the bugler sounded Taps, and the Marine Band, at slow tempo, played a final, dolorous chorus of "Eternal Father, strong to save. . . ." As his limousine returned across the bridge from Arlington Cemetery to Washington, RFK signaled the driver to leave the procession and circle the Lincoln Memorial. From the backseat, Kennedy peered up at the brooding statue of President Lincoln. Then he wordlessly told the driver to move on. On Monday night at the White House, he fled the room when Dave Powers and brother Teddy began singing, off-key, an old ballad they had sung together on the night JFK was reelected to the Senate in 1958:

> *. . . friends were dearer then,*
> *Too bad we had to part.*
> *Now I know a tear would glisten*
> *If once more I could listen*
> *To the gang that sang "Heart of My Heart."*

By midnight all the guests had finally gone. Only the late president's brother and his widow remained. "Shall we go visit our friend?" Robert asked. The black Mercury wound past the Lincoln Memorial, across the bridge, up the hillside of Arlington Cemetery to the knoll below the Lee Mansion. Behind them Washington fitfully slept. The two knelt in the darkness before a flickering flame and prayed.

ROBERT KENNEDY seemed devoured by grief. He literally shrank, until he appeared wasted and gaunt. His clothes no longer fit, especially his brother's old clothes—an old blue topcoat, a tuxedo, a leather bomber jacket with the presidential seal—which he insisted on wearing and which hung on his narrowing frame. To John Seigenthaler, he appeared to be in physical pain, like a man with a toothache or on the rack. Even walking seemed difficult to him, though he walked for hours, brooding and alone. He admitted to Seigenthaler that he could no longer sleep, and then seemed to regret his confession. He tried to anoint his wounds with daubs of black sarcasm. "Been to any good funerals lately?" he asked one friend. "I don't like to let too many days go by without a funeral," he told another. On many winter nights he arose before dawn and drove, too fast, in his Ford Galaxie convertible with the top down, sometimes to see his brother's grave. On Thanksgiving he could not bear to return to Hyannis Port. Instead, he went to Florida and played "vicious" touch football with his friends, recalled Pierre Salinger. Kennedy was always all-out to win; now he seemed bent on inflicting pain. He went to his office in a trance and did no work. He seemed indifferent when Jimmy Hoffa, for years his great white whale, was finally convicted (of jury tampering) in March. After all those months of hectoring prosecutors to "get moving" on organized crime, he appeared to lose all interest in the underworld on November 22. Kennedy had been discussing strategies for attacking the mob with Manhattan U.S. Attorney Robert Morgenthau poolside at Hickory Hill when the call came from Hoover. "I saw him often after that, but he never mentioned organized crime to me again," said Morgenthau.

His grief was understandable, and yet it seemed too overwhelming, so all-consuming. While sympathetic, his friends began to wonder as the weeks passed and Kennedy's gloom only deepened. True, Kennedy was a sensitive man who always seemed to feel more deeply than most. Some believed that RFK had so invested himself in his brother's life that a part of him had died with the president. Others saw a classic case of survivor's guilt. But Kennedy's guilt may have been less generic, more specific. Without question, he worried that his own aggressive pursuit of evil men had brought evil upon his own house. His close friends, like Mary Bailey Gimbel from Milton days, could sense the denial and read the clues. Gimbel noticed that RFK never used the word "assassination," and when he saw his brother's face on the cover of a magazine, he turned the picture over, as if he could not bear the sight. It was Gimbel who observed that RFK was affected most by one poem in the well-thumbed poetry collection he began lugging around after his brother's death—the Gérard de Nerval poem about the man who walked a lobster on a leash because the lobster knew "the secrets of the deep." Kennedy had his own deep secrets.

In 1975, when the assassination plots against Fidel Castro were finally exposed in congressional hearings, John McCone had a flash of recognition. He recalled standing with Kennedy at Hickory Hill in the first minutes and hours after he had learned of his brother's death. He had felt at the time that there was something troubling Kennedy that he was not disclosing. McCone had been taken aback when Kennedy asked him if the CIA had killed the president. In 1975, as he learned more about the anti-Castro intrigues and plotting that had been kept even from the CIA director, McCone began to suspect that Kennedy felt personally guilty because he had been involved, directly or indirectly, with attempts to kill Castro.

John Seigenthaler, too, sensed in the months after JFK's assassination that Robert Kennedy seemed haunted, as if he were holding something back. Kennedy's uneasy remorse was apparent to observant strangers. In February, RFK traveled through London on a trip to the Far East. At a dinner given by Ambassador David Bruce, he was seated next to Ann Fleming, the wife of Ian Fleming, creator of the James Bond spy series. Mrs. Fleming's recollection of the evening, recounted in a letter a few days later to a friend, is revealing of

Kennedy's mood and preoccupations at the time. RFK, she wrote, "either has a neck injury or suffers from furtive guilt, for he seemed unable to hold his head straight or look one in the eye. . . . He is obsessed by Ian's books," she reported. Kennedy grilled her, in a "humourless" fashion, she wrote, for facts about her husband and his espionage intrigues. RFK may have had more than fictional plots on his mind.

Kennedy's determination to find out who killed his brother, so purposeful in the first few hours after the shooting, seemed to shut down in the winter of 1964. Possibly, RFK did not want to learn where the trail led. Certainly, he had no interest in the public investigation of the death of the president, the Warren Commission. Although he knew more about the possibility of plots against the president than any other single person in the government, he offered virtually no help to investigators. Rather, he concealed what he did know. In June, Chief Justice Earl Warren wrote RFK and asked him if he had any "additional information" to offer, or information suggesting a "domestic or foreign conspiracy." "What do I do?" Kennedy scrawled in his tiny handwriting on a note, attached to Justice Warren's letter, from an aide who was suggesting that the commission would appreciate a "personal response." He took two months, until August, to answer and then fudged: there was nothing *in the Justice Department files*, he reported, to suggest a conspiracy. RFK never told the Warren Commission of his fears about Giancana, or Castro, or Hoffa, or the Cuban exiles. In September, the Warren Commission issued its findings: Lee Harvey Oswald, acting alone, had murdered President Kennedy. RFK later told an aide that he regarded the Warren Commission report as a public relations exercise to reassure the public. The public, at least initially, accepted the commission's conclusion. Though Kennedy gave lip service to the single-gunman explanation, he never quieted his own doubts.

Kennedy's restless mind continued to torment him. In the past, he had always used action as an outlet. Now, paralyzed by grief, unwilling to go where the facts might lead, he groped for meaning in other, less familiar realms. The intellectual indifference of his youth had long since given way to earnest self-improvement, the sort of learning one could get from reading Civil War histories and attending Hickory Hill seminars. Poetry and philosophy remained foreign territory. Kennedy the seeker ventured there next, accompanied by a knowing and elegant guide, his brother's widow.

Jacqueline Kennedy had leaned heavily on RFK on the day of JFK's death, just as she had through crises large and small reaching back to the death of her first child in 1956. In December and January, Robert Kennedy began to rely on her. The late president's mourners in chief continued to grieve together, sometimes at odd hours. Secret Service records show that they visited JFK's grave together at about midnight on November 25 and 27 and then again at 1:30 a.m. on December 4. In December, RFK began calling on the former first lady at her new house in Georgetown. Sitting before the fire in the gloom of winter afternoons, Jackie and RFK talked of many things, including Catholicism and spiritualism. RFK was struggling with the good God of his childhood faith. On a yellow sheet found in his papers from about this time, he had scrawled, "The innocent suffer—how can that be possible and God be just." And: "All things are to be examined & called into question—There are no limits set to thought." Jackie's own searches had begun earlier and taken her further. She had sought out Benedictine priests for a time in the 1950s to discuss her spiritual longings, and her search had broadened, into poetry and philosophy, back to the ancient Greeks.

Inevitably, Ethel had to put up with the chatter that her husband was spending too much time in the company of his brother's widow. Jackie had never been a favorite of the Kennedy sisters, Eunice, Jean, and Pat, who felt more natural kinship with the outgoing and athletic Ethel. Cultured and refined, Jackie had no use for practical jokes and touch football. But she was more intellectually curious, and more spiritually in tune with Robert Kennedy at this tortured moment, than was Ethel Kennedy, secure in her faith. Jacqueline Bouvier had more in common with her brother-in-law than first appearances might suggest. She was shrewd and, in her own way, very tough minded. The product of neglectful parents, she was—like Robert—a survivor from an early age. She and RFK were equally adept manipulators of public image. It had been Jackie who planted the seed of Camelot with presidential chronicler Teddy White for a *Life* magazine article a few days after JFK's death. RFK may not have liked the Camelot imagery—the Lancelot role was perhaps too close for comfort—but he appreciated and joined his sister-in-law's efforts. They made a formidable team. "Bobby gets me to put on my widow's weeds and go down to his [LBJ's] office and ask for tremendous things like renaming Cape Canaveral after Jack," Jackie told Charlie Bartlett. In time, RFK would outgrow his brother—he would come closer than JFK ever did to the myth of moral visionary that Bobby and Jackie worked so assiduously to create. But in the months after JFK's murder, RFK felt very small indeed, shrunken inside his brother's old coat, worn as a hair shirt, a literal reminder of his inadequacy. Jackie, too, needed the myth of her fallen husband to secure her own brittle identity. Together, the president's brother and widow were fused by the love of John F. Kennedy, however conflicted their feelings may have been at times.

It is impossible to know the intimate nature of the relationship between Robert and his brother's widow. There can be no doubt that they shared a deep affection and emotional bond. In their grief and yearning for solace, they may have shared more. Nonetheless, beyond gossip and somewhat questionable sightings of the two embracing, no evidence has emerged that would prove a physical relationship. J. Edgar Hoover was always on the prowl for indiscretion, yet RFK's FBI file reveals not even the rumor of an affair between them.

In March 1964, while Ethel and the children were skiing in Vermont, RFK accompanied Jackie, her sister, Lee, brother-in-law Stas Radziwill, and Charles Spalding to the Caribbean island of Antigua, where they stayed in Bunny (Mrs. Paul) Mellon's seaside villa. Ethel Kennedy was either confident enough or broad-minded and generous enough to permit her husband to travel with Jackie. The couple do not appear to have been cavorting on the beaches during their stay at the Mellons'. RFK was a sensualist who craved brilliant sunlight and the sea. But he appears to have spent much of the vacation holed up in his room reading a book given to him by Jackie, Edith Hamilton's *The Greek Way*. "I'd read it quite a lot before and I brought it with me," Jackie recalled. "So I gave it to him and I remember he'd disappear. He'd be in his room an awful lot of the time . . . reading that and underlining things." After he returned home, RFK gravely wrote Mrs. Mellon to thank her for providing him and the president's widow with a retreat: "It meant a great deal in Jackie's life as I know it did in mine. Without your wonderful kindness I am not certain Jackie could have borne the pain."

But it was RFK who found the most lasting relief from Hamilton's *The Greek Way*. The book, written thirty years before by a Bryn Mawr classicist, was a revelation to Kennedy. Hamilton's discussion of history and tragedy in fifth-century Greece—an age, as Robert Frost had proclaimed in a poem written for John F. Kennedy's inauguration, "of poetry and power." It is easy to imagine Kennedy, desperate for some meaning in senseless tragedy, transfixed by the morals extracted by Hamilton from the historians Herodotus and Thucydides and the playwrights Aeschylus, Sophocles, and Euripides. It is useful to read along, as it were—to read *The Greek Way* as Kennedy did that first time:

As Hamilton tells the story, in the beginning of the golden age of Athens, the Persians, mighty and rich, are undone by arrogance. "The gods who hated beyond all else the arrogance of power had passed judgment upon them. The time had come when the great Empire should be broken and humbled. Insolent assurance will surely, soon or late, be brought low. Herodotus says, just as Aeschylus writes,

> *All arrogance will reap a harvest rich in tears.*
> *God calls men to a heavy reckoning*
> *For overweening pride.*

Triumphant over the cruel East, Athens becomes the hope of the West. But Athens, too, succumbs to hubris and wrecks its empire in the Peloponnesian Wars. "The arrogance that springs from a consciousness of power was the sin Greeks had always hated most," Hamilton reminds. Yet at the height of empire the Greeks cannot resist the lure of foreign adventure and foolish wars—including one fought over a lesser neighboring island, Melos, conquered and enslaved for no real reason save proximity. Overextended, the Greek Empire gets bogged down in a wasting war with Sparta. "Powerful men pull the city down," writes Thucydides.

Reading these words in the cool dark of his room, as the brilliant light of the Caribbean illuminated the sea beyond—as the radiance of the Aegean had shone for the Greeks in an earlier millennium—Kennedy must have wondered if the great historians were speaking directly to him. Had the Kennedys, too, been brought down by hubris? Had RFK, in extending his brother's empire, pushed too far and too hard?

If Kennedy found damnation in the lessons of the historians, he found deliverance in the words of the poets. "Poetry confronts the inexplicable," writes Hamilton. First comes the acceptance of fate. In the plays of Aeschylus, "again and again the note of foreboding is struck. Some dreadful deed is impending— what, none may say, but any moment we may be face to face with it." Kennedy was well acquainted with such foreboding, and he had experienced the event not once, but three times with his own siblings. Reading Hamilton's description of Aeschylus' *Oresteia*, Kennedy may have found at least a measure of solace in learning that the fall of great houses is fated—and felt kinship with Agamemnon and the House of Atreus, doomed to repeat the sins of the fathers, generation upon generation. We cannot know exactly what he was thinking during the hours he absented himself from the other revelers (in Chuck Spalding's recollection, they drank too much rum and moodily listened to records on the verandah). We do know that RFK went on to buy all of Hamilton's books and many of the plays they describe; some of the dog-eared copies, full of underlinings and notations, still rest in the bookshelves of the bedroom he shared with Ethel at Hickory Hill.

The saving grace for Kennedy was the exaltation Greeks found in suffering. "In agony learn wisdom!" cries the herald in Aeschylus' *Prometheus*. The Greeks understood that "injustice was the nature of things," but that the awfulness of fate could be borne and redeemed through pain. By reading the great tragedies, Kennedy could find meaning (and relief) because "tragedy is nothing less than pain transmuted into exaltation by the alchemy of poetry," Hamilton writes. "Tragedy's one essential is a soul that can feel greatly." Few souls ever felt more than Robert Kennedy's. He committed to memory, and often quoted, the last passage from Hamilton's chapter on Aeschylus. The author has been describing Agamemnon's accursed fate, and the fate of the House of Atreus, to "visit upon the children the sins of the father." But "pain and error have their purpose and their use: they are steps on the ladder of knowledge," writes Hamilton, quoting Aeschylus:

> God, whose law it is that he who learns must suffer. And even in our sleep pain that cannot forget, falls drop by drop upon the heart, and in our own despite, against our will, comes wisdom to us by the awful grace of God.

Kennedy marked another passage, a reflection on Aeschylus himself. The poet was also a warrior; he had fought at Marathon, the site of the great victory of Athens over the Persian invaders at the beginning of the golden age. Aeschylus was not just a thinker but a doer. "Life for him was an adventure, perilous indeed, but men are not made for safe havens," writes Hamilton, paraphrasing the Greeks. "The fullness of life is in the hazards of life." It was time for Robert Kennedy to rejoin the living, to experience again the hazards of life, to feel, like the Athenians so many centuries before, "the overwhelming obligation to serve the state."

• • •

KENNEDY WAS TRYING, haltingly, to rejoin the world. Between existential pon-
derings, he missed temporal power. In February, he lamented to columnist
Murray Kempton that he could no longer call his brother. "It's strange to think
that you can't just pick up the phone," said Kennedy. He meant that he missed
not just his brother's voice, but his mandate. "What makes me sad is I see a
problem . . . and I can't do anything about it," said Kennedy, who was still attorney general and a member, mostly in absentia, of the Special Group
(Counter-Insurgency). In *The New Republic*, Kempton wrote a sympathetic
piece about RFK's mourning entitled "Pure Irish." Kempton was startled by
Kennedy's thank-you note: "I'm sure Jack liked it."

Once the goad of the bureaucracy and the executor of his brother's will,
RFK had become just another member of the president's cabinet, and not a favored one. That February, RFK received a stern letter from the Johnson White
House informing him that the Justice Department's record of hiring women
lawyers was "disappointing." The attorney general was required to do better
and instructed to file a weekly progress report. The missive was no different
from the sort of demands RFK had routinely placed on the federal bureaucracy
in his brother's name. (Just a few months before, RFK had angrily complained
to the president that the State Department's failure to hire more blacks for policy jobs "sticks out like a sore thumb.") But Kennedy was galled by the
peremptory tone of the letter and probably by its authorship; it was signed by
Ralph Dungan, a former member of Kennedy's Irish mafia who had stayed on
in the Johnson White House. Kennedy, who was paternalistic towards women
and did not regard them as victims of discrimination, replied to Dungan with
dripping sarcasm. He informed the White House aide that he would consider it
a "real favor if you would furnish me a list of girl lawyers who are qualified for
GS-15 [a high civil service rank] or above. I would also appreciate an outline of
your plan of how I am to hire them when there are no vacancies and there is an
economy drive. You people think of wonderful programs which we over here
want you to know we fully support. . . ."

Kennedy seemed to wander about a desolate landscape in the winter and
spring of 1964, lost in regret and, at times, churlish self-pity. But he was heading somewhere. His course was neither linear nor rational. The path he took
back into public life was costly: it exacerbated an already poisonous relationship with Lyndon Johnson into a bitter feud that would, in time, become a full-
scale civil war. Yet Kennedy responded to the personal; his animus against
Johnson, while foolhardy and corrosive, was powerful motivation to rejoin the
fray. Kennedy's exile was regenerative in another way. Driven from power, he
was able to identify with the powerless. He did not so much change as evolve:
he had always empathized with the downtrodden, especially when directly
confronted by their plight, and he would never, for an instant, lose his desire to
win. Yet from the wants of the needy and his own impatient desire to make
right the wrongs of the world, he began to find, in fitful fashion, a public voice
that was his own, and not his brother's.

In March, Kennedy made his first major speech since the assassination—a St. Patrick's Day address to the Friendly Sons of St. Patrick in Scranton, Pennsylvania. Typically, he turned the speech into an almost physical test of courage. Kennedy had been obsessively reading a melancholy Irish poem about the death of "the Liberator," Owen O'Neill. He planned to end the speech to the Friendly Sons with the last verse:

> *We're sheep without a shepherd*
> *When the snow shuts out the sky—*
> *Oh! Why did you leave us, Owen?*
> *Why did you die?*

Reading over the speech text, Kennedy's spokesman, Ed Guthman, cut out the poem. Kennedy asked why. "Because you'll never get through it," said Guthman. "I've been practicing in front of a mirror," Kennedy said. "I can't get through it yet—but I will." When Kennedy arrived in Scranton, enormous crowds broke through the police barricade and later lined the roads, standing, worshipfully or curiously, in a heavy, wet snowfall. Kennedy made it through the speech—barely, said Guthman—and on the plane flight back to Washington began talking about getting back into public life. But he knew the crowds were for his brother, not him. That same day, RFK had brought columnist Mary McGrory with him to see Jackie at her house in Georgetown. Kennedy had always been playful with McGrory, once throwing her over his shoulder and carrying her into the Justice Department. After an "excruciating" conversation at Mrs. Kennedy's, McGrory tried to cheer up RFK. "I said, 'Oh Bobby, you'll go on. You're young, rich, and good looking,' " recalled McGrory. "He just burst into tears and bawled."

While the prince brooded in exile, his liegemen dreamed of the Restoration. RFK's heir apparency had been a source of family teasing. After the 1960 election, his brother had jokingly given him a cigarette case inscribed, "When I'm through, how about you?" To the faithful, however, destiny required another Kennedy in the White House. In an occasional but seditious way, Kennedy gave heart to the plotters. "We must all stay in close touch and not let them pick us off one by one," he told Richard Goodwin and Arthur Schlesinger in mid-December. ("They" were LBJ and his followers.) In an irresponsible and potentially mischievous act of backdoor diplomacy, a Kennedy acolyte, New York painter William Walton, was sent to the Soviet Union to meet with RFK's old back-channel friend Georgi Bolshakov. At a Moscow restaurant in early December, Walton told Bolshakov that the Kennedys regarded LBJ as a "clever time-server incapable of realizing [President] Kennedy's unfinished plans." President Johnson, said Walton, was a tool of big business who would probably chill U.S.-Soviet relations. But the Soviets should take heart: RFK intended to run for president, probably in 1968. The Soviets, who considered RFK more of a hard-liner than his brother, were not noticeably moved. Regarding the Kennedy back channel as no longer useful, Ambassador Dobrynin dropped it.

Some of Kennedy's friends and advisers wanted him to begin the succession struggle right away. Eyeing the vice presidency as a stepping-stone, they wanted to force Lyndon Johnson to accept RFK as his running mate in the 1964 election. As usual, the most outrageously forward was Paul Corbin. While others had tiptoed about RFK in the weeks after the assassination, Corbin wanted Kennedy to snap out of his funk. Corbin, the ex-marine, always saw himself as Kennedy's shock trooper. Granting himself wide authority, he would declare "Bobby says," whether or not Kennedy knew what he was doing. Operating on his own initiative (but possibly with RFK's silent assent), Corbin went to New Hampshire in February to try to organize a write-in campaign for RFK in the first of the presidential primaries on March 10.

President Johnson was naturally furious and justifiably skeptical that Corbin was freelancing. He had kept on most of Kennedy's aides, but he felt nervous surrounded by men who wore PT-boat tie clips. His grievances against RFK were by now well established. The glad-handing Texan, who had loathed every minute of his humbling vice presidency, found it more convenient to blame the attorney general than President Kennedy. He railed that RFK had bugged his office and plotted to dump him from the ticket in 1964.* Without question, RFK had been openly rude to LBJ, while Hickory Hill guests enjoyed themselves too much at Johnson's expense. At a party in October, RFK had been presented, to great hilarity, with an LBJ voodoo doll. "Whatever happened to Lyndon?" hooted the merrymakers. On those rare occasions when she felt compelled to invite the vice president to Hickory Hill, Ethel put LBJ and Lady Bird at what she called the losers' table. The cutting gibes quickly came back to lacerate Johnson's thin skin.

As president, Johnson no longer had to suffer in silence. When he heard about Corbin's machinations, he summoned RFK into the Oval Office after a cabinet meeting on February 11. LBJ was direct: he wanted Corbin out of New Hampshire and fired from the Democratic National Committee. RFK tried to protest that Corbin had been appointed by President Kennedy, "who thought he was good." (A stretch: JFK disliked Corbin about as much as everyone else did.) Johnson ignored RFK's unsubtle sentimentality. "Do it," he commanded. Then he added, with words he had long suppressed, "President Kennedy isn't president anymore. I am."

---

* LBJ was sure that RFK was secretly feeding the Bobby Baker investigation in the hope that the scandal would drag down Baker's Senate mentor. Kennedy did suspect Johnson of corruption and may have looked for evidence to prove it. One former congressional staffer involved in the Baker investigation has claimed that RFK actively fed dirt on Johnson and Baker to the Republicans. But Kennedy's close friend Charles Bartlett recalled, "From my conversation with Bobby, I didn't frankly have the sense that Bobby was trying to use the Baker thing as a sword to destroy Johnson. In a conversation maybe a week or two before the assassination, I asked Bobby how the investigation was going. He had a lot of stuff about what Baker had done, investments he had made and this money, loans, etc., but he said he didn't think it really tied into Johnson at all. He said that very flatly." No doubt, RFK was also worried that the Baker investigation might lead back to Ellen Rometsch. It is impossible to know, of course, whether RFK was leveling with Bartlett.

Sitting there, in the office so recently occupied by his brother, Kennedy was shocked by LBJ's bluntness. "It was a bitter, mean conversation," he later recalled, ". . . the meanest tone I've heard." To Johnson, Kennedy angrily replied, "I know you're president, and don't you ever talk to me like that again." He turned and walked out. LBJ called the attorney general in his office that night and continued to insist that Kennedy get rid of Corbin. RFK defended Corbin as "harmless," a description rarely applied to the professional troublemaker, but revealing of Kennedy's determination to reward blind loyalty with blind loyalty. Decades later, old Kennedy aides continued to describe Corbin as "evil." Joe Dolan called him "Robert Kennedy's dark side." Corbin, who specialized in groundless accusations, once accused Dolan of taking a $10,000 bribe for selling a postmastership. Dolan went spluttering with indignation into the attorney general's office. RFK barely looked up from the newspapers. "You wouldn't come that cheap," Kennedy dryly remarked and went on reading.

To Kennedy, fealty counted. RFK, who referred to the president as "Johnson" and his late brother as "the president," could not understand how readily some of JFK's former aides transferred their allegiance to his successor. Dutybound men like National Security Adviser McGeorge Bundy believed that serving the new president was the responsible thing to do. For a time, quite unfairly, Kennedy regarded Bundy as traitorous. At the end of February, RFK blew up at Bundy over a seemingly trivial matter. At a White House meeting, Bundy gave more credit to Eisenhower than to JFK for the development of a new fighter plane. RFK must have said something angry or caustic, because Bundy wrote him the most painfully earnest letter of apology ("It disturbs me that we should ever have a difference about the service of the president's memory . . .") and promised "I'll try to find a way to make it up." A week later, he wrote RFK to say that he had made "informal inquiries" to see whether JFK could be awarded a posthumous Nobel Peace Prize. Ethel, too, felt let down by New Frontiersmen who stayed on to serve LBJ. Ambassador John Kenneth Galbraith sent RFK a copy of a memo he had written LBJ urging the president to make better use of his attorney general. "Show it to Ethel and tell her I still feel her teeth marks in my neck," wrote Galbraith. "Tell her seriously that her friends do better than she thinks."

Corbin's devotion was touching to RFK precisely because it was unwavering and unconditional. Hearing that Corbin had called in his condolences the night after JFK died, RFK at first made a sour face. He initially suspected Corbin of hypocrisy, since the inveterate agitator knew full well that the president had been angry with him for trying to smear Kenny O'Donnell on trumped-up corruption charges. But then RFK was told that Corbin had broken down weeping over JFK. Instantly moved, RFK forgave Corbin. Friends tried to warn Kennedy to be careful. At Hickory Hill, while changing for a tennis game in the early spring of 1964, columnist Rowland Evans told RFK that Corbin was causing him more trouble than he was worth. RFK abruptly cut Evans off: "When I want your advice, I'll ask for it." Most remained perplexed by Kennedy's stubborn defense of Corbin. But Ben Bradlee discerned the elemental bond of outsiderness: Robert Kennedy loved Corbin, he said, precisely because "no one else did."

Kennedy's hatred of LBJ was equally primitive and unreasoning. To be sure, their styles clashed. Johnson was all long-winded, arm-grabbing effusiveness, while Kennedy, terse to the point of silence, recoiled at touchers and clutchers. Even so, both had sympathy for the underdog and a keen instinct for deal-making and the art of the possible. They might, under other circumstances, have been allies. Yet by the spring of 1964 they were implacable foes. LBJ described Kennedy as "a little shitass" and "a grandstanding runt." RFK described LBJ as "mean, bitter, vicious—an animal in many ways." Cruelly, and with an unerring instinct for Kennedy's hidden vulnerabilities, LBJ remarked to Pierre Salinger that JFK's death had been "divine retribution" for the Kennedy administration's assassination plots.* Salinger fed the insult right back to Kennedy, who, choking with anger, pronounced it "the worst thing that Johnson has said."

How, then, can one explain Robert Kennedy's campaign to become LBJ's vice president? Through March, April, and May, he did nothing to discourage speculation that he would take the job if offered. If anything, he encouraged the chatter, while relishing polls that showed him the clear popular choice for the number two spot. There can be no doubt that Kennedy would have hated the vice presidency. Like a schoolboy who hazes because he was once hazed, Johnson would have tried to neuter Kennedy. Although Johnson said he would take anyone who could help him beat the Republicans in November, he was also widely quoted as saying that "whoever it is, I want his pecker in my pocket." Not likely Robert Kennedy's. In truth, a Johnson-Kennedy ticket was always impossible, for the simple reasons, as LBJ's brother, Sam, explained, "a) Lyndon hated Bobby," and "b) Bobby hated Lyndon."

One can only conclude that RFK's raw motivation for positioning himself as a vice-presidential candidate was perverse. He wanted to see Johnson squirm. Kennedy himself practically admitted as much in a confidential oral history given in May. "The one thing Lyndon Johnson doesn't want is me as vice-president," Kennedy said. "I think he's hysterical about how he's going to try to avoid having me or having to ask me. That's what he spends most of his time on, from what I understand: figuring out how he's going to avoid me." His friend Chuck Spalding understood that RFK enjoyed "nettling" Johnson: "The idea of Johnson and Bobby on the same ticket . . . in those sick days was almost too much. You couldn't help but consider that with a certain . . . relish."

RFK's "campaign" for the vice presidency in the spring of 1964 was an absurd spectacle, but at least, by personalizing politics, Johnson and the provocateur Corbin helped lure Kennedy back into the arena. In truth, Kennedy did not really know what he wanted to do. In between moments of despair—of want-

* LBJ mentioned the assassinations of Diem in Vietnam and Trujillo in the Dominican Republic, neither of which JFK authorized. Johnson did not know—yet—about the Castro plots.

ing, as he put it, to "go away"—he thought about running for U.S. senator from New York or governor of Massachusetts. Either job would give him an independent base from which to protect the Kennedy name and sally forth in pursuit of greater prizes. Still, both posts were elective, and he was not quite ready for pressing the flesh and jollying up local politicians. In early June, he abruptly offered to succeed Henry Cabot Lodge as U.S. ambassador to South Vietnam. His interest in Vietnam had never been pronounced. Nonetheless, serving in Saigon would both remove him from the physical reminders of his brother's presence and challenge him in a new hotspot. Lyndon Johnson was genuinely touched by Kennedy's offer of service. But he feared that RFK would be too much of an independent agent and rejected the idea.

On June 19, misfortune struck again. Teddy Kennedy suffered a broken back in the crash of a small plane outside Hartford, Connecticut. RFK's sense of doom hung over him as he rushed to his brother's bedside. That night, he lay in the grass outside the hospital, looking heavenward. "Somebody up there doesn't like us," he said to Walter Sheridan, adding, with painfully bleak sarcasm, "It's been a great year for giggles, hasn't it?" For a moment, his renewed zest weakened. He released a statement that he would not run for the Senate from New York. Privately, he explained to presidential adviser Clark Clifford that he wanted to spend more time with the recovering Teddy and help him campaign for reelection to the Senate from Massachusetts (the youngest Kennedy had been elected to fill an unexpired term in 1962).

Staring at the stars as he lay in the grass outside Teddy's hospital, bitterness rising within him, Kennedy could not help blaming the gods. But it was not like Robert Kennedy to resignedly accept fate. Defiance was more in his nature. He merely needed a prod.

A week after Teddy's accident, Kennedy left for Germany and Poland. The six-day trip served as a bracer and elixir, a journey among the oppressed and embattled that stirred his old empathies and helped him find his place as a tribune. Curiously, for someone so shy, he was revived by the tumult of a crowd.

Campaign-style baby-kissing and back-thumping appalled RFK. But he touched the sick and the old like a saint. On a quick trip to Chicago just before he left for Europe, he was accompanied by Ben Bradlee, then a reporter with *Newsweek*. Robert Kennedy had been wary and possibly even rivalrous with the dashing, wellborn friend of his late brother. Bradlee felt no great affection for RFK. Yet the newsman's gruffness melted as Kennedy toured a Catholic home for the aged:

He went from bed to bed, rubbing their hands, touching elbows, putting his head to their foreheads, comforting. I was skeptical, yet this was St. Francis of Assisi. These people were barely conscious, there was not a fucking vote in it. He got nothing out of it. Angie [Novello, RFK's secretary] said Bob is that way. He feels the same way about pigeons.

In Germany, Kennedy began by rededicating in the name of his brother the square where JFK had given his famous "Ich bin ein Berliner" speech.* He had spoken in the West Berlin *Platz* once before, in front of 150,000 people in February 1962. He had been so cold and stage-frightened that Ethel had come up behind him and rubbed his back while he stammered out his speech. The 70,000 Berliners who turned out this time, roaring with approval, came only for the echo of President Kennedy. But Poland was different. John Seigenthaler once remarked that RFK had a "strange fascination" with the Poles, whose country had been so often invaded but who endured, in part by their stubborn Catholic faith. Kennedy felt an affinity with a people constantly fighting back against feelings of loss.

The trip began badly. RFK went on an arranged visit to a Polish orphanage (to distribute copies of Charles Schulz's *Happiness Is a Warm Puppy*) only to discover that the children had all been temporarily removed by the communist government. At the U.S. embassy, Kennedy berated the stately, dignified U.S. ambassador, John Moors Cabot, for poor advance work. Cabot stoically endured the dressing down. The Brahmin diplomat was pained again the next day when Kennedy climbed on the roof of the ambassador's car to address vast crowds that would appear, spontaneously, from the narrow streets. While Ambassador Cabot vainly tried to signal Kennedy that the roof of the limousine was beginning to cave in, Kennedy playfully engaged the masses. With Ethel, he sang, in his reedy, off-key voice, "When Polish Eyes Are Smiling" in an ancient square in Cracow. Returning to the embassy for dinner—late as usual, keeping the dignitaries waiting—he roused the crowd at the expense of the unfortunate Cabot. "Would you like to come in with me?" he teased. "Yes! Yes!" the people cried. "Sorry, the ambassador says you can't come in," laughed RFK. Watching Kennedy make mischief, journalist and friend Joe Kraft was struck by Kennedy's animation and ease after so many months of depression. Feeling badly used, Ambassador Cabot indignantly offered his resignation, but for RFK, the crowds "got the juices flowing again," said Kraft. Kennedy had found, in his banter with the crowds, a speaking style that suited him far better than his mumbled set pieces on his brother's campaign trail. His speech-making ability would always be erratic, but Poland would be remembered as a place where Kennedy learned to feed off the crowd, to be as playful and blunt with five thousand people as he often was in private company. No longer concerned with embarrassing his brother, he was allowed to develop his own quirky style, quite different from his brother's rhetorical eloquence and cool detachment.

When Kennedy returned to Washington, he told his advisers that he

---

* RFK had actually used the line "Ich bin ein Berliner" before his brother made it famous in 1963. It was written for him by a foreign service officer, for some prepared remarks RFK delivered when arriving at Tempelhof Airport on his February 1962 trip. Perhaps because of RFK's poor delivery and an echoing airplane hangar, no one seems to have noticed.

would run for the Senate from New York after all. By now, the vice-presidential dance with Johnson was pure theater. In early June, when it became clear that Barry Goldwater, and not the more liberal Nelson Rockefeller, would win the Republican nomination, LBJ understood that Kennedy on the ticket might be a liability. Goldwater was strong only in the South, where Kennedy was weak. "I don't need that little runt to win," Johnson told his brother, Sam. "I can take anyone I damn please." LBJ formally delivered the news to RFK on July 29, reading from a prepared statement, while sitting stiffly behind his desk in the Oval Office, like a high school principal with a delinquent sophomore. Then the president met with some newsmen and mocked RFK gulping "like a fat fish" (Johnsonian make-believe: RFK had been calm). In a cruel loyalty test, LBJ made McGeorge Bundy tell Kennedy that he would have to announce that he had withdrawn on his own. Kennedy was miffed at Bundy, but finally said with a laugh to his staff, "Aw, what the hell, let's go form our own country."*

Kennedy continued to torment LBJ in his dreams. The president imagined Kennedy stampeding the Democratic convention in Atlantic City to secure a place on the ticket or even depose the president. "I didn't sleep two hours last night," he complained on July 23 to a crony, Texas governor John Connally (who had been badly wounded in JFK's car in Dallas in November). He was haunted by Kennedy's visage—"when this fellow looks at me, he looks at me like he's going to look a hole through me like I'm a spy or something." Actually, Johnson had Hoover to do the snooping for him. The FBI had removed his direct phone line to the attorney general as soon as JFK died and plugged into a more indulgent patron—Lyndon Johnson—at the White House. RFK was on to Hoover. "I understand that he sends all kinds of reports over to you about me," Kennedy pouted to LBJ in a phone conversation on July 21. Johnson played dumb: "Not any that *I* have seen. What are you talking about?" Kennedy mumbled, "Well, well, I just understand that—about me planning and plotting things." For the Atlantic City convention, Hoover dispatched a whole team of agents and wiretappers to keep tabs on Kennedy, who was supposedly conspiring with black activists to disrupt the convention.

He wasn't, though some of Kennedy's followers did urge him to stage a floor revolt. Kennedy wasn't interested. He did get off a last shot, with the help of his new poetry teacher. On the last night of the convention, Kennedy was scheduled to speak before a twenty-minute film memorializing the late president. None of the speech drafts include any lines from Shakespeare.† Yet when

---

* On July 2, LBJ signed the Civil Rights Act that RFK had first begun agitating for in spring of 1963. At the signing ceremony in the Oval Office, RFK hung back, sulking. Roy Reuther of the UAW pushed him forward, saying to LBJ, "Mr. President, I know you have reserved a pen for your Attorney General." Johnson blandly handed him a fistful. RFK got even in his own small way. He sent his civil rights assistant, John Doar, a framed photo of the signing ceremony and a pen. The inscription read, "Pen used to sign President Kennedy's civil rights bill."

† In an era when policymakers and journalists worried less about conflicts of interest, Kennedy had help writing the speech from four different working journalists: syndi-

he rose to address the convention, he stood waiting for twenty minutes for the applause to die down and concluded with a passage from *Romeo and Juliet:*

> *When he shall die,*
> *Take him and cut him out in little stars,*
> *And he will make the face of heaven so fine*
> *That all the world will be in love with night,*
> *And pay no worship to the garish sun.*

The allusion to the "garish sun" was obvious and galling to the followers of Lyndon Johnson. The suggestion to use it came at the last minute from Jacqueline Kennedy. Trumping the president with metaphorical allusions gave no peace to Kennedy. For fifteen minutes after the speech, he sat weeping on a fire escape outside the convention hall. Flying with him to New York that night, John Seigenthaler observed that RFK was "very depressed." Kennedy continued to complain about Johnson, asking Joe Alsop, "How much more do I have to take?" and calling the president "mean" in a way that Seigenthaler found "childlike." Kennedy needed to stop fretting about LBJ and turn to the unexpectedly stiff challenge of getting elected to the U.S. Senate.

---

cated columnist Charles Bartlett, *Nashville Tennessean* editor John Seigenthaler, Joe Kraft of *Harper's*, and Tony Lewis of the *New York Times*.

CHAPTER 16 SEARCHER

KENNEDY ANNOUNCED HIS CANDIDACY for the United States Senate from New York on August 22, 1964. He resigned as attorney general on September 2. On a sailing cruise with some friends in Maine, he carried what appeared to be a fourth-grade textbook on New York State history and geography. "Now where is the Hudson River again?" he would inquire in mock puzzlement. Though he had lived in the New York City suburbs until the age of twelve, he had no particular love for New York or feel for its murky melting-pot politics. "The politics in New York are no different from the politics in Massachusetts," he declared, "except that in New York they lie more."

This was bravado. Shy and tongue-tied and still in mourning, Kennedy was not a natural on the stump. His campaign organization was initially inept and always chaotic. He made the mistake of thinking that he could run on his brother's record, which he regarded as at least partly his own. But he had no real platform, other than vague promises to do more for New York. He was immediately branded a carpetbagger, a label that stuck when he took a busload of reporters to look at his old homestead in Bronxville and got lost. Never having hung from a subway strap, he had difficulty posing as the friend of the workingman. (Unaware that a token was required, he nearly impaled himself on the turnstile the first time he ventured underground.) Though he could hardly bear to admit it, he needed Lyndon Johnson's coattails to win. Robert Kennedy's 1964 Senate campaign can best be described as another learning experience. He was saved only when anger awakened him from melancholy.

Kennedy's own party did not embrace him warmly. The Democratic bosses in New York by and large supported RFK, but the rank and file were suspicious. After Kennedy accepted the party's nomination at a midtown Manhattan armory in early September, the Kennedy organization threw a celebration in a nearby hotel ballroom. Attractive young "Kennedy girls" in black dresses

and pearls were poised to welcome the grateful Democrats. Few came. Desperate to avoid the embarrassment of a half-empty hall, Kennedy aides flagged
down passing tour buses on Park Avenue, pulled off bewildered tourists from
Iowa and Ohio, and herded them into the ballroom to meet a Kennedy.

The novice candidate ran into particular resistance from Jewish reformers
who dominated the liberal wing of the party. Remembering Father Joe's sometimes thinly veiled anti-semitism, they regarded Kennedy as a hard-eyed Irish
punk who had collaborated with red-baiter Joe McCarthy. The New York establishment newspaper, the *Times*, attacked "ruthless" Robert with a series of edi-
torials, one unsubtly entitled the "Kennedy Blitzkrieg." Very thin-skinned
around reporters and editors he couldn't easily manipulate, Kennedy developed a lifelong resentment of the *Times*. He groused that the editors' idea of a
good story was "More Nuns Leave Church." Kennedy would later become, if
anything, pro-Semitic, but he had not forgotten, or entirely overcome, the unthinking prejudice of his youth. On a walking tour of a Jewish neighborhood in
Brooklyn on Rosh Hashanah in early September, Kennedy "was so nervous he
looked like he was going to have a heart attack," recalled Albert Blumenthal, a
West Side Democratic reform leader who was trying to help Kennedy find his
way in a strange land. Kennedy was not an easy or quick pupil. At an Orthodox
Jewish delicatessen, he wondered aloud why he couldn't get a glass of milk. Advised to wear a hat on a visit to a rabbi, he refused, mumbling to a friendly reporter that he didn't "want to look like fucking Calvin Coolidge." (Coolidge had
been famously photographed looking uncomfortable in an Indian war bonnet;
his example had made JFK forswear wearing funny hats.)

Kennedy's moodiness was obvious to voters. His speeches were flat or
screechy; missing was the banter he had so lightly shared with the Poles of Cracow. His TV ads were uninspiring until his aides had the good sense to film him
taking questions from students at Columbia University. One scene was edited
out of the commercials made from the film: A questioner asked Kennedy if he
agreed with the Warren Commission's finding that a single gunman shot JFK,
or whether he subscribed to any of the conspiracy theories. Kennedy was silent
for several minutes; the audience shifted uncomfortably. Finally, he snapped
back, "I've made my statement on that." He began to explain that in Poland,
four months earlier, he had told an inquiring reporter that he believed his
brother had been killed by a "deranged" person. Before he could finish,
Kennedy's voice cracked and his head dropped. He looked up again with tears
running down his cheeks. On the day in late September when the Warren
Commission report appeared, Kennedy canceled his campaign schedule. He
tried, unsuccessfully, to put his brother's death out of his mind. Campaigning
upstate the next day, he was warned by his aides that reporters were sure to ask
the reaction to the report. "Why?" asked RFK, his eyes suddenly glazing over.
"What are they going to do that for?" Predictably, the questions did come.
Kennedy mumbled, without conviction, that he accepted the single-gunman
verdict of the Warren Commission. Some days he wondered why he bothered
at all. "I don't know what difference it makes what I do," he said to an aide.

"Maybe we're all doomed anyway." Only Paul Corbin had the gumption to brace him: "Get out of this mysticism. Get out of your daze. . . . God damn, Bob, be yourself. Get hold of youself. You're real. Your brother is dead."

The Kennedy campaign was hardly the blitzkrieg the *Times* warned against. Behind schedule as usual one day, Kennedy chewed out his campaign manager, Steve Smith, husband of his sister Jean. "Steve, I want to tell you one thing. It wasn't like this when I ran my brother's campaign." Smith, who managed the family finances from the Kennedy office in the Pan Am building, tried not to get too excited about his in-laws' outbursts. (Years later, Smith was asked for some advice on how to be a Kennedy in-law. "Ask not what the Kennedys can do for you," he answered dryly. "Ask what you can do for the Kennedys.") A former hockey goalie with a low-key sense of humor, Smith referred affectionately to RFK as "the little fella" and tried to protect him from sentimental impulses. Smith banished Paul Corbin to New Jersey, where Corbin had so many phone lines installed that the police suspected him of running a bookmaking operation. Kennedy had himself to blame for the campaign's chronic lateness. With his obsessive work ethic, he demanded to be overscheduled but then, campaign adviser Justin Feldman complained, "slowed it down by shaking the hand of every nun he saw." Arthur Schlesinger was taken aback by the disorganization. Could Kennedy "conceivably have been the man who ran the allegedly well-organized and superbly-controlled presidential campaign in 1960?" he asked. "Well, that wasn't so hot either," Kennedy replied.

The huge crowds only seemed to remind him of his brother's popularity. In Buffalo, at the end of a long day of campaigning, motorcycle policemen were tipping over under the crowd surge. Looking down at the sea of people from a hotel window, Kennedy told Ed Guthman, "They're for him. They're not for me." As the crowds pressed around Kennedy's car, grabbing and clutching at him, *New York Times* reporter R. W. Apple watched his reaction:

> He looked terrified. You could see it in his eyes. These people were out of control, like pop-music crowds. Here was Jack come back. Bobby wore a small, bemused smile, but his eyes betrayed him. You could see him thinking, where is this going to stop?

Kennedy was worried that someone might get hurt. "He'd say, 'Careful, careful, they're going to get trampled.' "

And yet, Apple observed, "part of him was thrilled by" the tumult around him. The intense adulation, even if it was misplaced, could not help flattering and pleasing him. Consciously or not, he encouraged the jumpers and squealers. Hubert Humphrey, Johnson's running mate, drove with Kennedy through a vast throng in Westchester County. Kennedy complained to him about "too many young people pulling at him," Humphrey recalled. Humphrey, whose voluble earnestness concealed a wry sense of humor, replied that Kennedy could mitigate the problem by not standing on top of cars. As their limousine reached Manhattan, a woman tossed her shoes through the window. By the end of the motorcade, a girdle and a garter belt rested on the floor of the car. Humphrey said to RFK, "You're a magician. How'd you do that?" Kennedy laughed. "I'm a Beatle!" he told aides, half kidding of course, but smiling.

The adulation did not necessarily translate into votes, however. Many of the men and women who lined the streets to see RFK's family or surrogates were curiosity seekers. Kennedy was not wrong in his insecurity—a good portion of the campaign crowds had come not for his sake, but in remembrance of his brother. Fearful when Kennedy fell behind in the polls in September, the campaign scrambled to readjust. Word came down from campaign headquarters that "the candidate was to be referred to at all times as 'Robert F. Kennedy.' " "Bobby" sounded too much like "little brother." Speech coaches tried to improve RFK's flat or shaky delivery. His speeches were made slightly more substantive. RFK also got an unintentional boost from his opponent.

A month before election day, incumbent GOP Senator Kenneth Keating overplayed his hand. Kennedy had refused to attack the silver-haired, pink-faced, middle-of-the-road Keating, describing him as a nice man with a good voting record. But then Keating made the one charge guaranteed to inflame RFK: he attacked, albeit by insinuation, Ambassador Kennedy. In a naked play for Jewish votes, Keating falsely accused Kennedy, as attorney general, of signing off on a too-generous settlement of some claims against the General Aniline and Film Corporation. Describing General Aniline as a cartel that made Hitler's chemicals in World War II, Keating broadly hinted that Kennedy—like his father before him—was fronting for the Nazis. Kennedy was furious. To the relief of his aides, he began to hit back and to show more spark, abandoning his nasal monotone for a more natural and lively give-and-take with audiences. His competitiveness kicked in, along with his instinct for gamesmanship. He began to attack Keating's voting record, drawing on a fat stack of opposition research entitled "the Myth of Keating's Liberalism," prepared by Bill Haddad, the newspaperman who had worked as RFK's behind-the-scenes operative in the 1960 campaign. Haddad was useful in other ways. He owned a chain of small West Side newspapers. A reporter for one of the broadsheets "covered" Keating as a Kennedy spy, reporting regularly to Haddad on the GOP candidate's movements and meetings.

Slowly, the Kennedy campaign came around. The candidate increasingly found his voice. The vacant look was seen less often. Kennedy could be reticent in person, but he "was not shy in the streets," recalled campaign aide Jerome Kretchmer. Rather than brooding that he was a mere stand-in for his brother, Kennedy self-consciously used the family mythology to his advantage. Kennedy was no longer especially close to his mother (none of the children were), but he was respectful to Rose and some of their old bond remained. A veteran campaigner from the days of the Kennedy "teas" during JFK's congressional races, Mrs. Kennedy, a spry seventy-three-year-old, was a doughty trouper. On several occasions, she joined her son onstage. With a wink and a smile, RFK gently teased his mother for being strict and proper, and she played along, teasing back or playing the good-natured butt of his mild gibes. Their presence together reminded crowds that the Kennedys were a kind of American royal family, an institution worth preserving.

Keating's lead vanished. Falling behind in the polls as October wore on, he challenged Kennedy to a debate. Kennedy declined. He was fearful of taking on a man who looked like everyone's uncle, and he worried that he would betray his ignorance on issues affecting New Yorkers. Keating decided to hold a "debate" anyway, playing the old trick of debating an empty chair during a half hour of television time bought from the CBS affiliate. On the evening of the "debate," Kennedy met with his advisers at the family suite at the Carlyle Hotel to figure out what to do.

The atmosphere was tense and confused, recalled Peter Fishbein, a young lawyer and campaign aide who was in the room. Kennedy made two decisions. He called CBS and demanded to buy a half hour to respond to Keating. When the New York station balked, Kennedy picked up the phone and demanded to speak to the head of CBS, William S. Paley. Waking Paley in the Far East, where he was traveling on business, Kennedy swore, "Goddamn it! This is not fair!" Paley called CBS and ordered the local station to sell Kennedy the half hour. Then Kennedy demonstrated his political cunning. He decided to go to the studio just as Keating was beginning his phony debate and demand to be let onstage.

Kennedy was locked out of the studio—providing a good photo opportunity of the aggrieved challenger, banging to get in the door so that he could defend himself. Keating foolishly went on with the one-sided debate. Then, fearing an ambush by Kennedy, the incumbent panicked, fleeing out the back door as his aides knocked over chairs to slow down the stampeding press corps. The photographs were devastating. The distinguished, high-minded Keating was made to look silly and worse, as if he were the devious one, afraid of his challenger.

On election day, Kennedy won by 700,000 votes, 2 million less than LBJ's overwhelming margin of victory in New York. He had campaigned with Johnson in the final days. RFK's knuckles would turn white as the president threw a paw around his cringing shoulders and called him "ma boy." On election night, Kennedy pointedly failed to mention LBJ in his victory statement until he had named every low-level Democratic poll watcher in the state. Or so it seemed to President Johnson, who was watching on TV with growing fury. Kennedy was amiably deadpan with LBJ in a late-night phone call, telling the president, "Listen, I guess I pulled you through up here," but Johnson continued to brood. He complained in the morning to McGeorge Bundy that he had campaigned for RFK through "33 miles of Brooklyn . . . bragging on his brother" and that "If I'd kept my mouth shut, he would have been beaten. Very frankly, I thought last night it took him a long time to admit that the president had anything to do with it. . . . I just guess he can't bring himself to it." Caught in the middle, Bundy responded wearily, "Let's not start that war this morning."

To a friend, RFK had sounded rather morose. "If my brother was alive," he said, "I wouldn't be here. I'd rather have it that way." Kennedy ended his victory peroration with an inspirational quote from Tennyson's *Ulysses* that would become a trademark:

> *Come, my friends,*
> *'Tis not too late to seek a newer world.*

Kennedy had discovered the poem just that day. Tennyson's full text may reveal more than the fragment. As the romantic poet described the ancient Greek adventurer, Ulysses is an "idle king," tired of sitting about "mete[ing] and dole[ing] unequal laws unto a savage race." Though returned safely home to wife and son after his twenty-year odyssey from Troy, he longs to leave hearth and home and go back to sea, to danger and conflict. Ulysses is fatalistic but inexorably drawn to the journey: "It may be that the gulfs will wash us down; it may be we shall touch the Happy Isles, and see the great Achilles, whom we knew. . . ."

Kennedy had not even taken his seat in the Senate, but he knew that he would be restless there, meting out unequal laws with the other solons. He could not stop thinking of his own great Achilles. Two weeks later, on the anniversary of his brother's death, he wore his brother's bomber jacket with the presidential seal and brooded. He suddenly announced to his houseguest, John Seigenthaler, that he wanted to go to confession. On the way to church, he stopped off at his brother's gravesite, which was locked up. RFK hopped over the fence and shooed away the guard. It was obvious to Seigenthaler that Kennedy had made this trip many times before. At JFK's grave, RFK knelt and prayed. Walking back to the car, he seemed puzzled. He told Seigenthaler that his brother had called him two days before he died to wish him happy birthday. But now, Kennedy agonized, he couldn't remember a word his brother had said.

ROBERT KENNEDY was *"in* the Senate, but not *of* it," recalled Senate majority leader Mike Mansfield. "He did not become a member of the club," said Larry O'Brien, who had stayed on as the White House congressional liaison under Johnson. RFK lacked the patience and backslapping volubility to hang about the cloakroom swapping stories and favors with other lawmakers. The Senate is built on talk and courtesy. Kennedy was often silent or abrupt or just plain rude. He was not predictable: witty and playful one day, gloomy the next. A few senators, mostly relative newcomers like Fred Harris of Oklahoma and George McGovern of South Dakota, understood and admired him; others, particularly the old committee barons, were put off. The slow and meandering pace of legislation frustrated Kennedy. He wondered, "Why do they do all this bucking and filling? So much pleading and cajoling and all the rest," said O'Brien. Richard Goodwin, who had also stayed on with Johnson, writing some of his best speeches, understood the root of Kennedy's restlessness: "He hated all the talk after what he had done."

Kennedy found it hard to listen deferentially. As JFK's "Number One-

and-a-Half," he had run a secret war against Cuba and privately negotiated
with the Kremlin, but as a freshman senator, he was not senior enough to gain
a seat on the Foreign Relations Committee. Kennedy had been arguably the
most effective attorney general ever, transforming a sleepy bureaucracy into
an agent of change. Despite Hoover, he had swung the weight of the federal
government against organized crime and segregation in the South. But in his
three and a half years in the U.S. Senate, he lacked the seniority to pass any
major piece of legislation. While dutiful, he was often frustrated.

He tried to learn the local customs. He became a student of his younger
brother, Ted, who had slipped easily into the Senate club. The youngest
brother's virtual inheritance of JFK's seat in 1962 had put off veteran vote-
winners. But by playing follow the leader, doing his homework, and joining in
the jocular amiability of the cloakroom, Edward Kennedy had quieted the
snickering. "Baby Teddy"—seventeen years younger than Joe Jr., fifteen years
younger than Jack, seven younger than Robert—had always deferred to his
older brothers. Aboard the *Caroline,* Robert now sat in Jack's seat. In the Senate, however, Teddy was two years RFK's senior and without question the better nuts-and-bolts legislator.

Communicating by Kennedy shorthand, calling each other "Eddie" and
"Robbie," the brothers could shut out everyone around them. "It was as if the
two of them had . . . a really private world," said Dun Gifford, an Edward
Kennedy aide. As one tedious hearing dragged on into the late afternoon, RFK
fidgeted in his seat like a little boy waiting for the recess bell to ring. "Is this the
way I become a good senator—sitting here and waiting my turn?" he asked his
brother. Yes, replied Edward. "How many hours do I have to sit here to be a
good senator?" inquired Robert. Once, waiting to introduce an amendment
while two senators endlessly quibbled over a procedural matter, Kennedy could
not contain himself. "Oh forget it!" he exclaimed, flinging his papers into the
air and storming out the door. RFK pretended to be jealous of his brother's popularity with his colleagues and possibly he was. "If only I was a member of the
club, Teddy, the way you are, they'd take my amendments," RFK lamented, half
in jest. But he could not discipline himself to observe the ornate niceties of the
Senate or suffer its bigger fools. When Carl Curtis of Nebraska interrupted
consumer advocate Ralph Nader testifying on unsafe automobiles, Kennedy
chided him to listen first and criticize later.

> CURTIS: I have no objection to hearing his testimony, but when he
>   loses me with . . .
> KENNEDY: With big words?

Kennedy had even less tolerance for New York State politicians. His
brother gave him a book entitled, *"What I Know About New York Politics,* by
Robert Kennedy." The pages were blank. He enjoyed going to New York City
for the restaurants and, increasingly as time went on, the cultural offerings, but
"if we scheduled something in Buffalo or Rochester, he'd start moving around

trying to find some reason he didn't have to go," said Frank Mankiewicz, his press secretary. Kennedy's natural curiosity withered on the chicken-and-peas circuit. In September 1965, Joe Dolan, his administrative assistant, sent him a list of local groups that he was scheduled to address over the next month. Kennedy responded in his tiny scrawl, "I've never heard of half of these!" Tom Johnston, who ran his New York office, recalled, "It was very hard to get him to see an Albany politician or a labor leader. He was edgy and disagreeable with me if I pushed it. But he'd give [poet] Robert Lowell five hours." He made little effort to hide his contempt for favor-seekers and time-servers. Mankiewicz recalled Kennedy's acid sarcasm one night when he introduced a local Democratic ticket in Troy, New York. The candidates, sodden with drink in a dingy hall, stood for Kennedy's introduction. "There they are," said Kennedy. "Can't you just tell from their honest faces that they're doing a good job?" The reporters traveling with Kennedy burst out laughing.

At times, Kennedy seemed more interested in amusing the reporters with him than pleasing his audiences. Warren Rogers of *Look* recalled that, while delivering a forgettable speech to a bored audience in upstate New York, RFK interrupted his string of platitudes by mouthing, "Blah, blah, blah." The reporters again roared with laughter at this brazen in-joke, though the audience was baffled and probably embarrassed. Kennedy's courtship of the press was a careful, ongoing operation. Kennedy's daily schedules are studded with phone calls and meetings with favored journalists.

A few resisted the Kennedy treatment, but most reporters longed for an invitation to Hickory Hill. RFK wore out his first press secretary, Wes Barthelmes, a former paratrooper who couldn't take Kennedy's schedule. His successor, Frank Mankiewicz (son of Herman Mankiewicz, who wrote *Citizen Kane*), had the sense to see that Kennedy "didn't really need any PR advice" and limited his interventions to restraining Kennedy from lashing out when his feelings had been hurt, which was fairly often. The *New York Times* continued to nettle RFK. He muttered the old saw: "Anti-Catholicism is the antisemitism of the intellectuals." Among the angry letters he wrote—but never mailed—was one demanding to know why the *Times* failed to point out to readers that New York mayor John Lindsay was a Protestant.

In time, Kennedy did use the Senate effectively as a bully pulpit, as a platform to float new ideas, especially about ways to fight poverty. One of RFK's great qualities as a leader was his disdain for yes-men. He had never regarded himself as a visionary. He was a doer, an implementer. But he had the presence and wisdom to hire thinkers who would challenge and stir him. His in-house think tank was manned by two brilliant young lawyers, Peter Edelman and Adam Walinsky. Edelman, a former Supreme Court clerk, was cerebral and idealistic and calm. Walinsky, a Yale Law graduate, was passionate and bombastic—but very stimulating to Kennedy. Walinsky kept a poster over his desk which said, in Spanish, "When shit is gold the poor will have no assholes." Joe Dolan, Kennedy's administrative assistant, told him to take down the crude poster, but Walinsky, typically, refused. Walinsky and Kennedy were not intimate friends—Walinsky, while devoted, thought of Kennedy as sad and secretive. Kennedy rarely praised the young aide and routinely chastised him for inserting his own ego into his speeches. "Oh, Adam," RFK would sigh, in the same tone he would say, "Oh, Ethel." But Kennedy listened carefully to Walinsky and let him write the bulk of his words.

Ever in search of new ideas, Kennedy pumped Edelman and Walinsky, asking them almost every evening what to read and with whom to talk. But Kennedy, in 1965, was only episodically involved in the cause that would increasingly engage him in the last years of his life, the problem of the poor. When Lyndon Johnson was launching the War on Poverty in 1964–65, RFK was still distracted by mourning. In the early conception of Johnson's program, one can find traces of Kennedy's basic instincts and later thinking—his suspicion of bureaucracy, his dislike of welfare, his preference for local initiatives and personal responsibility over handouts and Big Government. But RFK played only a minor role in passing the great raft of initiatives—aimed at delivering better education, job training, legal rights, and health care to the poor—that swept through the Eighty-ninth Congress in the summer of 1965.

Kennedy did have personal as well as philosophical ties to the effort. Appointed director of the Office of Economic Opportunity, a Kennedy brother-in-law, Sargent Shriver, was Johnson's top general in the War on Poverty. (Shriver was independent-minded, however, no more or less loyal to RFK than he was to LBJ.) Some of the early thinking on ways to help the poor, especially through "community action," evolved from a Kennedy Justice Department program on juvenile delinquency run by RFK's old Milton chum, David Hackett. And LBJ claimed that he was fulfilling JFK's last wish, drawing his inspiration from the single word "poverty" found scrawled in the late president's papers from his final cabinet meeting.

Had he lived, President Kennedy would have made an unlikely crusader against poverty. On Tuesday, November 19, two days before JFK left for Dallas, White House economic adviser Walter Heller asked the president to describe his "current feelings" about launching an anti-poverty program. According to Heller's notes, JFK responded with his usual detachment and political prudence. "I am still very much in favor of doing something on the poverty theme to make sure we can get a good program," JFK said, "but I also think it's important to make clear that we're doing something for the middle-income man in the suburbs, etc. But the two are not at all inconsistent with each other. So go right ahead with your work on it." RFK, by contrast, was far more passionate about the poor. In between everything else he was doing, he had begun to educate himself in his own experiential way, summoning, for instance, a delegation of fifteen juvenile delinquents to his office to learn more about their motivations and alienation. On November 19, the same day as Heller's conversation with the president, RFK urged the president to read a memo from Dave Hackett calling for a "total attack" on the problems of poverty.

In the summer of 1964, Kennedy drafted a thoughtful memo urging LBJ to create jobs as the long-term cure for urban violence. But when Shriver and several aides called on Robert Kennedy during their planning sessions in 1964, they found him nearly catatonic. "He looked awful," recalled Frank Mankiewicz, who, before he joined Kennedy's Senate staff, had worked for Shriver at the Peace Corps. "He just sort of sat there. He was still in shock. He asked if what we were doing was what President Kennedy had in mind." Shriver's planning team, which included Hackett, assured him it was. "Fine," said RFK. Then he drifted back into his reverie.

Johnson, naturally, kept RFK at a distance. The president did not wish to allow RFK to take any credit for mounting the anti-poverty crusade (though he did blame him for some of its later failings). In any case, Kennedy was not ready to take a leading role. Though he had involved himself in poverty issues as attorney general, and had begun to make some crucial connections—between poverty and race, self-worth and crime—his education was incomplete, in hiatus while he grieved over his brother. His reactions were still mostly visceral. Touring Harlem in the spring of 1965, he could not get over the rat bites on the faces of little children. Yet, unlike Johnson, he was wary of quick fixes and had low expectations for federal largesse. He did not believe that creating new government agencies would do much. When the black ghetto of Watts in Los Angeles blew up in the summer of 1965, LBJ was shocked. The president, who had just succeeded in passing a program that promised billions to fight poverty, could not understand such ingratitude from the poor blacks he was trying to help. Kennedy, on the other hand, was not surprised at the explosion, and he was openly sympathetic to the rioters. He had been predicting trouble in the northern cities for two years. "A lot of those looters are just kids in trouble," he said. "I got in trouble when I was that age." He knew, partly from his own experience, that feelings of inferiority could sap initiative and provoke mindless violence. It is a reach to compare Kennedy's travails as the neglected little brother to the despair of ghetto dwellers, but Kennedy seemed to feel a direct kinship with the troubled youth of any time and place. As always, he personalized policy. After a briefing on the causes of juvenile delinquency in 1962, he had responded, "Oh, I see—if I had grown up in these circumstances, this could have happened to me." Over time, Kennedy's intuitiveness would make him an inventive and iconoclastic thinker on poverty, but in 1965 his thoughts were still directed inward.

DISPLAYS OF COURAGE had always been Kennedy's best offensive, his means of overcoming the insecurity of youth. Haunted by outsized notions of fate and hubris and possibly deeper demons after his brother's death, he turned again to danger as a rite of exorcism. Again and again, Kennedy tested himself against nature, climbing mountains and shooting white-water rapids, as if he could banish his mortality. He scaled forbidding heights and plunged into dangerous waters. He wanted to escape "the cold labyrinths of political life," said Richard Goodwin.

His first assault was on a mountain named after his brother. After Canada memorialized the fallen president with Mount Kennedy in the northern Rockies, the National Geographic Society suggested a climbing expedition by the surviving Kennedy brothers. Edward Kennedy's plane crash and back injury left RFK to do the honors, in late March 1965. At 13,900 feet, Mount Kennedy was the highest unclimbed mountain in North America. Climbing it would have been extremely difficult for any amateur. Kennedy carried an additional burden: he was deathly afraid of heights. His friends and family teased him for reckless vainglory. Alice Roosevelt Longworth, Teddy Roosevelt's acerbic grande dame daughter, suggested, "Bobby, why don't you just run around the airport and let them name that after you?" His mother's advice was, "Don't slip, dear." Unable to talk but still able to express himself, Joseph Kennedy Sr. took a photo of his eldest surviving son in climbing gear, crumpled it up, and hurled it across the room.

On the flight west, predictably, Kennedy read Churchill (who wrote that courage is "the first of human qualities because it is the quality which guarantees all others"). He was greeted at Seattle's airport by his guide, Jim Whittaker, the first American to climb Mount Everest. Whittaker was worried about his charge's lack of training. He had asked the senator's office whether Kennedy was in decent physical condition and received a cable, "He's wiry as hell," but Kennedy just looked small, sleepy, and vulnerable after dozing in his airplane seat. Uneasily, the strapping mountaineer asked Kennedy what he had been doing to get in shape. Kennedy replied that he had been running up and down the stairs at home, practicing yelling "help." "Oh boy," said Whittaker. As they hiked to base camp, Whittaker noted that Kennedy spent an inordinate amount of time just staring off into space.

Once on the mountain, Kennedy pressed. Bad weather threatened to delay the climb; Kennedy agitated to push on regardless of the conditions. As he led the expedition upward, Whittaker was surprised to hear the amateur's footsteps mushing along close behind and his high-pitched voice urging a faster pace. Once, Kennedy plunged through the soft snow into a crevasse, where he dangled from a rope, safe but shocked. On the second day, the party came to a nearly vertical ridge. To one side the mountain dropped straight down for six thousand feet. Kennedy later admitted that he was petrified and thought he would have to turn back. He heard Whittaker order, "Now you climb." Swinging his ice axe, he clambered up until he reached Whittaker just shy of the summit. The weather had turned brilliantly clear, and Whittaker asked if Kennedy wanted a photograph. "I don't care about the picture," Kennedy said. "Just get me the hell up the mountain."

Kennedy climbed the last fifty yards alone. Whittaker could see him reach the summit, drop to his knees, and cross himself. Then RFK reached into his pack and pulled out a flag with a family crest, three helmets on a field of green, designed by the Irish government for the Kennedy family in 1962. Kennedy jammed it into the snow, and then an American flag that was (to Whittaker's embarrassment) much smaller. RFK left some *PT-109* tie clips on the peak, along with a copy of JFK's inaugural address. He found no exultation in the experience. "I really didn't enjoy any part of it," he said. Whittaker was enthralled. He was "dumbfounded" by Kennedy's raw courage.

Whittaker was invited back to Hickory Hill and initiated into the cult of hyperactive competition. "Let's take a vote," Ethel announced. "Would we like Jim, if he hadn't climbed Mount Everest, would we have liked him anyway, or would we not have liked him?" The clan generously decided it would have liked him anyway. "It gets kind of right down to it," observed Whittaker, "but it's done in a funny, friendly manner. In all the things we did there was, in a sense, a testing." Whittaker began reading history books so that he could keep up at the dinner table. He was surprised to watch Kathleen, age fourteen, and a girl-friend, boxing—"really hitting, tears in their eyes"—and more startled when RFK said to his kids, "How many would like to see Jim and I fight?" At six feet five, 205 pounds, Whittaker was afraid that he would have to "really smash him [Kennedy] because he'd be after me." Fortunately, RFK thought better of the mismatch. Kennedy quizzed him about his conquest of Mount Everest, which had been dangerous and fatal to a couple of men in his party. "All this excited him," Whittaker said.

Politicking in upstate New York did not. That June, Joe Kempkes, a twenty-two-year-old man who had just graduated from college, was eating dinner with his parents in a restaurant in Buffalo, New York, when RFK walked in with the mayor and his entourage. During the glad-handing that followed, Kennedy caught the eye of young Kempkes ("my face looked like a map of Ire-land," Kempkes recalled, though his name is not Irish). With an almost imper-ceptible jerk of the head, Kennedy motioned Kempkes to follow him outside into the parking lot. From the trunk of his limousine, the senator from New York pulled a small white football. For five minutes, he played a forlorn game of catch with Kempkes. He explained to the star-struck young man that he was sick of hanging around mayors and politicians.

Back in Washington in late June, Kennedy spoke eloquently in favor of curbing the spread of nuclear weapons, suggesting negotiations with the Red Chinese (a very radical idea at this stage of the Cold War). The White House re-acted coolly—and the press wrote off Kennedy's initiative as one more skir-mish in the long-running battle between Kennedy and LBJ. A week later, Kennedy escaped again, this time to go white-water rafting in Utah with his family and new friend Jim Whittaker. A famous photograph showed Kennedy, white teeth flashing, his muscular brown arms paddling furiously, as he shot some rapids. Kennedy insisted on swimming in the rapids as well. "We'll lose him!" protested the guides. He went anyway.

In August, Kennedy went cruising off the coast of northern Maine with some friends aboard the *Palawan,* a yacht borrowed from Thomas Watson, the chairman of IBM. A gust of wind suddenly blew JFK's old bomber jacket off the deck and into the water. Without hesitating or apparently thinking, RFK went right over the side after his brother's jacket. The *Palawan* was sailing fast. The water temperature in the Bay of Maine was about 50 degrees. The captain quickly spun the wheel, but he seriously worried that Kennedy would drown in the icy water before he could bring the boat around. He estimated that Kennedy could last no more than twelve minutes. That was about how long it took to fish RFK, blue and shaking but holding the sacred garment, from the sea.

Over Labor Day, Kennedy took an even more harrowing swim. He had chartered a seventy-foot schooner, the *Nehris,* for a quick cruise off the New England coast with his children. Over the angry protests of the schooner's captain, he insisted on letting his children swim in water that the captain protested was shark-infested (the Kennedys promptly dubbed his boat "the Nervous"). The next day, the Kennedys, with most of their children on board, insisted on setting out in a thirty-knot near-gale and very heavy seas. After an hour and a half, they were hailed by a Coast Guard cutter with disturbing news: Kennedy's daughter Kathleen had fallen from her horse and suffered a head injury. Kennedy determined at once that he must go to her side. He dove into the raging sea and swam fifty yards to the cutter, his head disappearing under the breaking wave tops.

These dramatic feats captured small headlines, but little that he did on the floor of Congress attracted attention. In 1965, Kennedy was "impotent and frustrated . . . kind of floundering," recalled his friend Don Wilson of Time-Life. RFK wandered about, morose and distracted. Richard Goodwin was in New York, chatting with a woman he describes as "associated with the Kennedy administration" in the library of her New York apartment, when RFK wandered in one afternoon. He was wearing his brother's bomber jacket. He warily eyed Goodwin, who was still working for LBJ. "Let's go ice skating," he said abruptly. Goodwin didn't know how. As Goodwin clung to the rail on bended ankles, Kennedy swanned about the skating rink with the woman.

He needed something better to do than one-upping fickle speechwriters. In November, he went to South America for three weeks with an entourage of loyalists and journalists. His diplomatic hosts had scheduled the usual round of briefings and receptions. Kennedy went his own way. With crowds breaking through barbed-wire fences screaming "Kennedy! Kennedy!," clutching at him, ripping his suit, he embarked on an ecstatic journey among the poor. Moving from city to city in Peru, Chile, Argentina, and Brazil, he rarely missed a *barriada,* some so foul that his escorts stayed in their cars to avoid the stench. Kennedy walked through the mud and sewage, children clinging to his leg, in a transport of fellow suffering. In Concepción, Chile, he wanted to speak to students at the university. He was told that the communists would shout him down, that it was unsafe, that by Latin American custom the police stayed off campuses. But a Christian Democratic student told him that it would be considered a defeat if the communists kept him from speaking, thus guaranteeing his appearance. He was greeted by a hail of garbage and eggs as he walked in the hall. He went over to the communist section to shake hands. One of the students spat in his face.

The next morning at 4 a.m. he decided to visit the local mines. The manager was not happy to see him. "No, Mr. Kennedy, *please,*" he begged as Kennedy ignored his warnings and jumped, headfirst, into a mining car going into the dankest depths of the mine. After what he saw of working conditions there, he told a reporter, "I'd be a communist, too." Dick Goodwin, who had been invited along after the skating party, watched with wonder. Just four years before, Kennedy and Goodwin had plotted together to bring down Fidel Castro. Now RFK never mentioned Cuba, except to express his admiration for Che Guevara, Castro's ambassador of revolution, as a leader.

On November 20, his fortieth birthday, Kennedy was plunged back into gloom. In São Paulo, Ethel threw one of her parties to celebrate, holding up a toy plane she described as a U-2 sent by Lyndon Johnson to report on her husband's activities. Some guests started snapping party favors. Hearing the loud pop, Kennedy sank his head in his hands and said, "Oh no . . . Please don't." Two days later, on November 22, the second anniversary of his brother's assassination, he was possessed as he drove through the *barriada*. "Every child an education!" he cried. "Every family adequate housing! Every man a job!" On the plane, though, he buried his head in his arms.

He could not find enough adventure, test himself too much. He ventured out into the Amazon jungle in an ancient one-engine plane, surfed through rapids in a canoe, and—of course—went swimming in a piranha-infested stream, tossing a football with Goodwin, who couldn't wait to get out of the water. When he got home, the embassy sent Steve Smith at the Kennedy family office a bill for the repair of all the roofs he had dented climbing on top of embassy cars.

CHAPTER **17** CONSCIENCE

Robert Kennedy's trip to Latin America in November 1965 seemed to revive his interest in politics and public affairs. The crowds screaming "El presidente! El presidente!" were perhaps dreaming of his brother, but they were also shouting for him. He was feeling his way towards his own style of connecting with audiences, far more emotional than his brother's, closer to the people, particularly the poor. He was discovering the sustaining power of adulation, that he could feed off the hopes and needs of voters. Before an audience, where JFK was cool, RFK was hot. His politics were still fairly cautious—he was, like his brother, more moderate than liberal. But in the cauldron of a crowd, he began to feel the passions that would eventually embolden him to run for president. For now, he had to travel to Poland or Peru to truly experience the exaltation of the masses. The crowds in New York still made him feel more like a Beatle—or a stand-in for JFK. But the outpouring in the *barriadas* gave him a feeling of confidence.

In the winter of 1966, he began to define his own thinking on the important issues of the day—Vietnam and the crisis of the cities—and to speak out. He remained mindful, however, that his most attentive audience was Johnson and that every independent word or gesture fueled the president's immense resentment. The result, Kennedy understood, was counterproductive: if Kennedy was seen to be pressuring Johnson to take a certain course, the president's reaction was likely to be to head in the opposite direction. Given that LBJ was the commander in chief in an escalating war, Kennedy had good reason to be cautious.

Kennedy's attitude on Vietnam in 1964–65 was rooted in ambivalence. Withdrawing U.S. forces was out of the question. In September 1963, during the Kennedy administration's agonized debate over Diem, RFK had asked whether America shouldn't cut its losses and pull out. But he had let the question drop, and soon returned to the orthodoxy of the era, that America could not abandon its Asian ally to communism.* Still, he was increasingly dissatisfied with the way the Johnson administration chose to fight the war. Counterinsurgency was out of fashion by 1965. Under the influence of the Joint Chiefs, who preferred conventional means of warfare to fuzzy ideas about winning "hearts and minds," Johnson had gradually escalated the American military involvement. By the winter and spring of 1965, B-52s were raining bombs down on the Viet Cong and North Vietnamese while American ground troops were beginning to engage the elusive enemy.

Doubting the prospects for military victory, Kennedy wanted a negotiated peace. In April 1965, he privately suggested a bombing halt to LBJ. Johnson did stop the bombing—briefly—but signaled his disdain by referring to the moratorium as "Bobby Kennedy's bombing pause." If Johnson is to be believed, Kennedy was not passionate about the idea. According to Johnson's record of the conversation, Kennedy said that a bombing pause "would do no harm, and maybe something useful would come of it." Johnson promptly asked Congress for another $700 million to pay for his escalation of the war. Kennedy grudgingly voted for the measure, not wanting to "let down the boys at the front," as Arthur Schlesinger put it. In July, Kennedy made one last plea for counterinsurgency, for a war effort that relied not on bombing and conventional forces but on guerrilla fighters and economic and political reforms to win the allegiance of the peasants away from the Viet Cong. In a speech at the International Police Academy, he argued that struggles with communism to the Third World had demonstrated "beyond doubt that our approach to revolutionary war must be political—political first, political last, political always. Victory in a revolutionary war is won not by escalation, but by de-escalation." Taking umbrage at the implied criticism of LBJ's war effort, the White House reacted with consternation. Unwilling to force a confrontation, Kennedy drew back and did not formally address the subject of Vietnam again for months.

But he was quietly educating himself, or rather being educated by the persistent Adam Walinsky, his speechwriter and pot-stirrer. An early critic of the war, Walinsky stuffed RFK's briefcase at night with articles by I. F. Stone, the leftist pamphleteer whose newsletter mined government documents to do a better job than the mainstream press of exposing LBJ's attempts to hide the scale of the buildup in Vietnam. Kennedy read and absorbed the material. He realized that Johnson's escalation through 1965 was not bringing the North Vietnamese to the bargaining table or turning the tide of battle on the ground. He understood that progress could not be measured in "body counts," the inflated scorecard of enemy dead that the military used to beguile reporters. But

---

*Some of the Kennedy faithful have argued that JFK intended to pull out of Vietnam in his second term. In private conversation, President Kennedy may have voiced a wish to get out of Vietnam, but he was by no means committed. Asked in a 1964 oral history what JFK would have done if the South Vietnamese had been on the brink of defeat, Robert Kennedy answered, "We'd face that when we came to it."

Kennedy wasn't prepared to take on the administration's handling of the war in public, at least in a prepared speech.

Off-the-cuff remarks were a different matter. One of the qualities that attracted Walinsky to RFK was his boss's impetuousness, his willingness to cut through cant and "do the right thing." In 1964, while RFK was still attorney general and Walinsky was a junior lawyer at the Justice Department, an old pacificist, A. J. Muste, had wanted to stage a "peace march" from Canada to Guantánamo Bay, Cuba. Overreacting, the Johnson White House instructed the Justice Department to seek a court order to stop Muste. "Let me get this straight," said the attorney general. "You want me to sign [the papers requesting an injunction] so that an 80-year-old man can't walk 800 miles? Fuck it. I don't think he's a threat to the security of the United States." Walinsky was delighted. "When I heard that," Walinsky recalled, "that's when I knew he was my man." In the summer and fall of 1965, Kennedy declined to deliver Walinsky's fervent speeches denouncing the Vietnam War. But he didn't restrain his impulse to side with the dissenters. When college demonstrators started burning their draft cards, Kennedy defended their right. Kennedy scorned well-off college kids who, heedless of the poor boys who would have to die in their place, used draft deferments to avoid the war. But he applauded risky shows of moral outrage that could land a protester in jail. At a press conference at the University of Southern California in November, he said that he did not "agree personally" with the draft card burners, but if "a person feels that strongly . . ." A questioner broke in: "What about giving blood to the North Vietnamese?" Kennedy answered, "I think that's a good idea." Giving blood, he said, "was a good idea . . . in the oldest traditions of this country." The reaction around the country, still very pro-war in November 1965, was indignant. The *New York Daily News* suggested that if Kennedy wanted to help the North Vietnamese, "why not go whole hog? Why not light out for the enemy country and join its armed forces?"

Kennedy's extemporaneous remarks betrayed his disquiet. A close friend—and a principal architect of the war—was sharing some of the same unease. In the fall of 1965, Secretary of Defense Robert McNamara was beginning to anguish over Vietnam. Though he had recommended escalating the war, McNamara knew that the bombing was not working, that it was unlikely to break the will of the leadership in Hanoi. He kept his doubts well concealed from the public, but he shared them, at least to some extent, with Robert Kennedy.

The two men remained close. RFK had regarded McNamara as the star of his brother's cabinet, clearheaded and decisive and, like RFK, action-oriented. Kennedy and McNamara had bonded in every possible way, from doing the twist at Hickory Hill to leading the doves against the hawks during the Cuban Missile Crisis. RFK could be defensive about McNamara. At a Hickory Hill get-together, when NBC's Sander Vanocur questioned a dubious scheme by the secretary of defense to erect an electronic barrier along the DMZ to keep out the North Vietnamese, RFK hotly defended his friend, right or wrong. Vanocur was so taken aback by Kennedy's vehemence that he told his friend RFK, "I'll never discuss Robert McNamara with you again."

Kennedy and McNamara were both emotional men who concealed their feelings imperfectly. McNamara felt much closer to Robert Kennedy than he did to LBJ, though as a loyal servant of the president, he could not permit himself to show it. Thirty years later, McNamara was circumspect discussing his private talks with RFK in the fall and winter of 1965–66. "We talked often. We talked about all kinds of things," said McNamara. "My impression was that he was feeling his way. I recall that he was increasingly doubtful that we could win militarily. That coincided with my feelings." Did McNamara tell Kennedy what he knew about the war and about administration policy? McNamara became guarded. "With Bob, I would not have failed to tell the truth—I'm not sure how much truth. He knew I was in a difficult position. I loved them both [LBJ and RFK]. He [Kennedy] didn't want to make it any harder than it was. We steered away from anything like that. He knew I was determined to be loyal to both, and he didn't want to make it too difficult for me." Did McNamara have an impact on Kennedy's thinking about the war? "I don't have any doubt about it," said McNamara.

McNamara and Kennedy usually spoke privately, not in their offices or over the phone, but while walking out at Hickory Hill. (Kennedy feared that LBJ was bugging him.) Kennedy's aides watched this back channel with fascination. Peter Edelman recalled that RFK would often preface his remarks about the war by saying, "Well, Bob McNamara told me . . ." Richard Goodwin, who had resigned from the White House and now advised RFK informally while teaching and writing at Wesleyan University in Connecticut, believed that McNamara was quite open with Kennedy. "McNamara gave Kennedy copies of his memos to Johnson. I read them on the plane. He sent them to Bob *before* Johnson." (McNamara denied this.) Walinsky, however, believed that McNamara was not leveling with Kennedy about the disastrous course of the war, and another Kennedy staffer, Milton Gwirtzman, said that Kennedy suspected that McNamara was speaking out of both sides of his mouth. Kennedy was not shy about pressing McNamara, according to Dun Gifford, an Edward Kennedy aide who flew up to Hyannis on the *Caroline* with RFK and McNamara in the summer of '65. He recalled Robert Kennedy leaning forward in his seat (the seat once occupied by President Kennedy) and pressing the defense secretary: "Now what the hell is going on out there?"

With his mathematical approach, McNamara had concluded that the United States had only one chance in three of beating the North Vietnamese by military force. On December 27, 1965, he flew from Aspen, where he was skiing with his family, to the LBJ Ranch in Texas to try to persuade President Johnson to halt the bombing. (McNamara: "I have no doubt I discussed this with Bobby, without revealing confidential conversations with the president.") Johnson agreed to stop the bombing—for a short while. The Joint Chiefs, resenting an end run by their civilian boss, clamored to resume the air war. RFK made his own peace offering on January 18. He sent LBJ a copy of Bruce

Catton's *Never Call Retreat*, describing how Lincoln had stood up to his generals and meddlesome politicians during the Civil War. Johnson seemed moved, at least by self-pity. He had received RFK's letter during an hour when he was "alone, prayerfully alone," he replied. "I knew exactly how Lincoln felt." Johnson quoted from Catton when he met with congressional leaders a few days later. But at the end of January, the bombing resumed.

Congress was finally stirring over the war. Kennedy, lacking a seat on a policy-making committee, was relegated to a back bench. During hearings conducted by Senate Foreign Relations Committee chairman J. William Fulbright early in February 1966, RFK stood at the back of the hearing room. After watching Dean Rusk drone on about the communist menace on February 19, he finally announced at a press conference that the United States should seek a negotiated settlement of the war. He suggested, almost in passing, that the National Liberation Front, the political arm of the Viet Cong, should be invited to the table. But his wording was imprecise—he spoke of giving the NLF "a share of power." Apparently, he did not think he was proposing anything radical. He had checked his statement with McNamara, who saw no objection (McNamara had been privately telling LBJ that a coalition government was the only way out). After he made his remarks, Kennedy headed for a skiing vacation in Vermont with his family.

The White House reacted strongly. Johnson ordered his men to publicly renounce the seditious senator from New York. Sharing power with the NLF would be like "letting the fox into the chicken coop," declared Vice President Humphrey. General Maxwell Taylor was ordered to reverse an earlier statement expressing agreement with Kennedy's views. On *Meet the Press*, McGeorge Bundy skewered RFK by quoting President Kennedy on the dangers of national front governments. The *New York Daily News* lampooned "Ho Chi Kennedy." Kennedy's Senate office felt like a bunker under siege, Peter Edelman recalled. RFK rushed back from his skiing vacation to make clarifying statements that further muddled matters. At lunch with friendly columnist Rowland Evans he bitterly denounced former John F. Kennedy aides, such as Bundy, for disloyalty to the family. Obliged as a New York senator to attend a formal dinner for LBJ at the Waldorf-Astoria later that week, he chewed on a cigar and radiated disapproval of the guest of honor.

LBJ did not have to catch RFK's sullen look to suspect a conspiracy. He felt surrounded by spies and traitors. Not without foundation, he charged his press secretary, Bill Moyers, with maintaining a back channel to RFK. Mac Bundy was caught in the middle, accused of playing both sides by Johnson and Kennedy. (He resigned as national security adviser at the end of February, to become head of the Ford Foundation; Johnson regarded his glitzy farewell party in Georgetown, attended by RFK and Ethel, as final evidence of betrayal.) "The trouble with all you fellows," Johnson bellowed at Moyers and Bundy, "you're in bed with the Kennedys." Johnson's anti-Kennedy rants became so pronounced by the summer of 1966 that Bill Moyers began to think that Johnson was clinically paranoid.

Johnson's remarks were fed back to Kennedy by his various agents and freelancing troublemakers. The effect was to silence him on Vietnam. He was already having trouble explaining his brother's legacy. "I don't know what would be best: to say that he didn't spend much time thinking about Vietnam; or to say that he did and messed it up," he worried to a friend. Suddenly, he thrust his hand in the sky and beseeched, "Which, brother, which?" Kennedy did not wish to deepen the tragedy by engaging in a battle of pride with Lyndon Johnson. Desperate for a leader, the small but growing band of antiwar activists showed their disappointment. "While Others Dodge the Draft, Bobby Dodges the War," wrote I. F. Stone in October. Jack Newfield, a *Village Voice* writer who befriended Kennedy, badgered him about his silence at the end of 1966. Speaking off the record, Kennedy responded rather wearily:

> If I become convinced that by making another speech that I could do some good, I would make it tomorrow. But the last time I spoke I didn't have any influence on policy, and I was hurt politically. I'm afraid that by speaking out I just make Lyndon do the opposite, out of spite. He hates me so much that if I asked for snow, he would make rain, just because it was me. . . .

IT WAS CLEAR that Kennedy's only real hope of changing Lyndon Johnson's Vietnam policy was to topple Lyndon Johnson. A few romantics like Arthur Schlesinger began to entertain the idea of RFK's running in '68 as early as the summer of 1966, but, in June, Kennedy was still swearing that he backed LBJ "all the way" as the Democratic standard-bearer and planned to run for reelection as a U.S. senator in 1970. Kennedy had more hope of accomplishing something worthwhile in the War on Poverty, a crusade he endorsed in concept, if not always in the particulars of LBJ's programs. By 1966, Kennedy had broken out of his melancholic self-absorption and plunged into the problems of the poor. Characteristically, he became frustrated as a mere foot soldier in Johnson's war and decided to open his own front in an overlooked Brooklyn ghetto.

In the haze of retrospect, the later Robert F. Kennedy is regarded in many quarters as a fierce liberal who favored massive government intervention. The image is misleading. He started with some strong prejudices. In 1964, he told an interviewer, "What my father said about businessmen applies to liberals. . . . They're sons of bitches." He was ranting at that time against "soft" politicians like Adlai Stevenson, but even as his own politics moved leftward in the years ahead, he never shed his suspicion of liberals. Kennedy "defied labels," noted his legislative aide, Peter Edelman. RFK was indeed willing to spend large sums to help the poor and he believed that government had an inevitable and essential role, but he was highly skeptical of federal bureaucrats or local machine politicians as effective reformers. "When bureaucrats testified, he assumed they would obfuscate, and he worried about money sticking to the fingers of governors and mayors," said Edelman. Kennedy believed that handouts broke the human spirit and left the recipients of welfare listless and despondent. He favored from-the-bottom-up decision making over top-down central authority (in principle, at least; in practice, he liked to exercise some control from behind the scenes). Communities would have to be rebuilt by the people who lived there, he argued, or not at all. In 1966, he began to express these ideas and, more importantly, look for a concrete way to put them into action.

In his newfound zest for poetry and philosophy, Kennedy had discovered Ralph Waldo Emerson, the nineteenth-century transcendentalist. Friends noticed that he began carrying around a thin, well-worn, jacketless copy of Emerson's *Essays*. He was particularly drawn to Emerson's insistence on self-reliance and "self-trust." He underlined, "When you have chosen your part, abide by it, and do not weakly try to reconcile yourself to the world." Still painfully shy at times, easily stung by criticism, he understood that the lack of confidence could be demoralizing, paralyzing. By his own frenetic activity, he sought to avoid brooding. With all his privileges, life was still a struggle for Robert Kennedy. What must it be like, he wondered, for a poor black man in a ghetto like Harlem or Watts?

After the Watts riots had resulted in the death of 34 and more than 1,000 wounded in August 1965, he had summoned Adam Walinsky and Peter Edelman out to Hickory Hill to go swimming and discuss the poor. ("He kept bathing suits out there for people like us," said Walinsky.) Oblivious, in his way, to the incongruity of discussing anti-poverty policy while working on his tan, Kennedy demanded of his aides, "What are we going to do about these riots?" In a recent speech, he had stirred a fuss by dismissing tougher laws as the answer—by asking, as Walinsky put it, "What had the law ever done for Negroes?" In that speech, he had pointed out that New York State spent more on welfare than education. Walinsky, who shared Kennedy's skepticism about welfare, ventured that the answer was work: putting the poor to work rebuilding their neighborhoods. The dignity of work was a powerful selling point to Kennedy. He told Walinsky to start shaping a program for urban reconstruction, and he cautioned against grandiose or unworkable solutions.

Over the next several months Walinsky and Edelman drafted three speeches. They consulted RFK as often as they could catch him, once at a Georgetown dinner party as Kennedy's glitzy friends chattered in the background. Kennedy quoted Emerson to his two young aides, but he did not engage in lengthy philosophical discussions. "It wasn't the way he did things. He was too busy anyway," said Walinsky. The speeches, delivered over three consecutive days in New York at the end of January 1966, were "as momentous an event in the history of the welfare state as any," writes Michael Knox Beran in his elegantly written biographical essay on RFK, *The Last Patrician*. Beran wished to portray Kennedy as a seer, a visionary far ahead of his time, challenging liberal orthodoxies about work and welfare two decades before the Democratic Party began to seriously question the efficacy of Big Government. Kennedy was indeed mercifully free of cant, and he came to have a subtle and sophisticated feel for the difficult challenge of overcoming inner-city poverty.

But he did not sound a clarion call. Kennedy's message in his anti-poverty speeches in the winter of 1966 was not clear or striking, certainly not to the audiences listening to his speeches at the time (Jewish fund-raisers, black community activists, and labor organizers). He called for a massive jobs program, but it is a stretch to read into his words, as Beran seems to, a lofty and coherent vision of spiritual regeneration for the poor through personal responsibility and self-help. The speeches, taken as a whole, contain a good deal of 1960s liberal boilerplate. The first one, largely Edelman's work, extolled the virtues of racial integration and warned against isolating the ghetto. The second, a Walinsky-drafted call for rebuilding cities through "community action," was more Emersonian, but it had a certain dreamy quality in its ambition for urban renewal. The third was a fairly unremarkable plea for better education and job training. Kennedy's speeches do not begin to confront the problems that would vex later jobs-creation programs, like the extremely high cost-per-job and opposition of organized labor to unskilled workers horning in on their livelihoods. In emphasizing work over welfare, Kennedy's rhetoric was really no different from LBJ's marching orders to Sargent Shriver, his designated commander in the War on Poverty: "You tell Shriver, no doles." Or Shriver's own slogan: "A hand up, not a hand out." Still, Kennedy was more publicly explicit than most Democrats and moderate Republicans in his acknowledgment that welfare might actually be doing more harm than good. In February, in a speech to some editors in New York, he noted that conservatives had long derided welfare for destroying self-respect and lower incentive. Then he confessed:

> Most of us deprecated and disregarded these criticisms. People were in need; obviously, we felt, to help people in trouble was the right thing to do. But in our urge to help, we also disregarded elementary fact. For the criticisms of welfare do have a center of truth, and they are confirmed by the evidence. Recent studies have shown, for example, that higher welfare payments often encourage students to drop out of school, that they encourage families to disintegrate, and that they often lead to lifelong dependency. . . .

With his suspicion of bureaucracies, Kennedy also attacked Big Government as the solution. In a reflexive dig at LBJ's Great Society, he said, "There is not a problem for which there is not a program. There is not a problem for which money is not being spent. There is not a problem or a program on which dozens or hundreds of thousands of bureaucrats are not earnestly at work. But does this represent a solution to our problems? Manifestly it does not." Kennedy wanted a new approach. After the New York speeches, he wandered by Walinsky's desk. "Now listen," he said. "I don't want to just talk about it. I want to do something."

From time to time, Kennedy talked with his aides about the possibility of a local experiment—taking one community and trying to rebuild it as a model. Harlem, with its high profile, was an obvious choice, but too risky. Its local

bosses, Adam Clayton Powell and J. Raymond Jones, were political schemers
who fought to control any federal money coming into their communities.
Kennedy could never hope to work with them. Bedford-Stuyvesant, in Brooklyn, was a more promising proving ground. It was less well known, but larger
(with 400,000 residents—80 percent black, 15 percent Puerto Rican—about the
size of Cincinnati), and most important to RFK, it was not dominated by one
particular boss or faction who could act as a rival power base.

On a bleak winter's afternoon, February 4, 1966, Kennedy toured Bed-Sty,
driving past the crumbling tenements, looking mournfully at idle young men
hanging about. He met with some local civic activists who berated him. A
woman in a purple sweater shouted, "You white politicians come out here and
nothing changes. . . ." Kennedy rode back to Manhattan with Judge Thomas
Jones, a local civic judge and the highest-ranking black political figure in Bed-
Sty. Jones had refused to go on Kennedy's tour. "I told them I had already seen
Bed-Sty," he recalled. In the car, Kennedy asked Jones what he wanted. A swimming pool for kids in the summer, answered Jones. Kennedy turned to Tom
Johnston, the head of his New York office. "Work it out. Get them a swimming
pool." Back at his luxurious apartment at UN Plaza, overlooking the East River
and the distant outlying boroughs—middle-class Queens, decaying Brooklyn—Kennedy was angry at his reception in Bed-Sty. "I don't have to take that
shit. I could be smoking a cigar in Palm Beach," he said. Johnston recognized
the signs. From anger would come understanding and then a desire to do something. "We gotta do better than a swimming pool . . . ," Kennedy muttered.
How was not entirely clear. Johnston and Walinsky were told to start finding
ways to help Bedford-Stuyvesant rebuild itself. They were not given very explicit instructions by their boss, but they knew they had better produce something—that, to Kennedy, the greatest secular sin was not trying.

OVER THE TWO YEARS since he discovered Edith Hamilton, Kennedy's reading
had broadened to include Albert Camus. The French existentialist resonated
with RFK for some of the same reasons the Greeks caught his attention. Camus
helped Kennedy deal with pain and inevitability. Kennedy was immensely relieved to read Camus's message that the absurdity and seeming meaningless-
ness of life is not an end but rather a beginning, that because life is so
wretchedly unpredictable and uncontrollable, it is up to each man to start his
life anew each day. By marrying faith in action with the acceptance of suffering
and fate, Camus gave Kennedy a philosophical construct that fit precisely.
Kennedy was reading Camus's The Stranger (along with a volume by Winston
Churchill) when he flew to Canada to climb Mount Kennedy. He read and
reread Camus's Notebooks and Resistance, Rebellion, and Death, and had
Angie Novello type up his favorite quotes on index cards. Naturally, his friends
teased him when he pulled out his copy of Resistance. "That book is really depressing," he would say. "And long." (Actually, about 270 pages.) But he was
proud of his intellectual self-discovery. When Jack Newfield profiled RFK as
"The Existential Hero" in the somewhat raunchy men's magazine Cavalier,

RFK sent a copy to his father, though he ripped it out of the magazine so that his father wouldn't see the dirty pictures. Kennedy was incorrigibly romantic about those who defied the odds to follow their dreams and beliefs. In 1966, when the musical version of Cervantes's *Don Quixote, Man of La Mancha*, won a Tony Award on Broadway, he went to see it three times. He played a record of "The Impossible Dream" over and over at his apartment at UN Plaza, until guests became accustomed to the sound, like elevator music.

Always on the lookout for real-life existential heroes that winter of 1966, Kennedy found one in Cesar Chavez, who was organizing migrant farmworkers in California. His involvement followed a familiar pattern: at first, he grumbled, he didn't want to fly out to California to meet with some striking Mexicans. He was busy with Vietnam and getting something going on Bedford-Stuyvesant. But reluctantly, as a favor to his liberal activist friends in the United Auto Workers, he flew out to Delano, California, in mid-March. On the plane he complained to Peter Edelman, "Why am I dragging my ass all the way out to California?" As he listened to the workers describe their wretched conditions in the grape fields, and to the local police chief explain why he was arresting picketers—because they *might* riot—his emotions engaged. He lectured the hapless Delano sheriff: "This is the most interesting concept. How can you go arrest somebody if they haven't violated the law? . . . I suggest that during the luncheon period that the sheriff and the district attorney read the Constitution of the United States."

Over lunch, while the sheriff was supposed to be reading the Bill of Rights, but was more likely denouncing meddling by celebrity senators, Kennedy met Cesar Chavez in the parking lot. Chavez, stunned by Kennedy's edgy, angry performance at the hearings, held in a packed, stifling auditorium, whispered to his lieutenant, Dolores Huerta, "He shouldn't go so far because it's only going to hurt him." Kennedy sized up Chavez, a gentle, soft-spoken man about his own age—at once steely and beatific—who had been fighting wealthy farmers for fifteen years. "Time stopped," recalled Edelman. "The chemistry was instant." Each man immediately admired the other, saw in each other the same qualities of suffering and pride. Chavez had never seen such honest anger and sympathy in a white public official. Kennedy promised to help Chavez. He did, raising money, pushing for legislation to protect migrant workers, and badgering the IRS to stop using deportation threats to break the farmworkers' union.

ONE PARTICULAR PASSAGE from Camus's writing caught Robert Kennedy's attention. In his daybook, he scrawled:

> Perhaps we cannot prevent this world from being a world in which children are tortured. But we can reduce the number of tortured children. And if you believers don't help us, who else in the world can help us do this?

Kennedy's sensitivity to the suffering of children explains some of his fascination with the quote, which he used on the dedication page of *To Seek a Newer*

World, a collection of his speeches and thoughts published in 1967. But he was also animated by the lesson he had drawn from existentialism: that the way to deal with despair and the heaviness of fate was by acts of individual courage.

Nowhere was injustice more stark, or the prospect for change bleaker, than in South Africa in 1966. The country's white ruling class had stripped the blacks of freedoms and a chance to earn a decent living. Protest from the First World was muted; the United States government, like others in the West, regarded South Africa as an outpost against communism, which seemed to be gaining ground in the continent in the early and middle '60s. The reform movement within Africa was tiny and frightened. Margaret Marshall, a young student activist in South Africa at the time, recalled the loneliness:

> South Africa was in its most mean, oppressive period. It was a nasty time. There was real fear—the first reports of torture. The world seemed to have ignored us. We invited [UN Secretaries General] Dag Hammarskjöld and U Thant. No one came. Visitors who did would say, "I didn't realize it was so complicated." But Bobby Kennedy was different. . . .

Marshall's group, the National Union of South African Students (NUSAS), invited Kennedy to give the annual Day of Affirmation speech at the University of Cape Town in June 1966. Kennedy's interest was immediately piqued by the chance to speak out. He accepted the invitation—"as a dare," recalled his friend Lou Oberdorfer, "like climbing Mount Kennedy."

He had second thoughts. What if the South African regime used his appearance as an excuse to crack down harder? By indulging his own need to prove his courage and defiance, would he be putting others at risk? Kennedy's disquiet was played out during the drafting of the Day of Affirmation speech. He would tone down Adam Walinsky's heated prose, only to have his aide try to slip fiery words back in. When Kennedy finally blew up, Joe Dolan suggested that he get rid of Walinsky rather than struggle with him. "Oh, Sorensen was worse," Kennedy sighed, thinking of his brother's talented wordsmith who could be prickly, too, about defending his prose. Walinsky was not fired, but he was layered: Richard Goodwin was brought in to help craft the speech—which would be remembered as Kennedy's best.

The South African government regarded Kennedy's trip as a publicity junket and canceled the visas of forty journalists who planned to accompany him. No government official was at the Johannesburg airport to greet him when he arrived on Saturday night, June 4, shortly before midnight. A huge crowd broke through the glass doors and engulfed RFK, tearing off his cufflinks. Fistfights broke out between anti- and pro-apartheid demonstrators.

An anxious Margaret Marshall welcomed Kennedy on behalf of the students' union. She would be his guide for the next five days. "I was the vice president of NUSAS because all the men had been sent to prison," she recalled. Five days earlier, the president of the students' union, Ian Robertson, had been "banned"—forbidden to meet in a room with more than one person—for five years. "Robertson's banning terrified me," said Marshall. "I was twenty years old, thinking about the threat of no work, no passport, and no university." Kennedy appeared equally nervous. Stopping over in London, where he was interviewed by the BBC, he had seemed distracted. "We're only here on earth for a short time" he said, as he stared past the camera. With Marshall, he was tentative and solicitous. "He didn't walk in and say this is the way it's going to be," said Marshall. "He kept asking, 'Is this going to hurt anyone? I can do this, but is anyone going to pay the price for me?' He worried that he was going to put me at risk. I said, 'Don't protect me.' "

In the biting cold of a South African winter's day, a crowd of about 15,000 surged around the auditorium at the University of Cape Town. Loudspeakers were placed outside to relay the speech, but South African security forces cut the wires. An empty chair was left for the banned Robertson. Kennedy's eyes were glistening with tears as he rose to speak. On this Day of Affirmation, he spoke of personal freedom and the "sacred rights of Western Society" that separated "us and Nazi Germany . . . Athens and Persia." He warned against "the danger of futility: the belief there is nothing one man or one woman can do against the enormous array of the world's ills." Steadying his quavery voice, he declared that many of the world's great movements began with the work of a single man. "Few will have the greatness to bend history itself; but each of us can work to change a small portion of events, and in the total of all those acts will be written the history of this generation. . . .

> It is from numberless diverse acts of courage and belief that human history is shaped. Each time a man stands up for an ideal, or acts to improve the lot of others, or strikes out against injustice, he sends forth a tiny ripple of hope, and crossing each other from a million different centers of energy and daring those ripples build a current which can sweep down the mightiest walls of oppression and resistance. . . .

When he had finished, there was silence. Like a child, Marshall recalled, he looked around him, "as if to say, was the speech okay?" Then, with a rush, a roar of applause crashed over him. Marshall could see that he was immensely relieved, "high and exhilarated." For the next three days, he toured the country, increasingly emboldened. He stood on the roof of his car and led curious blacks in singing choruses of "We Shall Overcome." With Ethel, he set forth on walking tours, first of the upper-class neighborhoods, stopping black servants in the street to shake hands and say, "I'm Robert Kennedy from the United States and this is my wife Ethel." Frightened by an entourage of white people bearing down on him, one black man gave a yelp and ran away. As word of his visit spread, blacks crowded around to touch him—whites never touched blacks in South Africa—and began holding high the lucky hand that had shaken Robert Kennedy's. Kennedy insisted on visiting the black townships, quizzing Marshall all the while. (Kennedy: "Where's the fire station?" Marshall: "There isn't one.") On a visit into the bush to see Chief Albert Luthuli, a founder of the banned African National Congress, he played a record of his brother's civil rights speech in June 1963 (racial equality is "a moral issue as old as the Scriptures . . . as clear as the American Constitution . . ."). "Master, master!" cried the locals as they crowded around his car. "Please don't use that word," asked Kennedy, embarrassed. Meeting secretly with Ian Robertson, he taught the banned student leader how to jump up and down on the floor to disrupt electronic eavesdropping devices. Confronting conservative students who found biblical support for apartheid, he asked, "What if God is black?"

On the next-to-last night, Kennedy went to a raucous and unusual mixed-race party at the home of his hosts in Johannesburg, a wealthy South African couple, Irene and Clive Mennell. The party rolled on until 4 a.m. (Kennedy, as usual, rarely slept; Marshall recalled him stretched out on the floor of the plane, wearing eyeshades.) At 5 a.m., Irene Mennell went to Kennedy's room to awaken him for the day's events. The guest room was next door to the bedroom of Mrs. Mennell's two-year-old daughter, Mary. Kennedy had heard Mary crying in the pre-dawn darkness and gone to comfort her. Mrs. Mennell found Kennedy peacefully sleeping on Mary's bed, cuddled with the little girl.

By the last day, Kennedy was holding impromptu rallies with hundreds of blacks who crowded around his car as sullen security service men looked on. As they drove down streets lined with people on the way to the airport, Kennedy remarked to Tom Johnston, who had advanced the trip, "If we stayed here another couple of days we'd take over this place." He was being wry, but not entirely. On the plane, Kennedy began worrying about the people he had left behind. He needn't have. In just a few days, he had given heart to the struggling anti-apartheid movement. Margaret Marshall* remembered:

> He reminded us—me—that we were not alone. That we were part of a great and noble tradition, the re-affirmation of nobility in every human person. We all had felt alienated. It felt to me that what I was doing was small and meaningless. He put us back into the great sweep of history. Even if it's just a tiny thing, it will add up. He reset the moral compass, not so much by attacking apartheid, but by simply talking about justice and freedom and dignity—words that none of us had heard in, it seemed like, an eternity. He didn't go through the white liberals, he connected straight—by standing on a car. Nobody had done that. How simple it was! He was not afraid.

AFTER THE EXHILARATION of South Africa, Robert Kennedy had difficulty returning to small-bore political battles in New York and LBJ's Washington. The temptation was to travel the world some more, to seek the adulation of Soweto

---

* Marshall became a lawyer, moved to the United States, and married Anthony Lewis of the *New York Times*. She became a state court of appeals judge and in 1999 was confirmed as the first woman to serve as chief justice of the Massachusetts Supreme Judicial Court.

and Concepción and Cracow. He considered India and Eastern Europe. When Adam Walinsky protested that he had too much to do at home, Kennedy wrote back, "Adam, I'm not going anywhere this fall. I shall be hand in hand with you while we walk through the ghettoes of New York."

The mock-heroic style was only half in jest. Kennedy's poetry reading had not eclipsed his inclination for action and his insistence on results. His political weather eye had spotted New York City's tall, WASPy, charismatic mayor, John Lindsay, walking Harlem to keep peace on hot summer nights. "Bobby was jealous of John Lindsay," recalled RFK's friend William Walton. "He said rather sourly, 'He [Lindsay] really ought to stay in his office and do his work there.' " Kennedy expected Lindsay to challenge him for the Senate in 1970 (or the presidency in 1972). Envious of Lindsay's ease of manner, Kennedy suspected that the mayor was a lightweight. Already whipping himself up to picture Lindsay as a too-handsome phony, Kennedy needed some accomplishments. He needed to make a go of rebuilding Bedford-Stuyvesant.

The practical obstacles were formidable. Kennedy's idea of community action was not new, and earlier experiments had been a flop. The anti-poverty legislation passed by Congress and signed by Johnson in 1964 required "maximum feasible participation" by the residents of poor neighborhoods in community action agencies created to help deliver new federal services, like job training and health care. The leading anti-poverty thinkers of the time argued that the poor could not overcome poverty without assuming a degree of political power. Indeed, so-called empowerment was first suggested by Robert Kennedy's Justice Department—by David Hackett's project on juvenile delinquency. But the community action agencies, intended by the first wave of Great Society legislation to empower the poor, had become mired in rancor and controversy. The Black Power movement was just arriving in the inner city, and many CAAs were taken over by black militants, to the consternation of local elected officials. "What in the hell are you people doing?" Chicago's Mayor Daley protested to the Johnson White House. "Does the President know he's putting M-O-N-E-Y in the hands of subversives?" The CAAs did almost nothing to reduce juvenile delinquency or alleviate poverty.

Adam Walinsky referred to the community action agencies as "bitching societies." They failed, he believed, because they gave poor people the appearance of political power—essentially, a platform from which to shout—without any real economic tools or resources. The key to saving the inner city, he argued, was to attract outside investment, to prime the pump of small-scale capitalism and entrepreneurship. That meant, of course, finding some investors—some white businessmen willing to put their money into the ghetto.

This was Robert Kennedy's job, though he was not eager to become a supplicant before corporate tycoons. Kennedy inherited his father's disdain for businessmen, and the feeling was mutual. Most business leaders were Republicans who recalled the Robert Kennedy of the 1962 steel crisis, subpoenaing the expense accounts of the Big Steel executives. Kennedy had to find his kind of businessmen—broad-minded, far-seeing, and, above all, loyal to Kennedy. His first stop was André Meyer, the hard-nosed chairman of Lazard Frères investment bankers who was already a trustee of the Kennedy family investments and a financial adviser to Jackie Kennedy. A bit of a name-dropper, Meyer enjoyed the cachet of his acquaintanceship with the Kennedys. In early September, Kennedy met Meyer for breakfast at the Hotel Carlyle and asked him to be chairman of the board of a still-unformed Bedford-Stuyvesant corporation. Meyer, always a deal maker, agreed to serve on the board (though not as chairman) on one condition—that Kennedy take a stronger stand against the Vietnam War. The French-born Meyer had a vivid memory of Dien Bien Phu, the defeat of French forces by the Vietnamese in 1954. With typical urgency, Kennedy rounded up three other prominent businessmen with Kennedy ties— investment banker Douglas Dillon, CBS chairman William S. Paley, and IBM chairman Thomas Watson—all in one day. His pitch was practical, said a friend who was discreetly working behind the scenes to line up other business leaders and their money: "It wasn't moral obligation. It was: look at the chaos we're going to have if we don't do something."

The precise "something" they needed to do remained elusive. Kennedy had a group of businessmen who were willing either to invest some capital and know-how or find others to do it for them, but they knew little about the needs and wants of a Brooklyn slum. It wouldn't do for white businessmen simply to dictate to black community leaders in any event. But Kennedy and his advisers knew perfectly well that these impatient businessmen would never stand for sitting through harangues from resentful community activists.

The solution, first suggested by Tom Johnston, who ran Kennedy's New York office, was to create two boards—one for the black community leaders to propose ideas for redevelopment, and another for Kennedy's white business friends to provide professionalism and resources. The two-board concept was a prescription for rivalry and conflict, but it fit Kennedy's experience. Overlap, blurry lines of authority, and infighting were typical of Kennedy political campaigns. The idea of whites quietly pulling strings for black frontmen was neither new nor off-putting to Kennedy: in the summer of '63, his men at the Justice Department had successfully taken over the March on Washington.

The next challenge was to find some seed money. Businessmen would not invest until they could see a viable organization in place. To tap the federal treasury, Walinsky was put to work writing amendments to existing anti-poverty laws for "special impact programs," though without telling other senators exactly which program Kennedy had in mind. Dun Gifford, Senator Edward Kennedy's aide, described RFK's blunderbuss lobbying style:

He would say, "Look, I've been to Bed-Sty, I was there yesterday and these people don't have jobs. The unemployment rate is 25 percent in the major slums in the country and we just have to do something. These amendments are going to do it." And somebody would say,

"How?" And he'd say: "Well, it's going to do it. Don't worry about it, it's going to do it."

Congress voted $45 million for a vaguely worded national program of job training and economic development in blighted areas. But Kennedy also needed immediate funds to pay the overhead of the Bed-Sty Corporation, so he turned to the Ford Foundation. Wary of the costs and the untested assumptions, the Ford Foundation staff turned him down. Kennedy went over their heads to implore the new head of the Ford Foundation, McGeorge Bundy. RFK had always been edgy around Bundy, who lacked the requisite blind loyalty to the Kennedys. But Bundy was reassured that men such as Doug Dillon and Tom Watson were rallying behind Kennedy's idea. Bundy authorized a Ford Foundation grant totaling $750,000 to get the Bed-Sty Corporation off the ground. In his acerbic way, the Brahmin Bundy (whose nickname at Yale had been Mahatma) told colleagues, "It was worth a few hundred thousand dollars to show Bobby that businessmen don't have horns."

The Bed-Sty Corporation was launched at Public School 305 in Bedford-Stuyvesant on December 10. Kennedy presided proudly over captains of industry and civic-minded black housewives who eyed each other at the opening press conference. The corporation's small but brainy staff was already consulting with famous architects like I. M. Pei and Philip Johnson on the design of a "superblock" as an example of what could be done to rebuild the community. Kennedy permitted himself a moment of optimism. The Bedford-Stuyvesant Corporation was his kind of organization: small, anti-bureaucratic, seemingly democratic but in fact tightly controlled, operating outside the mainstream and proud of it. Kennedy's men saw themselves as dashing guerrillas—Swamp Foxes of the war on poverty—upstaging and outperforming the clumsy redcoats—LBJ's Great Society. They were at once an elite and anti-establishment. The model, in a way, was the family of Joseph P. Kennedy.

CHAPTER **18** GHOSTS

ROBERT KENNEDY CAMPAIGNED on behalf of other Democrats in the fall of 1966, but he looked, especially to Lyndon Johnson, like a man who was running for president in 1968. LBJ's polls were skidding that fall, dragged down by the war. Propped up by nostalgia for Camelot, Kennedy's were climbing. Harris and Gallup surveys in August showed voters narrowly favoring RFK over LBJ in 1968. As Kennedy toured New York with Johnson on August 21, the *Christian Science Monitor* reported, "Crowds Applaud LBJ, Squeal at Kennedy." In Berkeley and Iowa, they tore off RFK's *PT-109* tie pin and cufflinks (he had stopped wearing gold ones by now). The placards said "BOBBY IN '68; BOBBY IN '72; BOBBY ANYTIME." Kennedy essentially played his brother on the tour, one hand in his coat pocket, the other chopping at the air, as he urged vaguely, "We can do better," and "We've got to get this country moving again." Kennedy was popular in part because he risked nothing. Jack Newfield, RFK's new friend in the counterculture press, dismissed his speeches as "cotton candy."

He was characteristically ambivalent about the adulation. He was routinely denting the roofs of cars to display himself to the jumpers and screamers, yet still fretful that they were cheering for his brother. On a trip to Seattle, reporter Mary McGrory watched nuns waving BOBBY NOW! posters and clutching at him. "He seemed melancholy and detached, rueful about it," she recalled. "It was almost as if he was thinking, *now* you tell me. It seemed like the cheering might not be enough, or that it might not mean anything." Kennedy awkwardly exposed his moody introspection to Newfield a few days before the November elections, inviting him up to his apartment overlooking the East River and, with some embarrassment, asking if Newfield liked poetry. The reporter watched as Kennedy, silhouetted in the twilight against a neon Pepsi sign across the river in Queens, read to him from Emerson's "Fame."

Kennedy spoke in "an unmusical monotone," staring into middle distance, but he had memorized the last verse ("Go then, sad youth, and shine . . . And die to Fame a happy martyr").

Kennedy never let down his guard, his awareness—as Edith Hamilton describes the Greeks' foreboding—that "some dread deed is impending." He expected the sins of the past to return, and he was not disappointed. In December, Kennedy was embroiled in a series of controversies that pitted him against J. Edgar Hoover and LBJ, dredging up half-buried secrets and reopening half-healed wounds. The skirmishes damaged him politically and added to his large stores of self-doubt. They reawakened bitter memories that seemed to rest just behind his pale blue eyes.

Yet they also forced a collision that was long coming. There is an uneasy contradiction in Robert Kennedy's life and career in the first three years after his brother's death. He was eager to show physical courage, pushing himself to climb mountains and plunge into roiling waters. He could speak passionately about justice and fairness, bravely taking the message into worlds starved of morality and decency, from the slums of Brazil to the vineyards of California. He was willing as well to look for practical solutions to complex problems and, with the Bed-Sty project, showed more originality and insight than most anti-poverty warriors of the 1960s. Yet he shied from the greatest challenge: taking on Lyndon Johnson and the war in Vietnam. He had the uncritical support of many voters (and not a few reporters) as he traveled the country in the fall of 1966, and he served them pablum. In part, he was restrained by prudence, by the political side of his brain that rejected unwinnable struggles as acts of self-indulgence. But at a deeper level, he may have been afraid: fearful of repeating the mistakes of the past, of succumbing to hubris and letting his missionary impulse lead him, once more, into tragedy. It took a series of setbacks in the late fall of 1966 and early winter of 1967 to shake him from his moody caution. For Robert Kennedy, the path to enlightenment always began in the darkest part of the forest. He needed to suffer before he could experience exaltation.

The first flare-up reminded Kennedy of old Faustian bargains, his willingness to overlook questionable means in the pursuit of worthy ends. On December 10, 1966, just as Kennedy was announcing the creation of the Bedford-Stuyvesant Corporation at P.S. 305 in Brooklyn, Hoover's FBI was releasing a stack of documents showing that Kennedy had approved of the FBI's practice of "bugging"—breaking into homes and offices to plant illegal electronic eavesdropping devices—in criminal investigations.

The controversy over bugging had been building for some time. Hoover had assumed blanket authority to bug suspected criminals—without telling his nominal boss, the attorney general, every time. A bureaucrat, the FBI director had created a paper trail to cover himself. The trail pointed straight at RFK. Kennedy never stopped insisting (even to friends who knew better) that he was completely in the dark about Hoover's bugging campaign, but the evidence strongly suggests that RFK was not speaking truthfully—that he was aware that Hoover was bugging the mob, even if he did not wish to know the details.

Hearing tapes of recorded conversations between mobsters plotting to kill Chicago cops in the summer of 1963, Kennedy later argued that he had been mistakenly informed that the bugs had been installed by the local police. It appears more likely that Kennedy did not want to know about the FBI's bugs. At the very least, the attorney general displayed a notable lack of curiosity about the source of the FBI's intelligence on the mob.

Kennedy might have gotten away with the pretense of ignorance had not his enemies seen a potential weapon to use against him. The leak of the FBI's bugs on the mob's casino skimming operation in Las Vegas in 1963 spawned lawsuits from the casino owners for invasion of privacy, which sparked congressional hearings beginning in 1965. Senator Edward Long of Missouri, chairman of a Judiciary subcommittee, was a friend of Roy Cohn's and an ally of Jimmy Hoffa's Teamsters. Long "is out to get Bobby," LBJ's press secretary Bill Moyers told Richard Goodwin. "Johnson is egging him on." Kennedy successfully stonewalled, however, and Hoover was still unwilling to publicly disclose his electronic eavesdropping apparat. One of the lawsuits from the FBI bugs in Las Vegas reached the Supreme Court in the spring of 1966, and again Lyndon Johnson agitated to expose RFK's role. The president used his crony on the High Court, Abe Fortas, to urge the other justices to demand a fuller accounting from the Justice Department, in the hopes of embarrassing RFK. Still, Kennedy was able to slip away, despite an awkward confrontation with his friend and successor as attorney general, Nicholas Katzenbach. That spring, Katzenbach informed Kennedy that the Department of Justice would confess in its brief to the Supreme Court that the FBI bugging took place "under Departmental practice in effect for a period of years prior to 1963"—a bland way of saying that, for years, the FBI had bugged with the approval of attorneys general up to and including Robert Kennedy. In an angry letter to his old friend, Kennedy demanded that Katzenbach tell the Supreme Court that he, Kennedy, had no personal knowledge of FBI bugging, either in this case or in general. For all his toughness, Kennedy disliked unpleasant scenes with intimates. He made his assistant, Joe Dolan, read the letter over the phone to Katzenbach. When Dolan shied from the harsh language in the note and began to paraphrase, Kennedy, who was listening in, thumped his finger on the note to make sure Dolan stuck to his exact words. (Katzenbach was in a difficult spot: "I am absolutely persuaded that Bobby Kennedy did not know about the FBI buggings," he recalled. "I am also absolutely persuaded that any objective observer would believe that he did." In the end, the Justice Department brief was silent on RFK's personal role.)

Kennedy's luck at covering up ran out on December 10. The incriminating documents released by Hoover's aides included affidavits from FBI agents who claimed to have witnessed RFK listening to the tape recordings of FBI bugs. Kennedy was able to produce a carefully worded letter from his liaison to Hoover, Courtney Evans, supporting his claim of ignorance. (Kennedy himself dictated the letter to the pliable Evans, according to Dolan.) But the overwhelming evidence—and much of the newspaper coverage—seemed to side with Hoover's version. The old image of RFK as a hard-eyed bully reemerged. Herbert Block, the influential political cartoonist known as Herblock, began lampooning Kennedy as a ferret and a snoop. When Ethel Kennedy ran into Herblock at a party at Arthur Schlesinger's, she angrily poked the cartoonist in the stomach. Many Americans already believed that RFK was a ruthless man willing to wiretap and bug his foes. LBJ was pleased to remind them. In a jab at RFK in his State of the Union address in January, President Johnson proposed banning all wiretapping and bugging, except to protect national security. In the audience in the House chamber, Kennedy refused to clap with his colleagues, instead crossing his arms and pursing his lips.

He was already embroiled in a bigger controversy, one that compelled him to place personal loyalty over political common sense, and led him back into the painful arena of his brother's death. Kennedy had always been fierce in the defense of his family's name. He no longer came to blows over slurs against his father or brother, though he seemed ready to. Usually, he managed to protect the family honor more discreetly by manipulating reporters with a mix of candor and inclusion. Perhaps, he became overconfident. Certainly, he was especially sensitive to the memory of his brother, whose legacy he and his sister-in-law had done so much to enshrine. In any case, their efforts to control the Kennedy image backfired when Jackie Kennedy lost her customary cool in the fall of 1966 and angrily tried to block the publication of William Manchester's authorized account of the death of President Kennedy.

RFK himself was impossibly thin-skinned about any book on his brother or the Kennedy presidency. In 1966, his old friend Paul "Red" Fay wrote a breezy, affectionate memoir, *The Pleasure of His Company*. Fay made the mistake of showing the manuscript to RFK before publication, as a courtesy and a gesture of friendship. Kennedy demanded all sorts of small changes. "Mr. Kennedy shall not be called Joe, Big Joe, but Ambassador Kennedy or Joseph K," he wrote in his squiggly hand on the manuscript. Fay had quoted Ambassador Kennedy sniping at the rich of Newport, Rhode Island. "I would like to see Red Fay write this story if my father was not ill—I think it's an outrage," Kennedy steamed. Out came references to Frank Sinatra and to RFK's own high-pitched voice. He balked at letting JFK be quoted as describing Robert McNamara as "a real cold drink of water." When he was done slicing Fay's manuscript, RFK cut Fay. He refused to speak to Fay, once a Hickory Hill regular, at the funeral of their mutual friend Dean Markham, who died in a plane crash in September.

Kennedy was in a defensive mood early that fall. Determined to avoid sensational treatments of JFK's assassination, RFK and Jackie had commissioned a memoir, in the hopes of pre-empting other writers. The chosen author, William Manchester, was picked for his elegiacal prose and worship of the late president. (Jackie referred to Manchester as the author she "hired.") The publisher, Harper & Row, had brought out earlier Kennedy books, including *Profiles in Courage* and *The Enemy Within*. Manchester and Harper's had agreed to donate most of their earnings to the John F. Kennedy Library; unwisely, they also agreed to give the Kennedys final control over the manuscript. Manchester's first draft of *The Death of a President,* delivered to the publisher in early 1966, was powerful and moving but in places overwrought. It portrayed Lyndon Johnson as boorish, especially in contrast to the ever-graceful Kennedys. Knowing that the book would be read as a mean-spirited attack on LBJ, RFK and his lieutenants persuaded Manchester to cut or tone down some of the more lurid passages, like the opening scene, in which a blood-lusting LBJ takes an appalled John Kennedy out to shoot deer.

Jackie Kennedy, however, wanted to go much further than her brother-in-law. Upset that she had poured out too much personal detail about her children and her last hours alone with JFK, she wanted to spike the book altogether. She had become accustomed to getting what she wanted. "Anybody who is against me will look like a rat unless I run off with Eddie Fisher," she told Manchester in an icy whisper in September. In December, after months of anguished wrangling, she filed suit to stop publication of the book and the excerpts in *Look* magazine. Robert Kennedy knew the lawsuit was a poor idea. It just drew press attention to the controversy and set off a scramble among reporters to find—and highlight—the offending passages. The fight between Manchester and the Kennedys was played as tabloid Shakespeare, a juicy spat that spoke of larger struggles between the king and the pretender-in-exile. It was "the biggest publishing story since the New Testament," said NBC's David Brinkley, in the hyperbole of the moment.

Kennedy's loyalty led him to blindly support his sister-in-law, no matter how unreasonable or impolitic her demands. "My crazy sister-in-law," he said with a sigh to Frank Mankiewicz, but he would snap at anyone who called the president's widow "Jackie." "It's Mrs. John Kennedy," he corrected. Although his predominant mood was irritation at having been dragged into such a messy fight, his belligerent side also showed. At one point in August, Kennedy suggested to Manchester that he intentionally sabotage the *Look* magazine excerpts to keep them from being published. Manchester said he could not in good conscience. "Then give them to John," said Kennedy, looking at his friend and adviser John Seigenthaler, who was helping vet the manuscript. According to Manchester, Seigenthaler "smiled weakly." ("I don't remember that," said Seigenthaler. "But it was a very tough meeting. Bob in effect accused Manchester of betraying Jackie.")

The only good news about the Manchester controversy was that it pushed the bugging controversy off the front pages. The suit was settled, some changes were made in the manuscript, but the damage to RFK, coming on top of the bugging scandal, was great. Kennedy began to sink in the polls. A full 20 percent of voters polled by Gallup in March 1967 said that they thought less of Kennedy because of the Manchester dispute. According to a Harris poll, in the fall Kennedy led Johnson 53 percent to 47 percent. By March, he trailed 39 percent to 61 percent. LBJ exulted: "God, it just murders Bobby and Jackie both," he told Katzenbach. "It just murders them on this thing."

• • •

KENNEDY, HAVING MUTED his own attacks on Johnson, was becoming increasingly uncomfortable with his own reticence about the Vietnam War. "Maybe I will have to say something," he told Jack Newfield in December. "The bombing is getting worse all the time now." By the end of 1966, there were about 400,000 American troops in Vietnam. Some 33,000 had been killed or wounded. The war was costing more than $2 billion a month. The American people were still fairly hawkish: according to one poll, one in four was willing to use nuclear weapons to defeat Hanoi. Kennedy's young staffers and a few of his old friends, like Arthur Schlesinger, urged him to speak out. Kennedy had tried to curb the more insistent doves, like Adam Walinsky. "Okay, that's enough, Adam," he would say to Walinsky, who occasionally got carried away (the young legislative assistant once penciled a Hitler mustache on a photo of LBJ). Kennedy was so worried about LBJ's reactions that he would edit any reference to President Johnson out of his speeches, substituting "the Administration."

Kennedy continued to fear that by taking a strong position against the war, he would prolong it. "He really believed," said Peter Edelman, "that if he said, 'Cut down the bombing,' LBJ would step it up; if he said, 'Don't put troops in,' LBJ would put in 10,000 more." These were not wholly irrational concerns. Johnson's oversensitivity to Kennedy bordered on the pathological. Yet Kennedy's caution was also rooted in the meaning he had given his own experience, derived from the morality plays of the ancient Greeks, warning against the sin of overweening pride.

Premonitions did not save the Greeks from their fates, nor Kennedy from his. A collision with LBJ was unavoidable. That it happened by accident simply underscores the inevitability. Fleeing the Manchester affair, Kennedy traveled to Europe for ten days at the end of January for a mix of business and pleasure—debating at the Oxford Union, having cocktails with Shirley MacLaine and Catherine Deneuve. The *New York Times* reported that in Paris, he had canceled some of his appointments because of a "touch of the flu." The French press reported that he dined alone at a small Left Bank restaurant with Candice Bergen, the young actress. On his official calls, Kennedy met with Etienne Manac'h, a French foreign ministry official who specialized in East Asian affairs. Kennedy later said he had trouble following the translation. When he arrived home three days later, he walked into a storm. A State Department official had leaked to *Newsweek* that Manac'h had passed along to Kennedy a peace feeler from the North Vietnamese, expressing a willingness to negotiate after a bombing pause. Kennedy didn't know "what the hell they had been talking about," he later confessed. LBJ saw a plot: Kennedy had been traipsing around Europe as a meddlesome freelance diplomat, leaking phony peace feelers to put the pressure on the president.

On February 6, Kennedy was summoned to the Oval Office at 4 p.m. The president was stewing. He accused Kennedy of leaking the peace feeler story. The leak, Kennedy protested, came from the State Department. "It's not *my* State Department, God damn it," Johnson erupted. "It's *your* State Department" (an especially paranoid reaction considering that RFK loathed the State Department). Johnson insisted that the military was winning the war on the ground, but by giving comfort to the enemy, Kennedy was killing American soldiers, said Johnson. He had blood on his hands. Kennedy stood up to leave. "I don't have to take that from you," he said. Back in his office, he said to his staff, "You know, what I have just been through is just unbelievable. . . . Do you know what that fellow said? That marvelous human being who is the president of the United States?" He told Jack Newfield that LBJ had been "very abusive. . . . He was shouting and seemed very unstable."

Johnson's tirade was a turning point. Kennedy told friends that he no longer saw much point in muffling his criticism of LBJ, since the president wasn't listening to anything he said and simply assumed the worst. He decided to speak out more openly against the war, to call for a halt to the bombing and a push for negotiations. He instructed Walinsky to start drafting a speech. "I'm going to escalate this," he told Mary McGrory. The press soon began touting a fight. "RFK SETS MAJOR SPEECH ON BOMBING" ran a five-column front-page headline in the *New York Times* on February 17. Kennedy might have felt liberated, but of course he did not.

As he tried to break free, the past pulled at him. The assassination of John Kennedy burst back into the news that same day, in a story in the *New Orleans States-Item* that was widely picked up. The flamboyant New Orleans district attorney, Jim Garrison, claimed to have uncovered a conspiracy and promised arrests. One of his star witnesses, David Ferrie, a sometime pilot with shadowy connections to anti-Castro plotters, died two days later—a suicide, claimed Garrison (actually, a heart attack). The mainstream press treated all this intrigue with proper skepticism, but Garrison's heavy breathing grabbed many headlines nonetheless. The Kennedy assassination had become a source of growing fascination to conspiracy theorists—among them, though he would deny it, RFK.

Robert Kennedy did not like to contemplate the cause of JFK's death. As they drank iced tea on the patio at Hickory Hill one day in 1966, CBS producer Don Hewitt asked him, "Do you believe Lee Harvey Oswald by himself killed your brother?" Kennedy replied, "What difference does it make? It won't bring him back." He changed the subject. Gingerly, Richard Goodwin tried to engage RFK from time to time on the subject, but Kennedy would shy away. According to Goodwin, Kennedy never actually read the Warren Report, and if he saw a mention of the investigation in the papers, he would quickly flip the page. Still, he apparently continued to wonder if Lee Harvey Oswald was really the lone gunman. In October, as he talked until 2:30 a.m. with Arthur Schlesinger at P. J. Clarke's saloon in New York, he had admitted that he thought the Warren Commission had "done a poor job," but that he didn't want to criticize the investigation publicly and thereby "reopen the whole tragic business," according to Schlesinger's diary. His private questions persisted. He filed away odd scraps of evidence, like an FBI report that Marina Oswald, the assassin's widow, had been forced to have sex with her business manager ("Angie—keep," RFK instructed his secretary in his tiny handwriting). When the Garrison story broke in February, Schlesinger asked RFK what he made of the charges of conspiracy. "He thought Garrison might be onto something," Schlesinger wrote in his diary. Kennedy's favorite investigator, Walter Sheridan, had gone to work for NBC after leaving the Justice Department. Sheridan had initially told the network that he would not do any work on the Kennedy assassination, but then he checked with RFK. Kennedy asked him to look into Garrison's charges, so off Sheridan went to New Orleans, ostensibly working for the network, but reporting regularly to the senator from New York. Seeing Garrison's face on magazine covers as they walked past a newsstand, Kennedy asked his press secretary, Frank Mankiewicz, "Does that guy have anything?" Mankiewicz started to reply, and Kennedy interrupted, "I don't think I want to know." But he did, discreetly. He asked Mankiewicz to start collecting information. (Mankiewicz became virtually a buff, studying blown-up photographs of the Grassy Knoll.) Kennedy called his former press secretary, Ed Guthman, who had become the national editor at the *Los Angeles Times*. "Bobby wanted to know everything. He was very curious," recalled Guthman. "I put five reporters on it."

When Kennedy was nagged by a private upset, he was susceptible to random outbursts. On the night of February 26, he ran into Katharine Graham, the owner of the *Washington Post*, at a dinner party. The *Post* had published a mildly gossipy story about Jackie Kennedy two weeks earlier. Kennedy was rough with Graham, whose husband, Phil, a friend of the Kennedys, had committed suicide in 1963. "You have lost your husband, too," he said coldly. "You should know better." He immediately felt regret. "I obviously upset you and I hadn't meant to . . . ," he wrote Mrs. Graham. "I had just seen Jackie the day before and she was so upset and really crushed and I thought to myself that here was a girl who hadn't committed any great crime but who day after day was being attacked and pilloried in all kinds of scandalous ways." Kennedy was feeling tender and protective, referring to Jackie Kennedy and Katharine Graham, two of the more formidable women of the age, as "girls." He continued: "There is an old Irish poem which in the course of its very beautiful words says, 'How can there be a God when children suffer.' It seems to me we could apply it equally to girls."

On March 2, Kennedy wrote Mrs. Graham that he was about to "give a speech that will compound my difficulties." He was feeling restless and a little reckless. He had been up until 3:30 a.m. working on a Vietnam speech. At breakfast, sensing his mood, Ethel greeted him, "Hail Caesar." He drove to the Senate at eighty miles an hour in his convertible with the top down, even though the temperature was 30 degrees. At about twenty minutes to four, he rose in the back of a half-filled Senate chamber and began speaking in a quiet, tense voice. Remarkably, for a politician, he apologized. He had been involved in "many" of the decisions leading the United States into war. "I can testify," he continued, "that if fault is to be found or responsibility assessed, there is enough to go around for all—including myself." He said the war was a "horror" and called for a bombing pause to test Hanoi's sincerity about wanting peace. Perhaps Hanoi was sending conflicting signals about its willingness to negotiate, Kennedy conceded. But why not, as his brother had done in the Cuban Missile Crisis, seize on the most favorable?

Lyndon Johnson did everything in his power to drown out or distract attention from Kennedy. On the day of RFK's address to the Senate, he gave two unscheduled speeches, an impromptu news conference to announce that Soviets had agreed to arms control talks, persuaded friendly senators to keep talking to keep Kennedy off the evening news, and, finally, confirmed a rumor that his daughter Luci was pregnant.

Those were just his public acts. On March 3, the morning after his speech, RFK woke up to find himself accused, in a column by the widely read columnist Drew Pearson, of having masterminded the CIA's plot to kill Fidel Castro. "President Johnson is sitting on an H-Bomb," Pearson declared. His column disclosed that Johnson had received "an unconfirmed report" that Kennedy had signed off on an assassination plot that "backfired against his late brother." Aware that the Kennedys were trying to kill him, Castro had allegedly decided to kill President Kennedy. The column speculated that RFK's torment after JFK's assassination stemmed from more than "natural grief." Could Robert Kennedy "have been plagued by the terrible thought that he had helped put into motion terrible forces that indirectly may have brought about his brother's martyrdom? Some insiders think so," Pearson wrote.

Kennedy did not have to guess at the identity of those "insiders." The timing of the column was not a coincidence. Pearson had been sitting on the story since late January, when the columnist first went to LBJ with a fantastic tale of plotting and revenge. Johnson routinely would collect gossip "about horrible things that the Kennedys had done," according to his assistant Marvin Watson. Hoover always accommodated, passing along salacious detail. Kennedy, not surprisingly, retaliated in kind. "He had spies all over the Johnson administration," said his friend, columnist Rowland Evans. One was an executive mansion housekeeper who went over Johnson's books and fed tidbits of petty corruption back to Kennedy. RFK told Evans, for instance, that Johnson used U.S. Army soldiers to pick up around the LBJ Ranch. Kennedy and Johnson were old hands at subtly threatening blackmail. Each was well aware that the other was collecting damaging information that could one day prove useful. Neither one was inclined to fire the first shot. Robert Dallek, LBJ's biographer, compared the standoff to the nuclear mutual assured destruction (MAD) between the superpowers. Still, as his paranoia towards RFK grew, LBJ could not resist dropping the Mafia-Castro plot bombshell on Kennedy.

The conniving behind the March 3 Drew Pearson column, entirely hidden from public view, is revealing of the viciousness that underlay the Johnson-Kennedy rivalry. It also shows that while Kennedy did not like to speak or perhaps even think about his brother's assassination, the subject was often not far from his consciousness. The maneuvering began with mobster Johnny Rosselli, trying to collect an IOU for his brief service to his country, his participa-

tion in the CIA plots to kill Castro in the early '60s. By 1966, Rosselli was under
pressure from the FBI, which was using the immigration service to threaten
deportation proceedings. (J. Edgar Hoover wanted to force Rosselli to become
an informant against the mob; Rosselli feared that if he talked, he would be
murdered, as indeed he later was.) Rosselli went to his old CIA pal, William
Harvey, to intercede with the spy agency to protect him. As added insurance,
Rosselli's lawyer, Edward Morgan, fed the story to Drew Pearson for his popular column, "The Washington Merry-Go-Round." As Morgan spun Rosselli's
tale to Pearson, Castro had caught and tortured one of the CIA assassination
teams sent to kill him in 1963. A Mafia spy close to Castro heard the Cuban dictator say, "If this is the way they play the game, I will play the same way."
Rosselli hinted that Oswald was a pawn in a larger Castro-run plot to kill JFK.

Drew Pearson was a savvy practitioner of the muckraker's art. He had long
since worked out a protection racket with Lyndon Johnson. In return for holding off on stories that might hurt Johnson, Pearson was routinely rewarded
with stories about LBJ's enemies. In January, Pearson had gone to LBJ with this
assassination plot tale. A conspiracy theorist, LBJ was fascinated. "It's incredible!" he told the new attorney general, Ramsey Clark, on February 18, suggesting that the Justice Department should look into the matter. When RFK
attacked Johnson's war policy with his March 2 speech, LBJ encouraged Pearson to publish the Rosselli story the next day to embarrass RFK.

RFK scrambled to protect himself. The following day, March 4, he re-
trieved his files on his May 1962 CIA briefing on the assassination plots and
had lunch with the director of the CIA, Richard Helms. Contacted in 1999,
Helms said he could not recall what the two men spoke about over lunch, but
they undoubtedly discussed Pearson's column. Meanwhile, Johnson continued
to look for proof of RFK's involvement in the assassination plots. In mid-
March, the president instructed Helms to prepare a report on the plots against
Cuba. The spy agency's internal investigation, finished in May 1967 (but not
publicly released for another twenty-five years), is an astonishingly frank doc-
ument. It details many of the agency's nutty schemes, including plans to make
Castro's beard fall out. But, to LBJ's chagrin, it makes scant mention of Robert
Kennedy.

To a conspiracy theorist, this may suggest a cover-up, that Helms and the
CIA somehow contrived to protect RFK. But one of the principal CIA investigators who compiled the report, Scott Breckinridge, said that he received no instructions from Helms or anyone else at the agency to downplay Kennedy's
role in the plots. No partisan, Breckinridge simply never heard Kennedy cited
as a mastermind by any of the CIA officials he interviewed. That may be partly
because the agency men were reluctant to volunteer any more information to
the in-house investigators than was strictly necessary. But it was also because
Kennedy's involvement in the plots was in fact remote, largely insulated by
"plausible deniability." Lyndon Johnson never stopped looking for evidence
that would expose RFK on the Cuba plots. Lacking sources or fresh disclosures,
however, other reporters were unable to follow up Pearson's assassination plot

story, and it faded, not to surface again until the CIA plots were exposed in congressional hearings in the aftermath of Watergate in 1975.

Kennedy was fortunate. In a later, more aggressive and sensationalist age of journalism, Pearson's column would have set off a more determined hunt. But Kennedy could not escape his old fears that his involvement with Castro and the mob had somehow come back to hurt his brother. Even while he debated Vietnam and tried to look for new solutions to the problems of race and poverty, he was constantly dealing with the fallout from his past and the desire of his old enemies for revenge.

Kennedy himself was an obvious target for assassination plots. FBI bugs and taps had picked up threats from various mobsters and Hoffa's henchmen. Most were bluster. But right in the midst of Garrison's revelations and Kennedy's preparations for his antiwar speech in early March, the FBI received a threat that had to be taken seriously. One of Hoffa's goons, the head of the Teamsters Union in Puerto Rico, Frank Chavez, had sworn that he would kill RFK if Jimmy Hoffa ever went to prison. On March 1, 1967, the Supreme Court turned down Hoffa's last appeal of his conviction for jury tampering in Tennessee. That same day, Chavez and two other thugs, carrying guns, boarded a plane for Washington. Kennedy was warned and given armed guards. Hickory Hill was placed under surveillance. It later turned out that Hoffa himself talked Chavez out of shooting RFK. Fearful that he would never get out of jail if the Teamsters were caught trying to kill Kennedy, Hoffa demanded that Chavez turn over his gun. (A few months later, Chavez was murdered by his own bodyguard.)

Kennedy tended to be fatalistic about threats, generally refusing to use bodyguards or take much of any security precaution. But he could not free himself of the worry that his brother had been killed by a mobster whose real enemy was himself. In New Orleans, Walter Sheridan quickly determined that Jim Garrison was a fraud and a publicity seeker. He even brought a defector from Garrison's camp up to Washington, to Kennedy's Senate office in order to tell RFK, in person, that the New Orleans district attorney was not believable. Kennedy was only partly reassured. He doubted that the Cubans had killed his brother—but he continued to worry about the mob and about one mobster in particular.

Carlos Marcello, the don of New Orleans, had a fierce grievance against RFK. He was high on the list of Mafia bosses targeted by Kennedy in 1961, up there with Giancana and other "Top Hoodlums." During the first months of the Kennedy administration, Marcello had been deported from the United States, essentially kidnapped and left in the jungles of Guatemala. The mobster made his way back to the United States and hired a better lawyer, but he believed that the attorney general had been out to persecute him. He had reputedly vowed to get even. ("Don't worry about that little Bobby son of a bitch, he's going to get taken care of.") One night during the summer of '67, RFK, in a rare moment of disclosure, told Richard Goodwin that he thought his brother had been killed by "the guy from New Orleans," meaning Marcello. His suspicions may have been fed by something told him by Walter Sheridan, who had spent months looking into Marcello and his connections while working on the Garrison story. Sheridan, who, according to his wife, contemplated suicide when his hero RFK was killed in 1968, refused to talk about JFK's assassination until just before he died in 1996. Then he shocked his son, Walter Jr., by stating that he was "convinced" that President Kennedy had been killed by a conspiracy. Joseph Kennedy II, RFK's oldest son, had a similar experience. In the last year of his life, RFK told his son that the full truth about the Kennedy assassination would never be known. Young Kennedy had the impression that his father knew something others did not, though exactly what remained a mystery.

IN APRIL, Kennedy told Arthur Schlesinger that he feared his March speech calling for a bombing pause in Vietnam had only served to stiffen LBJ's determination to go in the opposite direction. A week later Johnson escalated the bombing. Schlesinger could feel RFK's despair. "An indefinable sense of depression hung over him," Schlesinger wrote in his diary, "as if he felt cornered by circumstance and did not know how to break out."

Unable to have any impact on the war—except perhaps to inadvertently prolong it—Kennedy saw himself as marginalized, frozen out. The more outside he felt, the more he identified with outsiders. As always, his feelings were never far below the surface. In March, during a speech at the University of Oklahoma, he was asked about student deferments from the draft. Kennedy said he was against them, that they were unfair to the poor who couldn't afford to send their kids to college. The crowd booed. Kennedy took the bait. How many, he asked, favored student deferments? The students cheered. How many wanted to escalate the war? Most raised their hands. "Let me ask you one other question," said Kennedy. ". . . How many of you who voted for the escalation of the war also voted for the exemption of students from the draft?" The audience responded with a "giant gasp," recalled Oklahoma senator Fred Harris. Kennedy liked to bait middle-class students, saved from the front lines by their deferments while the poor went to war.

Kennedy seemed hungry to share the experience of the dispossessed. "I wish I had been born an Indian," he told a group of Native Americans in March, smiling so that he would not appear to mawkishly pander. He told Newfield that he envied him for having grown up in the ghetto (Newfield had been raised in Bed-Sty). Such statements seem condescending, but they were not. Though Kennedy was capable of both posturing for political effect and overromanticizing his own whims and desires, there can be no doubt that his identification with the downtrodden was genuine. From boyhood, Kennedy had felt a kinship with the powerless, one that often showed as contempt for the powerful.

By the spring of 1967, RFK was fairly bristling. At about this time, a young *Newsweek* reporter, Jayne Ikard, accompanied Senator Kennedy on a tour of a hospital in the Bronx. His host, a doctor, was using the occasion to promote his own accomplishments. In the elevator, Kennedy harshly informed the puffed-up doctor, "I don't like inspection tours. This one just ended. Take me to the children." Kennedy had "gone into the elevator smiling and he came out smiling. He was cold as ice inside the elevator," remembered Ikard. Kennedy took the patients in the children's ward out for ice cream, as hospital administrators vainly protested that he was breaking the rules. (As usual, Kennedy had no money. His driver paid for the ice cream.)

"Kennedy needed children as much as they needed him," observed Mary McGrory, who often brought children from an orphanage out to swim at Hickory Hill. "It was total immersion on both sides," she recalled. In April, Kennedy, as a member of the Senate Labor Committee's newly created subcommittee on poverty, traveled to rural Mississippi to hold hearings. Appalled by the testimony, he went out into the fields. Kennedy was hardly new to scenes of want and deprivation, but he was still shocked by the living conditions of poor blacks in the Delta. The stench and vermin in the windowless shacks overwhelmed his senses. He sat down on a dirty floor and held a child who was covered with open sores. He rubbed the child's stomach, which was distended by starvation. He caressed and murmured and tickled. No response. The child was in a daze.

Kennedy was highly agitated when he returned to Washington that night. He walked in on his kids at dinner at Hickory Hill, "ashen faced," recalled Kathleen, his eldest daughter. "In Mississippi a whole family lives in a shack the size of this room," he announced to his nine children, ages fifteen to two (Ethel had just had a tenth, Douglas, born prematurely in March). "The children are covered with sores and their tummies stick out because they have no food. Do you know how lucky you are? Do you *know* how *lucky* you are? Do something for your country." In the morning, he went to see Orville Freeman, the secretary of agriculture, and angrily pointed out that under the food stamp program, people with no income still had to pay fifty cents per family member to buy food. "There are no people with no income," replied Freeman, fending him off. "We met them yesterday," said Kennedy. That night he flew to New York and saw Amanda Burden, the young wife of one of his New York aides, Carter Burden. "He grabbed me," recalled Amanda Burden. "He said, 'You don't know what I saw! I have done nothing in my life! Everything I have done was a waste! Everything I have done was worthless!' He was so shaken, so self-deprecating about his life. Mississippi was the worst thing, he needed to dedicate his life to this."

At congressional hearings on anti-poverty legislation in July, Kennedy called on child psychiatrist Robert Coles of Harvard, who had gone with a team of doctors to the Mississippi Delta, to describe the toll taken by poverty on children. At an earlier hearing, in November 1966, Kennedy had sat rapt as Coles described how small children lose their vibrancy when they develop a consciousness of the world's cruelties, how their faces shut off and become blank and impassive. Moved, Kennedy asked Coles to come for lunch in the Senate Dining Room. The two talked late into the afternoon, "in a reverie of their own," observed Peter Edelman. "Kennedy kept asking why, why, why," recalled Coles. "It was very personal. I realized that he was asking about himself."

Kennedy and Coles continued to talk from time to time, at first about poverty and children, then in a more personal vein. Coles, something of a renegade in his own profession, was well matched with Kennedy. Little by little in their conversations, often by indirection, Kennedy revealed glimpses of his own childhood to Coles. He described how his father had taught him to be tough; Coles sensed his fear of timidity and weakness. Coles was fascinated by Kennedy's childlike qualities, the way he loved ice cream and squirmed on a dais. He realized that, in an odd way, Kennedy had been saved by neglect. "To be overlooked was a privilege in the Kennedy family. Bobby was the only one who was truly in touch with his emotions, who was able to feel. The others were cut off from theirs, made to be adults, required to be stoic."

Kennedy's hypersensitivity could have been self-indulgent (and occasionally was). But as Coles perceived, Kennedy was able to turn "his quest for meaning into public good." It may be, that at some level, he fought with President Johnson because, as Coles put it, "he couldn't fight his father and brother." But the same psychic energy also motivated Kennedy to devote his life to service, to work now to end the war and help the poor.

To do so, he had to swallow some of his prejudices. One was against rich businessmen. In the summer of 1966, Kennedy had been invited by a friend, William Orrick, to the annual Bohemian Grove Encampment outside San Francisco, where wealthy tycoons became fraternity pranksters for a fortnight. Kennedy was put off by the spectacle of drunken captains of industry peeing on trees and telling dirty jokes. He made no effort to disguise his disdain. "He was very difficult," said Orrick. His friends tried to build bridges to the business community. IBM chairman Tom Watson, whom Kennedy had solicited for the Bed-Sty board, arranged a lunch in New York for Kennedy attended by corporate executives and financiers. "Bob was really nervous," recalled Burke Marshall, who had gone to work at IBM after the Justice Department. "His hands were shaking. He was terrible, all stiff. The businessmen sat like lumps. They had only come for Tom Watson."

Still, knowing that he needed allies in business, Kennedy tried to enlist their money in solving social ills. He believed that the only real hope for the inner city lay in attracting capital—in persuading business to invest in the inner city. He preferred legislation to create jobs over a guaranteed minimum income, a favorite liberal cause of the time, because his puritan ethic emphasized the dignity of work. In the summer of 1967, he introduced a bill to use tax breaks to lure investors into poor neighborhoods—a radical idea at the time, widely imitated decades later. Kennedy wrestled with the intricacies of the tax code. "Peter, help me, I got a D in Economics AA," he told Edelman. Kennedy was weak with facts and figures, unless they were "horror statistics," said Frank Mankiewicz, "like the number of babies born in South America who would not live for more than a year." But he pushed hard for innovative anti-poverty legislation using the tax code as a lever. The old barons who ran the tax-writing committees on Capitol Hill were not much interested. Kennedy also faced the reflexive opposition of Lyndon Johnson, who lobbied against the bill in the

Senate. That summer, Kennedy sponsored legislation to create two million public service jobs, but that, too, was sunk by the Johnson White House. LBJ complained that Kennedy was posturing. At any rate, there was no money: the Vietnam War was overwhelming LBJ's hope to have guns and butter and stealing from his Great Society.

Kennedy still had Bedford-Stuyvesant. The noble experiment of the Bed-Sty Corporation had gotten off to a wobbly start. The two-board idea—one (all-black) to design programs to meet the community's needs, the other (all-white) to provide resources and know-how—was bound to create resentment. The white board brought in glossy names, like architects I. M. Pei and Philip Johnson and urban planner Ed Logue, to design grandiose schemes—giant shopping centers, a garment district, a university annex. The talent descended on Bedford-Stuyvesant with "bewildering confusion and frightful energy," according to a 1969 Ford Foundation study. The experts were predictably greeted as "colonialists." None of their projects were built. The black board, meanwhile, was splitting apart. A three-way struggle broke out between Judge Thomas Jones, Kennedy's ally (he liked Jones's experience as a World War II combat officer); the so-called matriarchy, a group of very sharp-tongued, strong-willed women who ran the local civic group; and the black militants, who accused the women of "emasculating the community and denying [it] the model of black manhood." At a tumultuous meeting at the end of March 1967, Kennedy found himself playing referee.

He handled himself with aplomb, having long since learned how to take abuse. Actually, the militants were intimidated—and co-opted—by him. Sonny Carson, the head of Brooklyn CORE and the loudest of the group, was uncharacteristically subdued. He had seen the heads turn when Kennedy walked into a local church. "Man, it was like the Pope walked in. There was a strangeness that caused blacks to love him. He was this younger brother full of pain. That's how he got over," Carson recalled. "I thought, Oh my God, if I interrupt him, people will look at me like, 'What the fuck are you doing, man? You can't do that! That's Robert Kennedy!' " Kennedy asked Carson to serve on the board.

The revolt settled down with the appointment of a local hero, Frank Thomas, the deputy police commissioner and a onetime basketball star, as the staff director of the local, all-black board, which was renamed Restoration. But progress was slow. Demanding as ever, Kennedy would "look at a vacant block and say, 'I want a building there,' " recalled Eli Jacobs, the staff director of Development and Services, the white outsiders' board. "He'd come back a few weeks later and not understand why it couldn't be built." Meeting with the staff of the two boards at his UN Plaza apartment, RFK pounded the table. "I want *results*. Let's get the garbage picked up." Eager to please, Thomas would say, "We will do it, Bob. I will get it done." Jacobs would have to explain that since the Bed-Sty Corporation was not a government agency, there wasn't much they could do about the garbage, except complain to the New York City bureaucracy.

Kennedy lobbied, mostly in vain, to get corporations to invest in Bed-Sty. Only one company built a plant: Tom Watson's IBM, creating about four hundred jobs. One corporate executive told him, "Senator, the afternoon I walk into my board of directors and tell them that Bobby Kennedy was here today, and he thinks we should put a plant in Bedford-Stuyvesant, that is the afternoon they'll have me committed." Kennedy was discouraged by his failure to win over big business. His prejudices against businessmen were reinforced. But he refused to become a defeatist about Bedford-Stuyvesant. He liked to quote Camus's *Myth of Sisyphus.* "Well," he would say, smiling bleakly, "the boulder is at the bottom of the hill again." Then he would push. Over time, the corporation became, relatively speaking, a success. It did not transform Bed-Sty into a middle-class neighborhood, but it did loosen up mortgage money from white-owned banks and help create a stock of decent housing as well as some (but not many) new jobs. Three decades later, dozens of inner cities have community development corporations modeled after Robert Kennedy's original idea.

CHAPTER 19 COURAGE

IN THE SUMMER OF 1967, *Life* magazine commissioned novelist Saul Bellow to write a profile of Robert Kennedy. The novelist flew to Washington and spent a week following the senator on his rounds. The article never appeared. Kennedy kept going off the record to denounce LBJ, leaving him with little to write about. The famous novelist had never met Kennedy before and was taken aback by the ferocity of his emotions. "He never for a moment stopped thinking about his brother," Bellow recalled. "He seemed to be continually grieving. He was, literally, muscularly tense about it. His face was convulsed with some great emotional charge. He was nourishing his grief. It gave him energy. I never felt it was relief he wanted."

It was necessary, Bellow observed, for Kennedy to "connect his brother's death with an act of vengeance." The villain, naturally, was Lyndon Johnson. "When he spoke about LBJ," said Bellow, "he went off. He'd blow. 'What do you think about LBJ?' That would set him off. He just hated Johnson wholesale. He would spit fire." Mostly, though, Kennedy wanted to ask the questions. "He quizzed me. 'Tell me about H. L. Mencken.' Or Thorstein Veblen. *The Theory of the Leisure Class.* What was the *American Mercury?*" Kennedy seemed incapable of just passing time. The most routine tasks had to become self-improvement projects. Senator Kennedy would never take the subway from the New Senate Office Building to the Capitol; he had to walk. And while he exercised, he wanted to be educated. "With me, he figured he was getting favorable publicity and learning something, killing two birds with one stone," said Bellow. The searching questions never stopped. As they swam in the pool at Hickory Hill with some other houseguests, including Arthur Schlesinger, Kennedy turned to Bellow and gravely asked, "Tell me about alienation."

"No, don't," interjected Schlesinger, paddling by. Years later, Bellow laughed at the picture of Bobby Kennedy's pool afloat with intellectuals, competing for Kennedy's mind. At times, a battle seemed to rage for his soul as well, just as it would in later years for his memory and true legacy. Kennedy had become a vast screen upon which others projected their hopes and fears. The true believers wanted him to star in an epic for which he was not yet prepared.

By 1967, the legends were already half written. To his worshippers in the New York literati, he was a romantic anti-hero. He was, said Norman Mailer, a sheriff who could have been an outlaw. The Cold Warrior who wanted to kill Castro had become Che, the revolutionary in the hills. "He was driven to explore new worlds of thought and poetry, pleasures and the manifold varieties of human intimacy," wrote Richard Goodwin. The restless youth in the growing counterculture saw in him "the same incongruous combination of toughness, humor, and sensitivity they saw in other generational cult figures like [Jean-Paul] Belmondo, [Bob] Dylan, and [Humphrey] Bogart," wrote Jack Newfield. To liberals like Arthur Schlesinger, he was a voice of enlightenment who could save the Democratic Party from the madness of Lyndon Johnson. To Kennedy's loyal staff back in Washington, he was an irascible, moody boss who could save the whole world if he didn't spend too much time hanging around with celebrities. Why, they grumbled to each other, did Kennedy insist on staying with entertainer Andy Williams—"really a dopey guy," in Edelman's opinion—when he went, as it seemed he too often did, to Hollywood? They expected Kennedy to be a philosopher king.

Already by that summer, the struggle for RFK's political future had begun. The Young Turks like Walinsky and Goodwin were determined to depose LBJ. Walinsky had been beseeching Kennedy to run since the November 1966 elections. (Seeing the crowds turning out for Kennedy, Walinsky had exclaimed, "To hell with '68, let's go NOW!") In June, Goodwin sent Kennedy a translation from Homer about Achilles brooding in his tent after quarreling with Agamemnon. But most of JFK's old brain trust and all of the political pros counseled caution: it was not only heresy but folly to seek to oust a sitting president, even a very unpopular one like LBJ. Kennedy would tear apart the Democratic Party and allow the Republicans, possibly even the Lazarus-like Richard Nixon, to recapture the White House. The Vietnam War would go on and Kennedy's political career would be finished. The warring factions shared one faith: Kennedy must be president. The only issue was when.

Whether he was ready to lead the country was never seriously debated, except, perhaps, in RFK's own mind. Most of his career had been spent in supporting roles—with extraordinary powers, to be sure—but still not as the head man, the true leader. His brothers had been raised to rule. RFK had been expected to help out. He wanted to be his own man, but he remained his brother's keeper. Left holding his brother's coat; he was plainly ambivalent. He still wore JFK's old tweed topcoat everywhere—and then frequently left it behind and had to send a staffer from his office in search. He had been willing to do anything for his brother, and there had come a reckoning. Would there be another? Constantly self-mocking, he fretted about his reputation for ruthlessness, until even his friends found the refrain tiresome. "Although he joked about the word," wrote Theodore White, "it cramped his thoughts and public behavior." He liked crowds, but not back rooms. He still dreaded the backslapping bonhomie of the political clubhouse. "He recoiled at being touched," recalled Joe Dolan.

In the years since his brother's death, Kennedy had shown a capacity for growth, but the myth of his transformation, like most Kennedy legends, has been exaggerated. In some ways, one could argue, he retrogressed, albeit for the better. The hard shell he had put on to win his father's respect cracked open, allowing his vulnerability to show. The wants and needs of his boyhood could never be met. At some level, he still craved attention and needed to demonstrate that he mattered. Deep in his being, he was still the boy who plunged into Nantucket Sound because he couldn't swim and because no one in his family seemed to care.

The debate over whether RFK became a "new man" after his brother's death is in some ways unresolvable, if not fatuous. Those who knew him equally well before and after November 1963 could justly reach opposite, or nearly opposite, conclusions. Richard Goodwin: "He was always restrained by his brother's memory, it made him more cautious—I don't think he really freed himself until the day he died—but he did change. It happened to St. Augustine, so he knew it could happen to him. Internally, he changed a lot, from acute defiance to much more acceptance. He became less judgmental. He lost his dogmatism." David Hackett: "Did Bob change? No. He was a very complex person in 1943 and 1944 and a very complex person in 1968. . . . He did get less impatient, more philosophical, more fatalistic."

Kennedy's changes were real, but they were not radical, more an evolution than a transformation. There is no doubt that Kennedy embarked on a genuine intellectual journey when he began reading Edith Hamilton in 1964. The path led on to the ancient Greeks and Camus and Emerson. Kennedy often pulled copies of *The Greek Way* or Emerson's *Essays* from his pocket and read aloud to friends, who became accustomed to these odd recitations, delivered in a flat, unrhythmic voice with a mournful edge. But Kennedy's self-improvement had always been unrelenting; *before* his brother died, he listened to Shakespeare recordings while he shaved. Though increasingly well read, he was never facile or even articulate. After his week with Kennedy, Saul Bellow told a friend that RFK lacked the rigor and training to engage in true intellectual discourse. Kennedy aide William vanden Heuvel said that Kennedy made no pretense of playing the grand expositor: "He couldn't talk easily. He could recite from Aeschylus, but he did not try to explain it." Kennedy may have groped to find the words, said vanden Heuvel, "but he did have the feeling."

His thirst for new experience led him on expeditions into the counterculture, to sample its exotica and sit down with poets. He even grew his hair until it curled over his ears. But he remained, to the end of his days, essentially square. At RFK's forty-second birthday party at Hickory Hill, the Russian poet Yevgeny Yevtushenko, who had melodramatically described Kennedy's eyes as

"two blue clots of will and anxiety," proposed a toast—to Kennedy's comple-
tion of his brother's work. Yevtushenko wanted to smash glasses, according to
Russian custom. RFK suggested they find some cheaper goblets from the
kitchen. Dashed to the floor, the juice cups failed to break. Yevtushenko felt a
terrible foreboding. Kennedy, he said, "turned pale." Actually, as Arthur
Schlesinger pointed out, Kennedy was probably just tired and bored. On another evening, the poet Robert Lowell literally sat at Kennedy's knee. Goodwin
remarked on this show of poetical devotion, and Kennedy mumbled, "Yeah,
they're the first ones who turn on you, too." (True to prediction, Lowell became
a camp follower of Eugene McCarthy in 1968, but he did write a beautiful poem
about Kennedy when he died.)

Kennedy's experiments were just that, not conversions. He listened to Bob
Dylan, but more often to Broadway show tunes. He named sons born in 1965
and 1967 after pillars of the establishment—a hawkish chairman of the Joint
Chiefs of Staff, General Maxwell Taylor (Matthew Maxwell Taylor Kennedy),
and two patrician statesmen, Douglas Dillon and Averell Harriman (Douglas
Harriman Kennedy). In one memorable cross-cultural encounter, the beat poet
Allen Ginsberg was escorted into Kennedy's Capitol Hill office. The guru and
the senator talked past each other, in a gentle sort of way. Kennedy wanted to
know about politics: did Ginsberg think the hippies would ally with the blacks?
Ginsberg asked if Kennedy had ever tried "grass." RFK: "No, whatever that
means." Ginsberg chanted his Hare Krishnas for "the preservation of the
planet." Kennedy said, "You ought to sing it to the guy up the street," gesturing towards the White House. "He needs it more than I do." Kennedy was un-
nerved by open homosexuality. While working on his 1967 book, *To Seek a
Newer World*, "he absolutely could not deal with a homosexual copy editor at
Random House," noted Peter Edelman.

On his frequent trips to New York, Kennedy often went out late at night
with glamorous company. "There was a side to Kennedy that liked the bright
lights," said Edelman. "Bobby liked to party, and vanden Heuvel knew all the
social types," said Ronnie Eldridge, the Upper West Side Democratic activist
who was close to Kennedy. Vanden Heuvel's wife, Jean Stein, was a friend of
Andy Warhol's. The icon of pop held forth in a back room of a restaurant called
Max's Kansas City, a haven for artists and exhibitionists of all kinds. One night,
Kennedy appeared at Warhol's haunt, but the story, as told by actor Bob
Neuwirth to authors Jean Stein and George Plimpton for their memoir of the
'60s, *Edie*, shows the limits placed on Kennedy's fun:

> Bobby only stayed a few minutes because his bodyguard ordered him
> out of there. He had smelled something mysterious in the air. Bobby
> was having a good time. He was ready to boogie. [Former FBI agent]
> Bill Barry, his bodyguard, suddenly said, "Senator, we must leave."
> Bobby looked surprised and a little annoyed. "But I've just ordered a
> drink," he said. Bill Barry's voice hardened and he became urgent.
> "Senator, we must get out of here at once," and he whisked Bobby out
> of Max's. Apparently, he had smelled marijuana. . . .

While hardly a lothario in his brother's mold, Kennedy enjoyed teasing, flirtatious relationships with a number of young women. "He was always pleased when pretty girls found him attractive," said R. W. "Johnny" Apple, the *New York Times* political reporter, who often accompanied him between 1964 and 1968. "He'd preen a little and cock his head." It surprised Kennedy that women found him appealing. "Dave Powers [JFK's former personal aide] described Bobby dancing with Marilyn Monroe, like he couldn't believe his good fortune," said Goodwin. "When he was a kid girls would pay no attention. Now he had *the* girl in his arms." But he remained boyish and a little frightened: "Before dinner, he would seek me out," said Amanda Burden, the radiant young wife of his New York aide Carter Burden. The Burdens were prized guests on the social circuit, with or without RFK in tow. "Bobby would ask, 'What are you going to talk about?' He was very shy," said Amanda Burden. "It became a routine. It was a flirtation, but not really. We were both childlike in a way. He was sweet."

In some ways, said Goodwin, Kennedy found it easier to talk to the women than to the men around him. "The women didn't want something, or to compete with him. He needed to talk, and he couldn't always unburden himself to Ethel. It was very lonely to be a politician. You're never really with somebody," said Goodwin. "There's always a transaction going on." Kennedy's flirtations provoked the usual gossip. Kennedy watchers speculated that his marriage was strained, noting that while RFK was off on his search for meaning, Ethel stayed secure in her faith, so literal-minded that she reportedly objected to the teaching of evolution at her children's private school.

She may have felt uncomfortable about Kennedy's spiritual wanderlust. Many years later, Ethel watched a Jack Newfield film documentary that featured one friend after another describing how RFK had "grown" after JFK's death. "I don't like that part," she said to a friend, E. Barrett Prettyman Jr., who sat beside her through the screening. "She meant the idea that he had grown away from her," said Prettyman. She may have simply meant that she saw no need for him to "grow," since, in her eyes, he was very nearly perfect. In any case, Ethel was no stick-in-the-mud. She loved parties, entertained raucously and well, and was stylish in her bright minidresses, spawning imitators all over Georgetown. (Her spendthrift habits continued to exasperate her husband. When Kennedy moved into his suite in the New Senate Office Building in 1965, he told Edelman, "For God's sake, don't tell Ethel we're free to buy furniture. Tell her it's all government issue.") She was fearful about some things, especially of flying, after her parents died in a plane crash in 1955. Yet unlike her husband she refused to brood about fate. She lived in the present, determinedly upbeat and accepting of God's will. Believing that His will included another Kennedy in the White House, she was bold and unquestioning in her ambition for, and her belief in, her husband. Ethel Kennedy was one of the first to urge RFK to run against LBJ in '68. In the winter of 1967, she cabled RFK on his trip to Europe, "YOU MAY JUST HAVE TO DUMP OLE HUCKLEBERRY CAPONE." Kennedy's most intimate friends never doubted that Ethel remained at the center of her husband's universe. Mary Bailey Gimbel,

Kennedy's Milton crush and friend through the years, described RFK arriving at Hickory Hill after returning from New York. When Kennedy saw Ethel, "he'd light up," said Gimbel. She described the "paths of distress" on RFK's face; the "tension . . . sort of sliding away. . . . He *liked* being in that house with those kids and seeing her. It really pleased him." Gimbel believed that Ethel's "lack of introspection and sort of forthrightness was sort of a solace. . . ." It helped him deal with the "tangles" in his own head.

His Catholic faith became less absolute over time, and he was annoyed with the conservatism of the church hierarchy. On his trip home from South Africa in 1966, he had visited Pope Paul VI and urged him to become more interested in the plight of black Africa. The pope mumbled something about an interest in African art. In February 1967, Kennedy again visited the pope and lectured him that the Catholic Church in America needed to become more liberal and broaden its base beyond Irish and Italians to include Hispanics and other nationalities. Pope Paul cautioned that the church could not be changed by its "representatives in Los Angeles." Kennedy was not satisfied with these answers. But it is significant that RFK continued to seek out audiences with the pope, whom he described as "impressive" and "sensitive" in his diary.

Despite Kennedy's drift towards existentialism, he did not abandon his mother's faith. Nor, in his ventures into the counterculture, did he abandon a censorious moralism. On the 1965 trip to South America, he lectured an accompanying reporter against straying from his marriage. Carter Burden had avoided the draft in 1966 by having a baby. One morning in August 1967, Amanda found Kennedy playing with her infant. "Amanda," he said, "that was not a good reason to have a baby." Burden was "crushed" by his stern judgment. Truman Capote ran into Kennedy in the street sternly lecturing two small boys he had caught smoking cigarettes. The boys had to swear never to smoke again. "It was as if he was some sort of avenging angel who had fallen out of heaven upon them," recalled Capote. The boys promised and ran down the street, until one swung around and asked, "Can I have your autograph, Mr. Kennedy?" In a time of moral uncertainty, Kennedy did not lose sight of the right thing to do. The real question was whether he could summon the courage to do it.

KENNEDY WAS ADRIFT, like a boat in irons, unable to fall off and catch the wind. In late May, he exploded to Arthur Schlesinger, "How can we possibly survive five more years of Lyndon Johnson? Five more years of a crazy man?" Yet he ordered his speechwriters to strike any reference that might be interpreted as a criticism of the president. He would complain that the press reduced policy debates to a personal duel between the president and himself, and then heedlessly tell some friendly columnist or reporter (and there were dozens of them) how much he hated Johnson. The polls now showed Kennedy beating Johnson in 1968; depending on his mood, RFK would dismiss polls as "phony" or "something you really had to watch." The inner cities blew up during the "long hot summer" of 1967. President Johnson had to use paratroopers and tanks to quell the rioting in Detroit. Johnson seemed to regard the rioters as domestic Viet Cong. Watching the president speak on the riots without much apparent empathy for the poor people who had to live in the inner city, Kennedy complained to Mankiewicz, "It's over. The president's not going to do anything anymore. That's it. He's through with domestic problems, with the cities. . . . He's not going to do one thing. And he's the only one who can." Kennedy's own legislative efforts, a massive jobs bill and tax incentives to promote free enterprise in the inner city, were quickly sunk or outflanked by the White House.*

Though he brooded, Kennedy did not isolate himself. He never stopped questioning or looking for novel approaches. On the fringes of politics, a "Dump Johnson" movement was stirring. Its leader, Allard Lowenstein, was a friend of RFK's. Lowenstein was a creature of the '60s, a campus agitator and occasional lawyer who traveled around challenging the establishment from Stanford University to rural Mississippi to South Africa. Immensely charismatic, he was naturally drawn to RFK. Lowenstein became a "zealous" supporter, he recalled, after walking with Kennedy through a VA hospital in Queens in 1966 and watching him touch the maimed soldiers. Kennedy valued Lowenstein as a goad and a source of intelligence, a back channel into the New Left. In the summer and fall of '67, Lowenstein began seeing Kennedy "off calendar" at his office and at Hickory Hill. On an airplane flight in August, Lowenstein told Kennedy about his "Dump Johnson" campaign (more politely described as a "stop Johnson" effort). "If you want to run, we'll let you," the young activist teased the senator.

On September 26, Lowenstein went to Hickory Hill to make a more formal plea. Wearing bright green pants and a thin necklace of beads—half suburban, half hip—Kennedy welcomed Lowenstein, who kicked his shoes off and sat cross-legged on a chair, college bull-session style. Lowenstein laid out the "moral imperative" for Kennedy to run against Johnson, who he predicted could be forced out of the race. Kennedy did not disagree about Johnson. Indeed, he predicted that the president—"a coward"—would drop out on the eve of the Democratic convention. But Kennedy could not play the part of usurper. The reasons, as he explained them to Lowenstein, were entirely Shakespearean: His motives would be questioned. He would be accused of "ambition and envy." Johnson would see his challenge as a Kennedy family vendetta. Dis-

---

* Kennedy was becoming increasingly inattentive to the day-to-day work of the Senate. In the Eighty-ninth Congress, he had made 79 percent of the roll call votes. In the Ninetieth Congress through May 11, 1967, he made 71 percent, putting him in the lowest 10 percent of senators. On May 12, his administrative assistant, Joe Dolan, reported complaints that he was missing too many meetings of the New York delegation. He wasn't always paying attention on his visits upstate, either. On July 24, Dolan wrote Kennedy that a "girl in the North Country" had written to say that Kennedy "smiles with his lips but not with his eyes." By way of explanation, reported Dolan, "she says a number of people say that in your visits there you give an impression of not having your mind completely on the person you are talking to, being in a hurry to move on to the next person, the next town, etc."

couraged, Lowenstein wandered off to find another candidate. Most brushed him off. One, Senator Eugene McCarthy of Minnesota, did not. To little notice, McCarthy declared his candidacy in November.

Kennedy was still a creature of the establishment, still tied to its power-brokers. He was not willing to admit the degree of his disenchantment with the Vietnam War to his friends who were still working from within the Johnson administration. At about this time, the aging diplomat Averell Harriman, who was angling to become LBJ's peace negotiator, shook his finger at William Walton and said, "Your friend Bobby is not for cut and run like you are. He's more responsible than you are." When Walton reported Harriman's remark, RFK shrugged and remarked, "Little does he know."

Kennedy was deeply affected during these months by the personal disintegration of his friend Robert McNamara. Kennedy had always shared McNamara's sensitivity and bias for action and admired and envied other qualities Kennedy found lacking in himself: a commanding physical presence and crisp articulateness. Kennedy's most intense and greatest service had been arm in arm with McNamara, during the thirteen days of the Cuban Missile Crisis. Kennedy had looked to McNamara as a surviving link to his brother and as a wise counselor on the difficult problem of Vietnam. He was appalled by McNamara's collapse, which was obvious by August 1967. McNamara's wife, Margaret, was in the hospital with an ulcer—"Bob's ulcer," her friends said. Finishing his seventh year at the Pentagon, the secretary looked physically wasted and often verged on tears. Watching his jaw quiver in cabinet meetings, LBJ's aides wondered if McNamara was headed for a breakdown. So did LBJ. "We can't afford another Forrestal," the president said, thinking of the first secretary of defense, James Forrestal who, unable to cope with the pressures of his job, had jumped out of a hospital window in 1949. Johnson naturally blamed RFK for making McNamara feel like a "murderer." In late November, Johnson named McNamara as president of the World Bank, without telling him first. McNamara had been looking for a way out, but he was still caught off guard.

As soon as he heard about Johnson's shabby treatment of McNamara on that Monday, November 27, RFK headed straight for the office of the secretary of defense at the Pentagon. RFK urged his friend to go out with a "hell of a bang." Kennedy wanted Johnson's top Vietnam adviser to resign in protest against the war. McNamara has never disclosed the substance of their conversation, but apparently Kennedy was unpersuasive. Two nights later, Kennedy was gloomily having a drink with Arthur Schlesinger in the King Cole Bar at the St. Regis Hotel in New York at about 11 p.m., listening to Schlesinger complain about McNamara's failure to stand up to Johnson. "Wouldn't any self-respecting man have his resignation on the President's desk [in] half an hour?" Schlesinger asked. "Why does he fall in with LBJ's plan to silence him and cover everything up?" RFK said nothing. As they left the bar, Kennedy saw the headline on the first edition of the next morning's New York Times: "MCNAMARA TAKES WORLD BANK POST." Kennedy's mood grew bleaker. If a strong man like Bob McNamara could not defy Lyndon Johnson, how could he?

It was not necessary to visit bars with Kennedy late at night to know his true feelings. Anyone who had watched CBS's *Face the Nation* just three days earlier, on Sunday, November 26, could see the depths of his despair. The panelists, TV newsmen Martin Agronsky and Roger Mudd and Tom Wicker of the *New York Times*, kept badgering Kennedy: how could he oppose the war and still support LBJ? Kennedy squirmed in obvious discomfort. He did not want to be boxed into declaring his candidacy in 1968. Kennedy wobbled and weaved through the close questioning before letting loose an existential bleat:

> SENATOR KENNEDY: . . . I don't know what I can do to prevent that [declaring as a candidate in opposition to LBJ] or what I should do that is any different other than try to get off the earth in some way.

This was not the normal give-and-take of Sunday-morning talking heads. The host, Martin Agronsky, seemed shocked and backed off:

> MR. AGRONSKY: Senator, nobody wants you to get off the earth, obviously.
> SENATOR KENNEDY: I don't—
> MR. AGRONSKY: Nobody is trying to put you on the spot, really. . . .

But he was on the spot. His own staff and advisers and friends—and his conscience—kept him there. The Kennedy circle had begun meeting privately to discuss his options. At the first meeting, in New York in October, the consensus was against running. (The hotheads on Kennedy's staff, especially Walinsky, were not invited, and Kennedy himself stayed away to preserve deniability.) In December, a reprise with a slightly larger cast, including Kennedy, produced much turgid debate and no clear course of action. The strongest moral voice was Robert Kennedy's. He tried to rise above his own political prospects and ask what was good for the country. Whether or not he was sure of winning, Kennedy asked, was there not a case for trying in 1968? But he himself was resigned and fatalistic by the end of the meeting. "He supposed he would do nothing, and nothing would happen," Arthur Schlesinger recorded in his diary.

Kennedy's young staff kept up the pressure. "Time is running out," Walinsky had written him in November. Kennedy did not respond to Walinsky's urgings, recalled Esther Newberg, one of the staffers in Kennedy's Senate office. "His head would be down and his hands would be shoved in his pockets." So open about his emotions at times, he could utterly close down at others. "He had such a mask," recalled Newberg. "You couldn't read his face the way you could with so many others, really. He was almost glassy eyed sometimes." Kennedy's irresolution was becoming part of the public debate. HAWK, DOVE—OR CHICKEN? taunted a poster at Brooklyn College. Kennedy was not used to being mocked by college students. When Joe Dolan laughed at the poster, Kennedy sharply told him, "It's not funny." Closer to home, Jack Newfield wrote a biting piece in the *Village Voice* at the end of December. "If Kennedy does not run in 1968, the best side of his character will die. He will kill it every time he butchers his conscience and makes a speech for Johnson next autumn. . . . It will die every time a stranger quotes his own words back to him on the value of courage as a human quality." Newfield expected an argument from Kennedy when he saw him next, but Kennedy merely said, "My wife cut out your attack on me. She shows it to everybody."

Kennedy's wife, always his most fervent believer, was the most consistent advocate of a race for the White House. If she harbored private fears of becoming a widow, she did not discuss them, and her friends believed that she was able to banish morbid thoughts from her mind. She understood as well that her husband would regret it if he failed to try. In her cheery Camp Kennedy way, she enlisted the children to hang a "Run, Bobby, Run" banner from a bedroom window at Hickory Hill and to blast "The Impossible Dream" on the stereo at a meeting of Kennedy advisers in January. At Christmas, she sent out a coyly jokey card. On one side, the family posed under the inscription "Santa Claus in '67." On the other was a wryly smiling RFK. The caption read, "Would you believe Santa Claus in '68?" Never afraid to speak her mind, she tweaked the veterans of the New Frontier, like Ted Sorensen, who seemed to have become overcautious. "Why, Ted," she said as she listened to Sorensen outline all the reasons RFK should not run, "after all those high flown phrases you wrote for President Kennedy!"

Determined to be upbeat at all times, Ethel did not want to hear RFK's dirges. At dinner with Ethel and some friends in New York in January, RFK fretted, "I think if I run I will go a long way toward proving everything that everybody who doesn't like me has said about me . . . that I'm just a selfish, ambitious little SOB that can't wait to get his hands on the White House."

Ethel cut in. "You're always talking as though people don't like you. People do like you, and you've got to realize that," she said. RFK smiled. "I don't know, Ethel, sometimes in moments of depression, I get the idea that there are those around who don't like me." Kennedy was wisecracking, and the others around the table laughed, even though what he said wasn't particularly amusing. Kennedy could be genuinely funny and winning, and he worked hard not to show self-pity. But some of his humor was flat or dry to the point of desiccation. People laughed along in part the way they would in later years for Republican politician Bob Dole: they were relieved that somebody who had so obviously suffered could joke at all.

The Kennedy family went skiing over New Year's 1968, as always. RFK skied even more savagely than usual down the slopes of Sun Valley in Idaho. He interrupted his vacation to visit a nearby Indian reservation. In July, he had ended a white-water rafting trip down the Colorado with a visit to another reservation. Kennedy went from campfire singing and the sporting life to mournful discussions about hopelessness and high suicide rates in part because Native American reservations are close to the playgrounds of the wealthy in the West; but also because, at some level, he seemed to need to suffer. In California after the ski trip, he took Nicole Salinger, the young French wife of JFK's old press secretary, Pierre Salinger, with him to see an Indian school. The school seemed perfectly normal, Nicole Salinger recalled, except that the children had an eerie detachment: they were utterly unresponsive to other humans. "It was kind of embarrassing," said Salinger. Kennedy insisted on meeting alone with three or four teenagers. Salinger went with him. The three boys, who were "very turned inside and uptight . . . just opened up to him." For a few minutes, Kennedy was able to live in the realm of an alienated sixteen-year-old boy, which he inhabited naturally.

Then it was back to the familiar but somehow still alien world of politics. Kennedy had asked to meet with Jesse Unruh, the acknowledged leader of the California Democrats whose support would be critical to winning the state's primary in June. Unruh wanted a secret meeting; Kennedy preferred to meet openly in a restaurant, knowing that a secret meeting would inevitably leak and take on more import than he preferred. Kennedy wanted to find out what Unruh was willing to do; Unruh just wanted a poll. Afterwards, RFK told Edelman how much he hated "sitting and bullshitting" with politicians. Impatient as ever with empty small talk, Kennedy had alternated between moody silence and direct, yes-no questions ("Will I carry California?"). Edelman was a little surprised to hear Kennedy complain about greasing pols. "In the old days," Kennedy wearily explained, "I would have been able to leave Larry O'Brien behind after the meeting. He could talk the balls off a brass monkey."

The adviser RFK missed most was not Larry O'Brien but someone like the 1960 Robert Kennedy—a hard man who knew how to say no and to strike fear into laggards and plodders. "My problem is that I don't have anyone to be for me what I was for my brother," he told Edelman. His deeper problem, left unsaid, was that he was not his brother. In his heart he was still the campaign manager, not the candidate.

JFK's presence loomed over RFK in January 1968, embodied by two men, Theodore Sorensen and Edward Kennedy. "The Two Teds" were the advisers most firmly opposed to RFK's candidacy in 1968. RFK paid deference to Ted Sorensen, never his social intimate, but arguably his brother's closest adviser, JFK's "voice" of cool detachment and caution in the Kennedy White House. Ted Kennedy was the living reminder of family sacrifice. With Joe and Jack gone, if Robert fell, only Ted—"Baby Teddy"—would be left. EMK was, in effect, speaking for the family, always a powerful pull at any Kennedy. If stroke-stricken Joseph Sr., mute but still impassioned, had furiously crumpled up the photo of RFK in climbing gear ascending Mount Kennedy, how might he react to the news that Bobby was risking a presidential campaign that had a greater chance of ending in tragedy or failure than victory? "I know what Dad would have said," Ted told Richard Goodwin: "Don't do it."

Teddy Kennedy was a loyal party man who worried about splitting the Democrats apart in a secession struggle. Though he gave lip service, Robert Kennedy cared much less about party unity. He was a political loner who thought the party organization sclerotic, usually corrupt, and in any case something to work around, as he always had for his brother. Still, he knew that he would be accused of selfishness and arrogance if he ran. "It will be the bad old Bobby," Kennedy told writer Peter Maas, "trying to wreck the party because of his dead brother." RFK understood that the political obstacles to wresting the nomination from a sitting president in 1968 were huge. In that pre-reform era, the Democratic Party's nominating process (like the GOP's) was not very democratic. The party bosses—the mayors, the governors, the labor leaders—controlled most of the delegates at the party convention in August. With only fourteen primaries, voters played mostly an exhortatory role. An outsider could possibly force the hands of the bosses by sweeping the primaries, but the nomination would most likely be decided in "smoke-filled rooms" where favors—pork barrel and patronage—could be traded. Such a system vastly favored the incumbent. Though badly damaged by Vietnam, Johnson was sure to be a formidable deal maker in his own cause. Such certainly was the opinion of the experts. Kennedy's most disciplined political adviser in this period was probably Fred Dutton. A veteran of the '60 campaign who had handled the Kennedy administration's congressional relations for the State Department before returning to law practice after Johnson became president, Dutton regularly wrote precise, hardheaded memos that Kennedy read closely. To run for the presidency in 1968, Dutton wrote RFK in November 1967, would be "political suicide."

Robert Kennedy had not lost his deep streak of realism. He may have liked listening to "The Impossible Dream" on his stereo, but he preferred winning. In the political arena, he generally regarded tilting at windmills as self-indulgent. He understood political necessity and didn't try to dress it up. As attorney general passing on nominees for the federal bench, he had been required either to go along with a senator's choice, sometimes a hack supported by the local machine, or to hold out for some lofty jurist approved by the bar association. Joe Dolan recalled his terse instruction in one case in Pennsylvania: "Take the bad guy," said Kennedy. The faithful son still liked to repeat various sayings of his father. One was, "If there's a piece of cake on the table, eat it." Father Joe, the Wall Street investor who made millions by insider trading before it was outlawed in the '30s, taught his boys to be opportunistic, not quixotic, to go for the likely bet, not the long shot. In January 1968, the odds against beating LBJ looked very steep.

And yet . . . it was Robert Kennedy who liked to quote Dante that "the hottest places in Hell are reserved for those who, in a time of great moral crisis, maintain their neutrality." In his conclusion to his 1967 book, *To Seek a Newer World,* he warned against four great barriers to progress: "futility . . . expediency . . . timidity . . . and comfort." He exhorted poor blacks from the Mississippi Delta to South Africa not to give in to despair but to stand up for freedom. At critical moments in his own career he had *not* taken the safe course—he had defied his father to investigate labor racketeering and pushed his brother to make a moral argument for a civil rights bill.

Within forty-eight hours in January, two disparate acquaintances braced him with questions that framed the moral issue. One was Walter Lippmann, the aging pundit, who listened patiently to Kennedy outline his dilemma. "Well," said Lippmann, "if you believe that Johnson's reelection would be a catastrophe for the country . . . the question you must live with is whether you did everything you could to avert this catastrophe." The other was the fiery, leftish Greek film star Melina Mercouri. She asked him whether he wanted to go down in history as the senator who waited for a safer day.

Such arguments, the cool logic of a wise man and the dare of a melodramatic actress, would seem to be so compelling to someone of Robert Kennedy's temperament that it seems almost surprising that he hesitated as long as he did. One is left wondering if there were not some other reason that held him back.

In all the debates over whether or not to run in 1968, Kennedy apparently failed to mention two risks which must have weighed heavily on him. One was blackmail. RFK knew perfectly well that LBJ had been collecting dirt on him for years, aided all through JFK's presidency by J. Edgar Hoover. He knew from experience that Johnson could dredge up at any moment the whole bugging controversy and—worse—the secret, known only to a few, that Kennedy had authorized wiretaps on Martin Luther King. Kennedy was aware as well that LBJ had been fishing to learn more about the Kennedys' Cuba plots. He had read Drew Pearson's column in March 1967 charging him with hiring the mob to plot against Castro and had scrambled to put his files in order, consulting with CIA director Helms. How would voters feel if they knew that Kennedy, who castigated the Vietnam War as immoral, had run a secret program of subversion and assassination against Cuba? In columnist Pearson, the president had his own delivery vehicle, the best-read muckraker in America. Always careful to compartmentalize his secrets, Kennedy never mentioned any concern about blackmail to his administrative aide, Joe Dolan. Other former Kennedy aides acknowledged that blackmail was a risk (a real one, it turned out), but could not recall any discussions on the subject with Kennedy. Significantly, however, the one person who knew all of RFK's secrets—his faithful personal assistant, Angie Novello, who kept his records and took his phone calls—did admit to fearing that LBJ would try to smear her boss, though she could not quite bring herself to use the word. In 1969, she told Jean Stein and George Plimpton:

> I wanted Bob in the White House so badly, but I didn't want him to run in '68 because I was afraid of what certain people in high places would do. I was afraid they would do something mean and unheard of and I didn't want Bob hurt.

Novello continued, "I was afraid LBJ would . . ." She paused. "You know how vindictive he is! That if Bob threw in his hat . . ." She hesitated again, as if not wanting to spell out or contemplate the consequences. "That worried me," she concluded and changed the subject.

RFK's other great fear was the darkest and most unmentionable: that he would, like his brother, be murdered. He knew that he had many enemies, that he excited unreasoning emotions, that he had been the target of repeated threats, and that some of the threateners, like Teamster Frank Chavez, were dangerous. He was famous for ignoring death threats. In 1966, when Kennedy arrived to campaign in Billings, Montana, the FBI received a threat : "Kennedy dies at 4." Though RFK always insisted on an open car, Joe Dolan put him in a big black limousine rented from a funeral parlor. Kennedy turned to Dolan and inquired, "Where's my car?" "He was furious," Dolan recalled. In Wyoming there was another threat—a man had been seen on a roof with a gun—and Dolan insisted on hustling Kennedy out the back of the hotel. "Don't ever do that to me again," Kennedy angrily ordered.

Kennedy's defiance of danger was heroic, but also slightly compulsive. He seemed to be daring death as a way of coping with the dread of it. For RFK, courage was a shield, a defense against the demons of self-doubt. It had been all his life, from the first dive into Nantucket Sound to the subsequent plunges down frozen slopes and into icy waters from Utah to Maine and South America. We cannot know all the fears that lurked in Kennedy's head and heart, but judging from his obsession with courage, they were many and rarely quiet.

True courage is not fearlessness, recklessly riding towards the sound of the guns. It is overcoming fear, the kind of nameless dread that curls around the heart in the hours before dawn. For Kennedy to run for president in 1968 required every bit as much courage as it did for Lieutenant Joseph P. Kennedy Jr. to climb into the cockpit of a flying bomber on a secret mission over the English Channel in 1944—or for Lieutenant John F. Kennedy to swim every night out into the Japanese- and shark-infested waters looking for help to save the crew of his sunken PT boat. Not only moral courage, but raw physical courage.

AT THE END OF JANUARY 1968, Kennedy flinched. At a breakfast with fifteen reporters at the National Press Club on the thirtieth, he announced that he had no plans to oppose President Johnson for the Democratic nomination under "any conceivable circumstances." Press secretary Mankiewicz softened the statement to read "any foreseeable circumstances," but the damage had been done. He was brutally ridiculed on two prime-time comedy shows, *Rowan and Martin's Laugh-In* and the *Smothers Brothers Comedy Hour*, for, in effect, chickening out.

His office was a morgue. Adam Walinsky gave notice; Edelman said he probably would, too. Joe Dolan announced that he couldn't vote for Johnson and asked for a sabbatical. Kennedy put up no protests, meekly saying that he understood. Allard Lowenstein arrived to make a desperate plea. "I'm an unforeseen circumstance," he told Kennedy with customary bravado. In truth, Eugene McCarthy's insurgency seemed to be going nowhere in New Hampshire, and Lowenstein's "Dump Johnson" movement needed a better candidate. Kennedy tried to explain that the political obstacles were too great, that the powers-that-be would never abandon an incumbent president. Lowenstein wasn't listening. "The people who think that the future and the honor of this country are at stake because of Vietnam don't give a shit what Mayor Daley and Governor Y and Chairman Z think," he hotly declared. "We're going to do it, and we're going to win, and it's a shame you're not with us, because you could have been president." Lowenstein walked out. Kennedy ran after him and spun Lowenstein around with a hand on his shoulder. He was sorry, he said in a voice thick with emotion, he just couldn't do it.

Kennedy was catatonic for the next few days. He stopped returning phone calls and ignored his messages from Angie Novello. He just sat at his desk or paced. In Vietnam, a massive uprising by the Viet Cong and North Vietnamese regulars—the Tet offensive—had exploded, catching American forces completely by surprise. On February 8, Kennedy gave an antiwar speech that was, for once, completely unguarded in its criticism of Lyndon Johnson. He told IBM's Tom Watson that he now favored withdrawing all U.S. troops within six months "in any way possible." On a cold weekend at Hickory Hill, he huddled in the bathhouse by the pool with a few remaining stalwarts—as usual, a party was raging around them—and, staring down at the floor, once more said that he was not running. Richard Goodwin declared that he was going to work for Gene McCarthy. A report had filtered back that McCarthy, buoyed by outrage over the Tet offensive and a swelling army of "Clean for Gene" college kids knocking on doors, had suddenly surged to 40 percent in the polls in New Hampshire. Kennedy called a spy in the Johnson organization. Could the rumor be true? It was. Kennedy hated to see his natural allies among the young rallying to a different banner. "God, I'm going to lose them, and I'm going to lose them forever," he said.

He was already wracked with second thoughts. It galled him to think that Eugene McCarthy was wearing the crusader's mantle. When Marty Nolan, a *Boston Globe* reporter, told RFK that McCarthy seemed to be picking up support in New Hampshire, Kennedy muttered, "Gene's not all-Irish, you know." What? asked Nolan. "You know," said Kennedy, dead serious, "his mother's German. That accounts for his meanness." Nolan, who enjoyed a bantering relationship with RFK, shot back, "What accounts for yours?" Kennedy allowed himself a dry chuckle.

As always, his better angels competed with his baser instincts. He was carrying in his briefcase a letter from journalist Pete Hamill. In the broken-down homes of Watts, Hamill wrote, he had seen photographs of JFK hanging in the homes of the poor. This was "your obligation," wrote Hamill, "the obligation of staying true to whatever it was that put those pictures on those walls." Kennedy began looking for excuses to change his mind. There were many: on February 29, the Kerner Commission, appointed by the president after the summer of '67 riots, released its report on the causes of racial unrest in the inner cities, blaming "white racism." The White House essentially dismissed the report. In New Hampshire, George Romney, the presidential hope of GOP moderates, dropped out of the race, opening the way for Richard Nixon to secure the Republican nomination. Significantly, Fred Dutton reversed his earlier adamant opposition to RFK's candidacy. So did Kennedy's old friend Kenny O'Donnell. Their changes of heart counted for more with Kennedy than the harangues of his staff, long since discounted. Though Joe Dolan had taken leave from Kennedy's office, he had set up shop in Milton Gwirtzman's law office to begin quietly preparing for a presidential campaign, making briefing books, checking primary filing deadlines, and discreetly calling local political leaders, just in case RFK changed his mind. Kennedy knew about Dolan's activities and made no effort to stop him. By late February, Kennedy was randomly polling friends and acquaintances, asking if he should run. "What should I do?" he asked Amanda Burden. "Run," she said. "Really?" "Yes." He grabbed her arm. "Then I will!"

He wasn't just flirting. On Monday, March 4, he asked Dutton to approach his brother Ted and test his reaction to entering the race. It may seem peculiar that Kennedy needed a middleman to talk to his own brother, but RFK often used indirection in dealing with his own family. Dutton gingerly laid out the possibility, but the youngest Kennedy had already divined his older brother's intentions. "I think Bobby is going to run," he told Dutton. "The thing to do is to make sense of it."

And so Robert Kennedy backed into the race. There was no single moment, no one epiphany, no turning point. The Tet offensive, the president's indifference to the report of his own commission on racial unrest, the rebirth of Nixon, the changing opinions of his friends—all these were factors, but none was decisive. Kennedy's inner workings were far too complex to be simply charted; his decision making, certainly on a matter this momentous, was nonlinear. In a sense, the decision was inevitable. "He was always running for president," reflected Dolan. "He was the only senator to answer his out-of-state mail or to routinely schedule speeches in New Hampshire and Wisconsin [the first two primary states]." The life of a U.S. senator, with its quorum calls and cloakroom coziness, was always too confining for Kennedy. He felt himself drawn along on a greater tide. The fates could be slowed or diverted, but not stopped. Destiny is a grandiose word, but Robert Kennedy, small and slightly hunched and hand-wringing in the flesh, lived in an epic world of the mind and spirit, where fates clashed and destiny called—to him.

Back in the real world of politics, Kennedy faced a host of problems. The first was timing. If he announced before the New Hampshire primary a week away on March 12, he might be seen as "ruthlessly" trying to upstage McCarthy's children's crusade. At the same time, with accustomed realpolitik, Kennedy and his men figured that if McCarthy split apart the Democratic Party on primary day, the onus would be off RFK. Better to wait a week.

Second thoughts continued to weigh. On Saturday, March 9, Kennedy flew to Des Moines to attend the Iowa Democrats' traditional Jefferson-Jackson Day dinner, a gathering of pols including Democratic senators and governors from neighboring states. The conversation meandered, without directly focusing on the main question: was RFK running? After dinner, when the pols had left, Kennedy bitterly complained to two of his old friends and advisers, John

Reilly and John Seigenthaler, who were traveling with him. "What the hell were you guys doing in there?" he demanded. Reilly and Seigenthaler looked perplexed. Kennedy spluttered that they should have been pinning down the Democratic leaders to support an RFK candidacy. "I can't do that myself," said Kennedy. Had JFK lived, RFK would have been the one lining up support, demanding commitments. But Bobby Kennedy the candidate had no one to perform the role he played for his brother.

The next morning he flew to California to witness the end of a twenty-five-day hunger strike by Cesar Chavez. Away from the hacks, together again with his soulmate Chavez, he felt invigorated. The leader of the striking farm-workers had lost thirty-five pounds and was so weak he could barely talk. Kennedy sat beside him in unspoken communion. Then he climbed on the roof of a car and started shouting "Viva la huelga [Long live the strike]" in Spanish, Chavez later recalled, with a terrible Boston accent. The crowds tore at Kennedy. Chavez noted that his visitor's hands were bloody when they ceremoniously broke bread together. Kennedy had already decided to make his move: on the plane ride to Chavez's headquarters in Delano, he told Peter Edelman, "I'm going to do it. I've got to find a way to get McCarthy out. But I'm going to do it anyway." He called Ethel with the news. She was excited and optimistic. At one of the chaotic Hickory Hill confabs in February, Kennedy had beseeched Ethel, "What should I do?" She replied instantly, "Run. You'll beat him. Run. Do it." Listening to this exchange, Teddy Kennedy's aide Dave Burke quipped that there wasn't much point continuing the debate, Ethel had spoken. "She doesn't make all the decisions in this family," Kennedy said, but Burke could tell he was comforted by her absolute confidence. On Monday, RFK tried to win over the last doubter, Ted Sorensen, who told him that he would lose—but like all Kennedy loyalists, he would do whatever he could to help.*

On Tuesday, primary day in New Hampshire, Kennedy had lunch with his first real friend, David Hackett, and told the old Milton football hero that he was going to run. RFK seemed "relieved," recalled Hackett. But by late that night, over supper at "21" in New York, Kennedy's gloom had returned. In New Hampshire, Eugene McCarthy polled a remarkable 42 percent of the vote. Kennedy knew that he was going to have a very difficult time trying to persuade the triumphant McCarthy to drop out in deference to him. His concerns were confirmed after midnight in an awkward congratulatory phone call to the dragon slayer and his speechwriter, Richard Goodwin (who had not cut his

---

* In a last-ditch attempt to keep Kennedy out of the race, Sorensen approached the White House with what amounted to a deal: if the president would appoint a special commission to figure out how to extricate the United States from Vietnam, RFK would not run. For the next three days, Sorensen secretly negotiated with Johnson's new secretary of defense, Clark Clifford, who had transformed from hawk to dove in less than a month in office. Kennedy and Johnson forces later dismissed the negotiation as not serious—LBJ would not turn over his foreign policy powers to an outside commission, especially one with Robert Kennedy on it. But Sorensen has always maintained that the interest was real on both sides.

Kennedy ties; he was acting as a back channel to McCarthy's campaign). Hanging up the phone, Kennedy knew he had waited too long. "I think I blew it," he said.

At noon on Wednesday, he blurted to some reporters that he was "actively reconsidering" his decision not to run. The remark was a blunder; he succeeded only in appearing "ruthless" by stepping on McCarthy's headlines. The senator's staff struggled to write a statement congratulating McCarthy for his achievement. Kennedy balked. "I'm not going to make a national figure out of McCarthy," he insisted. One of Kennedy's aides had to point out that McCarthy "already *is* a national figure." Kennedy regarded McCarthy as "pompous, petty, and venal," while McCarthy regarded Kennedy as "a spoiled, unintelligent demagogue," writes Jack Newfield. In the weeks ahead, neither man would rise in the other's estimation. Kennedy was tortured with guilt that he had not jumped in the race sooner. Looking exhausted from a sleepless night, he met with a few senators in his office on Wednesday afternoon. He spoke "mechanically . . . as if he were at a press conference," said Senator George McGovern. "I'm just sure he was punishing himself inwardly for not having made the decision six months earlier. I think he died a thousand deaths" over McCarthy's upset in New Hampshire.

That evening the faithful gathered at Steve Smith's office in New York, ostensibly to debate one last time whether RFK should run, but really to begin discussing how. Dolan passed out the black books he had been compiling, listing key supporters state by state. The first page, "A" for Alabama, was blank. "Maybe he should reconsider again," muttered Dave Burke. Skeptical, Ted Kennedy joked, "Bobby's therapy is going to cost the family $4 million."

The senator's staff was told to reserve the Senate Caucus Room, where RFK had grilled Jimmy Hoffa and JFK had announced his presidential candidacy, for Saturday morning. On Friday night, the best Kennedy wordsmiths—Walinsky, Sorensen, and Arthur Schlesinger—met at Hickory Hill to write an announcement speech. They had to compete with a dinner party blaring in the dining room and the Kennedy children wrestling with the dogs and each other and dancing to the Jefferson Airplane in the living room. Fred Dutton compared the atmosphere to a discotheque; Jeff Greenfield, a young new speechwriter, felt as if he were on a scavenger hunt. The three principal speechwriters argued until after 3 a.m., when RFK went to bed. Sorensen finally won out, and produced a speech that sounded more like JFK than RFK. "Ted, this doesn't make any sense," Robert Kennedy said in the morning, peering at a paragraph after getting a haircut ("As short as possible," instructed Ted Kennedy). "But then," Kennedy added, "the whole thing doesn't make any sense." He seemed certain that he would lose, that in the end he would not be able to overcome Johnson's power or McCarthy's head start. But at least he had resolved to act.

After Kennedy's announcement—"I do not run for the presidency merely to oppose any man, but to propose new policies. . . ."—he flew to New York to march in the St. Patrick's Day Parade. Beforehand, he went to see Jacqueline Kennedy. Their relationship, tested by the Manchester controversy, was perhaps not quite as close as it had once been. But on this cloudy March day, Jackie Kennedy smiled and gently kissed RFK and wished him on his way. A few days later, she took Arthur Schlesinger aside at a dinner party. "Do you know what I think will happen to Bobby?" she said. "The same thing that happened to Jack. . . . There is so much hatred in this country, and more people hate Bobby than hated Jack. . . . I've told Bobby this, but he isn't fatalistic, like me." She knew perfectly well that her brother-in-law *was* fatalistic. Down on Fifth Avenue, on the St. Patrick's Day Parade route, Kennedy's old spokesman, Ed Guthman, quietly summoned Peter Maas, the writer, and a couple of other journalists friendly to Kennedy, to walk along close by RFK as he waved to the crowd. Maas realized that the newsmen had been formed into a kind of human shield. "Guthman was afraid some nut would take a shot at Bobby," Maas recalled.

CHAPTER 20 QUEST

THE DAY AFTER HE ANNOUNCED for the presidency, Kennedy flew to Kansas to deliver a long-scheduled speech, the Alfred M. Landon Lecture at Kansas State University. The setting was ideal for a raucous campaign kickoff. The KSU field house was packed with 15,000 well-scrubbed students—not bra burners and longhairs, but corn-fed farm kids from the heartland. They literally hung from the rafters, waving signs like "KISS ME, BOBBY." His voice flat and stammering, his right leg shaking, Kennedy began tentatively, but then cut loose, jamming his fist into the air while pouring out an antiwar diatribe and months of pent-up emotion. When he was done, drained after fifty minutes, "the fieldhouse sounded as though it was inside Niagara Falls; it was like a soundtrack gone haywire," recorded Jack Newfield. The next stop, before 17,000 at the University of Kansas, was more tumultuous. Jules Witcover, a reporter for the Newhouse news service who would write a vivid book about RFK's last campaign, *85 Days*, watched in awe from the press box: "It looked and sounded like some overly-done scene from a Hollywood movie of a Presidential campaign—the jumping young girls, the screams ricocheting off the distant field house walls." Witcover could see how Kennedy was feeding off the visceral response, "how he himself seemed to be pulled up on it like a small boy on a towering seaside breaker, riding it willingly, daringly, with evident exhilaration." Stanley Tretick, a photographer for *Look*, gaped at the hysteria and exclaimed, "This is Kansas, fucking Kansas! He's going all the fucking way!"

The first-wave euphoria soon wore off. RFK understood the odds. About half the delegates attending the 1968 Democratic convention would either be from the South, where RFK was still called "Little Brother," or controlled by Big Labor. George Meany, the head of the AFL-CIO, derisively referred to Kennedy as "that jitterbug." In the Senate, Kennedy had routinely antagonized visiting labor bosses by asking why their unions discriminated against

Negroes. Now Big Labor's money and organization—still formidable in the late 1960s—would be arrayed against him. "Businessmen distrust me," Kennedy told his friend Barrett Prettyman. "Can I do anything?" In March, Prettyman invited Alan Livingston, president of Capitol Records, to Kennedy's apartment at UN Plaza. The two men shook hands and sat down. "There was absolutely dead silence," Prettyman recalled. "Livingston didn't know what he was doing there. Afterwards, he said, 'What the hell was that all about?' I never brought another businessman."

"Who else could have brought together Big Business, Big Labor, and the South?" Kennedy boasted self-mockingly to Milton Gwirtzman. "And the Jews," added Gwirtzman. A week after Kennedy's red-hot launch, the *New York Times* counted 65 percent of the delegates solidly in the Johnson camp. Kennedy's true base was the poor minority and college-age population in a nation described by census expert Richard Scammon as "unblack, unpoor, and unyoung." Even the young had their doubts; many, loyal to McCarthy, were denouncing Kennedy as an opportunist. Kennedy's challenge was to create a coalition of the have-nots, quite a challenge in a nation where blue-collar workers, in full white flight from the cities, tended to be the most vehemently racist.

The Kennedy campaign had "no strategy," recalled Fred Dutton, one of its strategists. It did have plenty of egos. Kennedy's approach to staffing was "Rooseveltian," said Frank Mankiewicz, using a polite description for competitive mayhem. Kennedy told both Sorensen and Kenny O'Donnell that they were the campaign manager, though the real campaign manager was Steve Smith, unless it was Ted Kennedy—or, really, Bob Kennedy.* With a shrug, Kennedy decided to dispense with titles altogether and hold a free-for-all between his Senate staff, his brother Ted and his staff, and President Kennedy's former staff, none of whom got along particularly well. Sorensen insisted that "the bomb throwers," Adam Walinsky and Jeff Greenfield, be banned from the candidate's plane. Walinsky quarreled with everyone, but especially Fred Dutton, whom Kennedy asked to be his aide-de-camp on the campaign trail. Kennedy's advisers did share one virtue: they were not sycophants. Political candidates sometimes choose as their traveling companions soothing yes-men who can stroke wounded egos. In Dutton, Kennedy chose someone who was not afraid to deliver bad news.

Much was later made of the "new politics" of the Robert Kennedy campaign. Walinsky proclaimed the new age on day one: "Our strategy is to change the rules of nominating a president," he declared to reporters. "We're going to do it a new way. In the streets." As usual, however, Kennedy was traveling on two tracks. At about the same moment Walinsky was declaring the people's

---

* John Bartlow Martin, a late addition to the campaign, depicted the backbiting and confusing overlap in his journal in early April: "Schlesinger said Walinsky hates Sorensen (RFK previously told Arthur that Steve Smith would be campaign manager, Sorensen campaign director, and Kenny O'Donnell in charge of organizations, and that O'Donnell couldn't stand either of the other two)."

crusade, Kennedy was telling columnist Jimmy Breslin that the boss of old-fashioned big-city bosses, Mayor Daley of Chicago, was the key to victory. "Daley means the ball game," Kennedy said. The senator sent his old pal Kenny O'Donnell, no stranger to back rooms, to work on Hizzoner. In fact, the 1968 Kennedy campaign was a mishmash of old politics and new politics, as it had to be to have any chance of victory. The outcome depended on an imponderable: would the Daleys of the world, the party bosses who still controlled the nominating process, be swayed by the pandemonium of the Kennedy campaign or put off by it?

Kennedy needed first to find a true voice. His early speeches echoed his brother's—". . . and so I ask you, give me your heart, give me your hand, your help in this election"—a little too self-consciously. RFK's speech-making tended to be turgid or screechy, unless fatigue deepened his voice and made it softer and more resonant. (Kennedy's normal state—exhaustion—was in this sense a blessing.) In the early days of the campaign, he tended to shout, letting the crowd frenzy whip him up. Playing off Martin Luther King's 1963 speech at the Lincoln Memorial, Mankiewicz described RFK's exuberance as the "free-at-last syndrome." Kennedy was so relieved to be able to speak out that he literally yelled. The crowds yelled back. On a swing through California in late March, he was mobbed everywhere. More than once, Kennedy had to rescue small children from being trampled. Columnist Stewart Alsop, a middle-of-the-roader who was influential within the Washington establishment, compared the hysterical jumpers and screamers to Mao Tse-tung's rampaging Red Guard, which had been laying waste to China. Reporters traveling with Kennedy found it all, as one put it, a little "scary." Kennedy seemed to be blaming Johnson for whatever was wrong with the United States, not just the unwinnable war but rioting, draft-card burning, and drug addiction. In a speech delivered before a screaming crowd in Los Angeles he accused "the national leadership" of "calling upon the darker impulses of the American spirit." This was too much for some reporters. Richard Harwood of the *Washington Post* wrote an influential piece accusing Kennedy of playing the "demagogue."

Ethel Kennedy's response was to greet Harwood on the plane by crumpling up his newspaper and throwing it in his face. But Kennedy's staff knew that Harwood's piece reflected the temper not only of the press corps, who were generally sympathetic towards Kennedy, but also of many voters, who were less so. To Americans fearful of urban unrest—recalling the "long hot summer" of '67 and dreading a hotter one in '68—the Kennedy campaign looked like a "traveling riot," said Milton Gwirtzman, one of Kennedy's more sober-sided staffers. The campaign decided to consciously tone down the candidate's rhetoric. One solution was to send Gwirtzman himself out to write speeches that were sure to be duller than the ones crafted by Walinsky and Greenfield (Walinsky was blamed for the "darker impulses" speech, but it was actually secretly drafted by Richard Goodwin, who was still working for McCarthy but quietly helping out RFK).

Kennedy's clamorous campaign was offensive to the guardians of the fourth estate, but it was achieving one critical and somewhat unexpected outcome. In the White House, Lyndon Johnson heard the roar of the mob drawing closer. His advisers told him that he would probably lose the Wisconsin primary, on April 2, to McCarthy, but his true nightmare was a Kennedy restoration. "I felt that I was being chased on all sides by a giant stampede," he would later tell Doris Kearns Goodwin:

> . . . I was being forced over the edge by rioting blacks, demonstrating students, marching welfare mothers, squawking professors, and hysterical reporters. And then the final straw: The thing I feared from the first day of my Presidency was actually coming true. Robert Kennedy had openly announced his intention to reclaim the throne in the memory of his brother. And the American people, swayed by the magic of the name, were dancing in the streets.

For months, Johnson had been quietly contemplating not running for reelection. With his poll numbers dropping and the Pentagon asking for another 206,000 troops to throw into the void of Vietnam, Johnson decided the time had come to retreat with honor. On the night of March 31, he announced on nationwide TV that he was halting the bombing, calling for peace negotiations with the North Vietnamese—and no longer seeking reelection to the presidency.

Kennedy's plane was landing at La Guardia in New York just as Johnson was winding up his speech. The New York State Democratic chairman, John Burns, raced aboard the plane and breathlessly told Kennedy, "The president is not going to run." Kennedy stared at him. "You're kidding," he said. On the drive in from the airport, he seemed lost in thought. Finally, he said, "I wonder if he would have done this if I hadn't come in." At the UN Plaza apartment, Kennedy was "very, very quiet, much more so than he ever was," recalled John English, another local party leader. "When people would start to speak while he was watching TV, he'd glare at them." Ethel was more buoyant about Johnson's demise. "Well, he didn't deserve to be president anyway," she said. Kennedy disapproved of popping champagne corks, so she brought out a bottle of Scotch.

Kennedy asked for a meeting with the president—in effect, a truce. Johnson first vowed, "I won't bother answering that grand-standing little runt," but then he agreed to give RFK an audience. Kennedy came to the White House on April 3. After listening to the president filibuster for a while on the war, the Middle East, the budget, etc., Kennedy asked LBJ what he intended to do about the campaign. Stay out of it, said Johnson. "I am no king maker," he said, "and I don't want to be." Kennedy wasn't fooled. He understood that Hubert Humphrey would jump in the race with Johnson's behind-the-scenes support. But he wanted to at least put the president on record as declaring his neutrality. LBJ talked some more about how he had kept the faith with JFK. Kennedy tried to tell Johnson, "You are a brave and dedicated man," but he had difficulty spitting out the words. Johnson had to ask him to repeat them. When Kennedy left, LBJ met first with Vice President Humphrey to give him his secret backing, then, ominously, with his favorite muckraker, Drew Pearson. Johnson entertained the columnist with a history lesson—a distorted one—that blamed RFK for the Bay of Pigs. Pearson filed it all away, for later possible use. Johnson also met that day with Eugene McCarthy, who on April 2 had won the Wisconsin primary. The conversation was "almost pro forma and casual," McCarthy recalled. That is, until Robert Kennedy's name came up. Johnson said nothing, but drew the side of his hand across his throat.

Kennedy had at last toppled Johnson, but he knew that the Oval Office was not his sure reward. In the early-morning hours after Johnson's speech declaring that he would not seek reelection, Jim Whittaker, Kennedy's mountain guide and friend, had called and exclaimed, "Congratulations!" Kennedy wearily responded, "Jim, it isn't that easy." Johnson's withdrawal and offer of peace negotiations on Vietnam had deprived Kennedy of his most compelling issue. He had lost his voice to laryngitis, and his campaign organization was, in the blunt assessment of Fred Dutton, "a mess." With poetical condescension, Eugene McCarthy observed that "up to now, Bobby was Jack running against Lyndon. Now Bobby has to run against Jack. . . . It's purely Greek."

Kennedy was faced with a gauntlet of must-win primaries, beginning with Indiana on May 7 and ending with New York on June 18. On April 4, the day after his meeting with Johnson, he was scheduled to give his first Indiana speech on friendly ground—the heart of the ghetto in Indianapolis. On the plane, *New York Times* reporter Johnny Apple gave him some shocking news: Martin Luther King had just been shot in Memphis. Kennedy "sagged. His eyes went blank," recalled Apple. By the time he arrived in Indianapolis, King had been reported dead. Fearing a race riot, the chief of police advised Kennedy to stay out of the ghetto. Ethel begged him not to go. Kennedy sent her back to the hotel and went ahead. His police escort peeled off when he entered the ghetto.

A gray day had become a raw night. Kennedy arrived at the speech site—a wind-blown lot surrounded by tenements—in his brother's old overcoat with the collar turned up. About a thousand people milled about, most in a carefree mood. Adam Walinsky rushed up to hand his boss a hastily drafted speech, but Kennedy waved him off and pulled from his pocket some crumpled notes that he had written himself. It fell to Kennedy to tell the crowd that Martin Luther King was dead. There was a collective gasp and shouts of "No, no!" Remembering his own grief over his brother's death, Kennedy went on, a little clumsily at first, then powerfully and movingly:

> . . . For those of you who are black and are tempted to be filled with hatred and distrust at the injustice of such an act, against all white people, I can only say that I feel in my own heart the same kind of feeling. I had a member of my family killed, but he was killed by a white man. But we have to make an effort in the United States, we have to make an effort to understand, to go beyond these rather difficult times.

My favorite poet was Aeschylus. He wrote: "In our sleep, pain which cannot forget falls drop by drop upon the heart until, in our own despair, against our will, comes wisdom through the awful grace of God."

What we need in the United States is not division; what we need in the United States is not hatred; what we need in the United States is not violence or lawlessness; but love and wisdom, and compassion toward one another, and a feeling of justice toward those who still suffer within our country, whether they be white or they be black.

So I shall ask you tonight to return home, to say a prayer for the family of Martin Luther King, that's true, but most importantly to say a prayer for our own country, which all of us love—a prayer for understanding and that compassion of which I spoke. . . .

Let us dedicate ourselves to what the Greeks wrote so many years ago: to tame the savageness of man and to make gentle the life of this world.

Let us dedicate ourselves to that, and say a prayer for our country and for our people.

At the hotel, some of Kennedy's staffers were weeping. Kennedy himself was dry-eyed. "After all," he said sharply to Walinsky, thinking perhaps of his brother's assassination, "it's not the greatest tragedy in the history of the Republic." Especially after such an affecting speech, Kennedy's remark seemed a little heartless. He did call King's widow, Coretta, and offered to help (the Kennedy organization arranged to fly King's body back to Atlanta), but he did not appear to mourn. "I didn't get any clear feeling of deep emotion on his part. I really didn't, and it surprised me," said Don Wilson, a former *Life* magazine bureau chief and JFK administration official who was coordinating the campaign's advertising. The relationship between RFK and the civil rights leader had never been close. King had come to respect Kennedy and intended eventually to support him for president. But Kennedy still "made a face" when he was asked to defend King, said Frank Mankiewicz. Peter Edelman thought that RFK was "guilty over the wiretapping" and "didn't entirely trust" King.

More than sadness, King's death seemed to have aroused old fears in Kennedy. That night he wandered the halls of his hotel in Indianapolis, the Marriott (dubbed "the Marat/Sade" by Walinsky because staffers were tortured by phones always conking out). He stopped in at Walinsky's and Greenfield's hotel room, ostensibly to check on their speech for the next morning, but really to have some company. For the first time in the hearing of any staffer, he mentioned the name of his brother's assassin, Lee Harvey Oswald. He called him "Harvey Lee Oswald," just as the gunman had been misidentified in the first radio reports from Dallas. Greenfield realized that the name had frozen, at that moment, in Kennedy's brain. Sometime later, a sleepless, restless Kennedy knocked on the door of Joan Braden, an old friend who had worked on JFK's '60 campaign and had come to Indiana to help with RFK's effort. Braden was one of the women Kennedy liked to flirt with and, from time to time, confide in. On this night, according to Braden, he apparently revealed his true fear. "Joanie," he said, "that could have been me." At about 3 a.m., he returned to Greenfield's room and tucked in the young speechwriter. "You're not so ruthless," said Greenfield. "Don't tell anyone," said Kennedy.

The inner cities blew up on the night King died: riots in 110 cities (but not Indianapolis), 39 deaths, more than 2,500 injured. When Kennedy flew into Washington the next evening, he could see the smoke rising from the burned-out buildings along 14th Street. He wanted to walk the streets, but his aides argued against "grandstanding." He went anyway. Kennedy flew to King's funeral in Atlanta, and the night before endured hours of verbal abuse from various black civil rights leaders and celebrities, complaining about injustice and white oppression. He was used to it and listened in stoic silence. At about 1 a.m., John Lewis, a King disciple and veteran of many marches and beatings, took RFK and Ethel into the darkened church to view King's body. Kennedy wordlessly crossed himself. In the morning, he marched in the funeral procession. ("I said to myself, well, we still have Robert Kennedy," Lewis recalled.) To Karl Fleming, a *Newsweek* correspondent who watched RFK trudging along, slight and hunched in the heat, he seemed "defeated and quiet, quiet, quiet." But outside the church, he had quizzed Allard Lowenstein at length about King, saying he was sorry that he had never really known him. Kennedy was "surprised," recalled Lowenstein, to hear that King had a sense of humor.

King's assassination seemed to make Kennedy even more willful about ignoring threats against his own life. In Lansing, Michigan, one week after King was shot to death, police informed Kennedy's staff that a man had been seen on a rooftop holding a gun. Fred Dutton pulled the blinds in Kennedy's hotel room. "Don't close them," Kennedy instructed. "If they're going to shoot, they'll shoot." Dutton managed to hustle Kennedy out through the garage, but as the limousine sped past the front of the hotel Kennedy ordered, "Stop the car." Deliberately, he stepped out onto the open sidewalk and worked the crowd for several minutes. Fear hung over Kennedy's aides and the traveling press. "It stayed on our minds that Spring," recalled John Bartlow Martin. Kennedy's security was clearly inadequate. His bodyguard, former FBI agent Bill Barry, carried a gun, but Kennedy was always perched atop convertibles and reaching into crowds, no matter how hostile they seemed. Dutton, Dolan, and others often talked of beefing up the number of guards or at least riding in cars with roofs, but the candidate was resistant. (Barry eventually hired some plainclothesmen and didn't tell RFK.) "We're not going to start ducking now," Kennedy told Dutton. In his daybook, he quoted Camus: "Knowing that you are going to die is nothing."*

---

* Kennedy was also afraid of flying, especially in the rattletrap charters and single-engine puddle jumpers used by the campaign. Johnny Apple of the *New York Times* watched Kennedy's knuckles whiten as he gripped the armrest on takeoff. As usual, black humor was RFK's defense. After one aborted takeoff, Kennedy got on the P.A. system and announced to the reporters and staffers on the plane that, in the event of a fatal

For the first three weeks of April, Kennedy crisscrossed the country, drawing huge throngs, trying to prove his popularity to the bosses who controlled
the Democratic convention. "The crowds were savage," recalled John Bartlow
Martin, who was traveling with him as an adviser. "They pulled his cufflinks
off, tore his clothes, tore ours. In bigger towns, with bigger crowds, it was
frightening." In Kalamazoo, Michigan, a housewife reached in the car and
calmly removed Kennedy's right shoe, which she displayed to reporters as a
trophy of war. Kneeling on the seat of the car, his arms around Kennedy's waist
as the convertible inched along, Bill Barry desperately clung to the candidate as
the crowds grabbed at him. "Not so tight," Kennedy was heard to cry. "You're
going to break my back." Barry's knees were bloody; Ethel gave him a rubber
kneepad. One over-heated woman yanked Kennedy's head down by his tie; another pulled him out of the car altogether, breaking his tooth on the curb.
Kennedy's shyness would seize him at the beginning of a motorcade or mass
rally. He would grimace, tight-lipped, before plunging into a crowd—the same
grim face he wore before diving into icy rapids. As the crowd closed in around
him, he would just let his body go limp. "It was like he wasn't there," observed
Peter Fishbein, a young aide who traveled with the candidate. "His stare was
vacant." Once, when their car was nearly rolled by a wildly impassioned crowd
in California, Fishbein looked at Kennedy, who was limply waving and looking
far away. "Even for him, it could be scary," said Fishbein.

At the same time, Kennedy seemed to want and need to be touched. He
managed to find moments of communion in the hurly-burly. If he saw someone in a wheelchair, he would stop the motorcade—fifteen or twenty cars—and
get out to talk quietly to the disabled person. He did this so often that after a
while the cameramen stopped filming the event. He loved the children who ran
or bicycled alongside his car, squealing with glee. In Gary, Indiana, he scooped
up a ten-year-old boy and his four-year-old sister to ride with him. After a
stretch, he commanded his car to pull out of the motorcade and drive to the
children's home, a small frame house. He got out and sat on the porch, sipping
ice tea with their mother, while the motorcade waited. Kennedy exasperated his
schedulers by insisting on stumping on Indian reservations. "Why the hell are
we spending so much time with the Indians?" Dutton finally demanded.
Kennedy just glared at him.

During these weeks, Kennedy did find his voice. He toned down his rhetoric and settled on a theme of unity and reconciliation. He knew that his first primary test—in Indiana on May 7—would severely challenge his abilities as
peacemaker and coalition-builder. The midwestern state was conservative—
the Ku Klux Klan had been active in its southern counties—and suspicious of
outsiders. Kennedy regarded Indiana as "my West Virginia," the primary election that would make or end his campaign, just as West Virginia had for JFK in
1960. He had to beat not only McCarthy but also the LBJ/Hubert Humphrey
stand-in, Governor Roger Branigan, a favorite-son candidate who was popular

---

crash, he wanted to remind them that only his name would be in the headline. Everyone
else's would be down in the fine print.

and well organized. Kennedy's local guide was John Bartlow Martin, a well-known writer, former Stevenson aide, and native Hoosier. Martin had clear ideas about what Kennedy should and shouldn't do to win over voters who, by and large, regarded RFK as a "whippersnapper." In his journal Martin wrote:

> I thought that so far Kennedy had gone to too many universities in Indiana and had had too many mob scenes with youngsters scream-ing and tearing his clothes off. I thought that the ordinary Hoosier at home watching TV was sick of scenes of violence in Vietnam, or riot-ing in the cities after King was killed, and kids pulling Kennedy's clothes off. McCarthy on the other hand was running a low-keyed soft-spoken campaign which, while not ordinarily properly pitched at Indiana, might be effective by contrast with Kennedy's. Kennedy was too exciting. The people, I thought, did not want to be excited.

Kennedy did not rebuff Martin's counsel. "I have to stop looking like Frank Sinatra running for president," he conceded. In order to win the "back-lash vote," Martin urged Kennedy to run as a law-and-order candidate, re-minding people that he had been the nation's "chief law enforcement officer." Kennedy nodded. "I can go pretty far in that direction," he said. "That doesn't bother me." It bothered Kennedy's young aides, however. When Kennedy began pitching "law and order" on his Indiana campaign stops, Walinsky, Greenfield, and Edelman agonized back at headquarters. The impetuous Walin-sky would call out to Dutton with the candidate and say, "Well, Fred, he did it again." Dutton would temporize, "We have to get past Indiana," and Walinsky would seethe, "The whole nation is watching." Walinsky's more temperate col-league, Peter Edelman, recalled that these dustups "happened every morning, like clockwork." Walinsky and the others started writing limericks about how RFK had signed up with the KKK. The liberal-minded *New York Times* accused Kennedy of swinging right and, by implication, selling out.

The criticism was unfair. Kennedy did change his emphasis depending on his audience, stressing law and order with "backlash voters" and justice with inner-city blacks. Pleas for racial integration were notably absent from his speeches. He had not lost faith in integration as a tool of improving the for-tunes of blacks, but he made a "tactical" decision, said Edelman, not to alienate white blue-collar voters who were fearful of changing neighborhoods. Still, he challenged white middle-class audiences not to turn away from the problems of the poor, and he began to talk about fresh approaches to poverty, like pro-moting free enterprise over Big Government as the best hope for rebuilding the cities. These were ideas he truly believed in and had tried to put into effect in Bedford-Stuyvesant. If he sounded conservative on these matters, it was be-cause he was more conservative than his liberal advisers wished to believe. And, as usual, Kennedy positively delighted in baiting voters he found too smug.

On April 26, Kennedy spoke to an audience of medical students and doctors at the University of Indiana. His hands were shaking as he gripped the podium. His knuckles showed white, and his fingers played nervously along the fluted pedestal. He was visibly suffering from the flu. "He was in pain performing, and it was painful to see, like watching tics in a palsy ward," observed Peter Goldman, a *Newsweek* writer standing in the crowd. The students, almost all white and middle class, looking forward to prosperous careers, challenged Kennedy on his plan to provide more health care for the poor. "Where are you going to get all the money for these federally subsidized programs you're talking about?" one of the students demanded.

"From you," Kennedy replied. There were boos and hisses, but Kennedy hung in, quoting Camus on their duty to reduce the number of children who suffer: "If you do not do this, who will do this?" Just as a few in the crowd began to clap, Kennedy taunted them some more: "You sit here as white medical students, while black people carry the burden of the fighting in Vietnam." By the time he was done, Kennedy won grudging, but respectful applause.

He often gave ho-hum speeches and then came alive in the question-and-answer sessions. At a businessman's lunch in Vincennes, he talked about starving children. While his conservative audience listened unmoved, he trotted out one of his favorite statistics: "Do you know there are more rats than people in New York City?" Believing that rodents and New Yorkers shared many traits, a few of the locals began to chuckle. Kennedy froze. *"Don't . . . laugh,"* he commanded. The room grew silent.

Though Martin tried to steer Kennedy towards more middle-class concerns, he came to appreciate Kennedy's dogged attention to the poor, and began to notice that Kennedy's audiences did too:

> He went yammering around Indiana about the poor whites of Appalachia and the starving Indians who committed suicide on the reservations and the jobless Negroes in the distant great cities, and half the Hoosiers didn't have any idea what he was talking about; but he plodded ahead stubbornly, making them listen, maybe even making some of them care, by the sheer power of his own caring. Indiana people are not generous nor sympathetic; they are hard and hard-hearted, not warm and generous; but he must have touched something in them, pushed a button somewhere. He alone did it.

Some of Kennedy's appeal was ineffable, a matter of body language and emanations. One is struck, listening to scratchy recordings of Kennedy's speeches, how deeply mournful he sounded. Martin described Kennedy's strangely captivating aura of frailty, urgency, and humility:

> He always looked so alone, too, standing up by himself on the lid of the trunk of his convertible—so alone, so vulnerable, so fragile, you feared he might break. He was thin. He did not chop the air with his hand as his brother Jack had; instead he had a little gesture with his

right hand, his fist closed, the thumb sticking up a little, and he [would] jab with it to make a point. When he got applause, he did not smile at the crowd, pleased; instead, he looked down, down at the ground or at his speech, and waited till they had finished, then went on. He could take a bland generality and deliver it with such a depth of feeling that it cut like a knife. Everything he said had an edge to it.

Kennedy's edginess was effective with voters standing in a crowd, feeling his vulnerability and empathy. It was less appealing over television or radio. Kennedy in a surging crowd was too hot for the cool medium. Gene McCarthy, by contrast, had a languid, slightly professorial manner that was appealing to voters frightened by hyper-charged times. McCarthy, better than Kennedy, instinctively understood how to use TV and radio. He knew how to take advantage of "free media," making himself available for TV and radio interviews—sometimes just by showing up at the studio. Kennedy could fire up 1,200 people in a sweaty hall—and turn off ten times that many watching a ten-second film clip on the evening news. McCarthy didn't bother with showy and exhausting rallies, but, with his offhand sound bites, he could appeal to thousands and sometimes millions of voters over the airwaves. "Suddenly," wrote David Halberstam, "the Kennedy camp realized what had happened. There would be two minutes on television each night of Robert Kennedy being mauled, losing his shoes, and then there would be fifteen *free*—that was painful—minutes of Gene McCarthy talking leisurely and seriously about the issues."

Kennedy's "new politics" of the street looked outmoded compared to McCarthy's coolly limpid TV presence. Even the Kennedy campaign's clever advance work backfired. The favorite tricks of legendary advance man Jerry Bruno—packing too-small auditoriums, leading motorcades down narrow streets—would have worked to create the appearance of excitement for a worthy but dull candidate. But for Kennedy, who could (and did) transform sleeping villages into jumping mobs at midnight, Bruno's pyrotechnics were counterproductive. John Bartlow Martin tried to slow down the Kennedy machine—he vetoed the use of helicopters, saying they made the campaign look like an airborne assault in Vietnam. There was again talk of actively seeking smaller crowds—or intentionally boring them—but Kennedy couldn't help himself. "He wanted big crowds, and he was mad if he didn't get them," said Dutton. When RFK's speech was purposefully bland, he would mischievously stir up the crowd with wisecracks and provocations.

Kennedy fed off forces that could not be easily restrained and controlled. A few days before the Indiana primary, he went back to the District of Columbia, which was also holding a primary on May 7, and spent a day cruising the riot-torn streets. The mostly black crowds were so agitated they almost tipped over his car. On the plane back to Indiana, a shaken *Newsweek* reporter, Jayne Ikard, told Ted Sorensen, "You've got to turn it down." Sorensen, who had been the last holdout against running, just looked mournfully at her. "We can't," he said. "It's too late."

Taught public relations at his father's knee, Robert Kennedy, like all Kennedys, demanded close control over his public image. The campaign had a big and very expensive "paid media" apparatus to produce political ads. Money seemed to be no object: the campaign was spending about $1 million a week, more than any other political campaign up to that time. Don Wilson, the Time-Life man hired to oversee advertising and PR, later described his operation candidly as "very uncoordinated and pretty fouled up, really." Kennedy was chronically dissatisfied with his image makers, recalled Wilson. He hated his campaign poster, which, he complained, made him look "like the guitar player in a high school rock-and-roll band." (He was right; David Halberstam described the image as "both boyish and surly boyish.") Kennedy's answer to unsatisfactory media advisers was to hire more of them. At one time, Kennedy had the Papert advertising firm of New York, independent filmmakers Bill Wilson, Charles Guggenheim and George Stevens, and Richard Goodwin (who was trying his brilliant but novice hand at TV) all shooting and cutting film of one kind or another. "We spent money like water," recalled Gwirtzman. Kennedy was hard clay to mold. Though generally not camera shy, he froze up when reading a prepared text. Hollywood director John Frankenheimer (*The Manchurian Candidate, Seven Days in May*) was brought in to work with him. "He was very tense, rigid. I kept telling him, easy, easy, easy, just talk, don't give a speech," recalled Frankenheimer. "He said, 'I'm a lousy actor,'" Kennedy's dignity warred with his practicality. He understood the importance of good political ads, "but he was a little embarrassed by them," recalled Dutton.

As a boss Kennedy could be harsh. "These speeches are boring," he would tell young Greenfield, who learned not to wait for compliments. Martin was at first taken aback by Kennedy's mocking, almost derisive manner. At a meeting of all his advisers at Hickory Hill in April, RFK curled up on a couch, a small and almost childlike figure, while the competing egos jostled around him, loudly debating various subjects. But when he spoke up to render a decision, said Martin, "that ended it." Kennedy did not like formal meetings and had few. The BBC wanted to film a staff meeting, so there was one—and never another. Impervious to distinctions between the "old" politics of the back room and the "new" politics of the street, Kennedy demanded both. He wanted idealistic social activists and old-time fixers under his tent, though with his penchant for compartmentalizing, he usually did not tell one about the other. Sideswipes, and sometimes head-on crashes, were unavoidable. Dun Gifford, Ted Kennedy's aide, recalled a "steady, slow burn" between Kenny O'Donnell and Larry O'Brien (who had quit the Johnson administration to rejoin the Irish mafia) on the one hand and poor people's groups like Operation Breadbasket, Jesse Jackson's anti-poverty organization that was loosely allied with the Kennedy campaign. O'Donnell and O'Brien were trying to cultivate big-city mayors in New Jersey, Illinois (with special emphasis on Daley), and Ohio. According to Gifford, O'Donnell's staffers would call in the anti-poverty activists such as Jackson and say, "Would you please get those poor people out of the mayor's office because we're going to lose every fucking delegate vote in the state if you don't."

As always, the Kennedy family poured into the breach. RFK's sisters, Jean Smith and Eunice Shriver, revived the Kennedy tradition of ladies' teas. The teas may not have had quite the social cachet they enjoyed in JFK's early congressional campaigns, when they were seen as proof that Irish Catholics had arrived, but the Kennedy women had an aura of glamour that was attractive to suburban housewives. Even Stanislaw Radziwill, the former husband of Jackie's sister, Lee, came to Indiana to appeal to the Poles of northwest Indiana. He arrived well liquored and demanded an enormous hotel suite, but he was surprisingly effective as a speaker and crowd pleaser. Also in Kennedy campaign fashion, hotel bills were not always paid; many of the campaign bills were later settled at ten cents on the dollar.

Absent from the family road show was Jacqueline Kennedy. She had never liked campaigning even for her husband, and she was especially sensitive about her privacy by 1968. Upset by the violence of American culture, she was contemplating marriage to Greek shipowner Aristotle Onassis, in part as a way to insulate her children on a Greek island fortress. RFK was not happy about Jackie's friendship with Onassis and reportedly asked her to hold off marrying the Greek tycoon. But Jackie still felt enormous affection for RFK and worried that he would drive himself too hard. She sent a recipe for health-food milk shakes, full of nuts and grains, to keep his energy high. According to Fred Dutton, he drank "a couple" and went back to ice cream.

The other Kennedy missing from the campaign trail was JFK. Robert Kennedy never invoked his brother's name. "It would have been totally out of character," said Joe Dolan. "He did not want to trade off JFK's memory." Kennedy was painfully aware that some voters still turned out hoping to see JFK reincarnated in RFK. And he knew that the Kennedy myth, which he had done so much to enshrine, was politically useful, that it would win him votes. But he was much too proud, too determined to be recognized in his own right, to explicitly capitalize on his brother's memory by comparing himself in some way to the late president.

Though in some ways softened since his days as his brother's enforcer, Kennedy had not lost his zest for covert operations. The campaign used small payoffs to win votes in the black inner city and in white ethnic neighborhoods. The going rate was $25 per district leader, recalled Richard Wade, Kennedy's campaign organizer in Gary, but the local machine of Mayor Richard Hatcher tried to hold the price down to $15. Making such payments—"walking-around money"—was common practice in most urban elections. McCarthy's campaign was more scrupulous in Indiana, but partly because it had blown most of its campaign chest in Wisconsin. McCarthy was the recipient of "Stop Kennedy" money from the unions. Kennedy's old investigator, Walter Sheridan, resumed his familiar role of following the money; in Nebraska, the next primary state, he followed some of McCarthy's right back to a Teamster-controlled bank.* From the '60 JFK campaign, Boston Irish ward heelers fanned

---

* The Teamsters also apparently tried to buy peace with RFK. A Teamster leader came to Senator Edward Kennedy proposing that the Teamsters would give RFK $1 million

out across the country to build political organizations for the remaining primaries (Indiana, D.C., Nebraska, Oregon, South Dakota, California, New York). Inevitably, the ubiquitous Paul Corbin lurked, noisily, in the shadows. Using a pseudonym (he posed as a retired military officer), he barged into California to prepare for the winner-take-all showdown there on June 4. Corbin's typically devious game plan: to hire scrofulous-looking hippies to cheer for McCarthy in a bid to antagonize middle-class voters. Corbin instructed them to stare straight into the camera and snarl, "I *hate* Kennedy."

If Kennedy did not win in Indiana, there would be no need for far-flung secret agents. Kennedy wanted not only to defeat McCarthy, but to crush him, drive him out of the race. Hubert Humphrey could afford to essentially ignore the primaries. He had inherited Johnson's delegate base and enjoyed the formidable support of Big Labor. Kennedy, on the other hand, had to win everywhere and overwhelmingly. He could not afford to split up the remaining delegates with McCarthy and still be able to argue to the bosses that he was an unbeatable force.

On election night in the Hoosier state, May 7, the early returns were encouraging. The industrial city of Gary, with its large minority population, had gone heavily for Kennedy. With what Jack Newfield described as her "primitive honesty," Ethel exclaimed, "Don't you just wish that everyone was black?" The giddiness soon ebbed. Watching TV in his suite, Kennedy saw his percentage of the vote begin to dip—from 54 percent to 48 percent. He made a child's face and said, "Eecch." When ABC's Frank McGee, an Indiana native, announced that "Kennedy is not doing as well as expected," Kennedy replied to the TV set, "Not as well as *you* expected." Shortly after nine, the final returns flooded in: 42 percent for Kennedy, 31 percent for Governor Branigan, and 27 percent for McCarthy. A solid win, but not the knockout blow Kennedy had hoped for. Interviewed on TV, McCarthy laid on the nonchalance a little thick: he breezily remarked that it didn't really matter who finished first, second, or third. "That's not what my father told me," said Kennedy. (Kennedy called his father two or three times a week, to engage in gentle, animated, one-sided conversations with the stricken patriarch, who could only grunt "no.")

Kennedy's admiring press corps created the impression after Indiana that RFK had managed to forge a coalition of have-nots by winning both the black vote and the so-called backlash vote, blue-collar ethnics angry at '60s liberalism and fearful of racial unrest. A particularly influential column by Robert Novak and RFK's friend Rowland Evans declared "Kennedy's Indiana Victory Proves His Appeal Defuses Backlash Voting." The column noted that in Gary, "while Negro precincts were delivering around 90 percent for Kennedy, he was running 2 to 1 ahead in some Polish districts." Some later scholars have portrayed

---

and help him at the polls—if RFK would agree to go along with the recommendation of the U.S. Parole Board to shorten Jimmy Hoffa's prison sentence. Sitting in his bath at the end of the day, RFK told brother Ted, "Well, you tell so and so, that if I get to be president, then Jimmy Hoffa will never get out of jail and there will be a lot more of them in jail."

Kennedy's success with the backlash vote as a myth. They point to an over-looked analysis of the Indiana voting returns by Kennedy's own aides, vanden Heuvel and Gwirtzman, in their 1970 RFK biography, *On His Own,* which points out that RFK lost fifty-nine of the seventy white precincts in Gary. The evidence of RFK's appeal to lower-income and ethnic white voters is actually mixed. Another survey shows that Kennedy did carry the seven largest counties where Alabama governor George Wallace had run strongest in 1964, while Kennedy's own internal polls showed him faring well among most ethnic voters. Kennedy may have lost most of the white precincts of Gary, where racial tensions ran high, but throughout Indiana he still drew fervent crowds—black and white—in poor industrial areas. No wonder the reporters who traveled with Kennedy were impressed that a white candidate could be wildly cheered by angry blacks, then cheered with equal enthusiasm by blue-collar whites who professed to hate the blacks.

Kennedy had to win over another naturally wary group in his next primary a week later, in Nebraska. He was remarkably successful with hardscrabble farmers. There was a kind of sweetness to Kennedy's Nebraska campaign in the second week of May. Whistle-stopping by train, he used whimsical, self-deprecating humor that made plainspoken prairie folk laugh and banter back. He would joke that he came from the "great farm state of New York," and when a gust of wind blew away a piece of paper on which he had scribbled some notes, he quipped, "There goes my farm program." In Crete, Nebraska (population 3,546), he told a crowd of a thousand, "You probably wonder why I come to Crete. When I was trying to make up my mind whether to run for president I discussed it with my wife, and she said I should, because then I could get to Nebraska. So I said why should I get to Nebraska and she said, 'Because then you might have a chance to visit Crete!' " The crowd clapped and cheered. "All those who believe that, raise their hands," he said. All the kids did, and their parents laughed. It was corny, and it might have been condescending coming from a different political figure. But Kennedy so clearly liked the people he met, so obviously shared their hopes, that many were moved.

So were the reporters who traveled with Kennedy. The candidate could be defensive and thin-skinned, to be sure. He demanded a strict off-the-record rule on the plane and was furious when a reporter broke it to reveal Kennedy's use of sign language to save his hoarse voice. The reporter described Kennedy outlining an S with his finger to order a Scotch whiskey. Kennedy, who drank relatively little, either at home or aboard a campaign plane that fairly sloshed with alcohol (stewardesses served reporters and campaign aides their "usuals" all through the day and night), wanted to maintain an image of moral purity. Yet he was willing to allow trustworthy reporters to see him literally undress. Warren Rogers of *Look* magazine was routinely allowed to follow RFK into his hotel room, where the candidate would unself-consciously strip off his clothes, lie down on the bed, begin eating ice cream (chased with beer), and make phone calls. As he made the calls to various party leaders asking their support, RFK would make childlike faces of boredom or disgust at Rogers. Kennedy would close his eyes and wrinkle his nose like a little boy being given a dose of castor oil. The communication between candidate and reporter was sometimes entirely nonverbal. "I never covered a guy who would say *nothing* to you. Most politicians can't stop talking. If Kennedy didn't want to answer your question, he'd just stare silently at you," said Rogers.

Kennedy had a way of revealing himself, sometimes in unintentional but human ways, that was seductive to even the most hard-bitten press hounds. The experience of Richard Harwood of the *Washington Post* is illustrative. Harwood had started off on the wrong foot, as far as the Kennedys were concerned, by accusing RFK of demagoguery on his first campaign swing. On election day in Indiana, Harwood had played a ferocious game of touch football against RFK. A former marine and a good athlete, the *Post* reporter had beaten Kennedy for the winning touchdown. Kennedy had egregiously fouled Harwood on the play, clawing at his face before he caught the ball. Harwood blew up, calling the senator a "lousy player and a dirty one, too." So that afternoon, he was surprised to be invited by Ethel to join the Kennedys for drinks and to watch the returns. Suddenly, he found himself allowed in the inner circle, taken into confidence, made almost a family member. He was hardly the only newsman so treated. When Harwood arrived at Kennedy's suite that night of the Indiana primary, he found that Hays Gorey of *Time* had been invited as well. They knocked on the door. None other than Theodore H. White, the famous *Making of the President* chronicler, opened up and looked skeptically at his colleagues from the fourth estate. "No press," said White, who apparently had come to regard himself as something grander and more privileged. Harwood and Gorey pushed past White and entered the sanctum.

Harwood's treatment followed an old Kennedy pattern: the closed fist followed by the open hand. Harwood was no dupe. But drawn into Kennedy's world over the next month, joked with, asked for advice, made privy to the candidate's doubts, Harwood gradually dropped his newsman's reserve and lost his objectivity. On the day of the California primary, Harwood called his editor in Washington, Ben Bradlee, and asked to be taken off the Kennedy campaign. "I'm falling in love with this guy," the tough-guy reporter confessed.

Kennedy won convincingly in Nebraska, with 51.4 percent of the vote to McCarthy's 31 percent. Again McCarthy airily dismissed the results, "I don't think I have to win all [of the primaries]. Losing one or two doesn't make all that difference." McCarthy knew he was in much better shape in the next contest, in Oregon a week later. Kennedy's moment of realization may have come when one of his strategists reported back on an exchange with Congresswoman Edith Green, who was helping to run the Kennedy campaign in her home state. "Have we got the ghettoes organized?" the strategist asked. Mrs. Green, a bit indignant: "There are no ghettoes in Oregon." There were hardly any blacks—about one percent of the population. Oregon is "one giant suburb," Kennedy lamented. He worried to columnist Joe Kraft as he flew into Portland in the third week of May. "It's all white Protestants. There's nothing for me to grab ahold of." There were, on the other hand, Teamsters organizers with bad memories of Kennedy's persecution of Jimmy Hoffa and many gun enthusiasts who regarded Kennedy's support for gun control as subversive. Kennedy's problems were exacerbated by a weak organization in Oregon. Back in 1960, Congresswoman Green, a prickly and territorial local chieftain, had not wanted RFK, whom she regarded with suspicion, to come to Oregon to campaign for his brother. Now she specifically banned from the state RFK's chief advance man, Jerry Bruno, who could be abrasive and had previously tangled with the formidable Mrs. Green. The one time Kennedy could have used some tricks to pep up the crowds, his chief magician was nowhere to be found.

Kennedy had another worry, a threat he had long awaited. Lyndon Johnson had been quiet through the primary season, publicly sworn to impartiality. He was not a great fan of Hubert Humphrey's, whom he regarded as weak. He actually preferred Republican Nelson Rockefeller, chiefly because he regarded Rockefeller as the best hope to "stop Bobby." For weeks, Kennedy's traveling companion, Fred Dutton, had been waiting for Johnson to strike, expecting to see his fingerprints on a scurrilous report about RFK. Dutton knew Johnson's ways from firsthand experience. In 1964, while Dutton was the congressional liaison at the State Department, President Johnson had requested Dutton to put together a file of derogatory information on Barry Goldwater, LBJ's Republican opponent in November. Dutton delivered a packet of information, mostly about Goldwater's intemperate remarks, to the Oval Office. Johnson thumbed through the information and complained, "There's nothing about Las Vegas [where Goldwater supposedly had ties to gambling interests] or Goldwater's girls."

Dutton knew that LBJ had long kept a file on Robert Kennedy. Indeed, Johnson had been in the Oval Office less than two months when his lieutenants began asking the FBI for more information about the Ellen Rometsch case. Johnson had always been restrained from using this information on the assumption, probably correct, that Kennedy was keeping a file on *him*. Still, there was always the risk that mutual deterrence would break down, and that Johnson would succumb to the temptation to start lobbing small bombshells into the Kennedy camp. The first hints that Johnson might be stirring began in the nationally syndicated columns of Drew Pearson, LBJ's hatchetman, in early May, just before the Indiana primary. On May 3, Pearson rehearsed RFK's reputation for ruthlessness, dredging up an old (and probably apocryphal) quote from Father Joe that "Bobby hates the way I do." On May 22 came an allegation that RFK had paid off a witness in one of the Hoffa cases. Then on May 24 came the column intended to do real damage: for the first time, Pearson revealed that RFK, as attorney general, had authorized wiretaps on Martin Luther King. The timing—the weekend before a primary in a state with a strong civil liberties tradition, ten days before the climactic California primary that would require a massive black turnout to secure victory for RFK—was clearly mischievous.

The column was apparently a setup, a straight feed from the Oval Office. "Drew got it from Lyndon," said Jack Anderson, the investigative reporter who was Pearson's chief legman. "Drew got me to confirm it with the FBI. Of course it was timed." The paper trail circumstantially supports Anderson's account: FBI files show a Johnson go-between first asking Cartha DeLoach, J. Edgar Hoover's top assistant for public affairs, about rumors that Kennedy had tapped King on May 17; a Drew Pearson meeting with Johnson on May 18; and DeLoach speaking to Johnson on May 23, the day before the column appeared.

It is clear from the column that Pearson and Anderson were shown FBI documents detailing Kennedy's role in first asking for the taps in July 1963 and then signing off on them in October. But the muckrakers made one small, sloppy mistake that the Kennedy defenders were able to seize upon to cloud the issue. At one point in the column, the word "bugging" was used. Wiretaps on phones are different from "bugs," electronic eavesdropping devices planted in a room. Hoover was careful to get Kennedy's permission on specific taps; bugging was done without informing the attorney general. Hoover had bugged *and* tapped King (bugs in his hotel rooms, taps on his phones), but only the taps were authorized by RFK.

Pearson called the Kennedy campaign for a response to the column on Thursday, May 23, just before it went to press. A very anxious Peter Edelman delivered the news to Kennedy, who seemed reasonably unperturbed. He told Edelman not to worry: "There'll be a lot of that," he predicted. "I was on the cover of *Time* and now [Time-Life founder Henry] Luce is turning over in his grave. It's not so bad." But Kennedy moved quickly to try to defuse the bomb. He called his wisest legal adviser, Burke Marshall, the former head of the civil rights division, who had gone on to work for Tom Watson at IBM. A brilliant Yale-educated lawyer, Marshall pounced on the columnists' careless use of the word "bugging." He dictated some very lawyerly talking points emphatically denying that Kennedy had ever permitted the FBI to "illegally bug" anyone, while allowing that "in cases affecting the national security" the attorney general did follow long-established precedent and sometimes authorize wiretaps.

Marshall's talking points were so cleverly drafted and so convincing of Kennedy's essential innocence that they fooled Kenendy's own staff. A Kennedy aide—it is not clear which one—wrote on them, "Dr. King was never the target of electronic surveillance of any sort. His loyalty to the United States has never been questioned." This was not true, of course. Kennedy tapped King to find out if he was under the influence of the Kremlin. But Kennedy made no effort to set the record straight with his own staff. He simply refused to talk about the King taps, except to complain that the article was "unfair." Kennedy would "tell you about A, B, and C," said Edelman, "but not D, E, and F." Fred Dutton was unable to get Kennedy to tell him anything about the wiretaps. "With Bobby and JFK," he recalled, "you could only go so far, and then they'd clam up." Scrambling to figure out what to say to the press, campaign spokesman Pierre Salinger fuzzed up matters even more. He told reporters that Kennedy had never approved electronic "eavesdropping." Does that include wiretaps? a reporter asked. Salinger fell back on Kennedy's generic defense that he authorized taps only in cases of national security.

Thoroughly muddled by this pettifoggery and confusion of euphemisms—and generally sympathetic to Kennedy—the political reporters did not follow up on the wiretapping story. But the campaign was concerned that Pearson's column, widely syndicated, would be passed around in black neighborhoods. Kennedy's strategists concocted a back-channel mission to gather intelligence from black civil rights leaders and to soothe any resentment. Through a friend of Steve Smith's who had good contacts in the National Football League, the campaign recruited Buddy Young, a black pro athlete (he had been a running back for the Baltimore Colts), to fly to Memphis, where King's old organization, the Southern Christian Leadership Conference, was holding a convention. Young met with the Reverend Ralph Abernathy, who had succeeded the fallen King as head of the SCLC. What was the reaction of black leaders to the news that RFK had wiretapped the martyred Dr. King? "It was no surprise to us," recalled Juanita Abernathy, the Reverend Abernathy's wife. "We knew the pressure that Bobby was under from the FBI. I'm not saying it [the taps on King] wasn't a shock. It was. But we understood that people"—meaning white politicians—"only supported us to a point. His [the Reverend Abernathy's] reaction was, sure it's true, but politics is politics." Inside the campaign, Kennedy's black organizer, John Lewis, who had been beaten and arrested many times marching for civil rights, was sad but philosophical. "It's like someone telling you that your wife is sleeping with someone else," he told Frank Mankiewicz. "You love her so much you don't want to hear about it."

Kennedy had another worry: that McCarthy would try to exploit the issue. Within a couple of days, the McCarthy campaign began airing radio spots with the voice of a black man saying, "I used to be for Robert Kennedy but then I learned about how he bugged my brother Martin Luther King's phone." Kennedy's relations with McCarthy had grown increasingly bitter. Kennedy was determined to ignore McCarthy. Slighted and resentful, McCarthy began to sharply mock Kennedy in his public remarks. Sure of his intellectual superiority, McCarthy was eager to debate Kennedy, confident that he would be at once more facile and substantive than Kennedy in a verbal sparring match.

Kennedy did not want to debate. In part, he was hewing to the well-established political maxim that front-runners can only lose by debating. But personal insecurity was also at work. He feared McCarthy's verbal facility and his own lack of it. Kennedy and McCarthy were not far apart on the issues, but McCarthy had ways to touch Kennedy's sore spots. McCarthy had repeatedly declared that he would fire J. Edgar Hoover. Kennedy had been notably silent on the subject. Asked at a California rally staged by a liberal women's group whether he would sack the FBI director, Kennedy paused for a long time and mumbled that the problem was the institution, not the man. He was just ducking: Kennedy dared not antagonize Hoover. He knew what was in those files.

Kennedy did not like to fear anyone. On Friday, May 24, the day Pearson's column appeared, he went for a walk on the beach with Ethel and his dog Freckles, who had accompanied him everywhere on the campaign. The day was gray and the water temperature was 53 degrees, but Kennedy wanted to go swimming. Stripping to his drawers, he plunged in. Oregonians, who never swam until August, were mystified. They thought he was showing off, not realizing that he was compensating—or just swimming.

That same day, McCarthy issued a statement saying that he had bought a half hour of TV time for a debate. Some of Kennedy's staffers strongly urged their candidate to accept the challenge. Kennedy was no longer the front-runner in Oregon; polls showed the race neck and neck. McCarthy's barbs were beginning to sting. The ringleader of the pro-debate faction was Adam Walinsky. On Saturday, he managed to win over at least a partial convert from within the JFK old guard, Larry O'Brien. The normally cautious O'Brien agreed to go talk to the candidate.

It was late Saturday afternoon. Exhausted as usual, Kennedy was trying to take a nap, though apparently not a restful one—Peter Edelman, standing outside in the hall, could hear Ethel speaking forcefully to her husband from inside the suite. O'Brien knocked on the door. Kennedy was in a testy mood. Earlier in the day, he had snapped at Edelman for being slow to fetch his shoes in the next room (Kennedy staffers were expected to be valets; one Kennedy aide found himself holding the head of one of Kennedy's dogs as it threw up out the car window). With O'Brien, Kennedy was short tempered. He blamed the old Irish hand for allowing himself to be conned by the rash Young Turks. Debating McCarthy was a bad idea, Kennedy insisted. He specifically brought up Pearson's wiretapping article. What if McCarthy started asking him about *that*? O'Brien didn't know what to say; Kennedy wouldn't even tell him if the charges were true. Out in the hallway, Kennedy began to hear a commotion. Walinsky, Edelman, and Jeff Greenfield, waiting outside to hear the results of O'Brien's mission, were chatting and laughing. Kennedy flung open the hotel door. Standing in his boxers, he exploded at the young staffers. All they ever did, he shouted, was play the guitar. (Walinsky liked to strum Beatles' songs on the plane.) If they had nothing better to do, he seethed, they should go ring doorbells. Shaken and upset, Walinsky started towards Kennedy to apologize. Kennedy slammed the door in his face.

Kennedy almost ran into McCarthy the next day. Both were looking for voters at the Portland zoo. Bill Barry spotted McCarthy's entourage about fifty yards away and whispered in Kennedy's ear. The candidate said, "Let's get out of here," and he and Barry ran for the candidate's car. In a terrible scene, recorded by TV cameramen, McCarthy supporters ran after them shouting, "Coward! Chicken!" Making the most of Kennedy's embarrassment, McCarthy calmly strolled over to the Kennedy press bus and invited the reporters to follow his campaign.

The next day, election day, Joe Dolan, Kennedy's faithful administrative assistant who had been handling scheduling for the campaign, walked by Kennedy's car. Kennedy leaned out and crooked his finger at Dolan. "I had been avoiding him," Dolan recalled. Kennedy looked Dolan in the eye. "You think I'm going to lose," he said. "I know you are," said Dolan. "We don't have blacks and Chicanos and we do have gun nuts."

Kennedy lost Oregon to McCarthy by six points, 44.7 percent to 38.8 percent. It was the first election ever lost by a son of Joe Kennedy (not counting JFK's first try for the Harvard Board of Overseers). Kennedy might have been crushed, but he was gracious in defeat. He took the blame on himself and congratulated McCarthy (something McCarthy had not done for him after RFK won in Indiana and Nebraska). Arriving at the airport in Los Angeles, Kennedy slid into the front seat of a car alongside his brother-in-law Steve Smith. They had a typically cryptic Kennedy conversation. "What do you think?" said RFK. "I think you're gonna win," said Smith. "But you gotta debate the guy."

CHAPTER **21** LEGEND

WHEN JOHN BARTLOW MARTIN had joined the Kennedy campaign in April, he was startled by Kennedy's worn visage. The brown-blond hair was turning gray, and the once-boyish face was deeply lined. "He really did not look young," Martin wrote. "He aged more than he should have since his brother's death." Kennedy's body was still hard from headlong exercise, but varicose veins protruded from his legs. At dinner, Ethel Kennedy counted out his pills, about a dozen in all, mostly vitamin pills and medication for his damaged voice. By California, Kennedy was taking a massive vitamin B_{12} shot every other day. He was existing on about four hours of sleep a night. Columnist Joe Kraft had "never seen him look so bad, so tired; his blue eyes were standing out really like a death's head from his skull."

Kennedy was forty-two years old. He kept his tan, and he could still be boyish in his manner and enthusiasms. But he was an old man. He had lived a lifetime, really several lifetimes, of hard stress, self-imposed and inflicted by almost constant conflict. As he entered the contest of his life, he was living on the edge of exhaustion.

He was worried about neglecting his family. At the end of April, while he and Ethel were campaigning in Indiana, his son David, age twelve, was picked up by police near Hickory Hill for throwing rocks at passing motorists. Troubled by his son's vandalism, Kennedy spoke to his friend, child psychiatrist Robert Coles. Why, he asked Coles, would his boy throw rocks? Because he wanted to hit someone, answered Coles. But why throw rocks at strangers? Kennedy asked. Because he can't throw them at someone else, Coles answered. "Bob's eyes widened," recalled Coles. "He realized that David, the smallest and most sensitive of the boys, was a little like him, throwing rocks at strangers—or LBJ." Kennedy understood that a consolation of losing the presidential race would be more time at Hickory Hill. "If I lose," he told reporters, "I'll go home and raise the next generation of Kennedys." With Joe Kraft, he recalled what his father had told him in the summer of 1961, when RFK had felt over-whelmed by the burdens of running the Justice Department and helping JFK deal with the Soviets in Berlin. "You may solve the Berlin crisis or you may not solve the Berlin crisis," said Joe Sr., "but nothing you do is as important as rais-ing your family."

Ethel Kennedy had become pregnant with their eleventh child that spring. Kennedy's mood, often irascible, improved when Ethel was on the plane. Marie Ridder, a Kennedy friend who was working for campaign chronicler Theodore H. White, recalled watching Bob and Ethel try to find a moment of privacy on the tarmac at the Indianapolis airport. Usually, the Kennedys were not physi-cally demonstrative with each other—"they were buddies, not lovey-dovey," said *Life* photographer Bill Eppridge—but Ethel was flying back to Washing-ton, and Kennedy seemed to want to hold on to her. "They were holding hands," Ridder recalled. "He was sorry to see her go."

Lonely in his crowd of liegemen, Kennedy looked for small escapes. In late May, he slipped off to director John Frankenheimer's Malibu beach house with some Hollywood glitterati, including Shirley MacLaine, Warren Beatty, Jean Seberg and Seberg's novelist husband, Romain Gary. Unable to leave Kennedy alone, Gary accosted him: "You know, don't you, that somebody is going to kill you?" Kennedy fended him off with fatalism. "That's the chance I have to take," he said. Privately, he nurtured his fears. In his desk drawer, he tucked away a quote from Keats: "While we are laughing, the seed of some trouble is put into the wide arable land of events, while we are laughing, it sprouts, it grows, and suddenly bears a poison fruit which we must pluck."

At moments, he would drop his guard and indulge in despair. After a long day of campaigning in Indiana, he had said to Richard Goodwin, "If I get to be president, what can I do anyway? With Congress and the press, what chance do I have to make basic changes?" He wanted to be his own man, yet inevitably, in low moments, he compared himself unfavorably to President Kennedy. After losing his audience with a flat, rambling speech one night in South Dakota, he gloomily told George McGovern, "I just am not Jack."

Yet these were exceptions. For the most part Kennedy carried on, drawing strength in the upturned faces, letting the crowd's adulation bathe him and in-vigorate him. Late at night, he sometimes came down to the hotel bar to have a drink with the photographers, quizzing them, wanting to know what they saw in the crowds, recalled *Life*'s Eppridge. "He wanted affirmation," said the vet-eran photographer. As ever, Robert Kennedy wanted to believe that the crowds were there for him and not his brother.

California, with its melting pot, was more congenial than Oregon. Arriv-ing in Los Angeles the morning after the Oregon primary, Kennedy stood in his convertible while it crept through teeming black and Mexican neighbor-hoods. The cuff links long gone, his shirt was torn and soaked with sweat by the time the motorcade hit downtown in a rain of Jerry Bruno–generated confetti. On a swing through the same neighborhoods ten days earlier, he had lost both his shoes. A British journalist observed "the hooded weariness disappear[ing] from his face." More than once, Kennedy told Dutton in the seat beside him, "These are my people." He was being truthful. There had not been since Lincoln, nor has there ever been again, a white national politician so embraced by people of color.

The hardheaded Dutton was worried about the people watching on TV— white middle-class voters in places like Orange County who feared rioting blacks and the influx of Mexicans. Dutton and scheduler Joe Dolan agreed: an absolute minimum of campaigning in poor black or Hispanic neighborhoods. Dolan canceled a motorcade through Venice when he learned that the neighborhood was mostly black. Kennedy was depending on heavy black and Hispanic turnout to beat McCarthy's affluent suburbanites on primary day, but the New Politics of the street were, momentarily at least, retired for the Old Politics of the back room. In San Francisco, John Seigenthaler, who had taken leave from editing the *Nashville Tennessean* to help rescue the Kennedy campaign in northern California, was paying black ministers to turn out their flocks. Assemblyman Willie Brown was helping him set the price. (In his journal, John Bartlow Martin recorded Seigenthaler's description of the bargaining process: Brown "told him [Seigenthaler] that a certain preacher was coming in and not to go a cent over $250. Seigenthaler started low, at $100, the preacher asked $500, and 'we came in right on the button, $250.' ") Jesse Unruh's local political operation counseled against buying black ministers too early, lest they have to be bought again.

Kennedy was kept far removed from these tawdry, if commonplace, transactions. He bridled at personal shakedowns. At a meeting set up to win over New York party leaders in May, a Queens Democratic boss brazenly demanded, "What's in it for me?" Kennedy started to explain that he could represent the interests of the state of New York better than the other presidential candidates, but the Queens pol persisted, "No, no, what's in it for me?" Kennedy's "face flushed, his muscles tightened," recalled John English, the Nassau County Democratic leader. English tried to escort the man out of the room before Kennedy took a swing, but Kennedy grabbed English by the arm, spun him around, and spat out, "Don't you make any deals with him!"

Kennedy continued to practice his own brand of back-channel diplomacy. An off-the-record meeting was arranged in Oakland with the so-called Black Caucus, a group of black community leaders, some self-appointed. Kennedy brought along astronaut John Glenn, warning him, "This isn't going to be pleasant." The blacks jeered and taunted Kennedy and his entourage. A tall man in flowing robes who called himself "Black Jesus" was particularly vituperative. He denounced two of the blacks traveling with Kennedy, Olympic decathlon champion Rafer Johnson and Assemblyman Brown, as "Technicolor Negroes" and RFK as a "white pig." Johnson was upset and ashamed, but Kennedy told him not to worry, that the blacks needed to be able to yell at someone. "He had tremendous tolerance for intolerance," Johnson remembered.

Kennedy's advisers were determined that the candidate be well prepared for the climactic and long-delayed debate with McCarthy, scheduled for Saturday night, June 1. The format would be a panel of three journalists asking questions. Kennedy was handed "about two pounds" of briefing material on Friday night. Sprawled on the bed with his dog Freckles, he fell right asleep. "Freckles probably got more out of it," Dutton said. Saturday was set aside for all-day debate prep. Tag teams of advisers briefed the candidate, who listened, but not always closely. His hotel suite in the Fairmont overlooked San Francisco Bay. The day was sun-drenched, the air sparkling clear. Kennedy's eyes kept wandering to the view out the window. Walinsky would look up from his thick briefing book and see Kennedy, dressed in a silk kimono, curled up at the end of the couch, surrounded by advisers but "floating almost all alone."

Kennedy dutifully rehearsed his answer to the question of whether he had wiretapped Martin Luther King. He planned to fudge: He had never authorized any bugging, he would say. He had approved wiretaps when the national security was threatened, but he never discussed specific cases. "That's not good enough," interjected Richard Goodwin. "It's the only answer they're going to get," Kennedy said. He got up and walked out of the room for a few minutes. "Next?" he said when he returned.

Fortunately for RFK, McCarthy had prepared for the nationally televised showdown by having a couple of drinks and reciting poetry with Robert Lowell. Kennedy's opponent was himself increasingly distracted. McCarthy's staffers despaired that their candidate had fallen into a clutch of journalists and artists they bitterly nicknamed "the astrologers." At the debate, McCarthy's coolness verged on indifference. One of the press questioners, Bill Lawrence of ABC, asked Kennedy about wiretapping King. Kennedy delivered "an obvious set piece" that was "scarcely convincing," reported the British team covering the campaign for the London *Sunday Times*. But McCarthy didn't bother to follow up. Kennedy got off one cheap shot: when McCarthy suggested that the ghettoes needed to be "dispersed," Kennedy interjected, "You say you are going to take ten thousand black people and move them into Orange County?" He wooed the Jewish vote by endorsing more arms for Israel, and later complained to his own aides that he had "pandered" to voters who continued to regard him as an anti-Semite. That day, an olive-skinned, bushy-haired Palestinian-American named Sirhan Sirhan, who had seen an earlier TV report of Kennedy wearing a yarmulke outside a synagogue, bought a box of ammunition for his .22-caliber pistol.

The overhyped debate was regarded as anticlimactic, "a mutually pedestrian performance," wrote David Halberstam. For Kennedy, a draw was a win: he had exceeded expectations. McCarthy "didn't do his homework," Kennedy said. The next day the absentee father took his kids (six of them had come out to California) to Disneyland, where they rode Pirates of the Caribbean. On Monday came the final, grueling push: Los Angeles to San Francisco, back to Long Beach and Watts, and down to San Diego, 1,200 miles and all three major California TV markets. On the plane back to Los Angeles, he recovered from his near collapse during his last speech in San Diego, but he was reaching the limit of his physical endurance.

Kennedy spent his last night with his family at John Frankenheimer's Malibu beach home. Primary day dawned gray. A chill fog hung over the windswept ocean. Kennedy went swimming and took his kids. Young David was knocked down by a crashing breaker and trapped by the undertow. Kennedy dove in after him. When Kennedy emerged, holding the frightened boy, both father and son were scraped and bruised from bouncing off the pebbly bottom.

After lunch, Kennedy slept, stretched out across two chairs by the pool. Richard Goodwin, casually glancing out to the terrace as he went to the buffet, froze when he saw Kennedy:

> His head [hung] limply over the chair frame; his unshaven face was deeply lined, and his lips slightly parted. There was no movement. I felt a sudden spasm of fear. But it swiftly receded. He was sleeping, only sleeping. God, I thought, reaching for the food, I suppose none of us will ever get over John Kennedy.

After eighty days of nearly nonstop movement, Kennedy could only rest and wait. Shortly after 3 p.m., the campaign learned the results of the first network "exit polls": Kennedy 49, McCarthy 41. There was relief, although not so much from the candidate, who wanted to break the 50 percent mark to erase the stain of Oregon. At 6:30 p.m., it was finally time to head back into Los Angeles, to the victory celebration at the Ambassador Hotel, and to be interviewed by the networks before voters in the East, three hours ahead, went to bed. Frankenheimer daubed Kennedy's scraped and bruised forehead with some actor's makeup and Kennedy put on a blue pin-striped suit and a white shirt that made him look dashing—presidential.

The Royal Suite at the Ambassador was a jolly, noisy cocktail party of the favored. There were entertainers and celebrities and authors and journalists, on their second and third drinks. Kennedy learned that he had that day won a primary in South Dakota—Humphrey's native state—by over 50 percent. He was happy about the results in an Indian precinct: 878 votes for him, 9 for a Humphrey-Johnson slate, 2 for McCarthy. "Did you hear about the Indians?" he asked reporters.

Kennedy had won four out of five primaries, and he was about to win a fifth, with the second-largest number of delegates. He was expected to win the largest, his home state of New York, two weeks later. The inevitability of Kennedy's triumph—at the Democratic convention in August and in the presidential election in November—has long since hardened into myth. Robert Kennedy himself was more realistic. As the victory party roared on towards midnight in the Royal Suite, the candidate summoned Goodwin into the bathroom, where they could talk privately about the formidable challenges ahead.

"I've got to get free of McCarthy," Kennedy said. Kennedy knew that there was a risk of being embarrassed in the Empire State. The peace movement was strong in New York, and so was resentment against Kennedy, who was regarded by many party regulars as an inattentive senator. Kennedy was confident of winning in New York, but he needed to win overwhelmingly. He didn't want to have to spend the next two weeks, he told Goodwin, "on every street corner in New York" trying to shore up his support. Vice President Humphrey, not McCarthy, was the man he had to beat. In June and July, Kennedy wanted to be on the road, he said, chasing "Hubert's ass all over the country." Larry O'Brien, a true pragmatist and the most reliable delegate counter, had told Kennedy that winning the nomination would be an uphill struggle. While Kennedy had been getting his cuff links torn off in close primary battles in mostly small states, Humphrey had been methodically lining up delegates in big states like New Jersey, Pennsylvania, and Ohio—enough to secure the nomination, unless Kennedy could somehow shake them free.

Unfortunately for Kennedy, McCarthy showed no signs of wanting to abandon the field to his rival. If anything, the senator from Minnesota was likely to stay in the race just to spite Kennedy, whom he had come to despise. The time had come, Kennedy understood, for some more Old Politics. He had an audacious deal in mind. Goodwin still had ties to McCarthy, who had been reasonably understanding when Goodwin quit his campaign to rejoin Kennedy in April. Standing in the bathroom as the revelers caroused outside, Kennedy whispered to Goodwin, "I think we should tell him if he withdraws now and supports me, I'll make him secretary of state."

This was the sort of realpolitik that Mayor Daley (or Joe Kennedy) would understand and approve of. Kennedy called the Chicago mayor sometime before midnight, when the networks were projecting Kennedy with more than 50 percent of the vote (the final total—Kennedy 46, McCarthy 42—turned out to be closer). Some of the Kennedy faithful later reported that Daley at least "hinted" that he would throw his support to Kennedy. Kenny O'Donnell later told colleagues that he had made a promise to "Da Mare" that the campaign would not go into Cook County in return for the "understanding" that Daley would be with Kennedy "when it mattered." But it would have been uncharacteristic for the shrewd and cautious Daley to commit himself until he had a better fix on the odds.

Kennedy was much too honest with himself to believe that he had sewn up the nomination. But he was alive, he had survived defeat in Oregon, and he had won in a huge state that was a true cross section of the nation. Blacks and Hispanics had turned out overwhelmingly for Kennedy, voting in much greater numbers than usual. He had lost the suburbs (and, despite his debate pander, Orange County), but he had generated tremendous crowds and momentum. Nineteen sixty-eight was not an ordinary year in any sense. If he could continue to draw fervent crowds—and start massaging the bosses— Kennedy believed he could win.

He was upbeat when he called Kenny O'Donnell, who was back in Washington. "You know, Kenny, I feel now for the first time that I've shaken off the shadow of my brother. I feel I made it on my own," he said, according to O'Donnell. Others, too, noticed that Kennedy seemed "liberated," as Jack Newfield put it. "He was witty, relaxed, in control," wrote Newfield. Kennedy was "puckish" that evening with Jules Witcover and Bob Healy of the *Boston Globe*, as "elated as either of us had seen him anytime during the campaign," recorded Witcover. Dick Goodwin wrote:

> The change in Kennedy was startling. The frantic sense of the early campaign, the harsh, punched lines, defensively seeking assurance in assertion and command of fact, were gone. There was now an easy grace, a strength that was unafraid of softness. For the first time since he had announced his candidacy, Robert Kennedy reminded me of his slain brother.

Goodwin, too, felt that Kennedy had been freed—first by defeat in Oregon, then by winning on his own in California. "He looked like a president," Goodwin wrote. "And once a man had begun to look like a president, he has doubled his chances to be one."

Perhaps. But there is a rosy haze of nostalgia over these accounts by men whose memoirs helped create the Kennedy legend. A different picture of Kennedy in his hour of triumph was painted by Warren Rogers, the *Look* magazine reporter who had been granted near-complete access by Kennedy for a Teddy White–like treatment "in words and pictures" of the campaign. Rogers described Kennedy pacing about the suite "like a caged panther.

> For a while, he would sit on his haunches in a corner, scrunched into the angle of the walls and floor like a child being punished, and the people there, all close friends, would go to him one or two at a time, bend over and chat. And then he would bound up, holding his victory cigar at an awkward, unpracticed angle. He would prowl in circles around the room, punching a fist into a palm and announcing, to no one in particular, over and over: "I'm going to get Humphrey. I'm going to *make* him debate me! I'm going to chase his ass all around the country. . . ."

Hardly a picture of command presence. Rogers—no Kennedy detractor, by a long shot—observed that it was unusual for Kennedy to use a word like "ass" except in private. The newsman figured Kennedy was just "uncertain about how he was going to cope with the enormous tasks that still lay ahead." Kennedy was right to be worried—and true to his character to show it. He would have been putting up a façade if he glided about the room coolly and wittily taking congratulations, the way his brother might have.

Robert Kennedy was not Jack Kennedy. But in an era of profound anxiety and disillusionment with politicians and all authority figures, Kennedy's questing, sensitive persona had the ring of truth. Kennedy's greatest

strength—his connection with voters and his hope to be the man for his confused time—came from the very qualities that were *not* presidential, at least in
the way John F. Kennedy projected leadership. John Bartlow Martin came closest to capturing these ineffable virtues and how they set RFK apart from JFK.
"They were very different men," Martin wrote.

> Jack Kennedy was more the politician, saying things publicly that he
> privately scoffed at. Robert Kennedy was more himself. Jack gave the
> impression of decisive leadership, the man with all the answers.
> Robert seemed more hesitant, less sure he was right, more tentative,
> more questioning, and completely honest about it. Leadership he
> showed; but it had a different quality, an off-trail unorthodox quality,
> to some extent a quality of searching for answers to hard questions in
> company with his bewildered audience, trying to work things out
> with their help.

Americans were afraid in 1968, and they eventually voted their fears and
elected Richard Nixon. But Kennedy offered them a different vision: of honest
courage, the willingness to face up to that which is most troubling—social unrest, racial inequality, war. His life and bearing showed a willingness to keep on
trying while knowing that real answers to hard problems are not easy and may
never be found. We will never know what kind of president Robert Kennedy
might have been. He might have been rash, he might have tried to do too much,
and he might have blundered. He would have pushed some ambitious programs, like national health care and a gargantuan jobs bill that might easily
have been blocked or badly distorted by lobbyists and lawmakers. While candid, Kennedy could also be canny—he had learned to be, to survive as an underdog. He probably would have been devious in some ways, and it is not
impossible to imagine him abusing the power of his office. But he would have
surely tried to tackle the problems of poverty and discrimination, and he would
have tried to end the killing in Vietnam long before President Nixon did. RFK
could be cautious, out of prudence, cunning, or fear. Possibly, the clash of politics, of trying to seek radical solutions in a country that was more conservative
than liberal in 1969, would have paralyzed Kennedy or made him more timid
in deeds than words. Failure, in a divided country in a confused time, was probably more likely than not. Nonetheless, Kennedy's life story suggests that had
he failed, he would have failed trying his utmost to lift up the poor and the
weak.

IT WAS JUST BEFORE MIDNIGHT, time to go down to the ballroom and declare victory. The sweltering crowd erupted, blaring, screaming at Kennedy and Ethel,
who looked "little-girlish in an orange and white mini-dress and white stockings," recorded Jules Witcover. Kennedy made the usual jokes, then became serious. He called on his countrymen to end "the divisions, the violence, the
disenchantment. . . ." Kennedy, who always told his children to "love our

country" and who hated the war but could never understand draft dodgers, was a deeply sentimental patriot. "We are a great country, an unselfish country, and a compassionate country," he said. To end the divisions, to restore the faith, were his reasons to run for the presidency. "So my thanks to all of you," he wound up, "and now it's on to Chicago, and let's win there."

Kennedy's devoted bodyguard, Bill Barry, moved to clear the way. But Kennedy, with Ethel behind, was boxed in by teenyboppers screaming, "We want Bobby! We want Bobby!" He veered in a different direction, led by the hotel maitre d', through a back entrance into a dark corridor. Seeing his charge diverted, Barry turned and began to push his way through the crowds.

In the passageway, members of the kitchen staff reached out to shake Kennedy's hand. Kennedy, smiling, turned around to look for Ethel. As he did, his assassin, the mentally unstable, unemployed drifter named Sirhan Sirhan, raised a snub-nosed pistol and opened fire. One bullet entered Kennedy's brain through the soft tissue behind the right ear—a chance shot. "Pop. . . . Pop, pop, pop, pop, pop. . . ." Sirhan sprayed bullets around the room. Kennedy threw up his hands to his face, staggered, and fell backwards to the concrete floor. People ducked and screamed. Barry caught up, too late. He lunged towards the assailant. Sirhan "was standing with the gun when I hit him," Barry later testified. "I hit him. I hit him with the edge of my hand. He dropped the gun on the table. . . . I swung him around and hit him twice with my fist, two rights high on the cheek. . . . When I hit him the second time, I knew I was going to kill him. So I put a stranglehold on him. Then I wanted to go back to the senator. . . ."

Barry left Sirhan struggling with Roosevelt Grier, the massive former lineman of the Los Angeles Rams, and knelt down beside Kennedy. He put his jacket under his head. "I knew immediately it was a .22, a small caliber, so I hoped it wouldn't be so bad, but then I saw the hole in the senator's head, and I knew."

Sirhan somehow squirmed free and grabbed the gun. A mob tore at him, shouting, "Get the gun! Get the gun!" "Kill him! Kill him!" "No, don't kill him!" Rafer Johnson finally peeled Sirhan's fingers off the shiny black revolver, as if he was peeling a grapefruit. Ethel, who had been yanked back to safety in the melee, emerged from the crowd and knelt beside her husband. "Oh my God," she whispered. She lightly stroked his face and chest. He seemed to turn his head slightly to look at her. "Is everybody else all right?" he whispered. The emergency crew arrived and lifted Kennedy onto a stretcher. "Gently, gently," said Ethel. Kennedy was heard to cry, "Oh, no, no, don't. . . ." Then he passed out, never to awaken.

Back in the ballroom, "an awful sound" rolled "like a moan," recalled Jack Newfield. A woman in a bright red party dress, sobbing uncontrollably, came by him, screaming, "No, God, no. It's happened again." The moan became a wail; it sounded as if, Newfield wrote, a hospital had been bombed: "the sound was somehow the sound of the twice wounded." Inside the corridor where Kennedy had been shot, someone had laid a rose on the bloody floor. A sign reading "The Once and Future King" hung on the wall. It had apparently been left there from some earlier function, but as the death watch began, so did the mythologizing.

All through the night and next day, Frank Mankiewicz delivered desultory progress reports on the surgery and condition of the patient, but few held out any real hope that he would live, or live as more than a vegetable. Inside the hospital room, Kennedy lay unconscious, wreathed in tubes and wires. His eyes were blackened, his face bruised, recalled his heartsick son Robert Jr. Brother Ted knelt at the foot of the bed, praying. Ethel lay beside her husband, as if she were dying, too. The flat line in the monitor showed that his brain had ceased to function, but his fierce heart beat on.

Kennedy was pronounced dead at 1:44 a.m., June 6, 1968, not quite twenty-six hours after he had been shot. At the White House, Lyndon Johnson was pacing, demanding, "I've got to know. Is he dead? Is he dead yet?" Johnson had apparently been pondering another assault on Kennedy's reputation. On Tuesday, June 4, he had written on a slip of paper, "Cosa Nostra. Ed Morgan. Send in to get Castro. Planning—." Ed Morgan was the lawyer for mobster Johnny Rosselli who first approached Drew Pearson with his sensational story about RFK's alleged assassination plots against Castro. As the voters went to the polls in California on June 4, it seems that Johnson was looking for skeletons that he might rattle at the Kennedy campaign. Johnson remained obsessed by the Kennedy administration's anti-Castro plotting. RFK had been "running a damned 'Murder Inc.' in the Caribbean," LBJ told a magazine writer in 1972.

Paranoid as ever about Kennedy's legacy, Johnson showed his worst side and questioned whether RFK was entitled to be buried at Arlington Cemetery. His advisers managed to convince the president that denying Kennedy a final resting place beside his brother was not only "cruel," writes Jeff Shesol, a chronicler of the Kennedy-Johnson feud, but "politically reckless." Kennedy was not accorded a state funeral, unless one considers the Kennedy family a sovereign state.

For two nights and a day, Kennedy's body lay in the vaulted nave of St. Patrick's Cathedral in New York. Lines of mourners snaked for twenty-five blocks outside the cathedral, waiting in the wilting heat to pass by his coffin. On Saturday morning, at a wonderfully eclectic and moving mass, his thousands of odd-lot friends, the entitled and disenfranchised alike, gathered in the cool dimness. Rose Kennedy arrived early and sat alone, lost in thought. She had heard the news of the shooting on the television on Wednesday morning as she arose to attend morning mass. A little later, a photographer had seen her in the driveway of the house at Hyannis Port, bouncing a ball like a small child. Inside the house, Joseph Kennedy had wept uncontrollably. He was too sick and disabled to come to his son's funeral.

Unable to find their seats in the cathedral, Cesar Chavez and a few farmworkers stood—directly in front of the congressional delegation, blocking their view (not deliberate, but "just such a nice touch," recalled Peter Edelman). The congregants listened to Leonard Bernstein conduct a Mahler symphony and

Andy Williams sing, slowly and with surprising majesty, Kennedy's favorite anthem, "The Battle Hymn of the Republic." Edward Kennedy rose and gave a simple and powerful eulogy. "My brother need not be idealized, or enlarged in death beyond what he was in life," Kennedy said. Rather, he should be

> Remembered simply as a good and decent man,
> who saw wrong and tried to right it
> saw suffering and tried to heal it
> saw war and tried to stop it.

His voice breaking slightly, the only surviving Kennedy brother ended with the quote, loosely borrowed from George Bernard Shaw, that RFK used to conclude his stump speeches:

> Some men see things as they are and say, "Why?" I dream of things that never were and say, "Why not?"

On Saturday afternoon, June 8, Kennedy's body, like President Lincoln's 103 years before, was carried by a funeral train from New York to Washington. As they had for Lincoln, many thousands—perhaps, for RFK, a million people—lined the tracks. The coffin, on a bier close to the floor of the observation car, could not be seen by bystanders. So Kennedy's pallbearers lifted it up and placed it, a bit precariously, on chairs. Along the route of the train, Boy Scouts and firemen braced at attention; nuns, some wearing dark glasses, stood witness; housewives wept. Thousands and thousands of black people waited quietly in the heat, perhaps because they lived close to the tracks, but also because they had felt for Kennedy, and knew they would miss him. "Marvelous crowds," said Arthur Schlesinger, staring out the window as the train slowly rocked south. "Yes," said Kenny O'Donnell. "But what are they good for now?"

Inside the score of railway cars carrying a disparate mélange of family, friends—real and would-be—celebrities and secretaries, true believers and hangers-on, grief was observed in manifold ways. The Catholics, Frank Mankiewicz said, drank and told funny and sentimental stories. The Protestants weren't quite sure what to do, except to vaguely disapprove of anyone having a good time. The Jews wept—"they'd have torn their clothes if they'd thought of it," recalled Mankiewicz. Carter Burden, Kennedy's young aide in the New York office, came down to the last car and glimpsed Ethel, alone with her slain husband. "It was the only moment, then or since, that I saw her cry," he recalled. "She sat there, immensely still, and hunched over in a plain, straight-backed chair. She had a rosary in her hands, and her head was resting against the casket."

She collected herself. She wanted to greet the other mourners and thank them for coming and for sharing her husband's life. Roosevelt Grier told her that the train stretched for twenty cars. It was stifling hot. Was she sure she wanted to go? "We're going to go," she said, and she did. So did the eldest Kennedy son, Joe, sixteen, flashing his father's toothy smile and remembering "Kennedys don't cry." Seeing the two of them, determinedly gracious, just about everybody else broke down.

The trip from New York to Washington, normally about four hours, took twice as long. Two bystanders who had jumped on the tracks in Elizabeth, New Jersey, were killed by a train passing in the other direction. The food ran out, the water ran out; finally, the liquor ran out. The thousand or so passengers stumbled off the train at Washington's Union Station shortly after 9 p.m., to the booming drums of the Navy Band.

Down Constitution Avenue, past the Justice Department . . . to the Lincoln Memorial, where everyone sang "The Battle Hymn of the Republic" one last time . . . across the bridge to Arlington National Cemetery. A light rain had stopped. The moon hung heavy and full over the Potomac. By candlelight and TV light, the weary pallbearers—old friends like David Hackett, trusted aides like John Seigenthaler, family champions like Steve Smith—hoisted the casket and stumbled up the hill to the knoll where John F. Kennedy lay buried. A gravesite had been chosen for Robert about thirty yards away.

When Robert had helped design JFK's grave, he had disagreed with his brother's widow. RFK wanted a plain white cross. Jackie desired a grander and more elegant memorial. Today, President Kennedy's grave spouts an eternal flame, and a massive black slab bears his name. On a sweeping curve of marble are carved the heroic words of John F. Kennedy's inaugural address, "Let the word go forth from this time and place . . . that the torch has been passed. . . ." Beyond lies the federal city and the great, glistening monuments to Lincoln and Washington.

Robert Kennedy's resting place is to the side, down a narrow alley shielded by some small trees. On a block of marble facing his grave are carved fragments of his two best speeches, his peroration from the Day of Affirmation speech to the South Africans ("Each time a man stands up for an ideal . . . he sends a tiny ripple of hope . . .") and the lesson from Aeschylus he delivered in a slum in Indianapolis on the day Martin Luther King was shot ("In our sleep, pain which cannot forget falls drop by drop upon the heart until, in our own despair . . . comes wisdom . . ."). A small, plain white cross stands by a stone slab inscribed with his name and the years of his birth and death. In contrast to the grandeur of JFK's grave, the effect is unadorned and a little lonely. One thinks of his struggle to overcome fear and wonders what, if he had lived, he might have done.

SOURCE NOTES

I have relied, in roughly equal measure, on interviews with RFK's associates and the written record from various books and archives. Both oral history and contemporaneous documents have limitations. People tend to remember stories they have told about events, not the events themselves. And documents often mislead (sometimes intentionally) or fail to tell the whole story. The scholar who relies on documents often misses the human element, the hidden motivations and attitudes that are so critical to the making of history; the journalist who relies on interviews can be "spun" or entertained with tales that are too good to be true. I don't pretend to have steered entirely clear of either pitfall. But I have tried to avoid hagiography and conspiracy theory by doubling back and reexamining both the written and oral record, imperfect as they are, for inconsistencies and mythmaking. These notes are heavily annotated. They seek to untangle—or at least present—ongoing debates over what really happened in RFK's life. I deal with the most critical questions—the factual debates that really affect the general reader's understanding of RFK's character—directly in the text. Other controversies—of interest more to historians and students of Kennedy's life and times—I hash out in the notes that follow.

Abbreviations Used in Source Notes

FRUS   U.S. Department of State, *Foreign Relations of the United States*. Washington, D.C.: U.S. Government Printing Office, 1961–1963

JFKL   John F. Kennedy Library, Boston

JPK Papers Joseph P. Kennedy Papers, John F. Kennedy Library

LBJL   Lyndon Baines Johnson Library, Austin, Texas

LOC   Library of Congress
NA   National Archives
NSA   National Security Archive, Washington, D.C.
NYT   *New York Times*
OH   Oral History
RK   Arthur Schlesinger, Jr., *Robert Kennedy and His Times.*
                Boston: Houghton Mifflin, 1978.
RFK CF   Robert F. Kennedy "Confidential File," John F. Kennedy
                Library
SHO   United States Senate Historical Office, Washington, D.C.
STOH   Jean Stein and George Plimpton Oral Histories, John F.
                Kennedy Library

PROLOGUE

17   Grand Canyon rafting trip, June 1967: George Plimpton interview;
George Plimpton STOH; James Whittaker OH, JFKL; Art Buchwald interview;
NYT, July 1-2, 1967. Ed Guthman, who was also on the trip, said that "only children
under ten" were put on the helicopter (Buchwald said there were other adults, including himself), that the trip was "hard" but "not brutal," and that he did not recall Plimpton "reeling" or that Williams "had to be carried out on a donkey."
18   "It's getting like the Alamo": Edwin Guthman, *We Band of Brothers*,
p. 204.
18   "Can they hit Oxford, Mississippi?": *RK*, p. 506.
18   In his daybook: ibid., p. 813.
19   Courage was a moral test: See Edwin O. Guthman and Jeffrey Shulman,
eds., *Robert Kennedy: In His Own Words*, pp. 264.
19   "full of fascination": Kenneth P. O'Donnell and David F. Powers,
"Johnny, We Hardly Knew Ye," p. 404.
19   "A paratrooper": Hugh Sidey interview.
20   "He had a child heart": George Stevens interview.
21   "a little boy in his enthusiasms": Robert Coles interview.
21   "There's a little boy. . . .": Joe Dolan interview.
21   "Doom was woven. . . .": Robert Lowell, *History*, p. 174.
21   Gérard de Nerval: Peter Collier and David Horowitz, *The Kennedys*,
p. 316; Jean Stein and George Plimpton, *American Journey*, p. 191.
21   "Why, God?": Charles Spalding OH, JFKL.
21   "like a man on the rack": John Seigenthaler OH, JFKL.
22   Hamilton's *The Greek Way*: Edith Hamilton, *The Greek Way*, p. 108;
Collier and Horowitz, *Kennedys*, p. 533.
22   RFK and Henry V: *RK*, p. 820.
22   became an existentialist: Jack Newfield, *Robert Kennedy: A Memoir*, pp.
58–59.
22   quote from Dante: RFK foreword in John F. Kennedy, *Profiles in
Courage*, p. 11.
23   hands trembled: This may have been a case of genes, not nerves. Various
of RFK's children also suffer from trembling hands.

23   Joe Dolan and death threats: Joe Dolan interview. Ed Guthman recalled, "In the New York campaign [for U.S. Senate] in 1964, the FBI called almost every morning with a death warning for where we were going that day. There was no use telling Bob. I'd discuss what to do with a New York City police detective, Jim King, who was traveling with us. If we thought it was serious, I'd tell photographers who were traveling with us and they would encircle him as we passed through the 'danger' area. . . . There are photos where you can't see Bob for all the photogs surrounding him." Ed Guthman to the author, Feb. 7, 2000.

23   "Kennedy: Hawk, Dove . . . ?": ibid.

23   "This is your obligation": Newfield, *Memoir*, p. 209; Pierre Salinger, *P.S.: A Memoir*, p. 192.

23   jumpers and screamers: Jules Witcover, *1968*, p. 115.

24   "We were losing altitude. . . .": Fred Dutton interview.

24   last RFK rally: Bill Eppridge, Karl Fleming, George Plimpton, Fred Dutton, Richard Harwood, Marie Ridder, Roosevelt Grier, Stuart Bloch interviews. According to advance man James Tolan, Kennedy was warned there would be firecrackers in Chinatown. "I knew it was coming, he knew it was coming, Ethel knew it was coming, but everyone just stopped and froze." James Tolan OH, JFKL.

26   Feiffer cartoon: *RK*, p. 807.

27   "house had many. . . .": Robert Coles interview.

CHAPTER 1: RUNT

29   Joseph P. Kennedy was intensely preoccupied: *RK*, p. 31. "My work is my boys," said JPK: ibid., p. 12.

29   Portsmouth Priory description: William Ackerman Buell, "Maker of School and Benedictine Monk: The Life of John Byron Diman," *Bulletin of the Newport Historical Society*, no. 140 (Fall 1970). Portsmouth Priory School catalogues, 1933, 1940–41. Interviews with David Meehan, Frank Hurley, Pierce Kearney, Cleveland Thurber, Dom Damien Kearney, OSB; Peter Buckley to author, Aug. 18, 1997; Paul Wankowicz to author, Aug. 11, 1997; Dom Julian Stead, OSB, to author, Aug. 12, 1997; A. Nicholas Reggio to author, Aug. 5, 1997; A. Blake Brophy to author, Oct. 30, 1997.

29   Luella Hennessey recalled: Luella Hennessey interview.

30   Within his family: Jean Smith interview, Schlesinger Papers, JFKL. The best overall treatment of the Kennedy family dynamic is Doris Kearns Goodwin, *The Fitzgeralds and the Kennedys*. For a somewhat harsher, but compelling picture, see Nigel Hamilton, *JFK: Reckless Youth*.

30   "the most generous little boy. . . .": Lem Billings interview, Schlesinger Papers, JFKL.

31   RFK in group portrait: See frontispiece, Hamilton, *Reckless Youth*.

31   "never amount to anything": Mary Bailey Gimbel interview, Schlesinger Papers, JFKL.

31   "What I remember most vividly. . . .": Jack Newfield, *Robert Kennedy: A Memoir*, pp. 41–42.

31   "Mrs. Kennedy's little boy Bobby": David Meehan interview.

31   "like a Hollywood star": Pierce Kearney interview.

31   "He didn't invite friends. . . .": Cleve Thurber interview.

31   "not arrogant. . . .": Frank Hurley interview.

31   "He didn't look happy. . . .": Father Damian interview.

31   dropping things: Eunice Shriver interview. RFK's trembling hands were caused by a "family tremor" that also affected Edward and John Kennedy from time to time, according to a family source.

32   Rose wrote an anxious letter to Joe Sr.: *RK*, p. 33.

33   "He wasn't kidding": Luella Hennessey interview.

33   Kennedys' win-or-else ethic: Michael Knox Beran, *The Last Patrician*, pp. 5–6.

33   cheated by adding extra canvas: Carter Bacon interview.

33   "Yes but—It was symbolic. . . .": Michael Mooney to RFK, Aug. 10, 1966; RFK to Mooney, Aug. 8, 1966, RFK Senate Papers, JFKL.

33   "Democracy is all done. . . .": Goodwin, *Fitzgeralds and the Kennedys*, pp. 712-13.

33   "I listened to Daddy['s] speech. . . .": RFK to Rose Kennedy, undated [January 1941?], RFK Pre-Administration files, JFKL.

34   Rosemary Kennedy's operation: Goodwin, *Fitzgeralds and the Kennedys*, pp. 741–46.

34   Joseph Kennedy secretive man and Gloria Swanson: Laurence Leamer, *Kennedy Women*, pp. 193–203, 241; Goodwin, *Fitzgeralds and the Kennedys*, pp. 459, 483; Hamilton, *Reckless Youth*, pp. 27, 73–75, 351.

34   "very unsociable. . . .": Rose Kennedy to "Dear Children," Jan. 5, 1942, JPK Papers.

34   "I was so disappointed. . . .": Rose Kennedy to RFK, Jan. 12, 1942, *RK*, p. 41.

35   recommendations for mass: RFK also wrote that he had read "5 or 6 books" since his return to school. Rose Kennedy to Children, Feb. 2, 1942, JPK Papers.

35   To prepare himself: Pierce Kearney interview.

35   Bobby was capable of sudden, almost wild acts: Rose Kennedy, *Times to Remember*, p. 103; *RK*, p. 22. RFK was so bleak in this period that he failed to defend his little brother, Teddy, who, chubby and younger than most boys, was a target for bullies when he arrived at the school in May 1941. One day as his arm was being twisted, Teddy called out for help to RFK, who was passing by. "You've got to learn to fight your own battles," said RFK, who kept on going. Adam Clymer, *Edward M. Kennedy*, p. 14.

35   cliff jumping in France: Eunice Shriver interview.

35   "To say the descriptions. . . .": Kathleen Kennedy to RFK, Jan. 13, 1942, Schlesinger Papers, JFKL.

35   struggled to improve himself: RFK to Dad, undated [Spring 1942]. He was also having trouble with a skin condition, probably adolescent acne. A Palm Beach doctor recommended treatments three times a week, but RFK refused because it was "quite impractical" to miss athletics and "I really don't think my face is that bad." Over spring break, Rose despaired, "I still cannot seem to find a boy or a girl whom he likes here. . . . The Bath and Tennis is teeming with young people just about his age, but of course it is difficult to make a break when you do not know

anyone, and he does not seem to have a very strong inclination to bother." Rose Kennedy to Children, March 18, 1942, JPK Papers.

35 "Bob wanted to please his father. . . .": Frank Hurley interview.

36 "Bob would haggle. . . .": Father Julian (Dom Damian Kearney) interview.

36 friend caught using an automobile: John Gibbons interview.

36 cheating incident: interviews with Father Julian Stead, OSB; Paul Wankowicz; Dom Damian Kearney, OSB; David Meehan; Cleveland Thurber; Frank Hurley; John Gibbons; John Spelman; John Gilman; Mike Egan; Pierce Kearney; Nick Reggio.

37 leaves Priory: Rose to Boys, Sept. 10, 1942, JPK Papers. "They were also rather handicapped at the Priory on account of lack of money and I felt this year the food and accommodations might be even less good than other years. I also felt that he had the advantage of a Catholic School training for three years and as he had reached the age of seventeen under those circumstances he ought to be able to hold his own as far as religion is concerned." The only letter in RFK's file at Portsmouth that touches on his departure is a letter from Doris Walker, secretary to JPK, asking the school to return RFK's towels. Doris Walker to Francis Brady, Sept. 9, 1942, courtesy Father Damian Kearney.

37 Robert Kennedy at Milton: David Hackett, Samuel Adams, Tom Cleveland, and Herb Stokinger (football coach) interviews, and correspondence to author from classmates Arthur Nichols, Peter Knight, and Samuel Campbell.

38 "There were no ugly incidents. . . .": Joy Luke interview.

38 "like a bird in a storm": Mary Bailey Gimbel STOH.

38 "most robust": Rose Kennedy to Kathleen and Joe, March 14, 1944. As early as 1940, Jack wrote Joe Sr., "Bobby has increased in strength to such a degree that I seriously believe that he will be bouncing me around plenty in two more years." JFK to Dad [March–April 1940], JPK Papers.

38 "scatterbrained eloquence . . . calm ignorance . . . model boy": John Knowles, *A Separate Peace*, pp. 9, 13, 14.

39 "four feet behind. . . .": Mary Bailey Gimbel STOH.

39 questions about poverty: Fred Garfield interview.

39 "I used to lie in my bed. . . .": Richard N. Goodwin, *Remembering America*, p. 443.

40 T. E. Lawrence fascination: Goodwin, *Fitzgeralds and the Kennedys*, p. 424.

40 John Buchan: Garry Wills, *The Kennedy Imprisonment*, pp. 163–74.

40 Jack Kennedy found inspiration: Hamilton, *Reckless Youth*, p. 544; John Buchan, *Pilgrim's Way*, pp. 168, 60, 104, 232.

40 quoted Lord Tweedsmuir: Newfield, *Memoir*, p. 291.

40 "To try to come steaming out. . . .": *RK*, pp. 51–52. "I think he should go into that V-12 and stay there for a good long time. He's too young to be out here for a while. . . ." JFK to Dad, Sept. 1, 1943, JPK Papers.

40 On a visit to Norfolk: Hank Searls, *The Lost Prince*, p. 196.

40 Joins navy: Joseph Kennedy to Kick, July 3, 1943. "He'll be able to get his diploma from Milton, which is what I wanted him to do right along." JPK Papers. Joe Sr. sent Joe Jr. a newspaper photo. Joe Jr. wrote back, "He certainly didn't look too en-

thusiastic. If he got a gander at this mud flat [Joe's base in England], he'd need Pappy to hold his arm up." Joseph Kennedy Jr. to Mother and Dad, Nov. 9, 1943, JPK Papers.

41   "The folks sent me. . . .": Hamilton, *Reckless Youth*, p. 627; *RK*, p. 52.

41   Joe Jr. also patronized: Joseph Kennedy Jr. to Mother and Dad [March 1944], JPK Papers.

41   working on a farm: Joseph Kennedy to Jack, Aug. 7, 1943, JPK Papers.

41   PT-boat tie clip: Rose Kennedy to Children, Feb. 16, 1943, JPK Papers.

41   "all terribly excited. . . .": Rose Kennedy to Children, Aug. 25, 1943, JPK Papers.

41   "the battler of the wars. . . .": Joseph Kennedy Jr. to Family, Aug. 29, 1943, JPK Papers.

42   "Bobby was so bowled over. . . .": Rose Kennedy to Kathleen and Jack, Sept. 21, 1943, JPK Papers.

42   RFK and Fred Garfield: Fred Garfield interview; Garfield correspondence to author, June 1 and June 10, 1998.

42   "Rose handed them out. . . .": ibid.

42   news of Joe Jr.'s death: Hamilton, *Reckless Youth*, pp. 658–65; Searls, *Lost Prince*, p. 290. RFK's role as family peacemaker is hinted at in a letter from Kathleen after she married Billy Hartington, heir to the Duke of Devonshire. The marriage deeply upset Rose because the children would be raised in the Church of England, not as Catholics. Kick was very distraught at her mother's reaction. RFK must have written something encouraging because Kick wrote back, "Please tell Bobby that his telegram was the best that I got and Billy agrees wholeheartedly on this point." Kathleen Kennedy to Family, May 18, 1944, JPK Papers.

43   "He looked like death. . . .": Fred Garfield interview.

43   "Dad's kind of disappointed. . . .": RFK to David Hackett, Sept. 5, 1944, Hackett Papers, JFKL.

44   "Things are the same. . . .": RFK to David Hackett, Jan. 26, 1945, Hackett Papers, JFKL.

44   "He would have killed him. . . .": Richard Daly interview.

44   "I am not sure. . . .": RFK to David Hackett, March 13, 1945, Hackett Papers, JFKL.

44   melancholy weekend: RFK to David Hackett, April 20, 1945, Hackett Papers, JFKL.

44   flunked his aptitude test: *RK*, p. 58.

45   V-12 to seaman: JPK to RFK, May 11, 1945. RFK was discharged from V-12 on Feb. 1, 1946, Schlesinger Papers, JFKL.

45   aboard destroyer: *RK*, p. 60; shipmate Herbert Edgren interviewed by Emily Johnson.

45   "Forget Bobby. . . .": Lem Billings STOH.

45   "I enjoyed what you said. . . .": Rose Kennedy to Children, Feb. 12, 1946, JPK Papers.

CHAPTER 2: TOUGH

47   accompany his grandfather: Rose Kennedy, *Times to Remember*, p. 333.

47   Honey Fitz, RFK, and history: Doris Kearns Goodwin, *The Fitzgeralds and the Kennedys*, pp. 101, 110, 119, 129–30, 367.

48   family ambition: ibid., pp. 584, 306.

48   "I can feel Pappy's eyes. . . .": Paul Fay, *The Pleasure of His Company,* p. 152.

48   "It was like being drafted. . . .": Nigel Hamilton, *JFK: Reckless Youth,* pp. 674, 724, 753–54.

48   "old-time politicians. . . .": Thomas H. O'Connor, *The Boston Irish,* p. xviii.

49   1946 Democratic primary: Hamilton, *Reckless Youth,* pp. 764–66.

49   "My brother has more courage. . . .": Helen O'Donnell, *A Common Good,* p. 53.

49   "I can't see. . . .": Fay, *Pleasure of His Company,* pp. 156–57.

50   Billings and RFK in Latin America: Lem Billings interview, Schlesinger Papers, JFKL.

50   RFK sexual initiation: Billings interviewed by David Heymann; C. David Heymann, *RFK,* p. 41.

50   RFK and O'Donnell and Harvard: O'Donnell, *Common Good,* pp. 28–34.

50   RFK on Harvard football team: interviews with RFK Harvard teammates: Sam Adams, Edmond Davis, Robert Drennan, Emil Drvaric, Wally Flynn, Charles Glynn.

50   "our good friend Dick Harlow": JFK to Mother and Dad, [Fall 1939], JPK Papers.

51   "whale of a game. . . .": Joseph Kennedy to Jack, Oct. 15, Nov. 4, 1943, JPK Papers.

51   Father Feeney: *RK,* p. 66; Joe Gargan interview.

52   "odd sight": George Plimpton interview.

52   relationship with K.K. Hannon: K.K. Hannon interview. Eunice Shriver recalled Hannon, and that she had switched her affections from RFK to JFK after a night at the movies. "That's why you don't do the same thing with your older brother," she laughed. Eunice Shriver interview.

53   "not serious": Lem Billings STOH.

53   JPK letters to RFK: *RK,* pp. 58–59.

53   Bobby was a mouthpiece: Kenneth O'Donnell STOH.

54   Eunice Kennedy on RFK friends: Eunice Shriver interview.

54   "Oh, you tell him off. . . .": Kenneth O'Donnell OH by Sander Vanocur, by permission of Kenneth O'Donnell Jr., JFKL.

54   RFK after Harvard: *RK,* pp. 73, 81.

54   uncashed $1,000 check. Kenneth O'Donnell OH by Vanocur, JFKL.

55   paper route: Kennedy, *Times to Remember,* p. 116.

55   RFK known for rudeness: Gerald Tremblay OH, JFKL; Gerald Tremblay interview; O'Donnell, *Common Good,* p. 62.

55   "ready to punch someone. . . .": Allison Page interview.

55   Ralph Bunche: James W. Hilty, *Robert Kennedy: Brother Protector,* p. 54; Lester David and Irene David, *Bobby Kennedy,* p. 58.

56   RFK dove overboard: Kennedy, *Times to Remember,* p. 104.

56   Skakel background: David and David, *Bobby Kennedy,* pp. 50–51.

56   "turned the tide": Jean Smith interview, Schlesinger Papers, JFKL. In her thank-you note to Rose, Ethel praised Teddy as a "credit to the long and mar-

velous line of Kennedys" but barely mentioned RFK. Ethel Skakel to Rose Kennedy [1949], JPK Papers.

56   Joan Winmill: Joan Winmill Brown, *No Longer Alone,* pp. 10–51.

57   RFK and Ethel wed: *NYT,* June 18, 1950; *RK,* pp. 87–89.

57   Rose's parasol: Dominick Dunne interview.

57   "an unbelievable mess": O'Donnell, *Common Good,* p. 69.

58   "goodies and baddies": Laura Bergquist Knebel OH, JFKL.

58   "looked at Bobby. . . .": E. Barrett Prettyman interview.

58   RFK wedding and Mary Pitcairn: Mary Pitcairn Davis interview by Clay Blair, Clay Blair Papers, American Heritage Center, University of Wyoming.

58   RFK, O'Donnell, and 1952 campaign: Kenneth O'Donnell OH by Vanocur, JFKL; *RK,* p. 94.

59   "All this business. . . .": *RK,* p. 96.

60   JFK and Addison's disease: Hilty, *Protector,* p. 65; Goodwin, *Fitzgeralds and the Kennedys,* pp. 849, 861.

60   "Those who knew him. . . .": Kennedy, "Tribute to JFK," *Look,* Feb. 25, 1964.

60   Kay Halle: Goodwin, *Fitzgeralds and the Kennedys,* p. 837.

60   "by elimination. . . .": Kenneth O'Donnell OH by Vanocur, JFKL.

60   "Yes, Dad": Jean Stein and George Plimpton, *American Journey,* p. 43.

61   JPK and McCarthy: Richard Donahue interview.

61   RFK and JFK Senate campaign: Kenneth P. O'Donnell and David F. Powers, *"Johnny, We Hardly Knew Ye,"* pp. 96–99; Lawrence O'Brien, *No Final Victories,* p. 30; *RK,* p. 96; Richard Donahue interview.

61   blocking Governor Dever: Kenneth O'Donnell OH by Vanocur, JFKL.

62   "so we had to build. . . .": Edwin O. Guthman and Jeffrey Shulman, eds., *Robert Kennedy: In His Own Words,* pp. 442, 444.

62   RFK and women volunteers: Joe Gargan interview.

62   loan to *Boston Post* publisher: JFK told journalist Fletcher Knebel, "You know we had to buy that paper." Laura Bergquist Knebel OH, JFKL.

63   "the biggest run. . . .": Kenneth O'Donnell interview by Clay Blair, Clay Blair Papers, American Heritage Center, University of Wyoming.

63   JFK and Lodge: O'Donnell and Powers, *"Johnny, We Hardly Knew Ye,"* pp. 101–103; Goodwin, *Fitzgeralds and the Kennedys,* pp. 115–18; Kenneth O'Donnell OH by Vanocur, JFKL.

63   RFK on election night: Torbert Macdonald OH, JFKL.

64   entertaining Larry O'Brien . . . "the last Irish Puritan": O'Brien, *No Final Victories,* p. 34; *RK,* p. 97.

64   "I don't think [Jack]. . . .": *RK,* p. 96; Gerald Tremblay interview.

64   "Well, what are you going to do . . . ?": O'Brien, *No Final Victories,* pp. 41–42.

64   RFK and McCarthy Committee: *RK,* p. 106.

65   ". . . cord of wood": Stein and Plimpton, *American Journey,* p. 49.

65   RFK and McCarthy: Jean Smith, Pat Lawford, Eunice Shriver, David Hackett interviews, Schlesinger Papers, JFKL; John Galvin interview by Clay Blair, Clay Blair Papers, American Heritage Center, University of Wyoming; E. Barrett Prettyman interview.

65   RFK and Cohn: Roy Cohn STOH; Hilty, *Protector*, p. 78; *RK*, p. 105.

66   JPK and Hoover: Anthony Summers, *Official and Confidential*, p. 262; Hilty, *Protector*, p. 36.

66   "Bobby telephones his father. . . .": Rose Kennedy to Pat, June 2, 1954, JPK Papers.

66   "He came back not to fight. . . .": Roy Cohn STOH.

66   RFK clash with Cohn: *RK*, pp. 107, 113. The stress on RFK was obvious to his friends. "Decided after looking at Bobby for so long on TV that he needs a rest. . . .": Grace and Bill Smith to Mr. and Mrs. Robert Kennedy, undated postcard, RFK Pre-Administration files, JFKL.

chapter 3: MORALIST

67   RFK and football fight: Lawrence O'Brien, *No Final Victories*, pp. 45–46.

67   "bad doldrums": Lem Billings interview, Schlesinger Papers, JFKL.

67   RFK and O'Donnell fight: Helen O'Donnell, *A Common Good*, p. 105.

67   walked out of banquet: Ernest Hollings, who was at the banquet as a fellow honoree, recalled that RFK told him that he objected to Murrow's mistreatment of Senator John McClellan on a story involving the Marshall Plan. Ernest Hollings interview.

68   "That's pretty tough company. . . .": *RK*, pp. 107, 115.

68   godfather rumor: confidential interview; Jean Smith interviewed by Schlesinger, Schlesinger Papers, JFKL.

68   RFK at JFK's wedding: *RK*, p. 120.

68   RFK in Soviet republics: Mercedes Douglas interview. "Douglas thought he was fighting something in himself. He rejected everything. When he got sick, Douglas thought he brought it on himself because he was so anti. The doctor who finally treated him, a woman, said, "This is a very disturbed young man." See also Harris Wofford, *Of Kennedys and Kings*, pp. 32–37.

68   "woman of loose morals": Aleksandr Fursenko and Timothy Naftali, *"One Hell of a Gamble,"* p. 115. It was standard procedure for Soviet intelligence to seek to ensnare U.S. officials visiting the USSR with prostitutes. Professor Naftali said that the report was probably not disinformation, since he found it in intelligence briefing papers sent to Khrushchev, and thus meant to be reliable. Still, the particular choice of words—"woman of loose morals"—does not sound like an expression Kennedy would use.

68   "I was appalled. . . .": Angie Novello STOH.

69   run for White House: Gerald Tremblay interview.

69   work for AEC: John Graves interview.

69   "somewhere like Nevada": Charles Bartlett interview.

69   ". . . New Mexico": Rose Kennedy to Pat, June 19, 1953, JPK Papers.

69   urged him to run for attorney general: Kenneth O'Donnell OH by Sander Vanocur, JFKL.

69   "he hates like me": John Seigenthaler OH, JFKL.

69   RFK family man: James W. Hilty, *Robert Kennedy: Brother Protector*, p. 78; *RK*, pp. 118–19.

69   home at five-thirty: Ruth Watt OH, SHO.

69   RFK hits dog: Charles Spalding interview.

70   LaVern Duffy: LaVern Duffy interview with David Heymann, Heymann Papers, SUNY, Stony Brook, NY.

70   "Name one person. . . .": Edward Bennett Williams interview, Schlesinger Papers, JFKL.

70   Ethel's parents' death: Warren Rogers interview. Jerry Oppenheimer, *The Other Mrs. Kennedy*, p. 232. Oppenheimer quotes a Skakel family member doubting that George Skakel was about to convert.

71   RFK with Zurlo and Amato: John Doltz interview, Marty Pera interview. Doltz was a Bureau of Narcotics agent. Pera succeeded Amato as head of the international organized crime desk of the Bureau of Narcotics. Pera then worked directly with Kennedy on the Rackets Committee after Apalachin in 1957. Pera told the author that he believed RFK didn't really become engaged in the organized crime issue until Apalachin.

71   RFK riding with drug agents: Howard Diller interview. See C. David Heymann, *RFK*, pp. 98–101; Howard Diller and Mel Finkelstein interviews by David Heymann, Heymann Papers, SUNY, Stony Brook, NY. Marty Pera said that Kennedy was known for never picking up the bill when out joyriding with the cops.

72   Johnny Dio: O'Donnell, *Common Good*, p. 132.

72   preliminary look into rackets: *RK*, p. 138.

72   warned JFK not to campaign: In June, JFK wrote his father that the prospects for winning were "limited" but that "churning up" might get him recognition (JFK to JPK, June 29, 1956). Joe Sr. wrote back essentially leaving it to JFK to decide (JPK to JFK, Aug. 1, 1956), but wrote Eunice that JFK should not campaign for the spot. Joseph Kennedy to Eunice Shriver, Aug. 7, 1956, JPK Papers.

73   "Whew, is he mad!": Kenneth P. O'Donnell and David F. Powers, *"Johnny, We Hardly Knew Ye,"* p. 138.

73   V.P. effort fails: *RK*, pp. 131–32. Jack Kennedy persuaded Congressman Tip O'Neill to give up his seat as a delegate for RFK. O'Neill hated RFK, who treated the future Speaker of the House as a hack. According to O'Neill, when he complained to Joseph Kennedy that RFK never thanked him for giving up his seat, the elder Kennedy told him, "Never expect any appreciation from my boys. These kids have had so much done for them by other people that they just assume it's coming to them." O'Neill also said JPK told him, "When Bobby hates you, you stay hated." Thomas P. O'Neill, *Man of the House* (New York: Random House, 1987), p. 83.

73   "You're the luckiest man. . . .": Kenneth O'Donnell OH by Vanocur, JFKL.

73   ". . . Do you believe me now?": Peter Collier and David Horowitz, *The Kennedys*, p. 219.

74   "Bob learned what not to do. . . .": Newton Minow interview; Harrison Salisbury STOH.

74   RFK investigates Teamsters: *RK*, pp. 141–42; Robert F. Kennedy, *The Enemy Within*, pp. 3–20.

75   "He was really mad. . . ." . . . "feels it is too great. . . .": Jean Kennedy Smith interview, Schlesinger Papers, JFKL; *RK*, pp. 142–43.

75   Oedipal urge: Doris Kearns Goodwin interview, "Robert F. Kennedy, A Memoir," a film by Jack Newfield and Charles Stuart, Discovery Channel, 1998.

75   JPK's shadowy ties: See Doris Kearns Goodwin, *The Fitzgeralds and the Kennedys*, pp. 511–15; Hilty, *Protector*, pp. 129, 524–25. Professor Hilty has done a thorough review of the literature and found no solid evidence of JPK's ties to the mob. See also Chapter 8.

76   Rackets Committee formed: Kennedy, *Enemy Within*, p. 17.

76   JFK reluctance to join: *RK*, p. 143; Kennedy, *Enemy Within*, p. 24.

76   Kenny O'Donnell role: Helen O'Donnell interview. In his oral history for the Kennedy Library, Kenny O'Donnell gave this account: ". . . [RFK] felt he needed somebody down there [in Washington] to give him some protection who was a friend. I was very much against it, but I finally did get down. I presumed that Senator Kennedy knew all about it, but I got there and I found he didn't know all about it. And he was very unhappy because he had planned for me to run the 1958 campaign and he didn't want me in Washington. So we made some accommodation."

77   RFK and Cheyfitz: Evan Thomas, *The Man to See*, pp. 82, 106.

78   dinner at Cheyfitz's: John Bartlow Martin, "The Struggle to Get Hoffa," *Saturday Evening Post*, June 27, 1959 (a seven-part series; see also July 4, 11, 18, 25; Aug. 1, 8); Kennedy, *Enemy Within*, pp. 36, 43; Clark Mollenhoff, *Tentacles of Power*, pp. 148–49.

79   Hoffa arrested: Thomas, *Man to See*, pp. 106–108.

79   "jump off the Capitol": Kennedy, *Enemy Within*, pp. 60–62; Mollenhoff, *Tentacles of Power*, pp. 154–55; *RK*, p. 155.

80   Beck collapsed: *RK*, p. 148; Kennedy, *Enemy Within*, p. 33.

80   Hoffa trial: Thomas, *Man to See*, pp. 108–18.

80   "Come on now. . . .": Angie Novello STOH.

80   Sheridan to Joe Louis: Kennedy, *Enemy Within*, p. 60.

80   Hoffa hearings began: ibid., pp. 72–73.

80   ". . . bug the little bastard": Victor Lasky, *JFK: The Man and the Myth*, p. 107.

81   "absolute evilness": Kennedy, *Enemy Within*, p. 159.

81   "My first love. . . .": Martin, "The Struggle."

81   Hoffa acquittals: Kennedy, *Enemy Within*, pp. 157–58.

82   Kennedy exhausted: *RK*, pp. 158–59.

82   Apalachin: ibid., p. 167.

82   "didn't know anything. . . .": Edwin O. Guthman and Jeffrey Shulman, eds., *Robert Kennedy: In His Own Words*, p. 120.

82   Cockeyed Dunn et al.: Kennedy, *Enemy Within*, pp. 89, 249.

83   Giancana: ibid., p. 253.

83   "Would you tell us anything . . . ?": Senate Select Committee Hearings, 86th Congress, 1st session, June 9, 1959, pp. 18672–81.

83   tense questioner: RFK's overbearing style caused some concern within his own family. Joseph Kennedy sent JFK a letter from Sargent Shriver (married to Eunice Kennedy) quoting an editor at a Chicago paper to the effect that RFK was creating sympathy for the witnesses before the Rackets Committee by appearing vindictive and even vicious. JPK to JFK, March 14, 1957, Schlesinger Papers, JFKL.

83   ". . . grunted, 'Oh!' . . .": "Youthful Chief Counsel," *NYT*, March 13, 1957.

83   ". . . full of shit": Robert Green interview.

83   "He wasn't the angry man. . . .": *RK*, p. 150.

83   "Am very pleased. . . .": ibid.

83   "a little keyed up. . . .": Ruth Watt OH, SHO.

83   Kennedy office described: Martin, "The Struggle." "If at first you don't succeed" is from his uncut first draft in John Bartlow Martin Papers, LOC.

84   "I felt a little funny. . . .": Walter Sheridan STOH.

84   RFK and Seigenthaler: John Seigenthaler OH, JFKL and STOH.

84   RFK and staff: Martin, "The Struggle."

85   RFK refused to go easy: Myer Feldman interview. See "R. F. Kennedy Cites Influence Proposals," *NYT*, March 7, 1959.

85   Mundt and Goldwater complained about RFK: Mundt to Goldwater, Dec. 26, 1957; Goldwater to Mundt, Dec. 28, 1957; Mundt to Goldwater, Dec. 30, 1957; Mundt to McClellan, Dec. 24, 1957, Mundt Papers, Karl E. Mundt Archival Library, Dakota State University.

85   investigate the UAW: *RK*, pp. 175–83. Kenneth O'Donnell recalled that RFK was "cold and antagonistic" when he first met with the UAW and that he assumed the union had committed improprieties. Kenneth O'Donnell OH for *"Johnny,"* JFKL.

85   "no guts": RFK handwritten notes, Dec. 24, 1957, Schlesinger Papers, JFKL.

86   did not antagonize organized labor: At an off-the-record meeting of Nieman Fellows at Harvard in February 1959, Kennedy reported that he had "run into one situation where an important politician [a state leader] has turned against him on the Rackets issue, but he sees no spread of this." James Reston confidential memoranda, James Reston Papers, University of Illinois. But Kenny O'Donnell worried that by 1959, JFK's presidential ambitions did make him a target for labor unions. Kenneth O'Donnell OH by Vanocur, JFKL.

86   ". . . didn't know it was going to be good politics. . . .": Paul Schrade interview.

86   "It happened that. . . .": Clark Mollenhoff STOH.

87   Mayor Daley: Kenneth O'Donnell OH by Vanocur, JFKL; JFK to JPK [1959], JPK Papers.

JPK and O'Rourke: Stephen Fox, *Blood and Power*, pp. 329–30. Marty Pera, the Bureau of Narcotics agent assigned to work with RFK and the Rackets Committee on organized crime, said he never heard any talk or gossip about JPK mob ties among the Rackets Committee staff.

87   RFK's inquisitional style: The most famous statement of this argument is Alexander Bickel, "Robert F. Kennedy: The Case Against Him for Attorney General," *New Republic*, Jan. 9, 1961.

87   To his credit: Martin to Schlesinger, Oct. 19, 1975, Schlesinger Papers, JFKL.

88   ". . . newspapermen don't watch us as closely. . . .": uncut Martin manuscript, John Bartlow Martin Papers, LOC.

88   Sidey observed that RFK enjoyed: Hugh Sidey interview.

88   *Life* profiled RFK: "A Debut in a Burgeoning Family," *Life*, April 21, 1958.

88   "tickle-tumble": Martin to Schlesinger, Oct. 19, 1975, Schlesinger Papers, JFKL.

88   "And you are the worst!": Paul Fay manuscript for *The Pleasure of His Company*, Myrick Land Papers, Boston University.

88   "Grandpa [Joe Sr.] told me. . . .": Rose Kennedy to Ethel, Jan. 15, 1960; JPK Papers.

88   "This is just to remind you. . . .": Rose Kennedy to RFK, Feb. 19, 1958, JPK Papers.

89   "The hearings are great. . . .": Ethel Kennedy to Rose and Joe, [Summer 1957], JPK Papers.

89   "We're all sick to death. . . .": Ethel Kennedy to Rose and Joe, [1957], JPK Papers.

89   "I know how excited. . . .": Rose Kennedy to Ethel, Jan. 23, 1957, JPK Papers.

89   "were running for president. . . .": Ruth Watt OH, SHO.

89   Although overheated: See *NYT Book Review*, Feb. 28, 1960.

CHAPTER 4: MANIPULATOR

90   "understood": Rose Kennedy, *Times to Remember*, p. 383.

90   ". . . high whining. . . .": Paul Fay manuscript for *The Pleasure of His Company*, Myrick Land Papers, Boston University. At RFK's insistence, Fay cut the adjective "high whining" from the published book.

90   "the deb": Doris Kearns Goodwin, *The Fitzgeralds and the Kennedys*, p. 890.

90   JFK and RFK at Hyannis Port: Ruth Watt OH, SHO.

90   "Jack thought Bobby. . . .": Charles Spalding interview.

91   "Jack was the tough one. . . .": Charles Guggenheim interview.

91   "It really runs on. . . .": William Shannon, "Said Robert Kennedy, Maybe We're All Doomed Anyway," *NYT Sunday Magazine*, May 16, 1968.

91   JFK was cruising: See Peter Collier and David Horowitz, *The Kennedys*, pp. 258–59. But see also Goodwin, *Fitzgeralds and the Kennedys*, p. 907 ("The Kennedy family tried desperately to locate the chartered yacht. . . .").

91   "on Bobby's advice": Rose Kennedy to Pat, Aug. 26, 1956, JPK Papers.

91   Jackie on RFK ruthless myth: Collier and Horowitz, *Kennedys*, pp. 208–209; *RK*, pp. 133, 98.

91   chaotic Kennedy machine: Jean Stein and George Plimpton, *American Journey*, p. 68.

92   "The Kennedy operation was very loose. . . .": Fred Dutton interview.

92   ". . . inherit my enemies": Collier and Horowitz, *Kennedys*, p. 213.

92   Joe Kennedy's role: JPK did have some influence with the bosses, including Richard Daley of Chicago. John Reilly, who worked in the '60 campaign and later for RFK at Justice—and was close to Kenneth O'Donnell—said that it was generally acknowledged that Joseph Kennedy did produce New York's delegation at the Democratic convention through his close contacts with party bosses Charles Buckley and Eugene Keogh.

92   Kennedy spending and Steve Smith: Kennedy, *Times to Remember,* p. 362; Joe Dolan and Fred Dutton interviews.

92   "It's not the pope. . . .": Kenneth P. O'Donnell and Thomas F. Powers, *"Johnny, We Hardly Knew Ye,"* p. 120.

92   spending in primaries: James W. Hilty, *Robert Kennedy: Brother Protector,* p. 135; David Halberstam, *The Powers That Be,* pp. 316–28.

93   "Did they ask my brother Joe . . . ?": Thomas C. Reeves, *A Question of Character,* p. 193.

93   first test was Wisconsin: Helen O'Donnell, *A Common Good,* pp. 169–70.

93   RFK and Cronkite: Walter Cronkite STOH; Hilty, *Protector,* pp. 140–41.

93   Bill Rivkin story: Enid Rivkin interview.

93   "I don't understand it. . . .": Charles Spalding interview, Schlesinger Papers, JFKL.

93   "in shock": O'Donnell and Powers, *"Johnny, We Hardly Knew Ye,"* pp. 180–81.

94   "cheap, cunning politician": Kenneth O'Donnell OH by Sander Vanocur, JFKL.

94   Paul Corbin: John Seigenthaler interview; Charles Bartlett interview; Richard Wade interview; *RK,* pp. 196–97; Hilty, *Protector,* pp. 141, 527.

94   ". . . break the machine!": Stephen Smith interview, Schlesinger Papers, JFKL.

94   RFK entertained by rogue politics: RFK to Burke Marshall, Sept. 23, 1963, Burke Marshall papers, JFKL.

95   FDR Jr.: *RK,* p. 201; Justin Feldman interview; Richard Donahue interview.

95   Chafin, $35,000: Raymond Chafin and Topper Sherwood, *Just Good Politics,* pp. 127–45.

95   RFK astute about money: David Fox interview.

95   "divided . . . into little bundles": Richard Donahue interview. The bundles, up to $100, were paid to precinct leaders. The money was used to "keep their organizations going," said Donahue. At about this time, in one of his fawning letters to Sorensen, White wrote, "I like to think of myself as an innocent." Theodore H. White to Theodore Sorensen, April 15, 1960, Theodore White Papers, JFKL.

95   money not decisive: Charles Peters interview.

95   "Come down here, Jack. . . .": Hubert Humphrey, *The Education of a Public Man,* p. 207.

96   ". . . going to hit him": Joseph Rauh OH, LBJL.

96   ". . . Are you with us?": Enid Rivkin interview.

96   RFK meets LBJ: Horace Busby OH, JFKL.

96   LBJ calls RFK "sonny": Kenneth O'Donnell OH by Vanocur, JFKL.

96   Tommy Corcoran: Robert Dallek, *Lone Star Rising: Lyndon Johnson and His Times,* pp. 490–91.

96   RFK at LBJ ranch: ibid., p. 559.

96   ". . . it's slaughter": William vanden Heuvel and Milton Gwirtzman, *On His Own: Robert F. Kennedy, 1964–1968,* p. 246. Vanden Heuvel and Gwirtzman date the incident after the election.

97   JFK medical report: Jeff Shesol, *Mutual Contempt*, pp. 34–35.

97   "You'll get yours.": Bobby Baker, *Wheeling and Dealing*, p. 118.

97   "You just won't believe it": Edwin O. Guthman and Jeffrey Shulman, eds., *Robert Kennedy: In His Own Words*, pp. 20–21, 304; *RK*, pp. 206–11.

97   "If you do this. . . .": Paul Schrade interview.

98   wasn't the whole story: The best analysis is Shesol, *Mutual Contempt*, pp. 48–57.

98   didn't quite level with RFK: Hilty, *Protector*, pp. 158–61.

98   "I always suspected. . . .": Fred Dutton interview.

98   "Yesterday was the best day. . . .": Charles Bartlett interview.

99   "crazy": David Hackett STOH.

99   "You can rest in November": Theodore White, *The Making of the President, 1960*, p. 250.

99   "We're not going to say anything. . . .": John Singleton OH, LBJL.

99   "There will be no religious issue.": John Graves interview.

99   ". . . popularity contest. . . .": *RK*, p. 213.

99   Bruno and Tuck: Jerry Bruno interview, John Reilly interview. Bobby Baker alleged that Kennedy operatives cut LBJ phone lines; Bruno denied it.

99   H. L. Hunt donation: John Seigenthaler OH, JFKL.

100   "Don't fuzz it up": *RK*, pp. 215–16; Stein and Plimpton, *American Journey*, p. 90.

100   No blacks, no dinner: Scott Peek OH, SHO.

100   Congressman William Dawson: Sargent Shriver interviewed by Anthony Shriver, "Kennedy's Call to King," OH, JFKL.

100   "Bob didn't want. . . .": John Seigenthaler OH, JFKL.

100   "hauling coal": Joe Dolan interview.

100   Powell $50,000: Taylor Branch, *Parting the Waters*, p. 343.

101   RFK "turned on us. . . .": Wofford, *Of Kennedys and Kings*, pp. 18–19. In his private communications with campaign chronicler Theodore White, RFK was full of praise for his brother-in-law Shriver's contribution. He urged White to give Shriver more credit in early drafts. The mutual back-scratching in the correspondence between RFK and White is intense. See Theodore White to RFK, March 14, 1961; RFK to TW, March 23, 1961; TW to RFK, April 5, 1961, Theodore White Papers, JFKL.

102   RFK on King's arrest: Wofford, *Of Kennedys and Kings*, pp. 20–22; *RK*, pp. 216–18; Branch, *Parting the Waters*, pp. 364–65.

102   leaflets and handbills: Sargent Shriver interviewed by Anthony Shriver, "Kennedy's Call to King," OH, JFKL.

102   Many political analysts believe: "It is difficult to see how Illinois, New Jersey, Michigan, South Carolina or Delaware (with 74 electoral votes), could have been won had the Republican-Democratic split of the Negro wards and precincts remained as it was in 1956." White, *Making of the President, 1960*, p. 354.

102   "Mr. Vice-President. . . .": Wofford, *Of Kennedys and Kings*, pp. 25–26. Curiously, blacks in Atlanta did not switch over from Republican to Democrat. They did almost everywhere else, however. *Pittsburgh Courier*, Nov. 19, 1960.

102   What happened is more complicated: Ernest Vandiver interview; Griffin Bell interview; Ernest Vandiver OH, JFKL.

103   "Bob, it's nice to talk to you": Guthman and Shulman, eds., *In His Own Words*, pp. 70–71. Seigenthaler and Schlesinger: Schlesinger to Seigenthaler, June 14, 1976; Seigenthaler to Schlesinger, Nov. 9, 1976, Schlesinger Papers, JFKL. Ex parte concerns: Hilty, *Protector*, p. 174. A New York Democratic leader recalled RFK making calls to Vandiver from Long Island that day. John English OH, JFKL.

103   Vandiver broke his silence: Clifford Kuhn, " 'There's a Footnote to History!': Memory and the History of Martin Luther King's October 1960 Arrest and Its Aftermath," *Journal of American History*, September 1997; Jack Bass, *Taming the Storm*, pp. 168–71.

104   RFK lost control: John Seigenthaler interview.

104   "Sure I'm glad. . . .": *RK*, p. 218.

104   "That's the Kennedy family m.o. . . . .": Joe Dolan interview.

105   "They're the worst kind": Richard Wade interview.

105   "Bob thought he understood Daley. . . .": John Nolan interview.

105   confront religious issue: Theodore Sorensen interview.

105   Nixon debates: Christopher Matthews, *Kennedy & Nixon: The Rivalry That Shaped Postwar America*, pp. 148–49, 159.

106   Haddad role: William Haddad interview. Haddad also claimed that he picked up word that the Eisenhower administration was preparing a CIA-backed invasion of Cuba by Cuban exiles. He said he got a tip from a photographer in Miami. If true, his account gives further credence to a claim by Richard Nixon that JFK mousetrapped him in the debates, criticizing the Eisenhower administration for inaction on Cuba while knowing that Nixon could say nothing because his hands were tied by secrecy. Theodore Sorensen denied that Kennedy had been informed of the Bay of Pigs operation (Sorensen, *Kennedy*, p. 205). But see Seymour Hersh, *The Dark Side of Camelot*, pp. 168–84.

106   Sinatra gave campaign report on Nixon: John Seigenthaler interview.

107   "I'm doing all the work.": *RK*, p. 219.

107   "Oh, Bunny, you're president. . . .": White, *Making of the President, 1960*, pp. 15–18.

107   teasing Teddy: Richard Donahue interview.

107   RFK worried about Teddy: Kenneth O'Donnell OH by Vanocur, JFKL.

107   election returns: White, *Making of the President, 1960*, pp. 344–47; Hilty, *Protector*, p. 179.

107   One of the more persistent conspiracy theories: See Hersh, *Dark Side of Camelot*, pp. 130–68. Historian Michael Beschloss pointed out to me that Daley's citywide control counted for more than the mob-run wards, which were solidly Democratic in any case. Michael Beschloss interview. Sargent Shriver, who ran Illinois for Kennedy, said that Daley held back announcing the vote in Chicago until the early hours of Wednesday morning because the mayor figured that if he announced the Chicago tally before the downstate vote came in, the Republicans would cheat and inflate their votes in southern Illinois to top the Democrats in Chicago. Sargent Shriver interview.

108   "Ignore him": Sander Vanocur interview.

108   Jackie Robinson: Peter Maas interview.

108   "I don't know what Bobby does. . . .": Charles Bartlett interview.

108   JFK wore right makeup: Hilty, *Protector*, p. 177.

108   fend off extortion schemes: Hersh, *Dark Side of Camelot*, pp. 102–20.
108   coalfields of West Virginia: David Hackett interview; Stein and Plimpton, *American Journey*, p. 70.

CHAPTER 5: PROTECTOR

109   "I had to do something. . . .": *RK*, p. 228.
109   "Nobody's better qualified": John Seigenthaler OH, JFKL; Drew Pearson to RFK, Dec. 5, 1960, RFK Personal Correspondence, Attorney General Papers, JFKL.
109   *Times* editorialized: *NYT*, Nov. 23, 1960.
110   "This will kill. . . .": John Seigenthaler OH, JFKL.
110   In newsreel clips: NBC News, "RFK," May 1963.
110   "rueful and fatalistic": *RK*, p. 233.
110   William Rogers: Edwin O. Guthman and Jeffrey Shulman, eds., *Robert Kennedy: In His Own Words*, p. 73.
110   "roar of incredulity": Mortimer Caplin interview.
110   sense of disappointment: Anthony Lewis interview.
110   "I don't know why. . . .": Charles Bartlett interview.
111   "Oh, Mr. Kennedy! . . .": Warren Rogers, *When I Think of Bobby*, pp. 20–21.
111   "a bad impression": Louis Oberdorfer interview.
111   ". . . absolute disgrace. . . .": Joe Dolan interview.
111   JFK hinted: Joe Dolan interview. See Dennis J. Hutchinson, *The Man Who Once Was Whizzer White*, pp. 157–62, 173–79. White told U.S. District Court Judge Sven E. Holmes that he urged JFK to make RFK attorney general and suggested himself as a strong number two.
112   Go deal with them: William Geoghegan OH, JFKL.
112   "I don't think he knew. . . .": David Hackett STOH. Kennedy asked Hackett to head up what became the President's Commission on Juvenile Delinquency and Youth Crime in March 1961 after meeting with a youth gang worker in Harlem on a Sunday afternoon. The social worker took him to meet separately with black, Puerto Rican, and Italian gangs. RFK was puzzled why they resorted so frequently to violence, and decided to look into the question. Ed Guthman to the author, Feb. 7, 2000.
112   "His initial reaction was. . . .": Archibald Cox interview.
112   handwriting: Joe Dolan interview.
112   "a better sense. . . .": John Nolan interview.
112   "Almost done with that?": James Symington interview.
112   "special kind of stoicism. . . .": Joseph Kraft STOH.
112   Judge Keogh: Victor S. Navasky, *Kennedy Justice*, pp. 364–72; William Hundley interview; John Reilly interview.
113   Igor Cassini: Peter Maas interview.
114   ". . . we can't fix": Myer Feldman interview.
114   RFK spoiled: He was not altogether unself-conscious about being spoiled. He teased the Skakels, who were big present givers. "I want you to know

that I don't care what kind of present you give me for Christmas as long as it's big and expensive and with the name of the company at which you purchased it." RFK to George Skakel, Dec. 8, 1954, RFK Pre-Administration Papers, JFKL.

114   RFK rarely carried money: Courtney Evans STOH; John Reilly interview; confidential interview.

114   "Don't you think . . . ?": Peter Maas interview.

114   RFK leaving his coat: Ethel was an even bigger offender in this regard. FBI memo, June 10, 1964, FBI.

114   "It would be *extremely*. . . .": *RK*, p. 242.

114   "If you want to be secretary of state. . . .": Richard Reeves, "The People Around Bobby, "*NYT Magazine*, Feb. 12, 1967.

114   "Marlboro Men": ibid.

114   tossing a football: *NYT*, March 3, 1961.

114   ". . . seeing newspaper people": Guthman and Shulman, eds., *In His Own Words*, p. 50.

114   ". . . reporters are not your friends": confidential interview.

114   *Redbook* changes: RFK to EMK, Dec. 14, 1961, RFK Papers, JFKL.

115   "In a calculated way. . . .": John Seigenthaler interview.

115   *The Enemy Within: RK*, p. 262; "The Friends and Enemies Within," *Newsweek*, March 11, 1963; *NYT*, Sept. 23, 1961; Jones to DeLoach, March 24, 1961, RFK file, FBI. Schulberg did not think Kennedy was indulging his vanity. "He was offhand about it." Kennedy was very involved in the script, even writing some lines for it. Budd Schulberg interview.

115   "horror of wasting time": Paul O'Neil, "The No. 2 Man in Washington," *Life*, Jan. 26, 1962.

115   "Don't tell me what I can't. . . .": Blakey and Billings, *The Plot to Kill the President*, p. 196.

115   FBI overkill in communists: Guthman and Shulman, eds., *In His Own Words*, pp. 120–21.

116   courting Hoover: Jones to Nichols, July 20, 1955; RFK to Hoover, Aug. 31, 1956; Jones to DeLoach, July 13, 1960; JPK Sr. to Hoover, April 12, 1957, RFK and JPK files, FBI. JPK also instructed JFK to send a signed copy of *Profiles in Courage* to Hoover. Joseph Kennedy to Jack, Jan. 18, 1956, JPK Papers.

116   "allegations have been received. . . .": DeLoach to Hoover, July 13, 1960, FBI.

116   "Send memo to A.G.": Legat Rome to Hoover, Jan. 30, 1961, Hoover Official and Confidential files, FBI.

116   RFK and Justice Department gym: Rosen to Parsons, Feb. 1, 1961; Mohr to Malone, Feb. 1, 1961; Mohr to Edwards, Feb. 1, 1961 (see Hoover notation), RFK file, FBI.

116   "When I pick up this phone. . . .": Curt Gentry, *J. Edgar Hoover*, p. 477; William Sullivan, *The Bureau*, p. 53.

117   Mr. Hoover: See RFK to Hoover, June 22, 1964, RFK file, FBI.

117   dog was "lonely": Helen O'Donnell, *A Common Good*, p. 300.

117   ". . . A hysterectomy?": William Hundley interview; Gentry, *Hoover*, pp. 477-79.

117   replaced by William Parker: *RK*, p. 260.

118   "extremely reliable sources": For the most comprehensive discussion of RFK and Hoover and illegal eavesdropping, see Navasky, *Kennedy Justice*, pp. 69–94. Joe Dolan recalled: "Often, they tipped off bugs with the phrase, 'T-1 of known reliability, who is not available for interview and not available to testify.' "

118   RFK informed of FBI surveillance: A memo from Hoover to Byron White on May 4, 1961, clearly states, "In the interest of national safety, microphone surveillances are also utilized on a restricted basis, even though trespass is necessary, in uncovering major criminal activities. We are using such coverage in connection with our investigations of the clandestine activities of top hoodlums and organized crime." FBI files. On July 6, 1961, Courtney Evans, RFK's liaison to Hoover, wrote a memo to his superiors that Kennedy was "aware" of electronic surveillance on the mob. Evans to Belmont, July 6, 1961, FBI files. RFK was apparently curious to learn more. On July 12, 1961, RFK's phone log showed this message: "Courtney Evans called re: technical surveillance methods you inquired about." RFK phone logs, JFKL. According to Cartha "Deke" DeLoach, Hoover's assistant, "seventeen agents in New York and fourteen in Chicago" witnessed Kennedy listening to FBI bugs. In Chicago, "they shut the tape off when they learned that Giancana had given $25,000 to JFK's campaign." Cartha DeLoach interview. It is possible, as Burke Marshall suggested to the author, that the FBI agents were telling Hoover what he wanted to hear, not the truth.

118   played tapes from the bugs: William Sullivan, a top FBI official, told Curt Gentry that RFK was being "set up"—creating a record that he had heard the tape from a bug. Gentry, *Hoover*, p. 478. William Roemer, an FBI agent in Chicago, said he boasted to Kennedy about the FBI bug. Roemer, *Roemer: Man Against the Mob*, pp. 214–17. But Ed Guthman, who was present, said that the FBI agents "stated very clearly that they got the tape from the Chicago police." Ed Guthman to author, Feb. 7, 2000.

118   "You look old. . . .": David Ellis interview; Ellis to author, Aug. 7, 1999.

118   "He became a civil libertarian later.": William Hundley interview; Joe Dolan interview; Richard Donahue interview. Some of RFK's colleagues are skeptical about the claims that RFK knew nothing of the bugging. "It's hard to believe he didn't know," Robert Morgenthau, the former U.S. attorney in New York, told the author. "The FBI would drop pretty broad hints. They'd say about a source, 'He can't see, but his hearing is excellent.' " Robert Morgenthau interview.

118   Kennedy approved six hundred taps: Navasky, *Kennedy Justice*, p. 74; James W. Hilty, *Robert Kennedy: Brother Protector*, pp. 233–34. Myer Feldman, deputy counsel to President Kennedy, recalled that RFK pushed for legislation to give the attorney general broad authority to wiretap, but that JFK overruled him. Myer Feldman interview. But see *RK*, pp. 269–72. Victor Lasky, a persistent critic of the Kennedys, accused RFK of widespread use of illegal electronic eavesdropping. Because of his animus, Lasky may be an unreliable source, but he repeats a disturbing and possibly more believable story from an underworld figure who claimed that he was hired by RFK to wiretap the phones of newspaper reporters staying in Newport, Rhode Island, in September 1963 (Victor Lasky, *It Didn't Start with Watergate*, pp. 90–92).

118   "We knew you couldn't use it": William Hundley interview. The FBI

did, too. "We knew in our minds that it would be inadmissible," said Carla De-Loach. Carla DeLoach interview.

120   ". . . man-eating shark": Evan Thomas, *The Very Best Men: Four Who Dared: The Early Years of the CIA*, p. 237.

120   did not quiz Bissell closely: Guthman and Shulman, eds., *In His Own Words*, pp. 240–41.

120   "Hugh, do you have anyone in Cuba?": Hugh Sidey interview.

120   "I don't think it's going as well. . . .": Guthman and Shulman, eds., *In His Own Words*, p. 242.

120   "not a bit good": Bundy to JFK, April 18, 1961, *FRUS*, vol. X, p. 272.

121   "Then Bobby Kennedy called me up. . . .": Admiral Burke's conversation with Commander Wilhide, ibid., pp. 274–75.

121   "The shit has hit the fan. . . .": Scott Peek OH, SHO.

121   RFK emotional, JFK in tears: Michael Beschloss, *The Crisis Years*, p. 123; Thomas, *Very Best Men*, pp. 263–64; Richard Reeves, *President Kennedy*, pp. 94–95; Kenneth P. O'Donnell and David F. Powers, *"Johnny, We Hardly Knew Ye,"* p. 307.

121   RFK composed a memo to JFK: RFK to JFK, April 19, 1961, *FRUS*, vol. X, pp. 302–304. His handwritten editing is in the Schlesinger Papers, JFKL.

122   "We've got to do. . . .": Reeves, *President Kennedy*, p. 95.

122   "Bobby put his fist. . . .": Louis Oberdorfer interview.

122   RFK berates LBJ and Bowles: Guthman and Shulman, eds., *In His Own Words*, pp. 264–65. See Chester Bowles, "Notes on Cuban Crisis," *FRUS*, vol. X, pp. 304–306; *RK*, pp. 471–72.

122   Kennedy's tirade: Richard Goodwin, *Remembering America*, p. 187.

123   "I then became involved in every major. . . .": Guthman and Shulman, eds., *In His Own Words*, p. 249.

123   "Up until that time. . . .": Peter Collier and David Horowitz, *The Kennedys*, pp. 271–72.

123   "As my father always told me. . . .": RFK to McCone, May 2, 1962, RFK AG Personal Correspondence, RFK Papers, JFKL.

123   Grayston Lynch, Stanley Gaines: Grayston Lynch interview; Stanley Gaines interview.

124   "Bobby Kennedy sat there. . . .": Lynch claimed that no real transcript of the hearings was made, that a record—abbreviated and inaccurate—was created at the end of the day. Grayston Lynch, *Decision for Disaster: Betrayal at the Bay of Pigs*, pp. 149–50. For a partial record of the Taylor hearings, see Luis Aguilar, *Operation Zapata*. The full Taylor Report was finally declassified in April 2000.

124   The final report: Cuba Study Group to President JFK, *FRUS*, vol. X, pp. 575–606. The report clearly singles out the canceled air strikes, though it also reflects RFK's view that the president was not adequately briefed on the consequences. See especially p. 602.

124   Four American pilots: Janet Weininger; Jake Esterline interview; Jonathan Lewis (Bissell's research assistant) interview; Seymour M. Hersh, *The Dark Side of Camelot*, pp. 215–16.

124   "You're the kind of guy. . . .": *RK*, p. 448.

124   named a child after him: ibid., p. 808. The child is Maxwell Taylor Kennedy born in 1965. For a profile of Taylor, see *NYT*, Oct. 31, 1960. Taylor had other backers as well. McGeorge Bundy and Charles Bohlen wanted to make him head of the CIA. Mac to Mr. President, May 11, 1961, RFK CF.

125   "How could you send us . . . ?": Roberto San Román (Bob Perez) interview.

125   Abruptly, Kennedy rose: Rowland Evans interview.

125   "We will take action against Castro. . . .": Reeves, *President Kennedy*, p. 181.

CHAPTER 6: TESTING

126   lunch with MLK: Taylor Branch, *Parting the Waters: America in the King Years, 1954–63*, pp. 404–405.

126   "I won't say I lay awake. . . .": Peter Maas, "Robert Kennedy Speaks Out," *Look*, March 22, 1961.

127   There was little eagerness: Harris Wofford, *Of Kennedys and Kings*, pp. 93, 139; *RK*, pp. 286–93. Ed Guthman argued that RFK was well aware civil rights would be a big issue for the Justice Department; that Wofford was "too identified" with the civil rights movement; and that RFK chose Marshall because, as he told Guthman, "everyone told me he was the brightest young lawyer in Washington." Ed Guthman to author, Feb. 7, 2000.

127   quit in protest: Interestingly, RFK leaked his protest on May 16—the first day he focused on the Freedom Riders. *NYT*, May 17, 1961.

127   "We Catholics. . . .": Arthur Schlesinger to RFK, Dec. 12, 1961; RFK to A.S., Dec. 21, 1961, Name File, RFK CF.

127   University of Georgia: *NYT*, May 7, 1961.

127   reluctance to use troops: Nicholas Katzenbach OH, JFKL.

127   enforcement of voter registration laws: Branch, *Parting the Waters*, p. 382.

127   Martin Luther King Jr.: For King background, see ibid., pp. 27–142. The code name was for the Birmingham protest in 1963, p. 690.

128   King shared Kennedy's guilt: Jean Stein and George Plimpton, *American Journey*, pp. 108–109.

128   Burke Marshall on RFK and MLK: Burke Marshall interview.

128   JFK suddenly "discovered": Branch, *Parting the Waters*, pp. 404–408.

128   RFK and Freedom Riders: Edwin O. Guthman and Jeffrey Shulman, eds., *Robert Kennedy: In His Own Words*, p. 83; *NYT*, May 15, 1961.

128   Preoccupied with Bay of Pigs: Edwin O. Guthman, *We Band of Brothers*, p. 167; Burke Marshall OH, JFKL.

129   "Tell them to call it off!": Wofford, *Of Kennedys and Kings*, p. 125.

129   RFK and Greyhound: *RK*, p. 296.

129   "Bobby" as epithet: Branch, *Parting the Waters*, p. 444.

129   "Get those niggers!": ibid., p. 446.

129   "It's terrible! . . .": Guthman, *Band of Brothers*, pp. 170–71.

129   FBI stood by: Branch, *Parting the Waters*, p. 420.

129   RFK indignant: Guthman and Shulman, eds., *In His Own Words*, p. 87; John Seigenthaler OH, JFKL.

130   Jim McShane: John Reilly interview.

130   William Orrick: William Orrick OH, JFKL.

130   "I wonder which side. . . .": Joe Dolan interview.

130   First Baptist Church: *Life*, June 2, 1961.

130   King called the attorney general: David Garrow, *Bearing the Cross: Martin Luther King, Jr., and the Southern Christian Leadership Conference*, pp. 156–58.

130   "If they don't get here. . . .": Branch, *Parting the Waters*, pp. 459–61; Ed Guthman interview.

131   ". . . Kelsey's nuts. . . .": Richard Reeves, *President Kennedy*, pp. 131, 682.

131   "honkers": ibid., p. 63.

131   "It took a lot of guts. . . .": Branch, *Parting the Waters*, p. 476.

132   "They'll stay": Guthman, *Band of Brothers*, pp. 154–55.

132   "This is too much! . . .": Wofford, *Of Kennedys and Kings*, p. 156.

132   Thurgood Marshall: Lloyd Cutler interview. RFK did want to diversify the federal bench: "I would like to put a Mexican-American on the Bench—Montoya would be a big help to us. What do you think?" RFK to Larry O'Brien, April 24, 1962. The choice was blocked by Senator Clinton Anderson. LO'B to RFK, April 26, 1962, RFK CF.

132   "John, it's more important. . . .": Pierre Salinger, Edwin Guthman, Frank Mankiewicz, and John Seigenthaler, eds., *An Honorable Profession: A Tribute to Robert F. Kennedy*, pp. 20–21.

132   draft exemptions: Branch, *Parting the Waters*, pp. 478–80.

133   "a tubby, bouncy little guy": Charles Bartlett interview.

133   "engaging, clownish. . . .": James Symington interview.

133   Holeman passed on Bolshakov's interest: Aleksandr Fursenko and Timothy Naftali, *"One Hell of a Gamble,"* pp. 109–14; Ed Guthman interview.

133   "Look here, Georgi. . . .": Reeves, *President Kennedy*, pp. 137–38.

134   nuclear test ban treaty: Fursenko and Naftali, *"One Hell of a Gamble,"* pp. 112–14.

134   "They're not queer. . . .": Peter Collier and David Horowitz, *The Kennedys*, p. 264.

134   "rather a weak figure": Guthman and Shulman, eds., *In His Own Words*, pp. 38, 44. In August, RFK proposed to JFK that Bowles be removed and farmed out to international conferences. "I know it is difficult but there is no question that with Rusk and Bowles in the two top positions things are going to continue to flounder at the State Dept. Rusk is no detail man either and with both of them in those top jobs things are going to get steadily worse." Attorney General to President, Aug. 15, 1961, RFK White House files, RFK CF.

134   problems with back channeling: author's interview with Philip Zelikow, Timothy Naftali, and Ernest May.

134   "Stupidly, I didn't write. . . .": Guthman and Shulman, eds., *In His Own Words*, p. 260.

135   Kennedy brothers kept to themselves: author's interview with Zelikow, Naftali, and May.

135   How the back channel worked: Fursenko and Naftali, *"One Hell of a Gamble,"* pp. 114–24. See also Michael Beschloss, *The Crisis Years,* pp. 180–81. In his oral history (p. 258), RFK said that Bolshakov had signaled room for negotiation on a test ban treaty. The examination of the record by Naftali and Fursenko shows no basis for this optimism. Timothy Naftali interview. It is possible that RFK misread Bolshakov during his first conversation—a pitfall in back channels.

136   "We've had a good life. . . .": Seymour Hersh, *The Dark Side of Camelot,* p. 254.

136   "a one chance. . . .": Guthman and Shulman, eds., *In His Own Words,* pp. 276–78.

136   "How You Can Survive Fallout": *Life,* Sept. 15, 1961.

136   JFK Nantucket shelter: Beschloss, *Crisis Years,* p. 271.

137   "There's no problem. . . .": *RK,* pp. 428–30.

137   "LeMay believed in devastation": Paul Nitze interview.

137   "I don't want that man. . . .": Reeves, *President Kennedy,* p. 182.

137   Maxwell Taylor: Guthman and Shulman, eds., *In His Own Words,* p. 254; Maxwell Taylor OH, JFKL.

137   RFK and Acheson: See Guthman and Shulman, eds., *In His Own Words,* pp. 19, 273; Beschloss, *Crisis Years,* pp. 242–44.

137   Mikhail Menshikov: Reeves, *President Kennedy,* p. 195; Beschloss, *Crisis Years,* p. 255.

138   leaks to Higgins: RFK phone messages, July 25, 1961, Aug. 16, 1961, JFKL; *New York Herald Tribune,* July 27, 1961.

138   RFK might have signaled through Bolshakov: Beschloss, *Crisis Years,* pp. 262, 280–81.

139   Kennedys moved to disarm the face-off: Guthman and Shulman, eds., *In His Own Words,* pp. 259–60; Ray Garthoff, "Berlin, 1961," *Foreign Policy,* Fall 1991, pp. 142, 152. But see W. R. Smyser, *From Yalta to Berlin,* p. 437. Smyser casts doubt on this story. He notes that JFK never told any other adviser and Khrushchev never brought it up during the Cuban Missile Crisis, when he had reason to.

139   RFK and Bowles: David Halberstam, *The Best and the Brightest* (New York: Random House, 1972), p. 89; Wofford, *Of Kennedys and Kings,* pp. 366–75.

139   RFK's cables "boring": Susan Mary Alsop interview.

139   General Clay and RFK: Peter Wyden, *The Wall: The Inside Story of Divided Berlin* (New York: Simon & Schuster, 1989), p. 214.

140   "The Attorney General has not spoken. . . .": *RK,* p. 560. See Guthman and Shulman, eds., *In His Own Words,* p. 302.

140   quoting Mao: Reeves, *President Kennedy,* p. 232.

CHAPTER 7: GOAD

141   "Counterinsurgency might best be described. . . .": Robert F. Kennedy, *To Seek a Newer World,* pp. 116–17.

141   the Swamp Fox: *RK,* p. 465. At the time, Walt Disney was running a popular drama about Francis Marion, starring Leslie Nielsen.

141   "Kennedy didn't understand. . . .": David Murphy interview. See Mem-

orandum for the Record Re Psychological Warfare and Information Activities, Aug. 22, 1961, RFK White House files, RFK CF.

141   September 11 memo: Memo to the President, Sept. 11, 1961, RFK White House files, RFK CF.

142   "He thought that by making their cops. . . .": Charles Maechling interview. Maechling showed the author a draft of his article "Camelot, Robert Kennedy and Counterinsurgency: A Memoir."

142   RFK and CI group: Charles Maechling interview; Thomas Parrott interview. See also Maxwell Taylor OH, JFKL.

143   RFK not head of CI group: After General Taylor stepped down to become chairman of the Joint Chiefs of Staff, there was some consideration of making RFK head of the CI group, but "I can hear State scream," advised one of JFK's national security advisers, Robert Komer (R. Komer to McGeorge Bundy, July 13, 1962). The nominal head was Deputy Secretary of State Alexis Johnson, but "note AG's increasingly central role in this enterprise," wrote Komer to Bundy, Sept. 19, 1962, Robert Komer Papers, JFKL.

143   "God watches every sparrow. . . .": Jean Stein and George Plimpton, American Journey, p. 208. RFK remembers it as "if God could take care of the little swallows in the skies, He certainly could take care of a little country like that." Edwin O. Guthman and Jeffrey Shulman, eds., Robert Kennedy: In His Own Words, p. 324.

143   Inter-Agency Youth Committee: Lucius Battle interview. The committee was established on April 11, 1962, after RFK was accosted by "critical students" in Japan and Indonesia. Getting the agencies to pitch in was slow-going: ". . . none of our training programs in any field are particularly good. . . . There was general agreement on this score. . . . AG Kennedy thinks we tend to get bogged down in the business of our own agencies and that we should take a step back to take a look and see where we are going in the future." Minutes of IYC, Nov. 8, 1963, IYC files, RFK CF. One purpose of the committee was to recruit agents for the CIA—Cord Meyer, a top CIA official, sat on the committee. William Haddad interview.

143   "Well, shit. . . .": Thomas Parrott interview. Kennedy wanted to put Arthur Goldberg, the Secretary of Labor, on the Special Group (CI), but the other members balked, partly because Goldberg was too voluble. Kennedy invoked his brother's name, and opposition became to crumble. But General Taylor insisted: no to Goldberg. Afterwards, Parrott, the recording secretary, said to Taylor, "You won that one. But you can only do it once." "Don't I know it," said Taylor.

143   "wire typewriters to explode. . . .": Robert Amory OH, JFKL.

143   "bureaucracy at its worst": Attorney General's Comments on Cuban Refugees in U.S., April 22, 1963, "Cuba Crisis" file, RFK CF.

143   "It is just incredible to me. . . .": RFK to Mike Forrestal, July 29, 1963, Name Files, RFK CF.

144   Guatemala water cannons: Julian J. Ewell to RFK, March 19, 1962; RFK to President, March 19, 1962, White House files, RFK CF.

144   "Now one other thing. . . ." . . . " 'Course, we wouldn't want him. . . .": JFK presidential audiotapes, cassette F. The conversation is undated, probably May 1963. JFKL.

145   White House recordings: See Michael Beschloss, Taking Charge, p. 548. Though turned over to the Kennedy Library after Watergate in 1975, the tapes sat

in a vault under lock and key, available only to the Kennedy family for almost twenty years. Matters improved in the 1990s, and by the end of 1999 about half had been transcribed and made available for public review; the rest await declassification. During the years in family custody—first by RFK, then after his death by Senator Edward Kennedy—it seems that a few of the tapes were tampered with: two cut and spliced from August 1962, perhaps four more missing from June 1963. The Dictabelts of JFK's phone calls are in worse shape. The president's secretary, Evelyn Lincoln, taped over at least some of them, and some may be missing. Philip Zelikow and Ernest May, "Preface to the Complete Kennedy Tapes," vols. 1–3 (draft), courtesy Philip Zelikow, March 2000.

145 Special Group described: The Special Group was actually the old 5412 Committee that approved covert actions in the Eisenhower administration. Thomas Parrott interview.

145 "The Cuba matter. . . .": *RK*, p. 473.

146 "We were hysterical about Castro. . . .": Senate Select Committee to Study Government Operations with Respect to Intelligence Activities, *Alleged Assassination Plots Involving Foreign Leaders: An Interim Report* (Washington, D.C.: U.S. Government Printing Office, 1975), hereafter cited as *Interim Report*, p. 142.

146 "terrier of a man": Kai Bird, *The Color of Truth* (New York: Simon & Schuster, 1998), p. 193.

146 "It was almost as simple. . . .": Evan Thomas, *The Very Best Men: Four Who Dared: The Early Years of the CIA*, p. 270.

146 Bundy regarded Cuba: Bird, *Color of Truth*, p. 201.

146 Cuban threat: "Crisis in Latin America," *Life*, June 2, 1961.

146 Castro background: *Current Biography Yearbook 1970* (New York: H. W. Wilson, 1970).

147 "My idea is to stir things up. . . .": RFK's handwritten note is quoted in *FRUS*, vol. X, p. 666.

147 "condition of shock": John McCone Memorandum for the Record, Nov. 22, 1963, *FRUS*, vol. X, p. 685.

147 "get off his ass": *Interim Report*, p. 141.

147 "moving" on Cuba: Richard Bissell interview.

148 RFK seemed bored by civil rights: Burke Marshall interview.

148 "the most effective commander": Goodwin to JFK, Nov. 1, 1961, *FRUS*, vol. X, pp. 664–65.

148 "Eliminate my name": Goodwin to RFK, Nov. 22, 1961, RFK Assassination Records Review Board, NA.

148 Ed Lansdale: See Memorandum for the Record, *FRUS*, vol. X, p. 98; Thomas, *Very Best Men*, p. 57.

148 "I wondered what that youngster. . . .": Edward Lansdale OH, JFKL.

148 "I decided to lay it right on the line. . . .": Lansdale to RFK, Dec. 7, 1961, Assassination Records Review Board, NA.

149 Lansdale urged Kennedy: Lansdale to RFK, Nov. 30, 1961, *FRUS*, vol. X, p. 687.

149 "resented CIA resistance. . . .": McCone Memorandum for the Record, Nov. 29, 1961, *FRUS*, vol. X, p. 687.

149 botched missions: John McCone Memorandum for file, Dec. 27, 1961,

FRUS, vol. X, p. 201. Haynes Johnson, *The Bay of Pigs,* pp. 261–62. Roberto San Román placed the raid in late November.

149   Helms memo to McCone: Memorandum from the Chief of Operations in the Deputy Directorate for Plans (Helms) to Director of Central Intelligence (McCone), Jan. 19, 1962, *FRUS,* vol. X, pp. 719–20. Richard Helms interview.

150   Lansdale's 33 "tasks": Operation Mongoose (Lansdale) to the members of the Caribbean Survey Group, Jan. 20, 1962, *FRUS,* vol. X, p. 721.

150   "elimination by illumination": *Interim Report,* p. 142; Thomas Parrott interview.

150   "We don't have anything": Sam Halpern interview.

150   failed to get Helms fired: Richard Bissell interview.

151   "They want James Bond?": Sam Halpern interview.

151   "So you're our James Bond?": Thomas, *Very Best Men,* pp. 288–89.

151   "Take that silly headgear off": Edward Lansdale OH, JFKL.

151   RFK and Harvey: William Harvey testimony, Church Committee, Executive Session, July 11, 1975, NA.

152   Kennedys "fags" . . . RFK "fucker": David Corn, *Blond Ghost: Ted Shackley and the CIA's Crusades,* p. 82. Kennedy's continued aggressiveness can be seen in the minutes of the Caribbean Survey Group on March 25, 1962. At the meeting, attended by Helms, Harvey, and representatives of State and Defense, Kennedy pushed and prodded, at one point asking what the chances were of "kidnapping some key people in the communist regime." At that stage, the CIA could barely keep agents alive on the island. Minutes of March 25, 1962, Caribbean Survey Group Meeting, courtesy of Maria Torrez, FOIA request.

CHAPTER 8:   INTRIGUE

153   CIA abuses: *Interim Report,* pp. 71, 73, 85.

153   doctrine of plausible deniability: ibid., pp. 119–20.

153   RFK too noble: *RK,* p. 498.

153   Mainstream historians scoff: See, for example, Michael Beschloss, *The Crisis Years,* pp. 137–42.

154   "circumlocutious" terms: ibid.; *Interim Report,* pp. 94–95, 117.

154   early assassination plots: *Interim Report,* pp. 13–70 (Congo); 71–180 (Cuba).

155   plan to kill Castro . . . "given to believe": ibid., pp. 123–24; Beschloss, *Crisis Years,* p. 139.

155   Bissell and Mafia: Richard Bissell interview; *Interim Report,* pp. 80–81; William Roemer Jr., *Roemer: Man Against the Mob,* p. 158. Sandy Smith, who covered organized crime for the *Chicago Sun-Times* and then Time-Life and who probably had better access to organized crime figures than any other journalist of his time, told the author the mob did not treat the plots very seriously.

155   Giancana, McGuire, Maheu: *Interim Report,* pp. 77–79.

155   Hoover's May 22 memo: ibid., pp. 125–27.

156   RFK and Evans: ibid., pp. 126–29. See Courtney Evans testimony, Sam Papich testimony, Church Committee files, NA.

156   RFK busy, RFK and Maheu case: John Nolan interview; Herbert Miller interview.

156   "Bob would talk. . . .": Courtney Evans STOH.

156   Bissell's "circumlocutious" remarks: *Interim Report*, pp. 122–23.

157   "See No Evil": Lester David and Irene David, *Bobby Kennedy*, p. 127.

157   RFK "status" . . . Taylor "the President's interest. . . .": *Interim Report*, pp. 128–36.

157   JFK-Szulc meeting: John Nolan, later RFK's administrative assistant, thought the pressure to kill Castro came from wealthy friends of the Kennedys in Palm Beach. John Nolan interview; *Interim Report*, pp. 137–38; Tad Szulc interview.

158   Halpern "get rid" of Castro: Sam Halpern interview; *Interim Report*, pp. 83–84.

158   ZR/RIFLE: Seymour Hersh quotes Halpern as saying that Harvey told him the authorization for ZR/RIFLE came directly from JFK (Hersh, *The Dark Side of Camelot*, p. 192). Halpern says now he's not sure; Harvey could have said, more generally, "the White House." Harvey was explicit in his testimony to the Church Committee: Bissell told him the authorization came "from the White House." In a 1994 interview, Bissell told the author it came from the national security adviser, McGeorge Bundy.

158   "They never told me *not* to": Richard Bissell interview.

158   Rosselli and poison pills: *Interim Report*, pp. 83–84.

158   Helms and Harvey: ibid., pp. 100–104, 149–54. See Harvey and Helms testimony, Church Committee files, NA.

159   "You haven't lived. . . .": Richard Helms interview.

159   RFK and Harvey; McCone and "executive action"; and Lansdale: *Interim Report*, pp. 148–56. In notes of his interview with F.A.O. Schwarz, chief counsel of the Church Committee, Arthur Schlesinger wrote: "Assassination: Helms hinted that AWD [Allen Dulles] told JFK & that JFK sd [said] not to tell McCone." Schwarz told the author he had no recollection of telling Schlesinger this. Schwarz doubted Dulles told JFK anything about the assassination plots. In his testimony, Helms did come close to insinuating that McCone must have known about the plots, "McCone," said Helms, "was in this business up to his scuppers," F.A.O. Schwarz interview; Schlesinger Papers, JFKL; Helms Testimony, Church Committee files, NA.

159   Special Group plotting, Aug. 10, 1962: See, for instance, Richard Reeves, *President Kennedy*, pp. 335–37. It is interesting to note that one of the White House tapes that was apparently erased or tampered with was from a meeting on Cuba on August 22. Zelikow and May raise the question whether assassination plots were discussed. Philip Zelikow and Ernest May, draft of "Preface to the Complete Kennedy Tapes."

159   McNamara, Lansdale, Harvey, McCone: *Interim Report*, pp. 161–68.

160   Inga Arvad: Nigel Hamilton, *JFK: Reckless Youth*, pp. 426–56.

160   JFK, Sinatra, and "Show girls. . . .": SAC New Orleans to Hoover, March 23, 1960, Hoover Official and Confidential files, FBI; SAC LA to Hoover, April 1, 1960, Sinatra file, FOIA/FBI.

160   FBI informants: Summary of Informant Reports, Sept. 29, 1960, Sinatra file, FOIA/FBI.

160   Giancana claimed to "own": Evans to Parsons, March 13, 1961, House Assassination Committee Records, NA.

160   JFK drawn to the glitz: JFK's friend Charles Bartlett said that JFK had no affection for Sinatra. "He was just keeping him warm for Peter Lawford, to get jobs for his brother-in-law. The Rat Pack wasn't that amusing." Charles Bartlett interview.

160   Sinatra playing the piano: Joan Braden interview.

161   "You ought to meet this guy! . . .": John Reilly interview.

161   Sinatra at Hyannis Port: Beschloss, *Crisis Years*, p. 312.

161   RFK ordered it deleted: Paul Fay manuscript of *The Pleasure of His Company*, Myrick Land Papers, Boston University.

161   FBI learned from an informant: *Interim Report*, pp. 78–79, 127–28. It was the tip about Giancana's involvement in the plots that led Hoover to authorize the installation of a bug in Giancana's headquarters, the Armory Lounge, in Chicago. McAndrews to Belmont, Dec. 19, 1960, House Assassination Committee Records, NA.

162   Giancana: ". . . I know all about the Kennedys. . . .": SAC Chicago to Hoover, July 13, 1961, House Assassination Committee Records, NA; William Roemer Jr., *Accardo*, pp. 253–59. Interestingly, Hoover omitted Giancana's remarks about the "Kennedys" in his memo about the incident to RFK. Hoover to RFK, July 14, 1961, House Assassinations Committee Records, NA.

162   incessant pressure from RFK: Foley to Hoover, Feb. 7, 1961; Rosen to Parsons, Feb. 6, 1961; Hoover to SAC Chicago, Feb. 20, 1961, House Assassination Committee Records, NA.

162   "the face of a gargoyle. . . ."; personified evil: Kitty Kelley, *His Way*, p. 264.

162   "was violent, crazy. . . .": William Hundley interview.

162   April 1961, RFK, Hoover, and Sinatra: Hoover to Tolson, Parsons, Rosen, DeLoach, April 17, 1961, House Assassination Committee Records, NA.

163   Formosa and Giancana conversation: SAC Chicago to Hoover, Dec. 9, 1961, House Assassination Committee Records, NA. Roemer has a slightly different version of the Sinatra-Formosa exchange. Roemer, *Roemer: Man Against the Mob*, p. 189.

164   Joe Kennedy and organized crime: Hersh, *Dark Side of Camelot*, pp. 134–36, quotes a mob lawyer named Robert J. McDonnell setting up a meeting between Joe Kennedy and mobsters in 1959. G. Robert Blakey, a former Justice Department official who worked as counsel to the House Assassination Committee, believes there was a deal between the Kennedys and the mob to steal the Chicago vote in 1960. His conclusion, he said, is based on FBI eavesdropping not yet made public. Blakey interview. See G. Robert Blakey and Richard Billings, *The Plot to Kill the President*, pp. 367–98. Presumably drawing on transcripts from the FBI bugs, Blakey quoted Giancana telling Judith Exner, "Listen, honey, if it wasn't for me, [Kennedy] wouldn't . . . be in the White House." Blakey also quotes a December 21, 1961, conversation between Giancana and Rosselli. Rosselli told Giancana that Frank Sinatra had been in touch with the Kennedys. "He's [Sinatra has] got it in his head that they're [the Kennedys were] going to be faithful to him." Giancana replied, "In other words, then, the donation that was made. . . ." [presumably, a campaign donation through Sinatra]. Rosselli interrupted, "That's what I was talking about . . ."

(Blakey and Billings, *The Plot to Kill the President,* pp. 376–77). Also see the Rosselli-Giancana conversation quoted at pp. 382–83. Richard Mahoney, in *Sons & Brothers* (pp. 43–49), writes that Johnny Rosselli organized a meeting between Joe Kennedy and various Mafia figures in February 1959, at a restaurant in New York. Mahoney's source was a mob lawyer named Mario Brod who also apparently did some work for James Angleton of the CIA. Brod died in 1980. In 1999, I interviewed Cartha DeLoach, an assistant FBI director who saw any sensitive wiretap information coming to Hoover on JPK. DeLoach said that, before 1961, the FBI had "no idea" of any contact between JPK and organized crime. "And we would have—we would have heard it on a bug, plus through our informants." However, he said that FBI bugs in 1961 picked up Giancana boasting that he had contributed $25,000 to the Kennedy campaign. He said the FBI generally believed that Joseph Kennedy had solicited the contribution, but it had no proof.

164 A 1964 summary of FBI files: Summary of FBI Reports on Frank Sinatra, June 8, 1964, Sinatra file, FOIA/FBI.

164 December 11 memo to RFK: Hoover to RFK, Dec. 11, 1961, Hoover Official and Confidential files, FBI.

164 JPK stroke: *Washington Post,* Dec. 20, 21, 22, 1961; *NYT,* Dec. 20, 21, 22, 24, 25, 1961; *RK,* pp. 586–89. But see Collier and Horowitz, *The Kennedys,* pp. 287–89.

165 February 2 FBI bug: SAC Chicago to Hoover, Feb. 2, 1961, House Assassination Committee Records, NA.

166 Hoover heard rumors that he would be "eased out": Anthony Summers, *Official and Confidential: The Secret Life of J. Edgar Hoover,* p. 289.

166 Judith Campbell's calls to Evelyn Lincoln: Evans to Belmont, Feb. 23, 1962, House Assassination Committee Records, NA.

166 "association" with Giancana: Evans to Belmont, Feb. 26, 1962, House Assassination Committee Records, NA.

166 "My Dear Mr. O'Donnell": Hoover to O'Donnell, Feb. 27, 1962, House Assassination Committee Records, NA.

166 other memo to RFK: Hoover to RFK, Feb. 27, 1962, House Assassination Committee Records, NA.

166 RFK world tour: *Newsweek,* Feb. 19, 1962; *NYT,* Feb. 22, Feb. 25, Feb. 26, 1962.

166 RFK and Ethel in Rome: *Newsweek,* Feb. 26, 1962.

167 scurrilous story: SAC LA to Hoover, March 5, 1962, Hoover Official and Confidential files, FBI.

167 RFK accustomed to such gossip: Edwin O. Guthman and Jeffrey Shulman, eds., *Robert Kennedy: In His Own Words,* pp. 128–35.

167 girls in Palm Beach and El Paso: John Seigenthaler interview; Ed Guthman interview; Memorandum for Personal Files, Feb. 22, 1961, Hoover Official and Confidential files, FBI.

167 "Hire faster ambassadors": Kenneth O'Donnell OH, JFKL.

167 "I suppose every month. . . .": Guthman and Shulman, eds., *In His Own Words,* pp. 128, 134.

167 "freelance artist": Moore to Jenkins, Dec. 24, 1975, House Assassination Committee Records, FBI files, NA.

167   FBI discovered Campbell's calls: "Judith E. Campbell," March 20, 1962, Hoover Official and Confidential files, FBI.

168   courier between JFK and Giancana: See Liz Smith, "Judith Exner's Final Revelation About JFK," *Vanity Fair*, January 1997; Hersh, *Dark Side of Camelot*, pp. 299–336, also credits Exner. The arguments against are more persuasive. For one thing, neither Giancana nor JFK, misogynists both, would have trusted a mistress with anything so sensitive. See Ernest May and Philip Zelikow, "Camelot Confidential" and Hersh's reply, "May-Zelikow Confidential," in *Diplomatic History*, Fall 1998. According to historian Max Holland, Hersh's best source, Martin Underwood, who claimed to have seen Exner travel to meet with Giancana, has recanted. See Roemer, *Roemer: Man Against the Mob*, pp. 185–86. Roemer, the FBI agent assigned to handle Giancana's surveillance, also disputed Exner's story.

168   "bury the Kennedys": Evans to Belmont, March 15, 1962, House Assassination Committee Records, NA.

168   "Tell me what you think of this": Joe Dolan interview.

168   RFK coldly turned him away: John Seigenthaler interview. Lawford said RFK would not take Sinatra's calls. J. Randy Taraborrelli, *Sinatra*, pp. 264–68. But Peter Maas overheard Kennedy call Sinatra. Peter Maas interview. Maas said that Bill Hundley, chief of Justice's organized crime division, told him that the FBI report on Sinatra warned that Giancana could be a fellow houseguest.

169   "Johnny," said RFK: Red Fay quoted in Peter Collier and David Horowitz, *The Kennedys*, p. 295.

169   Sinatra seized sledgehammer: Kitty Kelley, *His Way*, p. 302.

169   president's calendar: "There isn't much to report today," wrote Evelyn Lincoln, JFK's secretary, in her daily log. She noted that the president left to have lunch with Hoover in the mansion at 1 p.m. and never returned to the Oval Office. President's office diary, July 22, 1962, Evelyn Lincoln Papers, JFKL.

169   "Get rid of that bastard. . . .": Taylor Branch, *Parting the Waters*, pp. 568–69.

169   "couldn't be more feeble. . . .": *RK*, p. 262.

170   RFK signed off: ibid., p. 360. David Garrow, *Bearing the Cross: Martin Luther King, Jr., and the Southern Christian Leadership Conference*, p. 195.

170   "I don't like getting into this. . . .": Callahan to Mohr, April 12, 1962, RFK files, FBI.

170   FBI agents to awaken reporters: *RK*, pp. 403–404; Guthman, *We Band of Brothers*, p. 233.

171   fencing between RFK and Hoover: *Interim Report*, pp. 128–32.

171   Miller and Maheu case: Herbert Miller interview.

171   RFK briefing on Castro plot and Hoover meeting: *Interim Report*, pp. 132–35.

172   "Never write it down": RFK to McCone, May 2, 1962, RFK Personal Correspondence, RFK Attorney General Papers, JFKL.

173   mole in the IRS: SAC Chicago to Hoover, Sept. 8, 1961, House Assassination Committee Records, NA.

173   Giancana learned to evade: According to a preliminary report on Giancana made by the IRS at Kennedy's behest in 1961, the prospects were "bright" for a prosecution. But Frank Kiernan, the Justice Department's organized

crime lawyer sent to Chicago to prosecute cases (who showed the author the IRS report), said, "The IRS was overly optimistic. Giancana was very well covered. He paid enough taxes to cover his living." Frank Kiernan interview. There is some indication that the U.S. attorney's office in Chicago was slow to take on Giancana, in part because of squabbles with the FBI. In July 1962, RFK told Courtney Evans that "the USAG office in Chicago was still his #1 problem in the field." Evans to Belmont, July 3, 1962, RFK files, FBI. In Washington, a staff attorney, Dougald McMillan, believed that Giancana could be indicted for extortion and crimes related to his gambling interests. But Jack Keeney, an organized crime division lawyer who reviewed the McMillan memo, said, "I didn't see any case there. These guys [the mafioso] were careful. The problem was proving anything independent of the FBI's tapes. None of us thought we had a case, except McMillan." Jack Keeney interview.

173   tax investigation of Sinatra: Nicholas Gage, "Ex-Aides Say Justice Dept. Rejected Sinatra Inquiry," *NYT*, Feb. 14, 1976. In 1961, Dougald McMillan made an oral case to RFK that Sinatra was mobbed up. Kennedy told him to write a memo. Robert Blakey interview. The memo, supplemented by additional evidence in 1963, is preserved in RFK's confidential files. It is a forty-eight-page grab bag of informants' reports. "Sinatra's indebtedness to 'the boys' [the mob] may be traced to a low spot in his career, when racket figures helped him out and started him on the road to his present position of eminence in the entertainment field." The evidence makes "a fairly strong case for the proposition that Sinatra is controlled by racketeers" and "under Giancana's control." McMillan saw a "prima facie pattern of irregular financial dealings on the part of Sinatra and [Sammy] Davis [Jr.], the reason for which could be the avoidance of Federal taxes, payments to racketeers who control them, or both." Dougald McMillan to Bill Hundley, Aug. 1, 1963, RFK "Frank Sinatra" file, RFK CF. But former U.S. attorney Robert Morgenthau, who heard the evidence, saw no case against Sinatra. Robert Morgenthau interview.

173   Recent scholarship in Soviet archives: Ernest R. May and Philip D. Zelikow, *Kennedy Tapes*, pp. 671–79; Aleksandr Fursenko and Timothy Naftali, *"One Hell of a Gamble,"* pp. 166–83.

174   Public believes conspiracy theories: Evan Thomas, *The Very Best Men: Four Who Dared: The Early Years of the CIA*, p. 12.

chapter 9: PLAY

175   "... ten minutes" ... "For two hours. ...": Rafael Quintero interview.

176   RFK refused to believe earlier intelligence: National Intelligence Estimates: The Situation and Prospects in Cuba, March 21, 1962, *FRUS*, vol. X, pp. 772, 774.

176   RFK knew invasion out of question: Note by U. Alexis Johnson on Guidelines for Operation Mongoose, March 14, 1962, *FRUS*, vol. X, p. 771.

176   Castro sentenced brigade: editorial note, *FRUS*, vol. X, p. 783.

176   San Román meeting with RFK: Roberto San Román interview; Haynes Johnson, *The Bay of Pigs*, p. 274.

177   San Román and RFK discussed assassination: Roberto San Román interview.

178   RFK and San Román and Williams: Haynes Johnson interview; John-son, *Bay of Pigs*, pp. 133, 288–91.

178   Special Group decided not to use Guantánamo: *Interim Report*, p. 150. Repeatedly, RFK eyed Guantánamo as a base for action or provocation. One won-ders about his sitting in Guantánamo Bay in the winter of 1946 as a bored sailor who missed World War II.

178   reluctant to pay Castro's demand: Kennedy wanted to negotiate a lower price. He was initially reluctant to give covert support to the private committee raising funds. Memorandum of Discussion, John McCone, July 3, 1962, *FRUS*, vol. X, p. 842.

178   Charles Ford: Charles Ford was interviewed by the Senate Select Intelli-gence Committee, Sept. 19, 1975, Church Committee files, NA; Sam Halpern inter-view. Charles Ford, aka Fiscalini, appears on RFK's calendar on September 24 and September 26, 1962, RFK Office files, JFKL. Seymour Hersh speculates that Fis-calini was part of the assassination plots. There is no evidence and Ford's testimony contradicts this theory. See Hersh, *The Dark Side of Camelot*, pp. 286–88.

178   "She is a wonderful woman": Johnson, *Bay of Pigs*, p. 223.

178   "I thought it was a compliment. . . .": Roberto San Román interview.

179   "First of all. . . .": Jean Smith and George Plimpton, *American Journey*, p. 163.

179   push-up contest at Hickory Hill: Theodore White has told various ver-sions of this story with different entrants in the push-up contest. Ibid.

180   "We're winning! . . .": ibid.

180   "wild, informal mixture. . . .": William vanden Heuvel and Bernard Gwirtzman, *On His Own: Robert F. Kennedy, 1964–1968*, pp. 179–80.

180   Ethel's color scheme: Barbara Howar interview.

180   Bobby Jr.'s zoo: John Cronin and Robert F. Kennedy Jr., *The River-keepers*, p. 80.

180   "watching you go by. . . .": Stein and Plimpton, *American Journey*, p. 164.

180   ". . . 'hellzapopping'!": ibid., p. 161.

180   Ethel loved pranks: Peter Collier and David Horowitz, *The Kennedys*, p. 284.

180   Ethel handed out pencil and paper: ibid.

180   José Torres: Stein and Plimpton, *American Journey*, p. 169; Warren Rogers, *When I Think of Bobby*, p. 81.

180   ". . . relax in a violent fashion": Gerald Tremblay OH, JFKL.

180   Justice Department aides played football: James Symington interview.

180   "Bobby would really chew you out. . . .": Paul Fay interview.

181   "If you were going out for a pass. . . .": George Plimpton interview.

181   "I think he liked me. . . .": George Plimpton STOH.

181   Jimmy Brown like: Stein and Plimpton, *American Journey*, p. 171.

181   travels with Brandon Grove: Brandon Grove interview. Grove permit-ted me to read and quote from portions of his memoir, *An Inch Ahead Lies Dark-ness*, which is awaiting publication.

182   "Well, get on it, Averell. . . .": Rowland Evans STOH.

182   RFK's Brumus: Rogers, *When I Think of Bobby*, pp. 93–95.

182   pawed Rusk: Robert Rusk interview. RFK had gone to see Rusk to tell

him to fire Deputy Secretary of State George McGhee, whom RFK described as "useless, worthless." Rusk said, "Don't you think this is perhaps personal?"

182   "How is he feeling?": Nicholas Katzenbach interview.

182   RFK and Judy Garland: Joseph Kraft STOH; Joseph Kraft OH, JFKL.

183   Hickory Hill dunkings: Stein and Plimpton, *American Journey*, p. 165; *NYT*, June 21, 1962; *U.S. News & World Report*, July 2, 1962.

183   Sarah Davis: Gerald Tremblay OH, JFKL; Tremblay reconfirmed his recollection in an interview with the author. Sarah Davis told the author, "I'm the one who was really mad. I was walking across the ramp in front of Arthur [Schlesinger], who jiggled the ramp. I looked in horror as Ethel went in. Ethel blamed me. We went up to her room to change her dress and she put on a wig. . . . She pushed me in the pool. I have no memory of Bobby being involved. Maybe Gerry remembers." Sarah Davis interview.

183   "They used to sail with road maps. . . .": Douglas Dillon interview.

183   Kennedy cruises: Stein and Plimpton, *American Journey*, pp. 172–73.

184   "All we ate. . . .": ibid., p. 175.

184   "If you got to a flat place. . . .": Marie Ridder interview.

184   "You go in there to win": Kathleen Kennedy Townsend interview.

184   "He had a ferocious forehand. . . .": George Plimpton interview.

184   "Ethel, what's the matter? . . .": Rowland Evans OH, JFKL.

184   RFK could be sensualist: See Michael Knox Beran, *The Last Patrician*, p. 148.

184   maintain his tan: Hugh Sidey interview.

185   "He didn't like anybody to gripe. . . .": Gerald Tremblay OH, JFKL.

185   concern for poor: Peter Edelman interview. William Haddad, RFK's special assistant who became Peace Corps inspector general, recalled visiting RFK's office sometime in 1963. David Hackett had brought in a contingent of minorities, including American Indians, to talk to the attorney general about the problems of the poor. Haddad, a liberal who had always thought of RFK as a conservative, was struck by RFK's personal, careful questioning. "I began to think, this is something else, this is a different guy," Haddad recalled. William Haddad interview.

185   Dunbar High: E. Barrett Prettyman OH, JFKL.

185   he walked slowly among the children: Patrick Anderson, "Robert Kennedy's Character," *Esquire*, April 1965.

185   "didn't want to hear. . . .": Gerald Tremblay OH, JFKL.

186   "She adored Bobby. . . .": Paul Fay interview.

186   RFK scribbled, from memory: vanden Heuvel and Gwirtzman, *On His Own*, pp. 180–81.

186   "always carried a rosary. . . .": Cronin and Kennedy, *The Riverkeepers*, pp. 83–84.

186   "Brumus gets lonely. . . .": *NYT*, Aug. 4, 1962.

186   "Dad, I think you have made your point. . . .": Paul Fay manuscript for *The Pleasure of His Company*, Myrick Land Papers, Boston University.

186   formal dining room at Justice: Victor S. Navasky, *Kennedy Justice*, p. 340.

187   A steady stream: Rogers, *When I Think of Bobby*, p. 59.

187   struggling to remember all their names: vanden Heuvel and Gwirtzman, *On His Own*, p. 181.

187   reluctant to hold his babies: Pat Lawford, *That Shining Hour*, p. 25.

187   tickle-tumble: Rogers, *When I Think of Bobby*, pp. 15–16.

187   growing up at Hickory Hill: Kathleen Kennedy Townsend interview.

187   martyred saints: Cronin and Kennedy, *The Riverkeepers*, p. 84.

187   RFK's tastes ran: Rogers, *When I Think of Bobby*, p. 89.

188   "That's the biggest bunch of bullshit. . . .": Richard Goodwin, *Remembering America*, p. 447.

188   "There was nothing precious. . . .": Rogers, *When I Think of Bobby*, p. 90.

188   JFK steered clear of entertainments: Collier and Horowitz, *Kennedys*, p. 288.

188   "That was a party to miss. . . .": Mary Bailey Gimbel STOH.

188   "Enough": Brandon Grove interview. (Ethel Kennedy told this story to Grove.)

189   "all thrown together. . . .": William Walton STOH.

189   "a realist brilliantly disguised. . . .": *RK*, pp. 600–602.

189   "polite, but not cozy. . . .": Susan Mary Alsop interview.

189   "I am the president. . . .": Charles Bartlett interview.

189   RFK "circling, watching. . . .": Letitia Baldrige interview.

189   Rose and RFK: Joe Gargan interview; William vanden Heuvel interview.

190   helping EMK get elected: Guthman and Shulman, eds., *In His Own Words*, p. 328; *RK*, p. 371.

190   RFK and Joe Sr.: Rita Dallas, with Jeanira Radcliffe, *The Kennedy Case*, pp. 109, 143.

190   "The only time. . . .": Joe Dolan interview.

190   ". . . good for Jack. . . .": Laura Bergquist Knebel OH, JFKL.

190   "Hey, Jackie. . . .": Rogers, *When I Think of Bobby*, p. 74.

190   RFK and Tretick: Stanley Tretick OH, JFKL; Laura Bergquist Knebel OH, JFKL. Kenny O'Donnell told the *Look* reporter, "The president blew his stack, but secretly he loved those pictures."

191   Gore Vidal: *RK*, pp. 594–96; George Plimpton, *Truman Capote*, pp. 378–79.

191   JFK's crutches: Kenneth P. O'Donnell and David F. Powers, *"Johnny, We Hardly Knew Ye,"* p. 88.

191   JFK's promiscuity: RFK was always on the alert. When he heard that *Look*'s Fletcher Knebel was digging around in St. Louis following rumors that JFK had secretly married a woman from there, RFK warned his brother, who summoned Knebel and threatened, "You print that story and I'll end up owning *Look* magazine." Laura Bergquist Knebel OH, JFKL.

191   Jacobson and FDA: Richard Reeves, *President Kennedy*, pp. 685, 699. Reeves examined an unpublished memoir of Jacobson's.

191   June 7 FBI lab report: Evans to Belmont, June 4, 1962; Conrad to Jevrons, June 7, 1962; Evans to Belmont, June 11, 1962, RFK files, FBI.

191   Marilyn Monroe: Reeves, *President Kennedy*, pp. 315–16; Barbara Leaming, *Marilyn Monroe*, pp. 411–12.

192   without flying too close: Donald Spoto, *Marilyn Monroe*, pp. 489–90. Spoto, Monroe's most reliable biographer, traces (pp. 599–611) the path of the con-

spiracy theories from the gossip columns through Norman Mailer's popularization of the myth in *Marilyn* (1973) to the most skillful conspiracy theory, in Anthony Summers's *Goddess* (1989). The most unreliable witnesses appear to be Jeanne Carmen (see Spoto, p. 472) and Robert Slatzer (Spoto, pp. 228–29). Richard Burke, a former aide to Senator Edward Kennedy, claimed that among the White House tapes erased are those containing conversations with Marilyn Monroe and Judith Exner. Burke is not a reliable source. Philip Zelikow and Ernest May, "Preface to the Complete Kennedy Tapes."

192   Monroe departed drunk: Ed Guthman interview.

192   "wonderful sense of humor": Spoto, *Marilyn*, p. 491.

192   questions on a napkin: Joan Braden interview.

192   "Bobby and I engaged. . . .": *RK*, pp. 590–91.

192   "cornered animal": Helen O'Donnell (daughter) interview.

192   Monroe declined to attend Glenn pool party: Spoto, *Marilyn*, p. 533.

192   went to see her new house: ibid. See p. 491, footnote 4.

193   Monroe upset: ibid., pp. 540–41.

193   "Bobby discovered girls": Helen O'Donnell interview.

193   attested to his presence: Spoto, *Marilyn*, pp. 560–61.

193   Dolan picked up RFK: Joe Dolan interview. RFK kept a file on Marilyn Monroe, but it contains nothing very interesting or revealing. One envelope, marked "Les Articles du France Dimanche re You Know Who!," contained a March 27, 1963, article from an unreliable French tabloid speculating that Monroe killed herself over unrequited love for RFK. The file also contained a letter from Don Shannon of the Paris Bureau of the *Los Angeles Times* jokingly asking, "My only question: how did you have the time?" Shannon writes that *France Dimanche* is "one of the leading organs of the pornographic press in Paris." In another envelope, marked "Himself," there is a copy of *Photoplay* from August 1963 including a Walter Winchell column knocking down the French story. Winchell concludes that there is "no proof that the married man [RFK] was the villain in Marilyn's life and a good many of his friends are now convinced that the overdose was an accident." RFK "Marilyn Monroe" file, RFK CF.

193   John Miner: John Miner interview. Miner said he is writing a book about his experience in which he will print the full transcript.

193   Peter Lawford: Peter Lawford interview by David Heymann, Heymann Papers, SUNY, Stony Brook, NY. Myer Feldman, deputy counsel to President Kennedy and a Washington lawyer, told the author that the Kennedy family asked him to check out the rumors about RFK and Monroe. "I talked to Lawford and Steve Smith. Bobby had no interest in Marilyn Monroe. Lawford was just getting even." Myer Feldman interview. Other friends of Lawford, including the writer Dominick Dunne, give more credit to his account.

193   girl in El Paso: Evans to Belmont, Aug. 20, 1962, Hoover Official and Confidential files, FBI.

194   ". . . for many, many years to come": *Seattle Intelligencer*, Aug. 7, 1962.

CHAPTER 10: CRISIS

195   Meredith inspired: Walter Lord, *The Past That Would Not Die*, pp. 38, 96.

195   "Boy, that's all we needed. . . .": Edwin O. Guthman and Jeffrey Shulman, eds., *Robert Kennedy: In His Own Words*, pp. 195–96.

196   as a souvenir: Taylor Branch, *Parting the Waters*, p. 648.

196   "loony": *RK*, p. 318.

196   financial pressure on Barnett: Senator Ernest Hollings interview.

196   Thomas Watkins: Bill Minor interview; Charles Clark interview; Charles Eagles interview. Minor, who covered Watkins for the *New Orleans Times-Picayune*, said, "Watkins was a double-dealer. I didn't trust him. He was not a good, solid negotiator. He thought the feds would go away. The back channel was a miscalculation."

196   "I did the work. . . .": Burke Marshall interview.

196   "Marshall had impeccable taste. . . .": Theodore White STOH.

196   Walter Lord: Walter Lord interview. Lord's notes for *The Past That Would Not Die* are in the Walter Lord Papers, JFKL.

197   "Bob may have thought. . . .": Burke Marshall interview.

197   "Bob used to do this. . . .": Nicholas Katzenbach interview.

197   tape-recorded conversations: Summary of telephone calls to Tom Watkins, Sept. 20, 1962, Burke Marshall Papers, JFKL.

197   deal between Marshall, RFK, and Watkins: Transcript of telephone conversation between Watkins and RFK, Sept. 27, 1962, Burke Marshall Papers, JFKL.

198   "I don't know if it would be embarrassing. . . .": Transcript of telephone conversation between RFK and Governor Barnett, Sept. 27, 1962, Burke Marshall Papers, JFKL.

198   JFK telephone calls to Governor Barnett: *RK*, p. 320; transcript of telephone conversations between JFK and Governor Barnett, Sept. 29, 1962, Burke Marshall Papers, JFKL.

198   "the last militant race rally. . . .": Branch, *Parting the Waters*, p. 659.

198   "That won't do at all!": Transcript of telephone conversation between RFK and Governor Barnett, Sept. 30, 1962, Burke Marshall Papers, JFKL.

199   RFK threw together a team: Guthman and Shulman, eds., *In His Own Words*, p. 169.

199   Katzenbach and communications: Nicholas Katzenbach interview; Joe Dolan interview. Dolan used a pay phone because he feared the university phones would be tapped.

199   Colonel Birdsong: Victor S. Navasky, *Kennedy Justice*, p. 170; Lord, *Past That Would Not Die*, pp. 144–45.

199   "Mandrake the Magician": Guthman and Shulman, eds., *Kennedy: In His Own Words*, p. 167.

199   "Go to Cuba. . . .": Lord, *Past That Would Not Die*, p. 202.

200   Robert E. Lee's tomb: Nicholas Katzenbach OH, JFKL.

200   RFK assembled marshals: Lord, *Past That Would Not Die*, pp. 198, 217.

200   state police to withdraw: It was never finally determined who ordered the highway patrolmen to withdraw. Barnett denied it, as did a state senator he dispatched as his lieutenant at Ole Miss. Lord, *Past That Would Not Die*, pp. 205–206.

200   riot described: ibid., pp. 202–208.

200   "throwing iron spikes": presidential audiotape transcript #26, p. 4, Sept. 30, 1962, JFKL.

200   "the worst night. . . .": Lord, *Past That Would Not Die*, p. 228.

200   Coach Johnny Vaught: presidential audiotape transcript #26, pp. 5, 7, 30, 34, JFKL.

201   "This reminds me a little bit . . . Yech!": ibid., pp. 7, 23.

201   shotgun blast: Lord, *Past That Would Not Die*, pp. 216–19.

201   "We've got to take care. . . .": Joe Dolan interview.

201   "is getting them all stirred up. . . .": Presidential audiotape transcript #26, pp. 29–30, JFKL.

201   "The attorney general announced today. . . .": ibid., p. 33.

201   "is so scared. . . .": ibid., pp. 52–54.

202   The answer was no: Guthman and Shulman, eds., *In His Own Words*, pp. 161–62.

202   "Hey, Nick? . . .": presidential audiotape transcript #26, pp. 56–57, JFKL.

202   Katzenbach not eager to fire: Lord, *Past That Would Not Die*, p. 220.

202   "Damn army!": presidential audiotape transcript #26, p. 58, and #26A, p. 7, JFKL.

202   marshals held fast: Lord, *Past That Would Not Die*, pp. 223–24.

203   "Sure is a great day": presidential audiotape transcript #26, p. 43, JFKL.

203   "You did terrific": presidential audiotape transcript #26A, p. 14, JFKL.

203   JFK chewed out: Guthman and Shulman, eds., *In His Own Words*, p. 162.

203   JFK's poll ratings: Richard Reeves, *President Kennedy*, p. 364.

203   troops state of alert: Branch, *Parting the Waters*, p. 670; Nicholas Katzenbach interview.

203   Operation Mongoose, JFK dissatisfied: Memorandum by DCI McCone, Oct. 4, 1962, *FRUS*, vol. XI, pp. 11–13; Minutes of Meeting of Special Group (Augmented) on Operation Mongoose, Oct. 4, 1962, Assassination Records Review Board, NA.

204   "learning to live with Castro": Memorandum of Discussion Between President's Special Assistant for National Security (Bundy) and DCI McCone, Oct. 5, 1962, *FRUS*, vol. XI, pp. 13–15.

204   "noise level": See McCone, Memorandum for File, Discussion in Secretary Rusk's Office at 12 o'clock, Aug. 21, 1962, Mary McAuliffe, *CIA Documents on the Cuban Missile Crisis, 1962*, p. 21. This document is also in *FRUS*, vol. X, p. 947.

204   RFK and McCone: Walter Elder interview; Guthman and Shulman, eds., *In His Own Words*, p. 14; Aleksandr Fursenko and Timothy Naftali, *"One Hell of a Gamble,"* p. 199.

204   McCone extrapolated: McCone Memorandum, "Soviet MRBM's—Cuba," Oct. 31, 1962, McAuliffe, *Cuban Missile Crisis*, p. 13.

204   "it was decided. . . .": Fursenko and Naftali, *"One Hell of a Gamble,"* p. 384, footnote 30.

204   RFK's anguished memo: Memorandum from RFK to JFK, April 19, 1961, *FRUS*, vol. X, pp. 302, 304.

204   "surface to surface": RFK wrote: "McNamara said that Cuba has substantial offensive capability—what are we prepared to do. Cuba building rapidly both offensive and defensive power. 60 MiGs are substantial offensive capability. <u>Surface to Surface. Invasion</u> [heavily underscored]. <u>Whittle Away. Ground.</u> [a slash through 'ground'] <u>Surface to Surface.</u>" Cuba ExCom Meeting RFK Notes, Sept. 9, 1962, RFK CF.

205   Operation Bingo: Possible Actions to Provoke, Harass, or Disrupt Cuba, February 1962, Califano Papers, Assassination Records Review Board, NA.

205   "Remember the *Maine*": Report by the Department of Defense and Joint Chiefs of Staff representative on the Caribbean Survey Group, March 13, 1962, Assassination Records Review Board, NA. For a paper trail of RFK's particular interest in staging a "Sink the *Maine*" provocation, the documents cited by Mark White, *The Kennedys and Cuba*, pp. 100, 110, 122, 140. RFK seems to have latched on to some contingency plans that originated in the Defense Department. In a discussion with McCone on July 18, RFK said he was disappointed by Mongoose and wanted "intensified effort, but seemed inclined to let the situation 'worsen' before recommending drastic action." RFK seems to be looking for a provocation, manufactured if necessary.

205   "the Attorney General queried. . . .": Memorandum for the File, Discussion in Secretary Rusk's office, McAuliffe, *Cuban Missile Crisis*, p. 21.

205   "stepped up" program: Memorandum of Meeting with President Kennedy by John McCone, Aug. 23, 1962, *FRUS*, vol. X, pp. 953–55. RFK wrote General Taylor that he favored the stepped-up program because "I do not feel that we know yet what reaction would be created in Cuba of an intensified program. Therefore, I am in favor of pushing ahead rather than taking any step backward." RFK to Taylor, Aug. 9, 1962, Assassination Records Review Board, JFKL. In other words, when in doubt, charge ahead.

205   Rusk canceled U-2 flights: National Security Action Memorandum, no. 181, Aug. 27, 1962, *FRUS*, vol. X, pp. 957–58.

205   ". . . No guts?": Fursenko and Naftali, *"One Hell of a Gamble,"* pp. 214, 385, footnote 54.

205   *Indigirka:* ibid., p. 213.

206   "exclusively defensive weapons. . . .": ibid., pp. 219, 386, footnote 10; Richard Reeves, *President Kennedy*, p. 366, puts the date as October 6. On Kennedy's daily diary there is an entry for Bolshakov on October 5. RFK Papers, JFKL.

206   RFK and Bolshakov: The Bolshakov back channel had been used to defuse a crisis in Laos in the spring of 1962. Michael Beschloss, *The Crisis Years*, p. 397. On June 19, 1962, RFK wrote President Kennedy that he met in his office with Bolshakov at 4 p.m. RFK noted that Bolshakov raised "troops in Thailand point." On July 11, RFK wrote Mac Bundy, "Georgi said that Khrushchev personally would be most appreciative if the U.S. government would pull its troops out of Thailand." After talking to JFK, RFK told Bolshakov that "within ten days we would start to withdraw troops." Memo for McGeorge Bundy from the Attorney General, July 11, 1962, RFK White House McGeorge Bundy files, RFK CF.

206   Bolshakov defects?: Warren Rogers interview.

206   Khrushchev and missiles . . . "Why not throw . . . ?": Fursenko and

Naftali, *"One Hell of a Gamble,"* pp. 185–86, 178, 171; Ernest May and Philip Zelikow, eds., *The Kennedy Tapes: Inside the White House During the Cuban Missile Crisis,* pp. 668–71. There is a long-standing academic debate over Khrushchev's motivations. I was influenced by Philip Zelikow's emphasis on Berlin, though his colleague Timothy Naftali cautions that the records of the Soviet Politburo during the crisis make no mention of Berlin, which seems odd if Khrushchev was so clearly linking the missiles in Cuba to a later showdown over Berlin.

207 Khrushchev's false message: Fursenko and Naftali, *"One Hell of a Gamble,"* pp. 193–94.

208 RFK had FBI examine wine: Reeves, *President Kennedy,* pp. 346–47, citing Bolshakov's articles in *New Times,* no. 5, 1989.

208 U-2 flights over Cuba: Fursenko and Naftali, *"One Hell of a Gamble,"* p. 221. See Anatoly Dobrynin, *In Confidence,* pp. 72–73; Justin Gleichauf, "Red Presence in Cuba: The Genesis of a Crisis," *Army,* November 1979.

CHAPTER 11: BRINK

209 "Oh shit. . . .": Dino A. Brugioni, *Eyeball to Eyeball: The Inside Story of the Cuban Missile Crisis,* p. 223.

209 football field: Robert F. Kennedy, *Thirteen Days,* p. 24.

209 photo-interpreters: *FRUS,* vol. XI, p. 29.

209 "Can they hit . . . ?": *RK,* p. 506. There was some dispute about the range of the MRBMs. The White House was told over 1,000 miles, but some CIA analysts scoffed at "PRBMs"—political range ballistic missiles—and put the true range at 600 miles. Later, intermediate-range missiles were found in Cuba with a range of 1,000 to 2,000 miles. Richard Reeves, *President Kennedy,* p. 379.

209 "It had all been lies. . . .": Kennedy, *Thirteen Days,* p. 27.

209 "He [Khrushchev] can't do this . . . !": Kai Bird, *The Color of Truth* (New York: Simon & Schuster, 1998), p. 227.

210 best in Robert Kennedy: For a withering critique of JFK's handling of the Cuban Missile Crisis, see Garry Wills, *The Kennedy Imprisonment,* chapters 21 and 22. Wills does give RFK—"the mean altar boy"—credit for restraining JFK.

210 "I had always had a feeling. . . .": Jean Stein and George Plimpton, *American Journey,* p. 135.

210 members of ExCom: Kennedy, *Thirteen Days,* pp. 30–31.

211 *The Guns of August:* ibid., pp. 127–28.

212 The plans included: Operation Mongoose Sabotage Proposals, Oct. 16, 1962, Assassination Records Review Board, Gerald Ford Library (courtesy NSA).

212 Kennedy pointedly asked: Memorandum for the Record, Richard Helms, *FRUS,* vol. XI, p. 45.

212 strategic balance and Berlin: Graham Allison and Philip Zelikow, *Essence of Decision: Explaining the Cuban Missile Crisis,* pp. 100–105. See also Barton J. Bernstein, "Reconsidering the Missile Crisis: Dealing with the Problem of American Jupiters in Turkey," in James A. Nathan, ed., *The Cuban Missile Crisis Revisited* (New York: St. Martin's, 1992), p. 65; and Raymond Garthoff, *Reflections on the Cuban Missile Crisis,* p. 142.

212   "We're going to take out those missiles.": For the 6:30 p.m. ExCom meeting on October 16, see Ernest May and Philip Zelikow, eds., *The Kennedy Tapes*, pp. 78–117.

213   "If we go in. . . .": Cuba ExCom Meeting RFK Notes, Oct. 16, 1962, RFK CF.

213   "We are going to have to act. . . .": Cuba ExCom Meeting RFK Notes, Oct. 22, 1962, RFK CF.

214   His voice became slightly quavery: JFK presidential audiotape #28A, JFKL.

214   "RFK was a hawk. . . .": Robert McNamara interview.

214   "I'm older": Joe Dolan interview.

214   RFK wanted open debate: Edwin O. Guthman and Jeffrey Shulman, eds., *Robert Kennedy: In His Own Words*, p. 18.

214   RFK on Rusk: ibid., p. 268.

214   "He sometimes wouldn't even sit. . . .": Stein and Plimpton, *American Journey*, p. 132.

214   "We all spoke as equals. . . .": Kennedy, *Thirteen Days*, p. 46.

215   "floating crap game": Dean Acheson, "Dean Acheson's Version of Robert Kennedy's Version of the Cuban Missile Affair," *Esquire*, February 1969; Douglas Brinkley, *Dean Acheson: The Cold War Years, 1953–1971*, pp. 159–60.

215   "their tail caught. . . .": Stein and Plimpton, *American Journey* (quoting Elie Abel), p. 134.

215   make a dove out of RFK: "Bobby couldn't stand Dean Acheson," said Lucius Battle, who had been Secretary of State Acheson's special assistant and later worked closely with RFK on the Inter-Agency Youth Committee. Lucius Battle interview. Ted Sorensen said that RFK was also influenced by the arguments of Llewellyn Thompson that it was unwise to back Russia into a corner, and by the difficulty of writing an ultimatum without taking other more moderate steps first. Theodore Sorensen interview.

215   "I now know how Tojo felt. . . .": Theodore Sorensen interview. In *Thirteen Days*, Sorensen, who compiled and edited the book from RFK's drafts and papers, has RFK pass the note to the president on the first day. In light of RFK's "sinking the *Maine*" comment, this seems hard to believe. I asked Sorensen about this matter in 1999. He now believes that RFK penned the note on Wednesday, the second day, as he was listening to Acheson argue for a surprise strike. The note was passed not to JFK, but to Sorensen himself. Theodore Sorensen interview.

215   "We tried Japanese as war criminals. . . .": May and Zelikow, *Kennedy Tapes*, pp. 115, 121.

215   "My brother is not going to be the Tojo. . . .": These words do not appear in the paraphrased record taken by the State Department note-takers (there are no tapes of the ExCom meetings on Wednesday and Thursday that were held at State). They were first quoted in Elie Abel, *The Missile Crisis*, p. 64.

215   so much poppycock: George W. Ball, *The Past Has Another Pattern* (New York: Norton, 1982), p. 291.

216   "Pearl Harbor in reverse. . . ." . . . "his brother's clichés": *Esquire*, February 1969.

216   "very slow death": May and Zelikow, *Kennedy Tapes*, p. 138.

216   a blockade beckoned as the least bad: Kennedy, *Thirteen Days*, p. 37; Theodore Sorensen interview.

216   "He knew there was no such thing. . . .": Douglas Dillon interview.

216   rude to Robert Lovett: Brugioni, *Eyeball to Eyeball*, p. 288.

217   Sympathetic to RFK's exasperation: Robert Lovett OH, JFKL.

217   "Minds and opinions. . . .": Kennedy, *Thirteen Days*, p. 43.

217   votes: Cuba ExCom Meeting RFK Notes [in envelope marked Oct. 16, but more likely Oct. 18 or 19], RFK CF.

217   "If we don't do anything to Cuba. . . .": May and Zelikow, *Kennedy Tapes*, pp. 177, 182.

217   "Those brass hats. . . .": Kenneth P. O'Donnell and David F. Powers, *"Johnny, We Hardly Knew Ye,"* p. 361.

217   "That's not what he said to us. . . .": Theodore Sorensen interview.

218   "Have another look. . . .": Bird, *Color of Truth*, p. 234.

218   Acheson-Kennedy confrontations: Record of Meeting, Oct. 19, 1962, *FRUS*, vol. XI, pp. 116–19.

218   ". . . a real turning point in history. . . .": Douglas Dillon interview.

219   October 22 notes: Cuba ExCom Meeting RFK Notes, Oct. 22, 1962, RFK CF.

219   RFK called JFK: Kennedy, *Thirteen Days*, p. 47. Brugioni says the call was placed Friday afternoon. Brugioni, *Eyeball to Eyeball*, p. 304.

220   Stevenson proposed swapping: Minutes of the 505th Meeting of the National Security Council, Oct. 20, 1962, *FRUS*, vol. XI, p. 134.

220   "so *untough*" . . . "Tell me which side. . . .": Michael Beschloss, *The Crisis Years*, pp. 463, 466, 449.

220   "everyone jumped on Stevenson": *RK*, p. 515.

220   Sacrificing the navy base: Kennedy, *Thirteen Days*, p. 50.

220   McNamara had predicted giving up Jupiters: See May and Zelikow, *Kennedy Tapes*, p. 166; Bernstein, "Reconsidering," p. 72.

220   RFK's blockade/ultimatum approach: Allison and Zelikow, *Essence of Decision*, pp. 343–47.

221   Sorensen drafted, then scrapped: Theodore Sorensen interview. The draft is in his papers, box 49, JFKL.

221   "weak and defensive": Abraham Chayes, *The Cuban Missile Crisis*, pp. 81–82.

221   Harriman suggestion: Rudy Abramson, *Spanning the Century: The Life of W. Averell Harriman*, p. 593.

221   Kennedy listening to Thompson: Theodore Sorensen interview; Guthman and Shulman, eds., *In His Own Words*, p. 18.

222   Bolshakov message: Aleksandr Fursenko and Timothy Naftali, *"One Hell of a Gamble,"* pp. 237, 249–52. Bartlett did not recall his role. Charles Bartlett interview.

222   "Get ahold of Georgi" . . . "That wasn't very subtly done. . . .": Beschloss, *Crisis Years*, p. 500. For a slightly different version see Reeves, *President Kennedy*, p. 408. There are various versions of Bartlett's meeting with Bolshakov. There may have been two meetings. One was apparently at his office at the National Press Club. See Fursenko and Naftali, *"One Hell of a Gamble,"* p. 251.

222   RFK, JFK discussed Bolshakov: May and Zelikow, *Kennedy Tapes*, p. 343. In March 2000, Zelikow showed me an updated transcript of this conversation from the unpublished manuscript of vol. 3 of *Presidential Recording Series: John F. Kennedy: The Great Crises* (Philip Zelikow and Ernest May, general editors). In *The Kennedy Tapes*, the authors heard RFK say, "We had lunch today with him [Bolshakov]." After listening to the tapes again, Zelikow concluded that RFK said, "He had lunch . . .", referring to Holeman.

222   Was RFK holding back?: Philip Zelikow interview.

223   evacuate cities?: May and Zelikow, *Kennedy Tapes*, pp. 338–39.

223   tactical nukes in Cuba: Fursenko and Naftali, *"One Hell of a Gamble,"* pp. 241–42. The rockets with tactical nuclear warheads were discovered on Thursday, October 25.

223   "meager and almost pathetic": Ball, *Past Has Another Pattern*, pp. 299, 304.

223   to be with their families: Joe Dolan interview.

224   "Going camping . . . ?": James Symington interview.

224   "I'm not going. . . .": Edwin O. Guthman, *We Band of Brothers*, p. 126.

224   "We are very, very close. . . .": Theodore Sorensen OH, JFKL.

224   "It looks really mean. . . .": May and Zelikow, *Kennedy Tapes*, p. 342.

224   RFK and Dobrynin: Anatoly Dobrynin, *In Confidence*, pp. 83–85; Kennedy, *Thirteen Days*, p. 66.

224   forces on alert: May and Zelikow, *Kennedy Tapes*, p. 347.

225   "His face seemed drawn. . . .": Kennedy, *Thirteen Days*, pp. 69–71. Kennedy's handwritten version of the scene appears almost verbatim in *Thirteen Days*. This portion of the book is preserved in RFK's confidential files under "Cuba Crisis 1962. Kennedy—Khrushchev letter, Etc. 6-4-2." Arthur Schlesinger urged RFK to make a record: "Now that the worst is over, may I plead in the interests of history and hope that you might be able to set down your impressions of this week while they are still fresh in your mind?" A.S. to RFK, Oct. 29, 1962, RFK Name File, RFK CK.

225   McCone interrupted: In *Thirteen Days*, RFK has McCone's message come after he looked at his brother. The transcript shows that McCone got a message that the Soviet ships had stopped and left the room to check it while JFK worried about the submarine. Then the CIA director returned and confirmed the good news. May and Zelikow, *Kennedy Tapes*, pp. 354, 357.

225   "We are eyeball to eyeball. . . .": Dean Rusk, *As I Saw It* (New York: Norton, 1990), p. 237.

225   Khrushchev challenged quarantine: May and Zelikow, *Kennedy Tapes*, p. 391.

225   *Joseph P. Kennedy, Jr.:* Fursenko and Naftali, *"One Hell of a Gamble,"* p. 426.

225   twenty-four missiles were ready for launch: ibid., p. 266.

225   reconnaissance planes also spotted: May and Zelikow, *Kennedy Tapes*, p. 472.

225   Khrushchev's anguished letter: ibid., p. 485.

226   George Ball thought the letter: Beschloss, *Crisis Years*, p. 523.

226   "He's scared": Reeves, *President Kennedy*, p. 411.

226   "a slight feeling of optimism": Kennedy, *Thirteen Days,* p. 90.

226   ExCom deliberated Saturday morning: May and Zelikow, *Kennedy Tapes,* pp. 494, 499, 503.

226   debate over answering Khrushchev: Allison and Zelikow, *Essence of Decision,* pp. 357–60.

227   "Well, now, this is much of an escalation. . . ?": JFK audiotape #41A, JFKL; May and Zelikow, *Kennedy Tapes,* pp. 520, 563, 570–80. May and Zelikow quote RFK as asking "A U-2 was shot down?" The voice sounded like JFK's to the author.

227   Bundy's recollections: McGeorge Bundy, *Danger and Survival: Choices About the Bomb in the First Fifty Years* (New York: Random House, 1988), pp. 432–44.

228   "there was very little time left. . . .": Memorandum for the Secretary of State from the Attorney General, Oct. 30, 1962, RFK Papers, JFKL, reprinted in Jim Hershberg, "More on Bobby and the Cuban Missile Crisis," *Cold War International History Bulletin,* nos. 8–9 (Winter 1996–97), pp. 274, 346. Robert McNamara doubted that RFK told Dobrynin it would take four months or so to remove the missiles. McNamara ordered their immediate removal. Robert McNamara interview.

228   Dobrynin cabled Moscow: His cable to the Soviet Foreign Ministry, Oct. 27, 1962, is reprinted in Jim Hershberg, "Anatomy of a Controversy: Anatoly Dobrynin's Meeting with Robert Kennedy, Saturday, 27 October, 1962," *Cold War International History Bulletin,* no. 5 (Spring 1999), pp. 75, 79. Dobrynin found RFK to be humorless and impulsive. In his cable to Moscow on October 25, Dobrynin judged RFK to be a hawk. JFK was "vacillating" but heeding the hawks, "particularly his brother." Dobrynin to Foreign Ministry, Oct. 25, 1962, quoted in *Cold War International History Bulletin,* nos. 8–9 (Winter 1996–97), pp. 287–88. At a conference in 1993, Dobrynin claimed to have met with RFK on Friday night as well, but there is no record in Soviet archives or RFK's papers. Theodore Sorensen interview; Timothy Naftali interview. See Dobrynin, *In Confidence,* p. 85.

228   A young boy . . . "God, Dave. . . .": Reeves, *President Kennedy,* pp. 420–21.

229   "Suppose we make Bobby. . . .": May and Zelikow, *Kennedy Tapes,* p. 628.

229   *Roman Holiday:* O'Donnell and Powers, *"Johnny, We Hardly Knew Ye,"* p. 386.

229   instructions to call: Dobrynin, *In Confidence,* p. 91.

CHAPTER 12: CAUSES

230   RFK gets news at horse show: Robert F. Kennedy, *Thirteen Days,* p. 109.

230   "In order to save the world. . . .": Ernest May and Philip Zelikow, eds., *The Kennedy Tapes,* pp. 630–32; Graham Allison and Philip Zelikow, *Essence of Decision,* pp. 361–62; Aleksandr Fursenko and Timothy Naftali, *"One Hell of a Gamble,"* pp. 259–60, 283–87.

231   saw Kennedy smile: Anatoly Dobrynin, *In Confidence*, p. 92.

231   ". . . day of the doves": May and Zelikow, *Kennedy Tapes*, p. 635.

231   Georgia O'Keeffe's painting: George W. Ball, *The Past Has Another Pattern* (New York: Norton, 1982), p. 49.

231   "felt like dancing. . . .": Don Wilson OH, JFKL.

231   "We lost! . . .": Richard Reeves, *President Kennedy*, p. 425.

231   "Tell them to stop that": ibid., p. 424.

231   "This is the night I should go. . . .": Kennedy, *Thirteen Days*, p. 110.

231   "Who knows where and when. . . .": Dobrynin to Foreign Ministry, Oct. 30, 1962, quoted in *Cold War International History Bulletin*, nos. 8–9 (Winter 1996–97), p. 304.

231   "Very privately. . . .": Dobrynin, *In Confidence*, p. 93.

231   In the draft of an RFK memo: Jim Hershberg, "More on Bobby and the Cuban Missile Crisis," *Cold War International History Bulletin*, nos. 8–9 (Winter 1996–97), p. 345.

231   Shaping history: Briefing James Reston of the *New York Times*, RFK stressed his anger that he had been deceived by the Kremlin's decision to put missiles in Cuba. "You have to figure—and I think the president does—that you're dealing with gangsters, and you have to wear your jock strap at all times," he told Reston. RFK also dissembled about political calculations. RFK and JFK were so worried about the fallout that they half joked that the president would have been impeached had he done nothing about the missiles. Yet Reston recorded after seeing RFK, "The effect of all this on domestic politics was never discussed . . . between the President and Bobby, even in passing." Notes on the Cuban Missile Crisis, October 1962, James Reston Papers, University of Illinois.

232   ". . . a pretty risky operation. . . .": Kenneth O'Donnell OH by Sander Vanocur, JFKL.

232   Bartlett was used: Charles Bartlett interview.

232   *Saturday Evening Post* article: Dec. 8, 1962. JFK took a more sober-minded view with James Reston, judging from Reston's column on October 29, the day after the crisis ended. According to Reston, Kennedy rejected the conclusion of hard-liners that the way to deal with Moscow everywhere in the world was to be "tough, as in Cuba."

232   He requested only one change: Robert W. Merry, *Taking On the World*, pp. 387–95. Among the myths launched by the *Saturday Evening Post* piece was the suggestion that RFK had dreamed up the "Trollope Ploy" to save the day—say yes to Khrushchev's first letter and ignore the second demanding a missile trade. The notion of the Trollope Ploy, a play on a Trollope plot in which a woman chooses to treat a flirtation as a proposal of marriage, came from McGeorge Bundy, and it is a little too elegant to explain the muddle and confusion of the debate on Saturday, October 27.

232   When Robert Kennedy was writing *Thirteen Days*: Adam Walinsky interview. The Kennedys may have been planning to use the secret tapings of the ExCom sessions to write a history of the Cuban Missile Crisis as a campaign book. In the summer of 1963, President Kennedy had transcripts prepared and passed along to Robert Kennedy. Timothy Naftali speculates that RFK was readying to write an account of the crisis to coincide with the 1964 elections. After his brother was assassinated, RFK used the transcripts to write *Thirteen Days*, which was pub-

lished posthumously in 1969. Timothy Naftali, "The Origins of '13 Days,' " *Miller Center Report,* Summer 1999.

232   Not until 1989 did Ted Sorensen: Barton J. Bernstein, "Reconsidering the Missile Crisis: Dealing with the Problem of American Jupiters in Turkey," in James A. Nathan, ed., *The Cuban Missile Crisis Revisited* (New York: St. Martin's, 1992), p. 96.

233   Kennedys have been accused: See *RK*, pp. 512–15. There is some evidence that Kennedy was prepared to publicly trade the missiles rather than bomb Cuba or invade. On Saturday night, he set up a back channel through Dean Rusk to the United Nations, just in case bilateral diplomacy failed. Raymond Garthoff, *Reflections on the Cuban Missile Crisis,* pp. 59–60.

233   "plain dumb luck": See Douglas Brinkley, *Dean Acheson: The Cold War Years, 1953–71,* pp. 170–73.

233   RFK did not like being called "Bobby": Burke Marshall OH, JFKL.

233   "Thank God for Bobby": Patricia Lawford, ed., *That Shining Hour,* p. 74.

233   "They hardly had to speak. . . .": Isaiah Berlin OH, JFKL.

234   "We discussed creating a provocation. . . .": Roberto San Román interview.

234   RFK approved this risky mission: Operation Mongoose Sabotage Proposals, Oct. 16, 1962, Assassination Records Review Board, Gerald Ford Library; May and Zelikow, *Kennedy Tapes,* p. 103.

234   "in view of the changed situation. . . .": William Harvey to Director of Central Intelligence, "Chronology of Matahambre Mine—Sabotage Operation," Nov. 14, 1962, Assassination Records Review Board, Gerald Ford Library.

234   "We were soldiers. . . .": Roberto San Román interview.

234   history of Matahambre raids: Harvey, "Chronology."

234   Cubans during missile crisis: Roberto San Román interview; memorandum of Mongoose meeting, Oct. 26, 1962, by John McCone, Assassination Records Review Board, JFKL. ("The Attorney General questioned using such valuable Cuban refugee assets to form teams to infiltrate Cuba at a time when security would be exceedingly tight, therefore operational results questionable and losses high. . . . Mr. Harvey's defense of the plan was not conclusive. . . .") See Memorandum for the Director from Marshall Carter, Oct. 25, 1962, Mary McAuliffe, *Cuban Missile Crisis,* p. 311. ("The Cubans are not owned by San Román but have been recruited and checked out by CIA. . . . Unfortunately, San Román, like other exile leaders, is looking out for the future of San Román.")

235   Harvey during the meeting: Charles E. Johnson interview, July 26, 1975, Church Committee files, NA; Sam Halpern interview.

235   "Harvey has destroyed himself. . . .": David Corn, *Blond Ghost: Ted Shackley and the CIA's Crusades,* p. 93; Thomas Parrott interview.

235   "I have just met Jack Armstrong. . . .": James Symington interview.

235   no longer useful to RFK: Thomas Parrott interview. See George McManus to Richard Helms, Nov. 5, 1962, Assassination Records Review Board, Gerald Ford Library.

235   Quintero meeting at Hickory Hill: Rafael Quintero interview.

236   Cuban prisoners release: *RK*, pp. 536–38; John Nolan interview.

236   Meeting on Cuban prisoners: Mike Miskovsky interview. JFK also

wanted to hold the situation in abeyance for six weeks because a deal on the eve of the election could be a "political issue." John McCone, Meeting with the President, Sept. 25, 1962, NSA.

237   "The laws we violated. . . .": E. Barrett Prettyman interview.

237   Cardinal Cushing produced $1 million: Cardinal Cushing OH, JFKL.

237   In a characteristic pose: Nancy Sheridan interview.

237   "All right you guys. . . .": Joe Dolan interview.

238   White House operators unable to find: Mary Bailey Gimbel STOH; David Hackett STOH.

238   Bolshakov's usefulness was finished: Dobrynin, *In Confidence*, p. 97; Fursenko and Naftali, *"One Hell of a Gamble,"* pp. 322–23.

238   The president's rhetorical gesture: Kenneth P. O'Donnell and David F. Powers, *"Johnny, We Hardly Knew Ye,"* p. 312.

238   Bundy wanted diplomatic overtures: *Interim Report*, p. 173

238   "We told them where to buy guns. . . .": Sam Halpern interview.

238   The agency bugged Artime's safe house: Corn, *Blond Ghost*, p. 97.

238   "Their camps were horrible. . . .": Grayston Lynch interview.

238   RFK and San Román: Roberto San Román interview.

238   Haynes Johnson observed at close hand: Haynes Johnson interview.

239   RFK feared denouncing: Richard Cull OH, JFKL.

239   "Bobby trusted Harry. . . .": Haynes Johnson interview.

239   Williams "reliable. . . .": John Nolan interview.

239   RFK urged JFK to act: RFK to JFK, March 14, 1963, Sorensen Papers, JFKL.

239   "Do you think there was any merit . . . ?": RFK to JFK, March 26, 1963, Assassination Records Review Board, JFKL.

239   On April 3, he suggested: Memorandum for Record, Meeting on Cuba, April 3, 1963, NA.

CHAPTER 13: THREATS

240   "madder he became": Victor S. Navasky, *Kennedy Justice*, pp. 96–97.

241   sent a tape-recorded message: Richard Reeves, *President Kennedy*, pp. 354–55.

241   Wofford quit: Harris Wofford, *Of Kennedys and Kings*, p. 166.

241   "Get them out of there!": Reeves, *President Kennedy*, p. 464.

241   "We did not philosophize. . . .": Burke Marshall interview.

241   "I don't think" . . . "Nobody paid any attention": Edwin O. Guthman and Jeffrey Shulman, eds., *Robert Kennedy: In His Own Words*, pp. 149, 202–203.

241   *". . . tell me what they want. . . .":* Roger Wilkins interview.

242   Birmingham city government: Taylor Branch, *Parting the Waters*, p. 711.

242   "Letter from Birmingham Jail": See James Melvin Washington, ed., *A Testament of Hope: The Essential Writings of Martin Luther King, Jr.* (San Francisco: Harper & Row, 1986), pp. 289–302.

242   April 25, Wallace meeting: *RK*, pp. 337–38; Guthman and Shulman, eds., *In His Own Words*, pp. 185–86; John Reilly interview.

242   Kennedy spoke guardedly: Marshall Frady, *Wallace*, pp. 153–75. The transcript is in RFK Attorney General Correspondence, Civil Rights file, JFKL. See p. 4.

242   Project C and children: Branch, *Parting the Waters*, p. 757.

243   "That's very interesting, Roger. . . .": Jean Stein and George Plimpton, *American Journey*, p. 118.

243   "The Negro leadership didn't know. . . .": cabinet meeting, May 21, 1963, JFK audiotape #88.6, JFKL.

243   "I talked to King. . . .": Branch, *Parting the Waters*, p. 769.

243   "knew some lawyers down there. . . .": Burke Marshall interview.

243   calling on Walter Reuther: Walter Reuther OH, JFKL.

243   May 10 deal: Guthman and Shulman, eds., *In His Own Words*, pp. 170, 194.

243   "Let the whole fucking city burn": *RK*, p. 330.

243   "Uncontrollable": White House meeting, May 12, 1963, JFK audiotape #86.2, JFKL.

243   sparks in the wind: Notebook of Edwin Guthman, Mother's Day 1963, Edwin Guthman papers, JFKL.

243   racial demonstrations: Branch, *Parting the Waters*, p. 825.

243   Daley predicted "a lot of trouble": White House meeting, May 20, 1963, JFK audiotape #88.4, JFKL.

244   May 24 meeting: *RK*, pp. 330–32.

244   jittery businessmen: Guthman and Shulman, eds., *In His Own Words*, p. 181.

244   stammered Smith: Stein and Plimpton, *American Journey*, pp. 119–21; Branch, *Parting the Waters*, pp. 810–11.

244   Barely able to contain his contempt: Kenneth Clark OH, Columbia Oral History Program.

244   whole experience had been excruciating: *Newsweek*, May 16, 1963; Jimmy Wechsler, "RFK and Baldwin," *New York Post*, May 28, 1963.

244   Baldwin's homosexuality: Adam Walinsky interview.

245   "He is a nice fellow. . . .": Branch, *Parting the Waters*, p. 812. The FBI's Hoover helped stir up RFK's irritation with Jones and Stanley Levison by sending the attorney general a memo that drew on a bugged conversation between Levison and Jones. Jones tells Levison that, at the confrontation at Baldwin's, one of the guests described RFK as "the worst illustration of white arrogant liberalism." The FBI memo reported that "Levison said that this was a good description of the Attorney General." "Re: Sit Ins; Birmingham Alabama; Racial Matters," May 27, 1963, Stanley Levison files, FBI.

245   black sweeping the floor: Burke Marshall OH, JFKL.

245   Johnson never forgave Kennedy: Jeff Shesol, *Mutual Contempt*, pp. 85–87; Jack Conway OH, JFKL.

245   "depth of anger" . . . Marshall scoffed: Nicholas Katzenbach interview; Burke Marshall interview.

245   told Guthman he'd feel as strongly: Branch, *Parting the Waters*, p. 812.

245   "He'd always talk about. . . .": Burke Marshall interview.

245   "The final lesson of the Cuban. . . .": Maxwell Kennedy, ed., *Make Gentle the Life of This World,* p. 159.

246   "He had a way of creating the impression. . . .": Louis Oberdorfer interview.

246   "Pretty good job. . . .": JFK audiotape #88.4, JFKL.

246   The president needed to send a true civil rights bill: Guthman and Shulman, eds., *In His Own Words,* p. 172. According to Ed Guthman, several of RFK's aides, including Lou Oberdorfer and Joe Dolan, began talking about the need for a civil rights bill on the way home from a negotiating session in Birmingham in late May. They presented their views to RFK in his office the day before he was to leave for a speech in Asheville, North Carolina. RFK summoned his aides to travel with him to Asheville, and the drafting work began on the plane. Ed Guthman to author, Feb. 7, 2000.

246   "Bull Connor's bill": Guthman and Shulman, eds., *In His Own Words,* p. 171.

246   Wallace confrontation: Nicholas Katzenbach OH, LBJL. The discussions on how to deal with Wallace were recorded by a Time-Life film shown on ABC: Robert Drew, "Kennedy v. Wallace: A Crisis Up Close." Details and color from the two-day crisis are taken from that film, courtesy Gregory Shuker (the producer).

248   went according to script: Guthman and Shulman, eds., *In His Own Words,* p. 193; *RK,* p. 341.

248   Kennedy lit up a cigar: Drew, "Kennedy v. Wallace: A Crisis Up Close."

248   "He just decided that day. . . .": Guthman and Shulman, eds., *In His Own Words,* p. 199.

248   "I think it would be helpful. . . .": Drew, "Kennedy v. Wallace: A Crisis Up Close."

248   "Every single person. . . .": Navasky, *Kennedy Justice,* p. 99.

248   President Kennedy had a few hours: Guthman and Shulman, eds., *In His Own Words,* pp. 175, 179, 199–200.

248   "in moral terms": Burke Marshall interview.

248   "Who among us . . . ?": *RK,* p. 348. *Public Documents of the President of the United States. John F. Kennedy, January, 1961–November, 1963* (Washington, DC: U.S. Government Printing Office, 1964), pp. 468–71.

249   "every four days . . ." . . . "Whenever I had the need. . . .": *RK,* pp. 348, 345.

249   Newfield recalled: Jack Newfield, *Robert Kennedy: A Memoir,* pp. 22–23.

249   "We're in this up to our neck.": Wofford, *Of Kennedys and Kings,* p. 176. Wofford contrasts JFK's remark with President Lincoln's statement that his "whole soul" was committed to ending slavery.

249   "Bobby" was a curse word: Branch, *Parting the Waters,* p. 819.

249   King began talking about a march: FBI, Re Martin Luther King Racial Matter, June 4, 1963, in Michael Friedly with David Gallen, *Martin Luther King, Jr.: The FBI File* (New York: Carroll & Graf, 1993), pp. 259–60.

250   Kennedy had authorized the tap: Branch, *Parting the Waters,* p. 568.

250   "King is so hot. . . .": JFK audiotape #88.4, JFKL.

250   "What if they pee . . . ?": John Reilly interview, Alan Raywid OH, JFKL.

Raywid, an assistant to John Douglas, the top Department of Justice official handling the march, recalled the quote as, "They're going to come on down here and shit all over the monument."

250   ". . . very badly organized": Guthman and Shulman, eds., *In His Own Words*, p. 227.

250   Justice Department steps to control march: John Reilly interview; Joe Dolan interview; John Douglas interview.

251   persuade King to cut off Levison and Levison's Communist Party background: David Garrow, *Bearing the Cross: Martin Luther King, Jr., and the Southern Christian Leadership Conference*, p. 195; Branch, *Parting the Waters*, pp. 210–12, 565. Solo was the code name for two FBI informers, Jack and Morris Childs. The Childses first reported on Levison in 1952, identifying him as a supporter of American communism; Levison's active involvement ended in 1955, and the FBI removed him from a list of "key" communists in 1957 (Garrow, *Bearing the Cross*, pp. 651–52, n. 34). According to Garrow, although Levison raised money for the Communist Party as early as 1946, there is no indication he actually joined the party. And in 1963, after listening to his wiretaps for a year, the New York office of the FBI concluded that "Levison is not now under CP discipline in the Civil Rights field." Cartha DeLoach, Hoover's assistant director, insisted to the author in 1999 that Solo—the Childses—told the FBI that Levison was a top Soviet operative as late as 1963. A 1996 book on Solo claims that Levison continued to meet with a KGB officer, Viktor Lessiovsky, stationed at the UN sometime after 1961. John Barron, *Solo: The FBI's Man in the Kremlin*, pp. 261–69. The Levison files made public by the FBI are still heavily redacted, so it is hard to know exactly what they contain. They do not appear to show much evidence of contact between Levison and Moscow or attempts to subvert King. One FBI memo notes that the bug installed in Levison's residence on March 20, 1962, was "discontinued" on July 25, 1964, "due to the limited information being obtained at that time which was probably attributable to the attempt by Levison to keep most secret his contacts with and concerning King." Baumgardner to Sullivan, May 25, 1965, Stanley Levison files, FBI.

251   Hoover simply claimed too secret: Branch, *Parting the Waters*, pp. 565, 697.

251   "When I left the attorney general's office. . . .": John Seigenthaler interview.

251   Levison and O'Dell: Garrow, *Bearing the Cross*, pp. 200–208; Branch, *Parting the Waters*, pp. 573–74, 583, 596–97, 675, 678. In Kennedy's files, there is a copy of King's letter asking Jack O'Dell to resign. The letter makes clear the resignation is for appearances only. Dora McDonald to RFK, July 3, 1963, RFK Name File, RFK CF. In fact, O'Dell was likely no more than a fellow traveler.

252   ". . . this is not getting any better": Branch, *Parting the Waters*, pp. 692, 679.

252   King needed Levison: Taylor Branch, *Pillar of Fire*, pp. 26–27.

252   "He sort of laughs. . . .": Guthman and Shulman, eds., *In His Own Words*, p. 143.

252   Kennedy's aides insisted: John Seigenthaler, Ed Guthman, Burke Marshall interviews. Marshall was told that an FBI agent in Moscow, a member of the

top echelon of the Communist Party, told the FBI that Levison was a paid Soviet agent in the United States, a major figure in the Soviet intelligence apparatus. Marshall told Arthur Schlesinger that he had no way of questioning this. He was told in "the most formal and emphatic manner." He believed it at the time. Marshall "wonders now [in 1973] whether the FBI made it all up." Burke Marshall interviewed by Arthur Schlesinger, Schlesinger papers, JFKL. Marshall told the author that he could not recall ever discussing the FBI's evidence against Levison with RFK. Burke Marshall interview.

253   RFK probed CIA: Sam Halpern interview; Dino Brugioni, *Eyeball to Eyeball,* pp. 311–13.

253   King and Kennedy in the Rose Garden and proof to Young: Branch, *Parting the Waters,* pp. 835–38; Stanley Levison interviewed by Arthur Schlesinger, Schlesinger papers, JFKL.

253   Hoover June 21 memo to JFK: Director, FBI, to Attorney General, "Christine Keeler; John Profumo. Internal Security—Russia—Great Britain," June 21, 1963. "Bow Tie" File, FBI.

253   Sidey nearly broke it over sex: Hugh Sidey interview; RFK to Sidey, April 23, 1963, courtesy Hugh Sidey.

254   RFK and *Journal-American:* Brian Horan, a son of James D. Horan, one of the investigative reporters who broke the story, told Seymour Hersh that Kennedy pressured the publishers to spike the story after one edition. Seymour Hersh, *The Dark Side of Camelot,* p. 394. However, Kingsley Smith, the publisher of the *New York Journal-American,* denied that the Kennedys pressured the paper into spiking the story in a letter to Senator John Williams of Delaware (Dec. 11, 1963). Smith said the story ran in all editions. Senator John J. Williams Papers, University of Delaware Library, Special Collections. Warren Rogers, who was working for Hearst at the time, recalled repeated calls from RFK that day asking about the story.

254   The newspapermen told him: Courtney Evans to Director, "Interview by the Attorney General with Dom Frasca and James Horan of the N.Y. *Journal-American,* July 1, 1963," July 3, 1963, Hoover Official and Confidential files, FBI. See also Director, FBI, to Attorney General, "Christine Keeler" et al., July 5, 1963, "Bow Tie" File, FBI.

254   "Have we learned . . . ?": Evans to Belmont, July 2, 1963, "Bow Tie" File, FBI.

255   Ellen Rometsch under suspicion: Evans to Belmont, July 3, 1963, Hoover Official and Confidential files, FBI; Wannall to Sullivan, July 3, 1963, Rometsch FOIA/FBI. "Pursue vigorously and thoroughly," Hoover wrote on the report.

255   sexual relations with JFK: Bobby Baker interview. Baker claimed that Thompson escorted Rometsch to the White House "frequently." Baker said that he met once with JFK and the president told him that Rometsch gave him "the best oral sex I ever had."

255   Senator Smathers: George Smathers interview.

255   Kennedy made "particular note. . . .": Evans to Belmont, July 3, 1963, Rometsch FOIA/FBI.

255   The FBI preliminary investigation: Wannall to Sullivan, July 12, 1963: "Investigation has not substantiated the security allegations against subject nor does she apparently have the high-level sex contacts she originally boasted of." Cartha DeLoach, one of Hoover's top aides, told the author that the FBI did have

some indications of spying by Rometsch, but he would not be specific. There is no evidence in Rometsch's FBI file to support this claim. He also claimed that FBI did believe that Rometsch had had sex with JFK. "My recollection is that we had considerable evidence of her going to the White House," but he could not recall specifics. For background on Rometsch, see Clark Mollenhoff, "U.S. Expels Girl Linked to Officials," *Des Moines Register*, Oct. 26, 1963.

256   Rometsch deported: Bobby Baker and John Graves interviews; "Baker Inquiry Is Asked If German Woman's Ouster by U.S. Involved Security," *NYT*, Oct. 29, 1963. In Drew Pearson's notes of an interview with Lyndon Johnson on Nov. 23, 1963, Pearson wrote, "Ken O'Donnell hustled Rometch [*sic*] out of town faster than anyone ever hustled before. JFK was lucky." Drew Pearson Papers, LBJL.

256   "It is a pleasure. . . .": Hoover to RFK, July 5, 1963; RFK to Hoover, July 23, 1963, Attorney General Correspondence, RFK Papers, JFKL.

256   Las Vegas bugging controversy: Cartha DeLoach interview; William Hundley interview; Herbert Miller interview; confidential source. "The hoodlums of Las Vegas had a direct line" into the Justice Department, Hoover wrote in a memo rehashing the event two years later. Belmont to Tolson, "N.Y. Times Article, July 18, 1965, Concerning Organized Crime," July 22, 1965, RFK files, FBI.

257   Guthman blocked the FBI publicity grab: Ed Guthman interview.

257   "I never saw such skullduggery. . . .": *House Assassination Committee Report*, vol. V, p. 448.

257   "If Bobby Kennedy wants to talk. . . .": SAC Chicago to Director, "Giancana," July 1, 1963, House Assassination Committee Records, FBI files, NA.

258   the attorney general would be much too afraid: At least one assistant U.S. attorney in Chicago wanted to force Giancana to testify. SAC Chicago to Director, "Giancana," June 29, 1963. But the Justice Department ordered the Chicago prosecutors to ask no questions. SAC Chicago to Director, July 16, 1963, Hoover Official and Confidential files, FBI.

258   "he was sorry he had put me to so much trouble. . . .": SAC Chicago to Director, July 17, 1963, Hoover Official and Confidential files, FBI; "FBI Ordered to Curtail Spying on Crime Chief," July 16, 1963, AP story in Hoover's Official and Confidential files, FBI.

258   Kennedy was "incensed": Evans to Belmont, July 16, 1963, House Assassination Committee Records, FBI files, NA.

258   "Backstage with Bobby": *Miami News*, July 15, 1963.

258   Bundy memo to RFK: Bundy to RFK, July 13, 1963, NSA.

258   ". . . float other rumors. . . .": Summary Record of NSC Standing Group Meeting, July 16, 1963, National Security Files, JFKL. In addition to everything else, RFK was urgently implored by Arthur Schlesinger to attend a critical meeting on Africa policy that afternoon. Arthur Schlesinger to RFK, July 16, 1963, RFK Name File, RFK CF.

259   FBI knocking down "training school" allegation: Branch, *Parting the Waters*, pp. 852–58.

259   Rometsch report: Rosen to Belmont, Oct. 26, 1963 ("the Attorney General was orally advised on 7/16/63 of the results of the investigation"). Rometsch FOIA/FBI.

259   Evans warned Kennedy: Evans to Belmont, June 25, 1963; Baumgardner to Sullivan, July 23, 1963, Hoover Official and Confidential files, FBI.

260   "the worst illustration. . . .": Friedly, *Martin Luther King*, p. 160.

260   "a pain in the ass. . . .": Ed Guthman interview.

260   a Senate staffer close to Goldwater: Jones to DeLoach, Aug. 9, 1963, Hoover Official and Confidential files, FBI.

260   Hoover ordered Evans to write a memo: Hoover to RFK, Aug. 14, 1963, Hoover Official and Confidential files, FBI.

260   Ervin's rhetoric was eloquent: James Clayton, "Sam and Bob Show Enters Fourth Week," *Washington Post*, Aug. 9, 1967.

260   "What have you been doing. . . ?": *RK*, p. 366.

260   RFK was standing beside: *NYT*, Aug. 10, 1963.

260   Phil Graham and James Landis: *Washington Post*, Aug. 4 and Aug. 3, 1963.

261   RFK treatment of Landis: Donald A. Ritchie interview; Justin Feldman interview; Donald A. Ritchie, *James M. Landis*, pp. 189–202.

261   "slum areas and was shown low-cost. . . .": SAC Chicago to Director, Aug. 23, 1963, RFK file, FBI.

261   Brave Heart: *NYT*, Sept. 14, 1963.

CHAPTER 14: WORN

262   FBI and suicide suggestion to King: David Garrow, *Bearing the Cross: Martin Luther King, Jr., and the Southern Christian Leadership Conference*, pp. 373–74.

262   "stricken" look: John Seigenthaler interview.

262   "great distress. . . .": Anthony Lewis STOH.

263   RFK *less* reason to tap MLK: Taylor Branch, *Parting the Waters*, p. 908.

263   martyrs for King's cause: ibid., p. 889.

263   "I thought you would be interested. . . .": ibid., p. 861.

263   "So you're down here. . . .": Marietta Tree OH, Columbia University. "The quote as remembered by Marietta doesn't sound much like RFK to me, but she is a respectable witness." Arthur Schlesinger to author, Oct. 18, 1999.

263   October 7 memo: Hoover Memorandum to RFK, Martin Luther King, Jr., Oct. 7, 1963, FOIA/FBI.

263   "drank four martinis. . . .": Bobby Baker interview.

263   RFK, Baker, and LBJ: In 1998, Burkett Van Kirk, a former Republican staffer on the Senate Rules Committee, told the author that in 1963, RFK had fed damaging information on Baker to the committee, first through a cutout, then directly. Van Kirk claimed he was picked up at his house in Westmoreland Hills and driven to Hickory Hill, where RFK greeted him at the door. RFK was alone, Van Kirk said. He gave Van Kirk paper purporting to show that Baker had corrupt deals with various government contractors. Van Kirk, who told this story to Seymour Hersh (*The Dark Side of Camelot*, pp. 406–407, 446, 447), also told it to the author but could not provide corroborating details. Kenny O'Donnell denied that the Kennedys fed damaging information on Baker. See the note on p. 454.

264   Baker called RFK: Bobby Baker interview. RFK's phone log for October 9 shows a call from Baker. (Phone logs are in RFK Papers, JFKL.) John Lane inter-

view. Lane, a lawyer who represented Baker, listened to the conversation. Baker had come to his office for advice.

264   RFK and King wiretap: Branch, *Parting the Waters*, p. 907, citing John Seigenthaler and Ed Guthman. The note to Evans, undated, is in FBI files. Ed Guthman recalled that RFK tapped King only as a "last resort" because King repeatedly refused to break off contact with Levison. RFK ordered the tap to "settle for once and all time" whether King was under communist influence. Ed Guthman to author, Feb. 7, 2000.

264   Mollenhoff letter: RFK to Mollenhoff, Aug. 23, 1957; Mollenhoff to RFK, Dec. 23, 1957, Mollenhoff Papers, Herbert Hoover Library.

265   "Kennedy kind of slumped. . . .": Fletcher Knebel OH, JFKL. Ray Mollenhoff, Clark's son, recalled that Mollenhoff was not reinjured by the fall and did not believe that Mollenhoff broke with Kennedy over the incident. Ray Mollenhoff interview.

265   RFK regarded Mollenhoff as disloyal: Clark Mollenhoff STOH.

265   Mollenhoff's personal diary: Mollenhoff Papers, Herbert Hoover Library.

265   Mollenhoff and Williams meeting: call from Clark Mollenhoff regarding Ellen Rometsch, Oct. 25, 1963; confidential memorandum to Senator Williams from Clark Mollenhoff, Oct. 28, 1963. "The FBI file shows allegations that Mrs. Rometsch claimed associations with the high level persons in the executive branch; however, the investigation is reported to have failed to verify White House associations. The FBI investigation was limited to a questioning of Mrs. Rometsch and some of her women associates. There was no questioning of members of Congress, congressional staff officials, or executive branch personnel relative to Mrs. Rometsch." Senator John J. Williams Papers, University of Delaware Library, Special Collections.

266   "reported to be furious. . . .": *Des Moines Register*, Oct. 26, 1963.

266   JFK's reaction to Rometsch story: Kenneth O'Donnell OH by Sander Vanocur, JFKL.

266   RFK asked FBI for help . . . "it was also alleged . . ." . . . "told me the President. . . .": Rosen to Belmont, Oct. 26, 1963. The FBI noted a call from Kenny O'Donnell on Saturday afternoon, October 26, asking to be briefed on Rometsch. At 5:15, RFK called and said there was no substance to the charges in Mollenhoff's piece and asked for an investigation "to resolve this particular allegation." At 9 p.m., O'Donnell called the FBI to provide Rometsch's address. DeLoach somewhat gleefully reported that an RFK aide, probably Guthman, called him five times trying to get help spiking stories in the *New York Daily News* and the AP. For JFK's interest, DeLoach to Mohr, Oct. 28, 1963, Rometsch FOIA/FBI.

267   phone logs: White House phone logs, Oct. 25–29, 1963, JFKL.

267   Rometsch and Duffy: Bobby Baker showed me a copy of the attorney general's calling card with the handwritten notation from RFK. It appears to be authentic. Baker has copies of correspondence between Duffy and Rometsch. See Hersh, *Dark Side of Camelot*, pp. 398–403.

268   Mansfield and Dirksen meeting: Mike Mansfield interview (he remembered the meeting but said he could not recall the substance of the conversation). Cartha DeLoach told the author that Hoover met with the congressional leaders—

and kept out any mention of JFK and Rometsch—"in order to save his job." Cartha DeLoach interview. For the best chronology, see Branch, *Parting the Waters,* pp. 911–14; Evans to Belmont, Oct. 28, 1963; Hoover memos to Tolson et al., Oct. 28, 1963 (3:05 p.m. and 3:51 p.m.), and Hoover to Tolson et al., Nov. 7, 1963, Rometsch FOIA/FBI. RFK had been "vacillating" over more wiretaps on King and his associates, according to Courtney Evans. Evans to Belmont, Oct. 21, 1963, and Evans to Belmont, "Communism and the Negro Movement," Oct. 25, 1963, FBI files.

268   Senate leaders quietly informed: Williams himself backed off because he "didn't like sex scandals," because "he would not want to be the vehicle to bring down JFK," and because, after interviewing Rometsch's roommate, Ingrid Luttert, he doubted that Rometsch had consorted with White House officials, including the president, according to Williams's biographer Professor Carol Hoffecker at the University of Delaware (interviewed by Mike Hill). According to Luttert's affidavit in the Williams Papers, she told the FBI that she did not know whether Rometsch had sex with high government officials. Eleanor Hoefer, Williams's secretary, said the senator "wasn't interested in digging up dirt like that. He wanted stuff that was easier to prove." Eleanor Hoefer interview. Williams heard about the Senate leadership order to the Rules Committee to stay away from sex in a conversation with Senator Carl Curtis, the ranking minority member, on December 30, according to a note in his papers dated January 10, 1964. Senator John J. Williams Papers, University of Delaware Library, Special Collections.

268   covered his tracks: Edwin O. Guthman and Jeffrey Shulman, eds., *Robert Kennedy: In His Own Words,* pp. 129–30.

268   "Boy, the dirt. . . .": Richard Reeves, *President Kennedy,* p. 628.

268   Hoover's reward: Hoover to Tolson et al., Oct. 28, 1963, Rometsch FOIA/FBI. "The Attorney General said all such rumors were unfounded and vicious." Hoover to Tolson et al., Oct. 29, 1963, Rometsch FOIA/FBI.

268   Bayard Rustin: Branch, *Parting the Waters,* p. 913.

268   "We have twenty Vietnams. . . .": Stanley Karnow interview; *RK,* pp. 701–712; Guthman and Shulman, eds., *In His Own Words,* pp. 399–400.

269   RFK and OP-PLAN 34A: Richard Shultz, *The Secret War Against Hanoi,* pp. 22, 35–40, 289–91, 316–17; RFK's friend General Maxwell Taylor gently tried to rein in RFK's enthusiasm for covert operations and counterinsurgency. Taylor recalled that RFK once asked, "Why can't we just make the entire Army into Special Forces?" Andrew F. Krepinevich Jr., *The Army and Vietnam,* p. 35; Victor Krulak interview. McNamara later said that 34A was "not worth a damn. It was a stupid thing to do."

270   "hovered for a moment": *RK,* p. 714.

270   meeting on coup rumors: Tape #117/A53, Oct. 25, 1963, draft transcript by George Eliades (courtesy George Eliades); Memorandum of Conversation with the President: Vietnam, Oct. 29, 1963, President's National Security files, JFKL. See Ken Hughes, "JFK and the Fall of Diem," *Boston Globe Magazine,* Oct. 24, 1999.

271   murdered Diem: *FRUS, 1961–1963,* vol. IV, p. 533.

271   AMLASH: CIA Inspector General, Report on Plots to Assassinate Fidel Castro, pp. 75–91, Church Committee files, NA.

271   FitzGerald in Paris: Sam Halpern interview; Evan Thomas, *The Very Best Men: Four Who Dared: The Early Years of the CIA,* pp. 285–304. For an example of

a sabotage operation, see From the Coordinator of Cuban Affairs to the Special Group: Modification of Proposed Infiltration/Exfiltration Operations into Cuba During November 1963, Nov. 8, 1963, Assassination Records Review Board, NA.

271   RFK's role on AMLASH: RFK phone log, Oct. 11, 1963, JFKL. On November 12, the president's top advisers on Cuba met. The president questioned whether the sabotage program was worthwhile. Rusk strongly argued that it was unproductive. FitzGerald only hinted at the AMLASH operation, discussing in general terms the CIA's attempts to stimulate "disaffection in the Cuban military and power centers." FitzGerald said the CIA was "in touch with three persons who are in the military or who have highly placed contacts in such circles." A senior official involved in AMLASH said FitzGerald consciously played down the operation because he knew most of the president's advisers opposed any action that would deepen U.S. involvement. See Minutes of the Meeting to Review the Cuban Program, Nov. 12, 1963, released by the CIA Historical Review Program, NA.

271   "Bobby probably would have gone. . . .": Richard Helms interview; Thomas, *Very Best Men*, p. 300.

272   "Des wasn't freelancing. . . .": confidential source. In his testimony before the Church Committee on September 11, 1975, Helms noted that "all of these desires for assassination weapons came from AMLASH himself, as I recall it. There's no evidence that they originated from anybody in the Agency." Helms said the weapons were given AMLASH to keep him on board, working with the agency. Helms also said that he had "no specific recollection of" whether RFK was briefed on FitzGerald's meeting with AMLASH on October 29, but said, "I would have thought he would have."

272   exploding seashell: Thomas, *Very Best Men*, p. 295.

272   bomb in Castro's car: David Ellis interview.

272   RFK and assassination: The closest thing to a "smoking gun" document is a memo of a conversation between President Gerald Ford and Henry Kissinger on January 4, 1975. Kissinger warns Ford that the press is starting to look at "dirty tricks" by the CIA. Kissinger has spoken to Dick Helms, who, according to Kissinger, warned that the stories "are just the tip of the iceberg." If more information comes out, "blood will flow," says Kissinger. "For example, Robert Kennedy personally managed the operation on the assassination of Castro." This memo, released by the Assassination Records Review Board in June 1998, is more ambiguous than it appears. Helms may have just been telling a Republican secretary of state what he wanted to hear. Helms has testified under oath that he never discussed assassination with either John or Robert Kennedy, though he assumed they wanted Castro killed. See Evan Thomas, "The Castro Plot Thickens—Again," *Washington Post* Outlook, June 28, 1998.

272   "talked about knocking off Castro. . . .": Joseph Califano interview. Califano's military assistant, Alexander Haig, told the author, "I have no doubt everything he [Califano] told you is true." Haig personally believed that RFK ordered the assassination plots. But Haig never heard RFK talk about assassinations in his presence. Alexander Haig interview.

272   "nor did I have the sense. . . .": Cyrus Vance interview.

272   RFK was paying little attention: John Nolan interview. He was, however, continuing to meet with Harry Williams. Williams told Haynes Johnson, "I was a

hundred percent for the elimination of Castro. My plan was the physical elimination of Castro. My own feeling is that Kennedy was ready to eliminate Castro."
Haynes Johnson notes of interview with Harry Williams, Spring 1992. On October
7, 1963, Nolan sent a note to RFK that Williams wanted to see him to get a "green
light" from Nicaraguan strongman Anastasio Somoza to form an anti-Castro
force. Nolan reported that Williams said he "has men and territory; needs weapons
and money. Harry feels this is the best plan currently being considered." Williams
was apparently becoming impatient. He told Nolan that he didn't know "whether
to go back into mining or work in Cuban affairs." Nolan to RFK, Oct. 10, 1963, Assassination Records Review Board, JFKL.

273   "Des's tone was. . . .": confidential source. There is no record of the call
in the White House phone logs, but FitzGerald was probably using a secure phone
known at the CIA as "the green line" that did not pass through the White House
switchboard. "If he was using the green line, there would be no record," FitzGerald's executive assistant, Sam Halpern, told the author.

273   Cubela's poison pen: CIA officials have always insisted that it was
meant to be for Cubela's self-defense. Cubela himself rejected the weapon as inadequate. Sam Halpern interview.

273   "They should kill the whole family. . . .": *House Assassination Committee Report*, vol. IX, pp. 42–43.

273   Hoffa and RFK: *RK*, p. 280.

273   "I think the bitterness. . . .": Gerald Tremblay OH, JFKL.

274   removing Dean Rusk: Guthman and Shulman, eds., *In His Own Words*,
pp. 7–10.

274   ". . . we might need Lee": RFK to Kenneth O'Donnell, Sept. 25, 1963,
RFK White House files, RFK CF.

274   pork: Attorney General to the President, Oct. 2, 1963, RFK White House
files, RFK CF.

274   "I hope I am not causing too much trouble. . . .": RFK to Terry Sanford,
Aug. 7, 1963, Burke Marshall papers, JFKL.

274   "play Mr. Host": Nicholas Katzenbach interview.

274   "worked this like a son of a gun. . . .": Richard Donahue interview.

274   get moving on Mozambique: RFK to McGeorge Bundy, Oct. 20, 1963,
RFK White House files, RFK CF.

275   sustagen: Janet Travell, M.D., to RFK, Nov. 5, 1963, RFK Name File,
RFK CF.

275   "two Bobbies": William Baggs to RFK, Dec. 11, 1963, RFK Name File,
RFK CF.

275   Paul Corbin: Charles Bartlett interview; John Seigenthaler interview.
See Hersh, *Dark Side of Camelot*, pp. 442–46. O'Donnell called Corbin "the
Rasputin of our Administration . . . what his relationship is with the Kennedys I
will never know. . . .": Kenneth O'Donnell OH, JFKL. Bartlett wrote RFK praising
him for agreeing to be Corbin's godfather. Charles Bartlett to RFK, July 29, 1963,
RFK Name File, RFK CF.

275   RFK birthday: Lester David and Irene David, *Bobby Kennedy*, p. 213;
Patrick Anderson, "Robert's Character," *Esquire*, April 1965.

275   RFK not be attorney general much longer: Ramsey Clark OH, JFKL.

275   "It's all going too perfectly": William Manchester, *The Death of a President*, p. 33.

chapter 15: MOURNER

276   "I have news. . . .": Robert Morgenthau interview; William Manchester, *The Death of a President*, p. 196.

276   Hoover's reaction: Manchester, *Death of a President*, p. 257.

276   "I thought they'd get. . . .": Edwin O. Guthman, *We Band of Brothers*, p. 244.

276   RFK called Bundy: Manchester, *Death of a President*, p. 258; Seymour Hersh, *The Dark Side of Camelot*, p. 452.

276   RFK ordered the Secret Service: Bundy told friends that RFK was dismantling the taping system when LBJ walked into the Oval Office. Robert Bouk, the Secret Service man who did the actual dismantling, told the author that RFK was not present.

277   "He had the most wonderful life": Manchester, *Death of a President*, p. 257.

277   RFK asked McCone: Walter Sheridan OH, JFKL.

277   "One of your guys. . . .": Haynes Johnson interview. On November 15, the attorney general was informed that angry brigade members were threatening to demand back the brigade flag they had given President Kennedy in January. See Califano to Nolan, Nov. 15, 1963; Helms to Director of Central Intelligence, Nov. 21, 1963, Assassination Records Review Board, JFKL.

277   Draznin and intelligence network: Ed Guthman interview. "RFK would visit IRS agents in Chicago, Los Angeles, New York, and Miami so he wouldn't have to depend on Courtney Evans."

277   "He was very subdued. . . .": Julius Draznin interview.

278   RFK and Jacqueline Kennedy: Manchester, *Death of a President*, pp. 378–87.

278   "He'll always help you" . . . "I'll share him with you": Manchester, *Death of a President*, p. 416. "I'll share him with you" was cut from the Manchester manuscript by Richard Goodwin. See "Modifications of Manchester book for *Look* Magazine, Nov. 28, 1966," Myrick Land Collection, Boston University Special Collections.

278   coffin closed: Manchester, *Death of a President*, p. 418.

278   new order had begun: Charles Bartlett interview.

278   "God, it's so awful" . . . "Why God?": *RK*, p. 611.

278   "Do you know . . . ?": Manchester, *Death of a President*, pp. 453–454.

278   "Now *yew* don't like. . . .": *RK*, p. 623; Charles Spalding interview.

278   RFK and LBJ in Oval Office: Jeff Shesol, *Mutual Contempt*, pp. 120–23. McGeorge Bundy had urged LBJ to take over the Oval Office right away as a show of continuity. LBJ had been reluctant. Bundy later blamed himself for inadvertently creating tension between LBJ and RFK. Steve Bundy interview.

279   "Boys don't wear. . . .": *RK*, p. 611.

279   "Bobby should take . . ." . . . Ethel's wig: Manchester, *Death of a President*, pp. 506–507.

279   "Bobby, don't forget. . . .": Rowland Evans OH, JFKL.

279   RFK surprised at crowd size: Manchester, *Death of a President*, p. 511.

279   JFK autopsy and adrenals: Dr. J. Thornton Boswell interview, Aug. 17, 1977, House Assassination Committee Records ("Dr. Burkley made clear that he didn't want a report on adrenal glands, wanting instead that that information be reported informally.") Asked about the condition of JFK's adrenals, Dr. James Joseph Humes, one of the navy pathologists, ducked the question. Dennis Breo, "JFK's Death—the Plain Truth from the MDs Who Did the Autopsy," *Journal of the American Medical Association*, May 27, 1992.

280   JFK's brain: Andy Purdy, "Search for Missing Autopsy Materials," Aug. 17, 1977, House Assassination Committee Records; R. Michael McReynolds, Records on the Assassination of John F. Kennedy, *Prologue* (Quarterly of the National Archives), Winter 1992 ("One stainless steel containing gross matter"). There is still considerable confusion over the autopsy and interment of JFK's brain. See Douglas Horne, "Questions Regarding Supplementary Brain Examination(s) Following the Autopsy on President John F. Kennedy," June 2, 1998, Assassination Records Review Board.

280   disposing coffin: record of phone conversation between RFK and Lawson Knott, Feb. 3, 1966; RFK to Knott, Feb. 11, 1966; memo for record ("Kennedy Casket"), General Services Administration, Feb. 21, 1966, Assassination Records Review Board.

280   RFK and *Profiles*: Robert F. Kennedy, "Foreword to the Memorial Edition," Dec. 18, 1963, in John F. Kennedy, *Profiles in Courage*.

280   "poverty" note: Nicholas Lemann, *The Promised Land*, pp. 135–42.

280   RFK on Sunday and Monday: Manchester, *Death of a President*, pp. 511, 516–18, 525, 555, 590, 602–603, 608–609, 618–20.

281   Rose and Joe Kennedy: ibid., pp. 208–209, 371–73, 500–502.

282   RFK in JFK's clothes: Ronnie Eldridge interview; Joe Dolan interview.

282   RFK in pain: John Seigenthaler OH, JFKL.

282   "Been to any . . . ?" . . . "I don't like. . . .": See *RK*, p. 613.

282   On many winter nights: Lester David and Irene David, *Bobby Kennedy*, p. 217; John Seigenthaler interview.

283   "vicious" touch football: Pierre Salinger OH, JFKL.

283   RFK indifferent when Hoffa convicted: William Hundley interview.

283   "I saw him often after that. . . .": Robert Morgenthau interview.

283   Gimbel on RFK: Mary Bailey Gimbel STOH.

283   McCone sensed RFK's guilt: David Belin, *Final Disclosure*, p. 217. See Max Holland, "The Kennedy Assassination: Why the Warren Commission Was Wrong—and Right," *American Heritage*, November 1993.

283   holding something back: John Seigenthaler OH, JFKL.

283   Ann Fleming: Ann Fleming to Clarissa Avon, quoted in Mark Amory, ed., *The Letters of Ann Fleming*, p. 336.

284   "What do I do?": HFR [Harold Reis] to the Attorney General, June 12, 1964; Earl Warren to RFK, June 11, 1964, Assassination Records Review Board, NA.

284   Warren Commission findings: See Max Holland, "The JFK Files: Cuba,

Kennedy, and the Cold War," *The Nation*, Nov. 29, 1993. The CIA also withheld information from the Warren Commission. Interviewed by Arthur Schlesinger, Fritz Schwarz, chief counsel of the Church Committee, offered an ambiguous recollection. According to Schlesinger's notes from January 12, 1976, "FAOS [Schwarz] thinks the CIA suppressed story before Warren Commission because blvd. RFK wd. be furious if he knew." Knew what? Interviewed twenty-three years later, Schwarz could not recall. F.A.O. Schwarz interview, Schlesinger Papers, JFKL.

284   Warren Commission public relations exercise: Frank Mankiewicz interview.

284   Jackie, RFK visit grave: Secret Service Daily White House Diary, Nov. 25, 27, Dec. 4, 1963, JFKL.

285   "The innocent suffer. . . .": *RK*, p. 617.

285   Benedictine priests: confidential interview.

285   seed of Camelot: Theodore White, *In Search of History*, pp. 518–25.

285   RFK joined in Camelot mythmaking: Peter Collier and David Horowitz, *The Kennedys*, p. 318.

285   ". . . widow's weeds. . . .": Charles Bartlett OH, LBJL.

285   physical relationship: Letitia Baldrige told the author "it was a needy relationship. They would talk in a way that Ethel could not. But Jackie was not attracted to Bobby Kennedy."

286   *The Greek Way*: *RK*, p. 618. RFK's sister Jean Smith told Arthur Schlesinger that "after 1953 he found consolation in Greek tragedy rather than religion; this was the expression of his character." Jean Smith interviewed by Arthur Schlesinger, Schlesinger Papers, JFKL.

286   thank-you letter: RFK to Mrs. Paul Mellon, RFK Name File, RFK CF.

286   "All arrogance. . . .": Edith Hamilton, *The Greek Way*, p. 108.

286   "Powerful men pull. . . .": ibid., pp. 110–15.

287   "again and again the note of foreboding. . . .": ibid., pp. 138, 149.

287   Spalding et al. drank too much: Charles Spalding interview.

287   still rest in the bookshelves: Maxwell Kennedy interview. Mary Bailey Gimbel had RFK's copy of *The Greek Way*, which she showed Collier and Horowitz. (See note to p. 316 at p. 533 in *Kennedys*.)

287   "In agony learn wisdom! . . ." . . . "God, whose law. . . .": Hamilton, *The Greek Way*, pp. 148, 139, 142, 156.

287   ". . . safe havens" . . . "The fullness of life. . . .": ibid., pp. 147, 136.

288   "It's strange to think. . . .": Murray Kempton, "Pure Irish: Robert F. Kennedy," *New Republic*, Feb. 15, 1964.

288   "I'm sure Jack liked it": confidential interview.

288   women lawyers: Ralph Dungan to Attorney General; RFK to Dungan, Feb. 19, 1964. RFK White House files, RFK CF.

288   ". . . sore thumb": Attorney General to the President, March 16, 1963, RFK White House files, RFK CF.

289   Scranton speech: Edwin O. Guthman and C. Richard Allen, eds., *RFK: Collected Speeches*, p. 103.

289   " 'Oh, Bobby, you'll go on. . . . ' ": Mary McGrory interview.

289   "When I'm through. . . .": Shesol, *Mutual Contempt*, p. 112.

289   "We must all stay in close touch. . . .": *RK*, p. 631. Schlesinger sent RFK a novel called *The Gay Place* by a former LBJ staffer billed on its jacket as all about

"politicians, mistresses, movie stars, grafters, reformers" in the White House. "Herewith the volume," Schlesinger wrote. "This is not reading for Ethel." A.S. to RFK, undated, RFK Name File, RFK CF.

289 Walton and Soviets: Walton also told the Soviets that the Kennedys believed JFK had been killed by right-wing plotters. Aleksandr Fursenko and Timothy Naftali, *"One Hell of a Gamble,"* pp. 344–46. For a less lurid version, see William Walton, Notes on a Visit to Moscow, December 1963, RFK Name File, RFK CF.

290 begin the succession struggle: Arthur Schlesinger called together the faithful right after the assassination. At the so-called Harvard lunch, there was already talk of an RFK-Humphrey ticket in '64. Manchester, *Death of a President,* p. 474.

290   Paul Corbin: *RK,* p. 651.

290   Corbin's actions: John Seigenthaler OH, JFKL.

290   PT-boat tie clips: Cecil Stoughton OH, LBJL.

290   RFK had bugged his office: *RK,* pp. 622–25.

290   feeding Baker investigation: Burkett Van Kirk interview; Charles Bartlett OH, LBJL. Kenny O'Donnell maintained, "Bobby Kennedy had no more to do with it than the man in the moon." Kenneth O'Donnell OH, JFKL. If RFK and JFK meant to find a scandal on LBJ as a means of dumping him, they changed their minds. JFK understood that a Baker investigation could backfire and lead the press back to Rometsch. According to O'Donnell's version of a conversation the president had with Senator George Smathers, President Kennedy hinted as much, while carefully maintaining his own innocence: "George, do you know how that would read if Bobby Baker was indicted tomorrow morning with the girl situation involved? *Life* Magazine would put 27 pictures of these lovely looking, buxom lasses running around with no clothes on, and 27 pictures of Bobby Baker and hoodlums and vending machines, and then the last picture would be of *me*. And it would say, 'Mess in Washington under Kennedy Regime,' and 99 percent of the people would think I was running around with 29 girls because they don't read the story, and I'm going to defeat myself."

290   "Whatever happened to Lyndon?": Shesol, *Mutual Contempt,* pp. 104–106.

290   LBJ and RFK on February 11: John Seigenthaler OH, JFKL; Edwin O. Guthman and Jeffrey Shulman, eds., *Robert Kennedy: In His Own Words,* pp. 406–407; Richard Goodwin, *Remembering America,* p. 248.

291   "You wouldn't come that cheap": Joe Dolan interview.

291   McGeorge Bundy believed: McGeorge Bundy OH, JFKL.

291   "It disturbs me. . . .": McGeorge Bundy to RFK, Feb. 29, March 5, 1964, RFK White House files, RFK CF. Bundy had to apologize again in July for giving a quote to Marquis Childs appearing to criticize RFK's trip to Poland. McG.B. to RFK, July 12, 1964, RFK White House files, RFK CF.

291   "Tell her seriously. . . .": J. K. Galbraith to RFK, July 21, 1964, RFK Name File, RFK CF.

291   RFK forgave Corbin: John Seigenthaler OH, JFKL.

291   "When I want your advice. . . .": Rowland Evans interview.

292   RFK loved Corbin: Ben Bradlee interview.

292   "a grandstanding runt": Shesol, *Mutual Contempt,* p. 3.

292   "an animal in many ways. . . .": Guthman and Shulman, eds., *In His Own Words*, p. 417.

292   Johnson on assassination: Robert Dallek, *Flawed Giant*, p. 136; *RK*, p. 649.

292   "a) Lyndon hated Bobby. . . .": *RK*, p. 650.

292   "The one thing Lyndon Johnson doesn't want. . . .": Guthman and Shulman, eds., *In His Own Words*, pp. 413–14. See Dallek, *Flawed Giant*, p. 129.

292   "nettling": Charles Spalding OH, JFKL.

263   RFK thought about Senate and governorship: Goodwin, *Remembering America*, p. 297. "What's Bobby Going to Do?" *Newsweek*, July 6, 1964. Kenny O'Donnell later said that he persuaded RFK to run for vice president as a stalking horse for Hubert Humphrey. Kenneth O'Donnell OH, JFKL.

293   RFK offered to go to Saigon: Michael Beschloss, *Taking Charge*, p. 405. Johnson also feared for Kennedy's safety in Saigon.

293   "Somebody up there. . . .": Lester David and Irene David, *Bobby Kennedy*, p. 238.

293   spend more time with Teddy: Beschloss, *Taking Charge*, p. 437.

293   "He went from bed to bed. . . .": Ben Bradlee interview.

294   "Ich bin ein Berliner": George Muller to James Reston, July 23, 1988, James Reston papers, University of Illinois.

294   RFK in Berlin: *NYT*, June 27, 1964; Warren Rogers, *When I Think of Bobby*, pp. 142–43.

294   "strange fascination": John Seigenthaler OH, JFKL.

294   RFK in Poland: Joseph Kraft STOH and OH, JFKL; John Moors Cabot OH, LBJL; John Mapother to author, July 27, 1998; John Nolan OH, JFKL.

295   Johnson told RFK no on V.P.: Shesol, *Mutual Contempt*, pp. 204–10.

295   LBJ made Bundy tell RFK: Don Wilson OH, JFKL.

295   haunted by RFK: Beschloss, *Taking Charge*, p. 468.

295   civil rights bill signing: Nicholas Lemann, *The Promised Land*, p. 185; *RK*, p. 645.

295   July 21 phone conversation: Beschloss, *Taking Charge*, p. 460.

295   Hoover dispatched a whole team: Cartha DeLoach, *Hoover's FBI*, p. 381.

295   speech drafts: See speech drafts for Aug. 27, 1964, RFK Papers, Attorney General Papers, JFKL.

296   "garish sun": John Seigenthaler OH, JFKL; William vanden Heuvel interview.

296   weeping after speech: William Dunfey OH, JFKL.

296   "How much more do I have to take?": RFK to Joe Alsop [August 1964], Joe Alsop Papers. LOC.

CHAPTER 16: SEARCHER

297   cruise in August: Mary Bailey Gimbel STOH; Rowland Evans OH, JFKL; Don Wilson OH, JFKL.

297   "The politics in New York. . . .": Albert Blumenthal OH, JFKL.

297   lost in Bronxville: Joe Dolan interview.

297   impaled himself on the turnstile: Lester David and Irene David, *Bobby Kennedy*, p. 264.

297   needed LBJ's coattails: Myer Feldman OH, Joe Dolan OH, JFKL; Joe Dolan interview; Don Wilson OH, JFKL; Milton Gwirtzman interview.

297   RFK not warmly embraced: Franklin D. Roosevelt Jr. STOH.

298   pulled tourists off buses: Ronnie Eldridge OH, JFKL; Ronnie Eldridge interview.

298   hard-eyed Irish punk: Milton Gwirtzman interview. "We had a giant problem with the Jews out here [on Long Island]. It was really bad." John English OH, JFKL.

298   "Kennedy Blitzkrieg": *RK*, p. 668.

298   "More Nuns Leave Church": Adam Walinsky interview.

298   RFK "was so nervous. . . .": Albert Blumenthal OH, JFKL.

298   ". . . fucking Calvin Coolidge": R. W. Apple interview.

298   RFK and Warren Report: Terry Smith, "Bobby's Image," *Esquire*, April 1965.

298   "What are they going to do that for?": Richard Wade interview.

299   ". . . Maybe we're all doomed. . . .": William Shannon, "Said Robert Kennedy, 'Maybe We're All Doomed Anyway,' " *NYT Magazine*, March 16, 1968.

299   "Get out of this mysticism. . . .": *RK*, p. 670.

299   "Steve, I want to tell you. . . .": Richard Reeves, "The People Around Bobby," *NYT Magazine*, Feb. 12, 1967.

299   "Ask not what the Kennedys. . . .": Joe Dolan interview.

299   Corbin banished to New Jersey: Gerald Tremblay OH, JFKL.

299   ". . . shaking the hand of every nun. . . .": Justin Feldman interview.

299   "conceivably have been the man. . . .": Arthur Schlesinger STOH.

299   "They're for him. . . .": Edwin Guthman interview.

299   "He looked terrified. . . .": R. W. Apple interview.

300   "You're a magician. . . .": Hubert Humphrey OH, JFKL; Milton Gwirtzman interview.

300   "Robert" not "Bobby": Richard Wade interview.

300   Keating and Ambassador Kennedy: Justin Feldman interview.

300   RFK hit back: *RK*, pp. 672–73; John Nolan OH, JFKL.

300   "was not shy in the streets": Jerome Kretchmer interview.

301   RFK, Keating, and debate: Peter Fishbein interview; John Seigenthaler OH, JFKL. Fishbein said that the idea to appear outside the door at the time of the debate was Kennedy's alone. Joe Dolan said that it was his idea, communicated to Kennedy through Steve Smith. Joe Dolan interview.

301   RFK and LBJ election: Richard Wade OH, JFKL; Shesol, *Mutual Contempt*, p. 231.

302   RFK discovered poem: William vanden Heuvel and Milton Gwirtzman, *On His Own: Robert F. Kennedy, 1964–1968*, p. 54. The point about the real meaning of Tennyson's poem was suggested to the author by Jon Meacham.

302   RFK at JFK's gravesite: Peter Collier and David Horowitz, *The Kennedys*, pp. 324–25.

302   "*in* the Senate. . . .": Mike Mansfield interview.

302   "He did not become a member. . . .": Lawrence O'Brien STOH.

302   "He hated all the talk. . . .": Richard Goodwin interview.

303   ". . . a really private world": Dun Gifford OH, JFKL.

303   "How many hours do I have to sit here . . . ?": vanden Heuvel and Gwirtzman, *On His Own*, p. 64.

303   "Oh, forget it!": Helen O'Donnell, *A Common Good*, p. 364. In another telling, by Richard Reeves (*NYT*, April 14, 1966), Kennedy exclaimed, "Oh hell, why don't you just flip a coin."

303   "If only I was a member. . . .": Dun Gifford OH, JFKL.

303   "With big words?": *RK*, p. 682.

303   *What I Know About New York Politics:* Milton Gwirtzman interview.

303   "if we scheduled something. . . .": Frank Mankiewicz OH, JFKL.

304   "I've never heard of half. . . .": Joe Dolan to RFK, Sept. 15, 1965, Dolan Papers, JFKL.

304   "It was very hard. . . .": Tom Johnston interview.

304   "Can't you just tell . . . ?": Frank Mankiewicz OH, JFKL.

304   "Blah, blah, blah.": Warren Rogers interview.

304   ". . . need any PR advice" . . . "Anti-Catholicism. . . .": Frank Mankiewicz interview.

304   Walinsky poster: Joe Dolan interview.

305   sad and secretive: Adam Walinsky OH, JFKL.

305   "Oh, Adam": Peter Edelman interview.

305   in search of new ideas: Frank Mankiewicz OH, JFKL.

305   RFK and the War on Poverty: Nicholas Lemann, *The Promised Land*, p. 149, and Adam Walinsky interview. Walinsky: "Kennedy was never part of the debate over the War on Poverty. He never saw Sarge [Sargent Shriver, Johnson's head of the War on Poverty and Kennedy's brother-in-law], who was sensitive to LBJ. Nobody at Labor was asking what Bobby thought, and Bob Kennedy didn't care what the Labor Department thought." See Shesol, *Mutual Contempt*, p. 239. RFK did testify in favor of community action in 1965, and he did show an early distrust of the bureaucracy. Besieged with requests from New York school administrators who wanted money for the 1965 Elementary and Secondary Education Act, Kennedy asked, somewhat skeptically, "Well, what are you going to do with it?"

305   RFK and Shriver: Shriver said he never talked to Kennedy about the War on Poverty. "I didn't need to. I knew more about it than he did." He said he stayed out of the RFK-LBJ rivalry. "I was not a participant in it. I was not trying to help or defend one or the other." Sargent Shriver interview.

305   Heller and JFK: Walter Heller, Confidential Notes on a Quick Meeting with President and Other Leading Members of the Kennedy Family, Tuesday, Nov. 19, 1963, RFK White House files, RFK CF.

305   "total attack": Attorney General to the President, Nov. 19, 1963, RFK White House files, RFK CF.

305   1964 memo urging job creation: Peter Edelman interview; RFK to the President, Aug. 5, 1964, RFK White House files, RFK CF.

306   "He looked awful. . . .": See Lemann, *The Promised Land*, pp. 123–87, for the best history of the War on Poverty and Kennedy's role.

306   Touring Harlem: Michael Knox Beran, *The Last Patrician*, p. 101.

306   "A lot of those looters. . . .": vanden Heuvel and Gwirtzman, *On His Own*, p. 80.

306   "Oh, I see. . . .": Lemann, *The Promised Land*, p. 129.

306   he turned to danger: As always, there was a political element in some of these adventures, or at least his advisers saw political possibilities. RFK often got shrewd memos from Fred Dutton on how to position himself. In April 1966—after RFK's year of living dangerously—Dutton wrote him with many suggestions, one of which was, "At least one major, exciting personal adventure or activity every six months or so, as mountain climbing, river boating, etc. . . . This outlet also moves you into the 'existential' politics that I believe will be more and more important in the years ahead." With an eye on the Jewish vote, Dutton recommended that RFK "live for four or five days on a kibbutz in Israel. This should be useful in New York. . . ." Dutton to RFK, April 6, 1966, Fred Dutton Papers, JFKL. RFK wrote on top to Joe Dolan, "Joe, as usual, Dutton has some good points."

307   "Bobby, why don't you . . . ?": Joan Braden interview.

307   RFK assault on Mount Kennedy: *RK*, p. 811; *NYT*, March 24, 25, 26, 1965; "The Climber," *Newsweek*, April 5, 1965; Robert Kennedy, "Our Climb Up Mt. Kennedy," *Life*, April 9, 1965; "Mt. Kennedy," *National Geographic*, July 1965; *Boston Globe*, March 23, 24, 25, 1965.

307   "I don't care about the picture. . . .": James Whittaker OH, JFKL.

308   ". . . All this excited him": ibid.

308   Joe Kempkes: Joe Kempkes interview.

308   RFK nuclear weapons initiative: Tom Wicker, "Kennedy and Johnson," *NYT*, June 24, 1965. The original idea seems to have come from Fred Dutton. Dutton to RFK, May 12, 1965, Fred Dutton Papers, JFKL.

308   white-water rafting: *NYT*, July 3, 4, 5, 1965; Jim Whittaker OH, JFKL.

308   *Palawan* incident: Rowland Evans interview. George Stevens, another friend who was also on board, recalled that Kennedy's dog Freckles went overboard, and Kennedy dove in to rescue him. George Stevens interview.

309   "the Nervous": O'Donnell, *Common Good*, p. 384.

309   RFK dove into sea: *Washington Post*, Sept. 2, 1965.

309   "impotent and frustrated. . . .": Don Wilson OH, JFKL.

309   "Let's go ice skating": Richard Goodwin, *Remembering America*, pp. 431–32.

309   RFK in South America: *NYT*, Nov. 12, 14, 18, 19, 22, 26, 28, 1965; *Newsweek*, Nov. 22, Dec. 6, 1965; Richard Goodwin interview; William vanden Heuvel interview; Goodwin, *Remembering America*, pp. 437–42; vanden Heuvel and Gwirtzman, *On His Own*, pp. 166–72; *RK*, pp. 694–98.

309   "No, Mr. Kennedy, *please*": Andrew Glass, "The Compulsive Candidate," *Saturday Evening Post*, April 23, 1966.

CHAPTER 17: CONSCIENCE

311   RFK wasn't ready: Adam Walinsky interview; *RK*, pp. 724–31.

312   JFK and Vietnam: See Fredrik Logevall, *Choosing War*, pp. 71–72.

312   "would do no harm. . . .": Lyndon Johnson, *The Vantage Point*, p. 136.

312   International Police Academy speech: *RK*, p. 730.

313   A. J. Muste: Adam Walinsky interview.

313   giving blood to North Vietnamese: Transcript of RFK press conference at USC, Nov. 5, 1965, RFK Senate Papers, JFKL; *New York Daily News*, Nov. 10, 1965.

313   RFK defended McNamara on electronic fence: Sander Vanocur interview.

314   "We talked often. . . .": Robert McNamara interview.

314   "Well, Bob McNamara told me. . . .": Peter Edelman OH, JFKL.

314   "McNamara gave Kennedy copies. . . .": Richard Goodwin interview.

314   both sides of his mouth: Milton Gwirtzman interview.

314   "Now what the hell . . . ?": Dun Gifford OH, JFKL.

315   "I have no doubt. . . .": Robert McNamara interview.

315   RFK letter to LBJ: RFK to LBJ, January 1966; LBJ to RFK, Jan. 27, 1966, LBJL.

315   LBJ quoted Catton: John Steele files, Jan. 26, 1966, LBJL.

315   RFK relegated to back bench: Kennedy planned a trip to Vietnam at McNamara's suggestion but called it off in February at the last moment when LBJ went to meet with South Vietnamese leaders in Hawaii. RFK believed that LBJ had intentionally upstaged him. Joseph Kraft STOH.

315   "a share of power": *NYT*, Feb. 20, 1966. The idea was apparently Goodwin's. Richard Goodwin, *Remembering America*, p. 454.

315   RFK checked with McNamara: Milton Gwirtzman interview. For McNamara's private views, see Averell Harriman memorandum, May 14, 1966, Harriman Papers, LOC.

315   bunker under siege: Peter Edelman OH, JFKL. Transcript of press conference, Feb. 22, 1966, RFK Senate Papers, JFKL; Jack Newfield, *Robert Kennedy: A Memoir*, pp. 124–25; Jeff Shesol, *Mutual Contempt*, pp. 289–91.

315   denounced Bundy for disloyalty: Rowland Evans OH, JFKL.

315   RFK chewed on cigar: *RK*, p. 737.

315   "That's the trouble with all you fellows. . . .": Shesol, *Mutual Contempt*, p. 298.

316   RFK on JFK Vietnam legacy: *RK*, pp. 738–40.

316   "If I become convinced. . . .": Newfield, *Memoir*, p. 128.

316   RFK running in '68: *RK*, p. 740.

316   backed Johnson: *NYT*, June 20, 1966.

316   ". . . They're sons of bitches": Edwin O. Guthman and Jeffrey Shulman, eds., *Robert Kennedy: In His Own Words*, p. 204.

316   "defied labels": Peter Edelman interview.

317   copy of Emerson's *Essays:* Newfield, *Memoir*, p. 26.

317   "self-trust": Michael Knox Beran, *The Last Patrician*, pp. 114–17.

317   RFK, Walinsky, Edelman discuss poverty: Adam Walinsky interview; Adam Walinsky OH, JFKL.

317   "as momentous an event. . . .": Beran, *Last Patrician*, p. 104.

318   RFK's anti-poverty message: "A Program for the Urban Crisis: A Series of Three Speeches," Jan. 20, 21, 22, 1966, in Edwin O. Guthman and C. Richard Allen, eds., *RFK: Collected Speeches*, pp. 168–76. He spoke to the Federation of Jew-

ish Philanthropies of New York, the Borough President's Conference of Community Leaders, and the United Auto Workers Regional Conference in New York.

318   LBJ, Shriver on welfare: Maurice Isserman and Michael Kazin, *America Divided: The Civil War of the 1960s*, pp. 109–10.

318   "Most of us deprecated. . . .": "Redirecting Government, Solving Problems," Feb. 7, 1966, in Guthman and Allen, eds., *Collected Speeches*, pp. 208–11. Kennedy showed a desire for results (and some healthy skepticism) in federal aid to education. In 1965, he drafted an amendment to require accountability tests to measure the progress of federally supported schools. *NYT*, Nov. 14, 1966.

318   ". . . I don't want to just talk. . . .": Adam Walinsky interview. In August, Kennedy began to aggressively attack the administration's efforts to counter poverty in the inner city as a "drop in the bucket." *Washington Post*, Aug. 16, 17, 18, 1966. In October, he urged the administration to spend more on the War on Poverty. *Congressional Record*—Senate, Oct. 3, 1966, p. 24794.

319   Bedford-Stuyvesant: Adam Walinsky OH, JFKL. For an excellent history of the Bedford-Stuyvesant project, see R. B. Goldman, "Performance in Black and White: An Appraisal of the Development and Record of the Bedford-Stuyvesant Restoration and Development and Services Corporation," Ford Foundation, February 1969, Burke Marshall Papers, JFKL.

319   ". . . We gotta do better than a swimming pool. . . .": Thomas Johnston interview; Judge Thomas Jones OH, JFKL.

319   sin was not trying: Wesley Barthelmes OH, JFKL.

319   Camus helped RFK: Jack Newfield STOH; Newfield, *Memoir*, pp. 58–59.

319   "That book is really depressing. . . .": Mary Bailey Gimbel STOH. See Albert Camus, *Resistance, Rebellion, and Death*.

319   *Cavalier* article: Jack Newfield STOH.

320   "The Impossible Dream": *RK*, p. 804.

320   RFK and migrant workers: Peter Edelman interview; William vanden Heuvel and Milton Gwirtzman, *On His Own: Robert F. Kennedy, 1964–1968*, p. 103.

320   "He shouldn't go so far. . . .": *RK*, p. 791.

320   RFK pushed for legislation for migrant workers: Guthman and Allen, eds., *Collected Speeches*, p. 199.

320   "Perhaps we cannot prevent this world. . . .": Maxwell Taylor Kennedy, ed., *Make Gentle the Life of This World: The Vision of Robert F. Kennedy*, p. 133; RFK, *To Seek a Newer World*, dedication page. The book was dedicated to "my children and yours."

321   ". . . But Bobby Kennedy was different. . . .": Margaret Marshall interview.

321   "as a dare": Louis Oberdorfer interview.

321   drafting Day of Affirmation speech: Joe Dolan interview. Kennedy got an important push from Allard Lowenstein, a young student activist and lawyer who impressed him greatly. Lowenstein convinced Kennedy he had to speak out boldly to make a difference. Walinsky's and Goodwin's first drafts and the final draft with RFK's handwritten edits are in RFK's Senate papers—Trips/Speeches, June 6, 1966, JFKL.

322   "Robertson's banning terrified me. . . .": Margaret Marshall interview.

322   "We're only here on earth. . . .": This clip is in a film on RFK made by Charles Guggenheim for the 1968 Democratic convention, courtesy Charles Guggenheim.

322   Kennedy delivered Day of Affirmation speech: Guthman and Allen, eds., *Collected Speeches*, p. 236.

322   "high and exhilarated": Margaret Marshall interview.

322   "I'm Robert Kennedy from the United States. . . .": Guthman and Allen, eds., *Collected Speeches*, pp. 235, 248.

323   "What if God is black?": *NYT*, June 9, 1966; *RK*, pp. 746–47.

323   cuddled with little girl: Irene Mennell interview.

323   "If we stayed here. . . .": Tom Johnston interview.

323   "He reminded us. . . .": Margaret Marshall interview.

324   ". . . I'm not going anywhere this fall. . . .": Adam Walinsky OH, JFKL. Walinsky pushed RFK to stick with Bedford-Stuyvesant. "If you make this work, it will be the 'Kennedy Plan' everywhere." Walinsky to RFK, undated [November 1966], Adam Walinsky papers, JFKL. RFK was drawn into New York politics upon his return from South Africa, campaigning hard for a reform candidate for the corrupt New York surrogate court, Sam Silverman. RFK was not above low means for high ends. According to William Haddad, RFK's sometimes troubleshooter, Haddad and a newsman sneaked into the Manhattan courthouse to purloin the files of the incumbent, Arthur Klein, and leaked the evidence of corruption in them to the newspapers. William Haddad interview.

324   RFK and Lindsay: William Walton OH, JFKL; Justin Feldman interview. After an official in the Lindsay administration was caught up in a corruption scandal, RFK joked, "If Mayor Daley looked like Lindsay, he'd be president. If Lindsay looked like Daley, he'd be in jail." Frank Mankiewicz interview.

324   ". . . hands of subversives?": Nicholas Lemann, *The Promised Land*, pp. 122–29, 164–67.

324   "bitching societies": Adam Walinsky OH, JFKL.

324   RFK and businessmen: Burke Marshall OH, JFKL.

325   RFK and André Meyer: Thomas Johnston interview; Cary Reich, *Financier: The Life of André Meyer* (New York: Morrow, 1983), pp. 247–50, 264–65, 267.

325   rounding up support for Bed-Sty: William vanden Heuvel interview; confidential source.

325   the two-board idea: Thomas Johnston interview.

325   "He would say. . . .": Dun Gifford OH, JFKL.

326   "It was worth a few hundred thousand dollars. . . .": Eli Jacobs OH, JFKL.

CHAPTER 18: GHOSTS

327   RFK New York tour with LBJ: *NYT*, Nov. 14, 1966.

327   RFK played JFK: Jeff Shesol, *Mutual Contempt*, pp. 344–46.

327   "cotton candy": Jack Newfield, *Robert Kennedy: A Memoir*, p. 170.

327   "He seemed melancholy. . . .": Mary McGrory interview.

327   RFK meeting with Newfield: Newfield, *Memoir*, p. 26.

329   RFK did not want to know: For the FBI's evidence of RFK listening to the tapes in Chicago, see Marlin Johnson to James Gale, Dec. 20, 1965; Gale to DeLoach, June 28, 1966; in New York: John Danahy to Gale, Dec. 22, 1965. Courtney Evans told the FBI that RFK was fully aware that the FBI was using bugs, but that it was a "cozy matter." DeLoach to Tolson, Dec. 24, 1965. Evans said Kennedy "couldn't help but know." Hoover to Katzenbach, Jan. 5, 1966. Evans told the FBI that Kennedy knew about the eavesdropping microphones, but not their location. De-Loach to Tolson, June 2, 1966. In Chicago, RFK said he didn't want to know the lo-cation of the microphones, that "they are all illegal," Gale to DeLoach, June 28, 1966. See also Gale to DeLoach, July 1, 1966. In January 1967, Joe Dolan told an FBI agent that "anyone with an ounce of sense would know that Senator Kennedy had full knowledge of all the technical devices being used by the FBI." SAC Wash-ington Field Office to Hoover, Jan. 17, 1967, Hoover Official and Confidential files, FBI.

329   Senator Long egged on by LBJ: *RK*, p. 760. The FBI also encouraged Long: "Senator Long thoroughly dislikes former AG Kennedy and will use such in-formation against Sen. Kennedy." DeLoach to Tolson, Jan. 17, 1966, Hoover Offi-cial and Confidential Files, FBI.

329   Abe Fortas: Juan Williams, *Thurgood Marshall*, pp. 325–26.

329   Katzenbach and bugging: Victor S. Navasky, *Kennedy Justice* (New York: Atheneum, 1971), pp. 357–58, and Nicholas Katzenbach interview. William Hundley, head of the organized crime section, told the author he believed RFK knew about the bugging. Katzenbach was more equivocal. "Hundley is right in this sense. Bobby never pursued it, he never said, 'I assume this is from the local police, you're not doing this, are you?' Maybe he was scared of what he'd find out, or naive. But that doesn't agree with Bobby wanting to know everything, and it doesn't agree with Bobby being angry and slamming down the receiver." Burke Marshall continued to believe RFK. The FBI affidavits were fictions written to please Hoover, he told the author. Burke Marshall interview.

329   RFK learned about Hoover releasing memos: *NYT*, Dec. 11, 1966.

330   Herblock and RFK: Gerald Tremblay interview. Fred Dutton, who often wrote savvy political memos to RFK, wrote him in December that "outside Wash-ington," the "old canard about you—'too zealous,' 'ruthless' . . . remains far more entrenched than I had thought." Dutton to RFK, Dec. 8, 1966, Fred Dutton Papers, JFKL.

330   LBJ proposed banning wiretapping: Tweaking Kennedy was the only reason LBJ mentioned wiretapping. See John Steele Papers, Jan. 12, 1967, LBJL.

330   RFK refused to clap: Shesol, *Mutual Contempt*, p. 353.

330   Paul Fay manuscript: Fay's manuscript is in the Myrick Land Papers at Boston University. See Box 5, no. 19.

330   Dean Markham plane crash: *NYT*, Sept. 25, 1966.

331   Manchester's *Death of a President:* The best account is *The Manchester Affair,* by John Corry. The author's father, Evan W. Thomas II, was the editor at *Harper's* for JFK's *Profiles in Courage,* RFK's *The Enemy Within,* and *Death of a President.*

331   "Anybody who is against me. . . .": William Manchester, *Controversy and Other Essays in Journalism*, p. 39.

331   Mrs. Kennedy filed suit: *NYT*, Dec. 17, 1966.

331   "My crazy sister-in-law": Frank Mankiewicz interview.

331   "Then give them to John": Manchester, *Controversy*, p. 33; John Seigenthaler interview.

331   "God, it just murders Bobby. . . .": Shesol, *Mutual Contempt*, p. 362.

332   "Maybe I will have to say something. . . .": Newfield, *Memoir*, p. 128.

332   LBJ escalated: Shesol, *Mutual Contempt*, pp. 368–69.

332   staffers and friends urged him to speak out: Schlesinger to RFK, Jan. 23, 1967, Schlesinger Papers, JFKL; Adam Walinsky to RFK, "RE: Gratuitous Advice," urged him to run for president in 1968 [Nov. 1966], Adam Walinsky Papers, JFKL.

332   Hitler mustache: Shesol, *Mutual Contempt*, pp. 308–309.

332   "He really believed. . . .": Peter Edelman OH, JFKL.

332   collision with LBJ was unavoidable: In an hour-long meeting that January 1967, *New York Times* columnist James Reston could feel RFK's desire to run against LBJ. "When I mentioned that the political world was now being run by a lot of technicians and mechanics, he [RFK] said, almost involuntarily, 'What a chance!' " Reston "came away feeling that nothing could prevent him from becoming President of the United States except the death of Lyndon Johnson [because Hubert Humphrey would automatically succeed him and be the Democrats' standard-bearer in 1968]. His peers in the Senate have given him a breadth and depth of knowledge he did not have before, and what is more important, a somewhat kindlier view of human frailty. He seems to have acquired the habit of hating when he was Attorney General. After the death of his brother, he was naturally filled with morbid miseries and inner discords. But he seems more patient and thoughtful today." RFK file, memo to record, January 1967, James Reston Papers, University of Illinois.

332   RFK in Europe: *NYT*, Jan. 29, Feb. 2, Feb. 5, 1967.

332   Candice Bergen: C. David Heymann, *RFK*, p. 418. William vanden Heuvel, who accompanied RFK to Paris, told the author, "The French press was right." The article appeared in *Paris Presse*, Feb. 4, 1967. They dined at Cri de Paris in Saint-Germain-des-Prés.

332   Paris peace feelers: *RK*, pp. 765–68.

332   February 6 RFK and LBJ meeting: Peter Edelman OH, JFKL; Adam Walinsky OH, JFKL; Frank Mankiewicz interview.

333   "very abusive": Newfield, *Memoir*, p. 132.

333   LBJ's tirade was a turning point: *RK*, p. 769.

333   "I'm going to escalate. . . .": Mary McGrory interview.

333   "RFK SETS MAJOR SPEECH. . . .": *NYT*, Feb. 17, 1967.

333   Garrison investigation coverage: *NYT*, Feb. 19, 21, 23, 1967; *Time*, March 3, 1967; *Newsweek*, "Carnival in New Orleans," March 6, 1967.

333   RFK and Goodwin, Hewitt: Richard Goodwin interview; Don Hewitt interview.

333   Marina Oswald: Hoover to Attorney General, Feb. 17, 1964, RFK Confidential file, House Assassination Committee Records, NA.

334   "He thought Garrison. . . .": *RK*, p. 616.

334   Sheridan reported to RFK: Nancy Sheridan interview.

334   "Does that guy have anything?": Frank Mankiewicz interview. My own view on the Kennedy assassination is that JFK was almost surely killed by a single gunman—Oswald—acting alone. It is impossible to rule out a conspiracy, and there are unresolved questions about the ties of Oswald's assailant, Jack Ruby, to the mob. But Oswald, an addled loner, made a most unlikely hit man for the mob. For the best treatment of the various conspiracy theories, see Gerald Posner, *Case Closed*.

334   "Bobby wanted to know. . . .": Ed Guthman interview.

334   RFK and Katharine Graham: Robin Douglas-Home, "Jacqueline Kennedy," *Washington Post*, Feb. 12, 1967; Katharine Graham interviewed by Henry Brandon; RFK to Katharine Graham, undated, Katharine Graham Papers.

334   RFK on day of Vietnam speech: *RK*, p. 771; Newfield, *Memoir*, p. 137.

334   RFK speech excerpts: *NYT*, March 3, 1967.

335   LBJ distracts from RFK speech: William vanden Heuvel and Milton Gwirtzman, *On His Own: Robert F. Kennedy, 1964–1968*, p. 254.

335   Drew Pearson column: "Washington Merry-Go-Round," *Washington Post*, March 3, 1967.

335   collect gossip "about horrible things. . . .": Marvin Watson testimony, Church Committee, May 8, 1976, Church Committee files, NA.

335   LBJ used army soldiers: Rowland Evans OH, JFKL.

335   MAD: Robert Dallek interview.

335   Johnny Rosselli story: See Staff Report of the Select Committee on Assassination, March 1979, pp. 153–56.

336   Edward Morgan and Drew Pearson: Washington Field Office Report from FBI investigation of Rosselli's Death, Aug. 24, 1976, House Assassination Committee Records, NA.

336   assassination plot tale: Jack Anderson interview. "Drew had been a critic of Lyndon—'Lying Down Lyndon,' 'Landslide Lyndon.' But he made peace with LBJ. He really worked him. Drew told me, 'Lyndon is the kind of fella I'd like to make peace with frequently.' "

336   "It's incredible!": Michael Beschloss, *Taking Charge*, pp. 561–64.

336   LBJ encouraged Pearson: Jack Anderson interview. Morgan's initial contact was with Pearson's legman, Jack Anderson.

336   RFK lunch with Helms: Richard Helms testimony, June 29, 1975, Church Committee.

336   Helms could not recall: Richard Helms interview.

336   CIA's schemes against Castro: See chronology in Book V, Church Committee Report, 1975.

336   Helms and CIA contrived to protect RFK: Gus Russo, *Live by the Sword*, pp. 429–31.

336   no instructions from Helms: Scott Breckinridge interview.

336   CIA men reluctant to volunteer: Max Holland interview.

337   Frank Chavez attempt on RFK: Walter Sheridan, *The Fall and Rise of Jimmy Hoffa*, pp. 406–407.

337   Sheridan investigated Garrison: Nancy Sheridan interview.

337   defector from Garrison camp: *New Orleans States-Item*, June 23, 1967. The investigator was William Gurvich.

337   Carlos Marcello: The Marcello story is an interesting case history of RFK's impact on the bureaucracy. The longtime INS commissioner General Joseph Swing feared that he would lose his job if he didn't move fast on Marcello. So while RFK did not actually order Marcello's abduction, he created the atmosphere in which a nervous bureaucrat overreached. Joe Dolan interview. See *House Assassination Committee Report*, vol. IX, pp. 69–86.

337   "the guy from New Orleans": Jack Newfield interview. Walter Sheridan's notes for his investigation of Marcello have never been publicly released. Nancy Sheridan told the author that they contain wiretap evidence linking Garrison and other New Orleans politicians with Mafia payoffs. Nancy Sheridan interview.

338   shocked his son, Walter Jr.: Nancy Sheridan interview; Walter Sheridan Jr. interview.

338   RFK told his son: confidential Kennedy family interview. Helen O'Donnell said her father, Kenneth O'Donnell, also believed that JFK was killed by a conspiracy. It is possible that these children were projecting their own fears.

338   "An indefinable sense. . . .": *RK*, pp. 776–77.

338   RFK at University of Oklahoma: Fred Harris OH, JFKL.

338   "I wish I had been born. . . .": *RK*, p. 793.

338   RFK envied Newfield: Newfield, *Memoir*, p. 90.

338   RFK and Bronx doctor: Jayne Ikard interview. She was unable to recall the date, but it may have been Kennedy's tour of Grasslands Hospital in January 1968. See Newfield, *Memoir*, p. 200.

339   "Kennedy needed children. . . .": Mary McGrory interview.

339   RFK in Mississippi: Jean Stein and George Plimpton, *American Journey*, pp. 279–80.

339   ". . . Do you know how lucky you are . . . ?": Kathleen Kennedy Townsend interview.

339   RFK and Freeman: Peter Edelman interview.

339   "He grabbed me. . . .": Amanda Burden interview.

339   RFK and Robert Coles: Peter Edelman OH, JFKL.

340   "his quest for meaning. . . .": Robert Coles interview.

340   "He was very difficult": William Orrick OH, JFKL.

340   "Bob was really nervous. . . .": Burke Marshall interview; Burke Marshall OH, JFKL.

340   "Peter, help me. . . .": Peter Edelman OH, JFKL.

340   "horror statistics. . . .": Frank Mankiewicz OH, JFKL.

341   RFK's bill was sunk: Fred Harris interview; Shesol, *Mutual Contempt*, pp. 331–32. See *Congressional Record*—Senate, July 12, 1967, p. 18443, and Sept. 27, 1967, p. 27083.

341   Bed-Sty's wobbly start: R. B. Goldman, "Performance in Black and White: An Appraisal of the Development and Record of the Bedford-Stuyvesant Restoration and Development and Services Corporation," Ford Foundation, February 1969, pp. 26–32, Burke Marshall Papers, JFKL. Thomas Jones OH, JFKL; Thomas Jones interview.

341   RFK and Sonny Carson: Sonny Carson interview.

341   progress was slow: Eli Jacobs OH, JFKL; Tom Johnston interview.

342   RFK and Tom Watson . . . "Senator. . . .": Newfield, *Memoir*, p. 98.

342   RFK refused to become defeatist: Burke Marshall OH, JFKL; Burke Marshall interview.

342   community development modeled after Bed-Sty: Shesol, *Mutual Contempt*, p. 250.

chapter 19: COURAGE

343   Bellow profile: Saul Bellow interview.

344   Norman Mailer: *RK*, p. 816.

344   "explore new worlds. . . .": Richard Goodwin, *Remembering America*, p. 450.

344   "the same incongruous. . . .": Jack Newfield, *Robert Kennedy: A Memoir*, p. 39.

344   "really a dopey guy": Peter Edelman OH, JFKL.

344 . determined to depose LBJ: Jules Witcover, *85 Days*, p. 32.

344   translation from Homer: Goodwin to RFK, June 9, 1967, RFK Senate Papers, Personal Correspondence, JFKL. Agamemnon also broods because he has failed to protect a friend in battle: "Then let me die, and soon, since I did not protect my dying friend." Ever the self-improver, Kennedy also asked for other translations of Greek plays by William Arrowsmith.

344   RFK, JFK, and tweed coat: Joe Dolan interview; Ronnie Eldridge interview.

345   "it cramped his thoughts. . . .": *RK*, p. 808.

345   "He recoiled. . . .": Joe Dolan interview.

345   "He was always restrained. . . .": Richard Goodwin interview.

345   "Did Bob change? . . .": David Hackett OH, JFKL.

345   Shakespeare recordings: John Reilly interview.

345   RFK lacked the rigor: Walter Pozen interview.

345   "He couldn't talk easily. . . .": William vanden Heuvel interview.

345   He even grew his hair: On November 11, 1967, Joe Dolan urged RFK to get a haircut: "Everybody in the country will be looking to see if you've had a haircut when you go on TV Sunday." On December 7, Dolan reported "from a friend's friend and admirer, 'I think the hair cut thing is bad—so many liberals I have talked to say how much they like him but why the hell won't he get a hair cut?' " Dolan to RFK, Nov. 11, Dec. 7, 1967, Dolan Papers, JFKL.

346   "two blue clots . . ." . . . "turned pale": *RK*, p. 818.

346   "Yeah, they're the first ones. . . .": Richard Goodwin interview.

346   Lowell poem: "Like a prince, you daily left your tower/To walk through dirt in your best cloth. . . ." Robert Lowell, *History*, p. 174.

346   He named sons: *RK*, p. 808.

346   Ginsberg encounter: ibid., p. 819.

346   homosexual copy editor: Peter Edelman OH, JFKL.

346   "There was a side to Kennedy. . . .": Peter Edelman interview.

346   "Bobby liked to party. . . .": Ronnie Eldridge interview.

346   "Bobby only stayed a few minutes. . . .": Jean Stein and George Plimpton, *Edie*, p. 275.

347   "He was always pleased. . . .": R. W. Apple interview.

347   "Dave Powers. . . .": Richard Goodwin interview.

347   "Before dinner. . . .": Amanda Burden interview.

347   "The women didn't want something. . . .": Richard Goodwin interview.

347   Ethel reportedly disapproved of teaching evolution: William Manchester, *Controversy and Other Essays in Journalism*, p. 47. Maxwell Kennedy said his older siblings dispute this story.

347   "I don't like that part. . . .": E. Barrett Prettyman interview; John Reilly interview.

347   "For God's sake. . . .": Peter Edelman OH, JFKL.

348   "he'd light up. . . .": Mary Bailey Gimbel STOH.

348   visited pope and Catholicism: *RK*, pp. 749–50, 766, 781; William vanden Heuvel interview; Michael Novak interview.

348   ". . . that was not a good reason. . . .": Amanda Burden interview.

348   boys smoking cigarettes: *RK*, p. 815.

348   "How can we possibly survive . . . ?": ibid., p. 777.

348   struck criticism of LBJ: Jeff Greenfield OH, JFKL.

348   polls "phony": Jeff Shesol, *Mutual Contempt*, p. 348; Peter Edelman OH, JFKL.

349   "It's over. . . .": Frank Mankiewicz OH, JFKL.

349   RFK's legislative efforts: Newfield, *Memoir*, pp. 105–106.

349   voting record: Dolan to RFK, May 12, July 24, 1967, Dolan Papers, JFKL.

349   Allard Lowenstein: See William Chafe, *Never Stop Running*, passim.

349   "zealous" supporter: Allard Lowenstein OH, JFKL. Lowenstein had hoped to convince RFK to make a bolder Day of Affirmation speech in South Africa. David Halberstam, *The Unfinished Odyssey of Robert Kennedy*, p. 167.

349   "If you want to run. . . .": Lester David and Irene David, *Bobby Kennedy*, pp. 280–81.

349   "ambition and envy": Newfield, *Memoir*, pp. 184–86.

350   Eugene McCarthy: Witcover, *85 Days*, p. 35.

350   RFK and Harriman: William Walton OH, JFKL.

350   RFK and McNamara: Shesol, *Mutual Contempt*, p. 391.

350   "We can't afford another Forrestal": John Roche OH, LBJL.

350   "murderer": Doris Kearns, *Lyndon Johnson & the American Dream*, pp. 320–21.

350   November 27 RFK meeting with McNamara: Deborah Shapley, *Promise and Power*, p. 439. Shapley quotes McNamara as saying that RFK urged him to go out with a "hell of a blast." Interviewed in 1999, McNamara said, "He may have talked to me. I don't recall it." Robert McNamara interview.

350   "Wouldn't any self-respecting man . . . ?": *RK*, p. 823.

351   *Face the Nation:* Transcript, Nov. 26, 1967.

351   At the first meeting in October: Pierre Salinger, *P.S.: A Memoir*, p. 285.

351   "He supposed he would do nothing. . . .": *RK*, pp. 829, 832–33.

351   "Time is running out": To: RFK, From: Adam Walinsky, "Gratuitous Advice Reconsidered," undated [November 1967], Milton Gwirtzman Papers, JFKL.

351   "His head would be down. . . .": Esther Newberg OH, JFKL.

351   "It's not funny": Joe Dolan interview.

352   "If Kennedy does not run. . . .": Newfield, *Memoir*, p. 195.

352   "My wife cut out. . . .": ibid., p. 196.

352   "Run, Bobby, Run": Helen O'Donnell, *A Common Good*, p. 401; Frank Burns OH, JFKL.

352   "Would you believe Santa Claus . . . ?": Frank Mankiewicz OH, JFKL.

352   "Why, Ted?": Frank Burns OH, JFKL.

352   "You're always talking. . . .": *RK*, p. 840.

352   visiting reservations: *NYT*, July 6, 1967, and Jan. 3, 1968.

353   Nicole Salinger and Indian school: Nicole Salinger STOH.

353   RFK and Jesse Unruh: Frank Burns OH, JFKL.

353   "sitting and bullshitting": Peter Edelman OH, JFKL.

353   "The Two Teds": Milton Gwirtzman OH, JFKL. In an interview with Adam Clymer, Ted Kennedy acknowledged his private fear that RFK would be killed. "We weren't that far away from '63, and that still was very much of a factor." Adam Clymer, *Edward M. Kennedy*, p. 105.

353   "I know what Dad would have said. . . .": Richard Goodwin interview.

353   RFK cared less about party unity: Joe Dolan interview.

354   ". . . the bad old Bobby. . . .": Peter Maas interview.

354   sweeping the primaries: In 1952, Estes Kefauver won all the primaries and lost to Adlai Stevenson. William vanden Heuvel and Milton Gwirtzman, *On His Own: Robert F. Kennedy, 1964–1968*, p. 267.

354   "political suicide": Fred Dutton to RFK, Nov. 3, 1967, Dutton Papers, JFKL.

354   "Take the bad guy": Joe Dolan interview.

354   "If there's a piece of cake. . . .": William vanden Heuvel interview.

354   Dante quote: John F. Kennedy, *Profiles in Courage*, p. 11.

354   "futility . . . expediency . . .": Robert F. Kennedy, *To Seek a Newer World*, pp. 230–33.

355   Lippmann and Mercouri: *RK*, p. 838.

355   careful to compartmentalize his secrets: Joe Dolan interview.

355   "I wanted Bob. . . .": Angie Novello STOH.

356   Kennedy's fears: RFK apparently did not widely discuss his fears with friends, but there were exceptions. Jesse Unruh, the California political powerbroker, told John Reilly that RFK did raise concerns about getting shot when they met in February 1968. John Reilly interview.

356   "Kennedy dies at 4": Joe Dolan interview.

356   RFK flinched, ridiculed on TV: Witcover, *85 Days*, p. 43; vanden Heuvel and Gwirtzman, *On His Own*, p. 294. In the early-morning hours of January 19, after presenting a prize at the New York Film Critics Awards (and being accosted by Mercouri), RFK hinted at his decision not to run in a conversation with George Stevens at the King Cole Bar. "Why does everyone think I have to be president?" Kennedy asked. "I have ten kids, there are many other things for me to do." George Stevens interview.

356   office was a morgue: Newfield, *Memoir*, p. 204.

357   "The people who think. . . .": Halberstam, *Unfinished Odyssey*, p. 9.

357   RFK was sorry: Jean Stein and George Plimpton, *American Journey*, pp. 223–24.

357   RFK was catatonic: Angie Novello STOH; vanden Heuvel and Gwirtzman, *On His Own*, p. 293.

357   "in any way possible": Tom Watson OH, JFKL.

357   Goodwin and McCarthy: Richard Goodwin, *Remembering America*, p. 481.

357   McCarthy surged in New Hampshire: Pierre Salinger OH, JFKL.

357   "God, I'm going to lose them. . . .": Joe Dolan OH, JFKL.

357   McCarthy "half-Irish": Martin Nolan interview.

357   "your obligation. . . .": Newfield, *Memoir*, p. 207.

357   Dutton and O'Donnell had change of heart: Witcover, *85 Days*, pp. 53–54.

358   Dolan briefing books: Joe Dolan interview.

358   "What should I do? . . .": Amanda Burden interview.

358   "I think Bobby is going to run. . . .": Witcover, *85 Days*, p. 54.

358   "He was always running. . . .": Joe Dolan interview.

358   onus would be off RFK: Fred Dutton STOH.

358   March 9 trip to Iowa: John Reilly interview.

359   RFK and Chavez: Cesar Chavez OH, JFKL.

359   "I'm going to do it. . . .": Peter Edelman OH, JFKL.

359   "What should I do?": David Burke OH, JFKL.

359   RFK tried to win over Sorensen: Witcover, *85 Days*, p. 63.

359   peace commission: Theodore Sorensen interview; Clark Clifford, Memorandum of Conference with Senator Robert Kennedy and Theodore Sorensen, March 14, 1968, Schlesinger Papers, JFKL.

359   "relieved": David Hackett OH, JFKL.

359   supper at "21": *RK*, p. 849.

360   "I think I blew it": vanden Heuvel and Gwirtzman, *On His Own*, p. 304.

360   "actively reconsidering": Witcover, *85 Days*, p. 66.

360   "I'm not going to make. . . .": Jeff Greenfield OH, JFKL.

360   "pompous, petty. . . .": Newfield, *Memoir*, p. 190.

360   "punishing himself inwardly. . . .": George McGovern STOH.

360   "Maybe he should reconsider again": David Burke OH, JFKL.

360   "Bobby's therapy. . . .": Newfield, *Memoir*, p. 220.

360   reserve Caucus Room: Frank Mankiewicz interview.

360   drafting announcement speech: Stein and Plimpton, *American Journey*, p. 231; Jeff Greenfield OH, JFKL.

361   ". . . more people hate Bobby. . . .": *RK*, p. 857.

361   human shield: Peter Maas interview.

CHAPTER 20: QUEST

362   "the fieldhouse sounded. . . .": Jack Newfield, *Robert Kennedy: A Memoir*, p. 234.

362   "how he himself seemed to be pulled. . . .": Jules Witcover, *85 Days*, p. 101.

362   "This is Kansas . . . !": Newfield, *Memoir*, p. 234.

362   "Little Brother": William vanden Heuvel and Milton Gwirtzman, *On His Own: Robert F. Kennedy, 1964–1968*, p. 267.

362   RFK routinely antagonized labor: *RK*, p. 806.

363   "There was absolutely dead silence. . . .": E. Barrett Prettyman interview.

363   "Who else could have . . . ?": Milton Gwirtzman OH, JFKL. Kennedy never did win over politically powerful Jewish leaders. Philanthropist Eleanor Guggenheimer gave him a dinner in the spring of 1968 "largely for Jewish leaders, and rich," recalled William Walton. "The purpose was to try to win them back from hating Bobby." The evening was "cold and unpleasant." RFK said of Guggenheimer, "Never leave me alone with that woman again." William Walton OH, JFKL.

363   RFK created a coalition: Witcover, *85 Days*, pp. 152–53.

363   "no strategy": Fred Dutton STOH. Joe Dolan argued that there was a strategy—the same one JFK used in '60: win a couple of big primaries and then appeal to the bosses for support.

363   "Rooseveltian": Frank Mankiewicz OH, JFKL.

363   RFK told Sorensen and O'Donnell: Milton Gwirtzman OH, JFKL.

363   Martin on campaign structure: John Bartlow Martin notes, April 10, 1968, John Bartlow Martin Papers, LOC.

363   dispense with titles: Jean Stein and George Plimpton, *American Journey*, p. 239.

363   "bomb throwers": Jeff Greenfield OH, JFKL.

363   Walinsky quarreled: Adam Walinsky OH, JFKL.

363   deliver bad news: Fred Dutton STOH.

363   Walinsky on strategy . . . "Daley means the ball game": *RK*, pp. 864–65.

364   O'Donnell and Hizzoner: Frank Mankiewicz OH, JFKL.

364   RFK echoed JFK: J. B. Martin Campaign Journal, p. 46, John Bartlow Martin Papers LOC.

364   RFK's speech-making: Jeff Greenfield OH, JFKL. "Bobby got carried away," recalled his advance man, Jerry Bruno. "He'd go way, way beyond the written speeches. The crowd reacted to him and he reacted to the crowd. This *never* happened with JFK." Jerry Bruno interview.

364   RFK compared to Mao Tse-tung: Robert W. Merry, *Taking On the World*, p. 461.

364   a little "scary": Witcover, *85 Days*, pp. 110–19.

364   "the national leadership": Edwin O. Guthman and C. Richard Allen, eds., *RFK: Collected Speeches*, p. 338.

364   "demagogue": Richard Harwood, "Crowd Madness and Kennedy Strategy," *Washington Post*, March 28, 1968.

364   Ethel's response: Richard Harwood interview.

364   "traveling riot": Milton Gwirtzman OH, JFKL.

364   Gwirtzman to write speeches: Peter Edelman OH, JFKL.

365   "I felt that I was . . ." . . . "The thing I feared. . . .": Doris Kearns, *Lyndon Johnson & the American Dream*, p. 343.

365   "I wonder if he would. . . .": Witcover, *85 Days*, p. 127.

365   ". . . he'd glare at them": John English OH, JFKL.

365   April 3 meeting: *RK*, p. 868. Notes on Meeting of the President with Senator Robert Kennedy, April 3, 1968, Schlesinger Papers, JFKL.

365   "You are a brave. . . .": *RK*, p. 869.

365   LBJ meeting with Humphrey: LBJ told Humphrey he would not help, and then proceeded to, advising on how to campaign and concluding that he would be "at the Vice President's disposal at any time of the day or night." Memorandum of Conversation, April 3, 1968, Walt Rostow, Schlesinger Papers, JFKL.

366   LBJ and Pearson: *RK*, p. 869.

366   LBJ and McCarthy: Eugene McCarthy, *Up 'Til Now*, p. 196.

366   "Congratulations!": Jim Whittaker OH, JFKL.

366   "a mess": Fred Dutton interview.

366   ". . . It's purely Greek": Newfield, *Memoir*, p. 245; *RK*, p. 870.

366   ". . . His eyes went blank": R. W. Apple interview.

366   RFK went anyway: Stein and Plimpton, *American Journey*, p. 255; Witcover, *85 Days*, pp. 54–55.

366   RFK drafted own remarks on King: Adam Walinsky interview. According to Jerry Bruno, Walinsky was not present. Bruno said RFK made up the speech in his head as he drove, in silence, to the rally. Dutton and Bruno were in the car with him. Mankiewicz said he handed RFK some speech notes. Mankiewicz interview.

366   "For those of you. . . .": Guthman and Allen, eds., *Collected Speeches*, pp. 356–57.

367   "After all. . . .": Adam Walinsky interview.

367   "I didn't get any clear. . . .": Don Wilson OH, JFKL.

367   MLK supported RFK: Stanley Levison STOH. RFK asked Burke Marshall to call King to keep him from endorsing McCarthy. Burke Marshall OH, JFKL. According to a McCarthy aide, after King died, the McCarthy campaign was given some indication that King's widow, Coretta, would endorse McCarthy. Richard Grandjean interview. But James Tolan, an advance man for RFK, claimed that Burke Marshall obtained a written endorsement from Coretta Scott King, though the campaign never used it publicly. James Tolan OH, JFKL.

367   "made a face": Frank Mankiewicz OH, JFKL.

367   "guilty over the wiretapping": Peter Edelman OH, JFKL.

367   "Harvey Lee Oswald": Jeff Greenfield OH, JFKL; Adam Walinsky interview.

368   ". . . that could have been me": Joan Braden interview. See also Joan Braden, *Just Enough Rope*, p. 155. Warren Rogers, the *Look* reporter who covered Kennedy, doubted this story because it was out of character for RFK. "Kennedy wouldn't have said, 'It could have been me.' He might have said, 'I wish it had been me' about his brother's death." Warren Rogers interview.

368   "grandstanding": John Bartlow Martin memo, April 10, 1968, John Bartlow Martin Papers, LOC; *RK*, p. 877, says he did walk the streets.

368   stoic silence: Stein and Plimpton, *American Journey*, pp. 259–60.

368   viewed King's body: John Lewis interview.

368   "defeated and quiet. . . .": Karl Fleming interview.

368   "surprised": Allard Lowenstein STOH.

368 "Don't close them. . . .": Fred Dutton interview; Stein and Plimpton, *American Journey*, pp. 291–92.

368 "It stayed on our minds. . . .": J. B. Martin Campaign Journal, p. 14, John Bartlow Martin Papers, LOC.

368 candidate was resistant: Fred Dutton interview; Joe Dolan interview.

368 quoted Camus: Maxwell Taylor Kennedy, ed., *Make Gentle the Life of This World*, p. 98.

368 afraid of flying: R. W. Apple interview.

369 "The crowds were savage. . . .": J. B. Martin Campaign Journal, p. 16, John Bartlow Martin Papers, LOC.

369 RFK's right shoe: *NYT*, April 13, 1968.

369 Barry clung to RFK: Witcover, *85 Days*, pp. 113, 133.

369 "It was like he wasn't there. . . .": Peter Fishbein interview.

369 RFK talked to disabled person: Charles Quinn STOH.

369 sipping ice tea: Witcover, *85 Days*, p. 149.

369 "Why the hell . . . ?": Fred Dutton interview.

369 "my West Virginia": John Bartlow Martin memo, April 10, 1968, John Bartlow Martin Papers, LOC.

370 "I thought that so far. . . .": J. B. Martin Campaign Journal, p. 12, John Bartlow Martin Papers, LOC.

370 "Well, Fred. . . .": Peter Edelman OH, JFKL.

370 RFK and KKK: J. B. Martin Campaign Journal, pp. 19–20, John Bartlow Martin Papers, LOC.

370 swinging right: *NYT*, May 3, 1968.

370 RFK stressing law and order: John Bartlow Martin pushed him pretty far. In "Memorandum for Insert in the Senator's Book, RE: Local Talking Points," Martin passed along advice from the congressman from Terre Haute: "Stay *away* from civil rights—just don't talk about it. In some counties south of Terre Haute, Negroes are not allowed out after dark." John Bartlow Martin Papers, LOC.

370 avoided integration: Peter Edelman interview.

370 If he sounded conservative: See Michael Knox Beran, *The Last Patrician*, pp. 202–203.

370 April 26 at University of Indiana: Guthman and Allen, eds., *Collected Speeches*, pp. 342–43; Peter Goldman interview.

371 "Do you know there are more rats . . . ?": Guthman and Allen, eds., *Collected Speeches*, pp. 381–83.

371 RFK and audiences: J. B. Martin Campaign Journal, p. 36, John Bartlow Martin Papers, LOC.

372 RFK contrasted with McCarthy: David Halberstam, *The Unfinished Odyssey of Robert Kennedy*, p. 204. Arthur Schlesinger wrote an incisive memo describing this phenomenon: The Old Politics and the New, John Bartlow Martin Papers, LOC.

372 advance man Jerry Bruno: See Jerry Bruno and Jeff Greenfield, *The Advance Man*, passim.

372 vetoed use of helicopters: J. B. Martin Campaign Journal, p. 33, John Bartlow Martin Papers, LOC.

372 "He wanted big crowds. . . .": Fred Dutton interview.

372   "You've got to turn it down": Jayne Ikard interview.

373   spent about $1 million a week: Herbert Alexander, author of *Financing the 1968 Election* (Lexington, MA: Heath, 1971), estimated that Kennedy spent $11 million in just over eleven weeks in 1968. In this pre–disclosure law era, it was hard to know how much candidates raised and spent, but Alexander had good sources, including Steve Smith. Alexander estimated that Gene McCarthy raised and spent about $2.5 million. Kennedy's campaign debt after he died exceeded $3 million. The Democratic National Committee picked up $1 million and creditors ate the rest. Herbert Alexander interview.

373   "very uncoordinated. . . .": Don Wilson OH, JFKL.

373   "both boyish. . . .": Halberstam, *Unfinished Odyssey*, p. 107.

373   "We spent money. . . .": Milton Gwirtzman interview.

373   "He was very tense. . . .": John Frankenheimer interview.

373   ". . . he was a little embarrassed. . . .": Fred Dutton interview.

373   "These speeches are boring. . . .": Jeff Greenfield OH, JFKL.

373   RFK curled up on couch: Charles Guggenheim interview.

373   "that ended it": J. B. Martin Campaign Journal, pp. 4–5, John Bartlow Martin Papers, LOC.

373   BBC film: Adam Walinsky OH, JFKL.

373   "steady, slow burn": Dun Gifford OH, JFKL.

374   teas: John Douglas interview. Jerome Kretchmer, who helped organize for RFK in Indiana, believed that Kennedy's mere presence on the campaign trail was a much greater factor than ideology or political positioning. Jerome Kretchmer interview. William Haddad recalled that RFK gave a very liberal speech to a group of wildly cheering—and conservative—Poles. "They didn't care what he said. They just wanted to see and touch a Kennedy." William Haddad interview.

374   Radziwill drunk: Richard Wade interview.

374   Jackie Kennedy absent: Joe Dolan interview, Fred Dutton interview. For reports on Onassis and RFK's reaction, see Peter Collier and David Horowitz, *The Kennedys*, p. 367; and Edward Klein, *Just Jackie*, pp. 190–91. When Jackie told him that she intended to marry Onassis, RFK supposedly joked that it would "cost me five states."

374   buying votes: Jerome Kretchmer OH, JFKL. "We used cash for a lot of things," recalled Kretchmer. "It wasn't just Gary but in Hammond and East Chicago." Kretchmer keeps a blank check, drawn on the Bank of Indiana and signed by the campaign treasurer, on his office wall. (He went to Indiana with three blank checks and used two.) In an interview with the author, he recalled a Kennedy cousin arriving with an attaché case full of cash. Richard Wade, who also worked on the campaign in Gary, saw a suitcase of cash, but recalled a different bagman, a New York lawyer he declined to identify.

374   "walking-around money": Gerald Dougherty OH, JFKL. Dougherty, who helped manage Indiana, estimated that McCarthy outspent RFK. But Richard Grandjean, McCarthy's campaign manager in Indiana, said the McCarthy campaign was low on funds, having spent most of the campaign chest in the Wisconsin primary. Richard Grandjean interview.

374   some of McCarthy's money from Teamsters: J. B. Martin Campaign Journal, p. 30, John Bartlow Martin Papers, LOC.

375   Paul Corbin: Frank Mankiewicz OH, JFKL.

375   "primitive honesty" . . . "That's not what my father. . . .": Newfield, *Memoir*, pp. 263–64.

375   RFK called his father: J. B. Martin Campaign Journal, p. 13, John Bartlow Martin Papers, LOC.

375   backlash vote: William vanden Heuvel and Milton Gwirtzman, *On His Own: Robert F. Kennedy, 1964–1968*, pp. 348–49. See Garry Wills, "Waiting for Bobby," *New York Review of Books*, Feb. 10, 2000.

376   where Wallace had run strongest: "Analysis of Indiana primary results," May 8, 1968, Schlesinger Papers, JFKL. An analysis for RFK by pollster Stanley Greenberg showed Kennedy running well among most ethnic voters, though not among East Europeans. "Voting Prediction Model: Kennedy and McCarthy in Indiana," Stanley Greenberg et al., May 14, 1968, RFK 1968 Papers, JFKL. An analysis by Lou Harris of the returns showed that among blue-collar voters generally, RFK had 48 percent to Branigan's 28 percent and McCarthy's 24 percent. By his law-and-order emphasis in the last five days of the campaign, RFK slipped significantly (from 40 to 27 percent) among affluent and well-educated voters. *Newsweek*, May 20, 1968.

376   Kennedy in Nebraska: Witcover, *85 Days*, p. 205.

376   S with his finger: Frank Mankiewicz interview.

376   RFK and Rogers: Warren Rogers interview.

377   RFK and Harwood: Richard Harwood interview; Fred Dutton interview.

377   "There are no ghettoes. . . .": Witcover, *85 Days*, pp. 197–200.

377   "It's all white Protestants. . . .": Kraft STOH.

378   Green and RFK: Kenneth O'Donnell OH by Sander Vanocur, JFKL.

378   Bruno and Edith Green: Joe Dolan interview. Green also banned David Hackett, who was running Kennedy's "boiler room" delegate-counting operation.

378   worried about LBJ: Robert Dallek, *Flawed Giant*, pp. 174, 543–44.

378   "There's nothing about Las Vegas. . . .": Fred Dutton interview.

378   "Bobby hates the way I do": Drew Pearson and Jack Anderson, "Voters Must Weigh Bobby's Know-How," *Washington Post*, May 3, 1968.

378   May 22 allegation: Pearson and Anderson, "Bobby v. Hoffa," *Washington Post*, May 22, 1968.

378   May 24 column: Pearson and Anderson, "Kennedy Ordered King Wiretap," *Washington Post*, May 24, 1968.

378   "Drew got it from Lyndon. . . .": Jack Anderson interview.

379   Pearson, DeLoach, and LBJ: Ed Wiesl Jr., son of LBJ's longtime confidant Ed Wiesl Sr., approached the FBI to ask if RFK had ordered the taps on King, saying, "Drew Pearson had found out about this matter and probably would print it to embarrass Bobby Kennedy." Cartha DeLoach told Wiesl that the bureau "had no brief for Kennedy, in view of the shoddy way he had treated the FBI; however we do not want to be involved in any political maneuvers." If the article was printed, the FBI should take a "no comment" position, advised DeLoach. "Right," wrote J. Edgar Hoover, DeLoach to Tolson, May 17, 1968, RFK file, FBI. DeLoach may have just been making a record of neutrality. Jack Anderson said he got explicit confirmation from DeLoach, who, according to White House records, spoke to Johnson on May

23, 1968. LBJ appointment calendars and phone logs, May 18, May 23, 1968, LBJL. DeLoach said he did not recall the incident. Cartha DeLoach interview.

379   Burke Marshall and RFK talking points: The talking points, "From Burke Marshall," are undated in the Arthur Schlesinger Papers, JFKL. Peter Edelman recognized his own handwriting on some of the marginal notes on the document—but not the passage stating "Dr. King was never the target. . . ." In his oral history, Burke Marshall says Kennedy asked him what to say and both men agreed to say nothing because tapping King was "inexplicable" in a political campaign. Burke Marshall OH, JFKL. Marshall told the author that he did not want to explain more because that would involve dragging in King's associates Levison and O'Dell. "I didn't see how we could get into it. It was too complicated, too intrusive." Burke Marshall interview.

379   Bobby never wanted to get into it: Fred Dutton interview.

379   Salinger fell back on: Witcover, *85 Days*, p. 212.

380   Buddy Young: confidential interview; John Reilly interview.

380   "It was no surprise. . . .": Juanita Abernathy interview.

380   "It's like someone. . . .": Frank Mankiewicz interview; John Lewis interview.

380   feared McCarthy would exploit issue: "It was the source of much discussion. . . . Everybody felt that it was hurting—it was hurting—and that it might be brought up during the TV debate." James Tolan OH, JFKL.

380   McCarthy radio spots: Halberstam, *Unfinished Odyssey*, p. 157.

380   liberal women's group on Hoover: Gary Ross interview.

380   RFK swimming in Oregon: Witcover, *85 Days*, p. 213.

381   RFK urged to accept debate: Jeff Greenfield OH, JFKL.

381   The ringleader: Witcover, *85 Days*, p. 213.

381   RFK trying to take nap: Peter Edelman OH, JFKL.

381   RFK and O'Brien: Larry O'Brien OH, LBJL; Lawrence O'Brien, *No Final Victories*, p. 241.

381   RFK slammed the door: Adam Walinsky OH, JFKL; Peter Edelman OH, JFKL; Don Wilson OH, JFKL.

381   Portland zoo: Witcover, *85 Days*, p. 217.

381   "I had been avoiding. . . .": Joe Dolan interview.

382   first election lost: *RK*, p. 907.

382   "What do you think? . . .": confidential source.

CHAPTER 21: LEGEND

383   "He really did not look. . . .": J. B. Martin Campaign Journal, p. 29, John Bartlow Martin Papers, LOC.

383   varicose veins: Warren Rogers interview.

383   vitamin B_{12}: Fred Dutton interview.

383   "never seen him look so bad. . . .": Jean Stein and George Plimpton, *American Journey*, p. 267.

383   son David arrested: *NYT*, May 3, 1968.

383   Why would his boy throw rocks?: Robert Coles interview.

383   "If I lose. . . .": Richard Goodwin, *Remembering America*, p. 536.

384   "You may solve. . . .": Joseph Kraft STOH.

384   Ethel Kennedy pregnant: *NYT*, Aug. 10, 1968.

384   "they were buddies. . . .": Bill Eppridge interview.

384   "They were holding hands. . . .": Marie Ridder interview.

384   "You know, don't you . . . ?": Pierre Salinger, *P.S.: A Memoir*, pp. 185–87.

384   Keats quote: John Cronin and Robert F. Kennedy Jr., *The Riverkeepers*, p. 87.

384   "If I get to be president. . . .": Richard Goodwin interviewed by Arthur Schlesinger, June 11, 1977, Schlesinger Papers, JFKL.

384   "I just am not Jack": Helen O'Donnell, *A Common Good*, p. 415.

384   "He wanted affirmation.": Bill Eppridge interview.

385   "the hooded weariness. . . .": Lewis Chester, Godfrey Hodgson, and Bruce Page, *An American Melodrama*, p. 335.

385   "These are my people": Fred Dutton STOH.

385   voters in Orange County: Fred Dutton interview.

385   Dolan canceled a motorcade through Venice: Joe Dolan interview.

385   "we came in right on the button. . . .": J. B. Martin Campaign Journal, p. 59, John Bartlow Martin Papers, LOC.

385   Jesse Unruh's operation counseled: John Nolan OH, JFKL; Frank Burns OH, JFKL.

385   RFK bridled at shakedowns: John English OH, JFKL.

385   Black Caucus meeting: Fred Dutton STOH.

385   "Black Jesus": His name was Curtis Lee Baker. He said he ran a "black protector" organization. Stein and Plimpton, *American Journey*, p. 306.

385   ". . . tremendous tolerance for intolerance": Rafer Johnson OH, JFKL.

386   "Freckles probably got more. . . .": Stein and Plimpton, *American Journey*, p. 311.

386   "floating almost all alone": Adam Walinsky OH, JFKL.

386   wiretap question: John Seigenthaler interview.

386   "the astrologers": Stein and Plimpton, *American Journey*, pp. 302–303, 312.

386   "an obvious set piece": Chester et al., *American Melodrama*, p. 346.

386   "You say you are going to take. . . .": Frank Mankiewicz said he gave RFK this line in debate preparation. Frank Mankiewicz interview.

386   "pandered" to voters: Jeff Greenfield OH, JFKL.

386   Sirhan Sirhan: Jules Witcover, *85 Days*, p. 218.

386   "a mutually pedestrian performance": David Halberstam, *The Unfinished Odyssey of Robert Kennedy*, p. 206.

386   McCarthy "didn't do his homework": Stein and Plimpton, *American Journey*, p. 314.

386   final push: See Prologue.

387   RFK and David in ocean: *RK*, pp. 912–13. Schlesinger said David bruised his head, but John Frankenheimer recalled that it was RFK himself.

387   "His head [hung] limply. . . .": Goodwin, *Remembering America*, p. 535.

387   daubed RFK's bruised forehead: John Frankenheimer interview.

387   "Did you hear about the Indians?": Witcover, *85 Days*, pp. 254–55.

387   Royal Suite: RFK often used the bathroom for conferences. "Everybody's always going to the bathroom in politics," said Jack English, the Nassau County Democratic chairman. "Carmine DeSapio is famous for that; won't talk to anybody *but* in the bathroom." Stein and Plimpton, *American Journey*, p. 228.

388   "on every street corner. . . ": Goodwin, *Remembering America*, pp. 536–37.

388   uphill struggle: Larry O'Brien OH, LBJL. Senator Fred Harris, who was chairman of United Democrats for Humphrey but also a close friend of RFK's, told the author in 1999, "I think Humphrey would have been nominated." Harris, who knew the reality of delegate counts, doubted that RFK would have been able to shake enough loose from the Humphrey column. Fred Harris interview. Melody Miller, who was one of RFK's "boiler room" girls counting delegates, said that RFK had enough delegates "up his sleeve" to prevent a first-ballot victory by Humphrey.

388   "I think we should tell him. . . .": Goodwin, *Remembering America*, p. 537.

388   Daley at least "hinted": *RK*, p. 914; Frank Mankiewicz interview. "It was, 'I'm with you,' though there may have been some contingency."

388   O'Donnell's "understanding": John Reilly interview.

388   uncharacteristic for Daley: According to Democratic Party insider James Rowe, Daley did not like RFK. James Rowe OH, LBJL. But Richard Wade, the urban planning professor who worked in three Kennedy campaigns (1960, 1964, and 1968), disputed this assessment. Wade knew Daley and met with him on the Wednesday after each Tuesday primary. Daley told Wade that "primaries count," meaning that if Kennedy won enough primaries, he couldn't be denied the nomination by the party bosses. Daley had been impressed by RFK's performance with blue-collar voters in Indiana and rural voters in Nebraska. Richard Wade interview.

388   "You know, Kenny. . . .": Lester David and Irene David, *Bobby Kennedy*, p. 316.

389   RFK seemed "liberated": Jack Newfield, *Robert Kennedy: A Memoir*, p. 293.

389   "puckish": Witcover, *85 Days*, p. 261.

389   "The change in Kennedy. . . .": Goodwin, *Remembering America*, pp. 537–38.

389   "For a while. . . .": Warren Rogers, *When I Think of Bobby*, p. 149. Hollywood screenwriter Budd Schulberg had a similar experience. Just before RFK went downstairs to address the crowd, Schulberg was summoned to RFK's room. The candidate was sitting off in a corner on the floor, smoking a cigar. He wanted to talk about Schulberg's workshop for poor black artists in Watts. "It always struck me as a little odd," said Schulberg. Impatiently pacing nearby, Jesse Unruh finally told RFK that he had to go downstairs or he'd miss prime time. Budd Schulberg interview.

390   "They were very different men. . . .": J. B. Martin Campaign Journal, p. 47, John Bartlow Martin Papers, LOC.

390   national health care: Richard Wade interview.

390 "little-girlish . . .": Witcover, *85 Days*, p. 261.

391 ". . . So my thanks to all of you. . . .": Edwin O. Guthman and C. Richard Allen, eds., *RFK: Collected Speeches*, pp. 401–402.

391 shooting scene: Witcover, *85 Days*, pp. 267–73. Paul Schrade, a UAW official who was also wounded, heard RFK ask, "Is everybody else all right?" There are various conspiracy theories about RFK's assassination. I was persuaded by Dan Moldea's *The Killing of Robert F. Kennedy* that they are bogus.

391 "an awful sound" . . . "The Once and Future King": Newfield, *Memoir*, pp. 299, 302.

392 His eyes were blackened: Cronin and Kennedy, *Riverkeepers*, p. 87.

392 Brother Ted knelt: Goodwin, *Remembering America*, p. 539.

392 "I've got to know. . . .": Jeff Sheshol, *Mutual Contempt*, p. 456.

392 "Cosa Nostra. . . .": President's Handwriting file, June 4, 1968, LBJL.

392 ". . . damned 'Murder Inc.' ": Leo Janos, "The Last Days of the President," *Atlantic Monthly*, July 1973.

392 "cruel": Shesol, *Mutual Contempt*, p. 457.

392 Rose Kennedy: Gail Cameron, *Rose*, pp. 282–84.

392 "just such a nice touch": Stein and Plimpton, *American Journey*, p. 29.

393 Ted Kennedy eulogy: The speech was written by Adam Walinsky with help from Milton Gwirtzman and Burke Marshall. Witcover, *85 Days*, p. 305.

393 million people lined the tracks: *RK*, pp. 1–2.

393 crowds along the tracks: Stein and Plimpton, *American Journey*, p. 64. The Stein oral histories give a vivid picture of the train trip and burial in Washington.

393 "they'd have torn their clothes. . . .": ibid., p. 61.

393 ". . . that I saw her cry. . . .": ibid., p. 127.

394 "We're going to go.": ibid., p. 157.

394 RFK wanted plain cross: Frank Mankiewicz interview.

BIBLIOGRAPHY

MANUSCRIPT COLLECTIONS

JOHN F. KENNEDY LIBRARY, BOSTON

Joseph Dolan Papers
Fred Dutton Papers
Peter Edelman Papers
Milton Gwirtzman Papers
David Hackett Papers
Nicholas Katzenbach Papers
Joseph P. Kennedy Papers
Robert F. Kennedy Papers (Pre-
    Administration; Attorney General;
    Attorney General Confidential;

Senate; 1968 Presidential
    Campaign)
Evelyn Lincoln Papers
Walter Lord Papers
Burke Marshall Papers
Arthur Schlesinger Jr. Papers
Adam Walinsky Papers
Theodore White Papers
White House Guard and Telephone
    Logs

LYNDON BAINES JOHNSON LIBRARY, AUSTIN, TEXAS

S. Douglass Cater Papers
Robert F. Kennedy file
Harry McPherson Papers
Mike Manatos Papers
Drew Pearson Papers

Presidential Daily Diary Log
John Steele Papers
Larry Temple Papers
Marvin Watson Papers
White House Famous Names File

FEDERAL BUREAU OF INVESTIGATION, WASHINGTON, D.C.

FOIA Files of the following: Sam Giancana, J. Edgar Hoover Official and Confiden-
tial files, Dr. Max Jacobson, John F. Kennedy, Joseph P. Kennedy, Robert F. Kennedy,
Martin Luther King Jr., Peter Lawford, Stanley Levison, Marilyn Monroe, Ellen
Rometsch, John Rosselli, Frank Sinatra

National Archives, Washington, D.C.

House Assassination Committee
  Records
Joseph Califano Papers

Jim Garrison investigation files
Records of the Central Intelligence
  Agency

Library of Congress, Washington, D.C.

Joseph Alsop Papers
William O. Douglas Papers
Averell Harriman Papers

James Landis Papers
John Bartlow Martin Papers

Herbert Hoover Presidential Library, West Branch, Iowa
Clark Mollenhoff Papers

Massachusetts Historical Society, Boston
Nigel Hamilton Papers

Myrick E. Land Papers, Boston University
Karl E. Mundt Papers, Dakota State University, Madison, South Dakota
C. David Heymann Collection, SUNY at Stony Brook, New York
Senator John J. Williams Papers, University of Delaware, Newark
Clay Blair Papers, American Heritage Center, University of Wyoming,
  Laramie
Katharine Graham Papers, Washington, D.C.

PERSONAL INTERVIEWS

Juanita Abernathy, Samuel Adams, Herbert Alexander, Susan Mary Alsop, Jack Anderson, R. W. Apple, Carter Bacon, Bobby Baker, Letitia Baldrige, Charles Bartlett, Lucius Battle, Griffin Bell, Saul Bellow, Michael Beschloss, Richard Bissell, G. Robert Blakey, Stuart Bloch, Robert Bouk, Joan Braden, Ben Bradlee, Scott Breckinridge, Jerry Bruno, Steve Bundy, Amanda Burden, Joseph Califano, Samuel Campbell, Mortimer Caplin, Sonny Carson, Charles Clark, Tom Cleveland, Robert Coles, Archibald Cox, Lloyd Cutler, Robert Dallek, Richard Daly, Edmond Davis, Sarah Davis, Cartha DeLoach, Howard Diller, Douglas Dillon, Joe Dolan, John Doltz, Richard Donahue, John Douglas, Mercedes Douglas, Julius Draznin, Robert Drennan, Emil Drvaric, Dominick Dunne, Fred Dutton, Charles Eagles, Peter Edelman, Herb Edgren, Mike Egan, Walter Elder, Ronnie Eldridge, David Ellis, Bill Eppridge, Jake Esterline, Rowland Evans, Paul Fay, Justin Feldman, Myer Feldman, Peter Fishbein, Karl Fleming, Wally Flynn, David Fox, John Frankenheimer, Stanley Gaines,

Fred Garfield, Joe Gargan, John Gibbons, John Gilman, Charles Glynn, Ronald Goldfarb, Peter Goldman, Richard Goodwin, Richard Grandjean, John Graves, Robert Green, Roosevelt Grier, Brandon Grove, Charles Guggenheim, Ed Guthman, Milton Gwirtzman, David Hackett, William Haddad, Alexander Haig, Sam Halpern, K.K. Hannon, Senator Fred Harris, Richard Harwood, Richard Helms, Luella Hennessey, Don Hewitt, Eleanor Hoefer, Carol Hoffecker, Max Holland, Senator Fritz Hollings, Barbara Howar, William Hundley, Frank Hurley, Jayne Ikard, Charles E. Johnson, Haynes Johnson, Tom Johnston, Judge Thomas Jones, Stanley Karnow, Nicholas Katzenbach, Father Damian Kearney, Pierce Kearney, Jack Keeney, Joe Kempkes, Kathleen Kennedy, Maxwell Kennedy, Frank Kiernan, Peter Knight, Jerome Kretchmer, John Lane, Anthony Lewis, John Lewis, Jonathan Lewis, Walter Lord, Joy Luke, Grayston Lynch, Peter Maas, Mary McGrory, Robert McNamara, Charles Maechling, Frank Mankiewicz, Senator Mike Mansfield, Burke Marshall, Margaret Marshall, Mike Marshall, Ernest May, David Meehan, Irene Mennel, Herbert Miller, Melody Miller, John Miner, Newton Minow, Mike Miskovsky, Ray Mollenhoff, Robert Morgenthau, David Murphy, Timothy Naftali, Jack Newfield, Arthur Nichols, Paul Nitze, John Nolan, Marty Nolan, Michael Novak, Louis Oberdorfer, Helen O'Donnell, Allison Page, Thomas Parrott, Marty Pera, Charles Peters, George Plimpton, Walter Pozen, E. Barrett Prettyman, Rafael Quintero, John Reilly, Marie Ridder, Don Ritchie, Enid Rivkin, Warren Rogers, Gary Ross, Robert Rusk, Pierre Salinger, Roberto San Román, Paul Schrade, Budd Schulberg, F.A.O. Schwarz, John Seigenthaler, Nancy Sheridan, Walter Sheridan Jr., Eunice Shriver, Sargent Shriver, Hugh Sidey, Senator George Smathers, Sandy Smith, Theodore Sorensen, Charles Spalding, John Spelman, Father Julian Stead, George Stevens, Herb Stokinger, James Symington, Tad Szulc, Cleve Thurber, Gerald Tremblay, Cyrus Vance, William vanden Heuvel, Ernest Vandiver, Burkett Van Kirk, Sander Vanocur, Richard Wade, Adam Walinsky, Paul Wankowitz, Senator John Warner, Janet Weininger, Roger Wilkins, Donald Wilson, Philip Zelikow

ORAL HISTORY TRANSCRIPTS

GEORGE PLIMPTON AND JEAN STEIN INTERVIEWS, JFKL

Samuel Adams, George Ball, Charles Bartlett, Lem Billings, Roy Cohn, Paul Corbin, Walter Cronkite, Fred Dutton, Rowland Evans, Charles Evers, Mary Bailey Gimbel, Jeff Greenfield, David Hackett, Joseph Kraft, Stanley Levison, Anthony Lewis, Allard Lowenstein, Clark Mollenhoff, Jack Newfield, Angie Novello, Lawrence O'Brien, Kenneth O'Donnell, George Plimpton, Charles Quinn, Franklin Roosevelt Jr., Nicole Salinger, Arthur Schlesinger Jr., Budd Schulberg, John Seigenthaler, Walter Sheridan, Charles Spalding, Maxwell Taylor, José Torres, William Walton, Theodore White, Andrew Young

JOHN F. KENNEDY LIBRARY, BOSTON

Samuel Adams, Robert Amory, Wesley Barthelmes, Isaiah Berlin, Albert Blumenthal, McGeorge Bundy, David Burke, Frank Burns, Cesar Chavez, Kenneth Clark,

Ramsey Clark, Richard Cardinal Cushing, Joe Dolan, Gerald Dougherty, Peter Edelman, Ronnie Eldridge, Rowland Evans, Myron Feldman, Dun Gifford, Mary Bailey Gimbel, Jeff Greenfield, Milton Gwirtzman, David Hackett, Fred Harris, Hubert Humphrey, Rafer Johnson, Judge Thomas Jones, Nicholas Katzenbach, Fletcher Knebel, Joseph Kraft, Jerome Kretchmer, Edward Lansdale, Robert Lovett, Allard Lowenstein, Frank Mankiewicz, Burke Marshall, Esther Newberg, John Nolan, William Orrick, E. Barrett Prettyman, Walter Reuther, Pierre Salinger, John Seigenthaler, Sargent Shriver, Theodore Sorensen, Charles Spalding, Maxwell Taylor, Gerald Tremblay, Stanley Tretick, Richard Wade, Adam Walinsky, William Walton, Tom Watson, James Whittaker, Don Wilson

LYNDON B. JOHNSON LIBRARY, AUSTIN, TEXAS

Charles Bartlett
David Burke
John Moors Cabot
Lawrence O'Brien
Joseph Rauh

John Roche
James Rowe
John Singleton
Cecil Stoughton

U.S. SENATE HISTORICAL OFFICE, WASHINGTON, D.C.

Scott Peek

Ruth Watt

COLUMBIA UNIVERSITY, NEW YORK CITY

Evan Thomas

Marietta Tree

FILM AND AUDIOTAPES

Audio Recordings of Presidential Telephone Conversations—JFKL, Boston
Audio Recordings of Presidential Telephone Conversations—LBJL, Austin, Texas
Robert Drew, producer, "Kennedy v. Wallace: A Crisis Up Close"
Jack Newfield and Charles Stuart, "Robert Kennedy"

BOOKS

Abel, Elie. *The Missile Crisis.* Philadelphia: J. B. Lippincott, 1966.

Abramson, Rudy. *Spanning the Century: The Life of W. Averell Harriman, 1891–1986.* New York: Morrow, 1992.

Aguilar, Luis. *Operation Zapata.* Frederick, MD: University Publications of America, 1981.

Allison, Graham, and Philip Zelikow. *Essence of Decision: Explaining the Cuban Missile Crisis.* New York: Longman, 1999.

Amory, Mark, ed. *The Letters of Ann Fleming.* London: Collins Harvill, 1985.

Andersen, Christopher. *Jack and Jackie*. New York: Avon, 1996.

Baker, Bobby, with Larry King. *Wheeling and Dealing: Confessions of a Capitol Hill Operator*. New York: Norton, 1978.

Barron, John. *Operation Solo: The FBI's Man in the Kremlin*. Washington, DC: Regnery, 1996.

Bass, Jack. *Taming the Storm*. Garden City, NY: Doubleday, 1993.

Belin, David W. *Final Disclosure: The Full Truth About the Assassination of President Kennedy*. New York: Scribner's, 1988.

Beran, Michael Knox. *The Last Patrician: Bobby Kennedy and the End of American Aristocracy*. New York: St. Martin's, 1998.

Beschloss, Michael R. *The Crisis Years: Kennedy and Khrushchev, 1960–1963*. New York: HarperCollins, 1991.

———, ed. *Taking Charge: The Johnson White House Tapes, 1963–1964*. New York: Simon & Schuster, 1997.

Blair, Joan, and Clay Blair Jr. *The Search for JFK*. New York: Putnam, 1976.

Blakey, G. Robert, and Richard N. Billings. *The Plot to Kill the President*. New York: Times Books, 1981.

Blight, James G., Bruce J. Allyn, and David A. Welch. *Cuba on the Brink: Castro, the Missile Crisis, and the Soviet Collapse*. New York: Pantheon, 1993.

Braden, Joan. *Just Enough Rope*. New York: Villard, 1989.

Branch, Taylor. *Parting the Waters: America in the King Years, 1954–63*. New York: Simon & Schuster, 1988.

———. *Pillar of Fire: America in the King Years, 1963–65*. New York: Simon & Schuster, 1998.

Brinkley, Douglas. *Dean Acheson: The Cold War Years, 1953–1971*. New Haven: Yale University Press, 1992.

Brown, Joan Winmill. *No Longer Alone*. Old Tappan, NJ: Revell, 1975.

Brugioni, Dino A. *Eyeball to Eyeball: The Inside Story of the Cuban Missile Crisis*, ed. Robert F. McCort. New York: Random House, 1990.

Bruno, Jerry, and Jeff Greenfield. *The Advance Man*. New York: Morrow, 1971.

Buchan, John. *Pilgrim's Way*. New York: Carroll & Graf, 1984.

Califano, Joseph A., Jr. *The Triumph & Tragedy of Lyndon Johnson: The White House Years*. New York: Simon & Schuster, 1991.

Cameron, Gail. *Rose*. New York: Berkley, 1971.

Camus, Albert. *Resistance, Rebellion, and Death*, tr. Justin O'Brien. New York: Knopf, 1961.

Chafe, William H. *Never Stop Running*. New York: HarperCollins, 1993.

Chafin, Raymond, and Topper Sherwood. *Just Good Politics: The Life of Raymond Chafin, Appalachian Boss*. Pittsburgh: University of Pittsburgh Press, 1994.

Chang, Laurence, and Peter Kornbluh, eds. *The Cuban Missile Crisis, 1962: A National Security Archive Documents Reader*. New York: New Press, 1992.

Chayes, Abram. *The Cuban Missile Crisis*. New York: Oxford University Press, 1974.

Chester, Lewis, Godfrey Hodgson, and Bruce Page. *An American Melodrama: The Presidential Campaign of 1968*. New York: Viking, 1969.

Clymer, Adam. *Edward M. Kennedy: A Biography*. New York: Morrow, 1999.

Collier, Peter, and David Horowitz. *The Kennedys: An American Drama*. New York: Summit, 1984.

Corn, David. *Blond Ghost: Ted Shackley and the CIA's Crusades.* New York: Simon & Schuster, 1994.

Corry, John. *The Manchester Affair.* New York: Putnam, 1967.

Cronin, John, and Robert F. Kennedy Jr. *The Riverkeepers: Two Activists Fight to Reclaim Our Environment as a Basic Human Right.* New York: Scribner, 1997.

Dallas, Rita, with Jeanira Ratcliffe. *The Kennedy Case.* New York: Putnam, 1973.

Dallek, Robert. *Flawed Giant: Lyndon Johnson and His Times, 1961–1973.* New York: Oxford University Press, 1998.

———. *Lone Star Rising: Lyndon Johnson and His Times, 1908–1960.* New York: Oxford University Press, 1991.

David, Lester, and Irene David. *Bobby Kennedy: The Making of a Folk Hero.* New York: Dodd, Mead, 1986.

DeLoach, Cartha. *Hoover's FBI: The Inside Story by Hoover's Trusted Lieutenant.* Washington, DC: Regnery, 1995.

Dobrynin, Anatoly. *In Confidence: Moscow's Ambassador to America's Six Cold War Presidents.* New York: Times Books, 1995.

Fay, Paul B., Jr. *The Pleasure of His Company.* New York: Harper & Row, 1966.

Fox, Stephen. *Blood and Power: Organized Crime in Twentieth-Century America.* New York: Morrow, 1989.

Frady, Marshall. *Wallace.* New York: Random House, 1996.

Fursenko, Aleksandr, and Timothy Naftali. *"One Hell of a Gamble": Khrushchev, Kennedy and Castro, 1958–1964.* New York: Norton, 1997.

Garrow, David. *Bearing the Cross: Martin Luther King, Jr., and the Southern Christian Leadership Conference.* New York: Morrow, 1986.

Garthoff, Raymond L. *Reflections on the Cuban Missile Crisis.* Washington, DC: Brookings, 1987.

Gentry, Curt. *J. Edgar Hoover: The Man and the Secrets.* New York: Norton, 1991.

Goodwin, Doris Kearns. *The Fitzgeralds and the Kennedys.* New York: St. Martin's, 1987.

Goodwin, Richard N. *Remembering America: A Voice from the Sixties.* Boston: Little, Brown, 1988.

Guthman, Edwin O. *We Band of Brothers.* New York: Harper & Row, 1971.

Guthman, Edwin O., and C. Richard Allen, eds. *RFK: Collected Speeches.* New York: Viking, 1993.

Guthman, Edwin O., and Jeffrey Shulman, eds. *Robert Kennedy: In His Own Words.* New York: Bantam, 1988.

Halberstam, David. *The Powers That Be.* New York: Knopf, 1979.

———. *The Unfinished Odyssey of Robert Kennedy.* New York: Random House, 1968.

Hamilton, Edith. *The Greek Way.* New York: Norton, 1930.

Hamilton, Nigel. *JFK: Reckless Youth.* New York: Random House, 1992.

Hersh, Seymour M. *The Dark Side of Camelot.* Boston: Little, Brown, 1997.

Heymann, C. David. *RFK: A Candid Biography of Robert F. Kennedy.* New York: Dutton, 1998.

Hilty, James W. *Robert Kennedy: Brother Protector.* Philadelphia: Temple University Press, 1997.

Humphrey, Hubert. *The Education of a Public Man: My Life and Politics.* Garden City, NY: Doubleday, 1976.

Hutchinson, Dennis J. *The Man Who Once Was Whizzer White.* New York: Free Press, 1998.

Isserman, Maurice, and Michael Kazin. *America Divided: The Civil War of the 1960s.* New York: Oxford University Press, 1999.

Johnson, Haynes. *The Bay of Pigs.* New York: Norton, 1964.

Johnson, Lyndon. *The Vantage Point: Perspectives of the Presidency, 1963–1969.* New York: Holt, Rinehart and Winston, 1971.

Kearns, Doris. *Lyndon Johnson & the American Dream.* New York: Harper & Row, 1976.

Kelley, Kitty. *His Way.* New York: Bantam, 1986.

Kennedy, John F. *Profiles in Courage* (memorial edition). New York: Harper & Row, 1964.

Kennedy, Maxwell Taylor, ed. *Make Gentle the Life of This World: The Vision of Robert F. Kennedy.* New York: Harcourt Brace, 1998.

Kennedy, Robert F. *The Enemy Within.* New York: Harper & Bros., 1960.

———. *Thirteen Days: A Memoir of the Cuban Missile Crisis.* New York: Norton, 1969.

———. *To Seek a Newer World.* Garden City, NY: Doubleday, 1967.

Kennedy, Rose. *Times to Remember.* Garden City, NY: Doubleday, 1974.

Klein, Edward. *Just Jackie: Her Private Years.* New York: Ballantine, 1998.

Knowles, John. *A Separate Peace.* New York: Macmillan, 1960.

Krepinevich, Andrew F., Jr. *The Army and Vietnam.* Baltimore: Johns Hopkins University Press, 1986.

Lasky, Victor. *It Didn't Start with Watergate.* New York: Dell, 1977.

———. *Robert F. Kennedy: The Myth and the Man.* New York: Trident, 1968.

Lawford, Patricia, ed. *That Shining Hour.* Hanover, MA: privately printed, 1969.

Leamer, Laurence. *The Kennedy Women: The Saga of an American Family.* New York: Villard, 1994.

Leaming, Barbara. *Marilyn Monroe.* New York: Crown, 1998.

Lemann, Nicholas. *The Promised Land.* New York: Knopf, 1991.

Logevall, Fredrik. *Choosing War: The Lost Chance for Peace and the Escalation of War in Vietnam.* Berkeley, CA: University of California Press, 1999.

Lord, Walter. *The Past That Would Not Die.* New York: Harper & Row, 1965.

Lowell, Robert. *History.* New York: Farrar, Straus & Giroux, 1973.

Lycett, Andrew. *Ian Fleming.* London: Weidenfeld and Nicolson, 1995.

Lynch, Grayston L. *Decision for Disaster: Betrayal at the Bay of Pigs.* Washington, DC: Brassey's, 1998.

Maas, Peter. *The Valachi Papers.* New York: Putnam, 1968.

McAuliffe, Mary S., ed. *CIA Documents on the Cuban Missile Crisis, 1962.* Washington, DC: Central Intelligence Agency, 1992.

McCarthy, Eugene. *Up 'Til Now: A Memoir.* San Diego: Harcourt Brace Jovanovich, 1987.

Mahoney, Richard D. *Sons & Brothers: The Days of Jack and Bobby Kennedy.* New York: Arcade, 1999.

Mailer, Norman. *Marilyn.* New York: Grosset & Dunlap, 1973.

Manchester, William. *Controversy and Other Essays in Journalism*. Boston: Little, Brown, 1976.

——. *The Death of a President*. New York: Harper & Row, 1967.

Matthews, Christopher. *Kennedy & Nixon: The Rivalry That Shaped Postwar America*. New York: Simon & Schuster, 1996.

May, Ernest R., and Philip D. Zelikow, eds. *The Kennedy Tapes: Inside the White House During the Cuban Missile Crisis*. Cambridge, MA: Harvard University Press, 1997.

Merry, Robert W. *Taking On the World: Joseph and Stewart Alsop—Guardians of the American Century*. New York: Viking, 1996.

Moldea, Dan E. *The Killing of Robert F. Kennedy: An Investigation of Motive, Means, and Opportunity*. New York: Norton, 1995.

Mollenhoff, Clark R. *Tentacles of Power: The Story of Jimmy Hoffa*. Cleveland: World, 1965.

Navasky, Victor S. *Kennedy Justice*. New York: Atheneum, 1971.

Newfield, Jack. *Robert Kennedy: A Memoir*. New York: Dutton, 1969.

O'Brien, Lawrence F. *No Final Victories: A Life in Politics—from John F. Kennedy to Watergate*. Garden City, NY: Doubleday, 1974.

O'Connor, Thomas. *The Boston Irish*. Boston: Northeastern University Press, 1995.

O'Donnell, Helen. *A Common Good: The Friendship of Robert F. Kennedy and Kenneth P. O'Donnell*. New York: Morrow, 1998.

O'Donnell, Kenneth P., and David F. Powers, with Joseph McCarthy. *"Johnny, We Hardly Knew Ye": Memories of John Fitzgerald Kennedy*. Boston: Little, Brown, 1972.

Oppenheimer, Jerry. *The Other Mrs. Kennedy: Ethel Skakel Kennedy: An American Drama of Power, Privilege and Politics*. New York: St. Martin's, 1994.

Plimpton, George. *Truman Capote*. New York: Doubleday, 1997.

Posner, Gerald L. *Case Closed: Lee Harvey Oswald and the Assassination of JFK*. New York: Random House, 1993.

Reeves, Richard. *President Kennedy: Profile of Power*. New York: Simon & Schuster, 1993.

Reeves, Thomas C. *A Question of Character*. New York: Free Press, 1991.

Ritchie, Donald A. *James M. Landis: Dean of the Regulators*. Cambridge, MA: Harvard University Press, 1980.

Roemer, William F., Jr. *Accardo: The Genuine Godfather*. New York: Donald I. Fine, 1995.

——. *Roemer: Man Against the Mob*. New York: Donald I. Fine, 1989.

Rogers, Warren. *When I Think of Bobby: A Personal Memoir of the Kennedy Years*. New York: HarperCollins, 1993.

Russo, Gus. *Live by the Sword: The Secret War Against Castro and the Death of JFK*. Baltimore: Bancroft, 1998.

Salinger, Pierre. *P.S.: A Memoir*. New York: St. Martin's, 1995.

——. *With Kennedy*. Garden City, NY: Doubleday, 1966.

Salinger, Pierre, Edwin Guthman, Frank Mankiewicz, and John Seigenthaler, eds. *An Honorable Profession: A Tribute to Robert F. Kennedy*. Garden City, NY: Doubleday, 1968.

Schlesinger, Arthur, Jr. *A Thousand Days*. New York: Fawcett, 1965.

Searls, Hank. *The Lost Prince*. New York and Cleveland: World, 1969.

Shapley, Deborah. *Promise and Power: The Life and Times of Robert McNamara*. Boston: Little, Brown, 1993.

Sheridan, Walter. *The Fall and Rise of Jimmy Hoffa*. New York: Saturday Review Press, 1972.

Shesol, Jeff. *Mutual Contempt: Lyndon Johnson, Robert Kennedy, and the Feud That Defined a Decade*. New York: Norton, 1997.

Shultz, Richard H., Jr. *The Secret War Against Hanoi*. New York: HarperCollins, 1999.

Smyser, W. R. *From Yalta to Berlin: The Cold War Struggle Over Germany*. New York: St. Martin's, 1999.

Sorensen, Theodore C. *Kennedy*. New York: Harper & Row, 1965.

Spoto, Donald. *Marilyn Monroe: The Biography*. New York: HarperCollins, 1993.

Stein, Jean, and George Plimpton. *American Journey: The Times of Robert Kennedy*. New York: Harcourt Brace Jovanovich, 1970.

————. *Edie: An American Biography*. New York: Knopf, 1982.

Sullivan, William C. *The Bureau: My Thirty Years with Hoover's FBI*. New York: Norton, 1979.

Summers, Anthony. *Goddess: The Secret Lives of Marilyn Monroe*. New York: Macmillan, 1985.

————. *Official and Confidential: The Secret Life of J. Edgar Hoover*. New York: Putnam, 1993.

Taraborrelli, J. Randy. *Sinatra: Behind the Legend*. Secaucus, NJ: Birch Lane, 1997.

Thomas, Evan. *The Man to See: Edward Bennett Williams: Ultimate Insider; Legendary Trial Lawyer*. New York: Simon & Schuster, 1991.

————. *The Very Best Men: Four Who Dared: The Early Years of the CIA*. New York: Simon & Schuster, 1995.

U.S. Senate. *Alleged Assassination Plots Involving Foreign Leaders: An Interim Report of the Select Committee to Study Government Operations with Respect to Intelligence Activities*. Washington, DC: U.S. Government Printing Office, 1975.

vanden Heuvel, William, and Milton Gwirtzman. *On His Own: Robert F. Kennedy, 1964–1968*. Garden City, NY: Doubleday, 1970.

White, Mark, ed. *The Kennedys and Cuba: The Declassified Documentary History*. Chicago: Ivan R. Dee, 1999.

White, Theodore H. *In Search of History: A Personal Expedition*. New York: Harper & Row, 1978.

————. *The Making of the President, 1960*. New York: Atheneum, 1961.

Williams, Juan. *Thurgood Marshall: American Revolutionary*. New York: Random House, 1998.

Wills, Garry. *The Kennedy Imprisonment: A Meditation on Power*. Boston: Little, Brown, 1981.

Witcover, Jules. *85 Days: The Last Campaign of Robert Kennedy*. New York: Putnam, 1969.

————. *1968: The Year the Dream Died*. New York: Warner, 1997.

Wofford, Harris. *Of Kennedys and Kings: Making Sense of the Sixties*. New York: Farrar, Straus & Giroux, 1980.

INDEX

PHOTO CREDITS

ABOUT THE AUTHOR

Evan Thomas is assistant managing editor of *Newsweek* in Washington, D.C. He is the author, with Walter Isaacson, of *The Wise Men: Six Friends and the World They Made* and the author of *The Man to See: Edward Bennett Williams: Ultimate Insider; Legendary Trial Lawyer* and *The Very Best Men: Four Who Dared: The Early Years of the CIA*. He lives in Washington, D.C., with his wife and two daughters.